Trends and Innovations in Marketing Information Systems

Theodosios Tsiakis
Alexander Technological Educational Institute of Thessaloniki, Greece

A volume in the Advances in Marketing, Customer Relationship Management, and E-Services (AMCRMES) Book Series

BUSINESS SCIENCE Reference
An Imprint of IGI Global

Published in the United States of America by
Business Science Reference (an imprint of IGI Global)
701 E. Chocolate Avenue
Hershey PA, USA 17033
Tel: 717-533-8845
Fax: 717-533-8661
E-mail: cust@igi-global.com
Web site: http://www.igi-global.com

Library of Congress Cataloging-in-Publication Data

Trends and innovations in marketing information systems / Theodosios Tsiakis, editor.
pages cm
Includes bibliographical references and index.
ISBN 978-1-4666-8459-1 (hardcover : alk. paper) -- ISBN 978-1-4666-8460-7 (ebook) 1. Marketing--Management. 2. Marketing. 3. Management information systems. I. Tsiakis, Theodosios, 1978-
HF5415.13.T7334 2015
658.800285--dc23
2015009416

This book is published in the IGI Global book series Advances in Marketing, Customer Relationship Management, and E-Services (AMCRMES) (ISSN: 2327-5502; eISSN: 2327-5529)

British Cataloguing in Publication Data
A Cataloguing in Publication record for this book is available from the British Library.

All work contributed to this book is new, previously-unpublished material. The views expressed in this book are those of the authors, but not necessarily of the publisher.

For electronic access to this publication, please contact: eresources@igi-global.com.

Advances in Marketing, Customer Relationship Management, and E-Services (AMCRMES) Book Series

Eldon Y. Li
National Chengchi University, Taiwan & California Polytechnic State University, USA

ISSN: 2327-5502
EISSN: 2327-5529

Mission

Business processes, services, and communications are important factors in the management of good customer relationship, which is the foundation of any well organized business. Technology continues to play a vital role in the organization and automation of business processes for marketing, sales, and customer service. These features aid in the attraction of new clients and maintaining existing relationships.

The Advances in Marketing, Customer Relationship Management, and E-Services (AMCRMES) Book Series addresses success factors for customer relationship management, marketing, and electronic services and its performance outcomes. This collection of reference source covers aspects of consumer behavior and marketing business strategies aiming towards researchers, scholars, and practitioners in the fields of marketing management.

Coverage

- Social Networking and Marketing
- CRM strategies
- Online Community Management and Behavior
- Cases on Electronic Services
- Cases on CRM Implementation
- Mobile CRM
- Data mining and marketing
- Ethical Considerations in E-Marketing
- Electronic Services
- E-Service Innovation

IGI Global is currently accepting manuscripts for publication within this series. To submit a proposal for a volume in this series, please contact our Acquisition Editors at Acquisitions@igi-global.com or visit: http://www.igi-global.com/publish/.

The Advances in Marketing, Customer Relationship Management, and E-Services (AMCRMES) Book Series (ISSN 2327-5502) is published by IGI Global, 701 E. Chocolate Avenue, Hershey, PA 17033-1240, USA, www.igi-global.com. This series is composed of titles available for purchase individually; each title is edited to be contextually exclusive from any other title within the series. For pricing and ordering information please visit http://www.igi-global.com/book-series/advances-marketing-customer-relationship-management/37150. Postmaster: Send all address changes to above address.

Titles in this Series

For a list of additional titles in this series, please visit: www.igi-global.com

Capturing, Analyzing, and Managing Word-of-Mouth in the Digital Marketplace
Sumangla Rathore (Sir Padampat Singhania University, India) and Avinash Panwar (Sir Padampat Singhania University, India)
Business Science Reference • copyright 2016 • 309pp • H/C (ISBN: 9781466694491) • US $200.00 (our price)

Strategic Customer Relationship Management in the Age of Social Media
Amir Khanlari (University of Tehran, Iran)
Business Science Reference • copyright 2015 • 333pp • H/C (ISBN: 9781466685864) • US $200.00 (our price)

Maximizing Commerce and Marketing Strategies through Micro-Blogging
Janée N. Burkhalter (Saint Joseph's University, USA) and Natalie T. Wood (Saint Joseph's University, USA & Edith Cowan University, Australia)
Business Science Reference • copyright 2015 • 354pp • H/C (ISBN: 9781466684089) • US $225.00 (our price)

Analyzing the Cultural Diversity of Consumers in the Global Marketplace
Juan Miguel Alcántara-Pilar (University of Granada, Spain) Salvador del Barrio-García (University of Granada, Spain) Esmeralda Crespo-Almendros (University of Granada, Spain) and Lucia Porcu (University of Granada, Spain)
Business Science Reference • copyright 2015 • 404pp • H/C (ISBN: 9781466682627) • US $200.00 (our price)

Engaging Consumers through Branded Entertainment and Convergent Media
Jose Marti Parreno (Universidad Europea de Valencia, Spain) Carla Ruiz Mafe (Universidad de Valencia, Spain) and Lisa Scribner (University of North Carolina Wilmington, USA)
Business Science Reference • copyright 2015 • 354pp • H/C (ISBN: 9781466683426) • US $205.00 (our price)

Handbook of Research on Integrating Social Media into Strategic Marketing
Nick Hajli (Newcastle University Business School, UK)
Business Science Reference • copyright 2015 • 440pp • H/C (ISBN: 9781466683532) • US $310.00 (our price)

Customer Relationship Management Strategies in the Digital Era
Süphan Nasır (Istanbul University, Turkey)
Business Science Reference • copyright 2015 • 322pp • H/C (ISBN: 9781466682313) • US $200.00 (our price)

Handbook of Research on Effective Advertising Strategies in the Social Media Age
Nurdan Öncel Taşkıran (Ondokuz Mayıs University, Turkey) and Recep Yılmaz (Ondokuz Mayıs University, Turkey)
Business Science Reference • copyright 2015 • 509pp • H/C (ISBN: 9781466681255) • US $335.00 (our price)

IGI GLOBAL
DISSEMINATOR OF KNOWLEDGE
www.igi-global.com

701 E. Chocolate Ave., Hershey, PA 17033
Order online at www.igi-global.com or call 717-533-8845 x100
To place a standing order for titles released in this series, contact: cust@igi-global.com
Mon-Fri 8:00 am - 5:00 pm (est) or fax 24 hours a day 717-533-8661

Table of Contents

Detailed Table of Contents

on behalf of customer needs. This chapter suggests that professionals must be clear with users to create confidence, in order to improve business practice. And users expect professionals to share and explain them their actions toward machines/systems, and listen to what they require. This is very important to marketing as a sustainable link with the company can be created.

This chapter reviews the many new tools the advent of AI agents has placed into the hands of marketers and consumers alike. AI agents are redefining the roles and rules of the marketing game. While once marketing was the interaction between marketing professionals and customers, AI agents are taking key roles on both sides. The chapter shows how Artificial Intelligence Marketing Agents have begun to proffer the marketer unprecedented marketing research and communication capabilities. However, at the same time AI applications are empowering the consumer to bypass or question the corporate marketing message. Virtual Personal Shopping Assistants (VPSAs) can learn consumers' tastes, predict their needs, and optimize their product purchases. VPSAs are able to instantly match a consumer's need against all accessible products that meet the consumer's expectations and price points. The chapter concludes with recommendations for marketers to recognize the primary role that the consumer's VPSA will play in the marketing game and adjust their marketing efforts accordingly.

Governments around the world have come to recognize the potential of new Information and Communication Technologies (ICT's) to reshape the ways in which they interact with citizens, businesses and other key stakeholders, hence the current move towards e-Government. A major goal of e-Government initiatives is to improve the quality of public service delivery through providing individuals and organizations with a coherent interface with government that has to be organized around their needs rather than the structure of government bodies. To that end, many governments have begun applying to their e-Government strategies the commercial concept commonly referred to as "Customer Relationship Management" (CRM), thus generating a new field of knowledge and related applications. This chapter discusses some of the key issues to implementing CRM in e-Government. It lays particular stress on the CRM capabilities of identifying and differentiating users, promoting take-up of e-Government and measuring the progress against its stated objectives. The conceptual framework will also be related to a case-study dealing with the Italian Revenue Agency, responsible for collecting tax and customs duties for government, which is developing a rich CRM program along with an ICT re-engineering process.

Despite alleged widespread adoption of Corporate Social Responsibility (CSR) and responsible business practices by organisations worldwide, questions still remain on the motives for such adoption; effects and/or benefits of CSR adoption as well as how stakeholders can tell genuine responsible businesses from those paying lip service and using the CSR tag as a 'means-to-an end'. The litany of jargon often used interchangeably including such terms as CSR, sustainability, sustainable marketing, responsible business practice and sustainable development among others further lead to scepticism on organisations' commitments to CSR and the resultant allegations of greenwashing and CSR tokenism. This undermines genuine attempts to be corporately-responsible, fuelling confusion for any new players wishing to adopt responsible business practices. This chapter uses the Information Systems (IS) landscape as a lever to dissect issues in both CSR theory and practice, offering some practical guidelines for implementation and operationalisation, while raising further questions for research.

Among the multiple forms of bonding which can help companies to build and maintain buyer-supplier relationships, digital bonds, i.e. ties between an industrial buyers and suppliers formed when the IT systems of the parties are shared and integrated, are increasingly recognized as a strategic mean of customer retention. Despite several studies have unveiled which factors enable and constrain the companies' adoption of IT systems, we still have limited knowledge of how different types of digital bonds can be strategically managed. In this chapter we first provide a digital bond matrix in which four different types of digital bonds are identified. Then the proposed matrix is empirically validated by analyzing four different case studies representative of each digital bond identified. Finally, the matrix is applied as a device to inform strategic actions and decisions that can/should be undertaken to improve firms' digital bonds portfolio.

This chapter reveals the role of customer relationship management (CRM) in the global business environments, thus describing the theoretical and practical concept of CRM; the components of CRM in terms of key customer focus (KCF), CRM organization, knowledge management (KM), and technology-based CRM; the significance of CRM in global business; the significance of organizational characteristics in CRM; and the implementation of CRM in global business. The achievement of CRM is vital for modern organizations that seek to serve suppliers and customers, increase business performance,

Today, companies are turning to social media as a source of marketing information. Comments posted on social network sites, tweets, and blogs provide a wealth of data for the improvement of marketing decision making. Thus, marketers are greatly interested in how marketing activities can affect certain social media metrics and to what extent each drives business performance. The purpose of the chapter is to elaborate on the performance outcomes of social media activities and the possibility to use data from these networks for marketing information systems. Thus, the chapter discusses the theoretical foundations of social media and develops dimensions for social media performance measurement. In addition, the integration of social media performance measurement into a marketing information system is discussed and implementation issues are critically evaluated. The chapter closes with an outline of further research directions and a conclusion.

The usage of online social networking has increased as more people use digital technology to access and store information. In this chapter, the way recruiting services are being used by online social networks is discussed. This chapter utilizes the theoretical framework of social cognitive theory to understand the factors affecting intentions to adopt online social networking recruiting services. The chapter discusses the role of online behavioral advertising, ethical orientation, social influencers and online privacy concerns to see who they affect behavioral intentions. The results of the study reported in the chapter extend current understanding about online recruitment to see how social networks are an important part of the adoption process. The chapter provides practical and managerial insights into the role of online social networking in the recruitment context.

Recently, the role of information technology facilitating the exchange of information in markets has enabled new pricing mechanisms between buyers and sellers. Such electronic marketplaces, specifically Internet-based markets have supported customization of marketing mix elements efficiently. In response to supply and demand fluctuations, prices change more dynamically and quickly in the Internet than in physical markets. This chapter focuses on the revolution in pricing of businesses driven by the Internet. Within this context, primary characteristics of online pricing and auctions are reviewed systematically from the both view of buyers and sellers interacting. Furthermore, this chapter evaluates the effects of Internet as a new pricing mechanism and future trends of pricing rules within this attractive option.

E-commerce is a growing phenomenon in Africa. One area of e-commerce that is growing at a very fast rate is online retailing. This is despite concerns that individuals often have in relation to online shopping being associated with more risk than traditional retailing. This chapter looks at practices of online retailers that help in mitigating online shopping risk and the influence of these on customers' levels of trust as well as on their intentions to re-purchase from specific online stores. The findings show that provision of adequate online product information and online store security has positive influence on customers' level of trust in an online store. The findings also show that trust in an online store has significant influence on customers' intentions to repurchase from a store. The findings have wide implications on successful management of online store outlets and these have been highlighted in the chapter.

During its history, the largest U.S. consumer-to-consumer online platform, eBay, had to overcome two major obstacles: Asymmetry of information and competition from Yahoo Auctions. This chapter examines two of the mechanisms used by eBay that may account for the company's success story: the seller's rating mechanism and the insertion fee structure. The first of these mechanisms seems to have played an important role in addressing the problem of asymmetry of information in consumer-to-consumer online commerce. In addition, the eBay rating may have served as a barrier to entry for competing platforms in the consumer-to-consumer online commerce. The second mechanism appears to have aided eBay in its competition with Yahoo Auctions in the U.S. online auction market.

Successful organizations continually operate in a state of innovation in terms of the offerings they produce, frequently introducing new products or modifying and improving existing products as needed and by the market. The means of conceptualizing, designing, and marketing new products is known as new product development. Successful new product development is a considerable challenge for any market oriented organization. The cost of designing and developing new products is increasing while the rate of success of new products is not. Marketing managers are constantly looking for ways to improve their new product development process. This necessitates, among other things, linking an organization's capabilities and resources with the new product demands of the markets they serve. This chapter considers some of the internal process any market driven organization should focus on to improve the likelihood that their new products will enjoy market success.

Preface

Marketing information system (MKIS) is an essential tool for translating raw data to useful information. Strategic information, domain knowledge, and guidance within systematic strategic analysis are vital for managers to support strategic operation of firms such as marketing strategy development. The recent advancements of information technology and systems have transformed the marketing function due to the ability through technological means to record, find and compare marketing information. It is fundamental to understand the nature, role and strategic value of marketing information in different organizations, appreciate the role of information in marketing strategy, planning, management, monitoring, control and moreover to examine that marketing information system is a tool that is designed to support managers to make decision about marketing.

Information is the most valuable asset of enterprises and creates economic value in firms along with operational and strategic advantages. It is essential to identify information and research requirements for business and marketing decisions. Marketing information systems (MkIS) are people, equipment, and procedures to gather, sort, analyze, evaluate, and distribute needed, timely, and accurate information to marketing decision makers. Thus exploring the value of marketing information systems is crucial to the success of firms. The proposed book aims to provide knowledge of the functional components and structure of MkIS, to analyze the technological needs for supporting the marketing management processes, to reinforce the execution of marketing management by managing information, and to integrate business analytics to marketing.

This book consists of a compilation of eighteen (18) chapters // contributions discussing the "Trends and Innovations in Marketing Information Systems". These chapters // contributions are written by thirty two (32) authors, from all over the world, including many internationally renowned and experienced researchers and specialists in several disciplines and integrate contributions from academe, research institutions, and industry.

The book is structured into four (4) sections:

Section 1: Strategic use of IT/IS & Technologies for Marketing (including chapters 1-6)
Section 2: Customer Relationship Management (CRM) (including chapters 7-8)
Section 3: Social Media & Social Networking (including chapters 9-12)
Section 4: Improving market performance through marketing (including chapters 13-18)

Chapter 1, "*Web 2.0 Technologies and Marketing*," by Dora Simões and Sandra Filipe introduces the book with an overview of the use of social media marketing by pre-adults, setting off from a case study of pre-adults of different courses at a Portuguese higher education school. The aim of the chapter is to evaluate longitudinally the types of social media used by pre-adults, the contexts in which they use each social media type, their opinions about the intentions of social media marketing and the influences of social media marketing on their brand knowledge, attitude and behaviour.

Chapter 2 "*Information Technology Communication: Main Challenges and Pitfalls to Marketing and Management. Evidence from Curitiba (in Brazil)*," by Adriane Setti, Marisa Cesário, Sílvia Fernandes and Júlio Mendes, analyze the communication defects between IT professionals and users of their products and services, and then discuss some pitfalls and challenges to management and marketing. It addresses the communication between IT professionals and users in the corporate environment of Curitiba (Brazil). Results lead to perceive a need of formal training and screenplay by IT professionals to serve customers, manage their careers and assist technology on behalf of users.

Chapter 3, "*Artificial Intelligence: Marketing's game changer*" by Edward Forrest, and Bogdan Hoanca, offers a discussion to the applications and technologies utilizing Artificial Intelligence (AI), especially AI agents, that have begun to proffer the marketer unprecedented marketing research and communication capabilities. However, at the same time AI applications are empowering the consumer to bypass or question the corporate marketing message. Virtual Personal Shopping Assistants (VPSAs) can learn consumers' tastes, predict their needs, and optimize their product purchases. VPSAs are able to instantly match a consumer's need against all accessible products that meet the consumer's expectations and price points. It is becoming increasing important for marketers to recognize the primary role that the consumer's VPSA will play in the marketing game and adjust their marketing efforts accordingly.

Chapter 4, "*Business Management and new technologies to Improve the services*" by Giuseppe Granata, deals with the key issues, of implementing CRM in e-Government. It lays particular stress on the CRM capabilities of identifying and differentiating users, promoting take-up of e-Government and measuring the progress against its stated objectives..

Chapter 5, "*The treacherous path of Corporate Social Responsibility (CSR) and the role of Information Systems in its implementation*" by Tabani Ndlovu, Amon Simba and Anastasia Mariussen, some of the key issues to implementing CRM in e-Government. It lays particular stress on the CRM capabilities of identifying and differentiating users, promoting take-up of e-Government and measuring the progress against its stated objectives..

Chapter 6, "*Managing Digital Bonds in the Buyer-Supplier Relationships*" by Jari Salo, Giuseppe Pedeliento and Robert Wendelin, aims to strengthen our limited knowledge of how different types of digital bonds can be strategically managed. In this chapter the authors, first provide a digital bond matrix in which four different types of digital bonds are identified. Then the proposed matrix is empirically validated by analyzing four different case studies representative of each digital bond identified. Finally, the matrix is applied as a device to inform strategic actions and decisions that can/should be undertaken to improve firms' digital bonds portfolio.

Chapter 7, "*The Role of Customer Relationship Management in the Global Business Environments*" by Kijpokin Kasemsap, explains the theoretical and practical concept of CRM; the components of CRM in terms of key customer focus (KCF), CRM organization, knowledge management (KM), and technology-based CRM; the application overview of CRM; the importance of organizational characteristics in CRM; and the implementation of CRM in modern organizations..

Chapter 8, "*Data-Driven Customer Centricity: CRM Predictive Analytics*" by Othman Boujena, Kristof Coussement, and Koen W. De Bock, enlighten our knowledge on Customer relationship management (CRM) as it becomes an important tool in the toolset of the marketer. It is the practice of using the huge volumes of historical customer data to predict future customer behavior. This chapter introduces the reader to the shift towards a data-driven customer centricity approach, where marketers act upon what they know, rather than upon what they think.

Chapter 9, "*Social media as marketing information systems: Co-creation in viral video advertising*" by Christos Karpasitis, and Antonios Kaniadakis, propose an understanding of Social Media as useful Marketing Information Systems, which increasingly support the e-marketing function. More specifically, they explore the changing role of customers who as they become increasingly engaged in the Social Media Ecosystem and form communities of interest around certain products, they assume a more active role in co-creating and spreading marketing messages. To demonstrate this process they discuss the case of branded videos that are developed as part of viral marketing campaigns.

Chapter 10, "*The Rise of Relationship Marketing with Social Media*" by Ana Margarida Barreto, relates the improvement of market performance through marketing, specifically relationship marketing, by taking into consideration the brand perspective and the consumer perspective. The chapter aims to describe how social media has brought big challenges to brands, especially the strong ones, with repercussions on their brand image and consequently their brand equity, and how relationship marketing can be the answer to these new challenges

Chapter 11, "*Social media performance measurement*" by Goetz Greve, discusses the theoretical foundations of social media and develops dimensions for social media performance measurement. In addition, the integration of social media performance measurement into a marketing information system is discussed and implementation issues are critically evaluated. The chapter closes with an outline of further research directions and a conclusion.

Chapter 12, "*The role of online social networking in the recruitment context*" by Vanessa Ratten, examines how recruiting services are being used by online social networks. Using a sample of 218 Pennsylvanian college students, the chapter integrates social cognitive theory to understand the factors affecting intentions to adopt online social networking recruiting services. The role of online behavioral advertising, ethical orientation, social influencers and online privacy concerns are investigated to see who they affect behavioral intentions. The results, provides practical and managerial insights into the role of online social networking in the recruitment context.

Chapter 13, "*Online Pricing and Auctions*" by Kalender Özcan Atilgan, discusses the revolution in pricing of businesses driven by the Internet. Within this context, primary characteristics of online pricing and auctions are reviewed systematically from the both view of buyers and sellers interacting. Furthermore, this chapter evaluates the effects of Internet as a new pricing mechanism and future trends of pricing rules within this attractive option..

Chapter 14, "*Risk management, trust and repeat online shopping intentions: A South African perspective*" by Mercy Mpinganjira, investigate the practices of online retailers that help in mitigating online shopping risk and the influence of these on customers' levels of trust as well as on their intentions to re-purchase from specific online stores. The findings of the chapter, reveal that provision of adequate online product information and online store security has positive influence on customers' level of trust in an online store. The findings also show that trust in an online store has significant influence on customers' intentions to repurchase from a store..

Chapter 15, "*The Rise of eBay: Confronting the Challenges of Asymmetry of Information and Competition*" by Mikhail Ion Melnik, is dealing with the phenomenon of online auctions and how they become synonymous with the name of eBay as further more with the hegemony over the U.S. online auction market. In addition to greater competition, online businesses operating in the consumer-to-consumer space also faced other challenges including asymmetry of information. The industry and particularly eBay were successfully able to overcome this challenge and turn it into a shield against potential competitors.

Chapter 16, "*Successful New Product Planning*" by Nicholas Grigoriou. The matter of conceptualizing, designing, and marketing new products is known as new product development. Successful new product development is a considerable challenge for any market oriented organization. The cost of designing and developing new products is increasing while the rate of success of new products is not. Marketing managers are constantly looking for ways to improve their new product development process. This necessitates, among other things, linking an organization's capabilities and resources with the new product demands of the markets they serve. This chapter considers some of the internal process any market driven organization should focus on to improve the likelihood that their new products will enjoy market success.

Chapter 17, "*Upgrading Marketing Research: Neuromarketing Tools for Understanding Consumers*" by Anka Gorgiev and Nikolaos Dimitriadis, focuses on the recent developments in the marketing industry resulting from the rise of neuromarketing. It offers analysis of the problems initiated by the traditional marketing research approaches and how these problems are being resolved by implementation of neuromarketing techniques. Concluding, the authors provide initial insights from a small scale qualitative research conducted among representatives from all segments of marketing industry..

Chapter 18, "*Examining the Brand Communication Tools that Impact Brand Preferences of Women Consumer buying intentions-Empirical Investigation of Middle East*" by A M Sakkthivel and B Sriram, aims to design a model of constructs of brand communication tools (direct and indirect) and test the impact of the same on brand preferences of women consumer buying intentions from Middle Eastern countries with specific evidences from Sultanate of Oman. The results revealed that both the communication tools found to have a significant impact. It is found that the direct brand communication tools have a higher impact over women buying intentions..

I thank all authors for their personal efforts, patient and willingness, as the whole process of writing, reviewing, rewriting, editing, and proofreading needs a lot of time.

Theodosios Tsiakis
Alexander Technological Educational Institute of Thessaloniki, Greece

Section 1
Strategic use of IT/IS and Technologies for Marketing

Chapter 1
Web 2.0 Technologies and Marketing

Dora Simões
University of Aveiro, Portugal

Sandra Filipe
University of Aveiro, Portugal

ABSTRACT

This chapter reports on the use of social media marketing by pre-adults, setting off from a case study of pre-adults of different courses at a Portuguese higher education school. Data were collected through a questionnaire available online and analyzed with descriptive statistical techniques. Based on the pointed outlines, the aim is to evaluate longitudinally the types of social media used by pre-adults, the contexts in which they use each social media type, their opinions about the intentions of social media marketing and the influences of social media marketing on their brand knowledge, attitude and behaviour. Tendencies around concepts, tools and levels of attraction by the audiences, with focus on relationship marketing in the 2.0 era are revisited. Furthermore, the chapter presents the perception of pre-adults about social media marketing, and contributes with critical information that might help cast light over recent theories and practices of social media marketing.

INTRODUCTION

Nowadays, companies are driven by a new environment characterized by highly intense competition, high concern for quality, excess production capacity and strong technological development. Therefore, marketing professionals have felt the need to satisfy, retain and engage their customers through an orientation towards long-term relationships. The relationship marketing paradigm and the requirement for its implementation on business organizations, to improve customer retention levels, are clearly recognized in the academic literature (e.g., Kumar & Reinartz, 2012; Payne & Frow, 2013; Peppers & Rogers, 2011).

On the other hand, web 2.0 technologies made it easier for business organizations to reach the consumers in actual global market. Web 2.0 has become a platform that is easily available to anyone with

DOI: 10.4018/978-1-4666-8459-1.ch001

Internet access, has increased communication for organizations, fosters brand awareness, often improves customer service, and serves as a relatively inexpensive platform for organizations to implement marketing strategy developments (e.g., Evans & McKee, 2010; Greenberg, 2010; Wikström &Wigmo, 2010).

Social media employee web-based technologies to create highly interactive platforms via which individuals and companies share, discuss, co-create, and modify user-generated content. The various types of Internet communications such as YouTube, Blogs, LinkedIn, Facebook, Second Life have attracted millions of users and their sites are used widely across the world. A new communication landscape appeared and prevails. Positive and negative communication about brands and companies happens, with or without their permission.

Thereby, the chapter reports on the use of social media marketing by pre-adult people (youngsters between 18 and 24 years old), setting off from a case study of students of different courses at a Portuguese higher education institution. The main objective is to evaluate longitudinally the use of social media by pre-adults and the influence of social media marketing in their brand knowledge, attitude and behaviour. Data were collected through a questionnaire available online collected in two moments in time, spaced by one year (January, 2013 and 2014) and analyzed with descriptive statistical techniques. Based on the pointed outlines, this research explores and analyzes four key issues:

1. What are the types of social media that they are using?;
2. In which contexts are they using each social media type?;
3. What are their opinions about the intentions of social media marketing?; and
4. How does social media marketing influence their brand knowledge, attitude and behaviour?.

The chapter begins with a background around the theme. After that, a state-of-the-art will be presented about the conceptualization of relationship marketing concepts and its intertwining with social media tools. It highlights that the development of a program for implementing and managing a successful customer relationship management system is an essential part of strategic marketing development, but obviously, could be a complex and longer process. The following section focuses on the methodological aspects of the empirical study, including the context of the case study used in the research and techniques for collecting and processing data. After that, the chapter follows with a statistical analysis of the data collected through questionnaire, i.e., the section is devoted to presenting and discussing the main results obtained. Concerns about the target audience, particularly, oriented on pre-adult people are considered. Furthermore, contributions with focus on the individual, like personality, social and cultural status are presented. Finally, the chapter ends with the main conclusions and future research directions.

BACKGROUND

The emerging capabilities of marketing information systems and, in particularly, of the customer relationship management subsystems have been configured as essential tools for translating data to useful information (e.g., Kotler & Keller, 2009; Turban, Aronson, Liang, & Sharda, R., 2007).

Additionally, the higher speed of Internet access and the emergence of the web 2.0 era (and now of web 3.0), giving users the possibility to read and write, in par with the use of mobile equipment, are providing a cheaper and faster form for the organizations to establish contact with customers as well as with potential ones. Social media is part of the phenomenon known as web 2.0, building on its ideological and technological foundations, which allow the creation and exchange of user-generated content (Kaplan & Haenlein, 2010; Peixoto, 2010; Zarrella, 2009; Xi & Doug, 2011; Portmann, 2012).

Kim, Jeong and Lee (2010, p. 216) define social web sites "as those Web sites that make it possible for people to form online communities, and share user-created contents (UCCs)". According to Kim et al. (2010, p. 228) social web sites could be used by Individuals, Businesses and Governmental users. Particularly in businesses, the same authors identify four application:

1. Marketing and customer relationship management;
2. Corporate intranets;
3. External peer networking;
4. Miscellaneous.

This chapter, focusing in the first application identifying by Kim et al. (2010), analyze not only the use by pre-adults of online communities by sharing user-created contents, but also the potential influence of marketing in this context.

There are many social web sites, usually designed as social media, which could be used. Some of those which seem to have more relevance in the context of customer relationship management are online social networks, blogs, podcasts, wikis, among others.

Boyd & Ellison (2008, pp. 211) define online social networks as "web-based services that allow individuals to

1. Construct a public or semi-public profile within a bounded system,
2. Articulate a list of other users with whom they share a connection, and
3. View and traverse their list of connections and those made by others within the system".

We could use such tools in interactions with customers - maybe in some sales, marketing and customer service applications. Nevertheless, these tools have to be used as enablers, not as drivers. Greenberg (2010) refers: blog "is a running account of events or thoughts or ideas that can be authored by one person or sometimes multiple people" (p. 127); podcast "is an audio file that uses RSS (Really Simple Syndication) to distribute the broadcast to subscribers or allow them to download it to computers or portable music devices" (p. 129). Wiki (corporate) "is a wiki (collection of web pages designed to enable anyone who access it to contribute or modify content, using a simplified markup language) used in an organizational context, especially to enhance internal knowledge sharing" (pp. 130, 131).

In the context of customer relationship management (CRM): blogs could be the sites for customers to collaborate with ideas and a way to link and collaborate with business partners and sale channels; podcasts could be powerful learning tools, for example, to explain the use of a feature of a product, could support efforts of marketing focused around of mindshare and leadership, and can also be helpful in the training of employees; corporate wikis can be used for projects management or marketing purposes, enabling collaboration between customers and employees and for consequent innovation; but they can also constitute a good repository for dynamic knowledge base. The use of these tools for CRM purposes means that the involvement of customers is vital to improve the customer commitment, and in consequence increase the rates of acquisition and retention.

Nevertheless, the possibility of it be supported in online collaborative environments, is putting tremendous challenges on organizations and their human resources. It is therefore important that agents involved be able to recognize it, a priori, as a philosophy and a strategy that must be understood and accepted, to be assumed (Greenberg, 2010; Simões & Filipe, 2013). With this goal in mind, social media marketing can contribute significantly to make it real and, above all, successful, as it refers to efforts to create contents that attracts attention and encourages readers to share it with their social networks. In short, social media marketing seeks to engage customers where they naturally spend their time (Evans & McKee, 2010).

According to Greenberg (2010) social CRM is "designed to engage the customer in a collaborative conversation in order to provide mutually beneficial value in a trusted and transparent business environment" (p. 121).

But, the customers are different, belonging to different segments of market. Assuming that, how to involve the customers in this collaboration? What are the types of social media that they are using? What are the contexts in which they use each social media type? What are their opinions about the intentions of social media marketing? How does social media marketing influence their brand knowledge, attitude and behaviour?

Based on the above, social media marketing provides an opportunity for brands to optimize interactions with actual and potential consumers. However, a deep knowledge of the consumer side is required (Egan, 2011; Peppers & Rogers, 2011). An analysis already conducted by consumer segments demonstrates that pre-adults are active users of social networks; additionally, pre-adults are the future target segments of different brands (e.g., Lenhart, Purcell, Smith, & Zickuhr, 2010). Focusing on this age group, this chapter contributes with critical information that might help cast light over recent theories and practices of social media marketing capabilities on consumer behaviour.

THE CHANGING PARADIGM OF RELATIONSHIP MARKETING ON THE WEB

The social media marketing is associated with Social CRM strategies and usually focuses on efforts to create content that attracts attention and encourages readers to share it on their social networking websites (Evans & McKee, 2010; Greenberg 2010). Lawrence (2011) and Woodcock et al. (2011) warn that to develop a good social media strategy, managers must realize that the technologies are now allowing people to be quickly connected, chat, create and collaborate with each other. Therefore, before engaging in social media marketing, companies need to identify what they want and do not want to achieve, and this requires a strategy on how to produce content (Chiang & Hsieh, 2011).

Relationship Marketing

The term relationship marketing was first introduced by Berry in 1983, stating that relationship marketing is to attract, maintain and enhance relationships with customers (Berry, 1995). However, the original conceptual background of this new approach is the contribution that arise from two main lines of research developed by the Nordic School of Services and Industrial Marketing and Purchasing Group (IMP). The emergence of relationship marketing has been interpreted as a paradigm shift required by all, and not restricted to marketing services (Grönroos, 1980) and industrial marketing (Jackson, 1985) where it was first recognized.

In fact, the academic and the professional marketing literature highlights, since the 90s, the concept of relationship marketing (Christopher, Payne & Ballantine, 1994; Grönroos, 1997; Morgan & Hunt, 1994) presenting it as a new paradigm, that focuses on building stable and lasting relationships with their customers, in contrast to the traditional approach oriented to promote transactions (Grönroos, 1997; Gummesson, 1998). An oriented value creation approach, which results in the development of personalized marketing to meet the needs of consumers, is expressed (Sheth & Parvatiyar, 1995; Peterson, 1995).

More recently, Gilaninia, Almani, Pournaserani, & Javad (2011) define relationship marketing as the creation, preservation and strengthening of relationships with customers and other stakeholders. This relationship has implications for marketing, since it must focus on retaining customers through the maintenance and intensification of relations based on the principle of win-win (Agariya & Singh, 2011).

Relationship marketing is also cited as the philosophical foundation of Customer Relationship Management (CRM). Berry (2002, p. 73) defined it as "a philosophy, not just a strategy, a way of thinking about customers, marketing and value creation, not just a set of techniques, tools, and tactics". Buttle (2009) and Payne (2005) uphold that CRM is a strategy supported on technology. Although the concept of CRM has arisen associated with the implementation and put into practice the philosophy of relationship marketing, in some literature these two concepts continue to be used interchangeably. However, considering the dates, we find that the references to the concept of CRM are all recent. Despite the definition of relationship marketing, the definitions given for CRM are far from a consensus. Essentially, it is difficult to say whether it is a strategy, a process, a technology, and some people still refer to it as a philosophy. Nevertheless, Greenberg (2010) clarifies all these ambiguities pointing that CRM is (or should be) all that, a philosophy and a strategy that encompasses a set of processes and that is supported by technology. From his definition of traditional CRM, Greenberg develops a social CRM concept, as: "a philosophy and a business strategy, supported by a technology platform, business rules, processes, and social characteristics, designed to engage the customer in a collaborative conversation in order to provide mutually beneficial value in a trusted and transparent business environment" (p. 34). Along with the management of customer information there should always be present the formation of relationships, whose ultimate goal of quality is the generation and sustainability of confidence. This state is the ultimate result that is expected from the formation of a successful relationship, going through other constructs, such as symmetry, equity, dependence, satisfaction, and commitment (Britton & Rose in Peppers & Rogers (2011)).

Social Media Marketing Supporting Relationship Marketing on the Web

The Internet used to be a static place, but recently it has become more flexible and increasingly its content is user-generated. In a conference brainstorming, Tim O'Reilly and Dale Dougherty noted that the web, far from having crashed after the dot-com collapse in the fall of 2001, was more important than ever, with exciting new applications and sites popping up with surprising regularity (O'Reilly, 2007). The concept of web 2.0 quickly spread worldwide.

Currently, there are numerous definitions of web 2.0; some are broader, others are more generic, but all agree on the fact that the whole structure of the platform is targeted to the user's browsing experience, to sharing and creating knowledge, the user quitting to be a mere receiver of information (Hayes, 2006; O'Reilly, 2007). Moreover, according to O'Reilly (2007): "Web 2.0 is the network as the platform, spanning all connected devices". Hayes (2006) denies that the future is in the web 3.0, real-time collaborative web. However, it is not yet a consensual definition.

Social media is part of the Web 2.0 phenomenon, building on its ideological and technological foundations, which allow the creation and exchange of user-generated content (Kaplan & Haenlein, 2010; Peixoto, 2010; Zarrella, 2009) such as share photos, videos, social bookmarks and create or manage blogs. It has become a platform that is easily available to anyone with Internet access; additionally, it has increased communication for organizations, fostered brand awareness and often improved customer service, and served as a relatively inexpensive platform for organizations to implement marketing plans (p.e. Evans & McKee, 2010; Greenberg, 2010; Wikström &Wigmo, 2010).

Social media includes various types of Internet communications. Mangold & Faulds (2009) identified the following several types: social networking sites (MySpace, Facebook, etc.); creativity works sharing sites (YouTube, Flickr, etc.); user-sponsored blogs (Cnet.com, etc.); collaborative sites (Wikipedia); virtual worlds (Second Life); commercial communities (eBay, Amazon.com, etc.); and business networks (LinkedIn). These new web sites have become increasingly popular with hundreds of millions of users worldwide, and are a new powerful marketing tool. Moreover, with social media, marketing is a two-way communication (Eley & Tilley, 2009).

Social media provides new ways to connect, interact and learn; it allows people with no special knowledge to post and share content with the world instantly; it is a place where customers set the rules and the word-of-mouth makes or breaks the product; it represents a diverse source of online information created, driven and used by consumers intending to inform each other about products, brands, services as well as problems they have encountered. An increasingly important role of social media for business is evident today. It is possible to perform integrated marketing activities faster and in a cheaper way. However, before accepting the social media practice, companies need to know what they want and/or what they do not want to achieve. Therefore, a strategy is needed on how to produce the social media content (Chiang & Hsieh, 2011).

McAlister-Holand (2012) refers that social media marketing (SMM) is very different from marketing on social networks (MSN): SMM requires a specific strategy to social channels and content tailored to those platforms; MSN is simply distributing traditional marketing messages through social media and a way to push out company offerings to anyone who can hear them. This is in line with social CRM strategies.

Lawrence (2011) and Woodcock et al. (2011) warn that, to develop a good social media strategy, the managers should realize that technologies are now allowing people to quickly connect, converse, create, and collaborate with each other. Moreover, it is a consensus that successful organizations in an emerging economy of virtual/online networks and information will be those able to identify, enhance, create, and evolve their knowledge assets. The online social networks could be a good tool to do it. This idea was already sustained by Gerbert et al. (2003) who claimed that to build good relationships with customers, it is necessary to serve each customer according to their preferences, which requires management of customer information.

Additionally, the emerging capabilities of customer relationship management systems enabling both reading as well as writing in online collaborative environments are putting tremendous challenges on organizations and their human resources (Greenberg, 2010; Peppers & Rogers, 2011). It is therefore important that agents involved be able to recognize it, a priori, as a philosophy and a strategy that must be understood and accepted, to be implemented (Buttle, 2009). In a broad sense, social media marketing can contribute significantly to this, as it refers to the process of gaining website traffic or attention through social media sites. Social media marketing programs usually center on efforts to create content that attracts attention and encourages readers to share it with their social networks (Evans & McKee, 2010).

The Pre-Adult People with an Active User Profile of Web

At the beginning of the third millennium, hundreds of millions of Internet users around the world have visited thousands of social web sites (Kim, Jeong & Lee 2010). Social web sites are the latest stages in the development of the Internet.

Actually social media represent 10% of the total time spent on the Internet (Pallis, Zeinalipour & Dikaiakos, 2011). The most widely used are Facebook, MySpace, LinkedIn, and Twitter (Smith & Kidder, 2010). Specifically the Facebook numbers reveal the degree of its rapid growth and an active community: daily active users were 802 million on mean for March 2014, an increase of 21% year-over-year; mobile daily active users were 609 million on mean for March 2014, an increase of 43% year-over-year (Facebook Reports, 2014).

This new trend goes beyond the personal Web pages (Smith & Kidder, 2010). It provides an opportunity for users to present themselves, to connect with their friends and find new friends.

Many scholars have studied the main motives or reasons on use of social network sites: to keep in touch (Joinson, 2008); to communicate with friends (Pempek, Yermolayeva, Yevdokiya & Calvert, 2009); information, friendship and connection (Bonds-Raacke & Raacke, 2010); pastime, affection, fashion, to share problems, sociability, and social information (Quan-Haase & Young, 2010); to relax and entertain, to sharing information, companionship, professional advancement, social interaction and pass time (Smock, Ellison, Lampe & Wohn, 2011); self-expression, media drenching and performance, passing time, information seeking, personal status, relationship maintenance, entertainment (Dogruer, Menevi§ & Eyyam, 2011); relationship maintenance, passing time and entertainment (Special & Li-Barber, 2012); maintaining long-distance friendships (Tosun, 2012); information sharing, freedom of communication, free flow of information, control of information, sense of equality and requirement for information and entertainment (Moradabadi, Gharehshiran & Amrai, 2012); social connection, social network surfing, wasting time and using applications (Giannakos, Chorianopoulos, Giotopoulos, & Vlamos, 2013); belonging, hedonism, self-esteem, and reciprocity (Pai & Arnott, 2012).

Nowadays, millions of youngsters and pre-adults are daily connected in social media sharing sites, wikis, blogs, and social networks, among others. Research findings suggest that more than 70% of Internet users worldwide, aged over 15 years, are members of at least one social network website, and also that mobile is the perfect accelerator for social media usage (Belleghem et al., 2012; Lenhart et al., 2010).

Therefore, it is important to note that there is a significant difference between younger and older adult behavior: younger users are more likely to use Facebook for news purposes (Glynn, Huge & Hoffman, 2012) and have a larger number of friends compared to older users and their friends are in their own age range (age ± 2 years) (Pfeil, Arjan, & Zaphiris, 2009). Further, younger and older adult have different levels of participation in the online platforms of web 2.0 services and require different levels of attention from marketers.

Li & Bernoff (2008) identify six user profiles: (1) creators - create publications on a blog/website, upload personal videos and music, and write articles and stories; (2) critics - comment on blogs and forums, publish and contribute to wikis and articles; (3) collectors - use RSS feeds, adding photos and links to websites; (4) joiners - conserve his profile/account; (5) spectators - feature a passive posture, taking behaviours such as reading blogs and comments, viewing videos and photos, and listening to podcasts; and (6) inactive - do not perform any of the activities described above. Of the six profiles identified, the creators stand out as the most appealing to marketers, because they easily tend to turn into opinion leaders. Therefore, it is necessary to optimize the efforts of social media marketing in this consumer profile.

The results of a study developed in Europe context by Gray & Jennings (2008) highlighted that young people are online every day, and are more likely to visit sharing and social network sites or use instant messaging. One in four youngsters are bloggers and daily users of social networking, and engagement with social media is high amongst young people (nearly half are creators and nearly half are critics), while the other users have adopted a more passive profile (spectators).

Particularly, in Portugal, a study by Bareme Marktest (2012) reported that 73.4% of households had at least one computer in use; 62.3% of residents aged 15 and over used the Internet (with higher penetration among men and people between 18 and 24 years); and 83.8% of residents accessing the Internet from their homes had accessed sites related to social networks (people between 15 to 24 years showed higher affinity).

Solutions and Recommendations

Consumers around the world are using social media. They search for information and learn about consumers' experiences through social network sites. These users are customers or potential customers for the companies, but also they are good or bad promoters.

If traditionally, consumers had adopted a more secluded profile on the Internet (e.g., view content or buy products and services), currently consumers are using social media to create, modify, share and discuss content with other users on the Internet. This active sharing can significantly affect a company's reputation, sales, and even survival (Kietzmann, Hermkens, McCarthy, & Silvestre, 2011). According to Kim & Ko (2012) social media can have a dramatic impact on a brand's reputation.

Some managers continue to avoid and ignore social media because they do not understand what they are and how to interact with them and do not yet have any idea of the impact that social media can give their organizations.

Moreover, social network sites are a good medium for managers to capture their target audience, because they can customize their marketing programs according to the setting, they can create brand communities, and they can communicate with their customers very effectively. Since this is a two way communication, marketers can recognize real consumer needs in a spontaneous way which allows them to better respond to consumer needs, and increment their level of satisfaction and loyalty to the brand.

In the context of customer relationship management, social media marketing provides an opportunity for brands to optimize interactions with actual and potential consumers. As explained earlier, analysis already conducted by consumer segments demonstrates that pre-adults are active users of social networks. However, there is a lack of research on the Portuguese context about the types of social media used by pre-adults, the contexts in which they use each social media type; the opinions about the intentions of social media marketing and the influences of social media marketing on their brand knowledge, attitude and behavior. This analysis can enable more efficient involvement of the customers in the collaboration with the marketers.

METHODOLOGY

In order to meet the research objectives previously explained, in this study it was decided to resort to quantitative research, through the case study method, whose empirical nature enables them to be achieved. It is to observe and analyze the behaviors and opinions (these being subjective in nature) of the people interviewed during the research. According to Ferreira & Serra (2009), a case study refers to stories or anecdotes of situations occurring in the real world, whether for an individual, group of individuals, company, group of companies, industry or country.

So is a research method that shows suitable when the subject under study is a unit to be analyzed deeply. It presents a detailed examination of an environment, a simple subject or a particular situation (Godoy, 1995). The fundamental purpose of the case study is to analyze intensively a given social unit, which can be, for example, a company, a brand, a group of people. It fits so well in this study because it analyzes and tries to get better understanding about the use of social media marketing by pre-adults, young pre-college adults. The case study also revealed suitable for an aspect of a problem to be studied in depth within a limited period of time (Moresi, 2003).

This study is confined to pre-adult people, with ages between 18 and 24 years, who attend courses at the Higher Institute of Accounting and Administration of the University of Aveiro (ISCA-UA). Data were collected through a questionnaire available online, and edited using the LimeSurvey software. The questionnaire circulated via institutional mail to all students with active enrollment. The process was repeated, in two consecutive years: 2013 and 2014. The questionnaires were available between January and March of each year, having reinforced the request at the beginning of each month for the periods indicated. Age was controlled through a targeted question in the questionnaire itself. Data were analyzed using descriptive statistical techniques using the SPSS 21.0 software.

The universe of around 600 pre-adults was encouraged to respond to the questionnaires anonymously. The same titled, "social media marketing and university students", was organized in four parts: (1) characterizing the use of the Internet, (2) characterization of the use of social media, (3) characterization of perception compared to programs social media marketing, and (4) characterization of pre-adult university students. Each of the four parts of the questionnaire consisted of six to eight closed questions. For most of the questions, the answers were pre-oriented in a Likert scale with 5 points. Thus, respondents receive a number of classifications or dimensions of attitude, for which were identified the intensity of agreement using a scale of evaluation points completely defined (e.g., 1- strongly disagree to 5 - strongly agree).

RESULTS

Following the methodology previously defined, we obtained a total of 139 valid answers in the first phase, and 128 in the second phase. Thus, we had a representation of the universe around 22-23%.

The pre-adult university students who responded to the questionnaire were in major number women, representing around 75% of respondents (Table 1).

In the light of the answers given, the households of the students are composed mainly by 3 or 4 elements, representing between 74,1% and 78,1% of them. In both the phases the mode is 4, which

Table 1. Frequency of respondents by gender

Phase	Gender		Total
	Female	Male	
1st	94 (67,6%)	45 (32,4%)	139
2nd	97 (75,8%)	31 (24,2%)	128

demonstrates there are more families with 4 elements. In addition, in both the phases, and regarding the enrollment status, more than 75% of pre-adults are students in full time. Only approximately one quarter refers to employed students.

Concerning the family residence, the results indicate that between 60,1% and 68,8% of the respondents live in the district of the university (Aveiro). This result is not surprising, since in recent years the tendency is for the young to look up a course in a university near their area of residence.

The Social Media Usage and Contexts

Although the study is mainly focused on the use of social media, we started by asking the students some questions about the kind of devices and their frequency of Internet access. This information will help us to better understand the results of the use of social media and its receptivity with respect to social media marketing.

With regard to the number of times and time spent on the Internet, the results confirm that most pre-adults (80.6% and 81.3%, in first and second phases, respectively) access the Internet daily, several times a day, and also in both phases, more than 85% of the respondents spend between 1 to over 6 hours a day surfing (see Table 2). Note, however, that the majority spent between 1 and 3 hours surfing, which seems a reasonable value. Despite that, the results appear to prove that nowadays Internet access occupies an important part of the days of our pre-adult university students.

Concerning the devices that pre-adults have and which of those they typically use to access the Internet, the answers show that almost all students have a laptop (99.3% and 98.4%, in the first and second phase, respectively) and preferably use this device to surf the Internet (96.4% and 97.7%). In second order appears the mobile phone (77.0% and 89.8%). In the second phase, more pre-adults confirm to have this device and the same phenomenon is verified to the use of that to access the Internet (despite only 40.3% saying they use it to access the Internet in the first phase of the study, one year after, this value turned higher to 65.6%). Nevertheless, this clearly confirms the tendency to an increase of users (particularly, pre-adult university students) using mobile devices to access the Internet. We highlight

Table 2. Frequency of respondents relative to their Internet access

How Often Do You Access the Internet? vs. What Time Do You Spend, on Average, Using the INTERNET?	Occasionally		Weekly (1-6 Days a Week)		Daily (Once a Day)		Daily (Several Times a Day)		Total	
	Phase									
	1st	2nd	1st	2nd	1st	2nd	1st	2nd	1st	2nd
[6, …] hours a day	0	0	0	0	0	1	25	24	18.0%	19.5%
[3, …, 6] hours a day	0	0	0	0	2	1	39	41	29.5%	32.8%
[1, …, 3] hours a day	0	0	0	1	14	12	44	32	41.7%	35.2%
[…, 1] hour a day	1	0	0	0	2	2	2	5	3.6%	5.45%
[2, …, 6] hours a week	0	1	2	3	2	1	1	2	3.6%	5.45%
[…, 2] hours a week	1	0	1	0	2	2	1	0	3.6%	1.6%
Total	1.4%	0.8%	2.2%	3.1%	15.8%	14.8%	80.6%	81.3%	139	128

the fact that a considerable number of respondents signed to having game consoles and portable music players, but very few claimed to use those to access the Internet (see Table 3). Moreover, in this case, the tendency was to a decrease on the consecutive years of the study.

Relatively to access to the Internet and considering the results presented earlier about the use of small mobile devices such as mobile phones, tablets, etc. to use Internet services, we wanted to know more from the pre-adults. So, based on a scale of 1 (“I strongly disagree”) to 5 (“I strongly agree”), we realized that many strongly agree that the use of these devices has substantial benefits (mean 4 and mode 5). The early perception is reinforced by the fact that the respondents agreed that the advantage of the portability feature overcomes any limitations related to the small size (mean and mode 3). Nevertheless, the pre-adults consider that most of the services that interest them do not yet provide appropriate applications for small mobile devices. In general, the respondents disagree with the opinion “I don’t feel the need to use them and have difficulty in using them for the purpose of Internet access”. Thus, small devices are viewed as an asset for their lives, and this perception was obtained in both phases of the study.

Furthermore, we wanted to know which the services the pre-adults use when they access the Internet. Using the scale from 1 (“I do not use”) to 5 (“I use very often”), the most signed issues, representing an mean between 4.25 and 4.72 and a mode of 5, were: display and use email; study or do research for the study; obtain information of different nature; and use social media (e.g. social networks, sharing sites, blogs, wikis, virtual worlds, etc.). Secondly: chat online by text or voice; listen to music or some radio station; and download music files, videos, games, etc., representing an mean between 3.62 and 3.98 and also a mode of 5 which indicates that those services were signed as used very often. The other sentences were classified in lower levels, showing that actions like reading a newspaper, watching TV, playing video games, purchasing new or used products (with mean around 2 and mode of 1) are the least taken (see Table 4).

Table 3. Frequency of respondents about devices that have and use to access to the Internet

Device	What Devices Do You Have?		What Devices Do You Typically Use to Access the Internet?	
	Phase			
	1st	2nd	1st	2nd
Personal computer	48 (34.5%)	40 (31.3%)	30 (21.6%)	25 (19.5%)
Laptop	138 (99.3%)	126 (98.4%)	134 (96.4%)	125 (97.7%)
Tablet	16 (11.5%)	33 (25.8%)	12 (8.6%)	26 (20.3%)
Mobile	107 (77.0%)	115 (89.8%)	56 (40.3%)	84 (65.6%)
Game console (p. e. PlayStation or Wii)	35 (25.2%)	23 (18.0%)	8 (5.8%)	2 (1.6%)
Handheld game console (p. e. PSP)	15 (10.8%)	11 (8.6%)	5 (3.6%)	1 (0.8%)
Portable music player	44 (31.7%)	32 (25.0%)	2 (1.4%)	0 (0.0%)

Table 4. Mean (and mode) use of the Internet for some purposes by respondents

How Often Do You Use the Internet for Each of the Following Purposes?	Mean (Mode)	
	1st	2nd
To display and use e-mail.	4.70 (5)	4.72 (5)
To study or do research for the study.	4.46 (5)	4.41 (5)
To obtain information of different nature.	4.28 (5)	4.30 (5)
To use social media (e.g. social networks, sharing sites, blogs, wikis, virtual worlds, etc.).	4.29 (5)	4.25 (5)
To chat online by text or voice.	3.65 (5)	3.98 (5)
To listen to some music or radio station.	3.62 (5)	3.89 (5)
To download music files, videos, games, etc.	3.78 (5)	3.63 (5)
To search in brand websites for information about new products, prices, etc.	3.13 (3)	3.17 (3)
To read newspapers.	3.18 (3)	3.01 (2)
To watch TV.	2.38 (1)	2.30 (2)
To play video games.	2.11 (1)	2.28 (1)
To purchase new products (e.g. books, music, clothes, etc.).	2.06 (1)	1.95 (1)
To purchase/sale used products (e.g. books, music, clothes, etc.).	1.57 (1)	1.66 (1)

In the context of this study, it's worth highlighting the fact that searching in brand websites appears slightly below the middle of the table (with mean and mode around 3), although the purchase of products must be less practiced between the pre-adults students. Therefore, the use of social media (e.g. social networks, sharing sites, blogs, wikis, virtual worlds, etc.) appears well classified, with the pre-adults pointing to use them very often. Furthermore, there are no relevant differences to enhance in the different stages of the study, in two consecutive years.

Centered now on social media activities performed the viewing of social network websites (e.g. Facebook, Twitter, LinkedIn, etc.) is definitely the most frequently activity performed (mean between 4.29 and 4.45, respectively, in 1st and 2nd phases, and with mode of 5 in both cases). Viewing photos or shared videos (e.g., YouTube, SlideShare, etc.) is another often performed activity (mean of 3.71 and 3.55, and mode of 5 and 4, respectively, in 1st and 2nd phases). Posting on social network websites or blogs is an activity moderately executed by the respondents (mean of 2.90 and 3.02 in consequent's years). The other activities such as to create and manage blogs or social network pages; to participate in discussion forums or communities; to share something created (e.g. YouTube, Flickr, etc.); to visit virtual worlds (e.g. Second Life, etc.); or to collaborate on wikis are less practiced. One more time, a Likert scale of 5 points was used, from 1 ("I do not") to 5 ("I do very often").

So, concerning profile in social network websites, Figure 1 shows that Facebook is definitely the website with more frequency of profiles by the respondents. In consecutive orders appear Google+, LinkedIn, Twitter, and Pinterest. In all these cases, the tendency in successive phases of the study was towards the growth of the number of users with defined profile. Websites Hi5 and Myspace, despite presenting relevant results in the first phase, showed a decreasing tendency. Orkut confirms to be a website with much smaller adhesion.

About the social network website with more profiles by the respondents, and when inquired about the frequency of performing activities on this website, more than 85% in both phases claimed to performing

Figure 1. Frequency of respondents that have a profile in social network websites

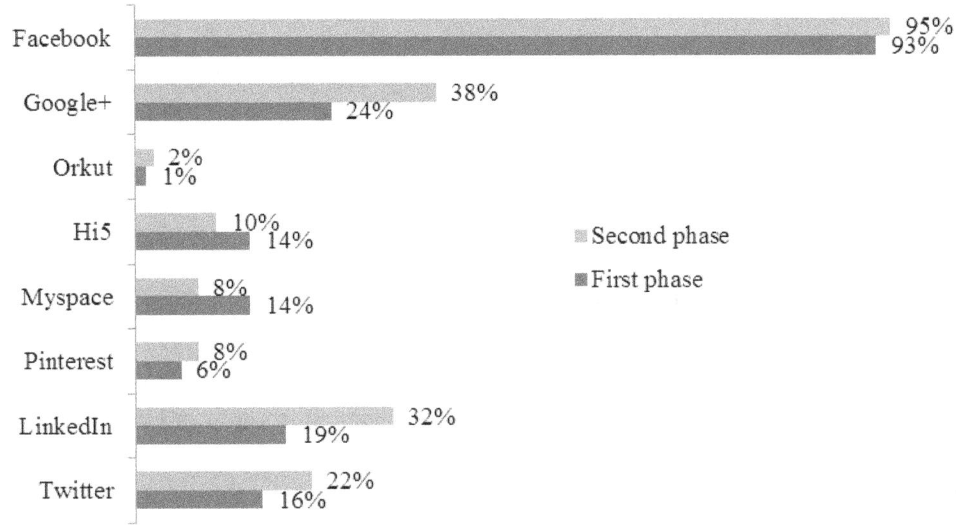

them from regularly to very often, still having more than 60% affirmed to performing them very often. A Likert scale of 5 points was used, from 1 ("Very rarely") to 5 ("Very often").With regards to the activities practiced, the results evidence that sending private messages to friends is the most performed activity (see Table 5). In second order appear, and with more evidence in the 2nd phase (higher mean value and mode of 5): following, without posting, the news in the pages of brands that they like. Highlight this fact, because in our sense this seems to confirm, one more time, the tendency of respondents to have interest in following brands through social networks websites. Very close it was refereed: following, without posting, pages of friends; and posting and sharing of news to friends' pages. Opposite to more interest demonstrated by brand pages, in last places appear posting to pages of brands that they like and sending private messages to pages of brands with products that they like. So, although, the respondents are following more and more social network websites of brands, they opt to doing this passively, without posting or sending messages. Again, a Likert scale of 5 points, from 1 ("Very rarely") to 5 ("Very often"), was used.

Table 5. Mean (and mode) of activities practiced on the social network website Facebook by respondents

What Is Your Degree of Agreement with Each Statement in Relation to the Activities that You Normally Practice on the Social Networking Website Facebook?	Mean (Mode)	
	1st	2nd
I send private messages to my friends.	3.74 (4)	4.07 (5)
I follow, without posting, the news in pages of brands that I like.	3.24 (3)	3,54 (5)
I follow, without posting, the pages of my friends.	3.32 (3)	3,38 (3)
I post and share news to the pages of my friends.	3.02 (3)	2.79 (3)
I post to pages of brands that I like.	2.38 (1)	2.04 (1)
I send private messages to the pages of brands with products that I like.	1.54 (1)	1.53 (1)

The results presented early are one more time reinforced by Figure 2, which displays that the answers of respondents about the activities practiced on Facebook, reveal an increasing tendency for pre-adults to adhere to be fans of brands pages.

Finally, and relatively to Internet and social media usage and contexts, we can conclude that essentially pre-adults demonstrate more and more appeal to use mobile devices to access the Internet. Also, they appear to be more interested in following the news of their preferred brands, by means of social network website Facebook. Although yet they don't use frequently to put postings or to send messages to brand websites administration, they seems to be attentive.

Social Media Marketing Perceptions

To meet the goals we set ourselves, we also inquired pre-adults' opinions regarding the intentions of social media marketing, and how social media marketing influences their brand knowledge, attitude and behaviour. The respondents were initially inquired about their situation towards brand pages on social networking websites. The answer analysis shows that the majority is fan of some or several brands, although some do not follow them continuously, or follow only a few brands they have a bigger interest in (84.2% and 85.2%, respectively, in the first and second phases of the study). Highlight the fact that 5% and 7%, in respective phases, mentioned that they follow continuously several brands. These results enhance the increasing tendency of interest by pre-adults in following the news from the brands through social networks websites. The main motivations pointed by respondents for becoming fans of a brand are presented in Figure 3.

Looking at the most voted sentences (in this question it was possible to sign several sentences), we can determine that in most cases one pre-adult becomes fan of a brand by his/her own initiative, because he/she is an admirer or customer of the brand. The following three most voted motivations, but very distant of the former, were "attracted by the possibility of obtaining a prize or promotional discount", "tip of an online friend" and "a link that I meet spontaneously while I surf the Internet".

Figure 2. Frequency of respondents that practice each activity on the social network website Facebook

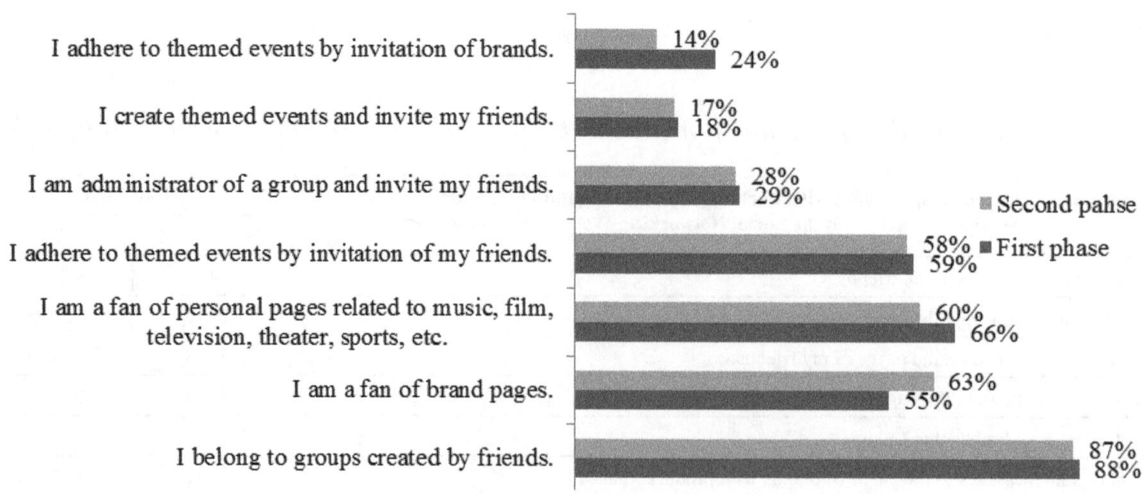

Figure 3. Frequency of respondents about main motivations for becoming fans of a brand on social network website

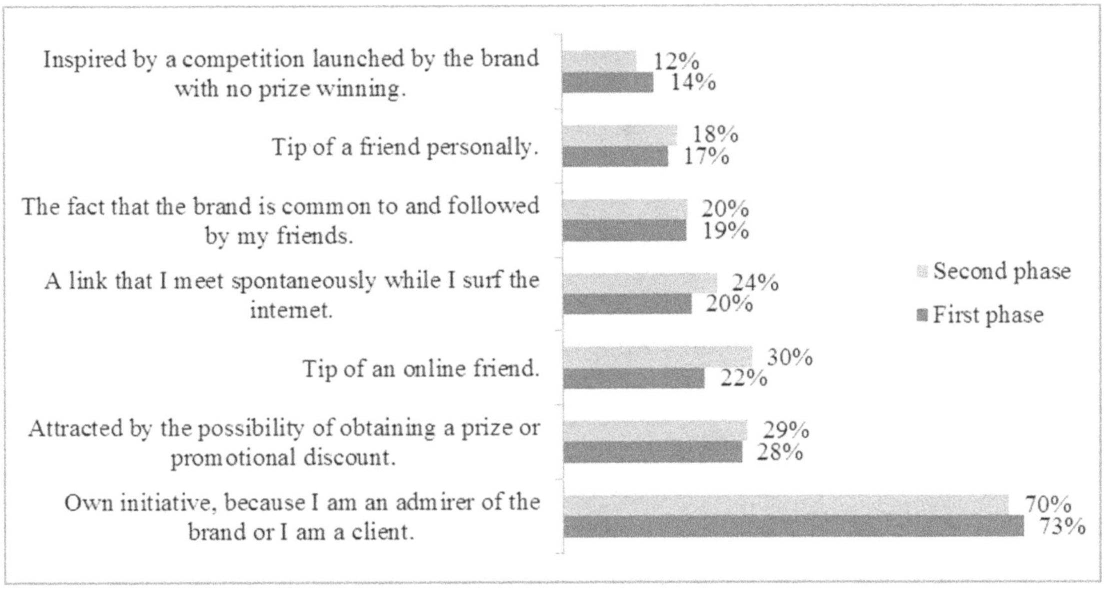

Additionally, the students were inquired about their opinion on the influence of social media marketing on brand awareness and customer retention. Having three alternatives, the answers are divided into "I think that it has advantages, but it must be applied following a carefully delineated marketing plan" (53.3% and 50.8%, respectively in consecutive phases) and "I think that it has many advantages, because people love to share what they do, and thus they can more easily induce the desire for a product or brand on other people" (46.0% and 49.2%). Only one person considered "I don't see any advantage because if anything goes wrong, the news spreads very quickly and that can be disastrous for the brand", in the first phase. In the second phase, this motivation wasn't pointed by anyone. Therefore, almost all respondents see advantages on the use, by business organizations, of social media marketing to brand awareness and customer retention, despite some of them enhancing the importance of adequately planning the strategy to implement.

The results exposed above are corroborated by the answers about on the use of social networking websites and other social media for dissemination and promotion of brands and products. Once again, almost all respondents consider this useful (92.8% and 97.6%, in consecutive phases), although some of them indicate that they sometimes feel that their privacy is invaded as well (46.0% and 39.8%). A minority (7.2% and 2.3%) feel very concerned, because they cannot even imagine that what they think and do on the Internet can be used to "hold" them to a brand.

Finally, the respondents were inquired about their level of interest, by subject, in brands on the Internet (see Figure 4). Once again, a scale of 5 points, from 1 ("None") to 5 ("Very high") was used. The analysis shows that the interests are higher in music (with mode 5), followed by fashion, reading, sport and travelling (with mode 4). Curiously, it's important to verify that the results, in terms of score, are very similar between the consecutive phases. Nevertheless, and as shown in Figure 4, a significant increasing tendency of interest of pre-adults in brands on the Internet in general. The means are all higher, except in relation to toys, games, and banking and business, but with a minimum difference.

Figure 4. Level of interest of respondents, by subjects, in brands on the Internet

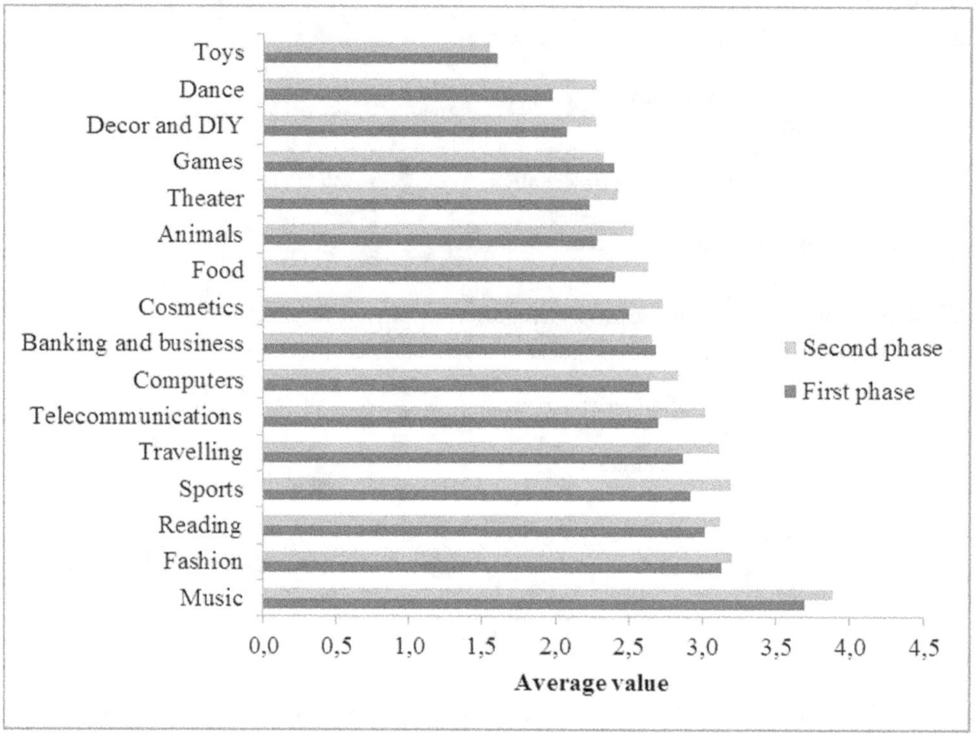

Solutions and Recommendations

Social media marketing plays a major role in modern marketing environment. Companies can communicate with their target audience very effectively through social media. Especially this is a good opportunity for international companies. However, marketers need more information about the use of consumers of social network sites in order to develop a better social media strategy.

Findings of this study provide information that the penetration rate of Facebook use is 93%, in January 2013, e 95%, in January 2014. If marketer is interested in using Facebook as a marketing tool, he should be aware of the motivations that drive Facebook use, and the perception of users about social media marketing.

Relatively to activities practice on the Facebook, sending private messages to friends is the most performed activity, closely followed by "following, without posting, the news to the pages of brands that they like". This confirms an increasing tendency towards interest in brands pages through social networks websites. Also very close appear "following, without posting, the pages of friends" and "posting and sharing of news to the pages of friends". Opposite to more interest demonstrated in brand pages, in last places appear posting to pages of brands that they like and sending private messages to pages of brands with products that they like. So, although, the pre-adults are following more and more the social network websites of brands, they opt to doing this passively, without posting or sending messages.

The opinions of pre-adults regarding the intentions of social media marketing and their situation towards brand pages on social networking websites, demonstrate that the majority is fan of some or several brands, although some do not follow them continuously, or follow only a few brands that have bigger interest. These results enhance nevertheless an increasing tendency of interest by pre-adults on following the news from the brands through social networks websites. In most cases one pre-adult becomes fan of a brand by her/his own initiative, because of being admirer or customer of the brands.

On respect of the influence of social media marketing on brand awareness and customer retention, opinions divide into "I think that it has advantages, but must be applied following a marketing plan carefully delineated" and "I think that it has many advantages, because people love to share what they do, and thus can more easily induce the desire for a product or brand on other people". Beyond that, almost all see advantages on the use, by the business organizations, of social media marketing to brand awareness and customer retention, despite some of them enhancing the importance of adequately planning the strategy to implement. They also enhance the importance of using social network websites and other social media for dissemination and promotion of brands and products. Nevertheless, some feel apprehension due to the invasion of their privacy.

In short, the main results show that pre-adults are fans of several brands, although they do not follow them continuously, or follow only a few of those in which they are more interested. They also show that the pre-adults consider the use of social media for dissemination and promotion of brands and useful products; although some have indicated that sometimes they feel that their privacy is invaded.

FUTURE RESEARCH DIRECTIONS

The work described above contributes to an on-going dialogue about the importance of social network sites, both for practitioners and researchers. In our opinion, many questions of this topic remain unexplored. Such questions will require large-scale quantitative and qualitative research. Methodologically, researchers' ability to make causal claims is limited by a lack of experimental and longitudinal studies. Although the situation is rapidly changing, scholars still have a limited understanding of who is and who is not using these sites, why, and for what purposes, especially outside the U.S.

Specifically, it is suggested to replicate the investigation of a representative sample of pre-adult, Portuguese or other nationality, and further study on the impacts of the actions of social media marketing in behavior towards brands. For example, relate the fact that pre-adults being fan of a brand to their level of satisfaction and loyalty to the brand.

The fields of relationship marketing and customer relationship management have matured over the past decade. We predict a continued evolution in these fields with the contribution of the social media sites, and the characteristics of the new generation of customers steeped on the new technologies.

Different organizational forms, new tools, newly available data and new technologies, and so forth, will be integrated into relationship marketing ideas. We hope that this chapter and the other papers in this topic provide the catalyst for other researchers to continue to move the theory and practice forward in this evolutionary process.

CONCLUSION

The results of the study show that the pre-adults access the Internet daily, several times a day, spending in general between 1 to over 6 hours a day surfing. This appears to prove that nowadays the Internet access occupies an important part of the days of our pre-adult university students. The study reveals a tendency to more and more use of small mobile devices (despite greater use of laptop, more pre-adults are using tablets and mobile phones) to access the web services. To note that, in second the phase, more pre-adults confirm to have this device and the same phenomenon is verified to the use of that for access to the Internet. Nevertheless, this clearly confirms the tendency to an increase of users (particularly, pre-adults university students) using small mobile devices to access the Internet. Most strongly agree that the use of these devices has substantial benefits, enhanced that the advantage of the portability feature overcomes any limitations related to the small size.

Concerning the web services used, the email is the most used; closed followed by study or research for the study; obtain information of different nature; and use social media (e.g. social networks, sharing sites, blogs, wikis, virtual worlds, etc.). Services like reading a newspaper, watching TV, playing video games, purchasing new or used products are the least used. Highlight the fact of although the purchase of products must be less practiced between the pre-adults, to search in brand websites appears well quoted.

With regard on social media activities performed, the view of social network websites (e.g. Facebook, Twitter, LinkedIn, etc.) is definitely the most frequently performed activity. This is followed by to viewing photos or shared videos (e.g., YouTube, SlideShare, etc.), posting to social network websites or blogs, creating and managing blogs or social network pages, participating in discussion forums or communities, sharing something created (e.g. YouTube, Flickr, etc.); visiting virtual worlds (e.g. Second Life, etc.); or collaborating on wikis are less practiced.

Relatively to having a profile on social network websites, Facebook is definitely the website with more frequency of profiles. In consecutive orders, but with significantly lowers rates, appear Google+, LinkedIn, Twitter, and Pinterest. In all these cases, the tendency in successive phases of the study was to towards the growth of the number of users with defined profile. With regards to the activities performed by our pre-adults on Facebook, the results show that sending private messages to friends is the most frequently performed activity, followed by: following without posting to pages of friends; following without posting news pages from brands they like; and posting and sharing news pages of friends. Last appear: posting to brand pages and sending private messages to pages of brands they like. Essentially, pre-adults manage their profiles belonging to groups created by friends; being fans of personal pages related to music, movies, television, sports, etc..; adhering to themed events; and being fan of pages of brands. A minority practice management groups or creating themed event activities. According to the six user profiles identified by Bernoff (2008) referred to in the literature review, these results have revealed that most pre-adults assume a profile of "critical" and "collector".

The results also show that the majority of pre-adults are fans of some or several brands, although they do not follow them continuously, or just follow the few which have more interest. In most cases, a pre-adult becomes a fan of a brand on its own initiative, because she/he is a fan or a customer's brand. The second motivation was the attraction by the possibility of obtaining a premium or promotional discount and the third motivation was the tip of an online friend (both with much lower values).

On the influence of social media marketing on brand recognition and customer retention, nearly all have advantages over its use by business organizations to brand awareness and customer retention. Some emphasize however the importance of proper strategic planning before implementation.

In addition, most respondents consider useful the use of social networks and other social media to publicize and promote brand and product websites, although some refer to feeling some fear for their privacy.

Consumers around the world are using social media. They search for information and learn about consumers' experiences through social network sites. As explained earlier, these users are customers or potential customers for the companies, but they can also be good or bad promoters. Companies can communicate with their target audience very effectively through social media. Especially this is a good opportunity for international companies. Moreover, social network sites are a good medium for managers to capture their target audience, because they can customize their marketing programs according to the setting, they can create brand communities and they can communicate with their customers very effectively. Since this is a two-way communication, marketers can recognize real consumer needs in a spontaneous way which allows them to better respond to consumer needs, and increment their level of satisfaction and loyalty to the brand. However, marketers need more information about the use of consumers of social network sites in order to develop better social media strategy.

As evidenced in the literature review, the social media marketing plays a major role in modern marketing environment and focuses on creating content that attracts attention and encourages readers to share it on their social networking websites.

Managers should realize that the technologies enable people to be quickly connected, chat, create and collaborate with each other and can contribute for the brand, positively or inversely negatively, and generate great challenges to organizations. Thus, organizations must be aware of the challenge that confront their brand today and prepared to develop a good social media strategy. Cumulatively, to build a good relationship with customers it is necessary for organizations to meet each client according to her/his preferences and recognize the relationship marketing as a philosophy that must be understood and accepted to be properly implemented.

Thus, this study provides some clues to marketing managers to recognize the importance and potential impact of the media associated with an appropriate marketing approach to relationship marketing.

REFERENCES

Agariya, A., & Singh, D. (2011). What really defines relationship marketing? A review of definitions and general and sector-specific defining constructs. *Journal of Relationship Marketing*, *10*(4), 203–237. doi:10.1080/15332667.2011.624905

Belleghem, S., Thijs, D., & De Ruyck, T. (2012). Social media around the word 2012. Retrieved from http://www.slideshare.net/InSitesConsulting/social-media-around-the-world-2012-by-insites-consulting

Berry, L. (1983). Relationship Marketing. In L. Berry (2002). Relationship marketing of services - Growing interest, emerging perspectives. *Academy of Marketing Science Journal*, *23*(4), 236–245. PMID:6410122

Berry, L. (2002). Relationship marketing of services: Perspectives from 1983 and 2000. *Journal of Relationship Marketing*, *1*(1), 59–77. doi:10.1300/J366v01n01_05

Bonds-Raacke, J., & Raacke, J. (2010). MySpace and Facebook: Identifying Dimensions of Uses and Gratifications for Friend Networking Site. *Individual Differences Research*, *8*(1), 27–33.

Boyd, D. M., & Ellison, N. B. (2007). Social network sites: Definition, history, and scholarship. *Journal of Computer-Mediated Communication*, *13*(1), 210–230. doi:10.1111/j.1083-6101.2007.00393.x

Buttle, F. (2009). *Customer Relationship Management* (2nd ed.). Burlinton, USA: Butterworth-Heinemann, Ltd.

Chiang, I., & Hsieh, C. (2011). Exploring the impacts of blog marketing on consumers. *International Journal (Toronto, Ont.)*, *39*(9), 1245–1250.

Cristopher, M., Payne, A., & Ballantine, D. (1994). *Relationship marketing* (2nd ed.). Burlinton, USA: Butterworth-Heinemann, Ltd.

Davenport, T. H., Harris, J. G., & Kohli, A. K. (2001). How do they know their customers so well? *MIT Sloan Management Review*, *42*(2), 63–73.

Dogruer, N., Menevi, I., & Eyyam, R. (2011). What is the motivation for using Facebook? *Procedia: Social and Behavioral Sciences*, *15*, 2642–2646. doi:10.1016/j.sbspro.2011.04.162

Egan, J. (2011). *Relationship marketing* (4th ed.). Harlow: Pearson Educational Limited.

Eley, B., & Tilley, S. (2009). *Online marketing inside out*. Melbourne: SitePoint.

Evans, D., & Mckee, J. (2010). *Social media marketing: The next generation of business engagement*. Indianapolis, Indiana: John Wiley& Sons, Inc.

Facebook Reports First Quarter 2014 Results (2014). Retrieved from http://investor.fb.com/releasedetail.cfm?ReleaseID=842071

Ferreira, M., & Serra, F. (2009). *Casos de estudo: usar, escrever e estudar*. Lisboa: Lidel - Edições Técnicas, Lda.

Giannakos, M., Chorianopoulos, K., Giotopoulos, K., & Vlamos, P. (2013). Using Facebook out of habit. *Behaviour & Information Technology*, *32*(6), 594–602. doi:10.1080/0144929X.2012.659218

Gilaninia, S., Almani, A., Pournaserani, A., & Javad, S. (2011). Relationship Marketing: A New Approach to Marketing in the Third Millennium. *Australian Journal of Basic and Applied Sciences*, *5*(5), 787–799.

Glynn, C., Huge, M., & Hoffman, L. (2012). All the news that's fit to post: A profile of news use on social networking sites. *Computers in Human Behavior*, *28*(1), 113–119. doi:10.1016/j.chb.2011.08.017

Godoy, A. S. (1995). Introdução à pesquisa qualitativa e suas possibilidades. *Revista de Administração de Empresas*, 35, 20-29.

Gray, S., & Jennings, R. (2008). How are young people using social media? Retrieved from http://www.slideshare.net/diusgovuk/how-are-young-people-using-social-media-presentation

Greenberg, P. (2010). *CRM at the speed of light: social CRM strategies, tools, and techniques for engaging your customers* (4th ed.). USA: The McGraw-Hill Companies.

Grönroos, C. (1980). Designing a long range marketing strategy for services. *Long Range Planning*, *13*(2), 36–42. doi:10.1016/0024-6301(80)90030-8

Grönroos, C. (1996). Relationship marketing: Strategic and tactical implications. *Management Decision*, *34*(3), 5–14. doi:10.1108/00251749610113613

Gummesson, E. (1998). Implementation requires a relationship marketing paradigm. *Academy of Marketing Science. Journal*, *26*(3), 242–249. doi:10.1177/0092070398263006

Jackson, B. (1985). Building customer relationships that last: How close can industrial markets get to their customers - and for how long? *Harvard Business Review*, *63*, 120–128.

Joinson, A. (2008). *Looking at, looking up or keeping up with people? Motives and uses of Facebook*. Florence, Italy: CHI.

Kaplan, A., & Haenlein, M. (2010). Users of the world, unite! The challenges and opportunities of social media. *Business Horizons*, *53*(1), 59–68. doi:10.1016/j.bushor.2009.09.003

Kietzmann, J. H., Hermkens, K., Mccarthy, I. P., & Silvestre, B. S. (2011). Social media? Get serious! Understanding the functional building blocks of social media. *Business Horizons*, *54*(3), 241–251. doi:10.1016/j.bushor.2011.01.005

Kim, A., & Ko, E. (2012). Do social media marketing activities enhance customer equity? An empirical study of luxury fashion brand. *Journal of Business Research*, *65*(10), 1480–1486. doi:10.1016/j.jbusres.2011.10.014

Kim, W., Jeong, O., & Lee, S. (2010). On social Web sites. *Information Systems*, *35*(2), 215–236. doi:10.1016/j.is.2009.08.003

Kumar, V., & Reinartz, W. (2012). *Customer relationship management: concept, strategy, and tools* (2nd ed.). New York, NY: Springer. doi:10.1007/978-3-642-20110-3

Lawrence, A. (2011). Is SCRM really a good social media strategy? *Journal of Database Marketing & Customer Strategy Management*, *18*(3), 149–153. doi:10.1057/dbm.2011.22

Lenhart, A., Purcell, K., Smith, A., & Zickuhr, K. (2010). *Social media & mobile Internet use among teens and young adults*. Washington, DC: Pew Research Center.

Li, C., & Bernoff, J. (2008). *Groundswell: winning in the world transformed by social technologies. Boston*. Massachusetts: Harvard Business Press.

Mangold, W. G., & Faulds, D. J. (2009). Social media: The new hybrid element of the promotion mix. *Business Horizons*, *52*(4), 357–365. doi:10.1016/j.bushor.2009.03.002

Marktest Bareme. (n. d.). Retrieved from http://www.marktest.com/wap/a/n/id~1a6a.aspx

Moradabadi, Y., Gharehshiran, M., & Amrai, K. (2012). What is the Motivation Student of Iranians for using Facebook? *Procedia: Social and Behavioral Sciences*, *46*, 5192–5195. doi:10.1016/j.sbspro.2012.06.407

Moresi, E. (2003). *Metodologia da Pesquisa*. Universidade Católica de Brasília - UCB.

Morgan, R., & Hunt, S. (1994). The commitment-trust theory of relationship marketing. *Journal of Marketing*, *58*(3), 20–38. doi:10.2307/1252308

O'Reilly, T. (2007). What is web 2.0: Design patterns and business models for the next generation of software. *Communications & Stratégies*, *65*, 16–37.

Pai, P., & Arnott, D. (2013). User adoption of social networking sites: Eliciting uses and gratifications through a means–end approach. *Computers in Human Behavior*, *29*(3), 1039–1053. doi:10.1016/j.chb.2012.06.025

Pallis, G., Zeinalipour-Yazti, D., & Dikaiakos, M. (2011). Online Social Networks: Status and Trends in New Directions in Web Data Management (pp. 213–234). New York, NY: Springer.

Payne, A., & Frow, P. (2013). *Strategic Customer Management: Integrating Relationship Marketing and CRM*. Cambridge University Press. doi:10.1017/CBO9781139057417

Peixoto, S. (2010). *Web Trends - 10 cases made in web 2.0. Gaia*. Comunicarte Publishing.

Pempek, T., Yermolayeva, Y., & Calvert, S. (2009). College students' social networking experiences on Facebook. *Journal of Applied Developmental Psychology*, *30*(3), 227–238. doi:10.1016/j.appdev.2008.12.010

Peppers, D., & Rogers, M. (2011). *Managing customer relationships: a strategic framework* (2nd ed.). Hoboken, New Jersey: John Wiley & Sons, Inc.

Peterson, R. (1995). Relationship marketing and the consumer. *Journal of the Academy of Marketing Science*, *23*(4), 278–278. doi:10.1177/009207039502300407

Pfeil, U., Arjan, R., & Zaphiris, P. (2009). Age differences in online social networking – A study of user profiles and the social capital divide among teenagers and older users in MySpace. *Computers in Human Behavior*, *25*(3), 643–654. doi:10.1016/j.chb.2008.08.015

Pordata. (n. d.). Retrieved from www.pordata.pt

Portmann, E. (2012). Towards an emergent semantic web. *Tiny Transactions on Computer Science*, 1.

Quan-Haase, A., & Young, A. (2010). Uses and Gratifications of Social Media: A Comparison of Facebook and Instant Messaging. *Bulletin of Science, Technology & Society*, *30*(5), 350–361. doi:10.1177/0270467610380009

Sheth, J., & Parvatiyar, A. (1995). Relationship marketing in consumer markets: Antecedents and consequences. *Journal of the Academy of Marketing Science*, *23*(4), 255–271. doi:10.1177/009207039502300405

Sheth, J., & Parvatiyar, A. (2002). Evolving relationship marketing into a discipline. *Journal of Relationship Marketing*, *1*(1), 3–16. doi:10.1300/J366v01n01_02

Smith, W., & Kidder, D. (2010). You've been tagged! Then again, maybe not: Employers and Facebook. *Business Horizons*, *53*(5), 491–499. doi:10.1016/j.bushor.2010.04.004

Smock, A., Ellison, N., Lampe, C., & Wohn, D. (2011). Facebook as a toolkit: A uses and gratification approach to unbundling feature use. *Computers in Human Behavior*, *27*(6), 2322–2329. doi:10.1016/j.chb.2011.07.011

Special, W., & Li-Barber, K. (2012). Self-disclosure and student satisfaction with Facebook. *Computers in Human Behavior*, *28*(2), 624–630. doi:10.1016/j.chb.2011.11.008

Tosun, L. (2012). Motives for Facebook use and expressing "true self" on the Internet. *Computers in Human Behavior*, *28*(4), 1510–1517. doi:10.1016/j.chb.2012.03.018

Wikström, E., & Wigmo, J. (2010). "Social media marketing: What role can social media play as a marketing tool?" Bachelor, Linnaeus University.

Woodcock, N., Green, A., & Starkey, M. (2011). Social CRM as a business strategy. *Journal of Database Marketing & Customer Strategy Management*, *18*(1), 50–64. doi:10.1057/dbm.2011.7

Zarrella, D. (2009). *The Social Media Marketing Book*. Sebastopol, Canada: O'Reilly Media, Inc.

Zhang, X., & Vogel, D. (2011). Electronic commerce in web 3.0: The evidence from emerging economics [IJCSIT]. *International Journal of Computer Science & Information Technology*, *3*(3), 240–254. doi:10.5121/ijcsit.2011.3317

KEY TERMS AND DEFINITIONS

CRM System: Information system incorporating a set of subsystems to support the diverse activities of Customer Relationship Marketing.

Customer Relationship Marketing: Strategic business process implemented in organization to keep an ideal mix of customer relationships.

Information System: Set of interdependent components (hardware, software, telecommunication networks, databases, human resources and procedures) that captures, processes, stores and disseminates information to meet some organizational goal.

Online Social Network: Web-based service that allows individuals to construct a public or semi-public profile within a bounded system, articulate a list of other users with whom they share a connection, and view and traverse their list of connections and those made by others within the system.

Relationship Marketing: Part of marketing strategy focused on the tasks necessary to build, develop and maintain long-term relationships with key stakeholders.

Social Media Marketing: One strategy developed and implemented to social channels with specific contents tailored to those platforms.

Social Media: Set of tools based on Internet technologies, as for example, blogs, podcasts, wikis and online social networks.

Social Web Sites: Web sites that allows individuals to form online communities and share user-created contents.

Web 2.0: The second generation of the World Wide Web that includes new features and functionality (technological improvements) that provide a level user interaction that was not available before.

Chapter 2
Information Technology Communication:
Main Challenges and Pitfalls to Marketing and Management – Evidence from Curitiba (in Brazil)

Adriane Setti
University of Algarve, Portugal

Sílvia Fernandes
University of Algarve, Portugal

Marisa Cesário
University of Algarve, Portugal

Júlio Mendes
University of Algarve, Portugal

ABSTRACT

Information technology (IT) changes introduce technical foreign terms in professionals' vocabulary which became part of many organizational routines. Communication problems result from the fact that the user (customer) not always dominates several terms. In this chapter, we analyze the communication defects between IT professionals and users of their products and services, and then discuss some pitfalls and challenges to management and marketing. It addresses the communication between IT professionals and users in the corporate environment of Curitiba (Brazil). Results lead to perceive a need of formal training and screenplay by IT professionals to serve customers, manage their careers and assist technology on behalf of customer needs. This chapter suggests that professionals must be clear with users to create confidence, in order to improve business practice. And users expect professionals to share and explain them their actions toward machines/systems, and listen to what they require. This is very important to marketing as a sustainable link with the company can be created.

INTRODUCTION

Interactivity has a vital importance and the option for using or not technical language should be conscious, as it is differential to understand and be understandable (Cassarro, 2011). IT professionals must be creative to be able to adapt to specific, local, regional and semantic situations. Thus, they need to know what the customer understands and, even more, what he really needs. The identity between parts

DOI: 10.4018/978-1-4666-8459-1.ch002

and the clarity of information open paths to strengthen confidence relations between the professional of computing and the user.

The stereotyped idea that the professional should treat the consumer as he would like to be treated seems so obvious that is practically not questioned; and the meaning is lost even before it is analyzed. For the reality of professionals focused during this study, which have personal marketing as a big ally, a continuing bond (loyalty) is created with the confidence in the service offered, based on communication clarity considering knowledge and vocabulary adaptation.

Considering that people do not only buy products, but also services (Madia de Souza, 2007), it is assumed that, in the information technology field, the search is not only for equipment or programs, but for security, information organization, and problem solving. As an effect, there is the demand for technical support and, sometimes, understanding support because there are still people that do not have an effective relation with technology. Some studies have demonstrated that technologies and innovations affording relative advantages, compatibility with existing practices and beliefs, low complexity, and potential observability, will be more extensively and rapidly understood or accepted than those with the opposite characteristics (Rogers, 1995). The user (client) not always dominates, or just does not know, several terms in the IT field. The understanding level of what is said or done can influence the level of confidence, making a difference in a negotiation (Gaete, 2010; Hanson, 2010; Partala & Kallinen, 2012).

From these initial considerations, the subject of study was defined: the communication processes in the IT field and its implications on management and marketing, whose research has both quantitative and qualitative analysis through an interdisciplinary approach involving management, marketing, information systems and communication. The general objective of this research is then to analyze the communication characteristics between IT professionals and the users of their products/services and the consequent impact on management and marketing performance. The relevance of this impact is related with the focus on the preparation of those professionals, not only in technical terms related to the technology, but also regarding their contact with users. The exploration of marketing concepts, such as sell to customer what he wants, is highly linked with communication through the power to get closer to user and promote his satisfaction what reflects upon management and organizational performance.

Thus, the present work is structured as follows: next section reviews main literature on the subject and formulates seven research questions to investigate; third section describes the methodology, the questionnaire designed, variables used, and sampling procedures. Then, fourth section presents answers' distribution and research questions' testing, summarizing the results obtained. The fifth section discusses implications for management and marketing, and sixth section concludes the study with some final considerations.

THEORETICAL FRAMEWORK

One deficiency was detected from previous researches (Wurman, 2005; Mattana et al., 2006; Kunsch, 2007; Cunha, 2009; Cassarro, 2011; Rezende, 2011; Silva, 2011): the user is not always familiar with technology or able to express himself; and the professional who deals directly with the public not always has the communication ability to guide the user. The care for complete training of future active professionals seeks turning them capable to explore and adapt the full power at their disposal. This study aims to highlight the importance of guiding individuals that play different roles in society, both IT users and professionals, to be able to maintain a clear and effective interpersonal communication.

There is the awareness that there must be a closer approach between population and technology, both in relation to individual or corporative performance, and there are proactive actions from some government strategies (Takahashi, 2000; Warschauer, 2006). Educational, organizational and government systems have expressed concern regarding the expansion of the IT area, not to become an isolation factor but of interaction and appropriation of information in society. There are numerous projects working on the comparison between traditional fields of education and IT field.

The organizational intelligence and strategic alignment of IT resources with business strategies and plans are nowadays the issues for more success in an organization, public or private. Thus, firm's strategic marketing should be complementary to the information systems planning (Rezende & Abreu, 2010; Polizelli & Ozaki, 2008). It is evident the close relation between the concepts of business intelligence, relationship marketing, information systems planning, and knowledge (Fernandes, 2013). The need is that the organizational intelligence be exercised, and the management of data and information add value to the product or service offered, aiming to make the difference to customers.

Organizations need to provide quality in their products and services, maintain service excellence and be alert to market changing conditions. Then, it is essential an accessible and transparent language in the communication with customers, anticipating their wishes and needs. In organizational terms, this study intends to encourage some thinking and development of interventional projects that aim at solving or overcoming noise in the communication process in the IT field. Some key issues for a successful management need always to be in vogue: communication skills; information understanding (an influent factor on reliability); etc.

It is interesting that many new technological terms and tools were absorbed from marketing and management such as: CRM (Customer Relationship Management), SEM (Search Engine Marketing); SEO (Search Engine Optimization), among others. And these have proliferated at a dizzying speed. Thereby, the purposed analysis will influence marketing information systems' strategy, due to its focus on professional's knowledge, not only in technical issues, but also regarding his semantic (understandable) contact with the user (Rezende & Abreu, 2010; Polizelli & Ozaki, 2008).

Technological learning by professionals may bring benefits to management such as: complex projects' expansion; their own training (identification of weaknesses/strengths); interactivity or interpersonal communication (which is different in business and education fields); customer's understanding of machine/system's operation (and realizing the benefits from its adoption); natural man-machine integration which improves management due to easier decision making from significant time reduction in problem solving (Rios, 2006; Costa, 2007; Gaete, 2010; Hanson, 2010; Allameh et al., 2011; Ignatius et al., 2012, Sun & Hsu, 2012; Miwa & Terai, 2012; Partala & Kallinen, 2012).

The conquest of future loyalty to products/services requires that users understand the machine or system's operation and realize the benefits from its adoption to analyze if a certain technology is needed in their lives. In the digital world, viral marketing (also known by word of mouth) is very strong, such as for example a social network's discussion on a service, what can be allied to satisfaction and trust (Giglio, 2010; Hanson, 2010; Matos, 2011; Liu, 2012). Thus, it is interesting to consider communication within different IT contexts. The spread of the internet ends up creating new options, and then a range of needs. The exploration of different users' profiles and distance-learning opportunities is just a small portion to be worked on.

CHALLENGES TO PROFESSIONALS

The search for relations between the fields of management and technology is growing due to the inevitable proximity among messages generated by technologies and administrative situations. It is important to consider the organizational and formal pressures, no longer limited in time and space, requiring new practices and understandings of this issue (Boar, 2002). If the information is the key element for manager's decision-making, it is indispensable that he understands the communication profile of the professional hired for the IT function. Trust and open communication should take place to clarify the user's needs and turn the IT professional able to know the reality he is going to work with and to indicate the most appropriate technology/system for it (Gordon & Gordon, 2006).

IT function will have, then, a new communication process built not exclusively on standard codes, but on the adaptation of those codes to user's own characteristics and differences. The major challenge is to know how to use IT on supporting decision-making, as an effective instrument of knowledge and citizenship building, considering that problems in the avalanche of information must be transformed into opportunities (Cassarro, 2011).

The manager must use IT to determine the necessary information for the effective development of activities (Gordon & Gordon, 2006) and must understand its relation with the information systems. It is primary the perception of how IT can gather technological and computational resources for storage, generation and use of information. These components interact and need the key element - the human resource (peopleware) - without which there would be no information systems functionality or use (Rezende, 2011). And on this interactivity, the basic principle of communication and marketing is to use the technology as a tool, not as a problem. Therefore, technology should not change the strategic planning of the company; the planning should choose the appropriate technology (Cassarro, 2011).

IT companies and professionals face the need of restructuring their relationship with society due the growing importance of technology and information. Also, IT tools and their explanation should be deeply explored since each individual's scholar level (Brynjolfsson, 2010; Hismanoglu, 2011; Hus, 2011; Klimova, 2011; Pineida, 2011; Silva & Pereira, 2011; Suduc et al., 2011; Eagle, 2012; Kolikant, 2012).

Inclusion and Exclusion

When considering that theory and practice (verbalization and action) are in an intrinsic relation, understanding it is essential to the IT professional otherwise it is possible to affirm this may cause an exclusion process (or unsuccessful negotiations). The choice by the inclusive (clear feedback communicated) way allows satisfaction and trust within the interaction with IT tools, including users with less technological experience. More clients and sustainable relations can be attained which influence management outcomes.

Besides the lack of bibliographical references associated to the IT professional's development, most studies related to this career are based on a personal motivation rather than on a career planning (Iizuka, 2003; Albertin, 2005; Reddy, 2006; Warschauer, 2006; Hanson, 2010; Naumann et al., 2010; Mirza & Al-Abdulkareem, 2011).

What this paper seeks to demonstrate is the unquestionable importance of communication processes in the IT field, both in terms of management and marketing. Facing the huge dissemination of technologies and information ('big data era'), vocabulary differentiation and human-machine interaction is not yet consolidated and the related professionals need to be aware of the inherent challenges and pitfalls.

Research Questions

Considering the objectives mentioned and the theoretical framework, main research questions (RQ) were addressed:

RQ1: Some technical terms of the vocabulary related with IT are not sufficiently clear
RQ2: It is important to consider the user's knowledge in IT field for a more efficient communication
RQ3: The IT professionals are prepared, in terms of communication, to assist the users
RQ4: It is important to build a screenplay (guide for conducting the approach to user) to capture the reality of each user
RQ5: The most qualified professional understands better the importance of user's assistance
RQ6: Problems tend to be solved when there is feedback from the user to the professional about the information system
RQ7: Professional and user believe that the professional already knows what to do and user does not need to participate

METHODOLOGY

The Questionnaire

This study addresses the communication between professionals of IT and its users in the corporate environment of Curitiba (Brazil). The underlying empirical approach examined responses from a sample of IT professionals (adults of both genders) with experience in the field and academic curriculum. It also examined responses from a sample of IT users (adults of both genders) which use platforms/systems/tools in that corporate environment.

The questionnaire, both for professionals and users, was divided in two parts. The first one gives information on the profile of each respondent. The profile variables include: gender, age, scholarship, charge/activity and action level. The second part is composed by 16 closed questions (both in the Professionals' questionnaire as well as in the Users' questionnaire) with a Likert response structure (1=totally disagree; 2=partially disagree; 3=partially agree; 4=totally agree). Not all the questions were used in the present work, as we worked only with the ones related with the objectives and research questions (RQ) formulated. The variables derived, most related with this research, are presented in Tables 1 and 2.

Sampling Procedures

The sample studied is composed by two sub-groups: one with IT professionals and the other with IT business users. Since it was not possible to be precise about the number of professionals in the city of Curitiba, linked to companies and autonomous (a common situation in the IT field), or about the number of users, the procedure for unknown populations is recommended (Stevenson, 2001; Neufeld, 2009; Luchesa & Chaves, 2011):

Table 1. List of variables from professional's questionnaire

Variable Number	Variable from Professional's Questionnaire
P1	In assisting the user, no need to keep explaining him all the details of the intervention in the system
P4	English terms cannot always be translated as there is no equivalent in Portuguese and translation can distort meaning
P5	Must have user's feedback, related with system/computer and communication process, for the necessary improvement
P6	It is important to consider the user's knowledge with respect to IT
P7	Sometimes an expression is so basic that IT professional does not realize that user may not know it
P8	Each client/user requires a different assistance approach
P9	In IT professional's academic graduation there was training on customer service/assistance
P10	The IT professional knows much better user's needs than the user himself
P11	System's complexity should be reduced to facilitate user's understanding
P12	Some terms reflect the real speed of IT changes and may not be sufficiently clear to users
P13	The use of technical terms streamlines communication processes in the IT field
P15	Over time IT professional realizes the importance of having a clear communication with the user
P16	The more qualified IT professional is, less contact with the user he has

Table 2. List of variables from user's questionnaire

Variable Number	Variable from User's Questionnaire
U1	By experience IT professional realizes user's needs despite he cannot explain them
U2	It is important to give feedback to IT professional concerning the system/computer and communication for the necessary adjustments
U4	Technology can be a source of benefits and job security
U6	Everyone should know IT well, not only the IT professionals
U11	The user strives to facilitate his interaction with the IT professional
U13	IT professional needs to consider user's reality in assisting him

$$n = \frac{z^2 p\left(1-p\right)}{e^2}$$

$$n = \frac{1.96^2 \times 0.5(1-0.5)}{0.05^2} = 384$$

where:

p = Estimative for the statistic unit percentage that verify the characteristic (usually the most conservative value used is 0.5).
e = Margin of error of the confidence interval.
z = Statistic value of confidence degree.

The dimension of this defined sample implies 384 questionnaires, both for professionals and users. Then, the questionnaire has been published online and an email with its link was sent to 500 IT professionals and 500 IT users, in order to obtain the necessary composition of the sample. We obtained 135 responses from professionals, equivalent to a 27.0% response rate (a response was then excluded due to some errors); and 108 responses from users equivalent to a 21.6% response rate (a total of 243 cases). Although these rates seem to be low, it is important to refer that other experiences with electronic surveys have already shown that this kind of research presents a response rate lower than 25% (Scornavacca Jr., Becker & Andraschko, 2001; Maier & Remus, 2002; Cohen, 2003; Graeml & Csillag, 2006; Antonelli & Santos; 2009; Silva, 2011).

Furthermore, the application of this research is restricted to Curitiba, unlike other studies that have a wider dissemination or a national level. Another aspect is that participation in the survey was completely voluntary; those who participated, after knowing the purpose, kindly accepted or not the invitation, in order to increase the probability of trusty answers which increase the study reliability. Also, the dimension of a sample must be at least four to five times bigger than the total of variables (Malhotra, 2006). In this research, considering that the questionnaire has 16 objective questions plus 5 open ones (totalizing 21 questions), the number of answers should be around 84 to 105. We obtained 108 from users and 135 from professionals, which mean a valid number to attend the requirements.

This research intends to increase the experience and knowledge around this bounded linguistic situation in which the researcher, based on some research questions, intensifies the analysis of the limits of this specific reality. The descriptive and exploratory researches are common when there is a concern with practical actions of the researcher (Sanchez, 1999; Barquette & Chaoubah; 2007; Gil, 2008).

RESULTS

Sample Characterization: IT Professionals

Regarding age group, it is observed that prevail younger people: 84.56% (44.85% up to 25 years old, and 39.71% from 26 to 35 years old) and only 15.44% are over than 35 years old (12.50% from 36 to 45 years old, and 2.94% from 46 to 59 years old). There were no respondents aged over 60 years old. Regarding gender, it is observed that 77.21% of the 135 respondents are male, demonstrating that there is still a strong predominance of male professionals in the IT field, which confirms the information presented on the Green Book (Livro Verde) (Takahashi, 2000).

Intersecting information about post-graduation level and last year of scholarship, 46% of professionals that participate in the survey have completed or almost completed their graduation. Thus, among the 135 professionals only 62 have post-graduation, what may reinforce that in the IT field, even without completed graduation, the professional is already inserted in the job market. Then some questions arise: does this mean the professional is somehow immature to deal with the user? Is there a trend of young people looking for post-graduation programs? Are post-graduates the older ones?

The prevalent charge or kind of activity among the respondent professionals is analyst (50.74%); followed by support/assistance (13.24%) and then supervisors (9.56%). The other significant portion (22.06%) is composed by professionals that work in diversified fields such as programming, development and management. According to their level of action, it is noticeable the predominance of operational professionals (61.94%), followed by tactical level (20.90%) and strategic level (17.16%).

Sample Characterization: IT Users

Regarding age group, respondent users are concentrated in two intermediate ranges: 39.81% in the group from 26 to 35 years old and 35.19% from 36 to 45 years old. We notice that, like in professionals, there were no respondents with age over than 60 years old. About gender, contrary to professionals, both men and women use IT similarly having almost the same percentage - 49.07% were male and 50.93% female.

A feature we highlight in users is their level of education: at one extreme there is the group with complete post-graduation (53.70%) and at the other extreme there is the group with high school (3.70%). As there was no obligatory orientation for disseminating the questionnaire, almost 75% of the respondent users having at least completed graduation may indicate that scholarship level influences the adoption of IT as a work tool. Concerning their action level, it is observed that the majority of users belong to the operational level (54.29%), while the others are divided between tactical (17.14%) and strategic (28.57%).

Table 3. Distribution of answers – professionals

Variables	Distribution of Answers
Professional's Age	
Up to 25 years	44.85%
From 26 to 35 years	39.71%
From 36 to 45 years	12.50%
From 46 to 59 years	2.94%
Over than 60 years	0%
Professional's Gender	
Male	77.21%
Female	22.79%
Professional's Scholarship	
Uncompleted graduation	26%
Graduation	23%
Specialization in progress	24%
Completed specialization	18%
Master's degree in progress	5%
Completed master's degree	4%
Doctorate in progress	0%
Completed doctorate	0%
Professional's Charge/Activity	
Owner/partner	4.41%
Supervision/coordination	9.56%
Analyst	50.74%
Support/assistance	13.24%
Other	22.06%
Professional's Action Level	
Operational	61.94%
Tactical	20.90%
Strategic	17.16%

Table 4. Distribution of answers – users

Variables	Distribution of Answers
User's Age	
Up to 25 years	16.67%
From 26 to 35 years	39.81%
From 36 to 45 years	35.19%
From 46 to 59 years	8.33%
Over than 60 years	0%
User's Gender	
Male	49.07%
Female	50.93%
User's Scholarship	
High School	3.70%
Uncompleted graduation	21.30%
Completed graduation	14.81%
Uncompleted post-graduation	6.48%
Completed post-graduation	53.70%
User's Action Level	
Operational	54.29%
Tactical	17.14%
Strategic	28.57%
User's Main Activity	
University teaching, coordination of courses and projects	23.13%
Administrative assistance, secretary, public service	18.5%
Accounting, management, banking, taxes	9.26%
Advocacy, registry	8.32%
Administrative analysis, systems analysis	7.38%
University internship	5.56%
Industry, engineering	4.62%
Human resources	1.84%
Other[1]	21.39%

These users' main activities are distributed in 9 categories, from courses/projects coordination to administrative analysis and others. Categories included are either autonomous such as lawyers and engineers, up to technical support such as teachers and supervisors. Responses emphasize that the highest percentage was concentrated in university teaching/coordination of courses and projects (23.13%) and the lowest in human resources (1.84%). The category 'Other' include: travel agency, marketing, sales, medicine, architecture, consultancy, etc. All these somehow use IT in their professional activities.

Research Questions' Verification

Average values and standard errors were used in order to verify the research questions proposed. Given the Likert response structure used in the questionnaire (1=totally disagree; 2=partially disagree; 3=partially agree; 4=totally agree), we can identify the average values indicating agreement (above 2.9) or disagreement (below 3.0). The consistency in the answers can be observed through the standard deviations.

The seven research questions previously formulated are tested here and resumed in Table 5.

In Table 5, we can see that in order to verify *RQ1-Some technical terms of the vocabulary related with IT are not sufficiently clear*, we used information from P4 and P12.These results indicate that IT professionals agree both with the existence of translation difficulties as well as with the difficulty related to the hurried evolution of technical language in this area.

In order to verify *RQ2- It is important to consider the user's knowledge in IT field for a more efficient communication*, we used information from P6, P8, U1, U11 and U13. These results show that the professional agrees both with the importance of considering user's knowledge in IT and with the need of changing the approach according to each user. And users strive to facilitate interaction with the professional who needs to consider the user's reality. Users do not agree that by experience the IT professional realizes user's needs despite not explained.

In order to verify *RQ3 - The IT professionals are prepared, in terms of communication, to assist the users*, we used information from P1, P9 and P15. These results reveal that IT professionals do not agree either with the lack of need in explaining all the details to users or with the existence of training on customer assistance in their academic graduation. Over time professionals realize the importance of having a clear communication with IT users.

In order to verify *RQ4 - It is important to build a screenplay (guide for conducting the approach to user) to capture the reality of each user*, we used information from P5 and P8. These results acknowledge that IT professionals agree both with having user's feedback related with the system and communication processes as well as with the need of consequent different assistance approaches.

In order to verify *RQ5- The most qualified professional understands better the importance of user's assistance*, we used information from P15 and P16. According to these data, as over time IT professionals realize the importance of having a clear communication with users, they do not agree that the more qualified they are, less contact with users they will have.

In order to verify *RQ6- Problems tend to be solved when there is feedback from the user to the professional about the information system*, we used information from P5, P11 and U2. These data indicate that, as well as IT professionals agree both with the need of having users' feedback and reducing system's complexity, users agree with the importance of giving their feedback to professionals concerning the system and communication processes.

In order to verify *RQ7- Professional and user believe that the professional already knows what to do and user does not need to participate*, we used information from P1, P10, U1, U4, U6 and U11. From

Table 5. Research questions' testing

RQ1 Testing	N	Average	Std. Dev.
P4: English terms cannot always be translated as there is no equivalent in Portuguese and translation can distort meaning	135	3.21	.907
P12: Some terms reflect the real speed of IT changes and may not be sufficiently clear to users	135	3.22	.816
RQ2 Testing	**N**	**Average**	**Std. Dev.**
P6: It is important to consider the user's knowledge with respect to IT	135	3.56	. 676
P8: Each client/user requires a different assistance approach	135	3.69	.480
U1: By experience IT professional realizes user's needs despite he cannot explain them	108	2.27	.903
U11: The user strives to facilitate his interaction with the IT professional	108	3.43	.726
U13: IT professional needs to consider user's reality in assisting him	108	3.83	.399
RQ3 Testing	**N**	**Average**	**Std. Dev.**
P1: In assisting the user, no need to keep explaining him all the details of the intervention in the system	135	2.56	.843
P9: In IT professional's academic graduation there was training on customer service/ assistance	135	2.39	1.072
P15: Over time IT professional realizes the importance of having a clear communication with the user	135	3.88	.324
RQ4 Testing	**N**	**Average**	**Std. Dev.**
P5: Must have user's feedback, related with system/computer and communication process, for the necessary improvement	135	3.77	.422
P8: Each client/user requires a different assistance approach	135	3.69	.480
RQ5 Testing	**N**	**Average**	**Std. Dev.**
P15: Over time IT professional realizes the importance of having a clear communication with the user	135	3.88	.324
P16: The more qualified IT professional is, less contact with the user he has	135	2.13	1.006
RQ6 Testing	**N**	**Average**	**Std. Dev.**
P5: Must have user's feedback, related with system/computer and communication process, for the necessary improvement	135	3.77	.422
P11: System's complexity should be reduced to facilitate user's understanding	135	3.41	.892
U2: It is important to give feedback to IT professional concerning the system/ computer and communication for the necessary adjustments	108	3.65	.517
RQ7 Testing	**N**	**Average**	**Std. Dev.**
P1: In assisting the user, no need to keep explaining him all the details of the intervention in the system	135	2.56	.843
P10: The IT professional knows much better user's needs than the user himself	135	2.30	.856
U1: By experience IT professional realizes user's needs despite he cannot explain them	108	2.27	.903
U4: Technology can be a source of benefits and job security	108	3.63	.540
U6: Everyone should know IT well, not only the IT professionals	108	2.92	.822
U11: The user strives to facilitate his interaction with the IT professional	108	3.43	.726

these results, as well as IT professionals do not agree both with the lack of need in explaining all the details and with knowing much better users' needs, users do not agree that by experience IT professionals realize users' needs despite not explained. Despite of agreeing that technology can be a source of benefits/job security and striving to facilitate their interaction with professionals, users do not agree that everyone should know IT well.

Summary of Results

The results are not completely independent from the Professionals' and Users' profiles. Regarding the professionals (Table 6), *P5 - Must have user's feedback, related with system/computer and communication process, for the necessary improvement* and *P10 - The IT professional knows much better user's needs than the user himself*, are correlated with the age of the professional. The older they are, the more they agree with these statements. And *P9 - In IT professional's academic graduation there was training on customer service/assistance*, is correlated with the gender. Thus, women agree more with that affirmation than men.

Table 6. Correlations Spearman's rho – professionals and users

Variable (Professionals)	Age		Gender	
	Correlation Coefficient	Sig.	Correlation Coefficient	Sig.
P1	-.060	.244	.057	.257
P4	.042	.313	-.006	.471
P5	**.162***	**.031**	-.079	.182
P6	.046	0.298	0.24	.389
P7	.461	.461	.009	.457
P8	.461	.449	.018	.416
P9	.014	.014	**.147***	**.044**
P10	**-.173***	**.023**	-.041	.319
P11	.055	.265	-.085	.163
P12	.099	.126	-.052	.276
P13	.062	.236	-.078	.185
P15	0.017	0.421	-0.018	0.419
P16	0.141	0.052	-0.079	0.180
Variable (Users)	**Age**		**Gender**	
	Correlation Coefficient	**Sig.**	**Correlation Coefficient**	**Sig.**
U1	.055	.287	-.057	.280
U2	.128	.093	.026	.394
U4	**-.265****	**.003**	**.176***	**.034**
U6	.083	.197	.080	.207
U11	.050	.302	**.191***	**.024**
U16	-.102	.148	.130	.090

* Correlation is significant at the 0.05 level (1-tailed).
** Correlation is significant at the 0.01 level (1-tailed).

Regarding the users (Table 6), *U4 - Technology can be a source of benefits and job security*, is correlated both with the users' age and gender, while *U11 - The user strives to facilitate his interaction with the IT professional*, changes only with the users' gender. We can conclude that younger women disagree more with the perception of job security provided by new technologies. We can also observe that women agree more with U11 than men.

From the research questions' verification (through analysis over the variables related with answers obtained in both questionnaires) the results about confirmations or discards are summarized in the following table:

Even though some respondent professionals are conscious that terms in English may cause problems in the user understanding, their use is so natural (or translation is not common) that they do not realize the problematics. This has management implications because, if information and communication are strategic issues (Kunsch, 2007), they should be clear and present immediate results. If the vocabulary is not fully compatible, the IT field is not fulfilling its function which is integrated in the organization to serve managers and support decision making (Stábile, 2001). IT is a strategic resource and therefore must adapt to different other functions, following the reality of each user for competitive advantage (Rostock, 2011). The results presented in this work demonstrate that respondent professionals recognize the importance of differenced treatment (consider the knowledge of each user), although it is not pursued in practice. But this is an essential factor for management and IT professional's career, in addition to making communication between parts more efficient (Limeira, 2005).

One problem highlighted by the results was the lack of professionals' training; asked about concrete approaches many did not answer the question or affirmed not knowing. They gave vague answers and some questioned the relevance of a strategy on assisting the customer. The respondent professionals working at the operational level refer unnecessary to explain the details of a system's intervention. This reflects a problem regarding the contact between professional and user (Rios, 2006).

Table 7. Research questions' summary

Research Questions (RQ)	Results
RQ1: Some technical terms of the vocabulary related with IT are not sufficiently clear	**Confirmed:** Based on the evidence that there is not enough clarity in communication, causing an uncomfortable situation to those who need IT services or products
RQ2: It is important to consider the user's knowledge in IT field for a more efficient communication	**Confirmed:** Once the majority of respondent professionals agree with the need to consider the user's knowledge in order to turn communication more efficient. This positioning is more theoretical[2] than practical (it reflects the problematics of this research)
RQ3: The IT professionals are prepared, in terms of communication, to assist the users	**Discarded:** As many respondent professionals start acting without sufficient training or preparation. The awareness of this issue occurs as time passes, what may undermine professional's performance
RQ4: It is important to build a screenplay (guide for conducting the approach to user) to capture the reality of each user	**Confirmed:** As respondent professionals consider important the adequate approach to know customer needs. Once more, a theoretical positioning is observed reinforcing this problematics
RQ5: The most qualified professional understands better the importance of user's assistance	**Discarded:** As the results did not highlight the relationship with this profile
RQ6: Problems tend to be solved when there is feedback from the user to the professional about the information system	**Confirmed:** Both respondent users confirmed the importance of giving their feedback and professionals recognize this importance
RQ7: Professional and user believe that the professional already knows what to do and user does not need to participate	**Discarded:** As respondent professionals do not agree both with the lack of need in explaining all the details and with knowing much better users' needs

Therefore, this kind of orientation is not pointed during the academic graduation, what has been discussed by Costa (2007) when defending that there is the need to combine technical expertise with leadership and communication skills. Implications on firm's IT management or professional's career may arrive, affecting marketing issues due to the risk that the professional is not able to sell what consumer really needs. Thus, it is advisable to consider including these orientations in professionals' graduation (Silva & Silva, 2003), considering that it is no longer good their isolation or individuality (Müller, 2009; Gaete, 2010), but their full interactivity. Discussing implications on the IT professionals' career is because of their strong trend to be liberal workers (Müller, 2009).

The responses of professionals pointed as favorable the following aspects: availability to the customer, security demonstration, clear communication, good contact network, indication of previous works, and appearance care. In this sense, it is clear the importance of personal marketing since it is common the IT professional to be autonomous (Müller, 2009), who himself might influence the customer to look for him and be motivated to use a technology.

Even without having a defined strategy (guide for preparing and conducting the approach), the respondent professionals consider customer feedback as a tool that indicates the necessary adjustments in terms of service. However, the purpose of this feedback is not clear and less is the collaboration intention as it is more likely a contact action than a feedback for corrective actions.

On the other hand, respondent users consider relevant the following aspects: clarity in communication, security demonstration and reliability, professional's ability to understand the customer, competence, efficiency, and cost-benefit relation. It is observed that the respondent users want their needs understood and answered; conditions that will basically encourage them to use IT (Bernardi, 2008) and turn them loyal. The user then recognizes the importance of maintaining contact with the professional. References and contact indications demonstrated to have an important role in choosing the IT professional, confirming that in the IT/IS environment 'viral marketing' (word of mouth) is common (Giglio, 2010).

In general, the respondent users make an effort to facilitate their interaction with professionals. Although ignorance is not necessarily punitive or considered an exclusion factor, IT knowledge is professionally differentiable (Bernardi, 2008; Romano, 2011). From the data obtained it is possible to realize that the user wants a more personalized interaction with the IT professional; he wants to be heard and also wants to hear confirming that he needs to understand technology (Rodrigues, 2008). The need of a more personal and less automatic relation arises, highlighting the maintenance of a partnership with the professional based on trust (Sousa, 2008).

The lack of reliability or clarity in information can affect reaching market goals. Disabled communication processes cause limitations that harm business once organizations, in order to become competitive, constantly need to rethink their informational structure, technological system's adequacy, and ways to attract and maintain customers.

Implications for Management and Marketing

Regarding the fulfillment of the overall objective of this research, occurs the verification of several management and marketing impacts from communication issues between IT professionals and users of their platforms/services. Those impacts are systematized bellow, having in mind the research questions (RQ) analyzed.

The confirmation of RQ1 has management implications, once the user may lose time or even have decision-making difficulties as he does not understand terms from the IT field in a clear way.

The confirmation of RQ2 has implications on firm and IT professional's career management, as the professional needs to gather information about the user in order to enhance communication efficiency and, consequently, reach his goals.

The discard of RQ3 has serious implications on: marketing, due to professional's unpreparedness in approach, relation and positioning strategies; and on his career's management as he lacks guidance to manage them what weakens his relationship with customer.

The confirmation of RQ4 has positive implications on IT professional's career management and, consequently, on marketing because one of the strategies of customer's approach contemplating his reality and gathering attendance issues should be a screenplay. Although IT professionals consider important to be prepared for customer's approach, the answers obtained show that they do not use this strategy perhaps due to lack of orientation in their own graduation process. This entails negative impacts, both for career management and personal marketing, because professional's performance and image is affected.

Despite of discarding RQ5, we can refer that it is expected that IT professionals develop a better approach to customers once they become more qualified. In the absence of such determination, negative implications on their career management will arise from fragilities of their relation with customers.

The confirmation of RQ6 has management implications as feedback from the user gives to professional the necessary guidance. Therefore, it is required that IT professionals are determinate in searching for feedbacks to know better how to manage the information received in order to plan strategies for future contacts.

The discard of RQ7 is positive as its underlying concern has direct implications on management. Self-confidence in communication can bring negative consequences to information management and decision-making. A professional that does not explain his procedures to the user will have implications on personal marketing as clients may disregard the professional whose performance is not efficient.

Thus, the importance of clear and efficient communication processes between IT professionals and users is confirmed since several management and marketing implications are evidenced, in both organizational and personal levels.

FUTURE RESEARCH DIRECTIONS

From this study, with evident management and marketing implications, it is possible to affirm that the situation requires:

- IT professionals technically prepared, with notions about communication processes and skills in inserting novelty from technologies into standardized behaviors;
- Assumption of lack of knowledge by the user in IT field until the opposite reality is confirmed;
- Empathy practice getting to know the user and develop trust;
- Emphasis on objective language, avoiding excessive technical terms;
- Understand the situation in order to offer the product or service customer really needs;
- Constant evaluation of issues related with the qualification of IT professional or team;
- Awareness of the importance of continuous transparency in communication processes;
- Identification of eventual internal problems that may affect the development of marketing and communication actions;

- Analysis of customer's reaction concerning messages sent by the company or by IT professionals in order to verify if his understanding was complete, partial or null;
- Measurement of customer's return to evaluate credibility and loyalty.

In the context of change, the elementary principles oriented to the market must be in harmony with concepts and working methods that emphasize the ability of dealing with social and cultural differences. Thus, if the techniques and marketing tools are designed to achieve business goals, they must be used to promote the minimization of misunderstanding concepts. A policy oriented to strategic communication turns the access to new markets easier, providing transparency and enabling vital partnership creation.

Clear communication has demonstrated its essential role so that the demand for specialized staff in organizations has grown. Then it is possible to get a balance between the awareness of socio-cultural reality and the ability to develop communication strategy and deal with multiple tools/ technologies. The key is dealing with a multicultural society, turning difficulties into opportunities, meaning that cultural differences should be reversed into positive marketing differentials. It is necessary to develop creative skills and remain alert to explore the opportunities innovations may offer. And also understand that communication processes in the IT field can be the expansion root for new management concepts, whose challenge is to establish a communication guide to diversity, identity and cultural exchanges.

In order to survive in this highly competitive society, both people and companies rely on information. Thus, opportune and personalized information is essential for situational knowledge and analysis, intelligent planning and decision-making.

CONCLUSION

From the results, we can perceive that the manner of how IT professional communicates with the user interferes with management because effective decisions cannot be taken without clear information. Both sides must be attained to get productive results for the organization. It is important that IT professionals incentivize effective communication processes with users because their performance tends to be autonomous and then they must manage their own career and care for personal marketing. Resuming previous main assumptions and testing, we can derive some strategic directives as following:

- The research acknowledges that the use of technical terms makes business communication harder due to the lack of specific knowledge by the user;
- The analysis allows to confirm that the IT professional does not realize actively the importance of being prepared for customer service (they generally do not present related training from academic graduation);
- The research indicates that both IT professionals and users make an effort to turn their interaction easier. However, it is still not sufficient for a trustful interaction;
- The study verifies the need of positioning strategies to: first, make professionals aware of these issues, and second guide them to explore and develop such skills.

We realize that new technologies and working methods, given the diversity of customer's areas of activity, impacts on the redefinition of many practices. Thereby opportunities are opened for new actions, strategic proposals and ways of managing business information. It is a challenge to create an effective communication process using IT technical language, and search for management tools capable of bridging both sides: vision of results by the customer and enterprise marketing goals with the objectives of IT professionals. The company that stands out by its efficient customer service and clear communication will certainly have more competitive elements than its competitors.

Each time more it is necessary to create or explore a strength that may become the differential over competitors. Cultural adequacy may take years to happen; so persistence is required. The results obtained show that IT professionals usually act by intuition, without formalization or orientation that give them more support and attendance parameters. Apparently, this behavior occurs without intention; in this way, many have worked it out by chance but others went wrong without even knowing exactly where the problem lies.

This research will have fulfilled a role if at least a portion of IT professionals be aware about the relevance of effective communication in the vitality of an organization or professional career. There are still gaps whose resolution depends on a commitment between awareness and action. Each professional must find his own way of working the communication process and, then, the personal marketing using his technical knowledge, personal experience and common sense to develop values such as understanding and contribution to business vision.

REFERENCES

Albertin, A. (2005). A tecnologia de informação e o indivíduo: Propondo um modelo de adoção de tecnologia para a inclusão digital (Report FGV n.11). School of Management, Getulio Vargas Foundation, Saint Paul, Brazil.

Allameh, S., Momeni, Z., Esfahani, Z., & Bardeh, M. (2011). An assessment of the effect of information communication technology on human resource productivity of Mobarekeh steel complex in Isfahan Iran. *Procedia Computer Science*, *3*, 1321–1326. doi:10.1016/j.procs.2011.01.010

Antonelli, S., & Santos, A. (2009). Uso da estatística para garantia da qualidade: Um survey com indústria de alimentos baseado no Seis Sigma. Proceedings of the Simpósio de Administração da Produção, Logística e Operações Internacionais. Annals FGV. School of Management, Getulio Vargas Foundation, Saint Paul, Brazil.

Barquette, S., & Chaoubah, A. (2007). *Pesquisa de marketing*. Saint Paul, Brazil: Saraiva Publisher.

Bernardi, P. (2008). Medindo a predisposição para a tecnologia [PhD Thesis]. School of Management, Getulio Vargas Foundation, Saint Paul, Brazil.

Boar, B. (2002). *Tecnologia da informação: A arte do planeamento estratégico*. Saint Paul, Brazil: Berkley Publisher.

Brynjolfsson, E. (2010). The four ways IT is revolutionizing innovation. Mit Sloan Management Review. Retrieved from http://sloanreview.mit.edu/article/it-innovation-brynjolfsson-article/

Cassarro, A. (2011). *Sistemas de informações para tomadas de decisões*. Saint Paul, Brazil: Cengage Learning.

Cohen, M. (2003). Uso da informação na economia de informação: Um estudo na indústria do Estado de São Paulo [PhD Thesis]. School of Management, Getulio Vargas Foundation, Saint Paul, Brazil.

Costa, A. (2007). Os paradoxos da carreira de tecnologia da informação no século XXI: Um estudo empírico exploratório [Master Dissertation]. School of Management, Getulio Vargas Foundation, Saint Paul, Brazil.

Cunha, A. (2009). A influência da linguagem no processo decisório. Retrieved from http://www.artigonal.com/gerencia-artigos/a-influencia-da-linguagem-no-processo-decisorio-1115309.html

Eagle, S. (2012). Learning in the early years: Social interactions around picture books, puzzles and digital technologies. *Computers & Education*, *59*(1), 38–49. doi:10.1016/j.compedu.2011.10.013

Fernandes, S. (2013). Main differentiating issues in aligning information systems with business performance. *International Journal of Information Systems in the Service Sector*, *5*(2), 17–29. doi:10.4018/jisss.2013040102

Gaete, L. (2010). Análise da resistência a sistemas de informação: A perceção dos gestores de tecnologia da informação acerca de sistemas ERP [Master Dissertation]. School of Management, Getulio Vargas Foundation, Saint Paul, Brazil.

Giglio, F. (2010). Implicações dos meios digitais na comunicação de marketing (XIII Semead -Management seminars). University of Saint Paul, Brazil.

Gil, A. (2008). *Métodos e técnicas de pesquisa social.* Saint Paul, Brazil: Atlas Publisher.

Gordon, S., & Gordon, J. (2006). *Sistemas de informação: Uma abordagem gerencial.* Rio de Janeiro, Brazil: LTC Publisher.

Graeml, A., & Csillag, J. (2006) An application of e-mail survey using a word form. Proceedings of the VIIth Annual Conference of Poms, Boston, USA.

Hanson, V. (2010). Influencing technology adoption by older adults. *Interacting with Computers*, *22*(6), 502–509. doi:10.1016/j.intcom.2010.09.001

Hismanoglu, M. (2011). The integration of information and communication technology into current ELT coursebooks: A critical analysis. *Procedia: Social and Behavioral Sciences*, *15*, 37–45. doi:10.1016/j.sbspro.2011.03.048

Hus, V. (2011). The use of ICT in the environmental studies subject. *Procedia: Social and Behavioral Sciences*, *15*, 3855–3860. doi:10.1016/j.sbspro.2011.04.385

Ignatius, J., Leen, J. Y. A., Ramayah, T., Kah Hin, C., & Jantan, M. (2012). The impact of technological learning on NPD outcomes: The moderating effect of project complexity. *Technovation*, *32*(7), 452–463. doi:10.1016/j.technovation.2012.03.003

Iizuka, E. (2003) Um estudo exploratório sobre a exclusão digital e as organizações sem fins lucrativos da cidade de São Paulo [Master Dissertation]. School of Management, Getulio Vargas Foundation, Saint Paul, Brazil.

Klimova, B. (2011). Making academic writing real with ICT. *Procedia Computer Science*, *3*, 133–137. doi:10.1016/j.procs.2010.12.023

Kolikant, Y. (2012). Using ICT for school purposes: Is there a student-school disconnect? *Computers & Education*, *59*(3), 907–914. doi:10.1016/j.compedu.2012.04.012

Kunsch, M. (2007). Comunicação organizacional na era digital: Contextos, percursos e possibilidades. *Signo y Pensamiento*, *51*(XXVI), 38–51.

Limeira, T. (2005) Marketing de serviços na indústria de tecnologia da informação: Novos desafios e oportunidades. Retrieved from http://bibliotecadigital.fgv.br/dspace/handle/10438/2920

Liu, S. (2012). The impact of forced use on customer adoption of self-service technologies. *Computers in Human Behavior*, *28*(4), 1194–1201. doi:10.1016/j.chb.2012.02.002

Luchesa, C., & Neto, A. (2011) Cálculo do tamanho da amostra nas pesquisas em administração. University central library, Curitiba, Brazil.

Madia de Souza, F. (2007). *O grande livro do marketing. M.* Saint Paul, Brazil: Books Publisher.

Maier, R., & Remus, U. (2002). Defining process-oriented knowledge management strategies. *Knowledge and Process Management*, *9*(2), 103–118. doi:10.1002/kpm.136

Malhotra, N. (2006). *Pesquisa de marketing: Uma orientação aplicada.* Porto Alegre, Brazil: Bookman Publisher.

Matos, C. (2011) Uma generalização empírica sobre comunicação boca a boca usando metanálise. Retrieved from http://www.scielo.br/pdf/rac/v15n5/a06v15n5.pdf

Mattana, L., Mota, M., Noro, G., Brito, I., & Rocha, S. (2006) Comunicação organizacional on-line: Aplicação estratégica e suas implicações na gestão de uma empresa de base tecnológica. Proceedings of the XXIX Communication Science Congress, University of Brasília, Brazil.

Mirza, A., & Al-Abdulkareem, M. (2011). Models of e-learning adopted in the Middle East. *Applied Computing and Informatics*, *9*(2), 83–93. doi:10.1016/j.aci.2011.05.001

Miwa, K., & Terai, H. (2012). Impact of two types of partner, perceived or actual, in human-human and human-agent interaction. *Computers in Human Behavior*, *28*(4), 1286–1297. doi:10.1016/j.chb.2012.02.012

Müller, E. (2009) O perfil motivacional e a inclinação de carreira do estudante e do profissional da tecnologia da informação [Master Dissertation]. School of Management, Getulio Vargas Foundation, Rio de Janeiro, Brazil.

Naumann, A., Wechsung, I., & Hurtienne, J. (2010). Multimodal interaction: A suitable strategy for including older users? *Interacting with Computers*, *22*(6), 465–474. doi:10.1016/j.intcom.2010.08.005

Neufeld, J. (2009). *Estatística aplicada à administração usando excel.* Saint Paul, Brazil: Prentice Hall Publisher.

Partala, T., & Kallinen, A. (2012). Understanding the most satisfying and unsatisfying user experiences: Emotions, psychological needs, and context. *Interacting with Computers*, *24*(1), 25–34. doi:10.1016/j.intcom.2011.10.001

Pineida, F. (2011). Competencies for the 21st century: Integrating ICT to life, school and economical development. *Procedia: Social and Behavioral Sciences*, *28*, 54–57. doi:10.1016/j.sbspro.2011.11.011

Polizelli, D., & Ozaki, A. (2008). *Sociedade de informação: Os desafios da era da colaboração e da gestão do conhecimento*. Saint Paul, Brazil: Saraiva Publisher.

Reddy, R. (2006). Robotics and intelligent systems in support of society. *IEEE Intelligent Systems*, *21*(3), 23–31.

Rezende, D. (2011). *Planeamento de sistemas de informação e informática: Guia prático para planear a tecnologia da informação integrada ao planeamento estratégico das organizações*. Saint Paul, Brazil: Atlas Publisher.

Rezende, D., & Abreu, A. (2010). *Tecnologia da informação aplicada a sistemas de informação empresariais*. Saint Paul, Brazil: Atlas Publisher.

Rios, L. (2006) Comércio eletrónico: Variáveis que influenciam a propensão à compra [Master Dissertation]. School of Management, Getulio Vargas Foundation, Rio de Janeiro, Brazil.

Rodrigues, E. (2008) A interação entre sistemas de informação e o trabalho no setor bancário no Brasil: Uma análise estruturalista [PhD Thesis]. School of Management, Getulio Vargas Foundation, Rio de Janeiro, Brazil.

Rogers, E. (1995). *Diffusion of Innovations*. New York, USA: Free Press.

Romano, R. (2011) Os impactos do uso de tecnologia da informação e da identificação e captura automática de dados nos processos operacionais do varejo [PhD Thesis]. School of Management, Getulio Vargas Foundation, Saint Paul, Brazil.

Rostock, F. (2011) O impacto da tecnologia da informação na geração de recursos competitivos nas empresas: Uma abordagem baseada em estudos de caso [PhD Thesis]. School of Management, Getulio Vargas Foundation, Saint Paul, Brazil.

Sanchez, F. (1999). *Metodologia para la investigacion en marketing y direccion de empresas*. Madrid, Spain: Ediciones Pirámide.

Scornavacca, E., Becker, J., & Andraschko, R. (2001) E-survey: Conceção e implementação de um sistema de survey por internet. Proceedings of the National Meeting of the Post-graduation Programs, Rio de Janeiro, Brazil.

Silva, A., & Silva, L. (2003) Representação mental sobre o atendimento dos profissionais de informática no CEFET. Proceedings of the XXIII National Meeting of Production Engineering, Ouro Preto, Brazil.

Silva, B. (2011) Decisões do uso da tecnologia da informação: Um estudo sobre o efeito das capacidades dinâmicas [PhD Thesis]. School of Management, Getulio Vargas Foundation, Saint Paul, Brazil.

Silva, B., & Pereira, M. (2011). Contributos da escola para a inclusão digital. *Innovación Educativa, 21*, 223–233.

Sousa, C. (2008). Difusão das tecnologias da informação e comunicação: Grupos estratégicos nas empresas portuguesas. *Tourism & Management Studies, 4*, 125–141.

Stábile, S. (2001) Um estudo sobre a desconexão entre usuários e desenvolvedores de sistemas de informação e sua influência na obtenção de informação pelo decisor [Master Dissertation]. School of Engineering, University of Saint Carlos, Saint Paul, Brazil.

Stevenson, W. (2001). *Estatística aplicada à administração*. Saint Paul, Brazil: Harbra Publisher.

Suduc, A., Bîzoi, M., Gorghiu, G., & Gorghiu, L. (2011). Information and communication technologies in science education. *Procedia: Social and Behavioral Sciences, 15*, 1076–1080. doi:10.1016/j.sbspro.2011.03.241

Sun, J., & Hsu, Y. (2012). An experimental study of learner perceptions of the interactivity of web-based instruction. *Interacting with Computers, 24*(1), 35–48. doi:10.1016/j.intcom.2011.11.001

Takahashi, T. (2000). *Sociedade da informação no Brasil. Green book*. Brasília, Brazil: Science and Technology Ministry.

Warschauer, M. (2006). *Tecnologia e inclusão social, a exclusão digital em debate*. Saint Paul, Brazil: Senac Publisher.

Wurman, R. (2005). *Ansiedade da informação 2: Um guia para quem comunica e dá instruções*. Saint Paul, Brazil: Cultura Publisher.

KEY TERMS AND DEFINITIONS

Feedback: Action or practice that allows business or professional to manage user suggestions and complaints in a controlled way.

Information Technology: The application of computers and communication equipment to store, retrieve, transmit and manipulate data, often in the context of a business or enterprise.

IT Professional: Related to a job that requires special education, training, or skills in the IT (information technology) field.

IT User: Related here with the term end user, used to distinguish the person for whom a hardware or software product is designed from the developers, installers, and providers of the product.

Screenplay: Here related with a script or execution guide for monitoring and then adjusting practice towards users' needs. Their feedbacks are considered in order to adjust the approach to each user's reality.

Technical Term: A term that has a specific meaning within a specific field of expertise (this should be defined, so that a non-technical receiver can both learn the term and understand how it is used).

Training: The acquisition of knowledge, skills, and competencies as a result of learning vocational or practical curricula. It has specific goals of improving one's capacity, productivity or performance.

User's Profile: A set of data associated with a specific user. It can be used to store a description of relevant characteristics which can be exploited taking into account the person's needs.

ENDNOTES

1 Travel agency, marketing, sales, medicine, architecture, consultancy, etc.

2 Related with the "agree" kind of answers.

Chapter 3
Artificial Intelligence:
Marketing's Game Changer

Edward Forrest
University of Alaska, USA

Bogdan Hoanca
University of Alaska, USA

ABSTRACT

This chapter reviews the many new tools the advent of AI agents has placed into the hands of marketers and consumers alike. AI agents are redefining the roles and rules of the marketing game. While once marketing was the interaction between marketing professionals and customers, AI agents are taking key roles on both sides. The chapter shows how Artificial Intelligence Marketing Agents have begun to proffer the marketer unprecedented marketing research and communication capabilities. However, at the same time AI applications are empowering the consumer to bypass or question the corporate marketing message. Virtual Personal Shopping Assistants (VPSAs) can learn consumers' tastes, predict their needs, and optimize their product purchases. VPSAs are able to instantly match a consumer's need against all accessible products that meet the consumer's expectations and price points. The chapter concludes with recommendations for marketers to recognize the primary role that the consumer's VPSA will play in the marketing game and adjust their marketing efforts accordingly.

INTRODUCTION

The idea of being able to call upon an all-knowing and all-powerful entity to answer your most important question or grant your greatest wish can be traced back through the centuries from the tales of Aladdin to the Oracles of ancient Greece. However, not until the emergence of the computer and its convergence with the internet, would the dream of instant answers to every personal query and concern move beyond wishful thinking. With the advent of the computer in the 1940's, visionaries such as Vannevar Bush foresaw the utility of amassing, collating and interlinking all of the information that was important and relevant to one's research and interests. In his 1945 treatise, "As We May Think," Bush conceived the development of a memory index or extender which he named the *"Memex"* – in which one could access,

DOI: 10.4018/978-1-4666-8459-1.ch003

retrieve, annotate, interconnect and share the world's record base. In 1958, John McCarthy expanded on Bush's idea of ready and hyperlinked access to a global database with his suggestion that software should be written and designed logically and follow the lines of deductive reasoning. In his 1958 paper "Programs with Common Sense," McCarthy argued that a computer program should be able to "draw immediate conclusions from a list of premises," the conclusions should be "either declarative or imperative sentences" and "when an imperative sentence is deduced the program takes a corresponding action." McCarthy's paper is regarded as the first to propose that software design, based upon "common sense reasoning ability," was the key to artificial intelligence. However, it would take four more decades before such AI applications would be realized. It was the mid 1990's, with the commercialization and diffusion of the Internet, exponential growth in computing power and advanced software sophistication that fully functional intelligent agents would come to pass. And, it was at this time that the nature and function of the "intelligent agent" was formally defined:

An intelligent agent is software that assists people and acts on their behalf. Intelligent agents work by allowing people to delegate work that they could have done to the agent software. Agents can, just as assistants can, automate repetitive tasks, remember things you forgot, intelligently summarize complex data, learn from you, and even make recommendations to you. (Gilbert, 1997)

Whether termed an agent or assistant or defined as artificial or virtual, these emerging applications are an amalgamation of many technologies-- voice recognition, linguistic sciences and natural language processing, machine learning, cognitive computing, analytical and predictive statistics, neural networking and deep-learning algorithms. With recent advances in deep-learning algorithms (which function better as more data is processed) and neurosynaptic chips (with a brain-inspired computer architecture that mimics one million neurons and 256 million synapses) the role and scope of intelligent agents has begun to far surpass simple voice based keyword searches or simple smartphone commands such as "turn on Bluetooth;" Indeed AI agents have come a long way from the 1990's when Blockbuster's in-store kiosks used a filtering algorithm to make film recommendations to members based on their rental history and "made such interesting recommendations as a pornographic film to kids and *Teletubbies* to grandparents living in the same household... or the first intelligent agent for the Macintosh ....silently threw everything it found in the trash" when a user used an incorrect name of the destination folder (Ansari, Essegaier, & Kohli, 2000). Today, it is hard to imagine anyone who has purchased online who has not been presented with recommendations from a marketer. The ability to understand and predict subscriber's tastes drives Netflix's user recommendations system, which in turn translates into customer satisfaction and subscription maintenance. In 2009 Netflix awarded its now famous Netflix Prize of $1,000,000, for the best collaborative filtering algorithm that could, based only on a user's previous ratings and the ratings by the general user community, predict the user's ratings for other films the user had not viewed. As AI agent technologies have continuously improved they have come to play an increasingly important role in marketing strategy and customer relationship management.

It has become standard practice to analyze a consumer's past and present consumption patterns and to make suggestions concerning current and future sales as well as cross- and up-selling. Advanced recommender systems are also taking into consideration more of the consumer's unique context, in terms of current location, current status and immediate needs. Yet, as sophisticated as the current recommender systems may be, the next generation of AI agents represent a paradigm shift in AI Marketing applications. Rooted in cognitive computing, advanced sensor technology and natural language interfaces, the next iteration of the AI Marketing agent is just beginning to emerge, and it fulfills the promise of that all-knowing and all-powerful entity that can obey and fulfill the consumer's ultimate command --"Tell me which brand is best to buy and why!"

This chapter's evaluation of the impact of AI technologies on Marketing will be multifaceted in scope. First, in order to clearly explain and fully prove the proposition that "Artificial Intelligence is Marketing's game changer," three factors will be addressed:

1. *What is Artificial Intelligence?*
2. *What is Marketing—or more specifically-- what is the Marketing Game?* and,
3. *What is changing?*

The impact of emerging AI technologies will be examined from the marketing practitioner's, as well as the consumer's perspective. Most notably will be a discussion of Virtual Personal Shopping Assistants (VPSAs) and the definitive role these applications will play within the ongoing paradigm shift in marketing's orientation from a marketer-driven-dominated arena to a consumer-centered-controlled marketing information system. Finally, the chapter will conclude with delineation of the research implications and social concerns of advanced AI agents' impact on marketing and commerce.

ARTIFICIAL INTELLIGENCE: MARKETING'S GAME CHANGER

What Is Artificial Intelligence?

First coined at a 1956 Dartmouth conference, the term AI has evolved over a half century of steady progress in building computers that can manipulate symbols (both logical and linguistic). According to the Google N-gram Project, the use of the term "artificial intelligence" peaked in 1989, even though AI systems would not enter mainstream media until the late 1990's. Before the 1990's, advancements in AI resulted mainly in academic papers and a small number of proprietary back office expert systems designed to automate key business decisions in logistics, procurement, operations management.

A number of developments brought AI into wider use in the 2000's. First, search engines evolved to include not just keyword searches, but more of the context (recent searches, longer term history of search preferences, social searching – aggregating searches geographically or by moment in time, searching for synonyms). Additionally, much work has gone into refining search results to make them more relevant for users, best exemplified by many of the Google proprietary algorithms. Search engines form part of the back end, the engine inside the AI system.

Another relatively recent development, natural language processing (NLP) systems are the front end to AI systems, and they allow users to interact with a computer in conversational language, not requiring a rigid syntax as do computer programming languages. NLP systems have matured beyond textual input, to the point where they can carry out reliable voice recognition, and they can parse and process natural language queries (for example in a search engine). Processing natural language takes considerable computing power, but continuous advances in computing technologies via Moore's Law have finally made sufficient computing power available in a cost effective package. Dedicated systems like IBM Watson rely on local hardware that occupies considerable physical space, but cloud technologies are increasingly used to move the computing power behind the scenes, allowing users to access it via handheld mobile devices. As an example, Apple's virtual personal assistant, Siri, relies on a voice or text interface on a thin client (a smartphone or tablet) that captures the raw user input and relays it to servers in the cloud for processing. The result of the processing is returned to the user in textual or sound format, giving the appearance that Siri resides in the mobile device, but without the hardware bulk apparent in the Watson system. Moore's Law allows the size of AI systems to shrink exponentially over time, and IBM's Watson has gone in two years from taking an entire master bedroom to the size of a pizza box (Upbin, IBM's Watson Now A Customer Service Agent, Coming To Smartphones Soon, 2013).

Moreover, intelligent agents are developing the sensors that early AI versions lacked. Using microphones, cameras, accelerometers and GPS in smart phones, AI systems are aware of the context around the user. They can detect emotions via voice analysis or facial expressions, and can detect whether the user is moving, stationary, or in a vehicle. They can tell whether the user is on an airport or in a coffee shop (Dwoskin, 2014). As GPS positioning accuracy continues to increase to possibly centimeter range (Boyd, 2014), AI systems will be able to detect exactly where the user is located in a particular store or room in a building, and will have increasingly accurate information about the context. This will allow marketers to pinpoint the customer's location down to the shelf or the individual product level. Finally, AI systems can tap into browsing histories, into contacts list and into data from other applications to create a data-rich profile of the user's preferences, current context and to be able to predict the most relevant response.

In addition, other advancements have made AI systems robust enough for general use. The development of AI systems had been plagued for many years by the so called Moravec's Paradox (Brynjolfsson & McAfee, 2014): high level reasoning was easy to automate, while basic sensorimotor skills (recognizing a face in an image, being able to pick up an egg from a basket without breaking it and the other eggs) were virtually impossible for a computer to do. A major advance of modern AI systems over the expert systems of the 1990's is the ability of intelligent agents to learn in real time. The expert systems developed in the 1990's were based on a set of predefined rules that were hardwired into the system and that had to be updated explicitly to avoid obsolescence. Instead, current AI systems learn from both structured and unstructured data, and are able to adapt and relearn as new data points are added. While expert systems tended to become obsolete as the environment changed, modern AI systems remain current as long as they have access to current data sets. Thanks to this ability to learn from data, it is easy for an AI system such as IBM's Watson --which can process 500 gigabytes of information (one million books) per second (Kawamoto, 2011)-- to branch out into a new field or to automatically stay current on the most recent knowledge.

To date, AI's greatest public recognition has been registered by IBM's Deep Blue victory over the world chess champion Gary Kasparov in 1997, and IBM's Watson victory over Jeopardy's all-time grand champions in 2011. It is now an establish fact that AI applications can meet and exceed human capabilities in many aspects where previously humans excelled. It is predicted that within the next decade the world will witness an AI "machine" pass the test laid down in 1950 by Alan Turing. That test deems an AI agent as intelligent when a human engaged in a "blind" conversation simultaneously with another human and the AI agent will not be able to discern which one is the AI agent. Accordingly, AI applications continue to emerge as a logical, economic and demonstrably superior alternative to its human workforce counterpart. Indeed, the on-going obsolescence of the human worker by computers and AI applications is advancing at such a pace that a recent Oxford University study (Frey & Osborne, 2013) found that out of 702 occupations evaluated, nearly half (47%) are at high risk of being fully or substantially computerized in the near future. Those first in line include most workers in transportation, logistics, office and administrative support and production-line-labor. The occupation with the absolute highest risk (at 99% probability of replacement) are "telemarketers"-- whose jobs "will become fully automated" as artificial intelligence, machine learning and interactive voice response systems are integrated and implemented. Ergo the question arises: What other impacts will AI have on Marketing and those that practice the profession?

What Is Marketing and More Specifically the "Marketing Game?"

Whether one examines the official American Marketing Association definition of Marketing (as "the activity, set of institutions, and processes for creating, communicating, delivering, and exchanging offerings that have value for customers, clients, partners, and society at large") or any of the 71 other definitions of Marketing that have been proffered (Cohen, 2011), it is clear that Marketing – in concept and practice—has been defined primarily from the seller's perspective. However, if one considers that the defining act of the marketing process is the phenomenon of exchange between a buyer and a seller, then Marketing is best defined as a game, wherein the buyer (consumer) and seller (marketer) attempt to maximize their cost/benefit ratio in the exchange of money for goods/services. Herein, the role and perspective of the consumer is equally as important as that of the marketer. The fact that the concept of Marketing has been relatively one-sided is attributable to the perceived passivity of the consumer in the marketing game. Marketing was something done to the consumer. Products were pushed. Communication was one way and intrusive. Jay Walker-Smith, president of the marketing firm Yankleovich estimated that the average consumer is bombarded with 5000 ads per day (Johnson, 2006), a number that makes it unlikely that most of the ad messages can stick in the mind of the recipient. Today, consumers are redefining the rules and their role in the game. Marketers no longer can simply buy consumers' interest, it must be earned. Howard Rheingold, a visiting professor at Stanford University and a worldwide authority on the social impact of the communication media, sees human attention as the scarce resource in a world where information will be increasingly commoditized (Rheingold, 2012). Communication should be interactive. Consumers increasingly rely on each other for product information and recommendations. Rather than the customer being targeted by the seller, it is the seller that is often sought out by the buyer.

It is already clear that the Internet and social media have radically altered not only the roles and relationships, but also the differential advantages held by marketer and consumers in the marketing game, as consumers can now find (via Google) and buy (via Amazon) anything, anytime, anywhere on the recommendation of friends and family (via FaceBook) or other customers (via Yelp) and tell the world about it in 140 characters or less (via Twitter). Artificial intelligence has already enabled marketers to understand qualitative input from surveys, in addition to the quantitative survey results. Using tools from companies like Luminoso Technologies and Kanjoya, Inc, marketers can automatically analyze text input on surveys and social media to understand meaning as well as the emotions of the subjects (Rusli, 2014). What is less clear, but arguably more significant, is the degree to which the next disruptive technology – Cognitive Computing -- will be the ultimate game changer. As the next and ultimate iteration of computing, Cognitive Computing is ushering in "the smart machine era" that (short of the singularity envisioned by Ray Kurzweil) "will be the most disruptive in the history of IT," as it "fulfills the earliest visions for what information technologies might accomplish — doing what we thought only people could do and machines could not" (Austin, 2013). *It* will " process sensory as well as transactional input, draw inferences from past experience, understand uncertainty, draw initial conclusions, interact with people in a natural, human-language like way and then modify conclusions according to feedback"... *It* will "solve problems like a human, have... advanced artificial intelligence algorithms and applications that mimic the brain's abilities for perception, action and cognition"....*It* will "interact with Humans... using advanced technologies like voice, gesture, and touch" and, *it* will "interact with other computers: leveraging the Internet of Things ...and respond to networks of other smart machines and devices that talk to each other, make decisions, and get work done autonomously" (Chamberlin, n.d.).

What Is Changing on the Marketers Side: Artificial Intelligence Marketing Agents (AIMAs)

Marketers are just now gaining access to an array of advanced AI platforms, services and technologies. The role and scope of marketing applications that AI is usurping ranges from the relatively simple adjustment of the style and delivery of promotional messaging to the complete coverage of customer relationship management services and interactions. Already Apple's Siri is a familiar companion to users of the iPhone. Google's AI stables include Google Now, a predictive assistant available on both mobile and desktop platforms. Microsoft's Cortana is the intelligent agent for Windows Phone 8.1 (unveiled in April 2014). The most recent addition to the AI family, Cortana inherits the friendliness and humor of Apple's Siri and the ability to anticipate the user's needs from the Google Now predictive assistant (Marshall, 2014). Cortana will learn the user's preferences and will learn to anticipate the user's needs, based on previous interactions, on geo-location information, and on current actions (for example, having a boarding pass ready as the user approaches the airport, when Cortana is aware of a previously made flight reservation). The search capabilities are based on Microsoft's Bing search platform. Unlike most other AI systems, Cortana will have a Notebook, where user preferences, reminders and contacts will be stored, and where the user will be able to review, add and delete information as an explicit privacy interface.

To date, rudimentary applications of artificial intelligence have been used to adjust images to make photos of human faces more memorable, more attractive or friendlier (Khosla, Bainbridge, Torralba, & Oliva, 2013), as well as to understand what makes images popular online (Khosla, Sarma, & Hamid, 2014). Accordingly, by monitoring social media responses, AI agents can modify campaign materials in real time, to maximize consumer interest and message retention. In addition, AI has been applied to the real time analysis of human emotions. Advanced image processing has matured to the point where emotion recognition can be done either via a webcam or using a camera in a physical setting (and emotion detection in verbal interactions has an even longer history) (Eaton, 2012). Using AI techniques, the user's reaction to a product or to an ad can be interpreted, and the stimulus can be modified accordingly. For pleasant or attractive stimuli, the viewer can be cajoled into completing a transaction, while for negative reactions the viewer can be offered more explanations (if the emotion detected is confusion or a blank stare), a different set of options (if positive and negative emotions are displayed) or a different offering altogether (if strong negative emotions are encountered).

Companies have already started to mine social media to understand emotions and preferences as expressed on social media sites. Bluefin Labs, acquired by Twitter in 2013, was one of the companies that started to mine Twitter postings to help companies understand how their customers perceive various product offerings. CBS was surprised to find out that lower rated shows sometimes generate more comments on Twitter, partly because the audience might be more inclined to use social media (or even because the type of show is more conducive to starting a discussion: competition shows tend to foster a more active audience) (Talbot, 2011). Bluefin also helped Procter & Gamble understand that the context is important for the way the message is perceived. The company aired the same product ad in two shows with similar viewer demographics and with similar ratings. The surprise outcome was that one show generated eight times more comments on social media than the other (Talbot, 2011). Bluefin Labs used AI to correlate the Twitter comments and public Facebook comments with the live feed of several TV channels, to understand which channel the posts refer to, as well as the type of content being shown. In 2011, Bluefin was able to process 1400 hours of TV programming per day, and more than 166.7 million comments (Arndt, 2011). By June 2012, the number of social media comments exceeded 100 million per month (Jannarone, 2012).The AI is able to distinguish between regular broadcasting (sports, reality TV etc.) and commercial breaks. The software attempts to understand emotions, and is able to handle the slang, shorthand text, as well as emoticons that are frequently used in social media (Talbot, 2011). On the other hand, the social media comments are far from representative of the entire TV audience. For example, in July 2012, Bluefin encountered comments from 8 million people on social media, out of the 115 million household TV sets then in the US (Jannarone, 2012).

Extrapolating on the marketing implications of emotion and facial recognition through webcam technologies, Burns (2013)asked a retail technology expert and expert in facial recognition technology to identify key applications for Google Glass. In this initial exercise to discern ideas that "would win you customers, intelligence, or other competitive benefits," an impressive range of applications were envisioned. To wit: If you are interested in *marketing research*, "forget focus groups," you will be able to share or *rent someone's feed* and spend an hour or day with the wearer, see what they see, how they live, how they work, shop or recreate. "With Google glass… you can *sell remotely*… log into a sales-person's Glass feed and view the object for sale – be it a house, car, product demo, campus tour…or any sale that requires a "walk around;" *Tourist Feeds*: take virtual vacations or participate in events through purchasing Google Glass feeds... sight-see, hike, attend fairs, amusement parks, concerts or any entertainment venue... Google Glass will enable products to interact (*Talking Products*) with shoppers by processing NFC [near field communication] tags, QR [quick response] codes or RFID [radio frequency identifier tags] to provide videos, coupons, promotions and suggestions …all by just picking up the product and viewing it… a wine bottle can recommend a food pairing, a shirt can suggest a tie, a food item can give a recipe and cooking lesson" (Burns, 2013).

Pricing is another traditional marketing endeavor where AI has made inroads, and where more changes are afoot. In online settings, prices can be adjusted on the fly, and Amazon has come under scrutiny when it attempted dynamic pricing, trying to squeeze a higher margin out of some of its customers (Gunderson, 2012). As some customers noticed, the prices for certain items would go up once the items were placed in the online shopping cart – and it is debatable whether this behavior depended on the item in cause, the identity of the shopper, or the time of the transaction (possibly related to a computer glitch or the practices of a third party selling the goods on Amazon). Amazon changes prices on a regular basis (in part to evaluate the price elasticity of the goods it sells), but now claims that it does so at the same time for all customers. Given the information the company has about particular shoppers (via their account history as well as the browser cookies and history), the company could use AI to adjust prices to possibly extract a higher profit margin out of the less price sensitive shoppers. While potentially lucrative, a practice like this is almost certain to lead to considerable backlash from customers. At the same time, more equitable price changes across the board could be done even in physical stores (Nusca, 2013), for example using the electronic price labels used in the Kohl's stores (Stross, 2013). These electronic labels allow much more accuracy in posting prices, but they also allow a company to put in effect a sale at a moment's notice. In particular, a product that is not selling well on a particular day, or an entire product category in a supermarket could be set on sale by an AI agent that monitors volumes of sales and introduces price promotions in real time.

Perhaps the most advanced demonstration of AI technology can be found in its application to customer relationship management services and interactions. Two years after demonstrating its ability to out-perform the smartest humans ever to play the game of Jeopardy, IBM has proffered its Watson Cognitive Computing application to marketers in the guise of the "Engagement Advisor." Envisioned as an intelligent technology whose services can apply to almost any industry, but especially those that receive many customer service inquiries, such as retailing, banking, insurance and telecommunications, the Engagement Advisor can supplement or supplant human customer-service representatives (Lohr, 2013). As described by Manoj Saxena, General Manager, IBM Watson Solutions:

Watson Engagement Advisor... available in hosted, on-premises, or cloud-based deployment models, learns from its interactions with consumers... "Watson can take questions in natural language, by typing it in or speaking, which makes for more natural conversations.... "Watson is also able to give you not just answers, but also the evidence and sources they're based on... Watson can provide omnichannel interactions; conversations begun on a smartphone, for example, can be picked up at the same point on a tablet later. (Schiff, 2013)

Now considerably smaller in size and faster than when it won Jeopardy in 2011, Watson's super Q&A capabilities are a perfect solution to the marketer's primary objective of creating, sustaining and growing one's relationship with their customers. Customers expect and demand immediate, knowledgeable and personal attention to their inquiries. A single point change in customer satisfaction can yield significant gains "in share of wallet, profitability, revenue, and relationship growth" (IBM Watson Engagement Advisor, Transforming the way people and organizations interact over the lifetime of their relationships, 2013). Engaged customers will spend up to three times more with a brand, and are two times more likely to recommend a company to others. Present levels of customer service are woefully inadequate, as half of the 270 billion customer service calls placed each year go unresolved (Upbin, 2013). Given its ability to scan, analyze and interpret over 200 million pages of structured and unstructured data in a matter of seconds and subsequently enter into a natural language conversation based on its interpretation of and conclusions drawn from its analysis-- the IBM Watson Engagement Advisor provides consumers with a depth of personalized and intelligent assistance that far exceeds what any human customer service agent could ever deliver.

Moreover, Watson's capability to interact, answer questions, and assist consumers with complex purchasing decisions and/or solve problems a consumer might be having with products will revolutionize marketing on other fronts as well. Its ability to analyze structured and unstructured data from credit cards, sales databases, social networks, location data, web pages will enable marketers to ascertain trends in consumer preferences and sentiments, calculate sales probabilities and "proactively and intelligently test, measure and optimize digital content, ads, website pages" (Fidelman, 2013). Applied to the task of media measurement, Watson is being utilized "to sift through and make sense of all the data advertisers receive about their Web, social media, print and television marketing campaigns... to optimize campaigns in real time across every marketing channel" (Lohr, 2013). In addition to being able to predict consumer trends and analyze consumer media consumption patterns, Watson has the ability to discern consumers' personalities through Psycholinguistic Analysis of the language consumers use when posting on social media sites and predict major events that are likely to happen in a consumer's life. "Amazingly, this tech doesn't even have to know a company's customer's social media accounts beforehand. It can figure them out on its own by sifting through what people post online with information in a company database"(Russell, 2014). And, as of November of 2014 with the introduction of Watson Analytics (as a web accessed freemium service) anyone can "aggregate, analyze, visualize and gain insight" from their own data sets).

What Is Changing on the Consumers Side: Virtual Personal Shopping Assistants (VPSAs)

From the consumers' perspective, the emergence of a virtual personal shopping assistant which can learn, predict and serve their tastes, needs and desires and optimize their product/service purchases is a welcome development. This virtual personal shopping concierge will be able to instantly match an immediate or imminent need against all accessible products that meet a consumer's expectations and price points. The savings in time will be significant, given that consumers are hard pressed to keep up with all the latest trends, specials and sales. Moreover, when they do enter shopping mode "50 percent of consumers spend 75 percent or more of their total shopping time conducting online research… as the current state of online and mobile shopping yields a time-consuming, inefficient experience, as consumers comb through websites for information, link by link, or enter keywords into search engines and hope for the best" (Natale, 2014). With one's own VPSA the global marketplace is monitored 24/7/365 and whether one is shopping or not, the consumer would be notified when any item of relevance is available. Once a potential product/service purchase is identified, the VPSA allows the consumer to "ask specific questions based on explicit needs and get expert, personalized, information-driven responses to guide buying decisions," thus creating "the same experience we have in real-world stores with great sales reps every day and is what's missing from digital retail" (Natale, 2014). An agent like IBM's Watson will be able to help a consumer through a complex purchase, for example a real estate transaction. Watson will be able to provide advice on the real estate market, including considerations about valuation, on the financing options available, on the architectural and regulatory restrictions on possible changes and improvements to the existing property, on the tax implications of the purchase, all with an eye to the consumer's financial situation, investment plans, and family situation.

Access to a personal, omniscient, omnipresent shopping assistant which can engage in real-time conversation to learn the consumer's needs, answer the consumer's questions and guide the purchase decisions is currently being developed in the form of Fluid XPS. A partnership between of IBM, North Face and Fluid Inc. building on IBM Watson's natural language interface and cognitive computing analytical abilities, "Fluid XPS will draw on data, (including the brand's product information, user reviews and online expert publications through IBM Watson) to provide consumers with informed recommendations according to their needs and desires. Consumers will receive valuable insights in making smart, satisfying purchases and be able to interact with Watson on desktops, tablets and smartphones for the first time" (Natale, 2014). In January 2014," Fluid's CEO presented a real life example comparing Fluid XPS with today's online shopping experience:

… trying to help his son purchase some equipment on line, they read and read product descriptions, they comparison shopped to find a great price, and, after hours of exploration, they walked away from

their computers without buying a thing. Instead they jumped in the car and went to REI. Why? Because they had questions and the only experts they had to consult with were themselves. Yelp isn't interactive. (Backaitis, 2014)

However, with Fluid XPS the experience for an individual "who plans to go camping in Patagonia and logs on to The *North Face's* website to gear-up ... wouldn't be that different from what happens in a physical store:"

... the concierge might ask the shopper a little bit about her/himself and what he/she might [be] looking for. Watson would then show him/her some things he/she might enjoy or need. In the case of someone who is about to go winter camping, Watson could suggest a sleeping bag for frigid weather. The shopper would be able to tell Watson things like "I think I'd be too warm in that" and then a new suggestion would be made. It sure beats shopping on most of today's retail sites that aren't much more than on-line catalogs from which you can electronically order. (Backaitis, 2014)

Of course, one of the concerns about a technology like Fluid XPS will be the level of trust the consumer needs to develop in the advice. Just as with a salesperson, an AI agent that seems pushy (up-selling or cross-selling) will not get a good response from the consumer. But with a person, the customer can tell if the salesperson is intending to manipulate, even with the most agreeable demeanor. In contrast, an AI agent will have no non-verbal clues that can engender trust, and will have more difficulty in building rapport and trust with the customer. However, IPsoft (2014) has just introduced an AI application that may address this concern in that it is touted as "The First Cognitive Agent Who Understands Like a Human:"

Amelia, our cognitive knowledge worker, interfaces on human terms. She is a virtual agent who understands what people ask – even what they feel – when they call for service.... Amelia is modeled on the human brain. For this reason, she becomes smarter with time. Her thought process can be explained in a sequence of steps:

If she understands your question, she responds to the inquiry.

If she knows the answer to the question, she executes the process to solve the issue.

If she does not know the answer to the question, she can find it by searching the web or your intranet.

If she cannot find the answer, she escalates the question to a human colleague. She then observes her colleague's actions and absorbs the information for future reference.

THE MARKETING GAME: NEW TOOLS, ROLES, AND RULES

The advent of AI agents has placed new tools into the hands of marketers and consumers alike, and subsequently has begun the redefinition of the roles and rules of the game. On the marketer's side, the standard approach of segmenting entire populations and assigning purchase probabilities and media exposure rates for such unrefined targets as "women 18-49 years old" are clearly antiquated. As Rugfelt

(2014) observed, "guessing what individual customers want, via researching large demographic populations, is no longer a viable marketing strategy...Amazon, Facebook, and Google are investing money in machine learning and artificial intelligence to predict what each of their customers want—even before they know... with the consumer more connected on more devices at all times of the day, there's more data available to collect and analyze."

Simultaneously, AI agents increase the knowledge and insight marketers have regarding consumers' product preferences and buying patterns, yet, render consumers less susceptible to the marketer's message and manipulation. As virtual personal shopping assistants search, evaluate, recommend and finalize purchases, the actual consumer is removed from the purchasing process. As marketers and consumers begin to fully avail themselves of the advantages that artificial-intelligence agents proffer, the nature and process of the facilitating exchange in marketplace will be dramatically altered. On the consumer's side, having a virtual shopping assistant that is fully informed of all available options, prices and evaluations greatly lessens the need or influence of the marketer's commercials or promo-tools. As the marketer is increasingly disintermediated, it will become increasing important for marketers to recognize the primary role that the consumer's VPSA plays in the marketing game and adjust their marketing efforts accordingly. Continuing to invoke the old moves in the new game will not only prove ineffective but counterproductive in gaining consumers' trust and patronage. Again, as Rugfelt (2014) observes, "today's marketers have more opportunities to analyze content and data to deliver campaigns that would benefit the marketer, but more important, the consumer." Furthermore,

... [b]ecause users will want their assistants to help them optimize their lives, they'll be willing to share lots of information with it. This way, marketers will be receiving a current, steady stream of relevant information while the assistant collects and learns how consumers behave, what they're doing, and what they want. Once this assistant has proven its relevance, users will trust it as an authority on the possible opportunities for themselves.

Accordingly:

Smarter marketing strategies ... should make room for more hypertargeted services offered to the consumer. Creating well-informed, relevant, and timely options that don't interfere with private digital spaces and respect the consumer's time and consideration will be a demand that will only increase.... We're already seeing marketing-driven apps powered and managed by individual consumers who self-serve by doing all the work a salesperson would help them with in-store. New AI-powered virtual assistants will exist to make consumers' individual lives more organized and improved—to take advantage of every discount, say, or to alert them when they're hitting their monthly spending limit. By using a Virtual Assistant app for advertising, the app can function as educational to consumers rather than feeling invasive, like other outdated forms of advertising, transforming the platform into a valuable service for the customer. (Rugfelt, 2014)

We are just beginning to contemplate the ramifications of only the initial iterations of artificial intelligence agents in the marketing arena. In the nascent stages of this paradigm shift in the marketing game the impact and effects of AI agents will be more experienced than understood. Albeit, one thing already is clear. Consumers are gaining access to information processing technology and techniques that were formerly the preserve of the marketing professional and have begun to fundamentally alter the informational asymmetries which were inherent in the marketing game. In the past the marketer controlled the channels of communication and distribution, positioned the product and set the price. The consumer was hit with over 3,000 messages a day that were placed in mass media vehicles that were targeted at a statistically similar gaggle of persons. The messages were intrusive and brief, designed as much to entertain as to inform, and provided the consumer with little more than a catch phrase in the guise of a slogan or jingle. With the advent of the internet and emergence of social media the communication pattern of the marketing game expanded from strictly "outbound" with the marketer doing all the talking, to "inbound" as well, wherein the consumer searches for, contacts, and transacts with the marketer. Social media has already fundamentally altered the pattern of behavior and communication that consumers employ as they search, evaluate and purchase products/services. Yet, however great and swift this change has been (given that social media is but a decade old), it could be said that the greatest change is still to come:

If you look out at the next five years, you'll see a super-convergence of major technologies coming together at one time—Big Data, the cloud, analytics, mobile, and social—creating a significant disruption in the market" (says Manoj Saxena, general manager of IBM Watson Solutions) who also noted the growing population shift toward consumers brought up amid digital technologies. "10,000 workers are retiring every day, soon to be replaced by millennials who have a whole different sense of how they want to interact [with brands]. (Schiff, 2013)

In light of this shift in the consumers' demographic and technographic profiles, a major re-ordering of marketing strategy is being evidenced. To assess the increased influence of social media, Simonson and Rosen (2014) draw upon the Influence Mix model. The model measures the three components that influence a person's decision to purchase a good or service: personal preferences, beliefs and experiences (P), influences from other people and sources (O) and the marketing message of the vendor (M). Since the three types of influence all compete for the customer's attention, this is a zero-sum game, where an increase in influence in one area will result in lower influence in another. Thanks to social media and to the increased availability of online reviews, the purchasing decision in many industries is more and more influenced by the O component, at the expense of the M component. Simonson and Rosen view this trend as weakening the power of brands, weakening influence of even past purchases and experiences with a brand, and an overall weakening of the powers of positioning and persuasion, traditional tools of the marketers. This trend is not across the board, as few customers will check social media when deciding what brand of tissue to purchase (so called O-independent purchases), but will be more prevalent for goods that have a social aspect or that are purchased less frequently, and for larger amounts (called O-dependent purchases). Sadly for marketers, the types of goods that are O-independent are in low margin, low differentiation, almost commodity product areas.

On one hand, this loss of control over the marketing message is bad news for marketers. Consumers disregard the marketing message in favor of online opinions from other customers with similar backgrounds and interests, something the company cannot easily control. On the other hand, the increased influence of the O lends itself to valuable and freely available market research information. Instead of positioning and persuading, Simonson and Rosen view marketing as moving to a model where marketers keep an eye on competitors' actions, view the reaction of the market, and make their own move in response. AI agents will review social media sites in real time, both about the company's actions and about the competitors', and will propose (or maybe even carry out) counteractions. A number of companies have positioned themselves to provide such services, for now driven less by AI and more by human brainpower: Bluefin Labs (acquired by Twitter), Radian 6 (now part of Salesforce), General Sentiment, Sysomos, Converseon, and Trendrr (Talbot, 2011). A company that has been successful in doing this type of quick response in the fashion industry is Zara (Gallaugher, 2013). The company strategy is to identify promising high end fashion trends and to produce low cost replicas, using a highly vertically integrated operations system to produce imitations of the latest fashion within two weeks of their public appearance. To identify trends, Zara currently relies on human input from sales staff on the store floor who interact with customers. Using AI agents, the company would be able to gather similar information even faster, to further shorten the product lifecycle.

Another intriguing avenue for marketing messages is in automated group recommender (AGR) systems. While the O-dependent decisions discussed above involve individual consumption of products and services, an entire category of hedonic offerings involves group consumption, for example artistic performances or fine dining. The challenge for such situations is that the decisions that are optimal for an individual are not optimal for the entire group. When a group of people must decide what movie to watch together or what bottle of wine to consume together, suggestions from an AGR can lead to decisions that are better for the group than a human-derived choice. Even when members of the group make individual decisions (for example making separate food choices for a restaurant meal together), AGRs can still provide value if group members share high quality social relationships among themselves (Hennig-Thurau, Marchand, & Marx, 2012). Such AGR tools could still be an avenue for marketers to aggregate preferences and to provide personalized advice the group could not otherwise gather on its own from online reviews.

From Mass Customization to Automated Mass Customization

Another area in which AI will change the marketing game is in product design and development. After almost a century of marketing to the mass of consumers (at best, segmented in large groups), information technology made possible a more personalized approach in the 1990's. Pioneered originally by companies like Dell Computer, this new approach involved the customer in the product definition. Instead of conducting market research and targeting some "best guess" product configuration to an entire customer segment, mass customization provided a wide set of options and allowed the customers to custom design the product that best fit their needs and their budget. For example, rather than purchase a standard configuration of a personal computer from Dell Computer, a customer could interactively configure online and in real time the personal computer's configuration: the CPU type and speed, the amount of RAM, the number and type of peripherals, until he or she found the best price/performance combination. More recently, Nike allowed customers to personalize athletic shoes using a vast menu of options. With the advent of AI agents, the customer could be abstracted from this process, because the AI agent will be able to carry out the transaction, personalizing the product based on its knowledge of the customer's preferences. This new capability will allow for a much larger set of options, which would not have been practical for human interactions. Moreover, with the advent of new technologies like 3D printing, more of the design could be outsourced to the customer's AI agent, not just a basic configuration with a set of standard options. For example, the AI agent could order a design for a coffee table that matches the style of other furniture in the customer's possession, of size and design that are not provided by the vendor. Indeed, when one considers the confluence and integration of AI technologies with 3D printing the ramifications are nothing short of revolutionary. When one combines the ability and convenience of producing one's own customized goods with the savings accrued through the elimination of labor, re-tooling, assembly, shipping and inventory carrying costs, the consequences are most ominous for any and all engaged in traditional manufacturing and dependent on the relative cost-efficiencies of out-sourcing. 3D printing not only renders factories obsolete but threatens whole country's economies as production is taken up by the consumer, distribution is de-globalized and marketing marginalized.

Your Artificial-Intelligence Marketing Agent vs. My Virtual Personal Shopping Assistant

In the final analysis, the ultimate winner of the marketing game comes down to a battle of the "bots." The marketer's bot that can find, read and analyze a consumer's every search, download, blogpost, picture, Facebook conversation, product evaluation, tweet, credit card purchase, media consumption preference and/or any and every other bit of information that can be gleaned in the infosphere about the consumer. With the ability to analyze the personality of the consumers, categorize their lifestyle and buying style, extrapolate all their information, the marketer can formulate the optimal marketing mix to sell, cross-sell and up-sell a consumer their product, as well as gain, sustain and cultivate consumers as life-long customers.

Meeting the Marketer's Bot in the marketplace/ring is the Consumer's Bot. In addition to knowing a consumer's tastes, needs and desires, the VPSA knows all past purchases, current preferences and future plans. Moreover, the VPSA has a 360 degree view of the marketplace and can provide a ranking and recommendation of all competitive and comparative products. Rather than pushing a single brand, as a marketer's bot, the VPSA more inclusively and objectively evaluates an entire evoked set of brands and proffers a recommendation aligned with and in the best interests of its master. No doubt, in the long run the VPSA should enable the consumer to gain the upper hand in the marketing game. This outcome appears inevitable, when one considers the latest advancement in Watson's AI skills- the ability to present reasoned arguments pro and con. In a recent demonstration (on April 2014), an example of Watson's new found debating capacity was evidenced. After scanning through its database of 15 terabytes of information on Wikipedia, Watson was asked to present arguments for and against the sale of violent videogames to minors. Watson's verbatim reply was:

I would like to raise the following points in support of the topic. Exposure to violent videogames results in increased physiological arousal, aggression-related thoughts and feelings as well as decreased social behavior. In addition, these violent games or lyrics actually cause adolescents to commit acts of real-life aggression. Finally, violent videogames can increase children's aggression.

On the other hand, I would like to note the following claims that oppose the topic. Violence in videogames is not causally linked with aggressive tendencies. In addition, most children who play videogames do not have problems. Finally, videogame play is part of an adolescent boy's normal social setting. (Borghino, 2014)

One can easily envision asking Watson for a reasoned argument for and against the purchase of any product. Watson having searched and analyzed every available customer review, user recommendation and *Consumer Reports* article in the world will deliver the consumer its verdict in a matter of seconds. For any purchase the consumer is considering all that is needed is a quick query of Watson: Watson what is the best brand? What is the best price?

CONSIDERATIONS AND RECOMMENDATIONS

To date, the application of AI agents has been principally developed by and has primarily served marketing professionals to augment and extend the traditional marketing toolset. It is already fairly common practice to use data driven advertising, where click-through rate or revenue generated are used as a metric to identify which one of two ads is more effective (Ayres, 2008). Using AI techniques, the ads themselves can be adjusted in real time to make them more memorable or possibly more effective at converting views into revenue, using techniques as outlined in (Khosla, Bainbridge, Torralba, & Oliva, 2013). Another use of AI agents has been in harvesting and interpreting the vast amounts of customer feedback available online on social media, knowing full well that the sites can have a critical role in shaping the customers' purchasing decisions. At outdoor equipment manufacturer LL Bean, existing marketing software flags products that have even a small number of one or two star ratings (out of five), for review by management. Products that have real flaws (as opposed to simply accidental flaws) are modified, discounted or discontinued (Simonson & Rosen, 2014). As discussed earlier, more advanced AI agents can cull information outside of the company's website, including social media sites, blogs, and other resources, to build a more complete picture of the perceived value of the company's product mix. The importance of obtaining this more complete picture is premised on the fact that the Influence Mix model predicts that in O-dependent industries (influences from other people and sources) the information available online will be more important than the marketer's commercial campaign.

This increasing realization that the influence and impact of the marketer's commercial campaign is on the wane is further exacerbated by the fact that it may eventually be dismissed altogether when the consumer's purchase cycle is fully maintained and conducted by a consumer's VPSA. As VPSAs become available they will increasingly serve as the primary product purchasing platform for consumers. Accordingly, corporate marketing efforts may in the end be better directed at VPSAs, rather than at human decision makers. Corporate marketers will need to address the VPSA directly, instead, or in addition to the human target.

If consumers increase their reliance on VPSAs, this will greatly reduce the success of some of the marketing techniques that rely on human traits: impulse buying (preference for a product that is immediately available over one that is less available), cognitive heuristics and limitations (preference for a simple choice over a more complex choice), sensory overload (responding to appetizing smells or to arousing imagery) and irrational decision making (including the inability to carry out complex calculations in one's head). In contrast, VPSAs will be closer to the *homo economicus* ideal, with essentially unlimited ability to uncover and compare choices, with the ability to follow the user's preferences and not be swayed by the commercial message, and with the power to negotiate with several merchants at the same time.

FUTURE RESEARCH DIRECTIONS

The role and scope of artificial intelligence in the marketing game is only in its nascent stage and its impact is predicted to increase exponentially. We have shown applications in marketing that will impact both corporate marketing systems (typically to improve on the traditional four P's of marketing), as well as those on the consumer's side.

Research on corporate marketing systems will need to focus on how to use AI to improve current marketing processes. A related, but important research area will involve the customer perceptions of these AI systems. Because AI agents will learn about consumers' habits and will be able to infer behaviors, trends and preferences that might be rather private, corporations will need to establish privacy policies that will reassure customers. In 2008, a controversial marketing campaign at Target sent pregnancy related coupons and offers to women, based on information mined from the purchasing patterns of these women. Since the customers had not registered to receive pregnancy related materials, several (including a 16 year old girl still living with her parents) viewed the materials as an invasion of their privacy (Hill, 2012). As more advanced AI systems are able to dig even deeper into the motives behind customers' purchases, companies will need to at least give the impression that they did not pry too deeply: Target resorted to mixing pregnancy related offers with other seemingly random offers, leading the consumers to believe the company was not targeting them for particular purchases.

The rise of VPSAs will have a considerable impact on how customers make purchasing decisions, but the whole concept is still in its infancy. As rational decision making agents, VPSAs will not be susceptible to the same types of marketing messages currently aimed at humans. Marketers will need to understand how to position their products and how to target a mixed audience of both humans and VPSAs. Future research will also need to consider how VPSAs will be created and deployed to gain the trust of consumers. By their "personal" nature, VPSAs will have considerable insights into what drives consumers' preferences. Will the VPSA's data be owned by the consumer, or also accessible to the manufacturer of the agent? How will the consumer know that there are no backdoors (corporate or governmental in nature) that can leak out private information from the VPSA? How will the security of the agent be ensured, even if no backdoors are present? A third party breaking into a VPSA will gain tremendous information about the agent's owner, private and confidential information about purchasing preferences, but also bank accounts and purchase histories that could give a thief access to valuable physical and virtual assets. Unless consumers are satisfied with the security levels available for VPSAs, the merits of the technology will not be compelling enough for it to become widely used.

Finally, a social concern is that the rise of VPSAs will lead for further social inequalities. Wealthier people, who will be more likely to afford a more expensive and capable agent, will have even more access to the best deals, the most up to date information, and the most efficient consumption processes. Despite the possible economic benefits of VPSAs, an unwise application of the technology has the potential to further deepen the digital divide, and to increase the inequalities that plague society. Further research might uncover ways in which such an outcome can be avoided.

REFERENCES

Amazon Prime Air. (n. d.). *Amazon.com*. Retrieved from http://www.amazon.com/b?node=8037720011

Ansari, A., Essegaier, S., & Kohli, R. (2000). Internet Recommendation Systems. *JMR, Journal of Marketing Research, 37*(3), 363–375. Retrieved from http://www.haas.berkeley.edu/Courses/Spring2000/BA269D/AnsariEssegaierKohli99.pdf doi:10.1509/jmkr.37.3.363.18779

Arndt, R. Z. (2011, November 7). Bluefin mines social media to improve TV analytics. *Fast Company*.

Austin, T. (2013). The Disruptive Era of Smart Machines Is Upon Us. *Gartner*. Retrieved from http://www.gartner.com/doc/2598620

Ayres, I. (2008). *Super Crunchers: Why Thinking-By-Numbers is the New Way To Be Smart*. Bantam.

Backaitis, V. (2014, January 12). Will IBM's Watson Change the Customer Experience? Beyond Customer Experience Management - What your CMS really needs to deliver. *CMS Wire*. Retrieved from http://www.cmswire.com/cms/big-data/will-ibms-watson-change-the-customer-experience-nrf14-023767.php

Borghino, D. (2014, May 9). IBM's Watson can now debate any topic. *Gigmag*. Retrieved from http://www.gizmag.com/ibm-watson-debate/31993/

Boyd, J. (2014, April 23). *Japan's Plan for Centimeter-Resolution GPS*. IEEE Spectrum. Retrieved from http://spectrum.ieee.org/aerospace/satellites/japans-plan-for-centimeterresolution-gps/

Brynjolfsson, E., & McAfee, A. (2014). *The Second Machine Age: Work, Progress, and Prosperity in a Time of Brilliant Technologies*. New York, New York: W. W. Norton & Company.

Burns, W. (2013, February 27). Nine Business Applications for Google Glass. *Forbes*. Retrieved from http://www.forbes.com/sites/willburns/2013/02/27/nine-business-applications-for-google-glass-love-ideasicle/

Bush, V. (1945, July 1). As We May Think. *The Atlantic*. Retrieved from http://www.theatlantic.com/magazine/archive/1945/07/as-we-may-think/303881/

Chamberlin, B. (n. d.). *Cognitive Computing Trends to Watch in 2014*. Retrieved from http://www.bill-chamberlin.com/downloads/cognitive-computing-a-2014-horizonwatching-trend-report/

Cohen, H. (2011, March 29). *72 Marketing Definitions*. Retrieved from http://heidicohen.com/marketing-definition/

Dwoskin, E. (2014, January 13). What Secrets Your Phone Is Sharing About You: Businesses Use Sensors to Track Customers, Build Shopper Profiles. *Wall Street Journal*.

Eaton, K. (2012, June 7). Does your phone know how happy you are? The emotion recognition industry comes giddily of age. *Fast Company*.

Epps, S. (2013, June 2). Five Ways Google Glass Will Change Marketing. *Forbes*. Retrieved from http://www.forbes.com/sites/onmarketing/2013/07/02/five-ways-google-glass-will-change-marketing/

Fidelman, M. (2013, September 4). IBM's Watson Set To Revolutionize Marketing. *Forbes*. Retrieved from http://www.forbes.com/sites/markfidelman/2013/09/04/ibms-watson-set-to-revolutionize-marketing/

Frey, C. B., & Osborne, M. A. (2013, September 17). *The Future of Employment: How Susceptible are Jobs to Computerisation?* Retrieved from http://www.oxfordmartin.ox.ac.uk/downloads/academic/The-Future-of-Employment.pdf

Gallaugher, J. (2013). *Information Systems: A Manager's Guide to Harnessing Technology, v. 2.0.* Flat World Knowledge.

Gilbert, D. (1997). *Intelligent Agents: The Right Information at the Right Time*. IBM Corp.

GoodGuide Delivered To Your Phone. (n. d.). Retrieved from GoodGuide: http://www.goodguide.com/about/mobile

Gunderson, L. (2012, May 11). Amazon's 'dynamic' prices get some static. *The Oregonian*.

Hennig-Thurau, T., Marchand, A., & Marx, P. (2012, September). Can Automated Group Recommender Systems Help Consumers Make Better Choices? *Journal of Marketing*, *76*(5), 89–109. doi:10.1509/jm.10.0537

Hill, K. (2012, February 2). How Target Figured Out A Teen Girl Was Pregnant Before Her Father Did. *Forbes*.

IBM Watson. (2014, January). Retrieved from IBM: http://www-03.ibm.com/press/us/en/presskit/27297.wss

IBM Watson Engagement Advisor, Transforming the way people and organizations interact over the lifetime of their relationships. (2013, May). *IBM*. Retrieved from http://www-03.ibm.com/innovation/us/watson/pdf/ibm_watson_engagement_brochure.pdf

iOS7 - Siri. (n. d.). *Apple Computers*. Retrieved from http://www.apple.com/ios/siri/

IPsoft. (2014). http://www.ipsoft.com/what-we-do/amelia/

Jannarone, J. (2012, September 17). When Twitter Fans Steer TV. *Wall Street Journal*.

Johnson, C. (2006, September 17). Cutting Through Advertising Clutter. *CBS News*. Retrieved from http://www.cbsnews.com/news/cutting-through-advertising-clutter/

Kawamoto, D. (2011, February 8). How IBM Built Watson, Its Jeopardy-Playing Supercomputer. *Daily Finance*. Retrieved from http://www.dailyfinance.com/2011/02/08/ibm-supercomputer-watson-jeopardy/

Khosla, A., Bainbridge, W. A., Torralba, A., & Oliva, A. (2013). Modifying the Memorability of Face Photographs. *International Conference on Computer Vision 2013*. Sydney. doi:10.1109/ICCV.2013.397

Khosla, A., Sarma, A. D., & Hamid, R. (2014). What Makes an Image Popular? *International World Wide Web Conference*. Seoul, Korea.

Kotler, P., & Keller, K. (2011). *Marketing Management, 14/E*. Prentice Hall.

Lohr, S. (2013, May 21). I.B.M. Puts Watson to Work in Business. *New York Times*. Retrieved from http://bits.blogs.nytimes.com/2013/05/21/i-b-m-puts-watson-to-work-in-business/?_php=true&_type=blogs&_php=true&_type=blogs&_r=1

Maitin-Shepard, J., Cusumano-Towner, M., Lei, J., & Abbeel, P. (2010). Cloth Grasp Point Detection based on Multiple-View Geometric Cues with Application to Robotic Towel Folding. *Proceedings of the International Conference on Robotics and Automation*. doi:10.1109/ROBOT.2010.5509439

Marshall, G. (2014, April 3). Cortana: everything you need to know about Microsoft's Siri rival. *Techradar*. Retrieved from http://www.techradar.com/us/news/phone-and-communications/mobile-phones/cortana-everything-you-need-to-know-about-microsoft-s-siri-rival-1183607

McCarthy, J. (1958). Programs with common sense. *Symposium on Mechanization of Thought Processes* (pp. 77-84). Teddington, England: National Physical Laboratory.

Natale, J. (2014, April 23). IBM Watson Group to transform the consumer shopping experience. Retrieved from http://phys.org/news/2014-04-ibm-watson-group-consumer.html

Nusca, A. (2013, October 2). The future of retail is dynamic pricing. So why can't we get it right? *ZDNet*.

Rheingold, H. (2012). *Net smart: how to thrive online*. Cambridge, Massachusetts: MIT Press.

Rugfelt, M. (2014, May 1). Artificial Intelligence's Impact on Marketing. *Direct Marketing News*. Retrieved from http://www.dmnews.com/artificial-intelligences-impact-on- marketing/article/344554/

Rusli, E. (2014, April 2014). Firms Use Artificial Intelligence to Tap Shoppers' Views: Analyzing Focus Groups, Surveys, Online Forums and Social Media Provides New Data. *The Wall Street Journal*.

Russell, K. (2014, February 4). IBM Is Using Watson To Psychoanalyze People From Their Tweets. *Business Insider*. Retrieved from http://www.businessinsider.com/ibm-watson-psychoanalyzes-tweets-2014-2#ixzz2sPUJ6cOw

Saxena, M. (2013, May 21). *How Cognitive Technologies Can Help Transform the Way Companies and Consumers Connect. A Smarter Planet.* Retrieved from http://asmarterplanet.com/blog/2013/05/connect.html

Schiff, A. (2013, May 21). Just Ask Watson: IBM Unveils the Watson Engagement Advisor. *Direct Marketing News*. Retrieved from http://www.dmnews.com/just-ask-watson-ibm-unveils-the-watson-engagement-advisor/article/294283/

Seamans, R., & Zhu, F. (2014). Responses to Entry in Multi-Sided Markets: The Impact of Craigslist on Local Newspapers. *Management Science*, *60*(2), 476–493. doi:10.1287/mnsc.2013.1785

Simonson, I., & Rosen, E. (2014). *Absolute value: what really influences customers in the age of (nearly) perfect information*. New York, NY: Harper Collins.

Stross, R. (2013, February 9). Digital Tags Help Ensure the Price Is Right. *The New York Times*.

Talbot, D. (2011, October 18). A Social-Media Decoder. *MIT Technology Review*.

Upbin, B. (2013, February 8). IBM's Watson Gets Its First Piece Of Business In Healthcare. *Forbes*. Retrieved from http://www.forbes.com/sites/bruceupbin/2013/02/08/ibms-watson-gets-its-first-piece-of-business-in-healthcare/

Upbin, B. (2013, May 21). IBM's Watson Now A Customer Service Agent, Coming To Smartphones Soon. *Forbes*.

Wagner, M. (2011, January 19). What Does IBM's Watson Mean for Marketing? *The CMO Site*. Retrieved from http://www.thecmosite.com/author.asp?section_id=1137&doc_id=203302

KEY TERMS AND DEFINITIONS

Artificial-Intelligence Marketing Agent: A customer-facing artificial intelligence system that automates a range of current marketing functions including ascertaining, anticipating and serving the customer's tastes, needs and desires.

Automated Group Recommender (AGR) System: Provides product/service recommendations optimized for an entire group of consumers.

Automated Mass Customization: The ability of organizations to customize offerings for individual customers automatically, using artificial intelligence systems that can elicit, process and respond to the customer's preferences.

Cognitive Computing: Simulation of the human thought process through application of machine learning algorithms to data mining, pattern recognition and natural language computer processing systems.

Intelligent Agent: A computer system that displays artificial intelligence (the ability to elicit and interpret inputs from humans and to respond in a meaningful manner, adapting to the situation as a human would do).

Marketing Recommendation Systems: Information systems that exhibit rudimentary artificial intelligence by considering the customer's purchase history, stated preferences and implied preferences and making recommendations that are likely to be acceptable to the customer. An example are the suggestions made on the Amazon.com website when viewing a product's page.

Virtual Personal Shopping Assistant: An artificial intelligence based computer system that learns the preferences of a human user and is able to automatically search, negotiate and present back to the human the most relevant products and services that would meet the user's needs.

Chapter 4
Business Management and New Technologies to Improve the Services

Giuseppe Granata
University of Cassino and Southern Lazio, Italy

ABSTRACT

Governments around the world have come to recognize the potential of new Information and Communication Technologies (ICT's) to reshape the ways in which they interact with citizens, businesses and other key stakeholders, hence the current move towards e-Government. A major goal of e-Government initiatives is to improve the quality of public service delivery through providing individuals and organizations with a coherent interface with government that has to be organized around their needs rather than the structure of government bodies. To that end, many governments have begun applying to their e-Government strategies the commercial concept commonly referred to as "Customer Relationship Management" (CRM), thus generating a new field of knowledge and related applications. This chapter discusses some of the key issues to implementing CRM in e-Government. It lays particular stress on the CRM capabilities of identifying and differentiating users, promoting take-up of e-Government and measuring the progress against its stated objectives. The conceptual framework will also be related to a case-study dealing with the Italian Revenue Agency, responsible for collecting tax and customs duties for government, which is developing a rich CRM program along with an ICT re-engineering process.

1. INTRODUCTION

The e-Economy has dramatically transformed the expectations of individuals and organizations towards service delivery. One-to-one, 24x7, cross-organizational, multichannel services, shaped by leading-edge customer service organizations, are now expected to be made available in a range of contexts, including interactions with Governments.

Governments worldwide are responding to these expectations of customer service through developing rich e-Government programs.

DOI: 10.4018/978-1-4666-8459-1.ch004

E-Government has been defined in various ways. Drawing on global sources, definitions of e-Government range from «utilizing the Internet and the world-wide web for delivering government information and services to citizens» [1] to «the use by governments agencies of information technology (such as Wide Area Networks, the Internet, and mobile computing) that have the ability to transform relations with citizens, businesses and other arms of government» [2]. In a more comprehensive way, the OECD defines e-Government as «the use of information and communication technologies, and particularly the Internet, as a tool to achieve better government (…) by enabling better policy outcomes, higher quality services, greater engagement with the citizens and by improving other key inputs identified»[3]. Also, the Gartner Group refers to e-Government as «the continuous optimization of service delivery, constituency participation, and governance by transforming internal and external relationships through technology, the Internet and the new media»[4].

The common theme behind these definitions is that e-Government involves using new information and communication technologies (ICT's) to improve and increase the ways in which governments interact with their stakeholders.

It should also be noted that e-Government does not equate to e-Governance, since "governance", on the one hand, and "government", on the other, point to different aspects of the relationship between government and its stakeholders. Governance stresses the way in which decisions are made, while government stresses the way in which these decisions are carried out: delivery of a service is a function of government, while determining whether or not to provide a service relates to governance. Accordingly, e-Government relates to the provision of government information and transactions using electronic means, whereas e-Governance is «a technology-mediated relationship between citizens and their governments from the perspective of potential electronic deliberation over civic communication, over policy evolution, and in democratic expression of citizen will»[5].

e-Government initiatives fall into three categories relating to the main types of interactions it can be applied to, namely: Government-to-Citizens, Government-to-Business and Government-to-Government.

Not detracting from the importance of Government-to-Government and Government-to-Business, this chapter will focus primarily on Government-to-Citizen applications of e-Government.

A major goal of e-Government initiatives worldwide is to improve the quality of service delivery to constituents. In order to achieve this goal, many governments have begun applying to their e-Government strategies the commercial concept commonly referred to as "Customer Relationship Management", thus generating a new field of knowledge and related applications.

However, the adoption of CRM in (e)Government and understanding the resultant advantages is in its relative infancy. So, there is still much to be learned on the subject and it is indeed what drives the current research.

Research Objectives and Methodology

This research is conceptual in nature and aims to contributing to the current knowledge on the strategies that government organizations undergoing e-Transformations should develop in order to manage the impact of these initiatives on the relationship with their "customers". More specifically, the objective of this chapter is to highlight the potential of e-Government, if coupled with a systematic and strategic customer relationship management process, to be an enabler of better service delivery.

The chapter proceeds as follows: first, it reviews the existing literature on CRM; then discusses some of the key issues to implementing CRM within the context of an e-Government initiative; next relates the conceptual framework to a case-study dealing with the Italian Revenue Agency, which is developing a rich CRM program along with a ICT re-engineering process.

The data used in the case-study are drawn from a variety of sources. First and foremost, a series of focused interviews were conducted with the Director of the Office of Planning and Audit (Roman branch of the Agency). The information gathered was supplemented with illustrative material issued by the Office of External Relations as well as a few quantitative data drawn on The Agency's on-line and off-line publications.

The paper will conclude by highlighting some possible insights to be gained from the research and making suggestions for future researches on the subject.

1. THE GOALS OF CRM AND NEW TECHNOLOGIES

Prior to moving into a detailed discussion of CRM in e-Government, it is essential to trace the origin of the concept and its most common applications.

Customer Relationship Management (CRM) is a managerial concept currently sweeping businesses worldwide, especially among the professional service sector businesses. CRM is commonly referred to as the holistic process a business perform in order to identify, attract, differentiate and retain customers.

Put this way, CRM seems to be nothing but the practice of the old-fashioned marketing concept with a view to selecting and managing the most profitable customer relationships.

The concept of IT-enabled CRM (also known as e-CRM) is relatively new, instead. It refers to the integration of sales, marketing, service, enterprise resource planning and supply chain management functions through business process automation, technology solutions and information resources such as to maximize the value of each customer interaction (Galbreath, Rogers; 1999; p. 162).

Information Technology is widely believed to be a critical enabler of CRM initiatives. Actually, CRM has many technologies at its core such as call centers, computer telephony integration, Internet storefronts, data warehouse, to name but a few [6]. CRM technologies are most commonly deployed in functional areas such as customer support and service, sales and marketing, in order to optimize profitability and revenue. Integration between CRM systems and Enterprise Resource Planning is also becoming common [7].

Some of the key benefits that CRM solutions may offer include: provide better customer service, cross sell products more effectively, help sale staff close deal faster and simplify marketing and sales process.

Though current CRM practices rely heavily on technology, CRM should not be viewed as a merely technological initiative (Kale, 2003, p. 44). Above all, CRM involves an organizational focus on the behaviour of and communication with, the customer. It includes the harnessing of technology for mining data related to customer preference and behaviour. Ultimately, it focuses on effectively turning these data into intelligent business knowledge to more efficiently manage customer relationships. All that considered, CRM can be best referred to as a whole-of-business strategy that aligns the activities a business perform around customer needs and circumstances and involves using technology as an enabling tool of the processes required to turn strategy into business results.

CRM, or rather IT-enabled CRM, is a relatively recent phenomenon and so is the literature on the subject.

To date, attention has been paid primarily to CRM in the business environment. Yet, the current efforts by governments to improve the quality of service delivery through increasing their customer focus have made CRM a significant consideration in government, too.

Enhanced quality of service delivery has been a major component of public administration reform over the past two decades and the use of ICT's to generate improvements has been a primary driver for e-Government initiatives worldwide. Indeed, given the emphasis in both policies and in commentary, more generally on online service issue and online service targets, one might assume this to be the only objective of e-Government (OECD, 2005, p. 34).

In the early stages of e-Government, however, governments merely focused on putting as many services on line as possible, most of which were organized around their own organizational structures rather than around constituents' needs.

Presently, governments are no longer pursuing that approach to e-Government. Indeed, e-Government initiatives being implemented today are primarily aimed at improving the quality of service delivery through re-organizing services around constituents' needs. As a result, governments are now attempting to adopt many of the service delivery and customer relationship management capabilities most commonly found among leading-edge customer service businesses.

The above considerations all argue for the significance of exploring the current CRM practices performed by government organizations with a view to improving their e-Service delivery models.

The starting point of any critical study on the subject should be to consider what CRM means to government. It should be noted that most definitions of CRM that have been provided in literature refer to the business environment, while there are few specifically relating to CRM in the public sector.

A working-definition comes from Accenture (2003, p. 15):

«CRM is a capability that allows government to dramatically improve its relationship with its customers through reorganizing services around customer intentions [need and circumstances]. It allows agencies to create an integrated view of the customer and use this information to coordinate services across multiple channels. CRM provides government with a set of tools and techniques that enable intelligent interactions:

- Based on information/insight about the characteristics, needs and preferences of customers;
- Encompassing all channels of interaction;
- Embodying a comprehensive history of the previous interactions with each customer;
- Encouraging customers to use the most appropriate channel;
- Enabling agencies to meet their objectives of improving services, reducing costs and improving program effectiveness.

CRM constitutes a more comprehensive, methodical approach to providing services that traditionally have been pursued in separate, ad hoc ways».

To others, CRM is primarily a technology, a «class of software designed to provide governments with the ability to manage their constituent relationships consistently, effectively and through a variety of channels» (Kavanagh, 2001, p. 35).

Of the above definitions, this paper adopts the former as best describing the gist and the purpose of CRM in the public sector. True that the CRM technologies that are now being adapted to the public sector may be important enablers of modernized public services or e-Governments, but on the other hand technology by itself will not suffice for governments to achieve the goal of improved service delivery. In the absence of a whole-of-government approach that integrate technology, people and processes, the success of these initiatives is unlikely.

Dealing with CRM and e-Government in the brief space of this paper requires a very narrow focus. The next section focuses on some of the CRM capabilities governments should develop in order to improve their e-Service delivery models, namely: identifying and differentiating users, promoting take-up of e-Government, measuring the progress towards its stated objectives.

2. E-GOVERNMENT: SELECT AND DIFFERENTIATING USERS

A basic CRM capability that is imperative for governments to develop is identifying what e-services need to be enabled, or improved, to what constituents, through what channels. This is quite similar to establishing product-market relationships in businesses, and may be viewed as the first key step to successfully implement e-Government initiatives.

At the very beginning, e-Government services were based on the structural characteristics of government agencies and civil servants, rather than on the needs of constituents. In such way, to access a service, constituents needed to know which agency provided it. This is hardly justifiable in modern government since it is entirely possible, by means of new information and communication technologies, to develop interfaces (most notably web-based interfaces) capable of shielding constituents from the machinery of government, while satisfying all the internal administrative concerns for completeness, timeliness and control (Marche, McNiven; 2003; p. 77).

Governments have now come to recognize the need for their e-Government services to be (re)organized around users' needs with a view to rendering consistently differentiated and, wherever possible, personalized services [8]. This is commonly referred to as either "citizen-centric", "constituent-focused" or "user-focused" approach to public service delivery.

e-Government has the potential to be an enabler of such a shift in service delivery: without the constraints of physical locations, distinct workforces and long-standing culture barriers that have historically impeded service integration or re-organization, e-Services could be organized from a constituent-centric perspective far more easily than can be done in the offline world.

Taking a user-focused approach to e-Government involves, above all, understanding who users actually are and what they want (Kost, 2004, p. 1).

As different people have different needs and expect specific e-Services to be enabled appropriately, governments need to develop a detailed view of their customer (constituent) base through gathering and analysing information about constituents in order to gain insights into their needs and practices and (re) shape their e-service offerings accordingly.

Recent studies found that high-performance government organizations around the globe actively use customer information to shape their services, channels and operations (Linder, Brooks; 2008; p. 82). They actually organize teams to gather data from many sources, including transactions records, satisfaction surveys and outcome studies, to develop insights into client needs and practices. Then they use these insights to understand different client segments and to design and target services, as well as to tailor delivery channels, such as to maximize the overall value they deliver.

Leading governments are also making moves towards a model of *proactively* identifying what services may be useful to constituents by involving them in developing their policies and initiatives (Accenture, 2003, p. 22). In such model, government agencies actively seek customer inputs through surveys, focus groups, workshops, committees, user groups and similar panels. These consultations cover not only the services that are being offered but also the processes and the channels required to deliver them. This represents a significant shift in public service delivery strategies where agencies have traditionally sought feedback only after implementing a customer service program.

Despite the widespread commitment referred to above, however, many government agencies are still struggling to develop a customer knowledge base, that is an organized collection of customer information. The trouble is not as much gathering information – agencies have multiple methods of collecting information about their customers – as translate this information into business intelligence.

Indeed, e-Government global surveys (Accenture, 2003, p. 21) indicate that many agencies are not very effective at optimizing the use of data to improve service delivery, especially as regards grouping customers into different sets based on specific wants/needs, using insights from grouping to tailor services to specific customer needs and/or deliver through preferred channels. In such cases, a more refined segmentation of their customer base would be a key issue for agencies to address in order to further tailor and target electronic service delivery.

What is also critical to government agencies is the capability to share customer information with other agencies.

Governments have a general reputation of functional insularity, which is often called "silos" or "stovepiping". It refers to the inability to integrate customer information and service provision across government agencies. This is to be traced back to both deeply entrenched cultures and practices, supported by the tradition of ministerial accountability, and to the fact that it was administratively very difficult to integrate systems and practices between agencies.

The existing CRM technologies (e.g. data warehouse) that are now being adapted to the public sector can play an important role in enabling inter-agency data sharing and the assembly of customer information towards the creation of customer knowledge. Yet, CRM technological initiatives – in both public and private organizations – usually imply the implementation of a customer-centric business strategy, a redesign of functional activities and a re-engineering of work processes around all customer touch points using technology as an enabler (Croteau, Li; 2006; p. 32).

Instead, until very recently, many government agencies have focused more on the technological aspects of CRM and less on pairing technology upgrades with changes in business processes that would have fully exploited new system capabilities. As a result, agencies have not realized all the benefits expected from their initiatives and are still struggling with integration issues.

3. PROMOTING THE E-SERVICES

Also inherent in a holistic CRM process is promoting take-up of e-Government services as they become available.

Extensive researches into citizen-to-government interactions found that even in countries with high percentages of e-Government usage and Internet penetration the telephone continues to be the predominant means citizens use to communicate with government (Accenture, 2005, p. 28).

A major barrier to e-Government take-up is citizens' perception that e-channels are not as easy to use as traditional channels (e.g. telephone, post/mail, in person). Security and privacy also figure among barriers but not as prominently as the widespread perception that traditional channels are more convenient [9].

It should also be noted that people do not necessarily know how or where to access e-Government services. Many perceive government as complex and unconnected and their knowledge of e-Services can be quite limited. As a result, potential users are often unaware of the electronic services that have been made available.

The above considerations all point to the need for governments to raise public awareness about e-Services and, all the more important, to educate people to use them.

There is, however, evidence that some leading countries are beginning to apply effective methods to drive e-Government take-up (Accenture, 2006, p. 36), namely:

- Strong pressure or mandatory use of e-channels for some services (e.g. requiring agencies to accept only electronic invoices from suppliers);
- Incentives for online use to encourage people to take more advantage of self-service. This is particularly common among revenues agencies (e.g. promising earlier refunds or offering extension of filing deadline for those who file electronically). Approaches of the kind, however, are not always easy to apply, especially in those countries that value individualism or believe that all citizens must receive the same service advantages irrespective of their ICT's abilities. In such contexts, any approach that appears too heavy-handed by the government or implies favourite treatments for a particular group may cause trouble;
- Marketing pull. Leading governments are also using a broad range of marketing tools, from basic and *ad hoc* campaigns (e.g. running a public service announcement on television) to more innovative ones, such as direct e-mail, outbound calls and website ads.
- High-touch push. Many governments' agencies are putting PC facilities and support in offices that offer counter services. Others arrange for road special shows or events staffed with personnel to help people use e-services. By providing people with means and support, they teach them how to get the most out of electronic service offerings, with a view to winning e-Government converts one by one.

What is also proving effective is the development of a single e-Government "brand" and a consistent way for users to navigate among e-Government services with a common look and feel (OECD, 2005, p. 38). A few governments, for instance, have created a single brand for web and DiTV based services, and besides are using it as the electronic response route in all government advertising.

Clearly, promoting take-up of e-Government is taking hold as a priority and, yet, many governments still find themselves confronted with the problem of a relatively low usage.

It goes without saying that the potential value gained from e-Government – in terms of improved public services, greater efficiency and cost savings – will not be realized if e-Government usage remains low. Not to mention that is costly to provide both traditional and electronic channels delivering the same content.

Actually, governments find themselves in a competitive situation that is their traditional channels are competing with the new electronic channels. Such competitive environment is foreign to the prescriptive service delivery approach traditionally used in government. No wonder, then, if governments struggle with developing the business processes and the "products" needed to prompt a sizable migration to e-services.

Yet, achieving this migration is increasingly important for governments to control the overall cost of e-Government.

The challenge stems at least in part from governments' relative inexperience with marketing, which has never been part of their organizational mind-set.

As noted earlier, government agencies are not always able to use customer data to create effective segmentation and, as a result, they fail to target the right message to various customer groups using the most effective communication and marketing techniques.

Improved customer segmentation is, again, what will deliver the customer insights required to developing and promoting the e-Services specific customer groups are more likely to use. This will create a higher value for those customers, thus stimulating their migration to e-Services, which in turn will increase agencies' return on investment.

4. EVALUATING E-GOVERNMENT

A final CRM issue to be addressed in the course of any e-Government program is evaluating the effectiveness of the program in meeting its service delivery objectives.

In the past, the imperative issue for governments worldwide was to put as many services and information on line as possible, moving from the assumption that simply getting services on line would undoubtedly deliver benefits both to governments and constituency. As a result, e-Government evaluations were largely based on availability targets (i.e. the number of government services being made available online).

Such simplistic approach to developing and evaluating e-Government programs no longer applies in the current e-Government landscape where governments have reached the point of having at least some aspects of all their services on line (although few have achieved a widespread adoption of such services). The challenge now facing governments is increasing e-Services uptake by making them more and more user-focused, which in turn relies, to a large extent, on governments' capability to properly evaluate the existing e-Service offerings so as to identify areas needing improvements.

The gap between what e-Government programs provide and the way people view and actually use these programs points to a problem governments have historically had in evaluating their performance. That is, government organizations tend to measure their performance in terms of inputs and outputs rather than on results constituents actually value.

True that the matter of value is complex both to public and private sector organizations. In the private sector, however, there are at least generally accepted ways of measuring it – such as shareholder value analysis – while no such measure exists to guide public managers. The reason for this is fairly clear: in the private sector, shareholder value is consistently measured in the same financial terms regardless of the industry, whereas the "constituent value" is going to vary depending on the service being delivered.

As to e-Government services, finding appropriate measures is particularly difficult when it comes to evaluating issues such as service quality or savings of user time rather than the more simple service availability.

Yet, such evaluations are far more important than measurements of provision, as the real value of e-Government is that it may help governments deliver improved customer service and make government operations more efficient. Governments have now come to recognize that truth and, as a result, they are beginning to measure the success of their e-Government programs less by simply service availability on line than by more value-added measures.

Particular stress is put on measuring service quality, as most governments regard the improvement of the quality of public services as a major goal of e-Government programs.

The quality of e-Government services is often assessed as customer satisfaction, most commonly measured through surveys or online questionnaires. The frequency of these surveys is key to monitoring the changes under way in users' needs and practices and thereby making continuous improvements to service offerings. Results from these surveys may also be used to update quality standards.

Other measures commonly used (in a call center environment) include average time taken to resolve requests, number of calls handled per day, call center abandon rates, percentage of requests resolved in first contact and the like.

Also, successful delivery of e-Government can be measured by users' take-up of e-Government services. Besides traditional metrics (e.g. Web sites hits and page impressions), monitoring and analysing patterns of usage, attitudes towards data use, seasonal variation, audience breakdown and use of search terms are all effective ways of understanding how and to what extent users consume electronic services.

It is self-evident that the above measurements should not be a one-time event, as users' expectations and habits are evolving rapidly in a changing service environment. Their increasing shills in using technology and their experience of interacting with the online commercial sector will inform their views on the quality and usefulness of e-Government services. It is, therefore, essential to implement an ongoing evaluation process of e-Services and use its findings to inform changes to the e-Government program. Such findings should also inform the development of government agencies' overall business objectives with a view to making total service delivery more user-focused rather than simply enlarged through the introduction of new channels/services.

5. BARRIERS AND DIFFICULT TO IMPLEMENT CRM IN E-SERVICE

Though inherently a managerial concept, CRM is largely believed to be applicable to government, considering that governments have the largest customer base than any other organization in the world and, therefore, have much to gain from an improved understanding of their customers. In particular, some say that CRM is a natural part of governments' broader focus on e-Government, given that the latter implies the transformation of public sector internal and external relationships through net-enabled operations, IT and communications, to improve government service delivery (Bittinger, 2001, p. 2).

There are, however, a number of factors that may act as barrier or deterrent to implementing CRM in government. Firstly, the dynamism associated with a wide-ranging diversity of customers is unique to the public sector and, therefore, it complicates the matter of gaining insights into customer needs and practices (Pan, Tan, Lim; 2006; p. 240). Moreover, within the civil service, citizens are compulsory members of these public agencies regardless of their business value. In fact, when applied to the private sector, CRM aims at targeting the most valuable customer in terms of potential profit, whereas in government everyone needs to be treated equitably.

Other major challenges governments are faced with are the digital divide and citizen privacy concerns. The former is commonly referred to as the gap between those who have access to, and the capability to use, ICT and the Internet, in particular, and those who don't. Because of that gap, many will not be able to benefit from CRM initiatives such as the web delivery of public services. Governments, in partnership with private industry, need to bridge this technology gap and provide a playing field for everyone.

As to privacy concerns, it is has been noted that some CRM technologies such as the cookies give the government too much monitoring capability (Pang, Norris; 2002; p. 44). For instance, some people are concerned that monitoring a taxpayer's visits to the Revenue Agency web pages about tax deductions might lead to audits.

In general, however, the privacy, security and confidentiality of users' records need to be maintained. To address this issue, many countries are currently enacting privacy acts covering use of personal information in private sector and by web site operators (Kannabiran, Xavier, Anantharaaj; 2004; p. 238).

Last, but not least, CRM requires an investment in technology and the business case for this investment is not easily made by government organizations, given that the main drivers of CRM in the private sector (i.e. customer retention and profitability) are foreign to the public sector. Yet, governments can leverage CRM technological initiatives through targeting routine and high-volume services, not least because of the efficiency gains that can stem from driving the manual processing out of them. This in turn would allow them to refocus resources on higher value activities such as handling no routine requests or introducing new services, thus delivering an improved experience to users.

That is particularly the case of Revenue Agencies that have historically been among the first government agencies to deploy new technologies, because of the relative ease of establishing a business case for faster revenue collection and increased compliance.

On the basis of such considerations, the next section discusses the case of the Italian Revenue Agency, which is developing a rich CRM program as a corollary of its e-Government initiative.

6. CASE-STUDY: THE ITALIAN REVENUE AGENCY

Constituted in 1999, the Italian Revenue Agency has been operating since January 1st, 2001.

The Italian Revenue Agency carries out all the functions regarding the management, assessment, litigation and collection of taxes.

The Italian Revenue Agency is non-profit public body acting under the supervision of the Minister of the Economy and Finance that maintains control over policy orientation. As such, the Agency takes full managerial and operational charge of its affairs and is autonomous as regards regulations, management, assets, organization, accounting and finance. However, its internal general directives must be submitted to the Minister for approval, both in legitimacy and merits.

The creation of the Revenue Agency has marked the beginning of profound changes in the Italian Tax Administration; before that, it was a process of the classic hierarchical bureaucracy, both time-consuming and not very efficient.

The avowed purpose of the Agency is indeed to ensure the highest level of tax compliance, through initiatives aimed at:

- Simplifying relationships with tax-payers;
- Improving help and information services;
- Increasing its action against tax evasion.

Also, the Agency aims at achieving the peak efficiency by innovative schemes of organization and planning.

Among the most prominent changes brought about with the creation of the Agency has been the implementation of the "Fisco telematico" project (Electronic Tax Service), which has led within the last few years to a broad range of e-Services now available for individuals and organizations to fulfil their tax duties.

The project has not been conceived as a merely technological initiative but has also been accompanied with a systematic and strategic customer relationship management (CRM) process to govern the repercussions of e-Transformation on the relationships with taxpayers. Particular attention has been paid to making e-Services user-friendly, to promoting them through proper communication and education activities and, finally, to setting appropriate measures of success, and the associated monitoring mechanisms, that accurately reflect what drives user satisfaction towards such services.

Apart from the project, CRM has increasingly become an essential element of the Agency's overall service delivery policy, to the point of making a formal pledge (the "Service Charter") to provide taxpayers with services that are more and more focused on their needs, continuously improved – notably, through seeking feedback from taxpayers – and, not least, delivered and coordinated through various channels of interactions (local offices, the Internet, contact centers, home delivery). All that with a view to improving the relationship with taxpayers by putting them firmly at the centre of the Agency's thinking and action.

Properly managed relationships with taxpayers are, however, all the more demanding when it comes to rendering services electronically, which requires specific issues to be addressed such as the digital divide, privacy concerns or the more simple public unawareness of e-Services.

The sections below trace the main features of the Agency's e-Service system, with particular stress on the CRM practices being performed to ease its usability, promote take-up and evaluate its progress against the Agency's service delivery objectives.

6.1 The e-Service System

The e-Services currently being provided by the Italian Revenue Agency fall into two categories [10]:

- The services for the use of small enterprises and every other taxpayer, accessible via the Internet, that made up the "Fisconline" service;
- The services specifically designed for medium and large companies and intermediaries (e.g. consultants, professionals, CAAF, banks and post offices), that can be accessed through the "Entratel" network [11];

Among the most significant services delivered through Entratel and Fisconline are:

- e-Filing of income tax returns;
- Online payments;
- Cadastral services;
- Request of tax refunds;
- Assignment of the VAT registration number;
- Fulfilments (registrations and payments) related to real estate contracts.

Besides, visitors to the Agency's web site (www.agenziaentrate.it) can access to tax information (particular attention has been paid to making the site easy accessible to disabled); interact with contact center operators; consult the "Tax Documentation" online databank containing all tax regulations as well as circulars and decisions issued by the Agency; calculate road tax; find out tax deadlines; book an appointment at local offices; get the tax code.

A very innovative online service is the "tax mail box". This allows taxpayers to check information on their own tax position (e.g. tax returns submitted, payments, personal assets).

Finally, taxpayers can make inquiries by using the Agency's "Web Mail" services. A Contact Centre automatically acknowledges receipt of all e-mails sent and provides the relating answers.

6.2 The e-Filing System

Not decrying the importance of the other e-Services, the e-Filing is indeed the most significant change to the tax administration process brought about by the ICT re-engineering effort.

To consider the e-Filing process takes on particular importance for the purposes of this paper. From that it can be gathered, at least in part, how the Agency has managed the impact of e-Transformation on the relationship with taxpayers.

To begin with, users are requested to make an application for accessing the e-Filing service. The access code is issued via the Internet or by the Agency's local offices as for the "Fisconline" and "Entratel" services, respectively.

The drawing up of the documents (e.g. income tax return, VAT declaration) itself is computer-aided, thanks to specialized software distributed by the Agency gratis. The Agency also makes available application programs which allow checking that the documents have been drawn up in accordance with the required specifications. The use of these programs is not mandatory, rather they are conceived to be a help for users to detect the presence of errors that will impede the acceptance of the documents, once they are sent.

The Agency has also enabled an e-Filing Helpline, active Mondays to Fridays from 9 am to 5 pm. With the filing deadline approaching, the Helpline is active from 8 am to 7 pm and the number of operators is increased accordingly. Besides that, web pages are available to users (on the Agency's site) that collect answers to frequently asked questions (FAQ). The information available on such pages are the result of a systematic analysis on the data gathered through the help desk, with a view to giving answers to problems of the same kind. Finally, there is a fax number specifically designed for solving problems related to the access codes and passwords.

Another feature unique to the e-filing process is the authentication of the documents, aimed at establishing the identity of the e-filer who is responsible for the referential data integrity. That requires users to enter their PIN number or generating the authentication codes through an application software (as for "Fisconline" and "Entratel", respectively).

Once the documents are sent, a receipt is given within 1 day to the "Fisconline" and 5 days to the "Entratel" users.

As for the documents taxpayers file through intermediaries, a pre-notification is sent electronically to the latter in event of irregularities, given that in some cases irregularities can be removed through enlightening on purely formal elements (e.g. payments made but not included in the filed documents). That is aimed at saving, wherever possible, the taxpayer from a notification of irregularity.

It is self-evident from the above account that the e-Filing service is far from being the electronic version of the traditional filing methods, as it implies a number of CRM technologies, and the underlying business processes, that have actually engineered a turnaround from obsolete, bureaucratic procedures to more efficient, customer-centric ones. That is all the more significant for those who want to e-file without the assistance of intermediaries, that are now provided with a range of software utilities and customer service such that they are very likely to succeed in their object.

The most valuable benefits that accrue to taxpayers from such customer managed process can be summarized as follows: lower risk of mistakes in filing documents, greater awareness of filing correctly, fewer notifications of irregularity from the tax administration (when one is assisted by intermediaries).

Obviously, the e-Filing system yields benefits for the Revenue Agency, too. First and foremost, the reduced number of mistakes compared to those founded in the documents filed in the traditional manner. This way, some of the resources focused on traditional service delivery methods can be directed elsewhere and, eventually, cost savings can occur.

6.3 Promoting e-Services through Marketing, Communication, and Education

Since the launch of its e-Service program, the Italian Revenue Agency has been performing an ever-increasing number of marketing, communication and education activities, with a view to stimulating the migration of taxpayers to the electronic environment.

Indeed, the Agency has been using a range of marketing means including Ad campaigns on radio, television and press, media interviews, special events and customer service personnel at branches. Most notably, the Agency is present with its own stand space at several trade fairs where visitors are shown how to use, and can actually use, e-Services (e.g. tax return filing, assignment of tax identification number, Tax Mail Box).

Initiatives of the kind are also performed by the Agency through arranging for special road shows or being present at national conferences. Moreover, with the filing deadline approaching, customer service personnel is made available in a few Italian municipalities, those which are a long way from the Agency's local offices, to help people to file electronically.

In the same line of action, the Agency is committed to informing taxpayers of any new e-Service that becomes available to them. That information is actually delivered through a variety of means, such as press releases, press conferences and its own magazines [12].

On the education front, a far-reaching initiative currently being developed by the Agency is the "Fisco e Scuola" project, which is more generally aimed at spreading knowledge of taxation in schools. Besides teaching students the rudiments of the subject, it includes training courses in the use of the electronic tax services, to be set in the Agency's local offices or/and in schools.

The above list of the Agency's communication and education activities is far from complete, as describing them all would go well beyond this scope of this paper. It is clear, however, that these activities are an integral part of the Agency's organizational mindset, thus concurring with the current e-Government best practices. Indeed, among governments worldwide there is a growing recognition of the need for marketing, communication and education to achieve a sizable uptake of e-Government services.

That understanding is all the more important with tax services that have big personal implications for citizens or perceived negative ramifications if used improperly.

6.4 Evaluating e-Services

The Italian Revenue Agency is steadily engaged in evaluating its e-Service offerings – most notably through seeking feedback from users – so as to identify areas needing improvements, set priorities and update quality standards.

Since 2004, the Agency has been carrying out customer satisfaction surveys with regard to the "Fisconline" and "Entratel" services [13]. That is meant as a tool for listening to users and gaining insights into their needs, expectations and satisfaction with the services, information and assistance they are provided with.

The interviews are carried out electronically by means of questionnaires accessible from the home pages of "Fisconline" and "Entratel".

Respondents are segmented into categories, namely: business, self-employed worker, employee, pensioner and others, as to "Fisconline"; professionals, experts, CAAF, labour unions, tax consultants, companies and other, as to "Entratel". That answers the need to gain insights into the requirements, expectations and practices of specific groups of users so as to tailor the respective e-Service offerings accordingly.

The interviews look into many aspects of the e-Services, including: easiness of navigating and applying for information from the site, clearness of instructions, easiness of service usage, service reliability, certainty of tax fulfilments, capability to simplify tax fulfilments and detect mistakes, timeliness in resolving disservices.

Also significant are the evaluations of the online assistance and call centers (those which are specifically designed for Fisconline and Entratel users). As especially regards the latter, the customer satisfaction is measured in terms of completeness of answers, politeness, percentage of requests resolved in first contact, waiting time and appropriateness of the servicing hours.

Finally, customer satisfaction is measured in overall terms with reference to each of the above groups of users.

Also, the Agency is careful to monitoring the levels of e-Services usage.

Actually, in the last few years there has been a widespread rise in the e-Services usage, which reflects a growing acceptance of such services on the part of taxpayers (see Table 1).

Of particular importance is the increasing number of individuals who e-file their tax returns (Personal Income Tax) without the assistance of intermediaries. This is arguably due to the variety of information service and aids (e.g. contact centers, software utilities, web pages) the Agency has made available to individuals in the last few years, thus enabling them to get the most out of e-Services.

That observation is corroborated by the answers returned to the questions about the reasons for using the "Fisconline" services. Of the reasons respondents cited, the handiness of these services is the greatest perceived benefit, closely followed by time savings and a greater awareness of filing correctly (see Figure 1).

Equally significant, ho waver, are the perceived benefits of the e-Transformation to intermediaries (see Figure 2).

Table 1.

The Agency's e-Services Usage	2007	2008	2009	2010	2011	2012
Individual Unico forms (Personal Income Tax) sent via the Internet by taxpayers	149.738	185.234	410.341	531.618	612.300	755.00
Individual Unico forms sent via the Internet by offices	806.988	1.931.820	2.097.081	2.507.625	2.760.300	2.860.121
Individual Unico forms sent via the Internet by banks and post offices	2.393.814	1.151.182	631.120	208.101	67.125	18.141
Other documents filed via the Internet	6.943.919	7.543.612	9.268.252	10.370.719	12.178.100	13.548.200
Number of taxpayers registered using on-line "Tax Box"	1.062.708	1.523.793	1.807.534	2.124.400	2.850.344	3.231.103
Number of online registrations and payments concerning real estate contracts (selling or renting)	4.153.325	5.333.700	5.929.829	6.980.230	7.450.300	8.100.787
On-line payments	2.254.410	2.472.759	3.360.131	4.206.736	5.430.203	6.301.989

Source: Our elaboration on the Agency's Books (2012 - 2007). Available at www.agenziaentrate.it.

7. CONCLUSION

This paper has explored how the business strategy commonly referred to as Customer Relationship Management (CRM) can be adopted by government organizations while developing e-Government initiatives. In doing that, the research has highlighted some of the CRM capabilities that are essential for governments to get the most out of these initiatives in terms of improved service delivery, greater efficiency and potential cost savings.

Most notably, what has emerged from our studying is that a well-conceived plan of marketing, education and evaluation activities is key to increasing the acceptance of the new IT-enabled service delivery methods on the part of constituency. The need for these activities is quite understandable considering that the targeted benefits of e-Government can only materialize in so far that e-Government services become preferred by a critical mass of users. Until then, traditional service delivery channels still need to be maintained and, as result, governments do not realize the potential benefits of e-Transformation to the full.

Yet, achieving a higher take-up will require a better understanding of different user requirements than has traditionally been the case, so as to developing and promoting the electronic services specific user groups are most likely to use. This is not without challenges for governments because of their relative inexperience with marketing and performance evaluation.

Besides, user-focused e-Government requires the employment of specially devised technologies (e.g. computer telephony integration, customer self-service websites, data warehouse) and the business case for these investments needs to be built on well-founded prospects of usage. With that understanding, governments had better focus their e-Transformation efforts on routine and high-volume services which are excellent candidates for electronic delivery, because of the efficiency gains that can stem from driving the manual processing out of them. This in turn would allow to redirect resources toward higher value activities such as handling non-routine requests or introducing new services, thus delivering an improved experience to users.

Figure 1.
Source: Our elaboration on the Agency's Book (2012). Available at www.agenziaentrate.it.

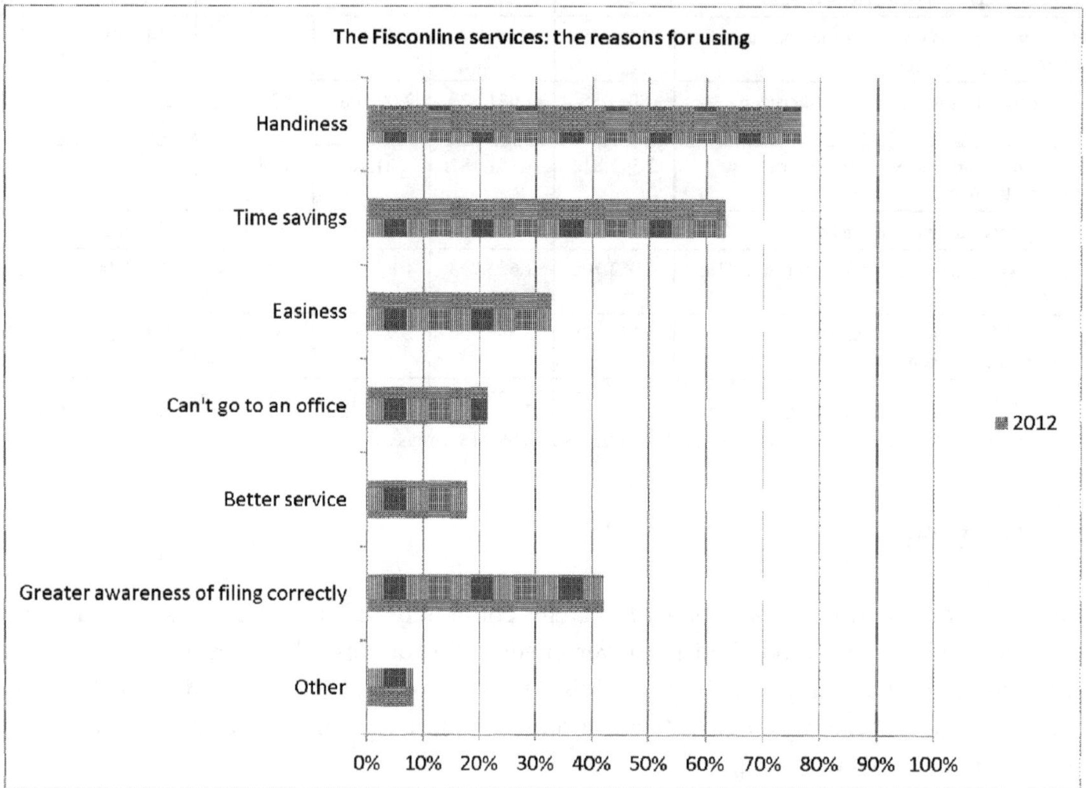

Source: Our elaboration on the Agency's Book (2012). Available at www.agenziaentrate.it

Figure 2.
Source: Our elaboration on the Agency's Book (2012). Available at www.agenziaentrate.it.

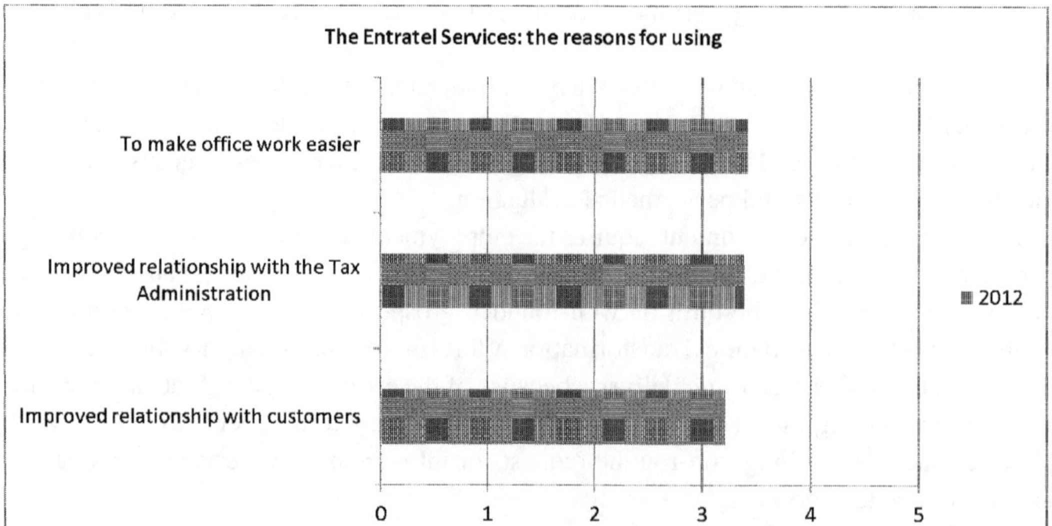

Source: Our elaboration on the Agency's Book (2012). Available at www.agenziaentrate.it

It is no accident that Revenue Agencies have historically been among the first in the public sector to deploy new technologies, because of the relative ease of establishing a business case for faster revenue collection and increased compliance.

In corroboration of the conceptual framework, this paper has studied the case of The Italian Revenue Agency, which typifies the journey of a public agency in implementing an e-Government initiative in conjunction with a systematic and strategic customer relationship management process.

While that case counts as empirical evidence of the notion that e-Government implementation should be accompanied by e-Transformation management through coherent marketing, communication and evaluation activities, we acknowledge the limitations of a single case-study in providing significant generalization.

Even so, our analysis has provided an unprejudiced account of the experiences and potential lessons gained from the transformation of the Italian Tax Administration, once a typical bureaucratic process, into one that possesses many of the CRM capabilities required to succeed in e-Transformation as well as any other reform initiative. In particular, what has proved effective in that case is the range of information and customer service enabled to make people familiar with e-Services, not to mention the attention paid to informing users of any new service being e-enabled and involving them in service improvement. Thus, the above limitations notwithstanding, our case-study provides at least some possible insights useful to identify similar practices in other organizations undergoing e-Transformations, so that they can be compared and benchmarked.

For future studies on the subject, three specific areas of research may be indicated to deepen the current knowledge of CRM strategies in e-Government. First, in-depth studies should be carried out on the subject of Marketing in government [14]. Also, particular attention should be paid to considering how government organizations can best evaluate the effectiveness of their e-Government programs in meeting their service delivery objectives. Finally, additional investigation is needed to ascertain to what extent the insights gained by private sector organizations, as to how CRM has been strategized within the context of e-Transformation, can be adapted to government organizations.

REFERENCES

Accenture. (2003). *CRM in Government: Bridging the Gap*. The Government Executives Series.

Accenture. (2004). *e-Government Leadership: High Performance, Maximum Value*. The Government Executives Series

Accenture. (2006). *Leadership in Customer Service: Building the Trust*. The Government Executives Series.

Bittinger, S. (2001). *Customer Relationship Management in e-Government*. Gartner Research Inc.

Collins, N. & Butler, P. (1995). "Marketing Public Sector Services: Concepts and characteristics", *Journal of Marketing Management*, (11), 83-96.

Collins, N., & Butler, P. (2002). The Marketplace, e-Government and e-Democracy. *Irish Marketing Review*, *15*(2), 86–94.

Croteau, A. M., & Li, P. (2003). Critical Success Factors of CRM Technological Initiatives. *Canadian Journal of Administrative Sciences*, *20*(1), 21–34. doi:10.1111/j.1936-4490.2003.tb00303.x

Galbreath, J., & Rogers, T. (1999). Customer Relationship Leadership: A leadership and motivation model for the twenty-first century business. *The TQM Magazine*, *11*(2), 161–171. doi:10.1108/09544789910262734

Gartner Group. (2000). Key Issues in E-Government Strategy and Management. *Research notes¸ Key issues*

Kannabiran, G., Xavier, M. J., & Anantharaaj, A. (2005). Enabling e-Governance through Citizen Relationship Management - Concept, Model and Applications. *Journal of Service Research*, *4*(2), 223–240.

Karimi, J., Somers, T. M., & Gupta, Y. P. (2001). Impact of Information Technology Management Practices on Customer Service. *Journal of Management Information Systems*, *17*(4), 125–158.

Kavanagh, S. (2001). Constituent Relationship Management Systems: A Primer for Public Managers. *Government Finance Review*, *1*(5), 35–39.

Kost, J. (2004). Analyze Government Transactions to Make Them Citizen-Centric. *Gartner Research, Research Notes*, 1-5.

Linder, J. C., & Brooks, J. D. (2004). Transforming The Public Sector. *Outlook*, *3*, 74–83.

Marche, S., & McNiven, J. D. (2003). E-Government and E-Governance: The Future Isn't What It Used To Be. *Canadian Journal of Administrative Sciences*, *20*(1), 74–86. doi:10.1111/j.1936-4490.2003.tb00306.x

OECD. (2003). *The e-Government Imperative, OECD e-Government Studies*. Paris, France: OECD Publication Services.

OECD. (2005). e-Government for better government. OECD e-Government Studies, Paris, France, OECD Publication Services.

Pan, S. L., Tan, C. W., & Lim, E. T. K. (2006). Customer relationship management (CRM) in e-government: A relational perspective, *Decision Support Systems*, 42, 237-250. Pang L. & Norris R. (2002), Applying customer relationship management (CRM) to government. *The Journal of Government Financial Management*, *51*(1), 40–45.

United Nations. (2005). *Global E-government Readiness Report*. From E-government to E-inclusion.

KEY TERMS AND DEFINITIONS

Business Management: The process of defining the goals of a company (either it public, private or private-social) and guidance of corporate management towards the achievement of these objectives by taking decisions on the use of available resources and, in particular, human resources.

Customer Relationship Management (CRM): Is commonly referred to as the holistic process a business perform in order to identify, attract, differentiate and retain customers. It is a term for methodologies, software and Internet capabilities to help manage enterprise customer relationships.

e-CRM: Refers to the integration of sales, marketing, service, enterprise resource planning and supply chain management functions through business process automation, technology solutions and information resources such as to maximize the value of each customer interaction.

e-Government: The continuous optimization of service delivery, constituency participation, and governance by transforming internal and external relationships through technology, the Internet and the new media.

e-Services: The set of services which can be taken via the Internet. Today they are used a lot by the government to offer its services to citizens.

Fiscoonline: A service for small and medium sized enterprises and every other tax payer, accessible via the Internet, to carry out transactions with Italian Revenue Agency.

Information and Communication Technology (ITC): Integration of information technology and those typical of communication, which creates an opportunity for interaction and sharing of knowledge through the use of modern technological tools and information.

Italian Revenue Agency: A non-profit public body acting under the supervision of the Minister of the Economy and Finance that maintains control over policy orientation. It carries out all the functions regarding the management, assessment, litigation and collection of taxes.

ENDNOTES

1 United Nations, *Global E-government Readiness Report 2005*. From E-government to E-inclusion, 14 - 15.

2 See http://www1.worldbank.org/publicsector/egov/definition.htm.

3 OECD, (2003) *The e-Government Imperative*, OECD e-Government Studies, 11-15.

4 GARTNER GROUP (2000) Key Issues in E-Government Strategy and Management, *Research notes*

5 MARCHE S. & J.D. MCNIVEN, (2003) E-Government and E-Governance: The Future Isn't What It Used To Be, *Canadian Journal of Administrative Science*, (20/1) 75 - 79

6 CRM applications are classified as either *operational* (e.g. for improving customer service, for online marketing and for automating the sales force), *analytical* (e.g. for building a CRM data warehouse, analyzing customer and sales data) and *collaborative* (e.g. for building Web and online communities, business to business customer exchanges and personalization service). Cfr. J. KARIMI, T.M. SOMERS, Y.P. GUPTA, (2001) Impact of Information Technology Management Practices on Customer Service, *Journal of Management Information Systems*, (17/4) 128.

7 It is important to distinguish between enterprise resource planning (ERP) applications, that are designed to support back-office operations, and customer relationship management (CRM) applications that deal with front-office operations. CRM applications are highly visible to customers, besides they enable the integration of front-office information with back-office systems.

8 An OECD (2005) study brings forward evidence of a trend toward *personalization* in government, especially as regards governments' web portals. The concept is about developing personalized services based on available constituent data within a context of a particular time, whereby services and information change as certain life events occur. Personalization, if well implemented, has obvious benefits for constituents as they may obtain more appropriate services and receive more relevant information, which should drive greater satisfaction towards e-Government. Still, personalization

has the potential to drive value for governments suggesting a better use of available constituent data to target e-Government service more accurately, thus improving the overall delivery strategy. The result should be an increased take-up.

The above trend, however, is recent and is not without challenges: first and foremost, the issue of privacy protection that results in legislative limits to how much personal information can be gathered. Cfr. *e-Government for better government*, OECD e-Government Studies, 2005, p. 36.

9 See also Accenture (2004), *e-Government Leadership: High Performance, Maximum Value*, The Government Executive 27.

10 To be exact, there is a third category of e-Services currently being provided by the Revenue Agency, namely the "Siatel" channel that allows (only) the State-owned agencies – such as the municipalities, provinces, regions, universities, consortium of municipalities in mountain areas, Local Health Authorities – to access the Tax Register.

11 That is a restricted network that can be accessed through a toll-free number or via the Internet at https://entratel.agenziaentrate.it. An access code, issued by the Revenue Agency, is required.

12 Among the magazines published by the Italian Revenue Agency is "Fiscooggi.it", the Agency's online magazine. It is an officially registered publication that integrates the documentation contained on www.agenziaentrate.it with real time updates on the activities of the Italian Revenue Agency and its central and peripheral offices, as well as with comments on tax regulations and laws.

13 It should be noted, however, that analogous evaluations are carried out with regard to all the other service delivery channels (i.e. the Agency's local offices, contact centers not specifically designed for e-filers).

14 Indeed, the existing literature on the subject of marketing in government refers, for the most part, to the marketing of electoral campaigns, while there is a shortage of writings specifically relating to the marketing of public sector services. Among the latter: Collins N., Butler P.(2002) The Marketplace, e-Government and e-Democracy, *Irish Marketing Review*, 86-94;

Chapter 5
The Treacherous Path of Corporate Social Responsibility (CSR) and the Role of Information Systems in its Implementation

Tabani Ndlovu
Nottingham Business School, UK

Amon Simba
Nottingham Trent University, UK

Anastasia Mariussen
Oslo School of Management, Norway

ABSTRACT

Despite alleged widespread adoption of Corporate Social Responsibility (CSR) and responsible business practices by organisations worldwide, questions still remain on the motives for such adoption; effects and/or benefits of CSR adoption as well as how stakeholders can tell genuine responsible businesses from those paying lip service and using the CSR tag as a 'means-to-an end'. The litany of jargon often used interchangeably including such terms as CSR, sustainability, sustainable marketing, responsible business practice and sustainable development among others further lead to scepticism on organisations' commitments to CSR and the resultant allegations of greenwashing and CSR tokenism. This undermines genuine attempts to be corporately-responsible, fuelling confusion for any new players wishing to adopt responsible business practices. This chapter uses the Information Systems (IS) landscape as a lever to dissect issues in both CSR theory and practice, offering some practical guidelines for implementation and operationalisation, while raising further questions for research.

DOI: 10.4018/978-1-4666-8459-1.ch005

INTRODUCTION

While there are more organisations purportedly adopting Corporate Social Responsibility (CSR) strategies today than there ever were (Nidumolu, Prahalad, & Rangaswami, 2009; Waddock, 2008), there still remains a myriad of questions regarding the genuineness or authenticity of such organisational strategies and requisite initiatives (McShane & Cunningham, 2012), the significance of the adopted organisational CSR initiatives (Matten & Moon, 2008) as well as the real purpose and effects of such undertakings (Fernando, 2010; Strugatch, 2011). There seems to be an upsurge of annual reports, corporate activities and CSR statements on company websites together with CSR claims posted via a host of other fora pitching organisations as virtuous and responsible (Hogan & Lodhia, 2011; Lozano, 2011).

This upsurge of various conceptions of responsible corporate behaviour causes confusion to the lay eye (Quiroz-Onate & Aitken, 2007), raising questions on whether such acclaimed responsible corporate behaviours actually bear any organisational and societal fruit or not (Brunner, Esch, & Kinscher, 2012). There are further doubts on how the intended and achieved results can be objectively appraised (Parisi & Hockerts, 2008; Wigley, 2008). The organisational virtuousness domain is littered with an array of such terms as CSR, sustainability, ethics, environmental management and responsible corporate behaviour among others, all sometimes used interchangeably. As a consequence, many businesses and stakeholders get lost in trying to decipher the meanings of these terms. They face a conundrum as to which conception to adopt as an embodiment of their own business initiatives in the area of responsible business practices (Baden & Harwood, 2013; Dahlsrud, 2008; Lozano, 2008). Added to the above, many stakeholders often find it difficult to judge whether their nominated organisations deliver on the CSR promises they make (Calabrese, Costa, Menichini & Rosati, 2013).

These and many other CSR-related questions have over the past three decades given rise to a multitude of academic discussions, which due to the complexity of the topic still seem to raise new rather than answer existing questions (Elliott, 2012). While this chapter concurs that providing definitive answers to these issues is difficult, if not impossible, its position is that creating a typology of extant CSR conceptions and clearly delineating implications thereof can be a driving force enabling understanding of CSR in general and specifically within a marketing context. To facilitate a better comprehension of what CSR in marketing is, as well as why and how marketers can bring it to life, this chapter focuses on CSR, its conception within a marketing environment, and the role IS can play in implementing and measuring CSR. This chapter therefore sets forth the following objectives:

1. To introduce more clarity to CSR terminology in use within a marketing context,
2. To outline rationale for pursuing CSR,
3. To provide guidelines for practical implications of CSR initiatives and highlight risks and opportunities in this area.
4. To show how information systems present opportunities for clearer conception, delivery and measurement of CSR results.

Pursuant to the above objectives, the chapter content is organised around four main discussions: CSR terminology, rationale for CSR adoption, practical CSR implementation as well as IS-reliant CSR management. The section below explores issues related to CSR terminology highlighting implications for theory and practice.

MAKING SENSE OF THE CSR JARGON

In spite of a considerable increase in research activity related to the concept of CSR and sustainable development, prompted by the recent global environmental, social and economic challenges (Morris, 2011), there is still no consensus on unified CSR terminology in literature. Instead, multiple interpretations of the same concepts are registered (Constanza & Patten, 1995; Ciegis, Ramanauskiene, & Martinkus, 2009; Mebratu, 1998; Theis & Tomkin, 2012). In an attempt to classify CSR-related concepts, establish the relationships between them and uncover existing concept duplications, Glavic and Lukman (2006) identify as many as 51 sustainability terms in environmental engineering alone. Some of the most widely used terms in the CSR field are sustainable development, sustainability, CSR and responsible corporate behaviour. These different conceptualisations are briefly discussed below.

Sustainable Development

Among the hundreds of 'sustainable development' definitions (Ciegis et al., 2009; Jochem, 2011; Pope, Annandale, & Morrison-Saunders, 2004), the definition developed in 1987 by the Brundtland Commission is the most cited conceptualisation. The inspirational WCED's (1987) definition presented sustainable development as the "development that meets the needs of the present without compromising the ability of future generations to meet their own needs". Although the above definition laid the invaluable ground for future sustainability and CSR research and brought the subject to the attention of wider audiences, it also became the main cause of sustainability and CSR research issues (Constanza & Patten; 1995; Theis & Tomkin, 2012). On one hand, it introduced more clarity to the meaning of sustainable development while on the other hand, it triggered a variety of different conceptualisations of CSR and sustainability aimed at further interpretation of the concept and its operationalization in different contexts (Faber, Jorna, & Engelen, 2005; Mebratu, 1998).

Sustainability

While 'sustainable development' and 'sustainability' are frequently used as two interchangeable terms or even synonyms, there exists a notable distinction between the two (Marsden, Kimble, Nellthorp, & Kelly, 2010; Marshall & Toffel, 2005; Theis & Tomkin, 2012). Unlike 'sustainable development' which refers to the process or "the development that continues" (Ciegis et al., 2009, p.29), 'sustainability' is explained as an aim and ability or "an aspiration, ideal and something one aims for" (Watson, Wienand, & Workman, 2009). Sustainable development when implemented, should ultimately usher in the ideal of sustainability. Organisations should therefore be looking to adopt sustainable business models in order to contribute towards the ideal of sustainability.

Defining Corporate Social Responsibility (CSR)

The debate regarding what constitutes CSR has not produced a uniform definition. The absence of a specific definition leaves CSR open to conflicting interpretations (Windsor, 2001). Broadly, the key question of CSR is: to what extent do the interests of business merge with the interests of society? In an attempt to clarify the concept of CSR, it is perhaps essential to begin with the works of the first and most prominent CSR writer Keith Davis (Carroll, 1999). Davis set forth his definition of CSR arguing that it is about "businessmen's decisions and actions taken for reasons at least partially beyond the firm's direct economic or technical interest" (Davis, 1960, p.70). Crucially, Davis (1960) categorically explained that CSR is a nebulous idea but it should be seen in a managerial context. Moving the discourse forward, Johnson, Whittington and Scholes (2011) suggested that CSR is mainly concerned with specific ways in which an organisation will move beyond the minimum obligations provided through regulation and corporate governance, and how the conflicting demands of different stakeholders will be reconciled. Consistent with this conceptualisation of CSR, Witcher and Chau (2014) explained it from the point of view of large organisations (especially Multi-National Corporations (MNCs)). They argued that MNCs have a responsibility to fulfil a corporate (and world) citizenship role by engaging in business activities that take into consideration the needs of various internal and external stakeholders.

Perhaps the last word on this can be left to McGuire (1963, p.144) who emphasised that, "the idea of social responsibilities supposes that the corporation has not only economic and legal obligations but also certain responsibilities to society which extend beyond these obligations". The idea of corporate social responsibility is therefore a discretionary one, left to each business to shape and align to both organisational as well as societal priorities if it is to be meaningful.

The challenge is that this discretionary nature of the concept has often been its undoing, resulting in tokenism or at worst green washing. Arguably, CSR contributes to a broader sustainability agenda and therefore can be seen as a subset of the latter.

Responsible Corporate Behaviour

Any organisation which is involved in producing and or trading either in goods or services must do so in a just and responsible manner. To this end Carroll (1999) noted four responsibilities of businesses: economic, legal, ethical and discretionary responsibilities. In his works there was a recognition that business organisations needed to look first to economics and produce products and services that society wanted, at a profit. This should be done in accordance with the law. In engaging in economic activities, a business organisation must do so in accordance with the generally held beliefs about behaviour in their respective society such as the notions of fairness and justice, together with discretionary responsibilities – purely voluntary obligations an organisation adopts, such as philanthropic activities (Witcher & Chau, 2014). Adding to the discourse on behaving in a socially responsible manner, Campbell (2007) agreed that corporate social behaviour is voluntary and dependent upon honourable people in authority. Ethical responsibilities are typically expected, but discretionary corporate socially responsible behaviour is not mandatory. The final decree on CSR should rest with government institutions specifically; they should intervene where organisations act irresponsibly. In reality, the above are vague and difficult to operationalise, resulting in patchy and varied conceptions and implementations of responsible corporate initiatives. Therefore, the notion of responsible business practices remains elusive even though different societies know when businesses act irresponsibly.

So by looking at a few conceptualisations of businesses attempting to act in a responsible manner, it can be seen that there are challenges in defining the concept of 'responsibility' and how this can be objectively operationalised to deliver to the CSR agenda. Questions arise as to how stakeholders can distinguish between genuine responsible businesses and their opposites as well as the benefits accruing from being a responsible business, especially considering the difficulties in navigating this terrain. This raises the question on why businesses should bother going down this path in the first place. The business case for adopting CSR is explored below.

WHY GO FOR CSR, REALLY?

CSR has traditionally been a discretionary initiative that organisations have adopted on a voluntary basis. This chapter argues that CSR initiatives are increasingly taking centre stage in business management to the extent that they are increasingly becoming a norm. Regardless of this, organisations appear to pursue CSR initiatives for a variety of reasons. Some of the reasons for the pursuit of CSR initiatives range from marketing and reputational reasons; risk mitigation reasons; responding to customer concerns; responding to regulatory and political pressures as well as addressing potential and internal employee concerns among others. Whatever the reasons may be, embarking on a CSR path comes at a cost for the respective organisation and may be seen as a drain on organisational resources (El Ghoul, Guedhami, Kwok, & Mishra, 2011). Alternatively, CSR may be viewed as an investment, aimed at generating goodwill for the implementing organisation.

Like any other investment, CSR initiatives need to be meaningful and effective, lest they be perceived to be a waste of valuable organisational resources. The sections below consider some of the rationales for the adoption of CSR initiatives together with their implications. While CSR and sustainability are often interchangeably used, the following paragraphs focus on CSR while acknowledging that this contributes to a broader, long term sustainability agenda.

CSR as a Marketing Tool

In a number of organisations, CSR initiatives may be designed as part of a broader marketing or reputational campaign, aimed at enhancing the image of the organisation or to competitively position a brand (Brüggenwirth, 2006). While there is absolutely nothing wrong with this inward-focused view, it is important that the organisation does not misrepresent its activities and make false claims (Dahl, 2010).

An exaggeration of claims or a misrepresentation of what the organisation actually does may amount to corporate green washing, defined by Furlow, (2010, p.1) as "...dissemination of false or incomplete information by an organization to present an environmentally responsible public image". Corporate green washing (whether by omission or commission) may have catastrophic consequences for a company's brand and long term reputation, destroying trust and potentially affecting competitiveness (Delmas & Burbano, 2011; Chen & Chang, 2013). It can be perceived as dishonesty and can mean that an organisation may find it difficult to engender trust among its wider stakeholder groups and particularly customers. Allegations of greenwashing cause doubt on the authenticity of not just the claims that the organisation makes with regards to its CSR credentials, but green washing also undermines the organisation's products and services and, therefore, may have detrimental effects on customer loyalty (Lyon & Maxwell, 2011).

To avoid such dismal outcomes, organisations adopting CSR initiatives as part of their marketing campaigns are well advised to ensure that they project honest CSR images and go on to deliver on the commitments they make. Underlying messages will help engender images of trust and breed believability, fostering customer loyalty to the brand and generating goodwill. This may in turn competitively position the company. Adoption of marketing-related CSR initiatives must not feel like a sneaky way to gain customer loyalty. To be meaningful, CSR initiatives must be intertwined with organisational strategic objectives and must be authentic. The initiatives must be embedded into long- term marketing and branding strategies and should ideally be a key part of the organisation's core values (Bebbington, Larrinaga, & Moneva, 2008; Brüggenwirth, 2006). This way, there is no separation between what the organisation actually stands for and what it does in practice, as well as the way it projects its image to the outer world. The organisation must genuinely care about the welfare of its stakeholders and be keen to ensure that its products and services are meaningful and do not cause harm to customers and other stakeholders. This will demonstrate that an organisation's CSR promises are true embodiments of its values and DNA rather than a mere means to an end.

CSR as a Risk Mitigation Tool

Quite a few organisations treat CSR as a risk mitigation tool and implement it as a "means to an end" (Kolstad, 2007, p.137). For example, even though some companies do not necessarily buy into the different CSR programmes, they realise that failure to adopt them may position them at a competitive disadvantage and, therefore, introduce CSR initiatives. Consequently, the authenticity of CSR initiatives borne out of this approach and how they are ingrained into the organisational practices may remain questionable (Lorenzo-Molo & Udani, 2013). It is believed that the commitment towards fully delivering on promises driven by risk mitigation may be weak, particularly when corporate resources are strained (Ellis & Bastin, 2011).

The genuineness of the initiatives may be tested when the organisation has to prioritise between other (often conflicting) demands, often relegating CSR to second best and implementing such initiatives only when it is convenient to do so (Bhattacharyya, 2010; Middlemiss, 2003). Examples of such prioritising and its effects on downgrading CSR importance can be found by looking at organisations that abandoned their CSR initiatives during the global recession because they could not afford to implement them as they focused on saving their core businesses (Ellis & Bastin, 2011). For these companies, the adoption of CSR initiatives would have clearly been an add-on and not core to what they do, undertaken only when conditions permitted. This puts the genuineness of the organisation's commitment to CSR in question.

CSR as a Response to Customer Concerns

Profit-oriented organisations exist to serve client needs for a return. As part of their strategic marketing pursuits, organisations regularly scan the market and gauge customers' reactions and appraise their offers in light of changing customer needs and the competitive environment (Kohli & Jaworski, 1993). Auditing the macro-environment in this way is designed to establish customer preferences, market trends and competing products among other things. Of late, responsible consumption, defined by Ozcaglar-Toulouse (2007, p.422-3) as "...the set of voluntary acts, situated in the sphere of consumption, achieved from the awareness of consequences judged as negatives of consumption on the outside world.." has gradually emerged as a growing trend in the business environment which many organisations respond to by developing innovative and sustainable offers (Webb, Mohr, & Harris, 2008). While this may sound like a reactive marketing gimmick, customer-oriented companies survive by responding to identified customer needs. Consequently, developing "green products" or adopting more responsible business practices to respond to customer needs should not be any different to the above. The distinction is that in this context, organisations respond to customer needs not with ordinary products, but rather, with innovative sustainable offers targeting specific niche needs (Schaltegger & Wagner, 2011). There is a rapidly growing number of organisations that uniquely position their sustainable offers by striking an equitable balance between their stakeholders' needs and profit motives. In this context, when organisations develop their products they aspire to establish their credentials by demonstrating a responsible approach to doing business. This is achieved by closely identifying and exploiting opportunities in niche areas within the

CSR arena. Challenges emerge when organisations integrate their responsibility claims only into their marketing messages and not into their core practical day-to-day operations, resulting in strategies appearing to be 'bolt-on'. Products and services considered sustainable ought to address economic, social as well as environmental concerns while offering prospects to improve livelihoods of stakeholders such as customers (Carroll, 1979).

CSR as a Response to Regulatory Pressure

Incidents of regulatory pressure on companies to adopt more responsible business practices are increasing. For instance, British Petrolium (BP), a large international oil and gas company, was pressured to clean up the Gulf oil spill and adopt more responsible oil drilling practices (Osofsky, 2011). In the finance sector, British bankers were accosted for what was perceived to be unethical bonuses (Gregg, Jewell, & Tonks, 2012). Elsewhere in the UK energy sector, the big six energy companies (E.ON, British Gas, NPower, EDF, Scottish Power and SSE) came under fire from the energy regulator, Ofgem for allegedly profiteering at the expense of poor customers (Greenberg, 2014). This prompted investigations by the regulator with aims to further reform the UK energy sector. These are just three examples of organisations succumbing to regulatory pressure and considering more responsible and sustainable approaches to doing business.

Although customers benefit from the protective oversight of the relevant regulators, there remains a question on whether businesses in this category can truly be socially responsible as their focus on CSR would have been brought about by pressure from their regulators and therefore externally-driven and 'bolt-on'. This raises questions on whether such CSR strategies and requisite initiatives would endure if regulatory pressure was removed. Further, this suggests that areas not picked up by respective regulators may remain questionable leading to customers getting less than desirable products and services.

CSR as a Strategy to Attract Talent or Address Employee Concerns

As the global race to attract talent gathers pace, most notable organisations keenly listen to employee concerns and reshape their credentials to attract and retain the best talent in an increasingly competitive global labour market. Adopting CSR has become one of the key differentiators for many employers (Bhattacharya, Sen, & Koschun, 2012). Research demonstrates that many skilled job seekers are beginning to select potential employers based on their CSR credentials among other factors (Lin, Tsai, Joe, & Chiu, 2012; Segal, Sobczak, & Triomphe, 2003). While more research still needs to be undertaken to establish the exact interplay of issues in this area, one can infer that less sustainable companies may find it difficult to attract top talent, especially since more responsible companies are perceived to be more likely to offer better working conditions and treat their staff more humanely (Locke & Romis, 2012). Besides using CSR credentials to attract new and retain current employees, organisations continuously engage their existing workforce in reshaping their CSR strategies, thereby engendering trust with such employees. Since CSR in organisations is best implemented through devolved structures involving those in the frontline, employees are regularly consulted on the latest CSR views and developments with their opinions communicated to the management on a continuous two-way basis (Jamali, 2008). Although the above portrays a somewhat gloomy picture of the current CSR practices, it also offers a number of valuable lessons. More specifically, from the various rationales of adopting CSR initiatives discussed above, this chapter advances two propositions as follows:

a) The more internally-derived the CSR strategies and initiatives, the higher their perceived authenticity and therefore the easier it is for the organisation to get stakeholder support;
b) The more externally-derived the CSR strategies and initiatives, the lower their perceived authenticity, as externally imposed CSR initiatives conjure a reactive approach and therefore potentially engender low authenticity and stakeholder trust.

The propositions above have been used to generate a model depicting the two-way correlation between the source of CSR strategies (i.e. whether externally imposed or internally driven) and their perceived authenticity (see Figure 1 below).

The model above implies that CSR strategies externally imposed by regulatory or political pressure tend to have less authenticity because they do not demonstrate the business' own voluntary undertaking. On the contrary, internally-derived CSR strategies may be perceived to be more authentic as they are voluntary, home-grown and instituted at the business' own volition in a proactive manner. Organisations seeking a sustainable marketing orientation are therefore well-advised to proactively devise CSR strategies if they are to gain traction with their stakeholders, lest they be viewed as merely responding to regulatory or other external pressure. The following sections suggest some practical guidelines as to how higher authenticity of CSR initiatives can be achieved.

TOWARDS A SUSTAINABLE BUSINESS PRACTICE

Ingraining CSR as Part of an Organisation's DNA

True CSR initiatives must be '*built-into*' the organisational strategies rather than be '*bolt-on*' i.e. they must not be added on as an afterthought (Galbreath, 2009; Maas & Boons, 2010; Sharp & Zaidman,

Figure 1. Correlation between CSR strategy source and perceived authenticity

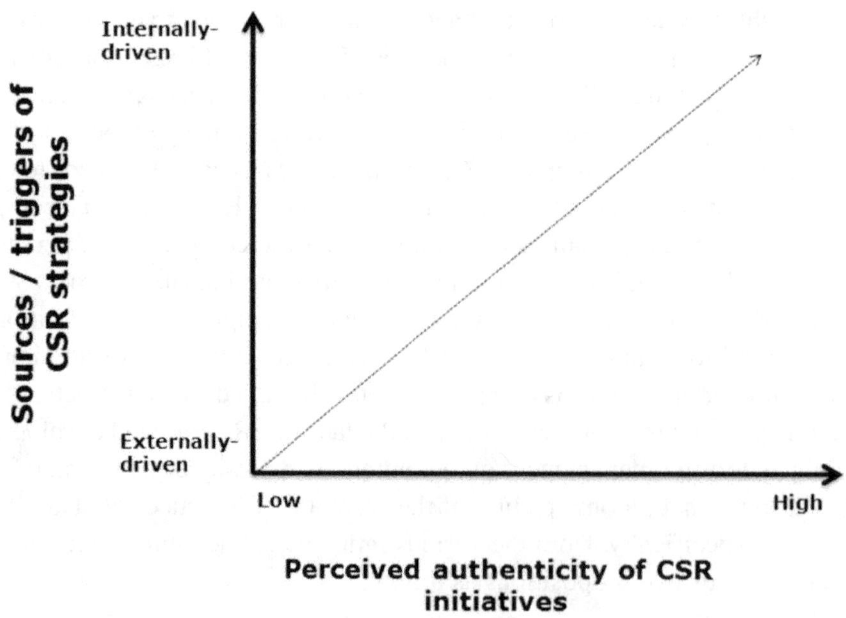

2010). Bolt-on CSR strategies give an impression of foisting, suggesting that they have not been in the original organisational design; that they may have been forgotten or that they may have consequently been viewed as burdensome and therefore not desirable, especially in the ever-busy work setting fraught with limited organisational resources. When developing long-term strategies in organisations, CSR thinking should be in the DNA of the business; it should be a part of the conception of all business strategies and should dictate how the business conducts itself while shaping the choice of opportunities pursued (Bhattacharyya, 2010; Carroll & Shabana, 2010; Sharp & Zaidman, 2010). Attempts to create separate CSR objectives outside organisational strategies are likely to create a rift between the business strategies on one hand and CSR strategies on the other. This rift will most likely relegate CSR strategies to second tier-level, only to be carried out when time and resources permit.

Proactive embedding of CSR principles by business managers into the strategies of an organisation potentially guarantee that such principles filter down into the nerve centre of the business, permeating every aspect of the business (Bonn & Fisher, 2011). In such instances, CSR is not how the organisation does business, it is the business. Most organisations which adopt this approach of embedding CSR into their operations do not have large CSR departments.

Instead, the implementation of CSR initiatives is devolved to the front line sections of the company with only a small CSR co-ordinating office. According to Arjaliès and Mundy (2012), such an approach minimises friction as those implementing CSR strategies are actively involved in shaping the formulation of the same. A values-driven CSR strategy is home-grown and thus, formulated as part of an organisation's broader strategy development. This fact is key as it determines the authenticity of CSR strategies and initiatives, engendering trust and buy-in among employees. The following sections give a brief overview of some of the actions that organisations ought to take in embedding CSR as part of their organisational DNAs and marketing strategies. The steps include (i) Clarification of CSR terminology, (ii) Creating a sense of urgency for change, (iii) Creating a shared vision, (iv) Facilitating internal communication and dialogue, (v) Developing a coherent CSR delivery programme, (vi) Aligning CSR initiatives with strategic business objectives as well as (vii) Measurement, controlling and assessing the significance of formulated CSR initiatives – Materiality. The steps form an iterative process of checking and realigning strategies to changing market conditions. These steps are summarised in Figure 2 below and discussed in more depth in the ensuing sections.

Clarify CSR Terminology

In light of the lack of universal CSR terminology, there is further need for organisations to internally map out the CSR terrain and clarify its jargon as a way of contributing to a better understanding and management of stakeholder expectations. An ideal approach is to create a CSR typology, outlining the different CSR conceptions and their implications for organisational strategy together with requisite outputs to different stakeholders for ease of appraisal.

Such a typology would allow each adopted concept to be measured using appropriate frameworks thereby engendering effectiveness and accountability. Undeniably, each organisation will need to draw up and adopt CSR strategies in line with its specific set of circumstances and its core business. It is key to highlight that the communication of a shared typology and sense of purpose among all involved in developing and delivering the adopted CSR programs is critical. This communication can be facilitated by the company's IS infrastructure, providing both ease of measurement as well as enhancing transparency of CSR outputs.

Figure 2. Steps involved in embedding CSR as part of the organisational DNA

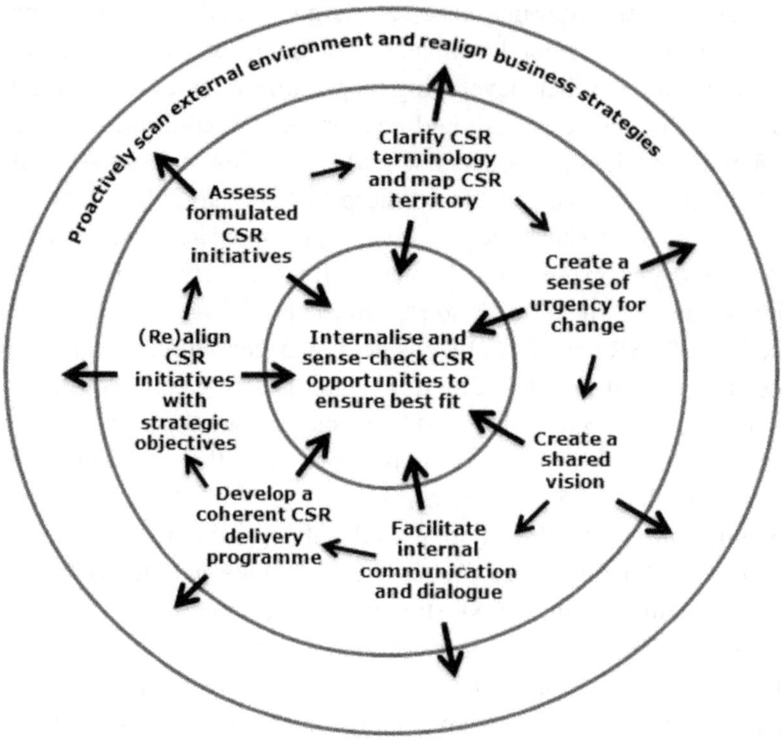

Create a Sense of Urgency

Adopting CSR initiatives often means moving the organisation from one state to another, creating the dreaded change that may threaten to unsettle many stakeholders as they leave their old comfort zones and may dread venturing into uncharted territory (Cramer, Van der Heijden, & Jonker, 2006). In order to convince various stakeholders to take such a leap, an organisation may have to significantly change its culture as well as carefully calculate the risks of the status quo. Stakeholders have to be reassured that change in favour of the CSR orientation potentially brings considerable benefits as opposed to the status quo. From that perspective, top management teams have to take a leading role in ensuring that various stakeholders who have an interest in the business are fully informed and understand the need and urgency for change (Cramer et al., 2006).

This should be carefully crafted to ensure that internal stakeholders can see the risks facing the organisation on one hand, versus the opportunities arising from the adoption of the proposed CSR initiatives on the other hand. Faced with a compelling need for change to adopt CSR initiatives or peril, top management teams have a choice on whether to create a burning platform to initiate an irreversible change process (Mirvis, 2011) or persuade employees to voluntarily rally behind the proposed CSR change programme. The burning platform analogy suggests creating a mandatory change agenda compelling employees to sign up to the change agenda or face whatever negative consequences management deem appropriate.

The burning platform option involves coercion and may breed ill-feeling which may in turn lead to half-hearted prisoner-like sentiments among employees who may not buy into the CSR programme (Othman, Darus, & Arshad, 2011). On the other hand, it ensures that every employee is mandated to participate. The alternative view is discretionary and allows those passionate with the initiatives to get involved. Each organisation will undoubtedly be operating within a particular cultural context and has to bear in mind the impact of their beliefs and values on their approach. Nations with very high power distance indices (Hofstede, 1984) may well be open to the burning platform approach where management create a compelling agenda for change, whereas those with less hierarchical and more equal societies (low power distance indices) may be more amenable to persuasion and personal discretion. Managers are therefore advised to take heed of their cultural environments in crafting their proposed CSR stakeholder engagement strategies and their requisite implementation approaches (Maon, Lindgreen, & Swaen, 2010).

Create a Shared Vision

The vision for the adoption of CSR initiatives is often coined at higher management levels while according to Weaver and Rotmans (2006), the implementation process is often delegated to lower levels of the organisation which usually lack insight into the vision of the top management team. This often ferments differences in scope and direction between the two levels of an organisation. As such, the disparity between these two layers of an organisation regarding the CSR vision may potentially threaten to derail the fledgling CSR initiatives. Consequently, the initiatives may be operationalised in a half-hearted manner, conjuring perceptions of box-ticking and CSR tokenism (Hine & Preuss, 2009). The result of the differences in understanding the objective of CSR initiatives on one hand and the appreciation of the practicalities of implementation on the other may damage internal stakeholder buy-in and compromise the credibility of the initiatives.

Employees may view the new initiatives as yet another fad, brought in by the '*out-of-touch*' management echelons who are often claimed to lack a detailed understanding of what happens on the ground (Seitanidi, 2009). In the circumstances, such strategies may be doomed to fail before they even take off. Clearly, this is not a desirable state for any organisation. CSR strategies and initiatives borne out of such divided organisational perspectives may not stand a chance as those implementing them may not even believe in them. The solution often lies with the creation of a shared vision and its communication across the organisation (Maon *et al.*, 2009). Strategies for sharing the CSR vision may take one-to-one meetings, team meetings, internal newsletters, memos, and staff addresses by company directors as well as an active employment of the organisation's various information systems. Sustained, consistent messages will go a long way in impressing upon internal stakeholders the drivers, importance and urgency of the proposed CSR change agenda, the specific objectives as well as a visible demonstration of the top management's support and commitment for the CSR initiatives (Jenkins, 2009).

Facilitate Internal Communication and Dialogue

A shared CSR vision is best engendered through an intensive internal communication programme, reliant on company's IS and aimed at creating an appropriate appetite for change and allowing stakeholders to collectively contribute towards, and to shape the CSR initiatives. Such an approach sounds unwieldy but creates buy-in while smoothening the CSR implementation process considerably. It offers stakeholders an opportunity to have their concerns heard and issues clarified before the implementation of CSR initiatives goes live. Clear and consistent communications must be employed in organisations intending to implement CSR to ensure that various stakeholders understand the need for change and are supported through the change process. CSR initiatives have to be interpreted and translated down to relevant, individual level issues such that each employee can see a personal reason for the proposed change and understand the exact role they have to play in contributing to the proposed CSR changes. This way, CSR adoption becomes a personal issue to each of the employees, albeit within the broader organisational collective.

In light of the above, it would be naive to assume that all employees will be converted into believers of any proposed CSR initiatives. Admittedly, any form of change in an organisation is likely to be treated with scepticism (Fenwick & Bierema, 2008). Nevertheless, as long as the proposed CSR strategy/vision has been well-crafted demonstrating the benefits of change versus the risks of the status, even the sceptics may have limited options but to endorse the programme, albeit with reservations. Understandably, their participation in and support of the programme may not be because of the promised benefits, but to avert any risks of doing nothing (Bebbington et al., 2008).

It is logical for the implementation of CSR initiatives to start by testing the viability of the proposed strategy. According to Khandelwal and Mohendra, (2010) this can be achieved by sharing anticipated benefits with key internal stakeholders and getting their views on board so as to secure their buy-in.

Develop a Meaningful CSR Delivery Programme

Once employees and other stakeholders are clear about the objectives of the proposed strategies and requisite initiatives, the strategies have to be integrated into a CSR programme to be treated as a holistic unit at higher levels of the organisation but parcelled out into different projects for implementation by various sections of the organisation. The parcelling out of the CSR projects ensures that different sections of the organisation are not burdened with trying to figure out aspects of the programme which may not directly relate to what they do at a local level. Each CSR project must be meaningful and should seek to exploit the interests and competencies of the teams involved (Maon *et al.*, 2010). It must clearly relate to the pursuits of the team implementing it and have the potential to bear realisable fruits for those working on it.

(Re)Align CSR Initiatives with Strategic Business Objectives

Pursuant to the above, it is important to note that adopted CSR objectives and requisite initiatives ought to align and be continuously realigned to the business' own objectives (Bhattacharyya, 2010; Lozano, 2008). In fact, one of the biggest let-downs for businesses attempting to adopt CSR-oriented strategies often emanates from a lack of alignment between the business' strategic objectives and the chosen CSR strategies and initiatives (Carroll & Shabana, 2010; Sharp & Zaidman, 2010). Failure to establish a "*built-in*" CSR strategy and aligning / realigning it to set strategic objectives of an organisation often causes friction between different sections of an organisation threatening to undermine the proposed CSR initiatives (Galbreath, 2009; Moore & Manring, 2009; Sharp & Zaidman, 2010). This often leads to conflicts around the deployment of scarce resources within an organisation (Bhattacharyya, 2010; Carroll & Shabana, 2010; Reinhardt, Stavins, & Vietor, 2008) and the prioritisation of the initiatives, given organisational resource constraints.

Assess Significance of Formulated CSR Strategies and Initiatives: Materiality

One of the key issues facing the development and implementation of CSR initiatives relates to the significance of such initiatives and the extent to which they align to the organisation's core business (McElhaney, 2009). This is often referred to as 'materiality' in CSR audit circles (Manetti & Becatti, 2009). Auditing for materiality ensures that organisations are judged not just on the quantity of what they do and disclose, but rather on the significance and extent to which they have gone towards addressing key issues around their core businesses. As discussed in earlier sections of this chapter, exaggerated claims or misrepresentations regarding an organisation's CSR initiatives may be tantamount to greenwashing (Vries, Terwel, Ellemers, & Daamen, 2013). Organisations need to carefully check their claims against actions actually implemented on the ground as a way of ensuring accurate and meaningful communication of their CSR outputs.

Each organisation seeking to implement CSR initiatives is therefore well-advised to ask itself key questions including: what is our core business and what impact does our business have on the environment, economy, society and broader stakeholders? Are those impacts negative or positive; what could we do that would leave positive imprints of our business among our stakeholders? Using our core competencies, what needs could we address within the communities that we operate in? How significant are the CSR activities that we have chosen to focus on in light of the scope of our organisational activities? What do our stakeholders consider to be the key issues that our business should concern itself with?

Answers to the above questions should give the organisation a clear idea of whether it is adopting a tokenistic CSR approach which may not endear the organisation to its various stakeholders or if it is proactively tackling significant challenges facing stakeholders. Depending on the size and scope of the operations of an organisation, expectations from stakeholders will vary (Carroll & Shabana, 2010). It would be unimaginative for a multi-national global giant to embark on considerably localised, low cost initiatives involving donations of a few clothing items when its operations are causing considerable suffering or causing environmental damage that affects many people (Frynas, 2005). Expectations of responsible business practices are slowly being mainstreamed, implying that businesses are increasingly expected to do more in the area of CSR. This is discussed in more detail below.

Be Proactive and Innovate

While the above discourse starts from the notion that CSR initiatives are voluntary, many stakeholders have come to accept responsible behaviour as a basic tenet of every business (Jamali, Safieddine, & Rabbath, 2008). This chapter asserts that gradually, CSR is being mainstreamed such that in the future, stakeholders may take it for granted that all organisations should by default be responsible (White, 2005). This is raising the bar for sustainable business practices and calls for organisations to continuously seek new and more innovative ways of differentiating themselves from their competitors. When business activities are anchored on CSR with every organisation expected to exhibit responsible business traits, there will be need for other differentiators to uniquely position organisations. Until then, many organisations continue to tout the CSR tune, despite the lack of clarity as to what this actually entails in practice and how stakeholders can appraise the implementation thereof (McWilliams, Siegel, & Wright, 2006).

Claims of responsible business conduct are becoming mundane with the evidence of CSR activities inclining towards similar antics that tend to be tokenistic at best and lacking innovation and strategic vision at worst (Frynas, 2005; Manteaw, 2008). There is therefore a compelling need for organisations to break away from the common CSR antics and embark on substantial, innovative and more meaningful initiatives that offer real-life changing opportunities for stakeholders. There is a dearth of commonly-touted CSR activities and unsurprisingly, reports of corporate malpractices continue to emerge despite glossy and impressive CSR credentials hung on the offending organisations' walls. CSR cannot just be a work uniform that organisations put on and take off as and when it suits. It has to be a way of life, a business ideology, underpinning the business' overall strategy.

INFORMATION SYSTEMS (IS) AS AN ENABLER FOR CSR

With developments in IT and Marketing Information Systems, there are increasing opportunities for organisations to develop and deploy more meaningful CSR initiatives with clearer measures to gauge successful implementation. Opportunities exist in information sourcing, sharing of best practice as well as data collection, reporting and dissemination of CSR results (Nasir, 2005). Further, developments in IT represent more efficient and environmentally-friendly approaches to implementing and managing CSR programs. Although there is yet more research required to fully flesh out and quantify opportunities in this area, CSR can greatly leverage off the use of such IS applications as market research aggregation, planning support tools, CRM systems, operational executive IS and other enterprise-wide systems and external information sources such as social networks and forums (Daniel, Wilson, & McDonald, 2003).

These systems can enable companies to understand the current CSR landscape more precisely, timely sense and proactively respond to the emerging internal and external CSR issues (Talvinen, 1995). Furthermore, these systems can help to establish effective communication channels between all stakeholders, support managers in their CSR decision-making, and engender adoption of responsible behaviour across the organisation (Daniel, Wilson, & McDonald, 2003; Nasir, 2005).

FUTURE RESEARCH DIRECTIONS

In business management and marketing, the concept of CSR covers a significantly large and well-researched topic area and it has not been possible to debate all its multi-faceted dimensions in this chapter. Consequently, this chapter only scratched the surface of the possibilities within the academic and practical field of CSR, which in-spite of the multitude of research still lacks common ground, illustrating numerous disputes and unanswered questions. One of the questions lacking consensus and introducing much confusion into the field is the CSR terminology. Further meta-analysis and interdisciplinary research is required to address this area and provide academics, as well as practitioners, with clearer and more operationalisable definitions of the key constructs. A more universal typology of CSR terminology, outlining implications of the jargon, will in turn enable a more user-friendly approach to CSR strategy formulation and requisite implementation. The meaning of CSR is changing in the context of globalisation and other emerging global issues. Future studies are therefore necessary to further shed light on implications of these changes to both the theory and practice of CSR.

CONCLUSION

This chapter has discussed three key themes: CSR terminology, rationale for CSR adoption as well as issues around practical CSR implementation. At the beginning of the chapter, concerns around the existing CSR jargon were discussed. It was established that the CSR landscape is littered with many terms often used interchangeably and causing confusion especially to those new to the terrain. The concept of responsible business practices and CSR was said to be vague, requiring clarification to enable firms to identify and adopt strategies commensurate with their type of business undertakings. To tackle this issue, while awaiting a better CSR conceptualisation, this chapter urged companies to clarify their understanding of key CSR constructs together with mapping their stakeholders' key concerns to enable timely operationalisation of CSR initiatives relevant to their specific business contexts.

The second discussion presented in this work focused on the rationale for pursuing CSR. Organisations were said to adopt CSR strategies for a variety of reasons, with their drivers for implementing CSR initiatives often clouding the authenticity of such CSR programmes. The chapter demonstrated that internally-derived initiatives were viewed as more authentic compared to externally-imposed CSR initiatives which it was argued, were reactive. To this end, the chapter proposed a framework (see Figure 1 on p.7) to capture the correlation between a source of CSR strategies and their perceived authenticity. While the model is conceptual and still needs empirical testing, it does raise pertinent points about proactive, internally-driven CSR strategies versus those imposed on the organisation by external forces. By waiting for other external forces to dictate CSR directions, organisations lose an opportunity to take leadership in the area and this may damage loyalty. The discussion considered the increased mainstreaming of expected responsible business practices and implications for future CSR initiatives. Following the discourse above, the recommendation is that in future, businesses may well have to seek more innovative CSR strategies as certain responsible practices may be taken to be the norm.

Finally, the chapter outlined some general guidelines for the practical implementation of CSR. It suggested that CSR should become a part of organisational DNA, highlighting the importance of aligning CSR strategies to the core business strategies. The chapter argued in favour of creating a sense of urgency for the adoption of CSR among an organisation's stakeholders. It further recommended that a shared vision be created and clearly communicated within the organisation. Lastly, the development of a CSR programme and a proactive assessment of the appropriateness of the CSR initiatives were proposed. Developments in Information Technology in general and Marketing Information Systems in particular were highlighted as key enabling platforms for enhanced CSR development, deployment and measurement of results. The chapter raised questions on whether CSR-triggered change should be coercive or voluntary, with suggestions for managers to consider the cultural contexts of their organisations when crafting and implementing CSR initiatives.

REFERENCES

Arjaliès, D. L., & Mundy, J. (2012, May). How firms use management control systems to formulate and implement CSR strategy: A levers of control perspective. *Proceedings of the EAA (European Accounting Association) Annual Conference*.

Baden, D., & Harwood, I. A. (2013). Terminology matters: A critical exploration of corporate social responsibility terms. *Journal of Business Ethics*, *116*(3), 615–627. doi:10.1007/s10551-012-1498-9

Bebbington, J., Larrinaga, C., & Moneva, J. M. (2008). Corporate social reporting and reputation risk management. *Accounting, Auditing & Accountability Journal*, *21*(3), 337–361. doi:10.1108/09513570810863932

Bhattacharya, C. B., Sen, S., & Korschun, D. (2012). Using corporate social responsibility to win the war for talent. *MIT Sloan Management Review*, *49*(2), 37–44.

Bonn, I., & Fisher, J. (2011). Sustainability: The missing ingredient in strategy. *The Journal of Business Strategy*, *32*(1), 5–14. doi:10.1108/02756661111100274

Brüggenwirth, B. (2006). The CSR brand positioning grid. In *Jonker, J & de White, J., Management Models for Corporate Social Responsibility* (pp. 140–146). Berlin: Springer Berlin Heidelberg. doi:10.1007/3-540-33247-2_17

Brunner, C. B., Esch, F. R., & Kinscher, N. (2012). Communicating corporate social responsibility: Empty promises or smart strategy? *Advances in Advertising Research*, *3*(1), 105–117. doi:10.1007/978-3-8349-4291-3_9

Calabrese, A., Costa, R., Menichini, T., & Rosati, F. (2013). Does corporate social responsibility hit the mark? A stakeholder oriented methodology for CSR assessment. *Knowledge and Process Management*, *20*(2), 77–89. doi:10.1002/kpm.1406

Campbell, J. L. (2007). Why would corporations behave in socially responsible ways? An institutional theory of corporate social responsibility. *Academy of Management Review*, *32*(3), 946–967. doi:10.5465/AMR.2007.25275684

Carroll, A. B. (1979). A three-dimensional conceptual model of corporate performance. *Academy of Management Review*, *4*(4), 497–505.

Carroll, A. B. (1999). Corporate social responsibility: Evolution of a definitional construct. *Business & Society*, *38*(3), 268–295. doi:10.1177/000765039903800303

Carroll, A. B., & Shabana, K. M. (2010). The business case for corporate social responsibility: A review of concepts, research and practice. *International Journal of Management Reviews*, *12*(1), 85–105. doi:10.1111/j.1468-2370.2009.00275.x

Chen, Y. S., & Chang, C. H. (2013). Greenwash and green trust: The mediation effects of green consumer confusion and green perceived risk. *Journal of Business Ethics*, *114*(3), 489–500. doi:10.1007/s10551-012-1360-0

Ciegis, R., Ramanauskiene, J., & Martinkus, B. (2009). The concept of sustainable development and its use for sustainability scenarios. *Inzinerine Ekonomika-Engineering Economics*, *2*(62), 28–37.

Costanza, R., & Patten, B. C. (1995). Defining and predicting sustainability. *Ecological Economics*, *15*(3), 193–196. doi:10.1016/0921-8009(95)00048-8

Cramer, J., Van Der Heijden, A., & Jonker, J. (2006). Corporate social responsibility: Making sense through thinking and acting. *Business Ethics (Oxford, England)*, *15*(4), 380–389. doi:10.1111/j.1467-8608.2006.00459.x

Dahl, R. (2010). Green washing: Do you know what you're buying? *Environmental Health Perspectives*, *118*(6), 246–252. doi:10.1289/ehp.118-a246 PMID:20515714

Dahlsrud, A. (2008). How corporate social responsibility is defined: An analysis of 37 definitions. *Corporate Social Responsibility and Environmental Management*, *15*(1), 1–13. doi:10.1002/csr.132

Daniel, E., Wilson, H., & McDonald, M. (2003). Towards a map of Marketing Information Systems: An inductive study. *European Journal of Marketing*, *37*(5/6), 821–847. doi:10.1108/03090560310465161

Davis, K. (1960). Can business afford to ignore social responsibilities? *California Management Review*, *2*(3), 70–76. doi:10.2307/41166246

Delmas, M. A., & Burbano, V. C. (2011). The drivers of greenwashing. *California Management Review*, *54*(1), 1–38.

El Ghoul, S., Guedhami, O., Kwok, C. C., & Mishra, D. R. (2011). Does corporate social responsibility affect the cost of capital? *Journal of Banking & Finance*, *35*(9), 2388–2406. doi:10.1016/j.jbankfin.2011.02.007

Elliott, J. (2012). *An introduction to sustainable development*. London: Routledge.

Ellis, L., & Bastin, C. (2011). Corporate social responsibility in times of recession: Changing discourses and implications for policy and practice. *Corporate Social Responsibility and Environmental Management*, *18*(5), 294–305. doi:10.1002/csr.254

Faber, N., Jorna, R., & Van Engelen, J. (2005). The sustainability of "sustainability" – a study into the conceptual foundations of the notion of "sustainability". *Journal of Environmental Assessment Policy and Management*, *7*(1), 1–33. doi:10.1142/S1464333205001955

Fenwick, T., & Bierema, L. (2008). Corporate social responsibility: Issues for human resource development professionals. *International Journal of Training and Development*, *12*(1), 24–35. doi:10.1111/j.1468-2419.2007.00293.x

Fernando, M. (2010). Corporate social responsibility in the wake of the Asian tsunami: Effect of time on the genuineness of CSR initiatives. *European Management Journal*, *28*(1), 68–79. doi:10.1016/j.emj.2009.08.002

Frynas, J. G. (2005). The false developmental promise of corporate social responsibility: Evidence from multinational oil companies. *International Affairs*, *81*(3), 581–598. doi:10.1111/j.1468-2346.2005.00470.x

Furlow, N. E. (2010). Greenwashing in the new millennium. *Journal of Applied Business & Economics*, *10*(6), 1–4.

Galbreath, J. (2009). Building corporate social responsibility into strategy. *European Business Review*, *21*(2), 109–127. doi:10.1108/09555340910940123

Glavič, P., & Lukman, R. (2007). Review of sustainability terms and their definitions. *Journal of Cleaner Production*, *15*(18), 1875–1885. doi:10.1016/j.jclepro.2006.12.006

Greenberg, M. R. (2014). Energy policy and research: The underappreciation of trust. *Energy Research & Social Science*, *1*(29), 152–160. doi:10.1016/j.erss.2014.02.004

Gregg, P., Jewell, S., & Tonks, I. (2012). Executive pay and performance: Did bankers' bonuses cause the crisis? *International Review of Finance*, *12*(1), 89–122. doi:10.1111/j.1468-2443.2011.01136.x

Hine, J. A., & Preuss, L. (2009). Society is out there, organisation is in here: On the perceptions of corporate social responsibility held by different managerial groups. *Journal of Business Ethics*, *88*(2), 381–393. doi:10.1007/s10551-008-9970-2

Hofstede, G. (1984). Cultural dimensions in management and planning. *Asia Pacific Journal of Management*, *1*(2), 81–99. doi:10.1007/BF01733682

Hogan, J., & Lodhia, S. (2011). Sustainability reporting and reputation risk management: An Australian case study. *International Journal of Accounting and Information Management*, *19*(3), 267–287. doi:10.1108/18347641111169269

Jamali, D. (2008). A stakeholder approach to corporate social responsibility: A fresh perspective into theory and practice. *Journal of Business Ethics*, *82*(1), 213–231. doi:10.1007/s10551-007-9572-4

Jamali, D., Safieddine, A. M., & Rabbath, M. (2008). Corporate governance and corporate social responsibility synergies and interrelationships. *Corporate Governance: An International Review*, *16*(5), 443–459. doi:10.1111/j.1467-8683.2008.00702.x

Jenkins, H. (2009). A 'business opportunity' model of corporate social responsibility for small-and medium-sized enterprises. *Business Ethics (Oxford, England)*, *18*(1), 21–36. doi:10.1111/j.1467-8608.2009.01546.x

Jochem, R. (2011). Sustainability modelling as an enterprise quality requirement. *Current Issues of Business and Law*, *6*(1), 129–140. doi:10.5200/1822-9530.2011.07

Johnson, G., Whittington, R., & Scholes, K. (2011). Exploring Corporate Strategy, 9th Edition. Place: Pearson Education Limited.

Khandelwal, K. A., & Mohendra, N. (2010). Espoused organizational values, vision, and corporate social responsibility: Does it matter to organizational members? *Vikalpa*, *35*(3), 19–35.

Kohli, A. K., & Jaworski, B. J. (1993). Market orientation: Antecedents and consequences. *Journal of marketing: A quarterly publication of the American Marketing Association, 57*(3), 53-70.

Kolstad, I. (2007). Why firms should not always maximize profits. *Journal of Business Ethics*, *76*(2), 137–145. doi:10.1007/s10551-006-9262-7

Lin, C. P., Tsai, Y. H., Joe, S. W., & Chiu, C. K. (2012). Modelling the relationship among perceived corporate citizenship, firms' attractiveness, and career success expectation. *Journal of Business Ethics*, *105*(1), 83–93. doi:10.1007/s10551-011-0949-z

Locke, R. M., & Romis, M. (2012). Improving work conditions in global supply chains. *MIT Sloan Management Review*, *48*(2), 54–62.

Lorenzo-Molo, C. F., & Udani, Z. A. S. (2013). Bringing back the essence of the "S" and "R" to CSR: Understanding the limitations of the merchant trade and the white man's burden. *Journal of Business Ethics*, *117*(1), 123–136. doi:10.1007/s10551-012-1513-1

Lozano, J. M. (2008). CSR or RSC? (Beyond the Humpty Dumpty syndrome). *Society and Business Review*, *3*(3), 191–206. doi:10.1108/17465680810907288

Lozano, R. (2011). The state of sustainability reporting in universities. *International Journal of Sustainability in Higher Education, 12*(1), 67–78. doi:10.1108/14676371111098311

Lyon, T. P., & Maxwell, J. W. (2011). Greenwash: Corporate environmental disclosure under threat of audit. *Journal of Economics & Management Strategy, 20*(1), 3–41. doi:10.1111/j.1530-9134.2010.00282.x

Maas, K., & Boons, F. (2010). CSR as a strategic activity: Value creation, redistribution and integration. *Innovative CSR: From Risk Management to Value Creation, 153*(172), 20.

Manetti, G., & Becatti, L. (2009). Assurance services for sustainability reports: Standards and empirical evidence. *Journal of Business Ethics, 87*(1), 289–298. doi:10.1007/s10551-008-9809-x

Manteaw, B. (2008). From tokenism to social justice: Rethinking the bottom line for sustainable community development. *Community Development Journal: An International Forum, 43*(4), 428–443. doi:10.1093/cdj/bsm015

Maon, F., Lindgreen, A., & Swaen, V. (2009). Designing and implementing corporate social responsibility: An integrative framework grounded in theory and practice. *Journal of Business Ethics, 87*(1), 71–89. doi:10.1007/s10551-008-9804-2

Maon, F., Lindgreen, A., & Swaen, V. (2010). Organizational stages and cultural phases: A critical review and a consolidative model of corporate social responsibility development. *International Journal of Management Reviews, 12*(1), 20–38. doi:10.1111/j.1468-2370.2009.00278.x

Marsden, G., Kimble, M., Nellthorp, J., & Kelly, C. (2010). Sustainability assessment: The definition deficit. *International Journal of Sustainable Transportation, 4*(4), 189–211. doi:10.1080/15568310902825699

Marshall, J. D., & Toffel, M. W. (2005). Framing the elusive concept of sustainability: A sustainability hierarchy. *Environmental Science & Technology, 39*(3), 673–682. doi:10.1021/es040394k PMID:15757326

Matten, D., & Moon, J. (2008). "Implicit" and "explicit" CSR: A conceptual framework for a comparative understanding of corporate social responsibility. *Academy of Management Review, 33*(2), 404–424. doi:10.5465/AMR.2008.31193458

McElhaney, K. (2009). A strategic approach to corporate social responsibility. *Leader to Leader, 52*(1), 30–36. doi:10.1002/ltl.327

McGuire, J. W. (1963). *Business and society*. New York: McGraw-Hill.

McShane, L., & Cunningham, P. (2012). To thine own self be true? Employees' judgments of the authenticity of their organization's corporate social responsibility program. *Journal of Business Ethics, 108*(1), 81–100. doi:10.1007/s10551-011-1064-x

McWilliams, A., Siegel, D. S., & Wright, P. M. (2006). Corporate social responsibility: Strategic implications. *Journal of Management Studies, 43*(1), 1–18. doi:10.1111/j.1467-6486.2006.00580.x

Mebratu, D. (1998). Sustainability and sustainable development: Historical and conceptual review. *Environmental Impact Assessment Review, 18*(6), 493–520. doi:10.1016/S0195-9255(98)00019-5

Middlemiss, N. (2003). Authentic not cosmetic: CSR as brand enhancement. *The Journal of Brand Management, 10*(4), 353–361. doi:10.1057/palgrave.bm.2540130

Mirvis, P. (2011). Unilever's drive for sustainability and CSR–Changing the game. *Organizing for Sustainable Effectiveness, 1*(34), 41–72. doi:10.1108/S2045-0605(2011)0000001007

Moore, S. B., & Manring, S. L. (2009). Strategy development in small and medium sized enterprises for sustainability and increased value creation. *Journal of Cleaner Production, 17*(2), 276–282. doi:10.1016/j.jclepro.2008.06.004

Morris, M. (2011). Sustainability: An exercise in futility. *International Journal of Business and Management, 7*(2), 36–44.

Nasir, S. (2005). The development, change, and transformation of Management Information Systems (MIS): A content analysis of articles published in business and marketing journals. *International Journal of Information Management, 25*(5), 442–457. doi:10.1016/j.ijinfomgt.2005.06.003

Nidumolu, R., Prahalad, C. K., & Rangaswami, M. R. (2009). Why sustainability is now the key driver of innovation. *Harvard Business Review, 87*(9), 56–64.

Osofsky, H. M. (2011). Multidimensional governance and the BP deepwater horizon oil spill. *Florida Law Review, 63*(5), 1077–1121.

Othman, S., Darus, F., & Arshad, R. (2011). The influence of coercive isomorphism on corporate social responsibility reporting and reputation. *Social Responsibility Journal, 7*(1), 119–135. doi:10.1108/17471111111114585

Ozcaglar-Toulouse, N. (2007). Living for "ethics": Responsible consumption in everyday life. *Research in Consumer Behavior, 11*(1), 421–436.

Parisi, C., & Hockerts, K. N. (2008). Managerial mindsets and performance measurement systems of CSR-related intangibles. *Measuring Business Excellence, 12*(2), 51–67. doi:10.1108/13683040810881199

Pope, J., Annandale, D., & Morrison-Saunders, A. (2004). Conceptualising sustainability assessment. *Environmental Impact Assessment Review, 24*(6), 595–616. doi:10.1016/j.eiar.2004.03.001

Quiroz-Onate, D., & Aitken, M. (2007). Business and human rights: A critical assessment of the notion of CSR and measurement. *Journal of International Trade Law and Policy, 6*(2), 79–90. doi:10.1108/14770020780000559

Reinhardt, F. L., Stavins, R. N., & Vietor, R. H. (2008). Corporate social responsibility through an economic lens. *Review of Environmental Economics and Policy, 2*(2), 219–239. doi:10.1093/reep/ren008

Schaltegger, S., & Wagner, M. (2011). Sustainable entrepreneurship and sustainability innovation: Categories and interactions. *Business Strategy and the Environment, 20*(4), 222–237. doi:10.1002/bse.682

Segal, J. P., Sobczak, A., & Triomphe, C. E. (2003). *Corporate social responsibility and working conditions*. Dublin: European Foundation for the Improvement of Living and Working Conditions.

Seitanidi, M. M. (2009). Missed opportunities of employee involvement in CSR partnerships. *Corporate Reputation Review, 12*(2), 90–105. doi:10.1057/crr.2009.7

Sekhar Bhattacharyya, S. (2010). Exploring the concept of strategic corporate social responsibility for an integrated perspective. *European Business Review, 22*(1), 82–101. doi:10.1108/09555341011009025

Sharp, Z., & Zaidman, N. (2010). Strategization of CSR. *Journal of Business Ethics*, *93*(1), 51–71. doi:10.1007/s10551-009-0181-2

Steiner, G. A. (1971). *Business and Society*. New York: Random House.

Strugatch, W. (2011). Turning values into valuation: Can corporate social responsibility survive hard times and emerge intact? *Journal of Management Development*, *30*(1), 44–48. doi:10.1108/02621711111098352

Talvinen, J. M. (1995). Information Systems in Marketing. Identifying Opportunities for New Applications. *European Journal of Marketing*, *29*(1), 8–26. doi:10.1108/03090569510075307

Theis, T., & Tomkin, J. (2012). *Sustainability: A comprehensive foundation*. Houston: Connexions.

Thompson, J., Scott, J. M., & Martin, F. (2014). *Strategic Management: Awareness and Change* (7th ed.). Hampshire, UK: CENGAGE Learning.

Vries, G., Terwel, B. W., Ellemers, N., & Daamen, D. D. (2013). Sustainability or profitability? How communicated motives for environmental policy affect public perceptions of corporate greenwashing. *Corporate Social Responsibility and Environmental Management*, *1*(2), 1–4.

Waddock, S. (2008). Building a new institutional infrastructure for corporate responsibility. *The Academy of Management Perspectives*, *22*(3), 87–108. doi:10.5465/AMP.2008.34587997

Watson, P., Wienand, N., & Worksman, G. (2009). Teaching sustainability: A valid methodology for addressing the associated problematic issues. *PWASET*, *41*(53), 2070–3740.

WCED (World Commission on Environment and Development). (1987). *Our common future*. Oxford: Oxford University Press.

Weaver, P. M., & Rotmans, J. (2006). Integrated sustainability assessment: What is it, why do it and how? *International Journal of Innovation and Sustainable Development*, *1*(4), 284–303. doi:10.1504/IJISD.2006.013732

Webb, D. J., Mohr, L. A., & Harris, K. E. (2008). A re-examination of socially responsible consumption and its measurement. *Journal of Business Research*, *61*(2), 91–98. doi:10.1016/j.jbusres.2007.05.007

White, A. (2005). *Fade, integrate or transform? The future of CSR* (Issue Paper). Business for Social Responsibility. Retrieved from www.bsr.org

Wigley, S. (2008). Gauging consumers' responses to CSR activities: Does increased awareness make cents? *Public Relations Review*, *34*(3), 306–308. doi:10.1016/j.pubrev.2008.03.034

Windsor, D. (2001). The future of corporate social responsibility. *The International Journal of Organizational Analysis*, *9*(3), 225–256. doi:10.1108/eb028934

Witcher, B. J., & Chau, V. S. (2014). *Strategic Management: Principles and Practice* (2nd ed.). Hampshire, UK: CENGAGE Learning.

ADDITIONAL READING SECTION

Burke, L., & Logsdon, J. M. (1996). How corporate social responsibility pays off. *Long Range Planning*, *29*(4), 495–502. doi:10.1016/0024-6301(96)00041-6

Moir, L. (2001). What do we mean by corporate social responsibility? *Corporate Governance*, *1*(2), 16–22. doi:10.1108/EUM0000000005486

Smith, N. C. (2003). Corporate social responsibility: Whether or how? *California Management Review*, *45*(4), 52–76. doi:10.2307/41166188

Turker, D. (2009). How corporate social responsibility influences organizational Commitment. *Journal of Business Ethics*, *89*(2), 189–204. doi:10.1007/s10551-008-9993-8

KEY TERMS AND DEFINITIONS

Bolt-On Strategies: Strategies reactively added on as an afterthought. Such strategies may easily be discarded when faced with resource constraints.

Built-In Strategies: Strategies developed as part of broader, long-term organisational plans.

Corporate Social Responsibility (CSR): A business philosophy emphasizing that organisations ought to take responsibility for their economic, social and environmental impacts and measure how successfully they do this.

Green Washing: An attempt by a business to gloss over its real sustainability performance by exaggerating or misrepresenting facts.

Responsible Consumption: A conscientious approach by consumers, seeking to minimise adverse consumption effects on the environment.

Responsible Corporate Behaviour: A conscientious business approach which goes beyond economic pursuits, seeking to demonstrate corporate citizenship and a strategic attempt to tackle the business' own impact on its environment.

Stakeholders: Various individuals and groups with vested interests in an organisation.

Sustainability: An aspiration, ideal and state one aims for.

Sustainable Development: Development initiatives that seek to meet needs of current consumers without jeopardising those of future generations.

Sustainable Development: Development that meets the needs of the present without compromising the ability of future generations to met their own needs.

Chapter 6
Managing Digital Bonds in the Buyer–Supplier Relationships

Jari Salo
Oulu Business School, Finland

Giuseppe Pedeliento
University of Bergamo, Italy

Robert Wendelin
Scania, Sweden

ABSTRACT

Among the multiple forms of bonding which can help companies to build and maintain buyer-supplier relationships, digital bonds, i.e. ties between an industrial buyers and suppliers formed when the IT systems of the parties are shared and integrated, are increasingly recognized as a strategic mean of customer retention. Despite several studies have unveiled which factors enable and constrain the companies' adoption of IT systems, we still have limited knowledge of how different types of digital bonds can be strategically managed. In this chapter we first provide a digital bond matrix in which four different types of digital bonds are identified. Then the proposed matrix is empirically validated by analyzing four different case studies representative of each digital bond identified. Finally, the matrix is applied as a device to inform strategic actions and decisions that can/should be undertaken to improve firms' digital bonds portfolio.

INTRODUCTION

Buyer-supplier relationships are a quasi-exchange mode between markets and hierarchies (Williamson, 1975) which are generally assumed to be cooperative and long-lasting (Morgan & Hunt, 1994). This research adopts an interactive perspective of buyer-supplier relationships where different types of bonds and bonding behavior have been identified and studied ((Hammarkvist, Håkansson, & Mattsson, 1982; Wilson & Mummalaneni, 1986; Johanson & Mattsson, 1987; Möller & Wilson 1995; Liljander & Strandvik, 1995; Wendelin, 2004; Salo & Wendelin 2013).

DOI: 10.4018/978-1-4666-8459-1.ch006

Bonding in industrial marketing is generally described as a gradually evolving process were two firms are tied together overtime (Geiger, Durand, Saab, Kleinaltenkamp, Baxter, & Lee, 2012). The degree of the tie is dependent on parties involved, relationship characteristics, existing bonds and contextual elements (Wendelin, 2011).

Among the multiple forms of bonding which can help companies in building, maintaining and developing buyer-supplier relationships, this research focuses on digital bonds (Salo & Wendelin, 2013), i.e. ties between an industrial buyer and an industrial supplier which are formed when the internal IT systems of the parties in a relationship are shared and integrated to form an inter-organizational system that enables and/or improves information exchange and transactions. In order for a digital bond to be formed in buyer-supplier relationships, a mutual investment of both parties involved to crate a shared IT architecture is required, as well as the usage of the IT system for business purposes.

Although the role that IT plays in business relationships is attracting an increasing scholar attention in multiple disciplines, such as industrial marketing (Reid & Plank, 2000; Sheth, 2007; Schubert & Legner, 2011; Janita & Miranda, 2013; Makkonen & Vuori, 2014), information systems (Rai & Tang, 2010; Rai, Pavlou, Im, & Du, 2012), operation research (Golicic, Davis, McCarthy, & Mentzer, 2002; Devaraj, Krajewski, & Wei, 2007; Sodero, Rabinovich, & Sinha, 2013) and supply chain management (Barua, Konana, Whinston, & Yin, 2004; Kärkkäinen, Laukkanen, Sarpola, & Kemppainen, 2007; Kim, Cavusgil, & Calantone, 2006) the major part of the entries available to date are mostly aimed at evaluating the impact of single isolated technologies on buyer-supplier relationships (Salo, 2006). Exemplars of such are electronic data interchange (EDI) (Stern & Kaufmann, 1985; Naudé, Holland, & Sudbury, 2000), internet based EDI (Angeles, 2000), websites (Leong, Ewing, & Pitt, 2002; Perry & Bodkin, 2002), electronic marketplaces (Grewal, Chakravarty, & Saini, 2010; Janita & Miranda, 2013), electronic auctions (Jap, 2002; Jap & Haruvy, 2008), extranets (Vlosky, Fontenot, & Blalock, 2000) and – just recently - mobile technologies (Yang & Järvenpää, 2005; Salo, 2012; Pan, Nam, Ogara, & Lee, 2013) and social media (Salo et al., 2013).

As a result, most of these studies are generally aimed at identifying which factors (endogenous and/or exogenous) enable and constrain the companies' adoption of the technology investigated.

In this research we adopt a broader stance and investigate buyer-supplier relationships from an interaction perspective, i.e. focusing on the impact that digital bonds play on the dyadic relationships between an industrial buyer and an industrial supplier.

Its purpose is twofold: first, by reviewing the literature to date, to determine what type of digital bonds exist in buyer-supplier relationships; second, to provide managerial directions on how different types of digital bonds can be strategically managed.

To reach these objectives different types of digital bonds in buyer-supplier interactions are described and categorized in a four entries matrix along two dimensions: the perceived importance of the relationship for the parties involved (Fiocca, 1982; Kraljic, 1983); and the level of complexity of the IT employed (Johnston & Vitale, 1988). The proposed matrix is then empirically validated through multiple case studies. Eight companies formed four relationships that are the cases studied in this research. Both buyers and suppliers were involved to increase the internal validity of the research findings drawn (John & Reve, 1982). Thus, altogether, sixteen interviews were conducted.

The results allowed to identify four distinctive types of bonds: "*oversized*" digital bonds, which emerge when complex IT systems are employed in less valued relationship; "*strong*" digital bonds, which are observed in buyer-supplier relationships characterized by a high perceived importance and complex IT systems employed; "*weak*" digital bonds, which were observed in situations in which a weak perceived importance of the relationship is assisted with simple IT; "*undersized*" digital bonds, which were found in situations in which a simple IT system is employed in important relationships.

In terms of managerial implications the research and the matrix advanced and tested help managers to coordinate their IT investments according to the importance of the relationship with their buyers and suppliers. Thus, the matrix proposed offers managers a valuable and "ready to use" diagnostic device to screen their relationships' portfolio, to identify areas of improvements, and to evaluate the efficiency and effectiveness of the digital bonds created via IT. The matrix can also be dynamically applied across the relationship life cycle with buyers and suppliers to evaluate how digital bonds can help to strengthen and improve strategic relationships.

This research contributes to the ongoing debate on relationship marketing in business interactions and networks, by underlining the role that digital bonds can play to favor the establishment of cooperative and collaborative relationships between industrial buyers and suppliers. The acknowledgment of the importance that digital bonds play in these relationships open the doors to the emergence of further studies on this topic.

The chapter is organized as follows. First, we provide a brief literature review on the use of IT in buyer-seller relationships. Second, the emergence of digital bonds is described and the matrix of digital bonds is presented. Third, the case study methodology employed is described. Fourth, case studies are used to depict the different areas of the digital bond matrix developed herein. Fifth, the managerial strategies are presented for each digital bond type followed by a discussion of results, managerial and research implications.

BACKGROUND

The Evolution of IT Systems in Business Relationships

Managerial and academic discussion has identified a number of ways to use IT in the business-to-business context. The development of IT systems and architectures to connect companies is largely due to the dramatic changes that occurred throughout the supply chains in recent years which led to rely on IT systems to reach higher levels of reactivity (Christopher, 2011).

Initially, in the late 1960s, IT was deployed within organizations to smoothen the inter-departmental communication processes and to enhance procedures such as bookkeeping and money transfer (Kaufman, 1966). The first inter-organizational information systems were Electronic Data Interchange (EDI) systems (Stern & Kaufmann, 1985). EDI can be defined as a system which involves the computer mediated exchange of business documents in a standard and automatically processable format between and among inter-organizational trading partners (Emmelhainz, 1993).

Since EDI systems were the first IT based tools that enabled both the buyer and the seller to be connected each other by means of a particular technology, this is where some of the first digital bonds appeared in the buyer-seller relationships.

EDI systems are designed for sharing business documents (e.g. invoices, purchase orders, shipping bills), product stocking numbers, and settlement information among a small number of firms (Shaw, 2000; Salo & Karjaluoto, 2006). EDI have been extensively used in many companies (Mukhopadhyay et al., 1995), especially large companies (Shaw, 2003) allured by exploiting the benefits offered by this IT system to obtain a potential competitive advantage (Mata et al., 1995). EDI in fact, provides a platform which allows business parties to reduce processing time, to improve speed and accuracy of inter-organizational communication, and to lead to cost savings (Mukhopadhyay, Kekre, & Kalathur, 1995; Mukhopadhyay, 1998).

Despite the benefits both buyer and supplier can enjoy by using EDI, these systems are relationship specific investment (Mukhopadhyay, 1998): thus, switching from one system to another is difficult and inhibited by the lock-in that occurs when firms invest in EDI systems that are developed and tailored to the specific needs of business parties. Nevertheless, early usage of EDI paved the way for information systems with less lock-in effects.

As depicted in Figure 1, the underlying technology of inter-organizational information systems has matured, which has enabled IT-facilitated commerce between business parties. EDI systems evolved into internet based systems (known as I-EDI) after the widespread of the web. Compared to EDI, I-EDI are featured for having less lock-in effects (Angeles, 2000). I-EDI systems are in fact often based on public domain software, i.e. does not require relationship specific investments to be developed and implemented, allowing faster communication and fewer costs compared to non internet based systems.

In addition, to these systems, extranets were developed. Extranets are extended intranets connecting a focal company with its customers, suppliers, and strategic partners in a seamless closed-user group (Maloff, 1997).

Extranets enable more plug-and-play type of relationships between business parties, since companies can add new connections if necessary, or drop connections when relationships cease to exist rather easily (Radosevich, 1997; Vlosky et al., 2000). While I-EDI extends traditional EDI, the extranet also makes other kind of activities possible by extending the amount and quality of information that can be exchanged between business parties.

Besides EDI, I-EDI and extranets, other IT based communication tools were developed and implemented to favor production planning and achieve higher levels of production performances.

Among these, manufacturing resource and planning systems (MRP) were used in modern factories to create bill-of-materials (BOM) and assist in the planning of production. These were internal system with an in-house focus, and connections to trading partners were not considered due to the immature IT infrastructure (Hodge, 2002; Møller, 2005). MRP systems evolved to second-generation systems (MRPII) with additional strengths including planning, analysis and forecasting as added features.

In the late 1990s and early 2000s, MRPs where made redundant when enterprise resource planning systems (ERP) were introduced (Møller, 2005). Kumar and van Hillegersberg (2000) defined ERP systems as "configurable information systems packages that integrate information and information-based processes within and across functional areas in an organization". Despite ERP systems are rather

Figure 1. Maturation of the buyer-seller relationship-specific information technology
Source: authors' elaboration

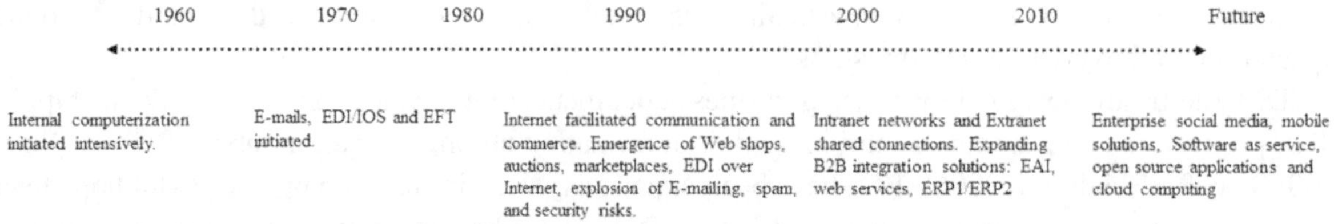

expensive, they allow companies to gain significant benefits such as improved customer service, better production scheduling, and reduced manufacturing costs if successfully implemented (Zhang, Lee, Zhang, & Banerjee, 2003).

Even with the advent of more complex ERP with many modules that assist intra-organizational processes in many ways, e.g. human resource management, accounting and finance, operations and logistics, etc. (Klaus et al., 2000), third parties were still excluded from the company's information backbone. It is argued that second generation ERP systems (ERPII) which are currently adopted, have been designed to enable an information infrastructure backbone where trading partners and additional third parties can be more easily added to a company's IT infrastructure. This is done in a secured and password protected manner in order to keep information accessible only to parties that are admitted to use it. ERP systems are becoming widely adopted and more expensive, and they are often crucial to the success of companies.

Other IT based systems to connect business parties in a more cost effective manner have emerged across the years. Six of those are discussed next.

First, as ERP systems are provided by competing software houses and are often mutually incompatible, the ERP adapters emerged. These adapters that connect competing ERP systems are offered as an easier solution for data exchange between business parties that have different systems. Nevertheless, several different types of adapters are needed since one adapter can only fit together two competing ERP software. Adapters are sometimes likened to enterprise application integration (EAI) and one type of application that can be integrated is ERP (Linthicum, 2000).

Second, third party integrators provide services (e.g. web services, software-as-a-service or cloud computing applications) in which two incompatible systems with their own information protocols are coded to understand each other with the help of a converter. Integrators provide this service to parties engaged in a relationship that are not willing to change their IT and/or are not able to afford the extra costs involved in the development of a relationship specific infrastructure (Chebbi, Dustdar, & Tata, 2006).

Third, simple radio frequency identification (RFID) systems are used to transmit the needed data between business parties (Yang & Järvenpää, 2005). This is a cost-effective and functional system in some areas of business, but only a limited amount of information can be transmitted. Systems based on RFID are often used by companies to track products in the supply chain in a cost effective and efficient manner and to keep up with logistical flows in and out the warehouses (Roberts, 2006). RFID has many applications also in consumer markets, e.g. paying tolls and small purchases (NFC - Near Field Communication application in mobile phones).

Fourth, mobile communication technologies provide easy and convenient access to the internet, and they are being used as effective information processing terminals. In the buyer-seller relationships, companies can exchange a wide variety of data ranging from mission critical steel processing information, to calling for pick-ups of ready products (Salo, 2012). Mobile systems are cost effective and flexible systems that can be used in many ways in buyer-seller relationships (Stender & Ritz, 2006), especially to speed up the sales process and enhance the sales force effectiveness in collecting and processing customers' orders. Sales force automation (SFA) systems are mobile based systems in which sales force personnel can input customer's orders wirelessly into the companies' enterprise databases via a PDA or smart phone (Aungst & Wilson, 2005).

Fifth, intelligent agent systems have been developed to solve complex information handling processes (Liu, Turban, & Lee, 2000; Papazoglou, 2001; Ketter, Collins, Gini, Gupta, & Schrater, 2012; Ngai, Peng, Alexander, & Moon, 2014). Systems based on intelligent agents follow preset rules and acquire information from other agents or systems based on those rules. For example, the steel industry is examining the use of intelligent agent systems to follow the progress of multisite production (Helaakoski, Kipinä, & Haapasalo, 2004). When a customer, such as a big oil company, wishes to know when their oil rig will be ready for installation, the steel company from which the oil rig was ordered can use intelligent agents to retrieve that information from its subcontractors. This of course requires subcontractors to have sufficiently advanced IT systems in place, and that employees input the relevant data into their IT systems after each work shift. Based on information that is retrieved by the intelligent agent, the steel company can give a more accurate estimate of the shipment date. This obviously saves time and money compared to a phone call to each of the subcontractors to hear their estimate on how many days, weeks of months the job would take.

Sixth – and last - are electronic commerce and auctions, which have also been used to help the buyer-seller relationships (Jap, 2002; Grewal et al., 2010). These have been cited many times as effective tools for the facilitation of buyer-seller relationships, but it seems that these systems can hinder and in some cases break existing buyer-seller relationships being price the most important factor in those exchanges (Wise & Morrison, 2000). The flexibility afforded by the relationship and the R&D that occurs in those relationships cannot be given a price tag. It is noted that raw materials and other easily procured items such as office supplies can be effortlessly acquired with electronic auctions and markets.

Each of the systems mentioned above have their own specific impacts on the potential and actual value creation of both the buyer and the seller. Every system enables a new way to coordinate and manage information; yet, binds companies to a certain technology or subset of technologies, which creates different digital bonds. To put it simply, not only the type of IT system applied in firms' interaction determines the nature of the bond created; but also the level of bond desired is assumed to be in line with the peculiar nature of each relationship.

Digital Bond Formation in the Buyer-Seller Relationships

Researchers have identified many different types of bonds that exist and evolve in buyer-seller relationships due to the need to reduce uncertainty and distance between trading partners (Hammarkvist et al., 1982; Johanson & Mattsson, 1987; Wilson & Mummalaneni, 1986; Liljander & Strandvik, 1995; Wendelin, 2004; Salo & Wendelin 2013). Without going into details on each type of bond, it can be stated that in many cases bonding is described as a gradually evolving process were two firms overtime are tied together. The degree of the tie is dependent on relationships parties, relationship characteristics, existing bonds and contextual elements in the bonding process (Wendelin, 2011). These contingencies that are discusses next, are particularly important in IT-related bonds that are characterized as digital bonds (Salo & Wendelin, 2013).

A digital bond emerges when two parties involved in a business relationship invest in IT in order to connect to another company or use their current IT resources to connect semi permanently (extranet, ERP integration etc.) to the other party.

Figure 2 illustrates the basic process of how digital bonds are formed in a buyer-seller relationship.

As the figure illustrates, a mutual investment to create a shared IT architecture (e.g. Extranet) or the mutual effort to adapt the partners' own IT to allow and favor communication. Is a prerequisite in order for a digital bond to be formed between business parties.

This requires existing trust and willingness to invest in the relationship in sight of the fulfillment of a common business objective (Morgan & Hunt, 1994). It can be stated that the digital bond is formed

Figure 2. Digital bond formation in a buyer-seller relationship

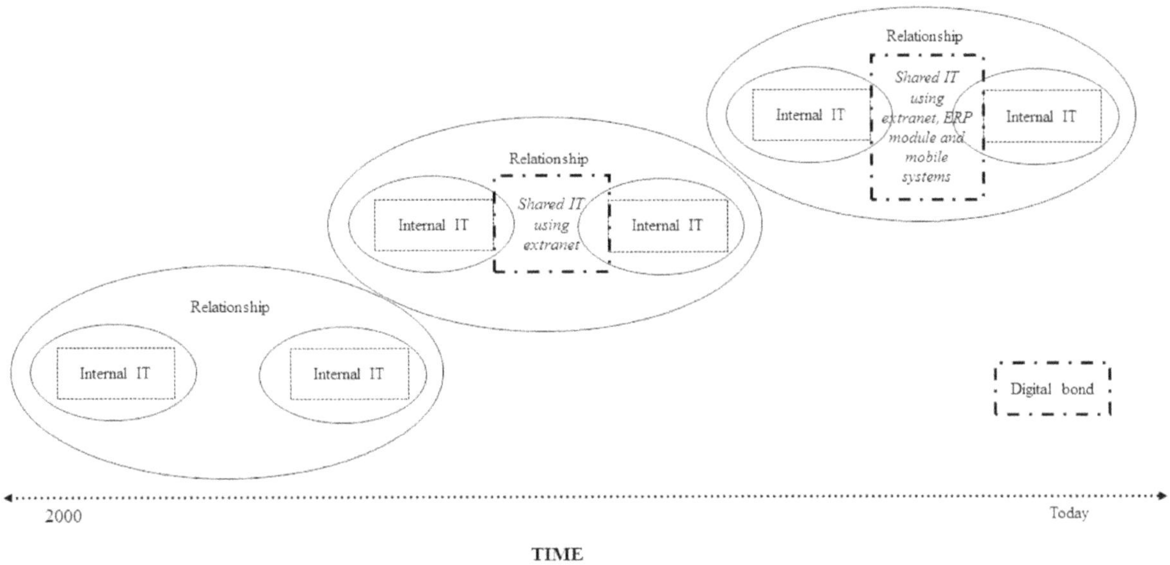

Source: adapted from Salo and Wendelin (2013)

when the internal IT systems of the parties in a relationship are shared and integrated to form an inter-organizational system that enables information exchange and transactions. Another possibility is to jointly buy or develop an inter-organizational system.

An inter-organizational system is created by joining a company's internal systems within a relationship to another business party's IT system. In order for the digital bond to emerge, the relationship specific information system must be used for digital business activities. If digital business activities are not conducted, then digital bond creation is not finalized. As a result, the digital bond is a hybrid IT that is built out of two or more shared and integrated IT, which is used for information exchange and transactions in a given relationship. A digital bond can be strengthened or weakened over repeated interactions (e.g. amount and quality of IT used, a number of connections with other companies, organizational levels using the IT systems that form the digital bond) between companies (Salo & Wendelin, 2013; Janita & Miranda, 2013).

Figure 3 presents a matrix in which the perceived importance of the relationship is divided into low and high (Fiocca, 1982; Kraljic, 1983). Perceived importance is the dyadic view of the relationship and does not solely represent the view of one company. Type of IT employed depicts the shared IT systems that are used in the relationship and can vary from simple to complex (Johnston and Vitale, 1988). Simple IT can consist of various internet-based applications such as extranet and I-EDI while more complex IT can be ERP, intelligent agents, mobile systems and traditional EDI.

Four different types of digital bonds are identified.

1. **Oversized digital bonds:** are formed when unimportant relationships are coordinated and managed with overly complex IT systems. An example of oversized digital bond can be the usage of ERP systems to handle simple invoice data processing or non-routine orders is an example of such overinvestment.

Figure 3. The digital bonds matrix
Source: authors' elaboration

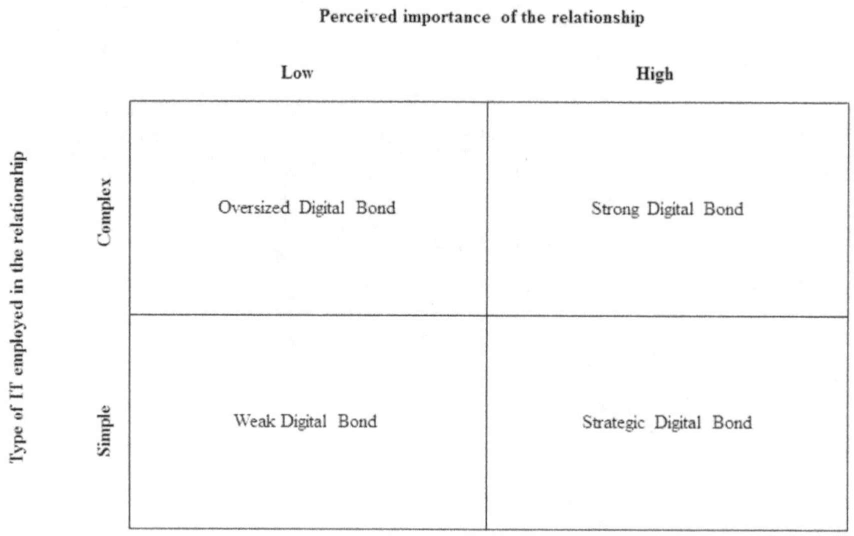

2. **Strong digital bonds:** are formed though sequential multi-level complex IT integration conducted purposefully in the relationship over time. Wal-Mart and many other retail companies are operating in this manner with their strategic suppliers. Similar behavior is observable in the automotive industry with Toyota as well.
3. **Weak digital bonds:** are formed when more simple and loose IT is employed (e.g. internet-based applications and adapters). For example, there are third parties that provide middleware or other plug-and-play type of IT that is leased from the third party. Untying these digital bonds is easier as data is stored and shared by the third party rather than by business parties on their own servers.
4. **Strategic digital bonds:** are information systems that are employed in a valuable buyer-seller relationship. As the relationship is important, it is suggested that this imbalance should be managed by additional IT investments in the relationship.

The analysis of the four type of digital bonds previously identified suggests that it is better to have strong connections also IT-wise in valuable buyer-seller relationships to take advantage over competitors. In a similar vein, an oversized digital bond is characterized by a large IT investment, but this investment should be reconsidered since the relationship itself is perceived by either buyer or seller as economically unimportant and/or strategically irrelevant.

Interactions between companies weaken or strengthen the digital bond depending on the underlying IT and the context and purpose of the relationship. Also the preceding conditions i.e. the type of buyer-seller relationship and the type of information systems connected, have an effect on the strength of the bond. Furthermore, information exchange that occurs between organizations and a high intensity of exchange further strengthens the digital bond. Strong bonds - as opposed to weak bonds - are formed over time when IT systems are adopted and continuously modified to meet companies' specific needs. IT is used intensively to solve problems in the relationship, as it provides real benefits to both parties involved. In practice, as there may be several IT systems in place that support communication in the relationship, it may be difficult to assess the existence, weakness, and even strength of a digital bond.

METHODOLOGY

This research employs systematic combining as research strategy (Dubois & Gadde, 2002) as it enables reconceptualization of the empirical data and theoretical framework. The case study approach is used in different areas such as sociology, psychology, history, anthropology, economics, management science, and political science (Yin, 1994). Yin (1994, p. 13) defines a case study as "an empirical inquiry that investigates a contemporary phenomenon within its real-life context, especially when the boundaries between phenomenon and context are not clearly evident". Since research on IT usage in buyer-seller relationships is an emerging study area (Makkonen & Vuori, 2014), in which the researcher has only some or no control over the events that are occurring in real-life, case study is suggested as a very appropriate research method (Stake, 1995) to achieve deeper understanding, solid contextual sense, and provocation toward theory building (Bonoma, 1985; Johnston, Leach, & Liu, 1999). The case selection is a pertinent stage in case research and advice on this matter is extensively provided in the literature (Eisenhardt, 1989; Pettigrew, 1990; Perry, 1998). The buyer-seller relationships analyzed were chosen based on theoretical sampling, in which the cases are selected so that they represent different types of digital bonds in which more or less complicated IT soultions are implemented in more or less valuable relationships.

Eight companies formed four dyadic relationships that are the cases studied in this research. Neither the identities of the companies, nor the respondents are revealed for reasons of confidentiality. The perspectives of both parties in the buyer-seller relationship are studied in order to be sure of the value of the findings (John & Reve, 1982). The main data source through which digital bonding and bond formation is described consists of interviews (Kumar, Stern, & Anderson, 1993; Arksey & Knight, 1999). The interviewees were accordingly asked to describe the history and current state of the relationship as accurately as possible. After that, they were asked to highlight the key people and events in the relationships. Finally, they specifically discussed the IT employed and how it has shaped the relationship. The choice of informants was based on the principle that information is best elicited from people who have knowledge of the phenomenon and who have been involved with the relationship.

Altogether, sixteen semi-structured interviews were conducted, each interview lasting from one and a half to two hours. Interviews have been conducted with personnel from logistics, product development, sales managers, buyers, suppliers, and other people involved in the cooperation between the companies. Key informants are critical for the success of case studies (Yin, 1994). The interviews were taped and transcribed. Qualitative data analysis was employed in order to thematize the material (Miles & Huberman, 1984). Field notes of the reactions of people have also been conducted. Taping and transcribing data and using field notes helped to achieve validity in qualitative research (Eisenhardt, 1989).

The researchers had in some cases also access to confidential internal and external documents regarding the cooperation between case companies. In addition to interviews, documents, minutes of meetings, industry reports and company visits were also used to triangulate the respondents' answers, as suggested in literature (Patton, 1987; Yin, 1994). The validity and reliability of the research was increased with the use of data triangulation (Denzin, 1978; Eisenhardt, 1989).

In the next paragraph each case is briefly described: in particular each case description reported below is basically aimed at identifying how digital bonds are formed in business relationships and problems that can arise due to the establishment of non optimal digital bonds.

DIFFERENT TYPES OF DIGITAL BOND

The Steel Mill Case - Oversized Digital Bond: Attempts to Rationalize the Employed ERP

Steel Mill is a large European steel producer with hundreds of off-the-shelf and tailored information systems. Besides producing steel, Steel Mill is also focused on further processing in an attempt to be more effective and competitive. One of the further processing activities is steel hardening, as hardened steel can be used for multiple purposes such as the assembly of military vehicles. Currently, the steel produced by Steel Mill is hardened by a relatively small workshop. From the workshop's perspective, Still Mill is a large customer. Thus, they have adjusted their IT systems to serve Still Mill at better and fits its needs and requirement. Still Mill in turn, has also re-configured its ERP system to match the needs of the workshop and favor the sharing of information and communication on the IT platform. Recently Still Mill have significantly increased the volume of steel to be hardened and trying to exploit the hardened still market. Due to the limited capacity of the workshop, Still Mill was forced to turn to other still workshops in order to satisfy the increasing demand of hardened still on its market. By increasing the number of suppliers, Still Mill was able to acquire the still hardened in a more cost effective way by increasing price pressure. The changing business climate of Still Mill have led to a situation in which the company was forced to evaluate the strength of the digital bonds established with the workshop across time, and to evaluate which kind of digital bonds should be established with the other workshops. As a result, they will downsize the ERP system and move to a simpler system, thereby rationalizing the oversized digital bond into a strategic digital bond from the workshop's perspective. This of course requires modification to the steel mill's IT infrastructure but also to the workshop's IT infrastructure, which has been adapted to the needs of the steel mill.

The Saw Mill Case - Strong Digital Bond: Attempts to Simplify the Employed Mobile System

Saw Mill is a European based company operating in the sawn goods industry. Saw Mill acquires raw material (logs) from individual forest owners and governments. Currently, logistics service providers (LSP) working in the wood transformation industry, have a fleet of trucks equipped by mobile tracking systems to track their vehicles and raw material moving. The LSP use the information stored through the mobile tracking system to plan routes effectively. Most of the critical information, from the Saw Mill's perspective, is stored in each device installed in the LSPs' trucks and in its servers. This makes complicated for Saw Mill to coordinate production, since the amount of warehoused raw material is kept at a minimum level. To close current orders and to be able to find capacity for new orders is tedious task. The IT employed is excellent for logistical needs of the company, but not for coordinating the Saw Mill's production. From the Saw Mill's perspective, the system is too complex, since they have to wait until each truck checks in to a mill area before they know the amount of raw materials arriving. Actions urge to be put forward to simplify the mobile system in use.

The Service Provider Case - Weak Digital Bond: Attempts to Keep the Status Quo by Using the Extranet

Service Provider operates in the EU and has specialized over the years to provide companies various services relating to events, meetings, trade shows, conferences and other corporate happenings. Service Provider organizes transportation, accommodation, facilities, catering and entertainment services for its customers. To this purpose Service Provider has by the time organized a network of hundreds of smaller subcontractors that provide the services they need for their customer. Only the biggest subcontractors are connected to the service provider via the extranet connection. Basically, the weak digital bond is currently sufficient, but as new players are entering the market formerly occupied almost solely by Service Provider, managers must focus their attention to the entrants. In this changing market, Service Provider is aiming to keep the status quo in the established relationships with its subcontractors. Most of the subcontractors are satisfied with the current business volume but some of them want to increase their share of business. However, forming a tighter digital bond with each of them is too expensive and complicated. Thus, Service Provider relies on the existing relationships and attempts to keep the volume of business high. In addition, the establishment of stronger digital bonds will be ineffective in preventing subcontractors to do business with upcoming new entrants.

The Manufacturer Case – Strategic Digital Bond: Attempts to Upgrade the Third Party Provided Internet Platform

E-auctions and marketplaces provide a convenient way to find new customers. However, these markets are global, and price is often the factor that closes the deal. The Manufacturer participated in some e-auctions and marketplaces to test if they could win some deals. This test was rather satisfactory as Manufacturer won a significant number of big deals using these systems. The share of customers from e-auctions and marketplaces rose rapidly in the Manufacturer's customer portfolio, and these customers became vital for the business due to investments in extra manufacturing capacity. Currently, intensive price competition and overcapacity is causing the manufacturer to lose deals to foreign competitors. It is in the Manufacturer's best interest to establish more enduring relationships by using channels other than electronic auctions or marketplaces. The first step is to establish a face-to-face relationship to favor the formation of trust and commitment, after which both parties can start planning and considering what type of digital bond is most appropriate to support the newly formed buyer-seller relationship.

DISCUSSION

The digital bond matrix depicted in Figure 3 and illustrated by the case studies, suggests that there are four distinctive types of bonds based on two dimensions. These dimensions are the importance of the relationships perceived by either buyer or seller (or both of them) and the type of IT employed in the relationship.

The matrix is used as a starting point to introduce different types of balancing or coping strategies within different types of bonds. These strategies are based on the inherent assumption that simple (e.g.

EDI, extranet, internet) and more complex (e.g. ERP, ERPII, intelligent agents or mobile systems) IT systems presented earlier, require different types of strategies when facing differences in the importance of the relationships.

Figure 4 details the managing strategies for each type of digital bond based on its unique characteristics. Each of these strategies are described next.

Rationalizing

Presents a situation in which an oversized digital bond emerges with complex IT employed in less valued relationship by either or both a seller or a buyer. Rationalizing refers to a management process where decision makers, after realizing that unnecessary IT systems are being used, takes measures to deploy more appropriate IT systems. Practically speaking, it might be difficult to increase the importance of a particular relationship, so it might be more justified to adjust the IT systems employed according to the importance of the relationship. Furthermore, managers can take actions before digital bond formation is initiated, by being aware of the importance of a relationship and of the complexity of IT systems employed. For example, attempts to integrate overwhelmingly popular ERP systems in order to coordinate multiple interfacing and overlapping tasks in the relationship, might cause an oversized digital bond to emerge and the need to afford costs that are not justified by the content and relative importance of the relationship. The Still Mill case is exemplary of the occurred emergence of an oversized digital bond that requires rationalization to deploy the most effective and less costly IT system to link Still Mill with an increased number of supplier of still hardening services, including the workshop with which the original IT system was deployed.

Figure 4. Managerial strategies for different digital bonds
Source: authors' elaboration

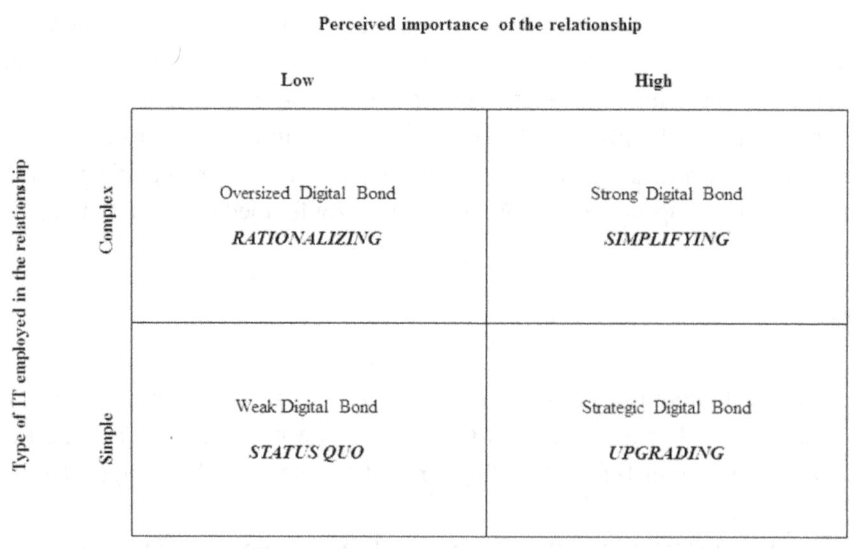

Simplifying

Presents a situation in which a strong digital bond emerges with complex IT systems employed in a highly appreciated buyer-seller relationship by either or both the seller and the buyer. The simplifying act refers to a decision making process where the management, after realizing that the IT system employed is too complex, takes measures to simplify the inter-organizational system. To this aim, Chief Information Officers and managerial personnel in the buying and in the selling organization might proactively attempt to balance the company's portfolio of digital bonds by avoiding the formation of strong digital bonds. In a highly appreciated relationship, parties may have overinvested in IT systems, thus making IT infrastructure management expensive and inefficient. For example, mobile systems used in buyer-seller relationships are rather expensive to tailor to each relationship and the benefits gained from such a customization are small. In addition, the use of multiple systems for same purposes is another strategy that causes unnecessary complexity of IT. The Saw Mill case presented above is archetypal of a situation in which the IT system is too complex and does not allow the buyer to have the information needed due to IT technical complexity. Even though the IT system applied offers real time access to information concerning the logistics of raw materials, since Saw Mill can have information of the amount of raw material arriving only when each truck checks in at a mill area, the company does not have access in advance all the information needed to program the production and to avoid an overstock of raw materials. Actions urge to be put forward to simplify the mobile system in use and allow Saw Mill to use the IT system in a more effective way.

Status Quo

Presents a situation in which a weak digital bond is formed with the employment of simple IT and with low perceived relationship importance. Status Quo strategy refers to actions to preserve the current state in the digital bond. When a weak digital bond is formed, both parties are satisfied with the benefits that the IT system employed brings. Practically speaking, new IT investment opportunities and development plans should be carefully planned and evaluated in order to avoid over-investing in IT since it is most likely that importance of the relationship is not going to increase without tremendous sales efforts or changes in the end product and market demand. A weak digital bond is formed for example, when parties are using extranet systems to coordinate the activities in the relationship. The Service Provider case displayed above is an example of weak digital bond that do not need to be strengthened as the establishment of stronger bonds will not lead to obtain any sort of advantage over upcoming new entrants in the competitive landscape.

Upgrading

Presents a situation where a strategic digital bond exists, IT employed in the relationship is simple, but the high perceived importance of the relationship triggers managerial actions. Upgrading refers to managerial actions to increase the IT investments in an important relationship where the current IT infrastructure does not meet one party or both party's needs. In practice, in this situation either the buyer or seller or sometimes both of them acquire significant returns on their IT investment due to the high importance of the relationship. The return itself might be monetary but might also be something else like reference value, pertinent information or a springboard for developing new products and services.

A strategic digital bond is formed for example, when the parties in the relationship have simple internet based systems that might be leased from a third party, used for extensive transactions and information exchange. The Manufacturer case previously analyzed, is an example of company that might be able to establish long lasting relationship with its customers investing in an IT system – other than e-auctions - which could favor the development of a mutual feeling of trust and commitment.

To clarify, in Figure 4, each of the digital bonds presents ideal situation in which the IT employed and the importance of the relationship is accurately known. This is practically speaking not always the case. The digital bond matrix and corresponding managerial strategies provide a managerial tool that can be used to identify digital bonds and evaluate whether the digital bond is desirable, whether additional investments should be conducted or whether the investments done in the past are unjustified in the present. The digital bond per se is not the desired outcome; rather are the business benefits – such as decreased coordination costs, increased innovativeness, improved service quality, image as a forerunner in the field - that are acquired are the key for digital bond management actions.

Instead of looking each digital bond type separately, a digital bond portfolio can be used to evaluate the amount and quality of the digital bonds a company has with its partners, suppliers and customers in order to manage digital bonds more effectively and in a costs-benefits fashion. When managing a portfolio instead of an individual bond, a more holistic view can be formed. Hence, managerial and IT resources can be directed to those digital bonds that deserve attention and action. Furthermore, when shifting the focus from an individual bond to a bond portfolio, both managers and academics can take the dynamic nature of digital bonds into consideration more easily.

The matrix of digital bonds and the derived managerial strategies provide a simplification of an overly complex management situation where the optimum is nowhere to be found. In practice, it is difficult to identify most of the different types of digital bonds that a company has, since many companies have hundreds of IT systems, not to mention the management of digital bonds in a portfolio.

CONCLUSION

This research aimed to increase the current knowledge on digital bonds, by identifying what type of digital bonds exist in buyer-seller relationships and especially how different types of digital bonds can be effectively managed. Based on a careful review of the most updated literature on business relationships and, in particular, on business bonds, the research presented a matrix of digital bonds. The matrix described four digital bond types and their emergence as a result of the type of IT employed and the perceived importance of the relationship by either seller or buyer or both. These are *oversized*, *strong*, *weak* and *strategic*. After defining each type of digital bond, managerial strategies were presented. For each digital bond type there is a specific managerial strategy depicting the managerial action required; *rationalizing* for oversized digital bonds, *simplifying* for strong digital bonds, *status quo* for weak digital bonds, *upgrading* for strategic bonds. Furthermore, multiple case studies were provided and briefly reported for each digital bond type in order to illustrate the managerial strategies in action. The research also discussed the importance of the portfolio of buyer-seller relationships in which companies are involved. These can be evaluated and managed with relationship portfolios that include digital bonds, in order to manage the interdependencies in the most effective manner.

Additionally, the dynamic nature of digital bonds and the need for constant evaluation and adjustment was also illustrated. The study contributes to the understanding of bonding in a buyer-seller relationship by depicting a digital bond matrix based on the type of IT used and the importance of the relationship.

For managers, the four strategies and the digital bond matrix help to coordinate the IT investments and other adaptations to be conducted in the buyer-seller relationships. Limitations for this research are the illustrative case studies that are employed to showcase each digital bond type. Salo and Wendelin (2013) used a longitudinal case analysis to depict how digital bonds emerge in buyer-seller relationships. Following this line of enquiry, future research could analyze in depth specific cases of information technologies and relational conditions that cause different types of digital bonds to emerge. This would help managers and academics to identify more accurately the technologies and relational conditions that lead to each digital bond type. Additionally, a relational bond audit (Wendelin, 2011) could be extended to cover digital bonds as well.

REFERENCES

Angeles, R. (2000). Revisiting the Role of Internet-EDI in the Current Electronic Commerce Scene. *Logistics Information Management*, *13*(1), 45–57. doi:10.1108/09576050010306396

Arksey, H., & Knight, P. T. (1999). *Interviewing for social scientists: An introductory resource with examples*. London: SAGE.

Aungst, S. G., & Wilson, D. T. (2005). A primer for navigating the shoals of applying wireless technology to marketing problems. *Journal of Business and Industrial Marketing*, *20*(2), 59–69. doi:10.1108/08858620510583650

Barua, A., Konana, P., Whinston, A. B., & Yin, F. (2004). An empirical investigation of net-enabled business value. *Management Information Systems Quarterly*, *28*(4), 585–620.

Bonoma, T. (1985). Case Research in marketing: Opportunities, problems and a process. *JMR, Journal of Marketing Research*, *22*(2), 199–208. doi:10.2307/3151365

Chebbi, I., Dustdar, S., & Tata, S. (2006). The view-based approach to dynamic inter-organizational workflow cooperation. *Data & Knowledge Engineering*, *56*(2), 139–173. doi:10.1016/j.datak.2005.03.008

Christopher, M. (2011). *Logistics and supply chain management* (4th ed.). New York: FT-Prentice Hall.

Denzin, N. K. (1978). *The research act: a theoretical introduction to sociological methods*. New York: McGraw-Hill.

Devaraj, S., Krajewski, L., & Wei, J. C. (2007). Impact of eBusiness technologies on operational performance: The role of production information integration in the supply chain. *Journal of Operations Management*, *25*(6), 1199–1216. doi:10.1016/j.jom.2007.01.002

Dubois, A., & Gadde, L. E. (2002). Systematic combining: An abductive approach to case research. *Journal of Business Research*, *55*(7), 553–560. doi:10.1016/S0148-2963(00)00195-8

Dubois, A., & Gibbert, M. (2010). From complexity to transparency: Managing the interplay between theory, method and empirical phenomena in IMM case studies. *Industrial Marketing Management*, *39*(1), 129–136. doi:10.1016/j.indmarman.2009.08.003

Eisenhardt, K. (1989). Building theories from case study research. *Academy of Management Review*, *14*(4), 532–550.

Emmelhainz, M. A. (1993). *EDI: a total management guide* (2nd ed.). New York: Van Nostrand Reinhold.

Fiocca, R. (1982). Account portfolio analysis for strategy development. *Industrial Marketing Management*, *11*(1), 53–62. doi:10.1016/0019-8501(82)90034-7

Geiger, I., Durand, A., Saab, S., Kleinaltenkamp, M., Baxter, R., & Lee, Y. (2012). The Bonding Effects of Relationship Value and Switching Costs in Industrial Buyer–Seller Relationships: An Investigation into Role Differences. *Industrial Marketing Management*, *41*(1), 82–93. doi:10.1016/j.indmarman.2011.11.013

Golicic, S. L., Davis, D. F., McCarthy, T. M., & Mentzer, J. T. (2002). The impact of e-commerce on supply chain relationships. *International Journal of Physical Distribution & Logistics Management*, *32*(10), 851–871. doi:10.1108/09600030210455447

Grewal, R., Chakravarty, A., & Saini, A. (2010). Governance mechanisms in business-to-business electronic markets. *Journal of Marketing*, *74*(4), 45–62. doi:10.1509/jmkg.74.4.45

Hammarkvist, K.-O., Håkansson, H., & Mattsson, L. G. (1982). *Marknadsföring för konkurrenskraft*. Malmö: Liber Förlag.

Helaakoski, H., Kipinä, J., & Haapasalo, H. (2004). An Agent architecture for steel product business network. In ICEIS (4), 467-470.

Janita, M. S., & Miranda, F. J. (2013). The antecedents of client loyalty in business-to-business (B2B) electronic marketplaces. *Industrial Marketing Management*, *42*(5), 814–823. doi:10.1016/j.indmarman.2013.01.006

Jap, S. D. (2002). Online reverse auctions: Issues, themes, and prospects for the future. *Journal of the Academy of Marketing Science*, *30*(4), 506–525. doi:10.1177/009207002236925

Jap, S. D., & Haruvy, E. (2008). Interorganizational relationships and bidding behavior in industrial online reverse auctions. *JMR, Journal of Marketing Research*, *45*(5), 550–561. doi:10.1509/jmkr.45.5.550

Johanson, J., & Mattsson, L. G. (1987). Interorganizational relations in industrial systems: A network approach compared with a transaction cost approach. *International Studies of Management & Organization*, *17*(1), 34–48.

John, G., & Reve, T. (1982). The reliability and validity of key informant data from dyadic relationships in marketing channels. *JMR, Journal of Marketing Research*, *19*(4), 517–524. doi:10.2307/3151724

Johnston, R., & Vitale, M. R. (1988). Creating competitive advantage with interorganizational information systems. *Management Information Systems Quarterly*, *12*(2), 153–165. doi:10.2307/248839

Johnston, W., Leach, M., & Liu, A. (1999). Theory testing using case studies in business-to-business research. *Industrial Marketing Management*, *28*(3), 201–213. doi:10.1016/S0019-8501(98)00040-6

Kärkkäinen, M., Laukkanen, S., Sarpola, S., & Kemppainen, K. (2007). Roles of interfirm information systems in supply chain management. *International Journal of Physical Distribution & Logistics Management, 37*(4), 264–286. doi:10.1108/09600030710752505

Kaufman, F. (1966). Data systems that cross company boundaries. *Harvard Business Review, 44*(1), 141–155.

Ketter, W., Collins, J., Gini, M., Gupta, A., & Schrater, P. (2012). Real-time tactical and strategic sales management for intelligent agents guided by economic regimes. *Information Systems Research, 23*(4), 1263–1283. doi:10.1287/isre.1110.0415

Kim, D., Cavusgil, S. T., & Calantone, R. J. (2006). Information system innovations and supply chain management: Channel relationships and firm performance. *Journal of the Academy of Marketing Science, 34*(1), 40–54. doi:10.1177/0092070305281619

Klaus, H., Rosemann, M., & Gable, G. G. (2000). What is ERP? *Information Systems Frontiers, 2*(2), 141–162. doi:10.1023/A:1026543906354

Kraljic, P. (1983). Purchasing must become supply management. *Harvard Business Review*, (September-October): 109–117.

Kumar, K., & van Hillegersberg, J. (2000). Enterprise resource planning: Introduction. *Communications of the ACM, 43*(4), 22–26. doi:10.1145/332051.332063

Kumar, N., Stern, L. W., & Anderson, J. C. (1993). Conducting interorganizational research using key informants. *Academy of Management Journal, 36*(6), 1633–1651. doi:10.2307/256824

Leong, E., Ewing, M., & Pitt, L. (2002). E-comprehension evaluating B2B websites using readability formulae. *Industrial Marketing Management, 31*(2), 125–131. doi:10.1016/S0019-8501(01)00184-5

Liljander, V., & Strandvik, T. (1995). The nature of customer relationships in services. In T. Swartz, D.E. Bowen, & S.W. Brown (Eds.), Advances in Services Marketing and Management (pp.141-167). London: JAI Press Inc.

Linthicum, D. S. (2000). *Enterprise application integration*. Addison-Wesley Professional.

Liu, S., Turban, E., & Lee, M. K. (2000). Software agents for environmental scanning in electronic commerce. *Information Systems Frontiers, 2*(1), 85–98. doi:10.1023/A:1010002205248

Makkonen, H., & Vuori, M. (2014). The role of information technology in strategic buyer–supplier relationships. *Industrial Marketing Management, 43*(6), 1053–1062. doi:10.1016/j.indmarman.2014.05.018

Maloff, J. (1997). Extranets: Stretching the net to boost efficiency. *NetGuide, 4*, 62–68.

Mata, F., Fuerst, W., & Barney, J. (1995). Information technology and sustained competitive advantage: A resource-based analysis. *Management Information Systems Quarterly, 19*(4), 487–504. doi:10.2307/249630

Miles, M. B., & Huberman, A. M. (1994). *Qualitative data analysis: An expanded sourcebook*. London: SAGE.

Møller, C. (2005). ERP II: A conceptual framework for next-generation enterprise systems? *Journal of Enterprise Information Management*, *18*(4), 483–497. doi:10.1108/17410390510609626

Möller, K., & Wilson, D. (1995). *Business Marketing and interaction and network perspective*. Boston: Kluwer Academic Publishers. doi:10.1007/978-94-011-0645-0

Morgan, R. M., & Hunt, S. D. (1994). The commitment trust theory of relationship marketing. *Journal of Marketing*, *58*(3), 20–38. doi:10.2307/1252308

Mukhopadhyay, T. (1998). How to win with electronic data interchange in information technology and industrial competitiveness. In C. Kemerer (Ed.), How IT Shapes Competition (pp. 91-106). Boston: Kluwer Academic Publishers.

Mukhopadhyay, T., Kekre, S., & Kalathur, S. (1995). Business value of information technology: A study of electronic data interchange. *Management Information Systems Quarterly*, *19*(2), 137–156. doi:10.2307/249685

Naudé, P., Holland, C., & Sudbury, M. (2000). The benefits of IT-based supply chains-strategic or operational? *Journal of Business-To-Business Marketing*, *7*(1), 45–67. doi:10.1300/J033v07n01_03

Ngai, E. W. T., Peng, S., Alexander, P., & Moon, K. K. (2014). Decision support and intelligent systems in the textile and apparel supply chain: An academic review of research articles. *Expert Systems with Applications*, *41*(1), 81–91. doi:10.1016/j.eswa.2013.07.013

Pan, Y., Nam, T., Ogara, S., & Lee, S. (2013). Adoption model of mobile-enabled systems in supply chain. *Industrial Management & Data Systems*, *113*(2), 171–189. doi:10.1108/02635571311303523

Papazoglou, M. P. (2001). Agent-oriented technology in support of e-business. *Communications of the ACM*, *44*(4), 71–77. doi:10.1145/367211.367268

Patton, M. Q. (1987). *How to use qualitative methods in evaluation*. London: SAGE.

Perry, C. (1998). Processes of a case study methodology for postgraduate research in marketing. *European Journal of Marketing*, *32*(9/10), 785–802. doi:10.1108/03090569810232237

Perry, M., & Bodkin, C. (2002). Fortune 500 manufacturer web sites: Innovative marketing strategies or cyberbrochures? *Industrial Marketing Management*, *31*(2), 133–144. doi:10.1016/S0019-8501(01)00187-0

Pettigrew, A. M. (1990). Longitudinal field research on change: Theory and practice. *Organization Science*, *1*(3), 267–292. doi:10.1287/orsc.1.3.267

Radosevich, L. (1997). Early adopters hail extranet benefits, dodge pitfalls. *InfoWorld*, *19*(23), 65–66.

Rai, A., Pavlou, P., Im, G., & Du, S. (2012). Inter-firm IT capabilities and communications for co-creating relational value: Evidence from the logistics industry. *Management Information Systems Quarterly*, *36*(1), 233–262.

Rai, A., & Tang, X. (2010). Leveraging IT capabilities and competitive process capabilities for the management of interorganizational relationship portfolios. *Information Systems Research*, *21*(3), 516–542. doi:10.1287/isre.1100.0299

Reid, D. A., & Plank, R. E. (2000). Business marketing comes of age: A comprehensive review of the literature. *Journal of Business-To-Business Marketing*, *7*(2-3), 9–178. doi:10.1300/J033v07n02_02

Roberts, C. M. (2006). Radio frequency identification (RFID). *Computers & Security*, *25*(1), 18–26. doi:10.1016/j.cose.2005.12.003

Salo, J. (2006), *Business relationship digitalization: a case study from the steel processing industry*, Doctoral dissertation, Oulu University Press, Oulu.

Salo, J. (2012). The role of mobile technology in a buyer-supplier relationship. *Journal of Business and Industrial Marketing*, *27*(7), 554–563. doi:10.1108/08858621211257329

Salo, J., & Karjaluoto, H. (2006). IT—enabled supply chain management. *Contemporary Management Research*, *2*(1), 17–30. doi:10.7903/cmr.76

Salo, J., Lehtimäki, T., Simula, H., & Mäntymäki, M. (2013). Social media marketing in the Scandinavian industrial marketing. *International Journal of Electronic Business Research*, *9*(4), 16–32. doi:10.4018/ijebr.2013100102

Salo, J., & Wendelin, R. (2013). Longitudinal analysis of digital bonding in buyer seller relationships. *Journal of Business-To-Business Marketing*, *20*(1), 1–19. doi:10.1080/1051712X.2012.719179

Schubert, P., & Legner, C. (2011). B2B integration in global supply chains: An identification of technical integration scenarios. *The Journal of Strategic Information Systems*, *20*(3), 250–267. doi:10.1016/j.jsis.2011.04.001

Shaw, M. (2000). Electronic commerce: state of the art. In M. Shaw, R. Blanning, T. Strader, & A. Whinston (Eds.), Handbook of Electronic Commerce (pp. 3-24). New York: Springer-Verlag. doi:10.1007/978-3-642-58327-8_1

Shaw, M. (2003). *E-Business Management*. New York: Kluwer Academic Publishers.

Sheth, J. N. (2007). Emerging research opportunities for doctoral students in b-to-b marketing. *Journal of Business-To-Business Marketing*, *14*(1), 13–22. doi:10.1300/J033v14n01_02

Sodero, A. C., Rabinovich, E., & Sinha, R. K. (2013). Drivers and outcomes of open-standard interorganizational information systems assimilation in high-technology supply chains. *Journal of Operations Management*, *31*(6), 330–344. doi:10.1016/j.jom.2013.07.008

Stake, R. (1995). *The art of case study research*. Thousand Oaks: SAGE.

Stender, M., & Ritz, T. (2006). Modeling of B2B mobile commerce processes. *International Journal of Production Economics*, *101*(1), 128–139. doi:10.1016/j.ijpe.2005.05.017

Stern, L., & Kaufmann, P. (1985). Electronic data interchange in selected consumer goods industries: an interorganizational perspective. In R. Buzzell (Ed.), Marketing in an Electronic Age (pp. 52-73). Boston: Harvard Business School Press.

Vlosky, R. P., Fontenot, R., & Blalock, L. (2000). Extranets: Impacts on Business Practices and Relationships. *Journal of Business and Industrial Marketing*, *15*(6), 438–457. doi:10.1108/08858620010349510

Wendelin, R. (2004). The nature and change of bonds in industrial business relationships [Doctoral dissertation]. Hanken School of Economics and Business Administration

Wendelin, R. (2011). Bond audit, a method for evaluating business relationships. *Journal of Business and Industrial Marketing*, *26*(3), 211–217. doi:10.1108/08858621111115930

Williamson, O. E. (1975). *Markets and hierarchies*. New York, NY: The Free press.

Wilson, D., & Mummalaneni, V. (1986). Bonding and commitment in buyer-seller relationships: A preliminary conceptualizations. *Journal of Industrial Marketing and Purchasing*, *1*(3), 44–58.

Wise, R., & Morrison, D. (1999). Beyond the exchange--the future of B2B. *Harvard Business Review*, *78*(6), 86–96. PMID:11184979

Yang, L., & Järvenpää, S. (2005). Trust and Radio Frequency Identification (RFID) Adoption within an Alliance. *Proceedings of the 38th Hawaii International Conference on System Sciences*. Hawaii, USA. doi:10.1109/HICSS.2005.643

Yin, R. (1994). *Case Study Research–Design and Methods*. London: SAGE.

Zhang, L., Lee, M. K., Zhang, Z., & Banerjee, P. (2003). Critical success factors of enterprise resource planning systems implementation success in China. *System Sciences - Proceedings of the 36th Annual Hawaii International Conference on* (pp. 10). IEEE. doi:10.1109/HICSS.2003.1174613

ADDITIONAL READING

Benson, J. K. (1975). The inter organizational network as political economy. *Administrative Science Quarterly*, *20*(2), 229–249. doi:10.2307/2391696

Berry, L. (1983). Relationship marketing of services – growing interest, emerging perspective. *Journal of the Academy of Marketing Science*, *23*(4), 236–245. doi:10.1177/009207039502300402

Blanning, R., & Bui, T. (2000). Decision Support Systems and Internet Commerce. In M. Shaw, R. Blanning, T. Strader, & A. Whinston (Eds.), *Handbook of Electronic Commerce* (pp. 53–75). New York: Springer-Verlag. doi:10.1007/978-3-642-58327-8_3

Bond, B., Genovese, Y., Miklovic, D., Wood, N., Zrimsek, B., & Rayner, N. (2000, October 4). *ERP is dead – long live ERP 2*. Gartner Group, RAS Services.

Chen, M., Chen, A. N., & Shao, B. M. (2003). The implications and impacts of Web services to electronic commerce research practices. *Journal of Electronic Commerce Research*, *4*(4), 128–139.

Clemons, E., Reddi, S., & Row, M. (1993). The impact of information technology on the organization of economic activity: The "move to the middle" hypothesis. *Journal of Management Information Systems*, *10*(2), 9–35.

Cooper, M., Ellram, L., Gardner, T., & Hanks, A. (1997). Meshing multiple alliances. *Journal of Business Logistics*, *18*(1), 67–89.

Davenport, T., & Prusack, L. (1997). *Information ecology. Mastering the information and knowledge environment*. New York: Oxford University Press.

Dedrick, J., Gurbaxani, V., & Kraemer, K. (2003). Information technology and economic performance: A critical review of the empirical evidence. *ACM Computing Surveys*, *35*(1), 1–28. doi:10.1145/641865.641866

Forrester, J. (1958). Industrial dynamics: A major breakthrough for decision makers. *Harvard Business Review*, *38*(July-August), 37–66.

Fuglseth, A.-M., & Gronhaug, K. (1994). Information systems as a secondary strategic resource: The case of bank credit evaluations. *Journal of International Management*, *14*(3), 269–280.

Garcia-Dastuge, S., & Lambert, D. (2003). Internet-enabled coordination in supply chain. *Industrial Marketing Management*, *32*(2), 251–263. doi:10.1016/S0019-8501(02)00269-9

Grönroos, C. (1994). From marketing mix to relationship marketing: Towards a paradigm shift in marketing. *Management Decision*, *32*(2), 4–20. doi:10.1108/00251749410054774

Gummesson, E. (1987). The new marketing- developing long-term interactive relationships. *Long Range Planning*, *20*(4), 10–20. doi:10.1016/0024-6301(87)90151-8

Johnston, R. B., & Mak, H. C. (2000). An emerging vision of internet-enabled supply chain electronic commerce. *International Journal of Electronic Commerce*, *4*(4), 1–24.

Lancioni, R. A., Smith, M. F., & Oliva, T. A. (2000). The role of the internet in supply chain. *Industrial Marketing Management*, *29*(3), 45–56. doi:10.1016/S0019-8501(99)00111-X

Lancioni, R. A., Smith, M. F., & Schau, H. J. (2003). Strategic Internet application trends in supply chain management. *Industrial Marketing Management*, *32*(3), 211–217. doi:10.1016/S0019-8501(02)00264-X

Negroponte, N. (1995). *Being Digital*. New York: Random House Inc.

Parvatiyar, A., & Sheth, J. N. (2000). The domain and conceptual foundations of relationship marketing. In A. Parvatiyar, & J.N. Sheth (Eds.), Handbook of Relationship Marketing (pp. 3-38). London: SAGE. doi:10.4135/9781452231310.n1

Porter, M., & Millar, V. (1985). How information gives you competitive advantage. *Harvard Business Review*, *85*(4), 149–160.

Rayport, J. E., & Sviokla, J. J. (1995). Exploiting the Virtual Value Chain. *Harvard Business Review*, *79*(Nov-Dec), 75–85.

Rokkan, A., Heide, J. B., & Wathne, K. H. (2003). Specific investments in marketing relationships: Expropriation and bonding effects. *JMR, Journal of Marketing Research*, *40*(2), 210–232. doi:10.1509/jmkr.40.2.210.19223

Ryssel, R., Ritter, T., & Gemünden, H. G. (2004). The impact of information technology deployment on trust, commitment and value creation in business relationships. *Journal of Business and Industrial Marketing*, *19*(3), 197–207. doi:10.1108/08858620410531333

Salo, J., Tikkanen, H., & Vassinen, A. (2010). Digital bonds in business relationships. Proceedings of the Industrial Marketing and Purchasing (IMP) annual conference, Budapest, Hungary.

Shapiro, C., & Varian, H. (1999). *Information Rules. A Strategic Guide to the Network Economy*. Boston: Harvard Business School Press.

Skjøtt-Larsen, T., Kotzab, H., & Grieger, M. (2003). Electronic marketplaces and supply chain relationships. *Industrial Marketing Management*, *32*(3), 199–210. doi:10.1016/S0019-8501(02)00263-8

Stephens, M., & Ramos, H. (2003). Who Moved My ERP Solution? *Journal of Information Technology*, *19*(1), 1–6.

Themistocleous, M., & Irani, Z. (2002). Towards a Novel Framework for the Assesement of Enterprise Application Integration packages. *Proceedings of the 36th Hawaii International Conference on Systems Sciences*. Hawaii, USA.

Van Hoek, R. (2001). E-supply chains – virtually non-existing. *Supply Chain Management*, *6*(1), 21–28. doi:10.1108/13598540110694653

Zablah, A. R., Bellenger, D. N., & Johnston, W. J. (2004). An evaluation of divergent perspectives on customer relationship management: Towards a common understanding of an emerging phenomenon. *Industrial Marketing Management*, *33*(6), 475–489. doi:10.1016/j.indmarman.2004.01.006

KEY TERMS AND DEFINITIONS

Bonding: A gradually evolving process were two firms are tied together overtime.

Digital Bond Matrix: Is a managerial tool that managers can use to screen and strategize their digital bonds' portfolio along the dimensions of importance of the relationship and complexity of IT systems employed.

Digital Bonds: Ties between an industrial buyer and an industrial supplier which are formed when the internal IT systems of the parties in a relationship are shared and integrated to form an inter-organizational system that enables and/or improves information exchange and transactions.

Information Technology (IT): Information technology is the application of computers and telecommunications equipment to store, retrieve, transmit and manipulate data, often in the context of a business or other enterprise.

Oversized Digital Bonds: Are bonds formed when unimportant business relationships are coordinated and managed with overly complex IT systems.

Strategic Digital Bonds: Are formed when highly important relationships are managed and coordinated by a simple IT infrastructure in the relationship.

Strong Digital Bonds: Are bonds formed when important business relationships are coordinated and managed with simple IT systems.

Weak Digital Bonds: Are formed when simple and loose IT is employed in buyer-seller relationships that are considered not particularly important.

Section 2
Customer Relationship Management (CRM)

Chapter 7
The Role of Customer Relationship Management in the Global Business Environments

Kijpokin Kasemsap
Suan Sunandha Rajabhat University, Thailand

ABSTRACT

This chapter reveals the role of customer relationship management (CRM) in the global business environments, thus describing the theoretical and practical concept of CRM; the components of CRM in terms of key customer focus (KCF), CRM organization, knowledge management (KM), and technology-based CRM; the significance of CRM in global business; the significance of organizational characteristics in CRM; and the implementation of CRM in global business. The achievement of CRM is vital for modern organizations that seek to serve suppliers and customers, increase business performance, strengthen competitiveness, and acquire routine success in global business. Thus, it is essential for modern organizations to consider their CRM applications, create a strategic plan to consistently investigate their dynamic promotions, and instantly respond to CRM needs of customers. Applying CRM will significantly improve organizational performance and accomplish strategic goals in the global business environments.

INTRODUCTION

CRM is one of the most famous strategies to identify customers and attract customer satisfaction (Pamsari, Dehban, & Lulemani, 2013). The use of CRM technology is expected to enhance organizational capability to sustain profitable customer relationships through the integration and sharing of information that influences the efficient interactions between organization and customers (Mohammad, Rashid, & Tahir, 2013), and the appropriate analysis of customer data (Mukerjee & Singh, 2009).

CRM is a major part of organizations' strategies to increase consumption of customers with the goal of profit maximization (vom Berg, Valdés, Memari, Barakat, & Gómez, 2014). CRM is one of the most complicated innovations in organizations (Keramati, Nazari-Shirkouhi, Moshki, Afshari-Mofrad, & Maleki-Berneti, 2013). CRM is a central perspective of business intelligence, and sales campaigns are

DOI: 10.4018/978-1-4666-8459-1.ch007

often used for improving customer relationships (Yao, Sarlin, Eklund, & Back, 2014). Ensuring customer satisfaction and maintaining long-term relationships with customers have become essential for survival among competitive service industries (Cheng, Yang, & Teng, 2013).

Maintaining long-term customer loyalty has been an important issue in the service industry (Hsieh, Chen, & Yuan, 2014). Strong customer relationship is an important perspective of proving the organization with competitive edge and maximizing organizational income (Jang, Kim, Lee, & Kim, 2013). A basic change in CRM thinking is needed to shift the focus of CRM from empowering organizations to empowering customers (Saarijarvi, Karjaluoto, & Kuusela, 2013).

The strength of this chapter is on the thorough literature consolidation of CRM. The extant literature of CRM provides a contribution to practitioners and researchers by describing a comprehensive view of the functional application of CRM to appeal to different segments of CRM in order to maximize the business impact of CRM.

BACKGROUND

Interest in CRM began to grow in 1990s (Ling & Yen, 2001; Xu, Yen, Lin, & Chou, 2002). The changing environment forces the companies to change their focus from customer acquisition to customer retention (Sheth, 2002) by building relationships with customers and adding more value to goods and services (Lindgreen & Wynstra, 2005). In the late 1990s, CRM is formed as a popular business term, which holds the same roots with relationship marketing and enhances the paradigm with the emerging information technology (IT).

The low level of success rates, the unsuccessful CRM implementations may lead to decrease in customer satisfaction and customer loyalty (Richards & Jones, 2008). As a result of the low success level of CRM, measurement models are proposed by both scholars and practitioners. The mentioned frameworks are classified into two groups: partial measurement model and holistic measurement model. The process of an organization is considered as one of the main components of CRM (Chen & Popovich, 2003; Mendoza, Marius, Perez, & Griman, 2007).

ROLE OF CUSTOMER RELATIONSHIP MANAGEMENT IN GLOBAL BUSINESS

This section reveals the theoretical and practical concept of CRM; the components of CRM in terms of KCF, CRM organization, KM, and technology-based CRM; the significance of CRM in global business; the significance of organizational characteristics in CRM; and the implementation of CRM in global business.

Concept of Customer Relationship Management

CRM refers to a firm's activities for establishing and maintaining relationships with its customers (Kalaignanam & Varadarajan, 2012). CRM is widely accepted as an effective approach for collecting, analyzing, and translating valuable customer information into managerial action (Ernst, Hoyer, Krafft, & Krieger, 2011). The concept of CRM has traditionally been considered as a set of philosophies, strategies, systems and technologies that will effectively manage the transactions of customers with organizations and the subsequent relationships with customers (Greenberg, 2010; Payne & Frow, 2006). The five perspectives of CRM include strategy, process, capability, philosophy, and technology (Zablah, Bellenger, & Johnston, 2004).

CRM is recognized as a customer-focused business strategy (Nguyen & Waring, 2013). CRM is used to attract and maintain long-term relationship and evaluation with customers (Mohebbi, Hoseini, & Esfidani, 2012), and to increase the acquisition and retention of customers by selectively initiating, building and maintaining appropriate relationships with customers (Payne & Frow, 2006). The rapid advancements in communication technology have greatly transformed the way relationships between organizations and their customers are functionally managed (Bauer, Grether, & Leach, 2002).

The digital linking of both people and things is becoming more and more popular (Britsch, Schacht, & Mädche, 2012). The advancement of Web technology like Web 2.0 drives many organizations to adjust their marketing strategy (Almunawar, Anshari, & Susanto, 2013). Ensuring customer satisfaction and maintaining long-term relationships with customers have become essential for survival among competitive service industries (Cheng & Yang, 2014).

CRM adoption has a positive effect on both customer satisfaction and organizational performance in business-to-business settings (Ata & Toker, 2012). The benefits that customers receive from organizations through this relationship should add value to their service experience provided by the core product offering (Wilson, Daniel, & McDonald, 2002; Zineldin, 2006), concerning social benefits, greater confidence, and special treatment (Dagger, David, & Ng, 2011). The positive financial return rates of CRM-related projects vary from ten to 30 percent (Brewton & Schiemann, 2003; Richards & Jones, 2008).

CRM is a contested concept (Ngai, 2005; Reijonen & Laukkanen, 2010). CRM is the technology and enterprise application (Harrigan, Ramsey, & Ibbotson, 2009; Ozgener & Iraz, 2006; Zwick & Dholakia, 2004). The aim of CRM is to build and maintain a profit maximizing portfolio of customer relationships (Zablah et al., 2004). CRM involves a high level of financial investment and the long-term commitment of an organization as enterprise resource planning (ERP), supply chain management (SCM), and other enterprise systems (Teo, Devadoss, & Pan, 2006; Nguyen, Sherif, & Newby, 2007). ERP system is functionally beneficial in providing management with the types of information in order to make critical decisions (Kasemsap, 2015).

CRM is a combination of people, processes and technology that seeks to understand an organization's customers (Chen & Popovich, 2003). CRM enhances customer loyalty and organizational performance (Hillebrand, Nijholt, & Nijssen, 2011). CRM involves identifying, attracting, developing and maintaining successful customer relationships in order to increase the retention of profitable customers (Bradshaw & Brash, 2001; Massey, Montoya-Weiss, & Holcom, 2001). Customer retention affects organizational profitability in that it is more efficient to maintain an existing relationship with a customer than create a new one (Payne, Christopher, Clark, & Peck, 1999; Reichheld, 1996).

CRM facilitates organizations to deploy organizational strategies by managing individual customer relationships with the support of customer databases and mass customization technologies (Verhoef & Donkers, 2001). Ciborra and Failla (2000) conceptualized CRM beyond a front office contact management system. Levine (2000) stated that CRM is the utilization of customer-related information or knowledge to deliver relevant products to customers. Kasemsap (2014a) indicated that whenever the organizations want to enhance their CRM performance, they would better adopt the appropriate brand loyalty based on the managerial perspectives of their organizational structure, environment, and context, thus aligning their customer value and customer satisfaction in modern business. Newell (2000) explored strategic methods for improving and maintaining customer retention in modern business.

An effective leadership of CRM is required in modern organizations (Galbreath & Rogers, 1999). Concerning CRM, executives and managers are influential in the authorization of expenditure, the monitoring of the organizational performance and the motivation of organizational members (Pinto & Slevin, 1987). In order to develop successful relationships with customers, organizations should focus on the economically valuable customers while keeping away and eliminating the economically invaluable aspects (Verhoef & Donkers, 2001). Social media systematically allows technological access to the data and video information for potential consumers in the knowledge-based organizations (Kasemsap, 2014b).

As organizations learn how to manage CRM, they develop a one-to-one relationship with customers, thus reducing cost efficiency and increasing profit efficiency (Krasnikov, Jayachandran, & Kumar, 2009). The correct data of customer is essential to successful CRM performance (Abbott, Stone, & Buttle, 2001). Technology plays an important role in CRM toward better business performance (Boyle, 2004). Ngai (2005) emphasized the importance of viewing CRM as a comprehensive set of marketing strategies for managing the relationships with customers related to the overall process of marketing, sales, service, and support in modern business.

Components of Customer Relationship Management

Kincaid (2003) defined CRM as a marketing construct made up of the four components in terms of marketing, sales, services, and support across the whole customer life cycle. CRM is related to the evidence of integrating people, processes, and technology through value chain to deliver customer value within business infrastructure (Kim, Choi, Qualls, & Park, 2004). The business philosophy is operationalized through an organizational strategy of CRM (Kim et al., 2004). CRM is a multidimensional construct consisting of four behavioral dimensions: KCF, CRM organization, KM, and technology-based CRM (Sin, Tse, & Yim, 2005; Yim, Anderson, & Swaminathan, 2004).

1. **Key Customer Focus:** KCF is positively correlated with the needs of selected key customers, through providing products and services that meet customers' needs and expectations (Ryals & Knox, 2001; Sheth, Sisodia, & Sharma, 2000). Payne and Frow (2006) stated that an important element that can enable the organization to be customer-focused is to adopt a cross-functional approach in which it delivers value to its customers. Webster (2002) indicated that the cross-functional processes and capabilities perform an important method of linking the organization to its customers, instead of relying on scattered uncoordinated individual contributions from organizational functions. At the strategic level, key customers and customer groups as part of the organizational mission are indicated (Lambert, 2010).
2. **CRM Organization:** The aim of CRM organization is to internalize the values that foster and facilitate orientation toward customers and fulfillment of their needs within the structure of organization. Chang and Ku (2009) stated that organizational structure plays an important role in the implementation of CRM, thus increasing organizational performance. Organizational structure influences knowledge flows and the costs of knowledge creation and exchange inside the organization (Weigelt & Miller, 2013).

CRM organization has a positive relationship with organizational performance (Akroush, Dahiyat, Gharaibeh, & Abu-Lail, 2011; Moreno & Melendez, 2011). Organizational structure involves the cross-functional teams, process teams, and customer-focused teams in modern business (Ryals & Knox, 2001;

Sheth & Sisodia, 2002). Regarding CRM organization, an organization-wide commitment is about the allocation of organizational resources in order to indicate customer requirement (Sin et al., 2005; Yim et al., 2004). Organizational structure facilitates communication through practical areas (Liu, 2007) as the information is valuable (Elmuti, Jia, & Gray, 2009).

3. **Knowledge Management:** Kasemsap (2013a) stated that the useful training programs are essential to help executives and managers establish their strategic skills for promoting employees' knowledge-sharing behavior. Organizational learning, organizational innovation, and organizational performance help organizations obtain sustainable competitive advantage in global business (Kasemsap, 2013b). Kasemsap (2013c) explained that organizations should recognize the significance of KM in maintaining knowledge creation and knowledge-sharing behavior to increase employees' performance.

Learning motivation is practically correlated with the learning transfer in global education (Kasemsap, 2013d). Organizational learning, KM, and knowledge-sharing behavior lead to better organizational performance (Kasemsap, 2013e). Kasemsap (2014c) described that KM, strategic orientation, and organizational innovation lead to improved organizational performance. Organizational learning is practically related to KM in modern organizations (Kasemsap, 2014d).

The techniques of transmission of knowledge regarding customers are the important resources that allow an organization to reinforce its positive connection with the customers, and gain competitive advantage (Croteau & Li, 2003; Shi & Yip, 2007). Customers' knowledge plays an important role in CRM (Mohammad et al., 2013). Organizations can utilize customers' knowledge to build and develop their relationship with customers (Zahay & Griffin, 2004). Customers' knowledge enables organizations to achieve competitive advantage in the global marketplace (Sin et al., 2005). Successful CRM is implied on effectively transforming customers' information into customers' knowledge (Plessis & Boon, 2004; Stringfellow, Winter, & Bowen, 2004).

Customers' knowledge is required to be shared and disseminated throughout organization (Ryals & Knox, 2001), because the potential of knowledge occurs when it is shared within the functions of organization in order to meet current customers and their expected requirements (Mohammad et al., 2013). KM helps organization succeed by building better customer relationships (Akroush et al., 2011; Sin et al., 2005; Yim et al., 2004). In addition, there is a positive relationship between KM and market effectiveness and financial performance (Sin et al., 2005), customer retention (Yim et al., 2004), and customer satisfaction.

Knowledge creation and knowledge utilization are the two behavioral dimensions related to management functions of KM (Zahra & George, 2002). KM is positively related to CRM, and can enhance organizational performance (Payne & Frow, 2006). Sin et al. (2005) explained that KM functions are reflected in CRM activities (i.e., capturing customer information about their needs and preferences; developing sound mechanisms for sharing customer knowledge to facilitate concerted actions by different departments; and acting on the knowledge generated and disseminated).

4. **Technology-Based CRM:** The advances in IT provide organizations with the ability to collect, store, analyze, and share customer information in ways that greatly enhance their ability to respond to the needs of individual customers and to retain customers (Butler, 2000). IT plays a central role in creating and maintaining a firm's competitive advantage (Kimble & Bourdon, 2013). CRM

makes the organizations profitable across a wide range of different customers (Goodhue, Wixom, & Watson, 2002). IT and information system play an important role in the development of CRM (Kincaid, 2003; Ling & Yen, 2001).

Data mining has great potential to improve the effectiveness of CRM (Han, Yang, & Wu, 2013). Governments and enterprises may infer collective tendencies and demands for scientific researcher in data mining and CRM to formulate appropriate training strategies and policies in the future (Tsai, 2011). Data mining is usually concerned on the construction of accurate models from data, which are usually applied to well-defined problems that can be independently formulated from other problems (Bella, Ferri, Hernández-Orallo, & Ramírez-Quintana, 2011). Leaders of global businesses should provide information and communication technology skills for organizational employees to enlarge their knowledge in the information age (Kasemsap, 2014e). Educational attempts to generate social networks should be systematically implemented for minimizing the lack of knowledge (Kasemsap, 2014f).

CRM can benefit from and contribute to the useful advancements of the Web mining research (Tuzhilin, 2012). Regarding the growing relevance of customer-oriented business strategies, IT investments in the field of CRM have considerably increased (Heidemann, Klier, Landherr, & Zimmermann, 2013). IT and information system can be used to support and integrate the CRM process to satisfy the needs of the customer (Akroush et al., 2011). Web 2.0 tools such as blogs, Wiki and other services, which are widely used by individuals, also have an effect on CRM systems (Askool & Nakata, 2011). Ngai (2005) stated that technology-based CRM supports the CRM effort in modern organizations, by managing the data required to understand customers.

Significance of Customer Relationship Management in Global Business

Customer relationship practices allow organizations to understand the expressed requirements of their customers, create customer value by sharing information and enabling the focused actions to serve customer requirements (Slater & Narver, 1995), and improve manufacturing performance (Reed, Lemak, & Montgomery, 1996). CRM enables organizations to collect customer feedback related to their products and services, thus adjusting their offerings based on feedback (Forza & Filippini, 1998; Slater & Narver, 1998). Quality problems can be reduced by including customer requirements in the new product and service design stage (Kaynak, 2003).

CRM efforts promote organizations to accumulate customers' information across various interactions and customize the offers to suit individual preferences (Mithas, Krishnan, & Fornell, 2005). This view of CRM enlarges the perception of perceived quality and affects customer satisfaction (Mithas et al., 2005). CRM innovation research studies have tended to incorporate a number of these innovation concepts into their research. Ozgener and Iraz (2006) explored the adoption of CRM, the purpose of the CRM adoption, and the aspects of management.

By recognizing customer requirements, organizations can eliminate excess components from their products (Reed et al., 1996). The improved product design can allow organizations to reinforce their product quality, reduce costs of defective production, and improve productivity (Reed et al., 1996). Samson and Terziovski (1999) stated that the practices of customer focus are positively correlated with operational performance and production performance. CRM processes are extensively investigated by academicians (Bueren, Schierholz, Kolbe, & Brenner, 2005; Payne & Frow, 2005).

Zablah et al. (2004) categorized the CRM processes into two types as the macro-level processes and micro-level processes. The macro-level process approaches CRM process as organization-wide process. Payne and Frow (2005) defined the macro-level processes as the strategic development, value creation, channel integration, KM, and performance evaluation. The micro-level processes focus on customer interaction management in order to maintain long-term customer relationships (Kohli et al., 2001). Scholars and practitioners proposed frameworks in order to measure CRM. The proposed methods are categorized into ten groups according to the application of CRM and the CRM measurement processes as follows:

1. **Indirect Measurement Models:** CRM plays an increasingly important role in an organization's marketing strategy (Baecke & den Poel, 2011). CRM is measured by brand building or customer equity terms and methods (Kellen, 2002; Richards & Jones, 2008). The components of brand equity, brand loyalty, brand awareness, perceived quality and brand associations are related to CRM activities. Customer equity is divided into three groups (i.e., value equity, brand equity and retention equity). Kasemsap (2014g) explained that organizations in emerging markets need to put more marketing attempts in creating brand management system in order to improve the marketing performance and gain strategic goals in global marketing.
2. **Measurement of Customer Facing Operations:** There is a need to expand the scope of the measurement methods commonly employed by management researchers and that a greater diversity of measurement methods would benefit the field by contributing to theory development and the pursuit of new areas of research (Scherbaum & Meade, 2013). Creating and sustaining customer value is a key competitive advantage for organizations because customers represent the largest source of cash flows for organizations (Mittal, Frennea, & Westbrook, 2014). Sales personnel have often been regarded as the main actor in the creation of customer intelligence (Turunen & Toivonen, 2011). The operational CRM systems automate the customer-related processes that why organizations evaluate process metrics in order to measure the success of CRM (Kellen, 2002).
3. **Critical Success Factors Scoring (CSFS):** CSFS uses the critical success factors as the basis for scoring (Mendoza et al., 2007). There are 13 critical success factors, and over 50 metrics defined in the management mode. Concerning the variety in the nature of the factors and the metrics, the model provides the options for each metric (Mendoza et al., 2007). Customer satisfaction is one of the critical success factors to many leading companies over the world (Nahm, Ishikawa, & Inoue, 2013). Customer satisfaction is acknowledged as a key determinant of the value a customer contributes to a firm (Eisenbeiss, Cornelißen, Backhaus, & Hoyer, 2014).
4. **Behavioral Dimensions of CRM Effectiveness:** Jain et al. (2003) identified the requirement for a tool focusing on behavioral dimensions for measuring CRM effectiveness. Jain et al. (2003) stated that behavioral dimensions of CRM effectiveness are categorized into ten characteristics (i.e., attitude, understanding expectations, quality perceptions, reliability, communication, customization, recognition, keeping promises, satisfaction audit and retention). To be effective innovators, firms must know their customers' customers and competitors better than their immediate customers do (Bohlmann, Spanjol, Qualls, & Rosa, 2013).
5. **CRM Scale:** CRM organization focuses on organizational structure, commitment of resource, and human resource management (Agarwal, Harding, & Schumacher, 2004). The technology-based CRM stresses organizational technology availability (Sin et al., 2005). KM involves the creation, transfer and application of knowledge in modern organizations. Organizational culture,

organizational learning, and KM significantly lead to better job satisfaction (Kasemsap, 2014h). Kasemsap (2014i) suggested that KM is positively correlated with job performance. Cooper et al. (2005) studied the advantage of, the importance of and the knowledge of CRM to organizations in the decision process.

6. **Relationship Quality (RQ):** Customer response is a crucial aspect of service business (Kim, Chae, & Olson, 2013). The quality of relationship between the customer and the vendor has been in the interest area of researchers (Dorsch, Swanson, & Kelley, 1998; Kumar, Scheer, & Steenkamp, 1995). The aim of RQ measurement model is to measure the issues that include customers' perception about the relationship. Roberts et al. (2003) suggested the dimensions of RQ in consumer services (i.e., trust in partner's honesty, trust in partner's benevolence, affective commitment, satisfaction, and affective conflict). Competitive intelligence is a function of customer orientation, customer-centric extra-role behaviors, and RQ (Hughes, Bon, & Rapp, 2013).
7. **Customer Measurement Assessment Tool (CMAT):** The questions and the score of the tool are based on the best practices of each assessment tool (Starkey, Williams, & Stone, 2002). Woodcock et al. (2003) categorized the CMAT into nine major areas (i.e., IT, people and organization, process, analysis and planning, the proposition, customer management activity in order to measure the marketing effect, customer experience, and competitor. Customer profitability measurement is an important element in CRM and a lever for improved marketing accountability in global marketing (Holm, Kumar, & Rohde, 2012).
8. **Customer Management Process (CMP):** CMP is a part of balanced scorecard (BSC) (Kaplan & Norton, 1992) is one of the major business processes focusing on customer management. The four sub-processes include customer selection, customer acquisition, customer retention, and customer growth (Kaplan & Norton, 1992). CMP measurement should be identified and utilized in organizations toward better business performance (Kaplan & Norton, 1992). The greater a sales team's customer knowledge creation capability is, the higher its customer relationship performance will be (Menguc, Auh, & Uslu, 2013).
9. **Relationship Management Assessment Tool (RMAT):** The co-creation of value is one of the key processes taking place within customer relationships (Baumann & Meunier-FitzHugh, 2014). RMAT tool is used to help executives and managers make self-assessments about the stages of relationships (Lindgreen, Palmer, Vanhamme, & Wouters, 2006). The important elements of RMAT are customer strategy, customer-interaction strategy, brand strategy, value-creation strategy, culture, people, organization, IT, relationship management process, learning, and KM (Lindgreen et al., 2006).
10. **CRM Scorecards (CRM-SC):** CRM-SC is the CRM performance measurement model based on BSC (Kim & Kim, 2009; Kim, Suh, & Hwang, 2003). BSC is originally developed in order to provide an outline for measuring organizational performance. BSC approach has been utilized in manufacturing industries, service industries and non-profit organizations (Kaplan & Norton, 2001). BSC model is broadly recognized by business writers as a breakthrough in performance measurement and reporting (Goulian & Mersereau, 2000).

BSC translates mission and strategy into objectives and measurable terms, viewed from the financial, customer, internal business process, and learning and growth perspectives, providing a balance between short-term objectives and long-term objectives, between desired outcomes, performance drivers of those outcomes, and between hard objective measures and soft subjective measures (Chang & Ku, 2009). In the CRM-SC, the components in each dimension are indicated to ensure that the relationships between the dimensions and the components are developed and maintained (Kim & Kim, 2009).

CRM adoption positively affects organizational performance in the global marketplace (Ata & Toker, 2012). Organizations have invested in CRM systems to gain competitive advantage (Smith & Chang, 2010). Organizations which pay more attention to a customer-centric approach can gain the benefit of implementing CRM systems. Refining and giving customer data back to customers may represent a future mechanism through which organizations develop their CRM performance to a new business level (Saarijarvi et al., 2013). An analytical CRM system should be developed to support customer knowledge acquisition (Xu & Walton, 2005).

Significance of Organizational Characteristics in Customer Relationship Management

Organizational capabilities include the people in organizations (their attitudes, culture, and identity), innovation ability and knowledge (Battor & Battor, 2010; Fletcher, 2002). Organizational elements have direct impact on the nature of the organization and its willingness to accept new ideas and change. Organizations that are open to accept new, challenging activities and embrace learning cultures and recognize the strength of their culture are likely to advance innovation and gain competitive advantage over their competitors (Denison, Lief, & Ward, 2004; Pansiri & Temtime, 2010).

A good collaboration within business networks is the basis for understanding the customer process and identifying customer needs (Heinrich, Zellner, & Leist, 2011). Organizations require the ability to absorb knowledge, transform it and use it to generate new knowledge, which promotes organizational innovation (Gray, 2006). The structure of organization is centralized where the executives' attitude, personality and values play a significant role in business decision making (Bruque & Moyano, 2007; Denison et al., 2004).

CRM means the basic change in the way that organizations are managed (Ryals & Knox, 2001), and business processes are conducted (Hoffman & Kashmeri, 2000). Organizations should pay the heightened attention to organizational challenges in CRM initiatives (Agarwal et al., 2004). Many studies have explored the CRM implementation in various industries such as hotels (Lo, Stalcup, & Lee, 2010), retailing (Minami & Dawson, 2008), financial services (Dimitriadis, 2010), tourism (Ozgener & Iraz, 2006), transport services (Cheng, Chen, & Chang, 2008), business markets (Gummesson, 2004), and public services (Pan, Tan, & Lim, 2006).

Chan (2005) stated that CRM involves the integrated business processes, organizational structures, analytical structures, and technological representation to present a unified view of a customer. Kim et al. (2003) stated that CRM effectiveness (CRME) consists of four customer-centric perspectives (i.e., customer knowledge, interaction, value, and satisfaction).

The key points of CRM include organizational structure, organization-wide commitment of resources, and human resources management (Agarwal et al., 2004) as follows:

1. **Organizational Structure:** CRM requires that the entire organizational work toward the common goal of forging and nurturing strong customer relationships. The customer relationships include the

establishment of process teams, customer-focused teams (Sheth & Sisodia, 2002), cross-discipline segment teams, and cross-functional teams (Ryals & Knox, 2001). The structural designs demand strong inter-functional coordination and inter-functional integration (Sheth et al., 2000).

2. **Organization-Wide Commitment of Resources:** The organization-wide commitment of resources should follow after crafting the design of organizational structure and integrating properly those involved components. Sales and marketing resources, technical expertise, as well as resources promoting service excellence should be functionally organized (Nykamp, 2001). The benefits of customer acquisition, development, retention, and reactivation are related to the organization's commitment of time and resources through key customer needs (Nykamp, 2001).
3. **Human Resource Management:** Regarding CRM, the strategy, people, technology, and processes are significant (Horne, 2003; McGovern & Panaro, 2004). Krauss (2002) stated the part of people is the most important aspect contributing to the success of CRM in modern organizations. The internal marketing brings in employees, the importance of service-mindedness, and customer orientation (Gronroos, 1990).

Strategic alignment of competitive strategies and dynamic capabilities may enable electronic businesses to create superior value for their stakeholders (Rashidirad, Soltani, & Syed, 2013). CRM is the business process that provides the structure for how relationships with customers are developed and maintained. CRM is a strategic, process-oriented, cross-functional, and value-creating process (Lambert, 2004; Payne & Frow, 2005). CRM is a method of achieving better financial performance (Boulding, Staelin, Ehret, & Johnston, 2005). The characteristics of CRM strategy involve six items (Donaldson & O'Toole, 2002) as follows:

1. **Emphasis on Quality:** Poor service is the dominant reason for losing business. The core product alone is no longer enough, and service quality is stressed as the key for business to be successful.
2. **Measuring Customer Satisfaction but Managing Customer Service:** This implies the understanding of different benefits that the prospect expects to manage the gap between expectations and performance after the purchase process.
3. **Investing in People:** Internal relationships are as important as external relationships. To implement relationship, orientation can come from the understanding of the defined objectives and the standardized meeting.
4. **Maintaining Dialogue with Customers:** Building long-term relationships is a significant factor in implementing CRM. Organizations adapting to customers' preferences have a higher propensity to retain them and make them loyal in modern organizations.
5. **Setting Realistic Targets and Assessing Performance:** Organizations must have an insight into customer perceptions of the various elements to reach business goals. The linkage among customer satisfaction, employee evaluation, and business performance data is very important in modern business organizations (Grigoroudis, Tsitsiridi, & Zopounidis, 2013).
6. **Relationship-Based Interfaces:** Customer loyalty and trust are increasingly recognized as crucial for businesses to gain a unique and advantageous position over their competitors (Azmat & Ha, 2013). This item is about connecting with both internal and external customers in a responsive and flexible manner. The processes of communication should be utilized and adapted to the individual customers' requirement.

Implementation of Customer Relationship Management in Global Business

Osarenkhoe and Bennani (2007) stated that CRM aims to lower costs by keeping customers rather than acquiring new ones. This has resulted in the currency of a number of terms such as customer retention, loyalty, and defection, which led to the emergence of economic arguments like customer profitability and lifetime value of customers. Thus, organizations have sought to improve their financial performance by increasing their customer retention rate (Bodenberg, 2001; Parvatiyar & Sheth, 2000). This point has led to the emergence of CRM as a management concept that provide the potential to positively impact the cost-revenue ratio by aligning the organization with its customers and focusing its resources on high-value customers (Geib, Kolbe, & Brenner, 2006).

Managing a successful CRM implementation requires an integrated approach to technology, process, and people (Chen & Popovich, 2003). CRM has evolved the advances in IT and organizational changes in customer-centric processes. Organizations implementing CRM will gain the rewards in customer loyalty and get the long-term profitability. The key factors to build a strong competitive position of organization are CRM and product quality (Zineldin, 2006). The effect of customer acquisition and retention orientations on customer knowledge and investment decisions is developed when an organization consistently implements a specific engagement strategy (Arnold, Fang, & Palmatier, 2011).

The implementation of CRM is widespread (Peppard, 2000) and more advanced (Ryals & Payne, 2001) in the financial services industry than in other industries. Effective business performance is achieved by improving the customer relationship by meeting diverse customer needs and increasing their involvement and participation in the marketing process (Bhattacharya & Bolton, 2000; Kim et al., 2004; Sheth & Parvatiyar, 1995). Customer and employee relationship-building actions affect organizational value through the mediator of customer satisfaction (Luo, Wieseke, & Homburg, 2012). CRM perspective leads to better business outcomes such as sales, profitability, and repetitive purchases in modern business (Christy, Oliver, & Penn, 1996). Successful CRM implementation depends on redesigning the organizational structure, the participation of all organizational members (Mohammad et al., 2013).

Organizations that implement CRM receive CRM benefits. Consumers who develop a strong relationship with an organization, and its offerings display a stronger sense of loyalty and intention to stay in the mutually beneficial relationship (Kim et al., 2004; Wulf, Odekerken-Schroder, & Iacobucci, 2001). Consumers continue to purchase the same products and services (Henning-Thurau & Klee, 1997; Reichheld, 1996). Improved customer retention and loyalty will reduce the marketing expenses (Christy et al., 1996; Sheth & Parvatiyar, 1995) because it costs less to serve loyal customers (Reichheld, 1996; Reichheld & Sasser, 1990).

FUTURE RESEARCH DIRECTIONS

The strength of this chapter is on the thorough literature consolidation of CRM. The extant literature of CRM provides a contribution to practitioners and researchers by describing a comprehensive view of the functional application of CRM to appeal to different segments of CRM in order to maximize the business impact of CRM. The classification of the extant literature in the domain of CRM will provide the potential opportunities for future research. Future research direction should broaden the perspectives in the implementation of CRM to be utilized in the knowledge-based organizations.

Practitioners and researchers should recognize the applicability of a more multidisciplinary approach toward research activities in implementing CRM in terms of KM-related variables (i.e., knowledge-sharing behavior, knowledge creation, organizational learning, learning orientation, and motivation to learn). It will be useful to bring additional disciplines together (i.e., strategic management, marketing, finance, and human resources) to support a more holistic examination of CRM in order to combine or transfer existing theories and approaches to inquiry in this area. CRM implementation scale components and their effect on customer satisfaction and loyalty from customers' perspectives can be a valuable research area in the future. An examination of linkages between CRM and business intelligence would seem to be viable for future research efforts.

CONCLUSION

This chapter revealed the role of CRM in the global business environments, thus describing the theoretical and practical concept of CRM; the components of CRM in terms of KCF, CRM organization, KM, and technology-based CRM; the significance of CRM in global business; the significance of organizational characteristics in CRM; and the implementation of CRM in global business. This chapter provided the information about requirement for management to be supportive of CRM innovation and technology, thus evaluating the available CRM resources (i.e., IT knowledge, skills, and infrastructure) in organizations, to recognize the importance of employees' contributions, and to be aware of organizational features practically appropriate to their organization's size and industry sector before managing the adoption and implementation of CRM.

This chapter extended the understanding of CRM adoption and implementation to help in building a greater understanding of the factors associated with such CRM adoption and implementation toward business success. Executives and managers should obtain the strategic business insights into CRM implementation which would help them in creating and maintaining successful CRM strategies in modern business. CRM becomes one of the most important competitive business strategies in the digital age, thus involving organizational capability of managing business interactions with customers in an effective manner. Through CRM, relationships with customers can be practically established and fostered as important resources in an attempt to improve customer retention and profitability. Applying CRM in the global business environments will greatly increase business performance and gain competitive advantage in the social media age.

REFERENCES

Abbott, J., Stone, M., & Buttle, F. (2001). Customer relationship management in practice: A qualitative study. *Journal of Database Marketing*, *9*(1), 24–34. doi:10.1057/palgrave.jdm.3240055

Agarwal, A., Harding, D. P., & Schumacher, J. R. (2004). Organizing for CRM. *The McKinsey Quarterly*, *3*, 80–91.

Akroush, M. N., Dahiyat, S. E., Gharaibeh, H. S., & Abu-Lail, B. N. (2011). Customer relationship management implementation: An investigation of a scale's generalizability and its relationship with business performance in a developing country context. *International Journal of Commerce and Management*, *21*(2), 158–191. doi:10.1108/10569211111144355

alem Mohammad, A., bin Rashid, B., & bin Tahir, S. (2013). Assessing the influence of customer relationship management (CRM) dimensions on organization performance: An empirical study in the hotel industry. *Journal of Hospitality and Tourism Technology*, *4*(3), 228–247. doi:10.1108/JHTT-01-2013-0002

Almunawar, M. N., Anshari, M. A., & Susanto, H. (2013). Crafting strategies for sustainability: How travel agents should react in facing a disintermediation. *Operations Research*, *13*(3), 317–342. doi:10.1007/s12351-012-0129-7

Arnold, T. J., Fang, E., & Palmatier, R. W. (2011). The effects of customer acquisition and retention orientations on a firm's radical and incremental innovation performance. *Journal of the Academy of Marketing Science*, *39*(2), 234–251. doi:10.1007/s11747-010-0203-8

Askool, S., & Nakata, K. (2011). A conceptual model for acceptance of social CRM systems based on a scoping study. *AI & Society*, *26*(3), 205–220. doi:10.1007/s00146-010-0311-5

Ata, U. Z., & Toker, A. (2012). The effect of customer relationship management adoption in business-to-business markets. *Journal of Business and Industrial Marketing*, *27*(6), 497–507. doi:10.1108/08858621211251497

Azmat, F., & Ha, H. (2013). Corporate social responsibility, customer trust, and loyalty: Perspectives from a developing country. *Thunderbird International Business Review*, *55*(3), 253–270. doi:10.1002/tie.21542

Baecke, P., & den Poel, D. V. (2011). Data augmentation by predicting spending pleasure using commercially available external data. *Journal of Intelligent Information Systems*, *36*(3), 367–383. doi:10.1007/s10844-009-0111-x

Battor, M., & Battor, M. (2010). The impact on innovation and performance advantages: Testing a mediated model. *Journal of Marketing Management*, *26*(9-10), 842–857. doi:10.1080/02672570903498843

Bauer, H. H., Grether, M., & Leach, M. (2002). Building customer relations over the internet. *Industrial Marketing Management*, *31*(2), 155–163. doi:10.1016/S0019-8501(01)00186-9

Baumann, J., & Meunier-FitzHugh, K. L. (2014). Trust as a facilitator of co-creation in customer-salesperson interaction: An imperative for the realization of episodic and relational value? *AMS Review*, *40*(1-2), 5–20. doi:10.1007/s13162-013-0039-8

Bella, A., Ferri, C., Hernández-Orallo, J., & Ramírez-Quintana, M. J. (2011). Using negotiable features for prescription problems. *Computing*, *91*(2), 135–168. doi:10.1007/s00607-010-0129-5

Bhattacharya, C. B., & Bolton, R. N. (2000). Relationship marketing in mass markets. In J. Sheth & A. Parvatiyar (Eds.), *Handbook of relationship marketing* (pp. 327–354). Thousand Oaks, CA: Sage. doi:10.4135/9781452231310.n12

Bodenberg, T. M. (2001). *Customer relationship management: New ways of keeping the customer satisfied*. New York, NY: The Conference Board.

Bohlmann, J. D., Spanjol, J., Qualls, W. J., & Rosa, J. A. (2013). The interplay of customer and product innovation dynamics: An exploratory study. *Journal of Product Innovation Management*, *30*(2), 228–244. doi:10.1111/j.1540-5885.2012.00962.x

Boulding, W., Staelin, R., Ehret, M., & Johnston, W. J. (2005). A customer relationship management roadmap: What is known, potential pitfalls, and where to go. *Journal of Marketing*, *69*(4), 155–166. doi:10.1509/jmkg.2005.69.4.155

Boyle, M. J. (2004). Using CRM software effectively. *The CPA Journal*, *74*(7), 17.

Bradshaw, D., & Brash, C. (2001). Managing customer relationships in the e-business world: How to personalize computer relationships for increased profitability. *International Journal of Retail & Distribution Management*, *29*(12), 520–529. doi:10.1108/09590550110696969

Brewton, J., & Schiemann, W. (2003). Measurement: The missing ingredient in today's CRM strategy. *Coastal Management*, *17*(1), 5–14.

Britsch, J., Schacht, S., & Mädche, A. (2012). Anything relationship management. *Business & Information Systems Engineering*, *4*(2), 85–87. doi:10.1007/s12599-012-0208-6

Bruque, S., & Moyano, J. (2007). Organisational determinants of information technology adoption and implementation in SMEs: The case of family and cooperative firms. *Technovation*, *27*(5), 241–253. doi:10.1016/j.technovation.2006.12.003

Bueren, A., Schierholz, R., Kolbe, L. M., & Brenner, W. (2005). Improving performance of customer-processes with knowledge management. *Business Process Management Journal*, *11*(5), 573–588. doi:10.1108/14637150510619894

Butler, S. (2000). Changing the game: CRM in the e-world. *The Journal of Business Strategy*, *21*(2), 13–14. doi:10.1108/eb040067

Chan, J. O. (2005). Toward a unified view of customer relationship management. *Journal of American Academy of Business*, *6*(1), 32–38.

Chang, H., & Ku, P. (2009). Implementation of relationship quality for CRM performance: Acquisition of BPR and organizational learning. *Total Quality Management*, *20*(3), 327–348. doi:10.1080/14783360902719758

Chen, I. J., & Popovich, K. (2003). Understanding customer relationship management (CRM): People, process and technology. *Business Process Management Journal*, *9*(5), 672–688. doi:10.1108/14637150310496758

Cheng, J. H., Chen, F. Y., & Chang, Y. H. (2008). Airline relationship quality: An examination of Taiwanese passengers. *Tourism Management*, *29*(3), 487–499. doi:10.1016/j.tourman.2007.05.015

Cheng, L. Y., Yang, C. C., & Teng, H. M. (2013). An integrated model for customer relationship management: An analysis and empirical study. *Human Factors and Ergonomics in Manufacturing & Service Industries*, *23*(5), 462–481. doi:10.1002/hfm.20343

Cheng, L. Y., & Yang, C. W. (2014). Conceptual analysis and implementation of an integrated CRM system for service providers. *Service Business*, *7*(2), 307–328. doi:10.1007/s11628-012-0160-z

Christy, R., Oliver, G., & Penn, J. (1996). Relationship marketing in consumer markets. *Journal of Marketing Management*, *12*(1-3), 175–187. doi:10.1080/0267257X.1996.9964407

Ciborra, C., & Failla, A. (2000). Infrastructure as a process: The case of CRM in IBM. In C. Ciborra (Ed.), *From control to drift: The dynamics of corporate information infrastructures* (pp. 105–124). Oxford, UK: Oxford University Press.

Cooper, M. J., Upton, N., & Seaman, S. (2005). Customer relationship management: A comparative analysis of family and nonfamily business practices. *Journal of Small Business Management*, *43*(3), 242–256. doi:10.1111/j.1540-627X.2005.00136.x

Croteau, A. M., & Li, P. (2003). Critical success factors of CRM technological initiatives. *Canadian Journal of Administrative Sciences*, *20*(1), 21–34. doi:10.1111/j.1936-4490.2003.tb00303.x

Dagger, T. S., David, M. E., & Ng, S. (2011). Do relationship benefits and maintenance drive commitment and loyalty? *Journal of Services Marketing*, *25*(4), 273–281. doi:10.1108/08876041111143104

Denison, D., Lief, C., & Ward, J. (2004). Culture in family-owned enterprises: Recognizing and leveraging unique strengths. *Family Business Review*, *17*(1), 61–70. doi:10.1111/j.1741-6248.2004.00004.x

Dimitriadis, S. (2010). Testing perceived relational benefits as satisfaction and behavioral outcomes drivers. *International Journal of Bank Marketing*, *28*(4), 297–213. doi:10.1108/02652321011054981

Donaldson, B., & O' Toole, T. (2002). *Strategic marketing relationship*. Chichester, UK: John Wiley & Sons.

Dorsch, M. J., Swanson, S. R., & Kelley, S. W. (1998). The role of relationship quality in the satisfaction of vendors as perceived by customers. *Journal of the Academy of Marketing Science*, *26*(2), 128–142. doi:10.1177/0092070398262004

Eisenbeiss, M., Cornelißen, M., Backhaus, K., & Hoyer, W. D. (2014). Nonlinear and asymmetric returns on customer satisfaction: Do they vary across situations and consumers? *Journal of the Academy of Marketing Science*, *42*(3), 242–263. doi:10.1007/s11747-013-0366-1

Elmuti, D., Jia, H., & Gray, D. (2009). Customer relationship management strategic application and organizational effectiveness: An empirical investigation. *Journal of Strategic Marketing*, *17*(1), 75–96. doi:10.1080/09652540802619301

Ernst, H., Hoyer, W. D., Krafft, M., & Krieger, K. (2011). Customer relationship management and company performance: The mediating role of new product performance. *Journal of the Academy of Marketing Science*, *39*(2), 290–306. doi:10.1007/s11747-010-0194-5

Fletcher, D. (2002). A network perspective of culture organizing and "professional management" in small, family business. *Journal of Business and Enterprise Development*, *9*(4), 400–415. doi:10.1108/14626000210450577

Forza, C., & Filippini, R. (1998). TQM impact on quality conformance and customer satisfaction: A causal model. *International Journal of Production Economics*, *55*(1), 1–20. doi:10.1016/S0925-5273(98)00007-3

Galbreath, J., & Rogers, T. (1999). Customer relationship leadership. *The TQM Magazine*, *11*(3), 161–171. doi:10.1108/09544789910262734

Garrido-Moreno, A., & Padilla-Meléndez, A. (2011). Analyzing the impact of knowledge management on CRM success: The mediating effects of organizational factors. *International Journal of Information Management*, *31*(5), 437–444. doi:10.1016/j.ijinfomgt.2011.01.002

Geib, M., Kolbe, L. M., & Brenner, W. (2006). CRM collaboration in financial services networks: A multi-case analysis. *Journal of Enterprise Information Management*, *19*(6), 591–607. doi:10.1108/17410390610708481

Goodhue, D. L., Wixom, B. H., & Watson, H. J. (2002). Realizing business benefits through CRM: Hitting the right target in the right way. *MIS Quarterly Executive*, *1*(2), 79–94.

Goulian, C., & Mersereau, A. (2000). Performance measurement-implementing a corporate scorecard. *Ivey Business Journal*, *65*(1), 48–54.

Gray, C. (2006). Absorptive capacity, knowledge management and innovation in entrepreneurial small firms. *International Journal of Entrepreneurial Behaviour & Research*, *12*(6), 345–360. doi:10.1108/13552550610710144

Greenberg, P. (2010). The impact of CRM 2.0 on customer insight. *Journal of Business and Industrial Marketing*, *25*(6), 410–419. doi:10.1108/08858621011066008

Grigoroudis, E., Tsitsiridi, E., & Zopounidis, C. (2013). Linking customer satisfaction, employee appraisal, and business performance: An evaluation methodology in the banking sector. *Annals of Operations Research*, *205*(1), 5–27. doi:10.1007/s10479-012-1206-2

Gronroos, C. (1990). *Service management and marketing: Managing the moments of truth in service competition*. Lexington, MA: Lexington Books.

Gummesson, E. (2004). Return on relationships (ROR): The value of relationship marketing and CRM in business-to-business contexts. *Journal of Business and Industrial Marketing*, *19*(2), 136–148. doi:10.1108/08858620410524016

Han, Y., Yang, F. Z., & Wu, G. (2013). Applying data mining to the customer relationship management in retail trade. *Social Media Retrieval and Mining: Communications in Computer and Information Science*, *387*, 116–124. doi:10.1007/978-3-642-41629-3_10

Harrigan, P., Ramsey, E., & Ibbotson, P. (2009). Investigating the e-CRM activities of Irish SMEs. *Journal of Small Business and Enterprise Development*, *16*(3), 443–465. doi:10.1108/14626000910977161

Heidemann, J., Klier, M., Landherr, A., & Zimmermann, S. (2013). The optimal level of CRM IT investments. *Electronic Markets*, *23*(1), 73–84. doi:10.1007/s12525-012-0096-0

Heinrich, B., Zellner, G., & Leist, S. (2011). Service integrators in business networks: The importance of relationship values. *Electronic Markets*, *21*(4), 215–235. doi:10.1007/s12525-011-0075-x

Hennig-Thurau, T., & Klee, A. (1997). The impact of customer satisfaction and relationship quality and customer retention: A critical reassessment and model development. *Psychology and Marketing*, *14*(8), 737–764. doi:10.1002/(SICI)1520-6793(199712)14:8<737::AID-MAR2>3.0.CO;2-F

Hillebrand, B., Nijholt, J. J., & Nijssen, E. J. (2011). Exploring CRM effectiveness: An institutional theory perspective. *Journal of the Academy of Marketing Science*, *39*(4), 592–608. doi:10.1007/s11747-011-0248-3

Hoffman, T., & Kashmeri, S. (2000). Coddling the customer. *Computerworld*, *34*(50), 58–60.

Holm, M., Kumar, V., & Rohde, C. (2012). Measuring customer profitability in complex environments: An interdisciplinary contingency framework. *Journal of the Academy of Marketing Science*, *40*(3), 387–401. doi:10.1007/s11747-011-0263-4

Horne, S. (2003). Needed: A cultural change. *Target Marketing*, *26*(8), 53–56.

Hsieh, Y. H., Chen, I. H., & Yuan, S. T. (2014). FCM-based customer expectation-driven service dispatch system. *Soft Computing*, *18*(2), 359–378. doi:10.1007/s00500-013-1063-1

Hughes, D. E., Le Bon, J., & Rapp, A. (2013). Gaining and leveraging customer-based competitive intelligence: The pivotal role of social capital and salesperson adaptive selling skills. *Journal of the Academy of Marketing Science*, *41*(1), 91–110. doi:10.1007/s11747-012-0311-8

Jain, R., Jain, S., & Dhar, U. (2003). Measuring customer relationship management. *Journal of Service Research*, *2*(2), 97–109.

Jang, J. H., Kim, S. W., Lee, Y. S., & Kim, J. (2013). The effects of relationship benefit on relationship quality and store loyalty from convergence environments: NPS analysis and moderating effects. *Electronic Commerce Research*, *13*(3), 291–315. doi:10.1007/s10660-013-9117-0

Kalaignanam, K., & Varadarajan, R. (2012). Offshore outsourcing of customer relationship management: Conceptual model and propositions. *Journal of the Academy of Marketing Science*, *40*(2), 347–363. doi:10.1007/s11747-011-0291-0

Kaplan, R. S., & Norton, D. P. (1992). The balanced scorecard: Measures that drive performance. *Harvard Business Review*, *70*(1), 71–79. PMID:10119714

Kaplan, R. S., & Norton, D. P. (2001). Transforming the balanced scorecard from performance measurement to strategic management: Part I. *Accounting Horizons*, *15*(1), 87–104. doi:10.2308/acch.2001.15.1.87

Kasemsap, K. (2013a). Strategic business management: A practical framework and causal model of empowering leadership, team cohesion, knowledge-sharing behavior, and team performance. *Journal of Social and Development Sciences*, *4*(3), 100–106.

Kasemsap, K. (2013b). Unified framework: Constructing a causal model of Six Sigma, organizational learning, organizational innovation, and organizational performance. *The Journal of Interdisciplinary Networks*, *2*(1), 268–273.

Kasemsap, K. (2013c). Innovative framework: Formation of causal model of organizational culture, organizational climate, knowledge management, and job performance. *Journal of International Business Management & Research*, *4*(12), 21–32.

Kasemsap, K. (2013d). Practical framework: Creation of causal model of job involvement, career commitment, learning motivation, and learning transfer. *International Journal of the Computer, the Internet and Management, 21*(1), 29-35.

Kasemsap, K. (2013e). Synthesized framework: Establishing a causal model of organizational learning, knowledge management, knowledge-sharing behavior, and organizational performance. *International Journal of the Computer, the Internet and Management, 21*(2), 29-34.

Kasemsap, K. (2014a). The role of brand loyalty on CRM performance: An innovative framework for smart manufacturing. In Z. Luo (Ed.), *Smart manufacturing innovation and transformation: Interconnection and intelligence* (pp. 252–284). Hershey, PA: IGI Global. doi:10.4018/978-1-4666-5836-3.ch010

Kasemsap, K. (2014b). The role of social media in the knowledge-based organizations. In I. Lee (Ed.), *Integrating social media into business practice, applications, management, and models* (pp. 254–275). Hershey, PA: IGI Global. doi:10.4018/978-1-4666-6182-0.ch013

Kasemsap, K. (2014c). Strategic innovation management: An integrative framework and causal model of knowledge management, strategic orientation, organizational innovation, and organizational performance. In P. Ordóñez de Pablos & R. Tennyson (Eds.), *Strategic approaches for human capital management and development in a turbulent economy* (pp. 102–116). Hershey, PA: IGI Global. doi:10.4018/978-1-4666-4530-1.ch007

Kasemsap, K. (2014d). The role of knowledge sharing on organisational innovation: An integrated framework. In L. Al-Hakim & C. Jin (Eds.), Quality innovation: Knowledge, theory, and practices (pp. 247–271). Hershey, PA: IGI Global. doi:10.4018/978-1-4666-4769-5.ch012

Kasemsap, K. (2014e). The role of social networking in global business environments. In P. Smith & T. Cockburn (Eds.), *Impact of emerging digital technologies on leadership in global business* (pp. 183–201). Hershey, PA: IGI Global. doi:10.4018/978-1-4666-6134-9.ch010

Kasemsap, K. (2014f). The role of social capital in higher education institutions. In N. Baporikar (Ed.), *Handbook of research on higher education in the MENA region: Policy and practice* (pp. 119–147). Hershey, PA: IGI Global. doi:10.4018/978-1-4666-6198-1.ch007

Kasemsap, K. (2014g). The role of brand management in emerging markets. In I. Samanta (Ed.), *Strategic marketing in fragile economic conditions* (pp. 167–184). Hershey, PA: IGI Global. doi:10.4018/978-1-4666-6232-2.ch009

Kasemsap, K. (2014h). The role of knowledge management on job satisfaction: A systematic framework. In B. Tripathy & D. Acharjya (Eds.), *Advances in secure computing, Internet services, and applications* (pp. 104–127). Hershey, PA: IGI Global. doi:10.4018/978-1-4666-4940-8.ch006

Kasemsap, K. (2014i). Unifying a framework of organizational culture, organizational climate, knowledge management, and job performance. In R. Perez-Castillo & M. Piattini (Eds.), *Uncovering essential software artifacts through business process archeology* (pp. 336–362). Hershey, PA: IGI Global. doi:10.4018/978-1-4666-4667-4.ch013

Kasemsap, K. (2015). Implementing enterprise resource planning. In M. Khosrow-Pour (Ed.), *Encyclopedia of information science and technology* (3rd ed., pp. 798–807). Hershey, PA: IGI Global. doi:10.4018/978-1-4666-5888-2.ch076

Kaynak, H. (2003). The relationship between total quality management practices and their effects on firm performance. *Journal of Operations Management*, *21*(4), 405–435. doi:10.1016/S0272-6963(03)00004-4

Kellen, V. (2002). *CRM measurement frameworks* (Working paper). DePaul University, Chicago, IL.

Keramati, A., Nazari-Shirkouhi, S., Moshki, H., Afshari-Mofrad, M., & Maleki-Berneti, E. (2013). A novel methodology for evaluating the risk of CRM projects in fuzzy environment. *Neural Computing & Applications*, *23*(1), 29–53. doi:10.1007/s00521-012-1216-7

Kim, G., Chae, B. K., & Olson, D. L. (2013). A support vector machine (SVM) approach to imbalanced datasets of customer responses: Comparison with other customer response models. *Service Business*, *7*(1), 167–182. doi:10.1007/s11628-012-0147-9

Kim, H. S., & Kim, Y. G. (2009). A CRM performance measurement framework: Its development process and application. *Industrial Marketing Management*, *38*(4), 477–489. doi:10.1016/j.indmarman.2008.04.008

Kim, J., Suh, E., & Hwang, H. (2003). A model for evaluating the effectiveness of CRM using balanced scorecard. *Journal of Interactive Marketing*, *17*(2), 5–19. doi:10.1002/dir.10051

Kim, J. W., Choi, J., Qualls, W., & Park, J. (2004). The impact of CRM on firm- and relationship-level performance in distribution networks. *Communications of the Association for Information Systems*, *14*(1), 632–652.

Kimble, C., & Bourdon, I. (2013). The link among information technology, business models, and strategic breakthroughs: Examples from Amazon, Dell, and eBay. *Global Business and Organizational Excellence*, *33*(1), 58–68. doi:10.1002/joe.21523

Kincaid, J. W. (2003). *Customer relationship management: Getting it right!* Upper Saddle River, NJ: Prentice-Hall.

Kohli, R., Piontek, F., Ellington, T., VanOsdol, T., Shepard, M., & Brazel, G. (2001). Managing customer relationships through e-business decision support applications: A case of hospital-physician collaboration. *Decision Support Systems*, *32*(2), 171–187. doi:10.1016/S0167-9236(01)00109-9

Krasnikov, A., Jayachandran, S., & Kumar, V. (2009). The impact of customer relationship management implementation on cost and profit efficiencies: Evidence from the US commercial banking industry. *Journal of Marketing*, *73*(6), 61–76. doi:10.1509/jmkg.73.6.61

Krauss, M. (2002). At many firms, technology obscures CRM. *Marketing News*, *36*(6), 5.

Kumar, N., Scheer, L. K., & Steenkamp, J. E. M. (1995). The effects of supplier fairness on vulnerable resellers. *JMR, Journal of Marketing Research*, *32*(1), 54–65. doi:10.2307/3152110

Lambert, D. M. (2004). *Supply chain management: Processes, partnerships, performance*. Sarasota, FL: Supply Chain Management Institute.

Lambert, D. M. (2010). Customer relationship management as a business process. *Journal of Business and Industrial Marketing*, *25*(1), 4–17. doi:10.1108/08858621011009119

Levine, S. (2000). The rise of CRM. *America's Network*, *104*(6), 34.

Lindgreen, A., Palmer, R., Vanhamme, J., & Wouters, J. (2006). A relationship management assessment tool: Questioning, identifying, and prioritizing critical aspects of customer relationships. *Industrial Marketing Management*, *35*(1), 57–71. doi:10.1016/j.indmarman.2005.08.008

Lindgreen, A., & Wynstra, F. (2005). Value in business markets: What do we know? Where are we going? *Industrial Marketing Management*, *34*(7), 732–748. doi:10.1016/j.indmarman.2005.01.001

Ling, R., & Yen, D. C. (2001). Customer relationship management: An analysis framework and implementation strategies. *Journal of Computer Information Systems*, *41*(3), 82–97.

Liu, H. Y. (2007). Development of a framework for customer relationship management (CRM) in the banking industry. *International Journal of Management*, *24*(1), 15–32.

Lo, A. S., Stalcup, L. D., & Lee, A. (2010). Customer relationship management for hotels in Hong Kong. *International Journal of Contemporary Hospitality Management*, *22*(2), 139–159. doi:10.1108/09596111011018151

Luo, X., Wieseke, J., & Homburg, C. (2012). Incentivizing CEOs to build customer- and employee-firm relations for higher customer satisfaction and firm value. *Journal of the Academy of Marketing Science*, *40*(6), 745–758. doi:10.1007/s11747-011-0290-1

Massey, A. P., Montoya-Weiss, M., & Holcom, K. (2001). Re-engineering the customer relationship: Leveraging knowledge assets at IBM. *Decision Support Systems*, *32*(2), 155–170. doi:10.1016/S0167-9236(01)00108-7

McGovern, T., & Panaro, J. (2004). The human side of customer relationship management. *Benefits Quarterly*, *20*(3), 26–33.

Mendoza, L. E., Marius, A., Perez, M., & Griman, A. C. (2007). Critical success factors for a customer relationship management strategy. *Information and Software Technology*, *49*(8), 913–945. doi:10.1016/j.infsof.2006.10.003

Menguc, B., Auh, S., & Uslu, A. (2013). Customer knowledge creation capability and performance in sales teams. *Journal of the Academy of Marketing Science*, *41*(1), 19–39. doi:10.1007/s11747-012-0303-8

Minami, C., & Dawson, J. (2008). The CRM process in retail and service sector firms in Japan. Loyalty.

Mithas, S., Krishnan, M. S., & Fornell, C. (2005). Why do customer relationship management applications affect customer satisfaction? *Journal of Marketing*, *69*(4), 201–209. doi:10.1509/jmkg.2005.69.4.201

Mittal, V., Frennea, C., & Westbrook, R. A. (2014). Managing customer value in business-to-business markets. *Marketing Review St. Gallen, 31*(3), 46–54. doi:10.1365/s11621-014-0362-y

Mohebbi, N., Hoseini, M. A., & Esfidani, M. R. (2012). Identification & prioritization of the affecting factors on CRM implementation in edible oil industry. *Journal of Basic and Applied Scientific Research, 2*(5), 4993–5001.

Mukerjee, K., & Singh, K. (2009). CRM: A strategic approach. *Journal of Management Research, 8*(2), 65–82.

Nahm, Y. E., Ishikawa, H., & Inoue, M. (2013). New rating methods to prioritize customer requirements in QFD with incomplete customer preferences. *International Journal of Advanced Manufacturing Technology, 65*(9-12), 1587–1604. doi:10.1007/s00170-012-4282-1

Newell, F. (2000). *Loyalty.com: Customer relationship management in the new era of Internet marketing*. New York, NY: McGraw-Hill.

Ngai, E. W. T. (2005). Customer relationship management research (1992-2002): An academic literature review and classification. *Marketing Intelligence & Planning, 23*(6), 582–605. doi:10.1108/02634500510624147

Nguyen, T. H., Sherif, J., & Newby, M. (2007). Strategies for successful CRM implementation. *Information Management & Computer Security, 15*(2), 102–115. doi:10.1108/09685220710748001

Nguyen, T. H., & Waring, T. S. (2013). The adoption of customer relationship management (CRM) technology in SMEs - An empirical study. *Journal of Small Business and Enterprise Development, 20*(4), 824–848. doi:10.1108/JSBED-01-2012-0013

Nykamp, M. (2001). *The customer differential: The complete guide to implementing customer relationship management*. New York, NY: AMACOM.

Osarenkhoe, A., & Bennani, A. (2007). An exploratory study of implementation of customer relationship management strategy. *Business Process Management Journal, 13*(1), 139–164. doi:10.1108/14637150710721177

Ozgener, S., & Iraz, R. (2006). Customer relationship management in small-medium enterprises: The case of Turkish tourism industry. *Tourism Management, 27*(6), 1356–1363. doi:10.1016/j.tourman.2005.06.011

Pamsari, M. B., Dehban, M., & Lulemani, H. K. (2013). Assessment of the key success factors of customer relationship management. *Universal Journal of Management and Social Sciences, 3*(4), 23–29.

Pan, S. L., Tan, C. W., & Lim, E. T. K. (2006). Customer relationship management (CRM) in e-government: A relational perspective. *Decision Support Systems, 42*(1), 237–250. doi:10.1016/j.dss.2004.12.001

Pansiri, J., & Temtime, Z. T. (2010). Linking firm and managers' characteristics to perceived critical success factors for innovative entrepreneurial support. *Journal of Small Business and Enterprise Development, 17*(1), 45–59. doi:10.1108/14626001011019125

Parvatiyar, A., & Sheth, J. N. (2000). The domain and conceptual foundations of relationship marketing. In J. N. Sheth & A. Parvatiyar (Eds.), *Handbook of relationship marketing* (pp. 3–38). Thousand Oaks, CA: Sage. doi:10.4135/9781452231310.n1

Payne, A., Christopher, M., Clark, M., & Peck, H. (1999). *Relationship marketing for competitive advantage*. Oxford, UK: Butterworth Heinemann.

Payne, A., & Frow, P. (2005). A strategic framework for customer relationship management. *Journal of Marketing*, *69*(4), 167-176. doi:10.1509/jmkg.2005.69.4.167

Payne, A., & Frow, P. (2006). Customer relationship management: From strategy to implementation. *Journal of Marketing Management*, *22*(1-2), 135–168. doi:10.1362/026725706776022272

Peppard, J. (2000). Customer relationship management (CRM) in financial services. *European Management Journal*, *18*(3), 312–327. doi:10.1016/S0263-2373(00)00013-X

Pinto, J. K., & Slevin, D. P. (1987). Critical factors in successful project implementation. *IEEE Transactions on Engineering Management*, *34*(1), 22–27. doi:10.1109/TEM.1987.6498856

Plessis, M. D., & Boon, J. (2004). Knowledge management in e-business and customer relationship management: South African case study findings. *International Journal of Information Management*, *24*(1), 73–86. doi:10.1016/j.ijinfomgt.2003.10.002

Rashidirad, M., Soltani, E., & Syed, J. (2013). Strategic alignment between competitive strategy and dynamic capability: Conceptual framework and hypothesis development. *Strategic Change*, *22*(3-4), 213–224. doi:10.1002/jsc.1934

Reed, R., Lemak, D. J., & Montgomery, J. C. (1996). Beyond process: TQM content and firm performance. *Academy of Management Review*, *21*(1), 173–202.

Reichheld, F. F. (1996). *The loyalty effect*. Boston, MA: Harvard Business School Press.

Reichheld, F. F., & Sasser, W. E. (1990). Zero defections: Quality comes to services. *Harvard Business Review*, *68*(5), 105–111. PMID:10107082

Reijonen, H., & Laukkanen, T. (2010). Customer relationship oriented marketing practices in SMEs. *Marketing Intelligence & Planning*, *28*(2), 115–136. doi:10.1108/02634501011029646

Richards, K. A., & Jones, E. (2008). Customer relationship management: Finding value drivers. *Industrial Marketing Management*, *37*(2), 120–130. doi:10.1016/j.indmarman.2006.08.005

Roberts, K., Varki, S., & Brodie, R. (2003). Measuring the quality of relationships in customer services: An empirical study. *European Journal of Marketing*, *37*(1-2), 169–196. doi:10.1108/03090560310454037

Ryals, L., & Knox, S. (2001). Cross-functional issues in the implementation of relationship marketing through customer relationship management. *European Management Journal*, *19*(5), 534–542. doi:10.1016/S0263-2373(01)00067-6

Ryals, L., & Payne, A. (2001). Customer relationship management in financial services: Towards information-enabled relationship marketing. *Journal of Strategic Management*, *9*(1), 3–27.

Saarijarvi, H., Karjaluoto, H., & Kuusela, H. (2013). Extending customer relationship management: From empowering firms to empowering customers. *Journal of Systems and Information Technology*, *15*(2), 140–158. doi:10.1108/13287261311328877

Samson, D., & Terziovski, M. (1999). The relationship between total quality management practices and operational performance. *Journal of Operations Management*, *17*(4), 393–409. doi:10.1016/S0272-6963(98)00046-1

Scherbaum, C. A., & Meade, A. W. (2013). New directions for measurement in management research. *International Journal of Management Reviews*, *15*(2), 132148. doi:10.1111/ijmr.12003

Sheth, J. N. (2000). Relationship marketing: Paradigm shift of shaft? In J. N. Sheth & A. Parvatiyar (Eds.), *Handbook of relationship marketing* (pp. 609–620). Thousand Oaks, CA: Sage. doi:10.4135/9781452231310.n23

Sheth, J. N. (2002). The future of relationship marketing. *Journal of Services Marketing*, *16*(7), 590–592. doi:10.1108/08876040210447324

Sheth, J. N., & Parvatiyar, A. (1995). Relationship marketing in consumer markets: Antecedents and consequences. *Journal of the Academy of Marketing Science*, *23*(4), 255–271. doi:10.1177/009207039502300405

Sheth, J. N., & Sisodia, R. S. (2002). Marketing productivity: Issues and analysis. *Journal of Business Research*, *55*(5), 349–362. doi:10.1016/S0148-2963(00)00164-8

Sheth, J. N., Sisodia, R. S., & Sharma, A. (2000). The antecedents and consequences of customer-centric marketing. *Journal of the Academy of Marketing Science*, *28*(1), 55–66. doi:10.1177/0092070300281006

Shi, J., & Yip, L. (2007). Driving innovation and improving employee capability: The effects of customer knowledge sharing on CRM. *Business Review (Federal Reserve Bank of Philadelphia)*, *7*(1), 107–112.

Sin, L. Y. M., Tse, A. C. B., & Yim, F. H. K. (2005). CRM: Conceptualization and scale development. *European Journal of Marketing*, *39*(11-12), 1264–1290. doi:10.1108/03090560510623253

Slater, S. F., & Narver, J. C. (1995). Market orientation and the learning organization. *Journal of Marketing*, *59*(3), 63–74. doi:10.2307/1252120

Slater, S. F., & Narver, J. C. (1998). Customer-led and market-oriented: Let's not confuse the two. *Strategic Management Journal*, *19*(10), 1001–1006. doi:10.1002/(SICI)1097-0266(199810)19:10<1001::AID-SMJ996>3.0.CO;2-4

Smith, M., & Chang, C. (2010). Improving customer outcomes through the implementation of customer relationship management: Evidence from Taiwan. *Asian Review of Accounting*, *18*(3), 260–285. doi:10.1108/13217341011089658

Starkey, M. W., Williams, D., & Stone, M. (2002). The state of customer management performance in Malaysia. *Marketing Intelligence & Planning*, *20*(6), 378–385. doi:10.1108/02634500210445437

Stringfellow, A., Nie, W., & Bowen, D. (2004). CRM: Profiting from understanding customer needs. *Business Horizons*, *47*(5), 45–52. doi:10.1016/j.bushor.2004.07.008

Teo, T., Devadoss, P., & Pan, S. (2006). Towards a holistic perspective of customer relationship management (CRM) implementation: A case study of the Housing and Development Board, Singapore. *Decision Support Systems*, *42*(3), 1613–1627. doi:10.1016/j.dss.2006.01.007

Tsai, H. H. (2011). Research trends analysis by comparing data mining and customer relationship management through bibliometric methodology. *Scientometrics*, *87*(3), 425–450. doi:10.1007/s11192-011-0353-6

Turunen, T. T., & Toivonen, M. (2011). Organizing customer-oriented service business in manufacturing. *Operations Management Research*, *4*(1-2), 74–84. doi:10.1007/s12063-011-0047-5

Tuzhilin, A. (2012). Customer relationship management and Web mining: The next frontier. *Data Mining and Knowledge Discovery*, *24*(3), 584–612. doi:10.1007/s10618-012-0256-z

Verhoef, P. C., & Donkers, B. (2001). Predicting customer potential value: An application in the insurance industry. *Decision Support Systems*, *32*(2), 189–199. doi:10.1016/S0167-9236(01)00110-5

vom Berg, B. W., Valdés, A. R., Memari, A., Barakat, N., & Gómez, J. M. (2014). Customer segmentation based on compensatory fuzzy logic within a sustainability CRM for intermodal mobility. *Soft Computing for Business Intelligence: Studies in Computational Intelligence*, *537*, 415–429. doi:10.1007/978-3-642-53737-0_27

Webster, F. E. (2002). Marketing management in changing times. *Marketing Management*, *11*(1), 18–23.

Weigelt, C., & Miller, D. J. (2013). Implications of internal organization structure for firm boundaries. *Strategic Management Journal*, *34*(12), 1411–1434. doi:10.1002/smj.2074

Wilson, H., Daniel, E., & McDonald, M. (2002). Factors for success in customer relationship management (CRM) systems. *Journal of Marketing Management*, *18*(2), 193–219. doi:10.1362/0267257022775918

Woodcock, N., Stone, M., & Foss, B. (2003). *The customer management scorecard: Managing CRM for profit*. London, UK: Kogan Page.

Wulf, K., Odekerken-Schroder, G., & Iacobucci, D. (2001). Investments in consumer relationships: A cross-country and cross-industry exploration. *Journal of Marketing*, *65*(4), 33–50. doi:10.1509/jmkg.65.4.33.18386

Xu, M., & Walton, J. (2005). Gaining customer knowledge through analytical CRM. *Industrial Management & Data Systems*, *105*(7), 955–971. doi:10.1108/02635570510616139

Xu, Y., Yen, D. C., Lin, B., & Chou, D. C. (2002). Adopting customer relationship management technology. *Industrial Management & Data Systems*, *102*(8-9), 442–452. doi:10.1108/02635570210445871

Yao, Z., Sarlin, P., Eklund, T., & Back, B. (2014). Combining visual customer segmentation and response modeling. *Neural Computing & Applications*, *25*(1), 123–134. doi:10.1007/s00521-013-1454-3

Yim, F. H. K., Anderson, R. E., & Swaminathan, S. (2004). Customer relationship management: Its dimensions and effect on customer outcomes. *Journal of Personal Selling & Sales Management*, *24*(4), 263–278.

Zablah, A. R., Bellenger, D. N., & Johnston, W. J. (2004). An evaluation of divergent perspectives on customer relationship management: Towards a common understanding of an emerging phenomenon. *Industrial Marketing Management*, *33*(6), 475–489. doi:10.1016/j.indmarman.2004.01.006

Zahay, D., & Griffin, A. (2004). Customer learning processes, strategy selection, and performance in business-to-business service firms. *Decision Sciences*, *35*(2), 169–203. doi:10.1111/j.00117315.2004.02338.x

Zahra, S. A., & George, G. (2002). Absorptive capacity: A review, reconceptualization, and extension. *Academy of Management Review*, *27*(2), 185–203.

Zineldin, M. (2006). The royalty of loyalty: CRM, quality and retention. *Journal of Consumer Marketing*, *23*(7), 430–437. doi:10.1108/07363760610712975

Zwick, D., & Dholakia, N. (2004). Consumer subjectivity in the age of Internet: The radical concept of marketing control through customer relationship management. *Information and Organization*, *14*(3), 211–236. doi:10.1016/j.infoandorg.2004.01.002

ADDITIONAL READING

Abbasi, M. R., & Torkamani, M. (2010). Theoretical models of customer relationship management (CRM). *Business Survey*, *41*, 19–35.

Alam, A., Usman Arshad, M., & Adnan Shabbir, S. (2012). Brand credibility, customer loyalty and the role of religious orientation. *Asia Pacific Journal of Marketing and Logistics*, *24*(4), 583–598. doi:10.1108/13555851211259034

Awasthi, P., & Sangle, P. S. (2012). Adoption of CRM technology in multichannel environment: A review (2006-2010). *Business Process Management Journal*, *18*(3), 445–471. doi:10.1108/14637151211232641

Bakanauskas, A., & Jakutis, A. (2010). Customer value: Determination in undefined environment. *Management of Organizations: Systematic Research*, *53*, 7–18.

Beldi, A., Cheffi, W., & Dey, P. K. (2010). Managing customer relationship management projects: The case of a large French telecommunications company. *International Journal of Project Management*, *28*(4), 339–351. doi:10.1016/j.ijproman.2009.12.004

Bhatnagar, V., & Ranjan, J. (2010). Principles for successful mobile CRM in organizations from data mining perspective. *International Journal of Electronic Customer Relationship Management*, *4*(3), 280–301. doi:10.1504/IJECRM.2010.035967

Duran, R. E. (2010). Extending CRM with mobile messaging: A case study. *International Journal of Business Innovation and Research*, *4*(1-2), 15–29. doi:10.1504/IJBIR.2010.029538

Eskafi, M., hossein hosseini, S., & Mohammadzadeh Yazd, A. (2013). The value of telecom subscribers and customer relationship management. *Business Process Management Journal*, *19*(4), 737–748. doi:10.1108/BPMJ-Feb-2012-0016

Gneiser, M. S. (2010). Value-based CRM: The interaction of the triad of marketing, financial management, and IT. *Business & Information Systems Engineering*, *2*(2), 95–103. doi:10.1007/s12599-010-0095-7

Guo, X. M., Wei Hao, A., & Shang, X. (2011). Consumer perceptions of brand functions: An empirical study in China. *Journal of Consumer Marketing*, *28*(4), 269–279. doi:10.1108/07363761111143169

Haq, I. U., Ramay, M. I., Rehman, M. A. U., & Jam, F. A. (2010). Big five personality and perceived customer relationship management. *Research Journal of International Studies*, *15*, 37–45.

Jamali, R., Moshabaki, A., Aramoon, H., & Alimohammadi, A. (2013). Customer relationship management in electronic environment. *The Electronic Library*, *31*(1), 119–130. doi:10.1108/02640471311299173

Jean, R. B., Sinkovics, R. R., & Kim, D. (2010). Drivers and performance outcomes of relationship learning for suppliers in cross-border customer–supplier relationships: The role of communication culture. *Journal of International Marketing*, *18*(1), 63–85. doi:10.1509/jimk.18.1.63

Jung Choo, H., Moon, H., Kim, H., & Yoon, N. (2012). Luxury customer value. *Journal of Fashion Marketing and Management*, *16*(1), 81–101. doi:10.1108/13612021211203041

Kassim, N., & Asiah Abdullah, N. (2010). The effect of perceived service quality dimensions on customer satisfaction, trust, and loyalty in e-commerce settings: A cross cultural analysis. *Asia Pacific Journal of Marketing and Logistics*, *22*(3), 351–371. doi:10.1108/13555851011062269

Kim, S. (2010). Assessment on security risks of customer relationship management systems. *International Journal of Software Engineering and Knowledge Engineering*, *20*(1), 103–109. doi:10.1142/S0218194010004591

Komunda, M., & Osarenkhoe, A. (2012). Remedy or cure for service failure? Effects of service recovery on customer satisfaction and loyalty. *Business Process Management Journal*, *18*(1), 82–103. doi:10.1108/14637151211215028

Liao, N. N. H., & Wu, T. C. H. (2009). The pivotal role of trust in customer loyalty, empirical research on the system integration market in Taiwan. *The Business Review, Cambridge*, *12*(2), 277–384.

Lukkari, P. (2011). Merger: Institutional interplay with customer relationship management. *Management Research Review*, *34*(1), 17–33. doi:10.1108/01409171111096450

Mainela, T., & Ulkuniemi, P. (2013). Personal interaction and customer relationship management in project business. *Journal of Business and Industrial Marketing*, *28*(2), 103–110. doi:10.1108/08858621311295245

Maklan, S., & Knox, S. (2009). Dynamic capabilities: The missing link in CRM investments. *European Journal of Marketing*, *43*(11), 1392–1410. doi:10.1108/03090560910989957

Munnukka, J., & Järvi, P. (2012). The price-category effect and the formation of customer value of high-tech products. *Journal of Consumer Marketing*, *29*(4), 293–301. doi:10.1108/07363761211237362

Osarenkhoe, A. (2009). The business culture of a firm applying a customer-intimate philosophy: A conceptual framework. *International Journal of Business and Systems Research*, *3*(3), 257–278. doi:10.1504/IJBSR.2009.026183

Padmavathy, C., Balaji, M. S., & Sivakumar, V. J. (2012). Measuring effectiveness of customer relationship management in Indian retail banks. *International Journal of Bank Marketing*, *30*(4), 246–266. doi:10.1108/02652321211236888

Ranjan, J., & Bhatnagar, V. (2010). Information security-enabled business process architecture for mobile CRM: The role of technology, planning, training and process. *International Journal of Networking and Virtual Organizations*, *7*(5), 452–464. doi:10.1504/IJNVO.2010.034924

Varela-Neira, C., Vazquez-Casielles, R., & Iglesias, V. (2010). Explaining customer satisfaction with complaint handling. *International Journal of Bank Marketing*, *28*(2), 88–112. doi:10.1108/02652321011018305

KEY TERMS AND DEFINITIONS

Customer Focus: An orientation of an organization toward serving its clients' needs.

Customer Relationship Management (CRM): A management philosophy according to which the company's goal can be best achieved through identification and satisfaction of the customers' stated and unstated requirement.

Customer Retention: An assessment of the product or service quality provided by a business that measures how loyal its customers are.

Customer Satisfaction: A degree of satisfaction provided by the goods or services of a company as measured by the number of repeat customers.

Information System (IS): A combination of hardware, software, infrastructure and trained personnel organized to facilitate planning, control, coordination, and decision making in an organization.

Information Technology (IT): A set of tools, processes, methodologies and associated equipment employed to collect, process, and present information.

Knowledge Management (KM): The strategies and processes designed to identify, capture, structure, value, leverage, and share an organization's intellectual assets to enhance its performance and competitiveness.

Organization: A social unit of people that is structured and managed to meet a requirement or to pursue collective goals.

Organizational Performance: An analysis of a company's performance as compared to goals and objectives.

Chapter 8
Data-Driven Customer Centricity:
CRM Predictive Analytics

Othman Boujena
Neoma Business School, France

Kristof Coussement
IESEG School of Management, France

Koen W. de Bock
IESEG School of Management, France

ABSTRACT

Customer relationship management (CRM) is becoming a very hot topic nowadays in academia and business environments. Indeed, companies are constantly searching for new innovative ways to create or maintain their competitive advantage. Due to the recent advances in Internet and technology, CRM predictive analytics is becoming an important tool in the toolset of the marketer. It is the practice of using the huge volumes of historical customer data to predict future customer behavior. This chapter introduces the reader to the shift towards a data-driven customer centricity approach, where marketers act upon what they know, rather than upon what they think.

INTRODUCTION

Within an economic context characterized by high competition and globalization, companies are investing in customer relationship management (CRM) to increase satisfaction and ensure loyalty. This priority is in line with the shift that marketing paradigm experienced from transactional or traditional approach to relationship one (Grönroos, 1995; Gummesson, 1997). In other words, the challenge is not any more on simply selling or converting customers but on developing value creating relationships. For a long time, achieving sales was the unique success indicator of marketing initiatives. This change in customer marketing is related to different factors like markets' evolution, the limited approach of 4P's that seems

DOI: 10.4018/978-1-4666-8459-1.ch008

to ignore the human dimension of marketing, the degree to which the 4P's could be replicated in different business models related to services or retailing and the development of marketing as a science and function within companies.

From theoretical point of view, relationship marketing (RM) refers to strategies and initiatives dedicated to the development and maintaining of long term and win-win relationships with customers. This definition covers some main elements like interactivity, time perspective and mutual benefits. Compared with previous dominant models, this approach is more focusing on demand and empathy. However, RM is not supposed to be only oriented toward the final customer but should consider other stakeholders that play a critical role in the success of company's marketing and strategy. For example, retailers have the opportunity to interact directly with customers by selling products and providing some services. Consequently, companies should develop strong relationships with their retailers given their strategic role in the chain.

As far as the difference between RM and CRM is concerned, CRM is simply considered as RM that uses technology for managing and interacting with customers. Even, CRM is also used in managerial context to describe technological solutions dedicated to customers' management.

While many CRM projects (70% on average) fail or do not manage to reach objectives, many academic calls are made to consider CRM first as a company strategy and orientation (Zablah, Bellenger, & Johnston, 2004). In fact, the decision to focus on the customer and align all processes for better satisfaction and loyalty should be a corporate and top management willingness and initiative. The way the company shape and implement customer management is supposed to be consistent with the brand DNA. In other words, the company must start from its business model, the claim and positioning of its brand to integrate customers' expectations and value creation mechanisms before designing the CRM strategy. According to Payne and Frow (2005), CRM is "an initiative that unites the potential of relationship marketing strategies and IT to create profitable, long-term relationships with customers and other key stakeholders. It provides enhanced opportunities to use data and information to both understand customers and cocreate value with them''.

Thus, CRM contribute to profitable relationships thanks to better customer knowledge that is enabled by data and information processing. This cycle is mainly facilitated by technology functionalities through the improvement of information collection, storage and diffusion processes. In general, CRM has three components: (1) organizational or strategic, (2) analytical and (3) operational as indicated in the Figure 1.

The strategic component of CRM refers to company's philosophy and approach of relationship marketing. It is about corporate culture, vision and employees' involvement in the process. The analytical component is related to the strategic usage of customer data to better understand, model and predict market responses. At this level, information can be related to customer identification or customer behavior. Finally, the operational level covers marketing automation (leads and marketing campaigns monitoring), sales force automation (SFA) (set of applications dedicated to help the sales force in its daily tasks and accounts' management) and service automation (front office interaction and after sale service through call centers or other channels).

Based on previous indications, it seems clear that the essence of developing relationships with customers relies on the capacity of companies in terms of favoring and building reliable knowledge. According to Day (1994), customer knowledge generation and market sensing are prerequisites for reaching customer satisfaction and customer value. Customer knowledge could be the result of internal processing of customer and market data but could also come from customers themselves (García-Murillo, Annabi, &

Figure 1. CRM components

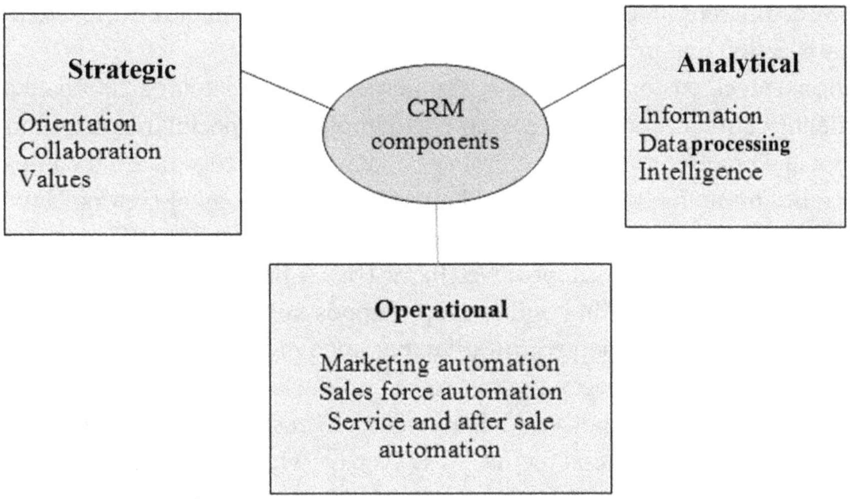

Correspondence, 2002). Nowadays, many companies use social media as a virtual space to interact with customers and collect valuable data about propositions, service evaluation or suggestions for innovation. Thus, the process of building profitable relationships goes through interactions with customers in order to gain a better and progressive understanding of changing needs, expectations and decision heuristics. Monitoring these interactions for intelligence reasons should take into account generated perceptions and emotions toward the company and/or the brand according to customer experience management principles. In fact, all customers' interactions with brand through the different touch points are supposed to convey a similar image to maintain the relationship.

Thanks to its structure, CRM implies the existence of a centralized data base that gathers marketing and customer information and makes it available and accessible for different partners within the company. Data users may be from marketing, sales or other departments like supply chain or finance. Technology facilitates functions integration within the company to provide a coherent face to the final customer. Many studies emphasized the positive impact of CRM at the organizational level but also operational level in terms of satisfaction, loyalty, processes effectiveness, sales cycle and prospection activities' optimization (Jayachandran, Sharma, Kaufman, & Raman, 2005).

However, the degree to which companies master customer knowledge capacities and processes depends on their stage in terms of CRM implementation cycle. Some companies are still facing many challenges to adopt CRM and make people use it while others come to deal with big data issues. Thus companies should find the virtuous cycle linking collection and analysis of customer data with organizational capacities and relationship management. This task is made complicated given channels multiplication online and offline and customer responses. Consequently, company's approach of knowledge should take into account the customer which should be the focus.

The idea of considering the customer at the center of all decisions and processes is not new in marketing. It is only about the famous "marketing concept''. Therefore, the idea is to align organizations on customer expectations and objectives seeking for satisfaction and loyalty. Customer experience should be designed in a way that ensures strong relationship and differentiated interactions. For this reason, the concept of customer centricity emerged during the last years and seems to represent one of the main priorities for many companies. It refers to a set of initiatives related to aligning organization and processes with customer satisfaction and profitability.

At the operational level, customer centricity implies an analytical approach of data allowing the segmentation and identification of profitable customers to implement special treatment initiatives for them. Thus, as a concept and practice customer centricity is not widely diffused within companies. In fact, the implementation relies on many organizational, human and technological factors. However, some good examples are generally mentioned as success stories in terms of operationalizing customer centricity. It is the case for companies like IBM, Zappos, Netflix or BBVA bank.

For example, as a shoe and clothing online shop, Zappos hold a mission of delivering happiness to customers. The company is then oriented toward experience provided to customers and integrates the emotional consequences related to receiving purchased products. Furthermore, Zappos relies on different levers mainly (1) involved and motivated employees, (2) customized and empowering services and (3) customer intelligence through social media. Also, Netflix which is a company providing on-demand Internet streaming media represents a business model that mobilizes internet for an optimized and empowered interaction with customers. The online interface is a valuable source of data on customers, their preferences, purchases records, etc. that is used by Netflix to better understand and then satisfy profitable customers. The capacity of identifying customer journey over channels and tracking shopping activities makes the customer moves from a source of discrete transactions to a continuous element changing through a life cycle.

Consequently, implementation of customer centricity is generally related to a better monitoring of customer lifetime value (CLV). In marketing, CLV refers to an estimation method consisting of predicting the net profit related to the whole future relationships with a customer. This approach allows contrasting expenses dedicated to acquiring customers with value provided by the customers through transactions. It is an economic analysis of relationships profitability that is supposed to identify the most valuable customers.

From CRM point of view, customer knowledge is the result of process starting from raw data which allows the identification of information which is converted to meaningful knowledge thanks to data mining. Generated knowledge is then supposed to be used as a relevant source for strategic and operational decision making and then value proposition. For this reason, customer knowledge is critical in sense it may influence many organizational initiatives.

As far as data management is concerned, researchers identified three different ways of using good quality information by companies: (1) data indicating how well the company is doing (sales amount, turnover, profits, etc.) and which is collected on a continuous basis, (2) data about markets (including customers) and environment and (3) functional data related to operations (prices, suppliers, etc.).

In addition to corporate, human and technological factors necessary for generating and monitoring knowledge, analytics methods are crucial in the process. In fact, company's capacity of capturing customers' behaviors and responses functions hinges on the degree to which adopted methods are adequate. One approach consists of examining the past to explain the future. This method generally relies on previous records of customer data. The other approach analyzes real time data through modeling and predictive methods. Thus, data set (declarative or behavioral) and methods will depend on decision type, customer life cycle and aroused questions in terms of CRM. For example, different approaches of data mining will be applied for marketing campaigns monitoring depending on the type of operations: acquisition, cross or up selling or retention campaigns.

To summarize, CRM is mainly about company strategy and practice relying on capacities in terms of customer knowledge. Analytical side of CRM seems to play a critical role in reflecting customer centricity through better understanding and treatment of profitable customers. At this level, predictive methods are important to reveal purchase patterns and customer behavior models.

PREDICTIVE ANALYTICS METHODS

A cornerstone of customer-centric marketing is predictive modeling, a part of analytical customer relationship management (CRM). Predictive modeling is the process of converting information from the customer database to consumer knowledge and insights by building and employing consumer prediction models (Blattberg, Kim, & Neslin, 2008). The predictive modeling process is intuitively easy: it uses past customer behavior information to predict future consumer behavior at the individual level. A prediction model links the customer information with future consumer behavior. Several predictive modeling applications are well studied in academia and practiced in a business environment. Table 1 provides a brief overview of the different applications along the customer life cycle, the most important of which are response modeling and churn prediction.

The purpose of predictive modeling is to target customers at the individual level. For example, churn prediction helps assign churn probability to a customer—that is, identifying whether the customer will end his or her relationship with the company. With this process, the firm can rank customers from highest to lowest probability to churn and accordingly develop retention programs to target these customers. This practice of targeted marketing actions is almost always better than random targeting (Burez & Van den Poel, 2007), because even slight changes in the retention rate can boost the company's profitability (Lariviere & Van den Poel, 2005).

Two key strategies help improve the quality of the prediction model. On the one hand, the marketing analyst could search information that captures a 360-degree view on the customer. Today, in addition to traditional transactional information, such as recency, frequency, and monetary value and socio-

Table 1. Overview of the different predictive modeling applications in the marketing domain

Customer Life Cycle	Customer acquisition	Prospect conversion	The process of managing customer prospects and inquiries to extend the current customer base.
	Customer development	Cross-selling	The task of selling additional products or services to existing customers to extend their current product portfolio.
		Up-selling	The task of extending/replacing existing products in a customer's product portfolio with an upscale extension/version; also referred to as NPTB (next-product-to-buy) modeling.
		Lifetime value modeling	The process of estimating the present value of future cash flows that a customer will generate according to the customer's relationship with the firm.
		Response modeling	The process of sending out targeted mailings to increase the response rate of catalog campaigns.
	Customer retention	Churn prediction	The process of identifying whether a customer will leave the company.
		Re-activation modeling	The process of activating "sleeping" customers or recapturing lost customers from the database.

demographic information, companies can use textual customer information such as client/company information (Coussement & Van den Poel, 2008b, 2009), website behavior information (Van den Poel & Buckinx, 2005), and social network information (Martens & Provost, 2011) to boost the quality of the prediction models. On the other hand, the marketing analyst could choose between different types of prediction models to optimize the prediction of future behavior. We investigate two types of algorithms: *single prediction methods* and *ensemble learners*. The latter combines the outcomes from various single prediction methods using an aggregation scheme, such as averaging aggregation into one final prediction.

In the remainder of this section, we examine the most popular single prediction methods—namely, logistic regression, generalized additive models, and decision trees—and ensemble learners. We explain these from a binary classification perspective, in which the analyst attempts to predict whether the customer will adopt some type of behavior, such as churn/no churn, response/no response, buy/no buy, etc.

Single Prediction Methods

Logistic Regression

Logistic regression is best explained from the popular generalized linear modeling framework, given as

$$E(Y) = \mu = h(X'\beta) \quad (1)$$

where Y is the customer behavior or dependent variable and E(Y) represents the expected value of Y; X'β is a linear combination of the data with the customer information summarized in X' and unknown parameters β, which we estimate; and h is a function that links the customer information to the customer behavior. As equation (1) shows, each outcome of the dependent variable Y is assumed to be generated from a particular distribution function. When the responses Y are binary (e.g. whether a customer's response is yes or no), the distribution function is the binomial distribution, and the interpretation of μ_i is then the probability, p_i, of Y_i taking on the value of one (i.e. customer i responded to the mailing). A logistic regression model is then obtained by applying the logit link function by

$$\text{logit}\{P(X)\} \equiv \log\left\{\frac{P(X)}{1-P(X)}\right\} = \alpha + \sum_{j=1}^{p} \beta_j^{'} X_j \quad (2)$$

where P(X) equals the probability that Y = 1 or the customer responded to the mailing given his/her characteristics. The parameter vector β is estimated from observations (y,x), usually by maximizing the likelihood function. More technical details on logistic regression appear in Hosmer and Lemeshow's (2000) book.

Logistic regression is a popular classification technique in several marketing-related predictive modeling settings, such as churn prediction (Coussement & Van den Poel, 2008a) and response modeling (Baesens, Viaene, Van den Poel, Vanthienen, & Dedene, 2002). Advantages of this technique include its ability to predict performance effectively (Coussement & Van den Poel, 2008a), its ease of use (Neslin, Gupta, Kamakura, Lu, & Mason, 2006), its capability to deliver justifiable and comprehensible prediction models, its availability in traditional software packages (e.g. SAS, IBM Modeler), and its capability to deliver closed-form posterior probabilities (Hosmer & Lemeshow, 2000).

Generalized Additive Models

A popular alternative to logistic regression is generalized additive models (GAMs). The GAM has proved superior in performance to logistic regression in a churn prediction setting (Coussement, Benoit, & Van den Poel, 2009). Compared with logistic regression, GAMs remove the linearity constraint and fit the data in a non-parametric way. In other words, the data themselves form the functional relationship between the customer characteristics and the customer behavior (Hastie & Tibshirani, 1986, 1990).

Assume that Y is the binary variable with a target label equal to 1 if the customer churned and 0 otherwise and that $X_1, X_2, \ldots, X_p$ summarize the customer behavior in a set of independent variables. Then, GAMs generalize the logistic regression principle by replacing the linear predictor $\sum_{j=1}^{p} \beta_j X_j$ in equation (2) with an additive component, where

$$\text{logit}\{P(X)\} \equiv \log\left\{\frac{P(X)}{1-P(X)}\right\} = \alpha + \sum_{j=1}^{p} s_j(X_j) \tag{3}$$

and $s_1(.), s_2(.), \ldots, s_p(.)$ are smooth functions. The most common smooth functions are smoothing splines for $s_1(.), s_2(.), \ldots, s_p(.)$ to estimate the non-parametric trend for the dependence of the logit on $X_1, X_2, \ldots, X_p$. A smoothing spline is the smooth (often) non-linear line through a set of noisy observations. Technically, a smoothing spline solves the following optimization problem: among all functions $\eta(x)$ with continuous second-order derivatives, find the function that minimizes the penalized residual sum of squares

$$\sum_{i=1}^{n} (y_i - \eta(x_i))^2 + \lambda \int_a^b (\eta''(t))^2 dt \tag{4}$$

where λ is a fixed constant and $a \leq x_1 \leq x_2 \leq \ldots \leq x_n \leq b$. Equation 4 consists of two parts. The first part is the goodness of fit, and the second part is a penalty term that penalizes curvature in the function by the smoothing parameter λ. The complexity of $\eta(x)$ is measured by λ and is inversely related to the degrees of freedom (df). If λ is small (i.e. the df are large), $\eta(x)$ is any function that allows an interpolation of the data; if λ is large (i.e. the df are small), $\eta(x)$ is closely related to a simple least squares fit. Literature suggests using the generalized cross-validation procedure to determine a good λ value (Wahba, 1990). However, several database marketing–related studies (e.g. Coussement et al. (2009)) follow Hastie et al.'s (2001) recommendation to use a λ corresponding to four degrees of freedom, because these authors find that a small number of degrees of freedom fits most data sets well. For more details on GAMs, refer to the work of Hastie and Tibshirani (1986, 1990) and Hastie et al. (2001).

GAMs have become popular tools in database marketing. First, they inject flexibility in the modeling process to better reconstruct the complex relationship between the customer information and the customer behavior, resulting in better prediction performance (Coussement et al., 2009) Second, statistically speaking, non-parametric methods perform worse when the number of independent variables increases, because the sparseness of the data inflates the variance of the estimates. This is often the case with predictive modeling in a database marketing setting, in which a great deal of customer information is typically tracked and stored in the transactional database. This problem is known as the "curse of dimensionality." However, GAMs avoid this problem, because additive models help approximate the multivariate regression function. Third, Coussement et al. (2009) show that GAMs deliver additional insight into the relationship between the customer information and the churn behavior. They show four different relationships: the U trend, the inverted U trend, the quasi-exponential trend, and the undefined, complex relationship. The main drawback of employing a GAM in a large-scale predictive modeling setting characterized by a large number of customer indicators is the excessive running time.

Decision Trees

In contrast with logistic regression and GAMs, decision trees are a predictive modeling technique that belongs to the stream of data-mining non-statistical techniques. Decision trees are popularly used in a variety of business setting, including to maximize online panel response rates (Neslin, Novak, Baker, & Hoffman, 2009) and to profile web user behavior for user identification (Yang, 2010). Murthy (1998) finds that more than 300 academic references employ decision trees, including recent applications in churn prediction (Neslin et al., 2006) and response modeling (McCarty & Hastak, 2007). The process of decision tree building is straightforward. A decision tree consists of a set of rules that divide a customer data set that is heterogeneous in terms of the dependent variable into smaller, more homogeneous sets of customers. The method is best explained by its construction phase. In this phase, all customers enter the decision tree at the start or root node at the top of the decision tree. This node runs a test that assigns customers to one of the lower-level or child nodes. The test is a logical question formulated in terms of the independent variable, chosen in such a way that it discriminates maximally between the levels of the dependent variable—for example, buyers and non-buyers. The result of the test determines which variable is used to split the root node into the lower-level child nodes. This process is repeated for subsequent child nodes until a terminal or leaf node is reached when the tree is fully grown or when the test no longer delivers significant splits. During prediction, the collection of unique paths between the root node and the leaf nodes makes up the rules used to generate predictions. All customers from the data set reaching the same leaf node receive the same prediction probability. Three popular decision trees are CHAID, CART, and C4.5.

- CHAID, or chi-square automatic interaction detection, is one of the most well-known decision tree algorithms in direct marketing (McCarty and Hastak (2007). Initially introduced by Kass (1980), CHAID builds decision trees in which more than two branches can be attached to a single node. These decision trees are called "non-binary decision trees." The name CHAID means that the chi-square test determines the next best split at each step in the tree. The tree stops growing when the chi-square test at the split at the lower step of the tree is no longer significant.
- In contrast with CHAID, CART, which stands for classification and regression trees (Breiman, Friedman, Olshen, & Stone, 1984; Steinberg & Colla, 1998), always splits the parent nodes into exactly two child nodes. The CART algorithm uses the GINI impurity index as the quality-of-split criterion. This means that the lower the GINI measure, the more homogeneous the distribution of the dependent variable is. The best split of a particular node has a GINI of zero, meaning that the variable perfectly separates the customers according to the levels of the dependent variable.

Technically speaking, for a response setting, if p_1 (p_0) is the proportion of responders (non-responders) to a mailing in node t with $p_1 = 1 - p_0$, the GINI impurity index (GI) in a binary classification setting is

$$GI = 1 - p_1^2 - p_0^2 \quad (5)$$

The best split is the one that maximizes the decrease in the GINI impurity measure between node t and the partitioned child nodes t_l and t_r,

$$\Delta(t,s) = G_{It} - p_l\, GI_{tl} - p_r\, GI_{tr} \quad (6)$$

where $\Delta(t,s)$ is the decrease in impurity using the splitting rule s; p_l and p_r are the probabilities of a customer going left and right; and GI_t, GI_{tl}, and GI_{tr} are GINI impurities of nodes t, t_l, and t_r. The tree is maximally grown and pruned by minimizing the loss of predictive accuracy (Breiman et al., 1984; Steinberg & Colla, 1998).

- Quinlan (1993) introduces another algorithm for decision tree induction called C4.5. C4.5 induces decision trees using the concept of gain ratio. Gain ratio is calculated as the reduction in entropy—or the measure of uncertainty—by splitting a node. For example, at the root node, it is highly uncertain to which group of the dependent variable a particular customer belongs; in contrast, the lower on the decision tree, the more homogeneous the customer groups become, and thus assigning a particular customer to one or the other group is more certain. C4.5 favors splits with the largest gain ratio—that is, the highest decrease in entropy. The tree is fully grown, and the pruning strategy is executed retrospectively (Quinlan, 1993).

Decision trees are popular techniques in predictive modeling because of their simplicity and transparency (Duda, Hart, & D.G., 2001). Their main drawback is that they are often not robust to changes in the data set, which often results in a loss in prediction performance. However, decision trees are considered the most popular single prediction method used in various types of ensemble learners, because they can inject diversity in the ensemble when small changes are enforced in the customer data set.

Ensemble Learners

Ensemble learning has received considerable attention in applied statistics (e.g. Ahn et al. (2007)), machine learning (e.g. Breiman (2001)), and pattern recognition (e.g. H. C. Kim, Pang, Je, Kim, and Bang (2003)) during the past 10 years. The rationale of ensemble learning is as follows: to achieve improved performance, models for supervised (e.g. classification, regression) or unsupervised (e.g. clustering) learning can benefit from combining several methods instead of focusing on just one. As such, ensemble classifiers, or multiple classifier systems (MCS), are a combination of many constituent member classification models, in which aggregate ensemble predictions are taken as combinations of the ensemble member outputs (Kuncheva & Rodríguez, 2007). The main factor defining the popularity of ensemble classification is the strong classification or ranking performance appearing in multiple comparative studies in various domains and applications (Bauer & Kohavi, 1999; Dietterich, 2000).

An ensemble improves classification performance over the individual classifier if accuracy and diversity are present among the ensemble members. That is, the constituent models need to have a certain level of expertise, and a certain level of disagreement must emerge among the ensemble members. Many different ensemble classifier algorithms have been proposed with varying strategies to maintain member accuracy and diversity. Most algorithms can be explained as configurations of the generic structure in Figure 2. Ensemble classifiers broadly differ along three structural dimensions of ensemble design: (1) the choice of the base classifier, (2) the treatment of the input training data, and (3) the aggregation strategy for the base classifiers. First, two broad strategies help identify the members of an ensemble. In hybrid ensembles, different types of algorithms are combined (e.g. Yu, Zhou, and Ting (2007)), while in non-hybrid ensembles, one classifier algorithm is chosen as the base classifier and replicated multiple times to obtain an ensemble (e.g. Breiman, 1996, 2001).

Second, many algorithms differ in terms of the treatment of the training data, used as input for each base classifier. Possibilities include data sampling schemes (e.g. Breiman (1996)), variable selection (e.g. (Ho, 1998)), or more complex data transformations (e.g. Kuncheva and Rodríguez 2007; Rodriguez and Kuncheva 2006). A third important element of any ensemble classifier algorithm is the fusion rule, used to aggregate ensemble members' outputs to ensemble predictions. A categorization between fusion rules for label outputs and fusion rules for continuous outputs is often made (Kuncheva, 2004). A well-studied and simple combiner is plurality voting, for example, implemented by default in bagging and random forest. The random subspace method (RSM) and GAMens implement average aggregation (sometimes referred to as the "mean combination rule"), which takes the average of the ensemble members' outputs. For both average aggregation and majority voting, weights can be assigned to ensemble members that score higher on a performance metric of choice to obtain weighted majority voting or weighted average aggregation (Kuncheva, 2004). Training error rates are often used as weights, but other metrics such as AUC, lift, or misclassification cost can be used as well. De Bock and Van den Poel (2010) conduct an experiment on the use of alternative weighting schemes in fusion rules in the context of churn prediction.

Figure 2. Generic ensemble classifier structure

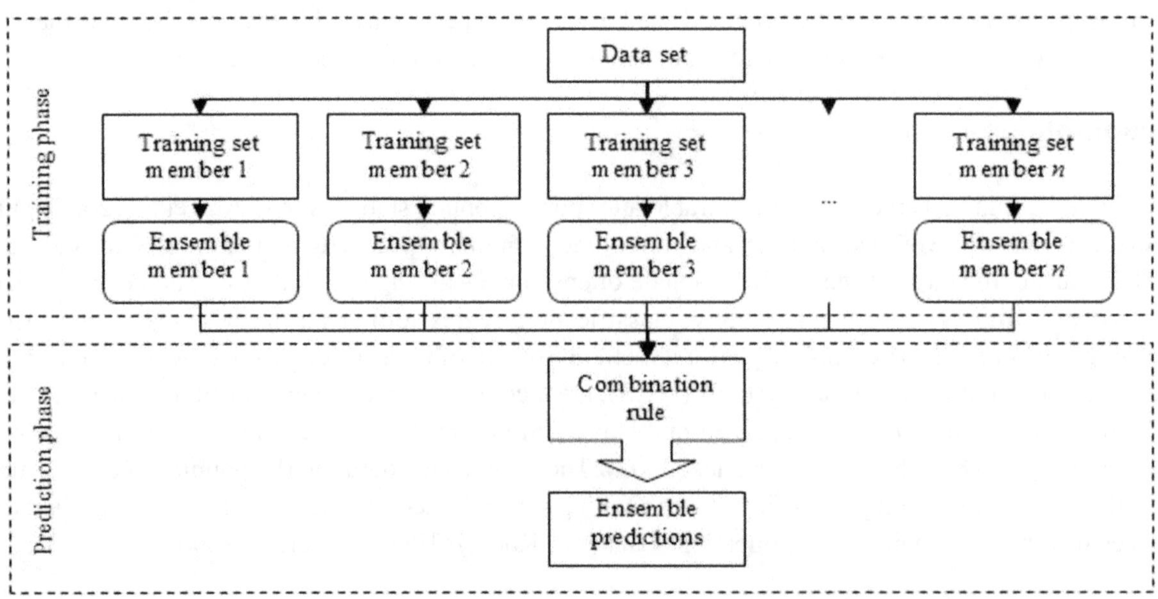

Algorithms

The most popular classifier ensemble schemes are non-hybrid and thus apply a base classification algorithm to differently permutated training sets. They are categorized into two classical ensemble schemes: bagging and boosting. *Bagging*, an acronym of bootstrap aggregation, was introduced by Breiman (Breiman, 1996). Although many variations have been proposed since its introduction (e.g. Bauer & Kohavi, 1999; Buhlmann, 2002), Breiman's original implementation is still a widely used ensemble classifier. It manipulates the training data using bootstrap sampling. Practically, to train a member of the ensemble, a bootstrap sample (with replacement) is drawn from an original training set. The bagged classifier is then obtained by means of majority voting of the individual classifiers' predictions. Theoretically, bootstrapping can induce significant differences in the constructed individual classifiers, which significantly improves the accuracy of the single classifier (Breiman, 1996).

Boosting has several variations (e.g. Merler, Caprile, & Furlanello, 2007; Zhang & Zhang, 2008), but its main idea can be traced back to the first practical boosting algorithm, *adaboost* (Freund & Schapire, 1997). In adaboost, each base classifier is trained either on reweighted versions of the training data, obtained by applying different weights, or on a resampled version of the training data, obtained from a sampling probability distribution to each of the training observations. During each iteration, the classifier is forced to concentrate on training observations that are difficult to predict correctly. When the maximum number of iterations is reached, predictions from all classifiers are combined through a weighted majority vote to produce the final classifier. Software implementations of bagging and adaboost are now present in most data-mining packages, such as WEKA (Frank, Holmes, Pfahringer, Reutemann, & Witten, 2009), R (Alfaro, Gámez, & García, 2006), and SAS Enterprise Miner.

As noted previously, in general diversity among member classifiers is a key driver of ensemble performance (Kuncheva & Whitaker, 2003). Several variations on the bagging and boosting methods have been proposed to further improve performance through an increase in diversity. Two popular strategies are (1) variations in training data and (2) the use of alternative base classifier algorithms. First, many studies have demonstrated the impact of variations of the input data used for the training of base classifiers. A related method to bagging is the RSM (Ho, 1998), also known as "attribute bagging" (Bryll, Gutierrez-Osuna, & Quek, 2003). In RSM, a random feature subset is sampled for the training of an ensemble member. Breiman (2001) combines bagging and a form of RSM in random forests. A random forest is an ensemble classifier that consists of randomized CART decision trees, in which bagging is combined with a random feature selection at each tree node. A software implementation of this algorithm is included in the randomForest R package (Liaw & Wiener, 2002). A closely related ensemble classifier is provided by Panov and Dzeroski (2007), who find that *subbag*, a combination of bagging and ordinary RSM, performs comparably to random forests. More recently, Rodriguez and Kuncheva (2006) proposed the *rotation forest*, an ensemble classifier based on rotations of the feature space using principal component analysis (PCA). Practically, a forest of decision trees is constructed in each iteration, the training set is divided into subsets, and PCA is applied to each subset. The purpose of a rotation forest is to increase the individual classifier performance and the diversity within the ensemble. Diversity is achieved for each classifier by applying feature extraction, while performance is increased by using all principal components and training the model on the entire data set. More details and the pseudo code for the algorithm appear in Rodriguez and Kuncheva's study (2006).

A second strategy to increase diversity among ensemble members is to vary or alter the base classifier algorithm. Many studies have proposed ensembles based on artificial neural networks (Hansen &

Salamon, 1990; Maclin & Shavlik, 1995; Opitz & Shavlik, 1995; Schwenk & Bengio, 2000) or support vector machines (H. C. Kim, Pang, Je, Kim, & Bang, 2002; H. C. Kim et al., 2003). Statistical regression techniques have also been used as base classifiers in ensemble settings. Finally, De Bock et al. (2010a) present GAMs as base classifiers in ensemble learners. Three algorithm variations (based on bagging, the RSM, and both) are proposed and compared. An experimental comparison reveals a significant increase of performance over decision tree–based equivalent algorithms. For a software implementation of this algorithms, refer to De Bock et al.'s (2010b) study.

Applications to Customer Intelligence

As noted previously, the classification technique used to create a predictive model in customer-centric marketing has a direct impact on the prediction quality and, thus, on the profitability of all subsequent marketing efforts to sustain customer retention, customer development, or customer acquisition (Neslin et al., 2006). Motivated by the suggested increase in classification performance, ensemble learning has received significant attention in analytical CRM literature during the past decade and especially in literature on churn prediction (De Bock & Van den Poel, 2011).

The first applications of ensemble learning to the prediction of customer churn emerged in data-mining and operational research–oriented journals at the beginning of the 21st century. For example, Mozer et al. (2000) conducted experiments on U.S. mobile carrier data and found that boosting was a viable strategy to improve the predictive performance of decision trees and neural networks. Hu (2005) found additional evidence of the potential of ensemble learning. Experiments on data from a financial services company compared a decision tree, a selective Bayesian network, and a neural network with two ensemble learning strategies (i.e. a boosted naive Bayesian network and a hybrid ensemble learner consisting of all benchmarked algorithms) and found that the ensemble learning strategy improved performance.

In their reference work, Lemmens and Croux (2006) introduced the use of ensemble learning to predict customer churn into the marketing literature stream. They compared logistic regression with two prominent strategies–namely, bagging and (stochastic gradient) boosting—to create non-hybrid ensembles of decision trees for an anonymous U.S. wireless telecom operator. Their results demonstrated that both ensemble learning algorithms significantly outperformed logistic regression. In another application of ensemble learning, Kim (2006) constructed non-hybrid ensemble learners of neural networks and logistic regression models using an adapted version of bagging, in which ensemble members are trained on random samples taken without replacement and with a size equal to half the number of instances in the calibration data set. Glady et al. (2009) created cost-sensitive churn prediction models based on customers' expected lifetime value using the adacost algorithm, a variant of adaboost. Finally, De Bock and Van den Poel (2011) conducted experiments on the use of rotation-based ensemble learners, transforming the input data of the ensemble members using feature extraction. They demonstrated favorable performance of this new approach over existing ensemble learners and single classifiers.

A popular non-hybrid ensemble classification algorithm that has received a great deal of attention in customer churn prediction is random forests. Larivière and Van den Poel (2005) introduced this ensemble learner to the churn prediction domain. Using data from a European financial services company, they found that random forests demonstrated superior prediction performance to logistic regression. Ample churn prediction research also shows that random forests outperform single classifiers in a pay television setting (Burez & Van den Poel, 2007, 2008) and in the newspaper publishing industry (Coussement &

Van den Poel, 2008a, 2009). However, in a fast-moving consumer goods retail setting, Buckinx and Van den Poel (2005) could not confirm the superiority of random forests to logistic regression and automatic relevance detection (ARD) neural networks. Prior research has also indicated that random forests are particularly suitable to deal with class imbalance, a frequently encountered issue in customer churn prediction. Burez and Van den Poel (2009) demonstrated that weighted random forests are superior in the presence of class imbalance. Xie et al. (2009) modified the random forest algorithm to be more robust to this problem. Their improved balanced random forests (IBRF) algorithm introduces cost-sensitive learning by iteratively altering the class distribution and increasing the importance of misclassified observations belonging to the minority class. Their experiments on data from a Chinese bank demonstrated performance improvements over conventional random forests and a selection of single classifiers.

Finally, two related applications of ensemble methods in analytical CRM are present in cross-sell analysis. Van Wezel and Potharst (2007) compared several classification algorithms in the construction of next-product-to-buy (NPTB) models. Although they observed no dominance of any method, ensemble methods consistently outperformed individual classifiers. Prinzie and Van den Poel (2008) proposed a novel ensemble classifier for multi-class classification, the random multinomial logit (RMNL), and applied it to NPTB modeling.

REFERENCES

Ahn, H., Moon, H., Fazzari, M. J., Lim, N., Chen, J. J., & Kodell, R. L. (2007). Classification by ensembles from random partitions of high-dimensional data. *Computational Statistics & Data Analysis*, *51*(12), 6166–6179. doi:10.1016/j.csda.2006.12.043

Alfaro, E., Gámez, M., & García, N. (2006). adabag: Applies Adaboost.M1 and Bagging.

Bühlmann, P. (2002, Jul 15-19). *Bagging, subagging and Bragging for improving some prediction algorithms*. Paper presented at the International Conference on Recent Advances and Trends in NonParametric Statistics, Iraklion, Greece. doi:10.1016/B978-044451378-6/50002-8

Baesens, B., Viaene, S., Van den Poel, D., Vanthienen, J., & Dedene, G. (2002). Bayesian neural network learning for repeat purchase modelling in direct marketing. *European Journal of Operational Research*, *138*(1), 191–211. doi:10.1016/S0377-2217(01)00129-1

Bauer, E., & Kohavi, R. (1999). An empirical comparison of voting classification algorithms: Bagging, boosting, and variants. *Machine Learning*, *36*(1/2), 105–139. doi:10.1023/A:1007515423169

Blattberg, R. C., Kim, B.-D., & Neslin, S. A. (2008). *Database marketing: analyzing and managing customers*. New York: Springer.

Breiman, L. (1996). Bagging predictors. *Machine Learning*, *24*(2), 123–140. doi:10.1007/BF00058655

Breiman, L. (2001). Random forests. *Machine Learning*, *45*(1), 5–32. doi:10.1023/A:1010933404324

Breiman, L., Friedman, J., Olshen, R. A., & Stone, C. J. (1984). *Classification and regression trees*. Belmont, CA: Wadsworth international group.

Bryll, R., Gutierrez-Osuna, R., & Quek, F. (2003). Attribute bagging: Improving accuracy of classifier ensembles by using random feature subsets. *Pattern Recognition*, *36*(6), 1291–1302. doi:10.1016/S0031-3203(02)00121-8

Buckinx, W., & Van den Poel, D. (2005). Customer base analysis: Partial defection of behaviourally loyal clients in a non-contractual FMCG retail setting. *European Journal of Operational Research*, *164*(1), 252–268. doi:10.1016/j.ejor.2003.12.010

Burez, J., & Van den Poel, D. (2007). CRM at a pay-TV company: Using analytical models to reduce customer attrition by targeted marketing for subscription services. *Expert Systems with Applications*, *32*(2), 277–288. doi:10.1016/j.eswa.2005.11.037

Burez, J., & Van den Poel, D. (2008). Separating financial from commercial customer churn: A modeling step towards resolving the conflict between the sales and credit department. *Expert Systems with Applications*, *35*(1-2), 497–514. doi:10.1016/j.eswa.2007.07.036

Burez, J., & Van den Poel, D. (2009). Handling class imbalance in customer churn prediction. *Expert Systems with Applications*, *36*(3), 4626–4636. doi:10.1016/j.eswa.2008.05.027

Coussement, K., & Van denPoel, D. (2009). Improving customer attrition prediction by integrating emotions from client/company interaction emails and evaluating multiple classifiers. *Expert Systems with Applications*, *36*(3), 6127–6134. doi:10.1016/j.eswa.2008.07.021

Coussement, K., Benoit, D. F., & Van den Poel, D. (2010). Improved marketing decision making in a customer churn prediction context using generalized additive models. *Expert Systems with Applications*, *37*(3), 2132–2143. doi:10.1016/j.eswa.2009.07.029

Coussement, K., & Van den Poel, D. (2008a). Churn prediction in subscription services: An application of support vector machines while comparing two parameter-selection techniques. *Expert Systems with Applications*, *34*(1), 313–327. doi:10.1016/j.eswa.2006.09.038

Coussement, K., & Van den Poel, D. (2008b). Integrating the voice of customers through call center emails into a decision support system for chum prediction. *Information & Management*, *45*(3), 164–174. doi:10.1016/j.im.2008.01.005

Day, G. S. (1994). The capabilities of market-driven organizations. *Journal of Marketing*, *58*(4), 37. doi:10.2307/1251915

De Bock, K. W., & Van den Poel, D. (2010). *Ensembles of Probability Estimation Trees for Customer Churn Prediction.* Paper presented at the 23rd International Conference on Industrial Engineering and Other Applications of Applied Intelligent Systems (IEA/AIE 2010), Cordoba, Spain. doi:10.1007/978-3-642-13025-0_7

De Bock, K. W., & Van den Poel, D. (2011). An empirical evaluation of rotation-based ensemble classifiers for customer churn prediction. *Expert Systems with Applications*, *38*(10), 12293–12301. doi:10.1016/j.eswa.2011.04.007

Dietterich, T. G. (2000). An experimental comparison of three methods for constructing ensembles of decision trees: Bagging, boosting, and randomization. *Machine Learning*, *40*(2), 139–157. doi:10.1023/A:1007607513941

Duda, R. O., Hart, P. E., & D.G., S. (2001). *Pattern classification* (second ed.): John Wiley & Sons Inc.

Frank, E., Holmes, G., Pfahringer, B., Reutemann, P., & Witten, I. H. (2009). The WEKA Data Mining Software: An Update. *SIGKDD Explorations*, *1*(1).

Freund, Y., & Schapire, R. E. (1997). A decision-theoretic generalization of on-line learning and an application to boosting. *Journal of Computer and System Sciences*, *55*(1), 119–139. doi:10.1006/jcss.1997.1504

García-Murillo, M., & Annabi, H. (2002). Customer knowledge management. *The Journal of the Operational Research Society*, *53*(8), 875–884. doi:10.1057/palgrave.jors.2601365

Glady, N., Baesens, B., & Croux, C. (2009). Modeling churn using customer lifetime value. *European Journal of Operational Research*, *197*(1), 402–411. doi:10.1016/j.ejor.2008.06.027

Grönroos, C. (1995). Relationship marketing: The strategy continuum. *Journal of the Academy of Marketing Science*, *23*(4), 252–254. doi:10.1007/BF02893863

Gummesson, E. (1997). Relationship marketing as a paradigm shift: Some conclusions from the 30R approach. *Management Decision*, *35*(4), 267–272. doi:10.1108/00251749710169648

Hansen, L. K., & Salamon, P. (1990). Neural Network Ensembles. *IEEE Transactions on Pattern Analysis and Machine Intelligence*, *12*(10), 993–1001. doi:10.1109/34.58871

Hastie, T., & Tibshirani, R. (1986). Generalized additive models. *Statistical Science*, *1*(3), 297–318. doi:10.1214/ss/1177013604

Hastie, T., & Tibshirani, R. (1990). *Generalized Additive Models*. London: Chapman and Hall.

Ho, T. K.Tin Kam Ho. (1998). The random subspace method for constructing decision forests. *IEEE Transactions on Pattern Analysis and Machine Intelligence*, *20*(8), 832–844. doi:10.1109/34.709601

Hosmer, D. W., & Lemeshow, S. (2000). Applied Logistic Regression (2nd ed.). John Wiley & Sons Inc.

Jayachandran, S., Sharma, S., Kaufman, P., & Raman, P. (2005). The Role of Relational Information Processes and Technology Use in Customer Relationship Management. *Journal of Marketing*, *69*(4), 177–192. doi:10.1509/jmkg.2005.69.4.177

Kass, G. V. (1980). An Exploratory Technique for Investigating Large Quantities of Categorical Data. *Journal of the Royal Statistical Society. Series C, Applied Statistics*, *29*(2), 119–127.

Kim, H. C., Pang, S., Je, H. M., Kim, D., & Bang, S. Y. (2002, Aug 10). *Support vector machine ensemble with bagging*. Paper presented at the 1st International Workshop on Pattern Recognition with Support Vector Machines, Niagara Falls, Canada. doi:10.1007/3-540-45665-1_31

Kim, H.-C., Pang, S., Je, H.-M., Kim, D., & Yang Bang, S. (2003). Constructing support vector machine ensemble. *Pattern Recognition*, *36*(12), 2757–2767. doi:10.1016/S0031-3203(03)00175-4

Kim, Y. S. (2006). Toward a successful CRM: Variable selection, sampling, and ensemble. *Decision Support Systems*, *41*(2), 542–553. doi:10.1016/j.dss.2004.09.008

Kuncheva, L. I. (2004). *Combining pattern classifiers: methods and algorithms*. Hoboken, New Jersey: John Wiley & Sons. doi:10.1002/0471660264

Kuncheva, L. I., & Rodríguez, J. J. (2007). Classifier ensembles with a random linear oracle. *IEEE Transactions on Knowledge and Data Engineering*, *19*(4), 500–508. doi:10.1109/TKDE.2007.1016

Kuncheva, L. I., & Whitaker, C. J. (2003). Measures of diversity in classifier ensembles and their relationship with the ensemble accuracy. *Machine Learning*, *51*(2), 181–207. doi:10.1023/A:1022859003006

Lariviere, B., & Van den Poel, D. (2005). Predicting customer retention and profitability by using random forests and regression forests techniques. *Expert Systems with Applications*, *29*(2), 472–484. doi:10.1016/j.eswa.2005.04.043

Larivière, B., & Van den Poel, D. (2005). Predicting customer retention and profitability by using random forests and regression forests techniques. *Expert Systems with Applications*, *29*(2), 472–484. doi:10.1016/j.eswa.2005.04.043

Lemmens, A., & Croux, C. (2006). Bagging and boosting classification trees to predict churn. *JMR, Journal of Marketing Research*, *43*(2), 276–286. doi:10.1509/jmkr.43.2.276

Liaw, A., & Wiener, M. (2002). Classification and Regression by randomForest. *R News*, *2*(3), 18–22.

Maclin, R., & Shavlik, J. W. (1995, Aug 20-25). *Combining the predictions of multiple classifiers: Using competitive learning to initialize neural networks*, Montreal, Canada.

Martens, D., & Provost, F. (2011). Pseudo-social network targeting from consumer transaction data. *Working paper CeDER-11-05 - New York University - Stern School of Business*.

McCarty, J. A., & Hastak, M. (2007). Segmentation approaches in data-mining: A comparison of RFM, CHAID, and logistic regression. *Journal of Business Research, 60*, 656-662. Doi:10.1016/j.jbusres.2006.06.015

Merler, S., Caprile, B., & Furlanello, C. (2007). Parallelizing AdaBoost by weights dynamics. *Computational Statistics & Data Analysis*, *51*(5), 2487–2498. doi:10.1016/j.csda.2006.09.001

Mozer, M. C., Wolniewicz, R., Grimes, D. B., Johnson, E., & Kaushansky, H. (2000). Predicting subscriber dissatisfaction and improving retention in the wireless telecommunications industry. *IEEE Transactions on Neural Networks*, *11*(3), 690–696. doi:10.1109/72.846740 PMID:18249796

Murthy, S. K. (1998). Automatic construction of decision trees from data: A multi-disciplinary survey. *Data Mining and Knowledge Discovery*, *2*(4), 345–389. doi:10.1023/A:1009744630224

Neslin, S. A., Gupta, S., Kamakura, W., Lu, J. X., & Mason, C. H. (2006). Defection detection: Measuring and understanding the predictive accuracy of customer churn models. *JMR, Journal of Marketing Research*, *43*(2), 204–211. doi:10.1509/jmkr.43.2.204

Neslin, S. A., Novak, T. P., Baker, K. R., & Hoffman, D. L. (2009). An Optimal Contact Model for Maximizing Online Panel Response Rates. *Management Science*, *55*(5), 727–737. doi:10.1287/mnsc.1080.0969

Opitz, D. W., & Shavlik, J. W. (1995, Nov 27-30). *Generating accurate and diverse members of a neural-network ensemble*, Denver, Co.

Payne, A., & Frow, P. (2005). A Strategic Framework for Customer Relationship Management. *Journal of Marketing*, *69*(4), 167–176. doi:10.1509/jmkg.2005.69.4.167

Prinzie, A., & Van den Poel, D. (2008). Random forests for multiclass classification: Random Multi-Nomial Logit. *Expert Systems with Applications*, *34*(3), 1721–1732. doi:10.1016/j.eswa.2007.01.029

Quinlan, J. R. (1993). *C4.5: Programs for machine learning*. Morgan Kaufmann Publishers.

Schwenk, H., & Bengio, Y. (2000). Boosting neural networks. *Neural Computation*, *12*(8), 1869–1887. doi:10.1162/089976600300015178 PMID:10953242

Steinberg, D., & Colla, P. (1998). *Classification and regression trees*. Salford Systems.

Van den Poel, D., & Buckinx, W. (2005). Predicting online-purchasing behaviour. *European Journal of Operational Research*, *166*(2), 557–575. doi:10.1016/j.ejor.2004.04.022

van Wezel, M., & Potharst, R. (2007). Improved customer choice predictions using ensemble methods. *European Journal of Operational Research*, *181*(1), 436–452. doi:10.1016/j.ejor.2006.05.029

Wahba, G. (1990). *Spline models for observational data*: Society for industrial and applied mathematics.

Xie, Y. Y., Li, X., Ngai, E. W. T., & Ying, W. Y. (2009). Customer churn prediction using improved balanced random forests. *Expert Systems with Applications*, *36*(3), 5445–5449. doi:10.1016/j.eswa.2008.06.121

Yang, Y. H. (2010). Web user behavioral profiling for user identification. *Decision Support Systems*, *49*(3), 261–271. doi:10.1016/j.dss.2010.03.001

Yu, Y., Zhou, Z. H., & Ting, K. M. (2007, Oct 28-31). *Cocktail ensemble for regression.* Paper presented at the 7th IEEE International Conference on Data Mining, Omaha, NE.

Zablah, A. R., Bellenger, D. N., & Johnston, W. J. (2004). Customer Relationship Management Implementation Gaps. *Journal of Personal Selling & Sales Management*, *24*(4), 279–295. doi:10.1080/08853134.2004.10749038

Zhang, C. X., & Zhang, J. S. (2008). A local boosting algorithm for solving classification problems. *Computational Statistics & Data Analysis*, *52*(4), 1928–1941. doi:10.1016/j.csda.2007.06.015

KEYWORDS AND DEFINITIONS

CRM: The acronym of Customer Relationship Management.

Customer Centricity: The science of engaging in a customer-focused business strategy.

Customer Lifecycle: The trajectory a customer follows from acquisition over development into retention.

Customer Relationship Marketing: The science of building and maintaining long-term relationships with customers.

Data Mining: The science of exploring and detecting recurring patterns in large quantities of data.

Ensemble Learning: A subdomain of data mining/predictive analytics that combines multiple predictive models into one prediction framework.

Predictive Analytics: The science of predicting future (consumer) behavior using past data.

Section 3

Social Media and Social Networking

Chapter 9
Social Media as Marketing Information Systems
Co-Creation in Viral Video Advertising

Christos Karpasitis
University of Central Lancashire, Cyprus

Antonios Kaniadakis
Queen Mary University of London

ABSTRACT

The chapter discusses the impact of the advent and dominance of Social Media in e-marketing. Drawing on concepts from the Social Sciences and the Information Systems field, we propose an understanding of Social Media as useful Marketing Information Systems, which increasingly support the e-marketing function. More specifically, we explore the changing role of customers who as they become increasingly engaged in the Social Media Ecosystem and form communities of interest around certain products, they assume a more active role in co-creating and spreading marketing messages. To demonstrate this process we discuss the case of branded videos that are developed as part of viral marketing campaigns. We show that branded videos constitute digital objects that combine certain content characteristics (visuals, sound, plot), which create cultural and emotional references that help engage customers and contribute to the video's virality in Social Media.

INTRODUCTION

Since the mid- 1990s many organizations have developed some form of Internet presence. Due to the vast expansion of ICT (information and communication technology) the Internet did not only revolutionize and restructure many sectors and provided new focus for business activities, but it has also generated opportunities and challenges for existing businesses and new entrants dealing in new direct relationships with customers (Gay et al, 2007).

Indeed, providers of both services and physical goods have recognized that the Internet is essential to their success as it offers a new virtual channel embedding many new marketing functions which can

DOI: 10.4018/978-1-4666-8459-1.ch009

clearly assist and institute a competitive advantage (Robins, 2000). These functions also enable companies or individuals to reach the global market as they supply the demands of both national and international markets. In this way their activities are no longer restricted by geographical boundaries. By using specific e-Marketing techniques, even small enterprises have now the prospect to access global markets and reach people from around the world.

It is clear, that the Internet offers companies the opportunity for online access to a global customer base. This also indicates that nowadays firms have a better chance of internationalizing more rapidly than they did ten years ago. By using the Internet, companies have the opportunity of quicker market diversification and entry into new markets. As Hollensen (2007) also argues, the Internet has made it possible for a company to make contact with large global customer group very quickly while, at the same time, the 'value' of the information offered is higher than ever.

Since the early days of the World Wide Web, scholars started pointing out the potential for the emergence of new forms of interactivity among businesses, customers and the market. That would eventually create a fundamentally dissimilar environment for marketing activities, compared to more traditional media (Hoffman et al, 1995; 1996).

More recently, with the advent and gradual dominance of what may be broadly understood as online Social Media or networks (i.e. Facebook, Twitter and Youtube), business interactions were transformed even more, opening up new possibilities for the emergence of a new type of marketing landscape. As the Economist (2009) reports, 'social networks are the new communication tool for business that offers the most powerful form of advertising'. Additionally, targeted emails with web links, search engine marketing techniques, search engine optimization (SEO), strategic placement of banner adverts and viral marketing campaigns are other methods that offer effective online communication and help companies in order to get more traffic to their sites.

As we can see, the business and marketing potential of the Internet have been acknowledged from its early days (i.e. the mid-1990s). It is only recently, however, with the emergence and growing importance of the Social Media, that businesses started approaching the Internet somewhat differently. We argue in this chapter that the past few years, businesses started using the Internet not simply as a platform of communication with customers and other businesses, but also as a marketing information system (MkIS) that generates useful information to support their marketing decisions. What is more, consumers have also started understanding the Internet not simply as a medium of communication and social interaction, but as a useful resource that supports a more active online consumer behavior. Indeed, consumers are not any more just passive recipients of marketing messages that in turn would lead them to purchase products and services; rather they are actively involved in the marketing function by sharing information with other customers, researching for prices, evaluating products and co-creating marketing messages.

In the following sections we shall discuss the case of branded videos that are created as part of viral marketing campaigns and try to show how they contribute to the growing importance of Social Media not just as virtual channels for communication but as MkISs that re-define both the marketing approaches of business as well as the behavior of consumers. More specifically, we make reference to the changing role of online consumers and the marketing-related challenges that this change poses to businesses. To better understand and theoretically conceptualize these changes we propose an understanding of the marketing function as a process of co-creation within a Social Media Ecosystem. We end the chapter with recommendations to practitioners and mapping directions for future research.

BACKGROUND

Defining e-Marketing

According to the Institute of Direct Marketing, e-Marketing is the use of the internet and related digital information and communications technologies to achieve marketing objectives (Gay et al, 2007). Mohammed et al. (2002), describes Internet Marketing as "the process of building and maintaining customer relationships through online activities to facilitate the exchange of ideas". Furthermore, Chaffey (2008) refers to digital/electronic communications as:

1. The use of Internet-based (TCP/IP) network technology for communications within an organization using an intranet; beyond the organization to partners such as suppliers, distributors and key account customers using password-based access to extranets and the open Internet where information is accessible by all with Internet access.
2. The use of web servers or websites to enable informational or financial exchanges as e-commerce transactions.
3. The use of other digital access platforms such as interactive digital TV, wireless or mobile phones and games consoles.
4. The use of e-mail for managing enquiries (inbound e-mail) and for promotion (outbound e-mail).
5. Integration of the digital access platforms and e-mail with other information systems such as customer databases and applications for customer relationship management and supply chain management.

Undoubtedly, the number of websites and online business activities has increased dramatically during the last 2-3 years. Nowadays, e-Marketing activities cover an essential part of any business strategy. What is also important to recognize is that Internet Marketing is rapidly becoming more and more popular than the traditional ways of advertising and promoting products.

As the Internet is a global phenomenon that connects individuals and organizations across borders, it is clear that it also plays a significant role in the whole process of globalization. For this reason, according to Gay et al. (2007) there are many issues that need to be considered before developing an international e-marketing strategy. Marketing planners must try to understand the different scenery of the international online environment as well as how it impacts upon the organization's marketing mix and related activities. It is remarkable that many online companies use international market entry strategies in a similar way to traditional offline businesses. Gay et al. (2007) continue by stating that the level of Internet adoption and complexity varies from country to country and this may well influence the strategies and countries selected. This is because different countries are influenced by different tastes, traditions, cultures, languages, legal aspects and environmental factors. See for example the studies by Hofstede and Mooij (2002) on the important role of national cultural values. In our age, Social Media can make a stand against these factors as they help organizations to collect, list and study most of this information for free.

From a consumer's perspective, buying from international sites offers a wider range or more exclusive products in better prices. Nevertheless, consumers may be concerned about the identity and reliability of an international online company. In addition, consumers may be concerned about the full cost of the purchase including imported and local taxes. Other issues may concern delivery times, cancelation and return policies. For these reasons, from the organization's point of view, study and understanding of the buyer's behavior, culture and values of the different markets are more than essential. As we shall argue in the following section the role of online consumers is changing as they are becoming part of an expanding ecosystem that generates and spreads useful quantitative and qualitative marketing information.

Social Media as Marketing Information Systems

Traditionally, consumers were using the Internet simply to expend content. However, nowadays consumes are utilizing online platforms such as blogs, sharing sites and social networks to modify, create, co-create, share, comment or discuss Internet content. According to Kietzmann et al. (2011), this represents the social media phenomenon. Other authors such as Kaplan and Haenlein (2010) define social media as "a group of Internet-based applications that build on the ideological and technological foundations of Web 2.0, and allow the creation and exchange of user generated content". Moreover, Ahlqvist et al. (2008) describe the social media phenomenon as one of the most remarkable developments in the Internet during the last few years. This might be because social media introduced substantial and pervasive changes to communication between organizations, communities and individuals. With more than 152 million blogs around the internet (Gaille, 2013), 4 billion online videos being watched everyday (Perez, 2012) and with almost 2.2 billion users on Facebook (Edwards, 2014), the social media phenomenon naturally arouses the interest of both business people and researches who want to know what's coming and how they should position themselves in the fast moving Social Media arena.

From a Business and Marketing perspective, it's true that online Social Media and networks (such as Facebook, Twitter, LinkedIn and Youtube) offer a new form of interaction between businesses and their customers. Also, this new form of interaction and communication gives the opportunity to increase revenue. For this reason, businesses are increasingly trying to find ways to promote products and services, connect with customers, and drive revenue through Social Media. Since successful marketing involves passing the right message to the right person at the right time, before using Social Media as an e-marketing tool, businesses need to consider which Social Media is the best for their case, their business objectives and their vision. While noting that innovation and change are rife, at this time, there are basically seven kinds of social media according to Mayfield (2008):

1. **Social Networks Such as Facebook and MySpace:** Sites that allow people to build personal web pages and then connect with friends to share content and communicate.
2. **Blogs:** Online journals with entries appearing with the most recent first.
3. **Wikis Such as Wikipedia:** Websites that allow people to add content or to edit the information on them, acting as a communal document or database.
4. **Podcasts:** Audio and video files that are available by subscription, through services like Apple iTunes.
5. **Forums:** Areas for online discussion, often around specific topics and interests.
6. **Content Communities Such as Flickr and Youtube:** Communities which organize and share particular kinds of content.
7. **Microblogging Sites Such as Twitter:** Sites that combine social networking with bite-size blogging, where small amounts of content (Updates) are distributed online.

All the available types of social media are implemented as marketing tools in many different ways. Companies, for instance, may study in depth the Social Media presence of their competitors as well as the existence of their target market in each one of the available Social Media, before making a decision on how to implement them in their marketing function. In addition, companies may review the different benefits that each one of the Social Media has to offer, and to study how these benefits could be connected with the company's aims and objectives. For example, a B2B company that aims on building relationships with other companies might prefer using LinkedIn instead of Facebook for the achievement of this goal since LinkedIn was purely developed for this purpos. Finally, by using social networks, companies may increase brand awareness globally (since social networks are not restricted by geographical boundaries), pass their messages easier and increase sales. We shall argue here however that the implementation of Social Media as marketing tools goes well beyond their affordances as platforms for brand awareness and direct advertising. They are increasingly understood as marketing information systems. The reason for this change, as we show in the following sections, is strongly related to the emergence of a new, more active and creative type of consumer, the Social Media user.

Indeed, Social Media have become the strongest and most popular communication channels for Internet users (Pelling and White 2009) and have emerged as primary online "hang outs" (Chu, 2011). By joining social networks like Facebook, users interact with each other and share information with ease and speed; this offers a promising platform for advertisers to build viral-driven, multidirectional communication with consumers (Holzner, 2008). As consumers increasingly turn to Social Media (e.g. Facebook groups, Blogs or Forums) as trusted sources of information and opinions, new opportunities arise to build consumer-brand relationships and viral advertising platforms. Below we discuss the changing role of online consumers as online social media users.

Changing Role of Consumers

The potential of the Internet as a marketing channel that would give businesses the opportunity to reach global audiences has been identified since its early days. However, the emergence and popularity of Social Media was a determining factor in engaging those audiences in a more active way with the Internet phenomenon. In comparison to more traditional marketing media, in Social Media, users are not passive consumers and receivers of marketing messages. They become actively involved in the creation, sharing and exchange of marketing messages (Hanna et al., 2011).

The use of user-generated content (UGC), for example, is one of the activities that prove the changing role of the consumers of the 21st century. As Van Dijck (2009) explains, with the emergence of many UGC sites, business interest has apparently shifted away from consuming activities and gravitated towards producing activities, giving users more power over content because they add business values. In particular according to Cha et.al (2009), UGC sites like Youtube, are creating new viewing patterns and social interactions, empowering users to be more creative, and developing new business opportunities. This occurrence is strongly connected with the "customer-made" phenomenon where businesses create marketing messages, goods, services or experiences in close cooperation with creative consumers, and in exchange giving them a direct say in what actually gets designed, processed, manufactured or developed (TrendWatching, 2006). In this way, customers contribute to their marketing strategies and advertising campaigns, which are part of a marketing activity called user-generated advertising.

A recent example of user-generated advertising is L'Oreal's "You Make The Commercial" contest where users were Armed with only a production kit and the challenge to create a 30 second commercial for either L'Oreal Paris Colour Juice or Studio Line "Hot" brands, Granite Bay's commercial, "Juicy,". The contest created so much excitement that every production kit was distributed in less than a week and the top 25 commercials posted for online voting received more than a quarter million votes in less than a month. Another example is Firefox's "Flicks" contest where Firefox was asking creative users to create and submit short videos about the power of the Web on mobile devices. Both L'Oreal's and Firefox's contests were asking users to share their productions in order to get votes. In this way, consumers helped companies to create a huge "buzz" about their products and services. Other similar examples of user-generated advertising are MasterCard's "Write a Priceless Ad", JetBlue's "Travel Stories" and McDonalds' "Global Casting".

What is important here is the fact that in most of the examples mentioned above, companies were asking consumers to vote in order to indicate the winners. This made users share their productions in Social Media, ask for votes and start a "buzz" around the campaigns. This brings us to another vital (for companies) consumer activity, which is called "content sharing". When people share/forward online content in social networks, most probably it means that they suggest it to their social neighbors and online friends. This helps companies increase their audience, become more popular and create a "marketing buzz". This view is also supported by Shi et.al (2010) who argue that content sharing in Social Media mimics word of mouth by face-to-face communication in our physical world. For this reason, Shi et.al (2010) also argue that content sharing is an integral part of the Social Media experience.

The other side of the coin of sharing information in Social Media is the awareness amongst consumers that Social Media constitute an important source of information about products. This awareness has led consumers to search in Social Media and other sites for products and product information before they make a purchase. Ten years ago, companies were reaching their consumers through print advertising, trade shows and other traditional marketing methods. Today, consumers start their shopping experience by searching on the Internet, in search engines, blogs and Social Media. They have the opportunity to compare prices and to look for other users' evaluations on products and services before making a buying decision. Indeed, we are all familiar with Amazon product evaluations and Trip Advisor's ratings on hotels and other hospitality services. Especially in times of economic crisis, as new research from Greece reports, consumers are making a more sophisticated use of the Internet tools available to them in order to access the best products in the best possible prices (IELKA, 2014).

Along with the examples of Amazon and Trip Advisor, another example of the importance of user rating and "trust" within the online market is the way that Ebay works where people can rate the services and products of each one of the sellers. Ebay, also included a feedback score for each seller which increases every time a buyer leaves a positive feedback for the seller's products or services. In this way, Ebay helps users getting what they really want by choosing and buying products and services from sellers who have good ratings, seem trustful and have a first-class selling history. To gain business value, then, organizations need to incorporate community building activities as part of their implementation of Social Media (Culnan et al, 2010).

In order to remain competitive, companies also realized that they need to be found online by consumers who were already searching for their products and services. In order to achieve this, companies started adopting a strong online presence in Social Media. Indeed, social media enable the creation of virtual customer environments (VCEs) in which communities of interest are formed around certain products or services (Culnan et al, 2010). As part of these communities, consumers as social media users are engaged in activities that would increase their trust towards a certain company and the products or services they are offering. For example, companies such as Microsoft, Cisco, Nokia, Volvo and Nike have established online customer forums. The forums range from simple online discussion groups to more sophisticated prototyping centers. In this way, companies use the information collected from these environments to develop new products and processes. By interacting with customers, for example, Nokia Corp. has tapped into pioneer design concepts. Similarly, AB Volvo has accelerated its product development by involving customers in virtual product concept tests while Microsoft Corp. has realized considerable savings by having "expert" customers provide product support services to other customers.

For all the above, we argue that Social Media is not only a medium of communication amongst the users; it is not simply a social "hang out" place (Chu, 2011). It is the space where a new "information economy" was created based on the building of trust amongst consumers which are social media users. In this economy, information is the new currency since users create, collect and share information. It is a space where the transmission of marketing messages does not any more follow a linear route from the advertiser to the potential consumer. It is rather based on the consumer's judgment, creativity and willingness to accept and share the message with their online friends.

In summary, the emergence and dominance of Social Media created new social spaces in which consumers assume a more active role. Indeed, as consumers are part of online communities, they are involved in a series of activities that generate and spread information about products and services, which disrupt the more traditional, linear, marketing function. Through their active engagement with Social Media, consumers become part of what may be understood as an emerging marketing information system, consisting of people (e.g. social media users) equipment (e.g. social media platforms) and procedures (e.g. sharing) (Armstrong & Kotler, 2007) which businesses need to embrace and integrate into their marketing practices.

Content Sharing in Social Media

As we have discussed in the previous sections, due to the changing role of consumers as generators and sharers of marketing and advertising content, Social Media can be understood in two ways: First, in the more conventional and popular sense, they can be perceived by businesses as a new way of reaching diverse customer audiences globally. This is the vision that was associated with the Internet as a whole since its infancy in the early to mid-1990s and indeed was in a sense realized by an increased Social Media presence by all kinds of businesses. However, as consumers become increasingly active in Social Media, by generating and sharing content and by their overall behavior in a Social Media context, there is a new emerging vision around these popular networking platforms. More specifically, they have become an important source of information that would help businesses make decisions to support their marketing practices and strategies. Nowadays, the amount of data that is generated by users' behavior and become available in Social Media is enormous. According to Kelly (2012), Facebook for example currently stores, accesses and analyzes more than 30 Petabytes (30000 Terabytes) of user generated data. Companies can collect internet analytics and insights about clicks, likes, comments, page visits, shares, demographic information and more. But which of these analytics are the most important for businesses? It seems that the answer to this question changes over the years. Initially, companies focused on the "number of clicks". More recently, they also started to measure "virality" and "attention" (Upworthy Insider, 2014). This shift shows that over the years, different "forms" of information become valuable and attract the attention of businesses and marketers. The speed however in which new valuable forms of information emerge and gain value shows that the marketing function is surrounded by rather high levels of fluidity and uncertainty. To put it more simply, the industry has not yet concluded with certainty on which form of information is valuable, how to measure it and how to interpret it for marketing purposes.

Nevertheless, recent research argues that "content sharing" in social networks has become a valuable information-generating consumer activity for Social Media marketing. In the previous section we discussed about user generated content sharing where companies, as part of their Social Media strategy, where inviting creative consumers to produce and share marketing content. There are times, however, when companies engage consumers to share content that they have created themselves, an activity that is known in Social Media marketing as "content marketing". Companies with huge online presence on Social Media like "Coca Cola", "Nike" and "American Express" create unique and interactive material that people want to share, and, in turn, new methods of content marketing mean new avenues to reach and converse with their customers. Carter and Marketo (2013) emphasize the importance of content sharing in Social Media marketing and the strong connections between content sharing, user engagement and content virality. "Number of shares", then, replaces "number of clicks" as valuable forms of information in e-marketing.

Generally speaking, debates around marketing are not only about how to use the internet to distribute your marketing message to diverse customers (i.e. function of the internet as an expanded marketplace), but also how to use information generated by online customer behavior (i.e. sharing, liking, commenting) in order to help companies create and release that marketing message in the first place. For example, by reviewing online content that was highly shared, Carter and Marketo (2013) found that highly shareable marketing messages do at least one of the following: Give, Advice, Warn, Amuse, Inspire, Amaze, Unite. Moreover, the Customer Insight Group (2011) argues that the key factors to influence sharing are:

1. Appeal to consumers' motivation to connect with each other – not just with your brand
2. Trust is the cost of entry for getting shared
3. Keep it simple
4. Appeal to their sense of humor
5. Embrace a sense of urgency

Indeed, all the above prove that "sharing" has become an important activity that makes online consumers active stakeholders of a company's online marketing strategy. However, all these changes and debates bring new challenges and rules to the "marketing game". Rules that companies and marketers need to study and adopt in order to remain alive and competitive.

Marketing as Co-Creation in the Social Media Ecosystem

The changing role of consumers in a Social Media context and the new challenges that disrupt the traditional marketing function pose a pressing need for new conceptualizations of Social Media marketing, one that acknowledges their role as MkIS. The uncertainty surrounding "what is important information" to support marketing strategies in a Social Media context and how to capitalize on the more active role of consumers, calls for an updated understanding of what is the impact of Social Media in the marketing function.

The new challenges for marketing in Social Media can be theoretically understood in the context of a new "ecosystem" (Kallinikos & Mariategui, 2011; Hanna et al, 2008). Indeed, drawing on theoretical insights from social studies of information systems and Social Media, we argue in this chapter that e-marketing in the Social Media era is not simply a task performed by a specific department of an organization. Instead, the e-marketing function is a process of co-creation that is performed within the broader

Social Media community, which we may theoretically conceptualize as an ecosystem. By ecosystem we understand an ensemble of stakeholders, processes, systems, operations and devices that make possible the production, mixing, and dissemination of digital content (Kallinikos & Mariategui, 2011). In reference to the changing role of consumers in the Social Media ecosystem, discussed earlier, they can now be understood as "digital consumers" who are accustomed to the fact that information-based digital content is readily accessible and interoperable (Deuze, 2007) and who are assuming a more active role in co-creating marketing content with companies and their specific brands.

For analytical purposes we shall understand the Social Media ecosystem as having technical, social and cultural/emotional constituents. The technical aspect refers to the functional interoperability amongst different Social Media platforms and the ways in which it is possible to link them together. One example is the fact that you can share Youtube videos on Facebook and Twitter or how the last two make possible the sharing of content and comments in these two platforms simultaneously. This functional interoperability makes possible the brand consistency, the content creation and the content sharing. The social aspect refers to the formulation of online communities around certain brands, products and services and how information about these are shared as part of social relations within and beyond those communities. One example, is how online communities of travelers discuss on Twitter about what is the best camera to use in their travels. Indeed, the online travel community Travel Talk On Twitter (or #TTOT) who also maintain a Facebook page, define themselves as "a social media travel event and a social travel hashtag on Twitter". What is interesting here is the understanding of an online community as an "event", which gives the community a high degree of ephemerality (e.g. the community does not necessarily require high degree of commitment from its members). Also, we may observe that hashtag, a symbol on our keyboard, has come to define the way we understand communities in a Social Media content. We are a hashtag on Twitter, means we are an online community that we express ourselves in the social space provided by a specific Social Media platform. Finally, the cultural/emotional aspect refers on how users co-create the marketing messages by linking the content characteristics of a digital object, such as, a video or a picture, with certain cultural references or emotions that were created elsewhere. A good example is the "cutesification" trend when brands achieve increasing shares in Social Media just because their marketing content appears "cute" to consumers (Heritage, 2013).

In a Social Media ecosystem, all these technical, social and cultural/emotional forces contribute to the creation of a social space in which digital consumers are creating, interpreting and sharing marketing content. The role of businesses and advertisers for the purposes of e-marketing would be to find ways to understand the behavior of the new digital consumers and successfully engage them in the process of co-creation of their marketing messages and campaigns. Understanding e-marketing as a process of co-creation between businesses and digital consumers helps us integrate our understanding of Social Media as e-marketing platforms but also as spaces where Social Media users can be engaged (Chu & Kim, 2011; Evans, 2010) and become part of a company's marketing information system.

MAIN FOCUS

Viral Marketing and Viral Videos

To demonstrate how e-marketing is performed in a Social Media ecosystem as a process of co-creation between marketing professionals and digital consumers we shall discuss in this section the case of viral video marketing. The case of viral videos and how they travel in Social Media is ideal in helping us illustrate the active role of digital consumers and how they are embedded in the marketing function for certain brands. We start by offering background information about viral marketing, its origins and its significance within a Social Media ecosystem.

During the last decade, providers of both services and physical goods have recognized that the Internet is essential to their success. Indeed internet offers a virtual channel embedding many new E-Marketing functions which can clearly assist and institute a competitive advantage (Robins, 2000, Gay et al., 2007). Viral Marketing is one such popular "new" technique which helps interacting and communicating with customers while increasing brand awareness through social networks (i.e. Facebook, Twitter, Youtube etc.) and public blogs. This is achieved by passing audiovisual marketing massages/buzzwords from one customer to another.

Viral marketing is also known as the "online word of mouth". More specifically, it refers to the word-of-mouth (WOM) empowered by the Internet (word-of-mouse) (Goldenberg et al., 2001), and to the broad buzz marketing (Thomas, 2004). This includes the marketing strategy behind it (Gruen et al., 2006) which is focused on advertising (Phelps et al., 2004) and branding (Dobele, et al., 2005). Indeed, Wilson (2000) describes viral marketing as any strategy that encourages individuals to pass on a marketing message to others creating the potential for exponential growth in the message's exposure and influence. In doing so, customers are recruited to be sales agents and spread the word about the product (Solomon et al, 2006). As a result, brand awareness is built quickly, sales are increased and marketing costs are kept lower than in traditional marketing techniques. Although the research landscape on viral marketing appears to be rather fragmented as it is characterized by dissimilar approaches, visions and terminologies (Camarero & San Jose, 2011), it is broadly accepted that as a type of unconventional marketing (Cova *et al.*, 2008), the viral marketing phenomenon drives people to receive and pass along original and creative messages (Southgate *et al.,* 2010) rapidly, and in an exponential manner (De Bruyn & Lilien, 2008). What is also broadly accepted, is that the more recent emergence and growth of online Social Media (Facebook, Youtube etc.), have moved viral marketing to another level (The Economist, 2008). One example that most people are familiar with, is the posting and sharing of videos on platforms like YouTube, Facebook and Twitter. More specifically, we are referring to online branded videos that are developed by advertisers as part of a marketing campaign of a product. This marketing activity is also known as video marketing or video advertising.

Since YouTube arrived on the scene, online videos have played a critical role in advertising and marketing. Entrepreneurs, business owners and even small companies are trying to take advantage of its power, no matter what their company's stage is. Leaders in every sector including retail, health care, banking, food and beverages and travel are sharing videos to demonstrate their products and services, to showcase their industry knowledge and to educate consumers. Furthermore, the fact that Cisco predicted that by 2017 online video will be used more widely than Twitter and Facebook (Roettgers, 2013) is also remarkable. According to Cisco's Visual Networking Index forecast, online video services had around 1 billion users worldwide in 2012. The company estimates that this number will almost double by 2017, reaching close to 2 billion users worldwide. That means that in four years, 81 percent of the world's internet users will also use online video services. In 2012, that number was still at around 58 percent. They also predict that:

- Online video will account for 69 percent of consumer internet traffic by 2017 (up from 57 percent in 2012).

- Mobile video will grow 16-fold from 2012 to 2017, and account for 66 percent of all mobile data traffic during that year.
- Internet-to-TV streaming will grow from 1.3 exabytes per month in 2012 to 6.5 exabytes per month in 2017.
- The number of web-enabled TVs in consumer's homes will grow from close to 180 million in 2012 to 827 million in 2017.
- Game consoles will become slightly less important as a way to bring internet video to the TV screen, while dedicated streaming boxes will see the biggest growth:

"Viral video", as a more specific form of viral marketing, describes a phenomenon in which online videos become extremely popular through rapid, user-led allocation (sharing) via the Internet and Social Networks. In other words, viral video refers to those videos which are viewed by a great number of people, normally as a result of knowledge about the video being spread rapidly through the internet population via online word-of-mouth (Burgess, 2008). Additionally, in his now-notorious post on the technology business weblog Techrunch, Greenberg (2007), defines viral videos as videos that have travelled all around the internet and been posted on YouTube, MySpace, Google Video, Facebook, Digg, blogs, etc. – videos with millions and millions of views. In other words, viral video is an e-marketing approach by which Social Media consumer audiences are engaged in order to share and spread marketing messages.

Co-Creation of Viral Video Marketing in a Social Media Ecosystem

Video Content Characteristics as Mechanism that Embed Marketing Messages

To understand how marketing messages are embedded in videos that are then shared in Social Media, we need to look at the individual content characteristics as the main constituents of brand videos. We argue that it is with a video's content characteristics that consumers are engaged and co-create the marketing message. More specifically, our focus will be on *visuals*, *sound* and *plot* as the main carriers of meaningful video messages.

Starting with visuals such as video graphics, there are numerous ways in which marketers can communicate their marketing video messages visually. Animation for instance (2D or 3D), is one of these ways that has affected the way of selling products (Callcott and Lee, 1994). The use of animation has affected the way of selling products. The reason that computer animation is so helpful in web advertising is because of its ability to grab the attention of the potential consumers (Sundar and Kalyanaraman, 2004). On the other hand, a more expensive, complex but realistic method of creating a marketing video is "live-action". This method involves recording live footage by using appropriate equipment (i.e. professional video cameras) and normally requires some actors. Both methods (animation and live action) have unique advantages to offer to marketers and entail different levels of viewers' response and engagement.

A great example of a brand video that went viral with more than 17 million views mostly because of its use of visuals is Dove's "Evolution of Beauty". For the specific video, Dove used a photography/animation technique called "Time Lapse" where a large number of images are used to make motion movie footage. The video starts with an ordinary woman entering and sitting down in a studio. Two harsh lights are switched on and the camera then switches to a time lapse sequence, showing a makeup and hair artist making the woman up and adjusting her hair, transforming her into an outstandingly beautiful billboard model. When the final physical adjustments of the woman's appearance have been made, the team members all move off-camera and a series of camera flashes begins as the photographer takes shots of the woman in various poses. One shot is selected from the batch and moved into a generic image editing software, where a series of "Photoshopping" adjustments are made to alter the woman's appearance even further, including, but not limited to: lengthening her neck, adjusting the curve of her shoulders, altering her hair and skin, and enlarging her eyes and mouth. The final image, now rendered almost unrecognizable, is then transferred to a billboard advertisement.

Indeed, visuals and graphics play an important role in the advertising industry. Advertisements for services and products are most effective when visuals stand out while upholding relevance to and transparency of the marketing message. Right visuals can attract the consumer's attention and increase the possibility that the viewer will buy the product or service. Additionally, effective use of color and visuals can increase attention and appeal to the consumer's emotions and behavior. Great examples are the visuals being used in Coca Cola's advertisements and the effective use of the red color which is stimulating and alerts consumers to pay attention. In fact, color is so important to a product's brand identity that the Supreme Court ruled in 1995 that a particular shade of color, such as Coca-Cola red, could serve as a legally defensible trademark (Lamancusa, 2003). By having all these in mind, someone could argue that visuals are as important as the marketing messages that they put across.

Another attention-grabbing video content characteristic is the audio. The audio used in marketing videos is normally a mixture of speech, sound effects and background music. Cooper (2013) emphasizes the importance of strategic audio branding while other studies in the digital sphere also point to the positive effects of audio on engagement. Furthermore, Lusensky (2011) explains that music strategy creates brand awareness and attention by involving the consumer in a conversation about the music. The power of sound, its suggestive capabilities and ability to reach into a consumer's emotions and imagination and take root, is maybe the most under-estimated of branding/advertising assets. Great examples of effective use of audio in marketing are the advertisements of Compare the Market and Coca-Cola. According to Smith (2013), the token response of "Simples" by Compare the Market's Meerkat entered the national vernacular. Additionally, Coca Cola's "Always Coca-Cola" audio signature proved that even one single creative execution has the power to be understood the world over. It is important to mention that both companies have remarked on the impact that the audio has made to their marketing.

In addition to audiovisual characteristics, another video content characteristic that is a main carrier of meaningful messages is the plot that the brand video follows. This content characteristic is strongly connected to a new marketing trend called "story advertising". According to Gossner (2013), story advertising is a new form of content marketing which involves producing advertising videos that present stories, normally with a beginning, a turning point and an end. Audi's "Prom", Volkswagen's "The Force", Old Spice's "The Man Your Man Could Smell Like" and Pepsi's "Uncle Drew" commercial series are all examples of successful advertising that use this new form of marketing.

Viral Videos as Digital Objects and the Process of Co-Creation

Some questions that may arise are: What happens after video developers and advertisers develop a brand video with the intention to become viral in Social Media and spread the marketing message to diverse audiences? How are Social Media users involved in the process of co-creation of the marketing message in the Social Media ecosystem? To answer these questions we suggest an understanding of videos as "digital objects (Kallinikos & Mariategui, 2011). More specifically, videos that are shared in Social Media in the familiar form of a youtube video constitute a substantially new breed of editable artefacts amenable to wide manipulation and revision. In relation to conventional objects, digital objects manifest an "openness", an "editability" and "expandability" and in this sense, they never achieve the definite closure of traditional objects (Kallinikos & Mariategui, 2011). What makes this openness possible is, to borrow a term from the Sociology of technology, the high degree of "interpretive flexibility" (Pinch & Bijker, 1992) that digital objects present.

This means that technological objects/artefacts may have different meanings and interpretations by various groups. Therefore, the attempt to embed a complete and fixed meaningful (marketing) message in a technological object like a digital video is more or less futile. It is an absolute certainty that the meaning of the initial message that is embedded in a video's content elements (sound, visuals, plot) is never fixed; rather it is altered, edited, re-interpreted as the video is shared in different Social Media contexts. More specifically, when a digital video goes viral in the ecosystem of Social Media, it generates a process by which Social Media users actively participate in the co-creation of the marketing message carried in this video, by placing a video's content elements (sound, plot, visuals) within different cognitive and cultural frameworks. For example, when a video is shared in a specific Social Media platform it generates comments, further shares, likes and so on, which contribute to the co-creation of the message that the video carries.

To get a closer look to this phenomenon we examined a brand video that recently went viral and how users contributed to the co-creation of the message that the video was carrying. To achieve this, we examined some of the comments that users were making while sharing the viral videos on Google+ (Google's social network) through Youtube.

Our example is a black and white brand video called "First Kiss" that was produced and released by a clothing company called "WREN". The brand video was released in March 2014 and was viewed more than 80 million times in less than 3 months. According to the company, for the video's purpose, 20 strangers were asked to kiss in front of the camera for the first time.

After analyzing the video comments and shares in Social Media we interestingly found that there were many users who were commenting about this video's visuals, sound or plot while sharing the video on Google+. Some of them where sharing it while commenting about the soundtrack (i.e. "what is the music used here?", "nice soundtrack", "I love the music"). Others where sharing it while commenting about the visual art (i.e. "I love the art behind this video", "oh it's black and white you know this is going to be such art"). Finally, some users were sharing it while commenting about the actors and the plot (i.e. "this is so cute", "actors or just strangers?", "the power of the first kiss").

In relation to the process of co-creating a marketing message, the "First Kiss" video is interesting because in the first instance the video itself has nothing to do with the product it advertises. Neither the plot or the sound and visuals directly convey a message that encourages people to buy clothes or makes any reference to what "WREN" sells. This means that the marketing message and the whole marketing function is to a large extent left to the Social Media users. At first, they contribute to the creation of the message by engaging in a process of interpreting the video by making reference to its content characteristics while sharing it in Social Media. In this sense, the video content characteristics (visuals, sound, plot) actually become the marketing message in the "First Kiss" video. In addition, since there are no additional details about the company or its products in the video, it is not until later and after pointed out by other viewers/users that the audience realizes that this is an advertising campaign by a clothing company.

The First Kiss video, therefore, shows that the specific advertising campaign demonstrates full awareness of the active role of Social Media users and engages them in creating the marketing message and also to create brand awareness. In terms of the former, the video content characteristics (visuals, sound, plot) actually become the marketing message while subsequently, consumers within the Social Media ecosystem share knowledge that creates the link between the specific video, the specific clothing brand and its products.

SOLUTIONS AND RECOMMENDATIONS

Advertising and marketing are changing more than ever, and it's the customers who are pulling the strings. As discussed earlier, the Internet has given customers ever-increasing powers to research, compare, and review brands, enabling both good and bad customer experiences to be broadcast to the world. This is proving challenging for many companies, who've always exercised so much control over their brand messages.

But many brands are harnessing the power of the Internet and "social proof" (also known as informational social influence) by optimizing user-generated content (UGC). These are the brands that understand the power of co-creation. For many companies, this means encouraging reviews of their products/ services and conversations around them. In our case, co-creation of the marketing message emerges from user comments, reviews and conversations about brand videos and their content characteristics. More specifically, by sharing and commenting on a video's content characteristics, Social Media users help create multiple cultural, emotional and cognitive contexts in which the marketing message is interpreted. These multiple interpretations help continuously co-create and re-create the marketing message and also act as motives for more users to engage in similar activities (viewing, sharing or commenting). In other words, they can help on creating a "buzz".

Therefore, the big challenge for marketing practitioners is: How can they "harness" the forces of co-creation of marketing messages in brand videos? What makes people co-create the marketing message and share/commend on a brand video? To answer such questions, businesses need to address certain issues. Below we provide just a few of them, based on what has been discussed in this chapter:

1. The creators of branded videos for viral marketing campaigns in Social Media need to carefully consider the combination of cultural, emotional and cognitive contexts on which the content characteristics of their videos will draw on and the impact that these will have on the videos' virality. For instance, a certain combination of music with a narrative and visual images may contribute more to a video's virality than an alternative combination. A particular music combined with a specific plot, for example, may provide to social media users the links for cultural references that will create an impression of a certain degree that would motivate these users to further share the video.
2. Businesses need to invest in developing communities of interest around their products and services. Interactions amongst members of such communities in Social Media are a powerful mechanism of co-creation. This basically means that businesses should aim to provide to their customers new opportunities for co-creation. Customer communities around certain products then, become platforms on which customers are engaged in a business' marketing function and co-create their marketing messages. Volvo's virtual product concept tests are great examples of developing such communities of interest.

3. Businesses should invest more in understanding the mechanisms by which viral messages are co-created in a Social Media ecosystem and the different technical, social, cultural and emotional ways in which online customers can be engaged. As we mentioned in this chapter, the Social Media ecosystem is evolving in a very fast pace. It changes continuously in ways that no one can accurately predict. Therefore, there is not one fixed recipe or road map about how to create a successful viral video campaign. What works today might not work tomorrow. Businesses need to constantly keep up to date with Social Media trends and identify technical, cultural and emotional ways to achieve virality. In so doing, businesses need to look beyond simple quantitative Internet metrics and analytics (i.e. Google analytics, number of clicks and shares) and more into qualitative information that may provide insights on how video virality works in a Social Media ecosystem.
4. An overall lesson from this chapter which encapsulates all the previous points, is that as customers become more active and more creative in Social Media, businesses should also become more creative in how they approach Social Media. They should not simply see them as a medium that helps them reach a broader customer base. Instead, they should understand them as an important part of their Marketing Information System. For this reason, they need to seriously consider new technical, social, cultural and emotional ways in which their organizational MkIS can "plug into" Social Media platforms and thus offer an extended scope in their e-marketing function.

FUTURE RESEARCH AND CONCLUSION

E-marketing as an academic field needs to start considering the role of Social Media as MkIS. Such an approach opens up a whole new field of study that shall combine theoretical insights and methods from a variety of disciplines, such as, marketing, information systems, social sciences, management and so on. More specifically, we may envision a significant contribution to information infrastructure studies. How can we approach Social Media as information infrastructures? What is the significance of such an approach for e-marketing? How can organizations balance their local circumstances with the challenges of a global landscape? (Rolland & Monteiro, 2002).

In what ways can Social Media constitute information infrastructures that would enable organizational transformation? (Timmermans, et al, 1996).

We are trying to answer these and other similar questions in subsequent publications and we recommend to the IS community to become engaged to this emerging research field. As we have shown in this chapter, industry practitioners have already started exploring the potential of Social Media as MkIS; the academic community needs to catch up and provide novel theorizations and understandings of the mechanisms that may turn a social networking platform into a useful tool for marketing practitioners. In so doing, we need to consider new methods of research, both quantitative and qualitative. In this chapter we propose that the IS community consider exploring "netnography" as an innovative method that could provide useful insights into the Social Media phenomenon.

The idea that the Internet can revolutionize marketing is not new. However, so far we have just perceived it as a communication channel that would help businesses reach diverse consumer audiences globally. In this chapter we have argued that we need to go beyond that and in the context of the impact of Social Media, we have attempted to reveal processes that help us understand it as a Marketing Information System. Basically, we have shown that what makes Social Media a useful MkIS is the changing role of consumers who increasingly assume a more active role as Social Media users and contribute to the co-creation and spreading of marketing messages. To this end, a theoretical understanding of Social Media as an ecosystem is essential as it provides the analytical space to explore social interactions and mechanisms of co-creation, as we have shown with the case of viral videos.

REFERENCES

Ahlqvist, T., Back, A., Halonen, M., & Heinonen, S. (2008). Social Media Roadmaps: Exploring the futures triggered by social media. VTT Research Notes 2454, Espoo, Finland.

Armstrong, G., & Kotler, P. (2007). *Principles of Marketing* (12th ed.). New York: Prentice-Hall.

Burgess, J. (2008). All Your Chocolate Rain Are Belong to Us?' Viral Video, YouTube and the Dynamics of Participatory Culture. In Video Vortex Reader: Responses to YouTube (pp. 101-109). Amsterdam, Institute of Network Cultures.

Callcott, M. F., & Lee, W. N. (1994). A content analysis of animation and animated Spokes - characters in television commercials. *Journal of Advertising*, *23*(4), 1–12. doi:10.1080/00913367.1943.10673455

Camarero, C., & San Jose, R. (2011). Social and attitudinal determinants of viral marketing dynamics. *Computers in Human Behavior*, *27*(6), 2292–2300. doi:10.1016/j.chb.2011.07.008

Carter, B., & Marketo. (2013). Contagious Content: What people share on Facebook and why they share it. Retrieved from http://www.marketo.com/_assets/uploads/Contagious-Content.pdf

Cha, M., Kwak, H., Rodriguez, P., Ahn, Y., & Moon, S. (2009). *I Tube, You Tube, Everybody Tubes: Analyzing the World's Largest User Generated Content Video System*. Barcelona, Spain: Telefonica Research.

Chaffey, D. (2008). E-Marketing. In M. J. Baker & S. Hart (Eds.), *The Marketing Book* (pp. 502–524). London: Butterworth, Heinemann. doi:10.1016/B978-0-7506-8566-5.50029-7

Chu, S. C. (2011). Viral Advertising in social media: Participation in Facebook groups and responses among college-aged users. *Journal of Interactive Advertising*, *12*(1), 30–43. doi:10.1080/15252019.2011.10722189

Chu, S. C., & Kim, Y. (2011). Determinants of consumer engagement in electronic word-of-mouth (eWOM) in social networking sites. *International Journal of Advertising*, *30*(1), 47–75. doi:10.2501/IJA-30-1-047-075

Cooper, L. (2013). Wired for Sound. *Marketing Week*. Retrieved from http://www.marketingweek.co.uk/trends/wired-for-sound/4006678.article

Cova, B., Giordano, A., & Pallera, M. (2008). Marketing non convenzionale. Il Sole 24 Ore, Milano.

Culnal, M., J., McHugh, P. J., & Zubillaga, J. I. (2010). How large U.S. Companies can use twitter and other Social Media to gain business value. *University of Minnesota*, 9(4), 243-259.

De Bruyn, A., & Lilien, G. L. (2008). A Multi-Stage Model of Word of Mouth Through Viral Marketing. *International Journal of Research in Marketing*, *25*(3), 143–225. doi:10.1016/j.ijresmar.2008.03.004

de Mooij, M., & Hofstede, G. (2002). Convergence and divergence in consumer behavior: Implications for international retailing. *Journal of Retailing*, *78*(1), 61–69. doi:10.1016/S0022-4359(01)00067-7

Deuze, M. (2007). *Media work*. Malden, MA: Polity.

Dobele, A., Toleman, D., & Beverland, M. (2005). Controlled infection! Spreading the brand message through viral marketing. *Business Horizons*, *48*(2), 143–149. doi:10.1016/j.bushor.2004.10.011

Edwards, J. (2014). Facebook Inc. Actually Has 2.2 Billion Users Now – Roughly One Third of the Entire Population of Earth. *Business Insider*. Retrieved from http://www.businessinsider.com/facebook-inc-has-22-billion-users-2014-7

Evans, D. (2010). *Social Media Marketing: The next generation of user engagement*. Indianapolis, Ind: Wiley Pub.

Gay, R., Charlesworth, A., & Esen, R. (2007). *Online Marketing: A customer-led approach*. New York, NY: Oxford University Press.

Goldenberg, J., Libai, B., & Muller, E. (2001). Talk the network: A complex systems look at the underlying process of word of mouth. *Marketing Letters*, *12*(3), 211–223. doi:10.1023/A:1011122126881

Gossner, M. M. (2013). From Content Marketing to Story Advertising? *Social Media Today*. Retrieved from http://socialmediatoday.com/martinmeyergossner/1876956/content-marketing-story-advertising

Greenberg, D. A. (2007). The Secret Strategies Behind Many Viral Videos. *Techcrunch*. Retrieved from http://www.techcrunch.com/2007/11/22/the-secret-strategies-behind-many-viral-videos/

Gruen, T. W., Osmonbekov, T., & Czaplewski, A. J. (2006). eWOM: The impact of customer-to customer online know-how exchange on customer value and loyalty. *Journal of Business Research*, *59*(4), 449–456. doi:10.1016/j.jbusres.2005.10.004

Hanna, R., Rohm, A., & Crittenden, V. L. (2011). We're all connected: The power of social media ecosystem. *Business Horizons*, *54*(3), 265–273. doi:10.1016/j.bushor.2011.01.007

Heritage, S. (2013). The cutesification of everything makes me want to strangle an elf., *The Guardian*. Retrieved from http://www.theguardian.com/commentisfree/2013/nov/24/cutesification-of-everything-elf-twitter-funny

Hoffman, D. L., Novak, T.P., & Chatterjee, P. (1995). Commercial Scenarios for the Web: Opportunities and Challenges. *Journal of Computer-Mediated Communications,* 1(3). Retrieved from http://onlinelibrary.wiley.com/doi/10.1111/j.1083-6101.1995.tb00165.x/full

Hoffman, D. L., Novak, & Thomas, P. (1996). A new marketing paradigm for electronic Commerce. *The Information Society*. Retrieved from http://www.bus.umich.edu/FacultyResearch/ResearchCenters/centers/Yaffe/downloads/Complete_List_of_Working_Papers/anewmark.pdf

Hollensen, S. (2007). Global Marketing, Chapter 20: Global e-marketing. *Pearson*. Retrieved from http://wps.pearsoned.co.uk/ema_uk_he_hollensen_globalmark_4/64/16425/4204992.cw/index.html

Holzner, S. (2008). Facebook Marketing: Leverage Social Media to Grow Your Business. Indianapolis, IN: Que.

IELKA. (2014). 10 Recessionary habits changing the Greek consumer in the retail sector. Retrieved from http://www.ielka.gr/?p=1712

Insider, U. (2014). What uniques and pageviews leave out (and why we're measuring attention minutes instead). Retrieved from http://blog.upworthy.com/post/75795679502/what-uniques-and-pageviews-leave-out-and-why-were

Kallinikos, J., & Mariategui, J. C. (2011). Video as Digital Object: Production and Distribution of Video Content in the Internet Media Ecosystem. *The Information Society*, *27*(5), 281–294. doi:10.1080/01972243.2011.607025

Kaplan, A. M., & Haenlein, M. (2010). Users of the world, unite! The challenges and opportunities of social media. *Business Horizons*, *53*(1), 59. doi:10.1016/j.bushor.2009.09.003

Kelly, J. (2012). Taming Big Data: A Big Data Infographic. *Big Data, Wikibon*. Retrieved from http://wikibon.org/blog/taming-big-data/

Kietzmann, H. J., Hermkens, K., McCarthy, P. I., & Silvestre, S. B. (2011). Social media? Get serious! Understanding the functional building blocks of social media. *Business Horizons*, *54*(3), 241–251. doi:10.1016/j.bushor.2011.01.005

Lamancusa, K. (2003). Emotional Reactions to Color, *Creative Latitude*. Retrieved from http://www.creativelatitude.com/articles/articles_lamacusa_color.html

Lusensky, J. (2011). *Sounds like Branding: Using the power of music to turn customers into fans*. Heartbeats International.

Mayfield, A. (2008). *What is Social Media?* Retrieved from http://www.icrossing.com/sites/default/files/what-is-social-media-uk.pdf

Mohammed, R., Fisher, R. J., Jaworski, B. J., & Paddison, G. (2002). *Internet Marketing: Building Advantage in the Networked Economy*. Boston: McGraw-Hill/Irwin.

Pelling, E., & White, K. M. (2009). The Theory of Planned Behaviour Applied to Young People's Use of Social Networking Websites. *Cyberpsychology & Behavior*, *12*(6), 755–759. doi:10.1089/cpb.2009.0109 PMID:19788377

Perez, S. (2012). YouTube Reaches 4 Billion Views Per Day. *Techcrunch*. Retrieved from http://techcrunch.com/2012/01/23/youtube-reaches-4-billion-views-per-day/

Phelps, J. E., Lewis, R., Mobilio, L., Perry, D., & Raman, N. (2004). Viral Marketing or Electronic Word-of-Mouth Advertising: Examining Consumer Responses and Motivations to Pass Along Email. *Journal of Advertising Research*, *44*(4), 333–348.

Pinch, T., & Bijker, W. (1992). The social construction of facts and artifacts: or how the sociology of science and the sociology of technology might benefit each other. In W. Bijker & J. Law (Eds.), *Shaping Technology/Building Society* (pp. 17–50). Cambridge, MA: MIT Press.

Robins, F. (2000). The e-marketing mix. *The Marketing Review*, *1*(2), 249–274. doi:10.1362/1469347002529134

Roettgers, J. (2013). Online video will be more popular than Facebook and Twitter by 2017. *Gigaom*. Retrieved from http://gigaom.com/2013/05/29/online-video-will-be-more-popular-than-facebook-and-twitter-by-2017/

Rolland, K. H., & Monteiro, E. (2002). Balancing the local and the global in infrastructural information systems. *The Information Society*, *18*(2), 87–100. doi:10.1080/01972240290075020

Shi, Z., Rui, H., & Whinston, A. (2010). Information sharing in social Broadacst: Evidences from Twitter. *Proceedings of the 21st Workshop on Information Systems and Economics*. New York, NY.

Smith, J. (2013). The Importance of audio branding, *IAB*. Retrieved from http://www.iabuk.net/blog/the-importance-of-audio-branding

Solomon, M. R., Marshall, G. W., & Stuart, E. W. (2006). *Marketing: Real People, Real Choices*. Upper Saddle River, New Jersey, USA: Pearson Prentice Hall.

Southgate, D., Westoby, N., & Page, G. (2010). Creative determinants of viral video viewing. *International Journal of Advertising*, *29*(3), 349–368. doi:10.2501/S0265048710201221

Sundar, S. S., & Kalyanaraman, S. (2004). Arousal, Memory, And Impression – Formation effects of animation speed in Web Advertising. *Journal of Advertising*, *33*(1), 7–17. doi:10.1080/00913367.2004.10639152

The Economist. (2008). Viral Marketing. Retrieved from http://www.economist.com/node/12677019

The Economist. (2009). Friends for Sale: What is a Facebook friend worth? Retrieved from http://www.economist.com/node/14460087

Thomas, G. M. (2004). Building the buzz in the hive mind. *Journal of Consumer Behaviour*, *4*(1), 64–72. doi:10.1002/cb.158

Timmermans, S., Bowker, G., & Star, S. L. (1996). Infrastructure and organizational transformation: classifying nurses' work. In W. Orlikowski, G. Walsham, M. Jones, & J. DeGross (Eds.), *Information technology and changes in organizational work* (pp. 344–370). London: Chapman and Hall.

TrendWatching. (2006). Customer – Made: time to tap into the global brain. Retrieved from http://trendwatching.com/trends/CUSTOMER-MADE.htm

Van Dijck, J. (2009). Media, Culture & Society: Users like you? Theorizing agency in user-generated content. *Media Culture & Society*, *31*(1), 41–58. doi:10.1177/0163443708098245

Wilson, R. F. (2000). The six simple principles of viral marketing. *Web Marketing Today*. Retrieved from http://library.softgenx.com/Children/marketing/ViralMarketing.pdf

KEY TERMS AND DEFINITIONS

Co-Creation: When the meaning of value and the process of value creation are shifting from a product- and firm-centric view to personalized consumer experiences.

Content Sharing: The sharing of online content which includes information, photographs, music and videos.

Ecosystem: A community of interacting organisms and their physical environment.

E-Marketing: The use of the Internet and related communication technologies to achieve marketing objectives.

Marketing Information System: A marketing information system (MkIS) is an information system (IS) designed to support marketing activities.

Online Brand Video: A brand's marketing video that was released online for marketing objectives.

Social Media Marketing: The process of gaining website traffic or attention through social media sites.

Social Media: Websites and applications that enable users to create and share content or to participate in social networking.

Social Proof: A psychological phenomenon where people assume the actions of others in an attempt to reflect correct behavior for a given situation.

User-Generated Content: The production of content by the general public rather than by paid professionals and experts in the field.

Viral Marketing: A marketing technique whereby information about a company's goods or services is passed electronically from one Internet user to another.

Viral Video: A viral video is a video that becomes popular through the process of (most often) Internet sharing, typically through video sharing websites, social media and email.

Chapter 10
The Rise of Relationship Marketing with Social Media

Ana Margarida Barreto
New University of Lisbon, Portugal

ABSTRACT

The mission and concern of the proposed chapter is to contribute to the improvement of market performance through marketing, specifically relationship marketing, by taking into consideration the brand perspective and the consumer perspective. In addition, the proposed chapter aims to describe how social media has brought big challenges to brands, especially the strong ones, with repercussions on their brand image and consequently their brand equity, and how relationship marketing can be the answer to these new challenges.

INTRODUCTION

New information and communication technologies (ICT) in general, and the Internet in particular, continue to grow in importance and to affect buying habits, entertainment, and user relationships. This phenomenon is not exclusive to one generation, but to all, with greater or lesser incidence. To illustrate, let's consider the following data: from 2000 to 2012 the Internet grew 566.4% (data from internetworldstats.com), in 2010 there were 2.4 billion Internet users (*idem*), corresponding to 34.3% world penetration. With regard to the popular SNS Facebook, in March 2013 there were 665 million daily active users. Also, in May 2013, there were more than 554.000.000 Twitter users, and in the year 2010, 25 billion tweets were sent (Twitter).

Neglecting these facts may undermine the success of any organization, whether private or public, from the services industry, or consumer goods, a political party, or nongovernmental organization. This is because the Internet is not only a digital space where a growing world population joins, but it is also an easy tool for communication or business purposes. In addition, the adoption of e-business is positively related to four measures of performance: business efficiency, sales performance, customer satisfaction, and relationship development (Wu *et al.*, 2003).

DOI: 10.4018/978-1-4666-8459-1.ch010

Effectively and efficiently using the Internet as a strategic channel requires a combined domain of various marketing practices. First, given the interactive nature of the channel, the Internet allows the establishment of interactive relations with different audiences, large-scale, synchronous, or diachronic, individualized and personalized (interactive marketing). Organizations committed to talking with and listening to the public can enjoy the constant enrichment of their databases (database marketing) and may later, based on the collected information, target their audience and customize their future messages (direct marketing) and take advantage of various resources (like text, sound, video, and image) at low cost. These messages, along with a set of actions that aim at sharing and collaborative construction of the brand or its products/services with their audiences, will help to foster a sense of closeness between the brand and customer (impacting the trustworthiness of the latter). In addition, they also provide the ability for the brand to immediately detect and act upon situations of crisis or discontent, avoiding the powerfully negative word of mouth (WOM) (relational strategy).

The perception that the future of marketing walks hand-in-hand with the evolution of ICT has aroused the interest of scholars worldwide who seek to explain this symbiotic relationship and to come out with new marketing concepts.

In 2001, Coviello, Milley & Marcolin added a fifth element to the theoretical classification of empirically validated marketing practices (transactional marketing, marketing database, interaction marketing and network marketing), made by the study group's "Contemporary Marketing Practices", in 1997. The concept introduced was e-Marketing (eM), defined as using the Internet and other interactive technologies to create and mediate dialogues between a company and its customers.

The designation of eM has been used deliberately in order to avoid the term "interactive," so that there was no confusion with the concept of interaction marketing. eM includes and is based on interactive technologies related with the management of customer relationships, sales activity, research, analysis and planning (see Brady, Saren, Tzokas, 2002). Using the words of Reedy, Schull & Zimmerman: "They are all online or electronic activities that facilitate [the] production and marketing of products or services to meet the desires and needs of the consumer. The electronic marketing improves the overall marketing program that, in turn, enables the company's objectives in e-commerce "(2001, pg. 26).

The eM concept combines within itself the practice of different types of marketing, such as database marketing, networking, and interaction marketing (Coviello et al., 2001), or, according to Rublescki (2009), the tools of traditional marketing with electronic resources.

Other denominations have been advanced to explain this phenomenon, like: cyber-marketing, digital marketing, communication and online marketing, web marketing (marketing done in a Web environment, according to Rublescki, 2009), and "one to one marketing". Some have even suggested that the word marketing be altered to "markITing" so that could reflect the widespread use of ICT in contemporary marketing practice (Brady et al., 2002).

Another concept that combines relational marketing and the use of new technologies is "customer relationship marketing" (CRM). CRM is defined as "cross-functional integration of processes, people, operations and marketing resources enabled by information technology and applications" (Payne & Frow, 2005, pg. 168). Although it is often confused with relationship marketing (Sheth & Parvitiyar, 2001), CRM is dedicated exclusively to the management of customer relationships, while relationship marketing can be applied to all stakeholders (Ryals, Payne, 2001; Chen, Ching, 2007).

To characterize marketing executed in an online environment as eM, dependent or driven by a relational strategy, seems to be conceptually the more correct option to describe the response to the demands of a 2.0 market, since it combines the traditional marketing mix ("4Ps"), with interactivity (dialogue), fostered by the databases (databases), and with the perspective and needs of current consumer ("4Cs"), guided by a relational strategy (Rublescki, 2009). In fact, the verification of the increasing use of eM by organizations and the reduced use of traditional methods makes the practice of eM a fait accompli nowadays, which means that eM can be seen as an established practice in most companies and no longer a novelty. For Brodie, Winklhofer, Coviello, and Johnston (2007), the success of eM comes from its coexistence with traditional practices, rather than it emerging as an independent practice.

From a marketing perspective, the Internet is not only important for its implementation growth, but also because it has empowered consumers and given them more control over information.

In the early days of the Internet, communication between organizations and users followed a communicational model represented by the "one-to-many" model. That is, the organization produced the message and the target received it; the organization informed and the target was informed.

With the emergence of the Web 2.0, roughly in 2004, the Internet suffers a qualitative evolution. New softwares with odd features are included to the existing supply (for example, blogs and social network sites), promoting the participation and interaction among users in equal circumstances.

It can be said that the democratization comes into the world of the Internet, and consequently, the communication paradigm "one-to-many" is replaced by the pattern "many-to-many." In other words, the information disseminated in the digital space ceases to have only one source, controller and selective, to have multiple, with or without anonymity. The society of information gives way to the society of knowledge, the era of production to the era of collaboration.

As a result, in the complex web of the network of the networks, users realized that their "voice" can be transmitted easily and free of charge, and, most importantly, be heard by many without geographical barriers. This loss of control over the information disseminated by companies in relation to their brands and themselves brings a new consciousness to Internet users – one that is selective, critical, and informed and that demands to be heard and demands greater transparency on the part of organizations.

The combination of these two factors (loss of control of information disseminated and the empowerment of clients) becomes indispensable in the application of a relational and interactive strategy between organizations and their customers with the support of new information and communication technologies.

Relationship Marketing

This shift from transactional marketing, represented by the marketing mix (where the goal is to increase market share and guidance is given to the product), to relationship marketing (where guidance is given to resources and their strategic capabilities with the aim of creating value and customer satisfaction), emerged from the need to initially supplement and then replace a simplistic model – which was incomplete and not sufficiently oriented towards the market and that also ignored the human factor (Grönroos, 1994; Sanchez Gil & Mollá, 2000 ; Constantinides, 2006[1]).

Relationship marketing is not a new approach, for it was planned for more than three decades (see for instance Grönroos, 1996) and the term was already being used in 1983 by Leonard Berry, in his book "Relationship Marketing" to explain a new way to ''attract, retain and - in the multi-service organizations – enhanc[e] customer relationships'' (p. 25). Research on relationship marketing began in the context of service industry (Egan, 2003) business-to-business (B2B) interaction (Morgan & Hunt, 1994).). In fact, in the 1970s two marketing schools were pioneering conceptual contributions to the relationship marketing approach - the Nordic School of Service, an expert in marketing services, represented by the researchers Christian Grönroos and Evert Gummson, among others; and the Industrial Marketing and

Purchasing (IMP) Group, geared to industrial marketing, which highlights the work of the investigator Håkansson. Only later was relationship marketing extended to the market of consumer goods in order to prove the validity, not only of consumer-company relationship, but also that of consumer-brand.

According to Blomqvist, Dahl & Haeger (1993), in relationship marketing each customer is considered as an individual or unit, the company's activities are predominantly targeted at existing customers based on interactions and dialogues, and the company aims to achieve profit through decreasing the turnover of customers and strengthening relationships with them. In the words of Berry (2002), relationship marketing is "a philosophy not only a strategy, a way of thinking about customers, marketing and value creation, not just a set of techniques, tools and tactics" (p. 73).

Many other definitions of relationship marketing have been presented over the last years, which have questioned whether it is a new area of marketing, or a new strategy, paradigm, or school. Some of these descriptions can be found in a compilation by Gummesson (1999).

It seems clear that relationship marketing guidelines suggest a change in marketing direction in favor of creating and establishing relationships that go beyond the transactional. However, it may be radical to say that relationship marketing emerged as a new paradigm that replaced the previous one.

It is true that traditional marketing needed to be revised or even replaced by a more current strategic and operating vision, one that is more realistic and effective or, as suggested by Gummesson (1999), for a new concept that focuses on the value of relationships and interactions. It is equally certain that in this sense relationship marketing emerged as a long-sought solution. Still, it is wrong to think that traditional marketing, in an operational perspective, as a paradigm, is entirely inadequate or has been entirely replaced. The combination of the four inter-relational factors of the marketing-mix (promotion, placement, price, and product) continues to make sense today. Moreover, the study by Pels (1999) discovered that firms employ a marketing approach that involves the joining of traditional marketing practices with the relational. More recently, Brodie, Coviello & Winklhofer (2008) claimed it to be possible to find a combination of different marketing practices and that successful companies are those able to be flexible and adapt to different opportunities. In other words, in practice, business-to-consumer approaches can be both relational and transactional, depending on the consumer or the product category (Garbarino & Johnson, 1999; Szmigin & Bourne, 1998). This means that relationship marketing, up to now, has not became a paradigm. What could be said instead is that marketing is going through a paradigm shift and relationship marketing is a driver of that shift, but not the only one.

Therefore, relationship marketing should be viewed as a marketing strategy that proposes the transfer of a self-centered management to a systemic view that places the organization as a network of relationships within which interactions are established (as a society).

With relationship marketing the customer is no longer seen as part of an anonymous homogeneous mass but rather ascends to the position of an individual seen as a collaborator and a co-producer. Following this idea, Wind and Rangaswamy (2000) propose the concept of "*customerization*." As mentioned by Gummesson in his book Total Relationship Marketing (2008), the "RM/CRM spotlight is on the individual, on the segment of one. It's one to one marketing. But focus is also on groups of like-minded people, affinity groups. The group members share a common interest, they want a relationship with the supplier, its products and services, and even with each other" (p. 16).

This unique relationship between brands and individuals is inimitable by the competition, providing an added value to the product or service and a competitive advantage to the organization.

For this to happen, companies have to be prepared to build and maintain a win-win relationship that both players want while knowing beforehand that the results are not immediate. Moreover, companies must take the customers' reasons to participate into account in this emotional dialogue. That is, the factors that contribute to engagement with the brand, specifically, trust, loyalty, and satisfaction. In fact, studies show that in general the longer the relationship the greater the profit. This is due to two effects resulting from loyalty: reduction of marketing costs and increase of customer share (Gummesson, 2002). To support this idea, Gummesson (1999) introduced the concept of Return on Relationship (ROR), a net financial result obtained in long-term relationships with the network of the company.

Thanks to the development of new technologies, it's now easier to apply a relationship marketing strategy. Indeed the development of new technologies and the resulting impact caused in the market and in the role of consumers, "demand" on the part of organizations for greater involvement and dialogue with their audiences.

In order to accomplish the defined goals, companies need to understand that they should listen to and know the target audience, as well as monitor and learn to adapt to social change. In doing so marketers will be able to get economic advantages (Reichheld, 1996; Blackston, 2000; Winer, 2001; Dowling, 2002), retain their customers, and convert them into brand ambassadors who will support the organization in obtaining new clients.

Thus, brands should no longer be seen only as properties of companies (Pino, 2007a). Rather it becomes necessary to have strategies which may not necessarily generate more immediate sales, but that may cause an attitude of approach between the public and the brands (Pino, 2007b).

According to Ndubisi (2003) the only sustainable growth strategy for an organization is through a mutual symbiotic relationship with customers, which will allow them to understand customers' needs more clearly and to create added value to the organization's products/services. This way, there will be increased customer retention and long-term relationships that can lead to higher revenues and reduced costs (Gummesson, 1999, p. 7).

The application of this relational approach should not be uniform but flexible to each case; it should be an approach, which can be deployed at different levels of the relationship and adapted to the audience (in form and in message) and to the new times.

By way of example, and using the words of Meadows-Klue (2008), "relationship marketing for the Facebook generation requires thinking and acting differently" (pg.245). The modification of the traditional roles of sender and receiver in the context of the Internet has changed the tone used to talk to customers. McWilliam (2000) adds that communication managers need to understand the foundations of dialogue that could lead to a strong relationship and redefine their own messages in the online context. The communication should no longer come from above, but from the same level. Companies should talk to their customers as friends do. "When brands talk about relationships in marketing, and searching for the "love" they want customers to share, most do this through the lens of a relationship between parent and infant. But now our infant has grown up" (Meadows-Klue, 2008, pg. 250). Companies are the ones that must adapt to customers and not the reverse (Wind & Mahajan, 2001).

Even though it is a strategy that aims at the growth or consolidation of an organization, it is wrong to think that relationship marketing is a foolproof recipe that can be applied blindly in any context or with any recipient. That is to say that the investment made in different contexts and with different targets does not imply obtaining similar results (Adjei, Griffith & Noble, 2009). As suggested by O'Malley and Tynan (2000), the expectation of getting an exclusive relationship may prove to be a fallacy. Even the possible value of revenue that can be obtained by a client (customer life value) has been called into question (Kellstadt & Sheth, 2002) revealing that some customers are not profitable in the long-term scenario (Reinartz & Kumar, 2000) and that relationship marketing can have diminishing returns (Hibbard, Brunel, Dant & Iacobucci, 2001).

This has made considerable impact on the applicability and feasibility of a theoretical framework of relationship marketing from the standpoint of the consumer. As regards Fournier *et al.* (1998, pg.43) "relationship marketing is powerful in theory but problematic in practice."

It is up to companies to have the sensitivity to determine the best measure to be adopted and to know how to prepare the organization as a whole, to respond before, during, and at the end of the relationship. It is also necessary to understand that the results of relationship marketing require time to determine. Finally, relationship marketing, to be effective, needs to take into account the relational mood of consumers.

Brands Reaction to Social Media

In 2004, a new terminology came into our lives, coined by Dale Dougherty, and popularized by O'Reilly Media and MediaLive International[2] intended to designate a second generation of communities and services based on Web platforms or social networks: the Web 2.0. New softwares with odd features (like blogs, wikis, podcasting, social network sites, etc.) were included to the existing supply, promoting participation and interaction among users in equal circumstances. Consequently, and more or less at the same time, appeared the concept of Web 1.0, referring to the previous generation.

These new softwares are commonly defined as Social Media. This form of media ''describes a variety of new sources of online information that are created, initiated, circulated and used by consumers intent on educating each other about products, brands, services, personalities, and issues'' (Blackshaw & Nazzaro, 2004, p. 2). According to Kaplan & Haenlein (2010), social media "is a group of Internet-based applications that build on the ideological and technological foundations of Web 2.0, and that allow the creation and exchange of User Generated Content" (p.61). As illustrated by Table 1, social media are numerous and varied.

For Meadows-Klue (2008) "within the Web 2.0 DNA, there is the creation of platforms that connect people together (social networks), the ability to produce and then share content with others (social media), the success in architecting frameworks for participation (rather than producing all the content), and extracting and processing some of a community's knowledge and then sharing it back (collective intelligence)" (p. 247).

From a commercial standpoint, social media is attractive to marketers and communication managers for the fact that consumers are at the center of discussions and talk about their consumption habits on

Table 1. Classification of Social Media by social presence/media richness and self-presentation/self-disclosure

		Social Presence / Media Richness		
		Low	**Medium**	**High**
Self-presentation/ Self disclosure	**High**	Blogs	Social network sites (e.g. Facebook)	Virtual social worlds (e.g. Second Life)
	Low	Collaborative projects (e.g. Wikipedia)	Content communities (e.g. YouTube)	Virtual game worlds (e.g.World of Warcraft)

Source: Kaplan, Haenlein (2010)

SNS using WOM and buzz marketing solutions to disseminate their messages in a strategic and effective way, benefiting from users' levels of credibility among members of their personal network. In fact, since the impact of WOM on sales was confirmed, by influencing consumers' opinions and by providing a new venue for companies to reach consumers with lower costs, it has been proposed by some researchers that businesses should embrace and facilitate WOM activities (Rosen, 2000; Godes & Mayzlin 2004; Liu, 2006; Duan, Gu & Whinston, 2008), confirming the viral potential or social effect social network sites (SNS) can have on benefit companies (Iyengar, Han & Gupta, 2009).

It is also suggested that social media can provide an excellent opportunity to leverage brand equity, specifically by the level of engagement, due to their online interactivity characteristic and the fact that personalized communication (possible on this type of website) generates the most positive outcomes, while mass-marketing and "push" messages generate the least (Jameson, 2010).

Social media has also disadvantages that should be considered in any marketing communication plan. Schrage (2000), for instance, stresses the difference between traditional markets and high-tech markets: high-tech markets are highly dynamic markets where brand attitude can be quickly built and destroyed with long lasting effect on future performance.

Social media has only been embraced by enterprises within the last few years and for that reason the effectiveness perception of this type of websites from the business point of view is still little studied in the academic literature, thus causing the need to directly contact companies to gather information. For this reason, this chapter combines the information collected in books and scientific journals on the subject of SNS with information obtained from companies, particularly from agents directly involved in the management of SNS.

To gather data, 90 of the largest Portuguese companies were contacted whose area of activity oscillates between the area of services and products, listed on the 2010 edition of the 1000 largest Portuguese companies from the Portuguese magazine "Revista Exame" and the Portuguese journal "Expresso". An online survey was sent to the heads of marketing and communication departments of the selected companies. Since the disclosure of the requested information could compromise the success of their strategic plans and consequently their interest to participate, anonymity was guaranteed through the absence of any identifier that could correspond the answers with the entity represented by the participant. 92% of the respondents claimed using SNS.

In the questionnaire distributed to the Portuguese companies, they were asked, by way of an open question, which are the main disadvantages when using SNS? As indicated in Table 2, 23.5% of the answers referred to the existence of negative comments from consumers. Followed by the lack of control of the content posted by consumers, the need for an immediate response, and the need for relevant content (17.6%). 11.7% stressed the company's exposure and the need for a policy of transparency as two other disadvantages. Participants also identified as limitations the lack of preparation to deal with the customer in this new environment and the need for constant monitoring (6%). Other cited concerns regarding the use of SNS were: the ability to distinguish from the competition on the SNS; the creation of a conversation (one-to-one communication) between the brand and the target, capable of adding value to the brand; the constant need for actualization and the capability to predict mass reactions to the messages; the facility to create and destroy a brand in these online spaces; the establishment of a close relation between the brand and the target; the amplification of the WOM phenomenon; and the need for resources to be and to follow the evolution of the medium.

Table 2. Seven main disadvantages when using SNS for Portuguese companies

Seven Main Disadvantages When Using SNS	
Negative comments from consumers	23.50%
Lack of control of the content posted by consumers	17.60%
Need for an immediate response	17.60%
Need for relevant content	17.60%
Company's exposure and the need for policy of transparency	11.60%
Lack of preparation to deal with the customer in SNS	6%
Need for constant monitoring	6%

Despite all the difficulties, 92% believed that SNS are not hype, but will remain in the future. As one of the respondents commented: "[b]eing on social network sites will be in the short term, as essential as being present in the press or on the radio".

These answers reflect a shift in the communication process between organizations and users. A change observed and recognized by 75% of the communication managers that answered the survey.

On SNS, for instance, consumers will be open to interact with brands as long as they are given the freedom to express themselves and the power to control the relationship and influence the brand. If a brand is not interested in evolving in response to consumer feedback it is not recommended to engage on these websites (Jameson, 2010). As was noted by 92% of the survey participants, SNS have empowered consumers.

On the other hand, 67% of the respondents also believe that SNS have also empowered brands, and 59% see SNS as a source of information about their target, a way to establish a closer relation with it (59%), and as providing an opportunity to conduct direct one-to-one communication with their target (58%).

When questioned why they decided to use SNS, participants replied that it is a reality with an important role in a well-conceived communication plan, specifically to spread a message. Others mentioned the fact that SNS are a trend with low costs. In addition, SNS allows brand's exposition in an online place frequented by many users, favoring brand notoriety. As noted previously, participants also stress the fact that SNS favors the establishment of a relationship with their target (especially the younger cohort), helps them engage with it, and are a source of information and feedback. Finally, participants reported that they use SNS because they are interested in testing the return generated by these new platforms compared to traditional media.

Social Media from the Consumer Perspective

Since its inception, SNS such as Facebook, MySpace and LinkedIn have become digital spaces capable of attracting millions of users in various age groups on a worldwide scale (Boyd & Ellison, 2007; Lenhart & Madden 2007), and the applications and features of these types of websites have changed the way Internet users communicate and interact with members of their social networks. This has led to meaningful changes in the media landscape (Cooke & Buckley, 2008), and the burgeoning of a new form of computer-mediated communication around the world connected by Internet, where the many-to-many, one-to-many and one-to-one communication models prevail (Barreto, 2013).

The main question that stands out is "why are online social networks so popular?" This is a question that can be answered through a multidisciplinary point of view, including sociological, psychological, biological and even technological perspectives.

First of all, human beings like to be informed. This conscious or unconscious information need (for more information see for instance Taylor, 1962) supports people in the two roles they play as members of society - as citizens and consumers (Moore & Steele, 1991), and varies considerably from individual to individual, because they are inherently different and belong to different social groupings.

On the other hand, social interaction per se is also a human need and an unavoidable occurrence. The following findings are representative of this biological need and its effects: people who have close connections with others are not only happier but are also mentally and physically healthier than people who lack stable and meaningful social support (McAdams, 1986). Loneliness shows up in measurements of stress hormones, immune function, and cardiovascular function (Hawkley et. al., 2006); lack or loss of interpersonal relationships also leads to negative emotional experiences such as anxiety, depression and feelings of isolation (Baumeister & Tice, 1990; Simpson, 1987); forming and maintaining social bonds is positively correlated with happiness in life and positive life outcomes (Baumeister & Twenge, 2003; Myers, 1992); finally, interaction with others is a natural behaviour that according to recent research from the University of Padova appears as early as week 14 of gestation (Castiello et al., 2010).

From a sociological point of view, human beings are inherently driven by a desire to form and maintain interpersonal relationships (Baumeister & Leary, 1995; Bowlby, 1969, 1973; Maslow, 1968; McClelland, 1951; Murray, 1954; Stevens & Fiske, 1995). This need for social inclusion can also be seen as a way to survive prevalent since the early days (Caporael & Brewer, 1995; Wilson, 1978), when rejection from the group would have meant death to the hominids. Since then, the survival value of interdependence has evolved into a set of internal mechanisms that propel human beings into social groups (Stevens & Fiske, 1995) and predispose them to relate with others, to experience affective distress when social relationships are denied or dissolved, and to experience pleasure or positive affects from social contact and relatedness (Baumeister & Leary, 1995). For Abraham Maslow (1968), when people could not meet this need of belonging, their need for self-esteem would not be satisfied either. In other words, without being first accepted as part of a group or by others, self-esteem doesn't develop properly. That is why people develop social bonds with relative ease under even the most adverse circumstances (Tajfel, 1970) and why the frequency with which adolescents use SNS can influence their social self-esteem and well-being (Valkenburg, Peter & Schouten, 2006).

SNS not only answer these needs for being informed and for social inclusion, but also facilitates them, by unifying different social networks in which the individual belongs, and by making it easy to catch up with them quickly (Silverthorne, 2009). This fact is supported by previous research that suggests that most SNS primarily support pre-existing social relations, although exceptions exist. That is, people interact on this type of websites with other people who are already part of their extended social network (Boyd & Ellison, 2007). When Danah Boyd (2007) asked some teenagers the reason why they chose to be part of the SNS MySpace, the answered she got was, "cuz that's where my friends are" (p.9). When she asked what they do on the site, they answered, "I don't know… I just hang out" (p.9).

These reactions lead us to one of the other reasons for the success of SNS – the social influence, which is defined as the change in an individual's thoughts, feelings, attitudes, or behaviors that results from interaction with others who are perceived to be similar, desirable, or experts (Rashotte, 2006). This is particularly true among adolescents (Urberg et al., 2003).

Another explanation that supports the endorsement of SNS is the social comparison theory, suggested by Festinger (1954). According to this theory individuals evaluate their own opinions and desires by comparing themselves to others perceived to be reasonably similar to them. The advantage of SNS is that they make this comparison process easy.

The principle of homophily can also be applied to explain the adoption of SNS by many users. Since we like and tend to spend time with people with whom we identify (Lazarsfeld & Merton, 1954; McPherson, Smith-Lovin & Cook, 2001), SNS have impacted both the efficiency of maintaining and acquiring desired relationships.

Furthermore, SNS are unique websites that enable users to articulate and make visible their social networks. This can result in connections between individuals that would not otherwise be made, between ''latent ties'' (Haythornthwaite, 2005) who share some connection.

Finally, SNS are relatively easy and enjoyable to use (Pinho & Soares, 2011). The type of design of the SNS is also crucial as it influences the level of adoption. Lorenzo-Romero et al. (2011) have also predicted that the perceived usefulness of SNS have a direct impact on the intention to use them, and an indirect impact through attitude. Another conclusion drawn from their study is that ease of use has a negative influence on perceived risk, although perceived risk is not a significant determinant of how useful SNS are perceived to be.

A summary of the aforementioned reasons for social network sites popularity can be found in Figure 1.

Despite all the reasons for using SNS, it is the ongoing levels of activity of the network users that determine the site's continuing success (Stroud, 2008). What attracts users to the site is a continually changing digital content (e.g., messages, pictures, photos, music, videos, blogs) generated by other users (Trusov et. al. 2006). And even though the mainstream media provides stories of online evidence

Figure 1. A multidisciplinary perspective to the popularity of social networks sites

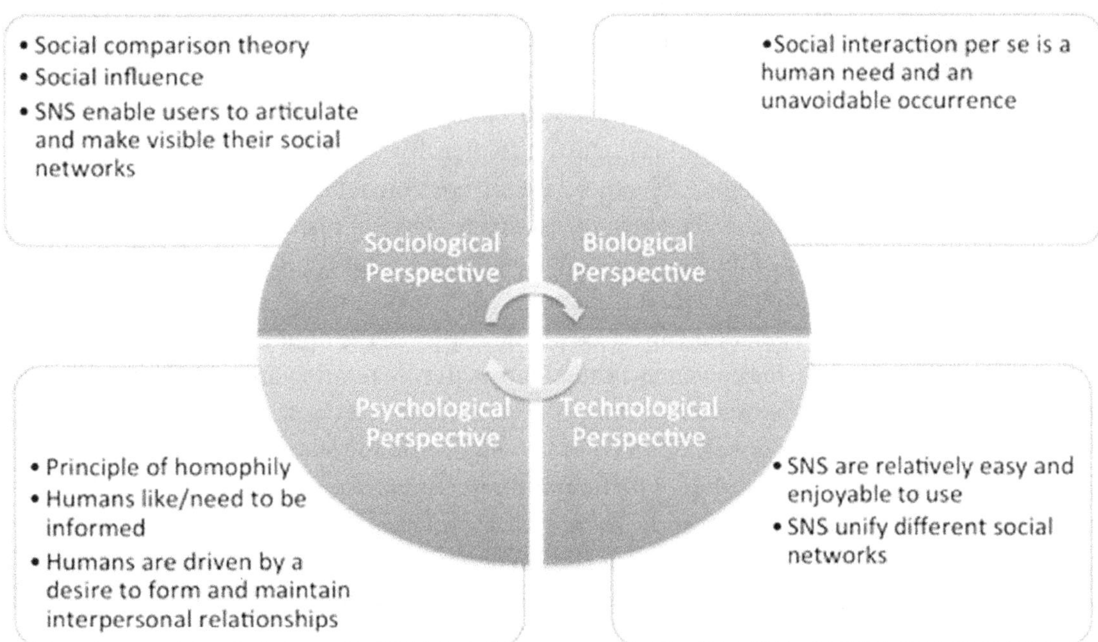

that SNS can be used against users in job interviews, users continue to publish personal data suggesting that their desire for identity is worth the calculated risk (Kent, 2008). Moreover, users trust both the data found on individuals' profiles and the wisdom of publishing data about themselves (Dwyer, Hiltz & Passerini, 2007).

What Makes People Connect with Brands?

By knowing why consumers develop and maintain relationships with brands, relationship literature advances by understanding which constructs should be measured, and brands find new ways for improving their performance and consequently strengthen their competitiveness.

According to the findings from Lab42's study (2012) concerning the SNS Facebook, users find brand pages highly valuable – in fact, 87% of people on Facebook "like" brands. The major motivations for users to like a brand on Facebook are: to get access to promotions and discounts; because they are loyal consumers or they trust the brand; because a friend has liked the brand; or even to help out a friend. In addition, 82% of people think Facebook is a good place to interact with brands; 75% feel more connected to a brand on Facebook and 50% of consumers think a brand's Facebook page is more useful than a brand's website.

However, 46% of users that liked a brand have no intention to buy from the brand, whether because they just wanted to have a free item, or because they can't afford the brand's products (Lab42's research, 2012). In this case, consumers can actually achieve self-actualization, even though they do not even consume the tangible product, since the value also lies in the brand, rather than only in the commodity (Wilson & Morgan, 2011).

On the other hand, consumers also find reasons to "unlike" a brand on this website, specifically when brands post too frequently; when consumers stop liking the brand; when they have a bad customer experience; or if they feel embarrassed to like it publicly. Regarding the last reason, it is worth mentioning that the three main categories social media users find most embarrassing are: adult novelty items, diet/weight loss products and health and wellness products or services.

As for the reasons given for not liking a brand, they are the following: brands clutter the user's newsfeed (47%), consumers don't want to be contacted (36%), they have concerns about privacy (30%) and because they use the SNS only to post things relevant to their lives (27%).

For Ashworth, Dacin & Thomson (2009), there are six possible relationship functions: knowledge – a relationships exists because it helps the consumer to make sense of his or her situation; utilitarian – a relationship based on the ability of the brand to consistently and reliably aid in the achievement of other goals, that is, the relationship is fostered (or terminated) based on rewarding (or punishing) consequences of that relationship; hedonic – a relationship based on the ability of the brand to directly inspire a variety of positive affective reactions in the consumer; value-expressive – a relationship based on the consistency of the values associated with the brand and the values central to the consumer (similar to the concept of "identification" as it has been conceptualized in the relationship literature), meaning, consumers are externally motivated to form relationships with brands for the social acceptance that comes from creating an image that others value and respect; social-adjustive – a relationship that exists because consumers' association with the brand creates a desired impression or to receive social approval; and finally, affiliation – a relationship that serves individuals' basic needs for friendship and belonging.

CONCLUSION

Whatever name we can call, there is no doubt that new technologies have brought a change in marketing practices, since traditional concepts and practices were insufficient in our days, as expected (Mintzberg et al., 1995:7, Bruce et al. 1996; Venkatesh, 1998).

These days there is still a common misunderstanding supporting the idea that to have a site in social media is merely to have a presence on a popular website where a large number of users converge. Nothing could be further from the truth. Social media is not about technology, but about people. It's about building relationships with your target audience and being able to meet the needs of both.

It is important not to confuse connection with relationship. Brands and consumers/clients can be connected to the same channel and yet not have any kind of relationship. Relationships are not an immediate and spontaneous outcome of brand presence in SNS. Establishing relationships with customers is much more than merely aspiring to a precise number of likes, friends, followers or fans.

The main advantage of a brand having a SNS page is the possibility of interaction between the brand and its followers, which can in turn lead to engagement. Hence, SNS have risen as a solution for companies interested in implementing a relationship marketing strategy.

Despite all the recognized benefits, some brands have not been exploring the full potential of the SNS Facebook. For instance, even though consumers are willing to engage with brands, the latter fail to promote engagement and use SNS merely as an informative channel. Perhaps this occurs because brands do not feel ready to engage in a relationship with consumers, or perhaps they do not even know how to begin doing so. As claimed by Wilson and Morgan (2011), "if brands are to be considered like people, by people, they should enjoy friendships with people and to assume that brands can reproduce identical friendships, to the ones enjoyed by consumers, at the same physical and emotional level may be a step too far" (p. 4).

Brands win when their consumers are engaged, for they act as brand advocators by recommending the brand products or services to their friends, who in turn also make recommendations to their friends (earned advertising). In other words, engagement is the key word, and for that brands first need to know their audience, how they behave, what they like, and what they expect from brands. To meet this challenge, it is essential to "hear" the audience. As brands start to hear them, soon they will be in the same line/ singing the same tune.

Furthermore, companies should bear in mind that it is not enough for consumers to merely like or follow their brand. Rather, they have to give them reasons to visit the brand profile page and interact with it/them, otherwise the "likes" have little value. Companies should also be customer-focused, that is, they should know their target well, which can be achieved by talking and listening to them, and by acting in accordance with the information gathered.

Social media is not another advertising platform, therefore companies should avoid the "campaign mentality" when using it. Instead, they are useful instruments that can add value to a brand whenever companies are willing and committed to engage in strategic and long-term thinking/relationships.

Still concerning the SNS users, it is important to understand that not only consumers can follow the brand activity. Stakeholders are also aware of the brand's activity and, consumers' perceptions about the brand and can therefore be influenced by what they see.

Thus, the key to success lies in how to use the knowledge gained from listening, which means that data mining, supported by new technology, becomes crucial. At the moment a brand can achieve engagement with its audience, it can then get the desired relationship. But remember that relationships are not static - they evolve and it takes work to maintain them.

REFERENCES

Adjei, M. T., Griffith, D. A., & Noble, S. M. (2009). When do relationships pay off for small retailers? Exploring targets and contexts to understand the value of relationship marketing. *Journal of Retailing*, *85*(4), 493–501. doi:10.1016/j.jretai.2009.09.001

Ashworth, L., Dacin, P., & Thomson, M. (2009), Why on earth do consumers have relationships with marketers? Toward understanding the functions of brand relationships. Handbook of brand relationships (pp. 82-106).

Baumeister, R., & Leary, M. (1995). The need to belong: Desire for interpersonal attachments as a fundamental human motivation. *Psychological Bulletin*, *117*(3), 497–529. doi:10.1037/0033-2909.117.3.497 PMID:7777651

Baumeister, R., & Tice, D. (1990). Anxiety and social exclusion. *Journal of Social and Clinical Psychology*, *9*(2), 165–195. doi:10.1521/jscp.1990.9.2.165

Baumeister, R., & Twenge, J. (2003). *The social self.* Handbook of Psychology. doi:10.1002/0471264385.wei0514

Berry, L. L. (2002). Relationship marketing of services—Perspectives from 1983 and 2000. *Journal of Relationship Marketing*, *1*(1), 59–77. doi:10.1300/J366v01n01_05

Blackshaw, P., & Nazzaro, M. (2009). Consumer-Generated Media (CGM) 101: Word-of-mouth in the age of the Webfortified consumer. In W.G. Mangold, & D.J. Faulds (Ed.). Social media: The new hybrid element of the promotion mix. *Business Horizons*, *52*(4), 357–365.

Blackston, M. (2000). Building Brand Equity by Managing the Brand's Relationship. *Journal of Advertising Research*, *40*(November/December).

Blomqvist, R., Dahl, J., & Haeger, T. (1993). [Relationship Marketing: Strategy and Methods for Service Competition] (In Swedish). Göteborg, Sweden: IHM Förlag.

Bowlby, J. (1969). Attachment and loss: Vol. 1. *Attachment*. New York: Basic Books.

Bowlby, J. (1973). Attachment and loss: Vol. 2. *Separation: Anxiety and anger*. New York: Basic Books.

Boyd, D. (2007). Why Youth (Heart) Social Network Sites: The Role of Networked Publics in Teenage Social Life. In D. Buckingham (Ed.), *MacArthur Foundation Series on Digital Learning – Youth, Identity, and Digital Media Volume*. Cambridge, MA: MIT Press.

Boyd, D., & Ellison, N. B. (2007). Social network sites: Definition, history, and scholarship. *Journal of Computer-Mediated Communication*, *13*(1), 210–230. doi:10.1111/j.1083-6101.2007.00393.x

Brady, M., Saren, M., & Tzokas, N. (2002). Integrating information technology into marketing practice–the IT reality of contemporary marketing practice. *Journal of Marketing Management* 18.5(6), 555-577.

Brodie, R., Coviello, N., & Winklhofer, H. (2008). Investigating Contemporary Marketing Practices: A Review of the First Decade of the CMP Research Program. *Journal of Business and Industrial Marketing*, *23*(2), 84–94. doi:10.1108/08858620810850191

Brodie, R. J., Winklhofer, H., Coviello, N. E., & Johnston, W. J. (2007). Is e-marketing coming of age? An examination of the penetration of e-marketing and firm performance. *Journal of Interactive Marketing*, *21*(1), 2–21. doi:10.1002/dir.20071

Bruce, M., Leverick, F., Littler, D., & Wilson, D. (1996). The changing scope and substance of marketing - the impact of IT. Proceedings from the European Academy of Marketing Conference - Marketing for an Expanding Europe, Budapest (Vol. 1, 185-204). University of Economic Science.

Castiello, U., Becchio, C., Zoia, S., Nelini, C., Sartori, L., Blason, L., & Gallese, V. et al. (2010). Wired to Be Social: The Ontogeny of Human Interaction. *PLoS ONE*, *5*(10), e13199. doi:10.1371/journal.pone.0013199 PMID:20949058

Chen, J., & Ching, R. (2007). The effects of Information and Communication Technology on Customer Relationship Management and customer lock-in. *International Journal of Electronic Business*, *5*(5), 478–498. doi:10.1504/IJEB.2007.015446

Constantinides, E. (2006). The marketing mix revisited: Towards the 21st Century marketing. *Journal of Marketing Management*, *22*(3-4), 407–438. doi:10.1362/026725706776861190

Cooke, M., & Buckley, N. (2008). Web 2.0, social networks and the future of market research. *International Journal of Market Research*, *50*(2), 267–292.

Coviello, N., Milley, R., & Marcolin, B. (2001). Understanding IT-enabled interactivity in contemporary marketing. *Journal of Interactive Marketing*, *15*(4), 18–33. doi:10.1002/dir.1020

Dowling, G. (2002). Customer Relationship Management: In B2C Markets, Often Less is More. *California Management Review*, *44*(3), 87–104. doi:10.2307/41166134

Duan, W., Gu, B., & Whinston, A. B. (2008). The Dynamics of Online Word-of-Mouth and Product Sales—An Empirical Investigation of the Movie Industry. *Journal of Retailing*, *84*(2), 233–242. doi:10.1016/j.jretai.2008.04.005

Dwyer, C., Hiltz, S., & Passerini, K. (2007). *Trust and Privacy Concern Within Social Networking Sites: A Comparison of Facebook and MySpace*. AMCIS.

Egan, J. (2003). Back to the Future: Divergence in Relationship marketing Research. *Marketing Theory*, *3*(1), 145–157. doi:10.1177/1470593103003001008

Festinger, L. (1954). A theory of social comparison processes. *Human Relations*, *7*(2), 117–140. doi:10.1177/001872675400700202

Fournier, S., Dobscha, S., & Mick, D. (1998). Preventing the premature death of relationship marketing. *Harvard Business Review*, *76*(1), 42–43. PMID:10176918

Garbarino, E., & Johnson, M. (1999). The Different Roles of Satisfaction, Trust and Commitment for and Transactional Consumers. *Journal of Marketing*, *63*, 70–87. doi:10.2307/1251946

Godes, D., & Mayzlin, D. (2004). Using online conversations to study word-of-mouth communication. *Marketing Science*, *23*(4), 545–560. doi:10.1287/mksc.1040.0071

Grönroos, C. (1994). From Marketing Mix to Relationship Marketing: Towards a Paradigm Shift in Marketing. *Management Decision*, *32*(2), 4–20. doi:10.1108/00251749410054774

Grönroos, C. (1996). Relationship marketing: Strategic and tactical implications. *Management Decision*, *34*(3), 5–14. doi:10.1108/00251749610113613

Gummesson, E. (1999). *Total Relationship Marketing*. London: Butterworth-Heinemann.

Gummesson, E. (2002). Relationship marketing and a new economy: It's time for de-programming. *Journal of Services Marketing*, *16*(7), 585–589. doi:10.1108/08876040210447315

Hawkley, L. C., Bosch, J. A., Engeland, C. G., Marucha, P. T., & Cacioppo, J. T. (2006). tT Loneliness, Dysphoria, Stress, and Immunity: A Role for Cytokines. *Cytokines: Stress and immunity*: 67.

Haythornthwaite, C. (2005). Social networks and Internet connectivity effects. *Information Communication and Society*, *8*(2), 125–147. doi:10.1080/13691180500146185

Hibbard, J., Brunel, F., Dant, R., & Iacobucci, D. (2001). Does relationship marketing age well? *Business Strategy Review*, *12*(4), 29–35. doi:10.1111/1467-8616.00189

Iyengar, R., Han, S., & Gupta, S. (2009). Do friends influence purchases in a social network? *Harvard Business School Marketing Unit Working Paper* 09-123.

Jameson, K. (2010). Flying high in a new age: An investigation into building airline brand equity through the interactivity of social media. Leeds Metropolitan University, April.

Kaplan, A. M., & Haenlein, M. (2010). Users of the world, unite! The challenges and opportunities of Social Media. *Business Horizons*, *53*(1), 59–68. doi:10.1016/j.bushor.2009.09.003

Lazarsfeld, P. F., & Merton, R. K. (1954). Friendship as a social process: A substantive and methodological analysis. In M. Berger, T. Abel, & C. H. Page (Eds.), *Freedom and Control in Modern Society. 18- 66*. Van Nostrand, New York.

Lenhart, A., Madden, M. (2007), Teens, Privacy, & Online Social Networks. *Pew Internet and American Life Project Report.* Washington.

Liu, Y. (2006). Word of Mouth for Movies: Its Dynamics and Impact on Box Office Revenue. *Journal of Marketing*, *70*(July).

Lorenzo-Romero, C., Constantinides, E., & Alarcón-del-Amo, M. D. C. (2011). Consumer adoption of social networking sites: Implications for theory and practice. *Journal of Research in Interactive Marketing*, *5*(2), 170–188. doi:10.1108/17505931111187794

Maslow, A. H. (1968). Toward a Psychology of Being. New York: John.

McAdam, D. (1986). Recruitment to High-Risk Activism: The Case of Freedom Summer. *American Journal of Sociology*, *92*(1), 64–90. doi:10.1086/228463

McClelland, D. C. (1951). *Measuring motivation in phantasy: the achievement motive*. Psycnet APA.

McPherson, J., Smith-Lovin, L., & Cook, J. (2001). Birds of a feather: Homophily in social networks. *Annual Review of Sociology*, *27*(1), 415–444. doi:10.1146/annurev.soc.27.1.415

McWilliam, G. (2000). Building Stronger Brands through Online Communities. *Sloan Management Review*, *41*(3).

Meadows-Klue, D. (2008), Falling in Love 2.0: Relationship Marketing for the Facebook Generation. *Journal of Direct, Data and Digital Marketing Practice*, 9(3).

Mintzberg, H., Quinn, J., & Ghoshal, S. (1995). *The Strategy Process* (European ed.). London: Prentice Hall.

Moore, N., & Steele, J. (1991). *Information-intensive Britain: a critical analysis of the policy issues*. London: Policy Studies Institute.

Morgan, R., & Hunt, S. (1994). The Commitment–trust Theory of Relationship Marketing. *Journal of Marketing*, *58*(3), 20. doi:10.2307/1252308

Myers, D. G. (1992). *The pursuit of happiness*. New York: Morrow.

Ndubisi, N. O. (2003). Service quality: Understanding customer perception and reaction, and its impact on business. *International Journal of Business*, *5*(2), 207–219.

O'Malley, L., & Tynan, C. (2000). Relationship marketing in consumer markets–rhetoric or reality? *European Journal of Marketing*, *34*(7), 797–815. doi:10.1108/03090560010331225

Payne, A., & Frow, P. (2005). A Strategic Framework for Customer Relationship Management. *Journal of Marketing*, *69*(4), 167–176. doi:10.1509/jmkg.2005.69.4.167

Pels, J. (1999). Exchange relationships in consumer markets? *European Journal of Marketing*, *33*(1/2), 19–37. doi:10.1108/03090569910249157

Pinho, José Carlos Martins, & Soares, A.M. (2011). Examining the technology acceptance model in the adoption of social networks. *Journal of Research in Interactive Marketing*, *5*(2), 116–129.

Pino, C. (2007a). *El Anunciante en la Era de la Saturación Publicitaria: Nuevas Herramientas de Comunicación*. Ámbitos.

Pino, C. (2007b). Nueva Era en la Comunicación Comercial Audiovisual: El Marketing Viral. *Pensar la Publicidad*, *1*(2), 63–76.

Rashotte, L. S. (2006). Social Influence. In G. Ritzer, & J.M. Ryan (Ed.), The Blackwell Encyclopedia of Sociology (Vol. 9, pp. 4426-4429). Oxford: Blackwell Publishing.

Reedy, J., Schullo, S., & Zimmerman, K. (2001). *Marketing eletrônico*. São Paulo.

Reichheld, F. (1996). *The Loyalty Effect*. Boston: Harvard Business School Press.

Reinartz, W. J., & Kumar, V. (2000). On the profitability of long-life customers in a noncontractual setting: An empirical investigation and implications for marketing. *Journal of Marketing*, *64*(4), 17–35. doi:10.1509/jmkg.64.4.17.18077

Rosen, E. (2000). *The Anatomy of Buzz: How to Create Word-of-Mouth Marketing*. New York: Doubleday Currency.

Rublescki, A. (2009). Webmarketing e cibercliente: o Marketing em tempos de "4Ps+ 2Ds+ 4Cs". *Biblioteca On-line de ciências da comunicação–BOCC*.

Ryals, L., & Payne, A. (2001). Customer Relationship Management in Financial Services: Towards Information-enabled Relationship Marketing. *Journal of Strategic Marketing*, *9*(1), 3–27. doi:10.1080/713775725

Sánchez, M., Gil, I., & Mollá, A. (2000). Estatus del marketing de relaciones. *Revista Europea de Dirección y Economia de la Empresa*, *9*(3), 47–64.

Schrage, M. (2000). A Go-Go Dot-Com? Not if its stock went-went. *Adweek Magazines' Technology Marketing,* 20(12), 32.

Sheth, J. N., & Kellstadt, C. H. (2002). The future of relationship marketing. *Journal of Services Marketing*, *16*(7), 590–592. doi:10.1108/08876040210447324

Sheth, J. N., & Parvatiyar, A. (2001). Customer Relationship Management: Emerging Practice, Process and Discipline. *Journal of Economic and Social Research*, *3*(2), 1–34.

Silverthorne, S. (2009). *Understanding Users of Social Networks. September 14* (pp. 1–2). Harvard Business Knowledge.

Simpson, J. A. (1987). The dissolution of romantic relationships: Factors involved in relationship stability and emotional distress. *Journal of Personality and Social Psychology*, *53*(4), 683–692. doi:10.1037/0022-3514.53.4.683

Stevens, L. E., & Fiske, S. T. (1995). Motivation and cognition in social life: A social survival perspective. *Social Cognition*, *13*(3), 189–214. doi:10.1521/soco.1995.13.3.189

Szmigin, I., & Bourne, H. (1998). Consumer in relationship marketing. *Journal of Consumer Marketing*, *15*(6), 544–557. doi:10.1108/07363769810240545

Tajfel, H. (1970). Aspects of national and ethnic loyalty. *Social Sciences Information. Information Sur les Sciences Sociales*, *9*(3), 119–144. doi:10.1177/053901847000900305

Taylor, R. S. (1962). Process of Asking Questions. *American Documentation*, *13*(4), 391–396. doi:10.1002/asi.5090130405

Trusov, M., Bodapati, A. V., & Bucklin, R. E. (2006). *Your members are also your customers: Marketing for Internet social networks* (Working Paper). University of California, Los Angeles.

Urberg, K. A., Luo, Q., Pilgrim, C., & Degirmencioglu, S. M. (2003). A two-stage model of peer influence in adolescent substance use: Individual and relationship-specific differences in susceptibility to influence. *Addictive Behaviors*, *28*(7), 1243–1256. doi:10.1016/S0306-4603(02)00256-3 PMID:12915166

Valkenburg, P. M., Peter, J., & Schouten, A. P. (2006). Friend networking sites and their relationship to adolescents' well-being and social self-esteem. *Cyberpsychology & Behavior*, *9*(5), 584–590. doi:10.1089/cpb.2006.9.584 PMID:17034326

Venkatesh, A. (1998). Cybermarketscapes and consumer freedoms and identities. *European Journal of Marketing*, *32*(7/8), 664–676. doi:10.1108/03090569810224065

Wilson, J., & Morgan, J. (2011). Friends or Freeloaders & quest; Encouraging brand conscience and introducing the concept of emotion-based consumer loss mitigation. *Journal of Brand Management*, *18*(9), 659–676. doi:10.1057/bm.2011.4

Wind, J., & Rangaswamy, A. (2000). Customerization: The Next Revolution in Mass Customization (MSI Report No. 00-108). Marketing Science Institute, Cambridge, MA.

Wind, Y., & Mahajan, V. (2001). *Digital Marketing: Global Strategies from the World's Leading Experts*. Edição de John Wiley and Sons.

Winer, R. S. (2001). A Framework for Customer Relationship Management. *California Management Review*, *43*(4), 89–105. doi:10.2307/41166102

Wu, F., Mahajan, V., & Balasubramanian, S. (2003). An analysis of e-business adoption and its impact on business performance. *Journal of the Academy of Marketing Science*, *31*(4), 425–447. doi:10.1177/0092070303255379

KEY TERMS AND DEFINITIONS

Brand Engagement: Expression of positive attitude from consumers towards brands, based on positive feelings and experiences, trust and satisfaction.

Relationship Marketing: A philosophy embedded on marketing strategy about value creation, through sustainable and long-term win-win relations with the company publics.

Social Media: Internet-based applications that allow the creation and exchange of User Generated Content, following the one-to-many, the one-to-one or many-to-many communication patter.

Social Network Sites: Web-based services of user generated content with three main functions: personal, social and, in some cases, "infomercial".

Web 2.0: Designation of a second generation of communities and services based on Web platforms promoting participation and interaction among users in equal circumstances.

ENDNOTES

1. Constantinides also adds other factors responsible for the weakness of the transactional approach.
2. What is Web 2.0," by Tim O'Reilly. Published on the O'Reilly website on September 30, 2005: http://www.oreillynet.com/pub/a/oreilly/tim/news/2005/09/30/what-is-web-20.html

Chapter 11
Social Media Performance Measurement

Goetz Greve
Hamburg School of Business Administration, Germany

ABSTRACT

Today, companies are turning to social media as a source of marketing information. Comments posted on social network sites, tweets, and blogs provide a wealth of data for the improvement of marketing decision making. Thus, marketers are greatly interested in how marketing activities can affect certain social media metrics and to what extent each drives business performance. The purpose of the chapter is to elaborate on the performance outcomes of social media activities and the possibility to use data from these networks for marketing information systems. Thus, the chapter discusses the theoretical foundations of social media and develops dimensions for social media performance measurement. In addition, the integration of social media performance measurement into a marketing information system is discussed and implementation issues are critically evaluated. The chapter closes with an outline of further research directions and a conclusion.

INTRODUCTION

Social media have irreversibly changed the way people communicate. A recent McKinsey survey of 1469 C-level executives reveals that while a majority list digital marketing and social media as a top ten priority on their strategic agendas and expect social media to deliver value for their firms, only a few have begun any systematic engagement with consumers via these media (Brown & Sikes, 2012). The primary reason for this reservation among managers to fully accept social media as a platform for marketing investments has been a lack of understanding of how firm actions in social media influence consumer engagement, and in the end, impact sales (Divol, Edelman, & Sarrazin, 2012). Thus, understanding of word-of-mouth in social media and measuring the performance of marketing actions in social media are key business priorities for today's customer relationship management (CRM).

Consequentially, a new concept of CRM, called Social CRM, has emerged that attempts to incorporate the technological and social changes resulting from the introduction of social media. This new view of

DOI: 10.4018/978-1-4666-8459-1.ch011

CRM incorporates a collaborative and network-focused approach to managing customer relationships. Social CRM can be defined as "a philosophy and a business strategy, supported by a technology platform, business rules, processes and social characteristics, designed to engage the customer in a collaborative conversation in order to provide mutually beneficial value in a trusted and transparent business environment. It's the company's response to the customer's ownership of the conversation" (Greenberg, 2010, p. 34). Social CRM is not a replacement for CRM, but is rather viewed as an extension that incorporates the social functions, processes, and capabilities that address the interaction between the customer and the company as well as the interaction between customers and/or users. However, with the diffusion of social media Social CRM is closely referred to customer management with the help of social networking sites. Social networking sites are applications that enable users to connect by creating personal information profiles, inviting friends and colleagues to have access to those profiles, and sending e-mails and instant messages between each other (Kaplan & Haenlein, 2009, p. 63). Hence, social networking sites are increasingly viewed as important manifestations of interactivity among members. Interestingly, customers are demanding the same level of interactivity with their business counterparts as compared to their peers (Rainie, Purcell, & Smith, 2011). This shift in expectations is challenging companies to implement marketing strategies and actions for social media and to facilitate customer-firm interactions in social media.

The diffusion of social networking sites also stresses the importance of word-of-mouth in marketing as interaction and collaboration are key features of social networks (e.g., Facebook, and LinkedIn), and online communities (e.g., Wikipedia, YouTube, and Flickr). Social networking sites provide constant connectivity among consumers (Jansen, Zhang, & Sobel, 2009) and marketers are focusing on leveraging these social interactions among customers to achieve benefits for their customer relationships. In today's connected world, online content is an integral part of a customer, and sharing online content can have a big impact on sales and the development of customer relationships (Chevalier & Mayzlin, 2006; Godes & Mayzlin, 2009). For companies it is of fundamental importance to make customers share their opinions among others. Thus, seeding strategies for initiating word-of-mouth are gaining importance. Seeding to key influencers with a strong network may be the winning approach because these people are more likely to pass the word to others (Hinz, Skiera, Barrot, & Becker, 2011, p. 55). Furthermore, firms should take the social networks of their customers into account when trying to predict and manage customer churn (Nitzan & Libai, 2011, p. 35).

Thus, for Social CRM it is of fundamental importance to measure performance outcomes of marketing activities in social media. Hence, the main objective of the chapter is to first, lay the foundations of social networks, social media and word-of-mouth. Second, to develop a framework for social media performance measurement, and third, to discuss implementation issues for the integration of social media performance measurement into a marketing information system.

THEORETICAL BACKGROUND: SOCIAL MEDIA AND SOCIAL NETWORKS

Put simply, social media is a medium for storing or retrieving information. From a sociology perspective, social media correspond to social networks. Social networks are social structures made up of a set of actors (i.e. individuals, groups or organizations) based on a set of dyadic ties (Wassermann & Faust, 1994). Combined, "social media are communication systems that allow their social actors to commu-

Figure 1. Types of social media (visualization based on Kaplan & Haenlein, 2010)

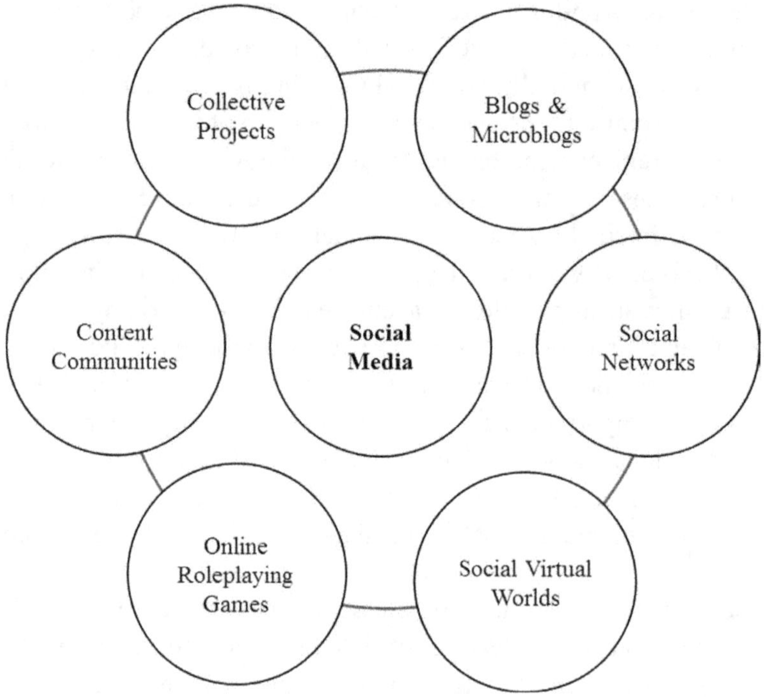

nicate along dyadic ties" (Peters, Chen, Kaplan, Ognibeni, & Pauwels, 2013, p. 282). Social media in the online context can be described as a group of Internet-based applications allowing the creation and exchange of user generated content (Kaplan & Haenlein, 2010). They classify social media into six different groups (see figure 1): collective projects (e.g., Wikipedia), blogs and micro-blogs (e.g., Twitter), content communities (e.g., Youtube), social networks (e.g., Facebook), online role-playing games (e.g., World of Warcraft), and social virtual worlds (e.g., SecondLife).

In the social sciences, a network is defined as a network of interactions or relationships, where the nodes consist of actors, and the ties consist of the relationships or interactions between these actors. Networks can have few or many actors, and one or more kinds of relations between pairs of actors. The size of a network can be determined in terms of the number of nodes of the network. The density of a network is the number of actual ties in the network divided by the number of all the ties that could be present. In an undirected network, the degree of a node is the number of ties that such a node has (see figure 2).

In directed networks, it must be distinguished between incoming ties (in-degree) and outgoing ties (out-degree). The out-degree of an actor is often a measure of how influential the actor may be. Also, the connections of an actor's neighbors can be important, even if the actor is not directly connected to them. To capture this aspect of how individuals are embedded in networks, one approach is to examine how far an actor is from other actors. The distance between two actors is the minimum number of ties that takes it to go from one to another.

Companies aiming at designing marketing actions and measuring the resulting performance in social media must understand the basic architecture and metrics of social network analysis.

Figure 2. Undirected network

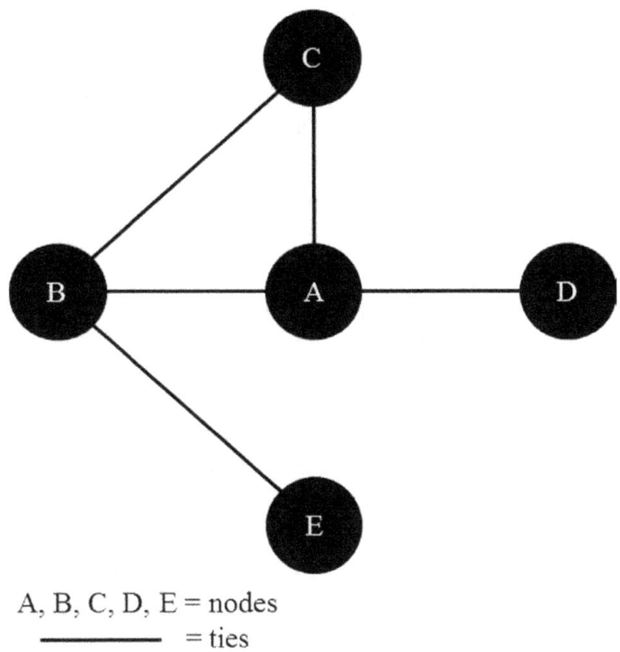

SOCIAL MEDIA AND WORD-OF-MOUTH

Social networks have been studied fairly extensively over two decades in the general context of analyzing interactions between people, and determining the important structural patterns in such interactions. In recent years research has focussed on online social networks. Online social networks have rapidly grown in popularity, because they are no longer constrained by the geographical limitations of a conventional social network in which interactions are mainly bound to face-to-face interactions or personal relationships. In addition, social networks are extremely rich, in that they contain a huge amount of content such as text, images or video for further analysis. Generally, social networking sites are just online equivalents of offline social networks. Managing relationships in social networks means managing customer interactions initiated by word-of-mouth (WOM) within a social media channel. Thus, a central aspect of social media performance measurement is about understanding word-of-mouth marketing.

Word-of-mouth marketing is the volitional influencing of consumer-to-consumer communications by marketing instruments (Kozinets, de Valck, Wojnicki, & Wilner, 2010, p. 71). The diffusion of social media channels on the internet with its reach and transparency is empowering CRM managers who are interested in managing WOM through e.g. targeted one-to-one seeding or viral marketing campaigns, with the internet allowing detailed measurement and management of Social CRM activities. Godes and Mayzlin (2009) distinguish between endogenous WOM and exogenous WOM. The former is characterized by conversations that occur naturally among consumers as a function of their experiences with the product. In contrast, the latter refers to WOM created as the result of the firm's actions. Consumers in social media channels can be regarded as active coproducers of firm-initiated WOM.

WOM in an online context can be defined as "a statement made by potential, actual, or former customers about a product or company, which is made available to a multitude of people and institutions via the Internet" (Hennig-Thurau, Gwinner, Walsh, & Gremle, 2004, p. 39). Thus, WOM communications are co-produced in consumer networks. Before the diffusion of social media on the internet, WOM has been modeled as a conversation between one consumer and another without direct prompting, influence, or measurement by marketers (Arndt, 1967). Most recent, marketers directly influence the consumer or opinion leader through targeted one-to-one seeding and viral marketing campaigns. In a network model structure, e.g. in social media, WOM messages do not flow unidirectionally, but rather are exchanged bidirectionally among members of the social network (see figure 3).

SOCIAL MEDIA AND CUSTOMER ENGAGEMENT

Customer engagement may be manifested cognitively, affectively, behaviorally or socially. The cognitive and affective elements of customer engagement incorporate the experiences and feelings of customers whereas the behavioral and social elements capture the participation by current and potential customers, both within and outside of the exchange situations (Vivek, Beatty, & Morgan, 2012). In other words, customer engagement shows up as actions or rather behavior. An engaged customer will perform certain actions that a disengaged customer will not. What engaged customers do largely depends on what companies allow and what technology enables. Some examples of actions that engaged customers can perform are: they provide ideas and suggestions, they do some of the work, they collaborate, co-create, they buy, they recommend a brand or product to family, friends or colleagues and they provide feedback (Iqbal, 2011).

Hollebeek (2011) generally defines customer engagement as the level of expression of an individual customer's motivational, brand-related and context-dependent state of mind characterized by a degree of activation, identification and absorption in brand interactions. Another recent analysis about customer engagement is done by van Doorn et al. (2010), who suggest that customer engagement behaviors go

Figure 3. Network coproduction model (Adapted from Kozinets et al, 2010, p. 71)

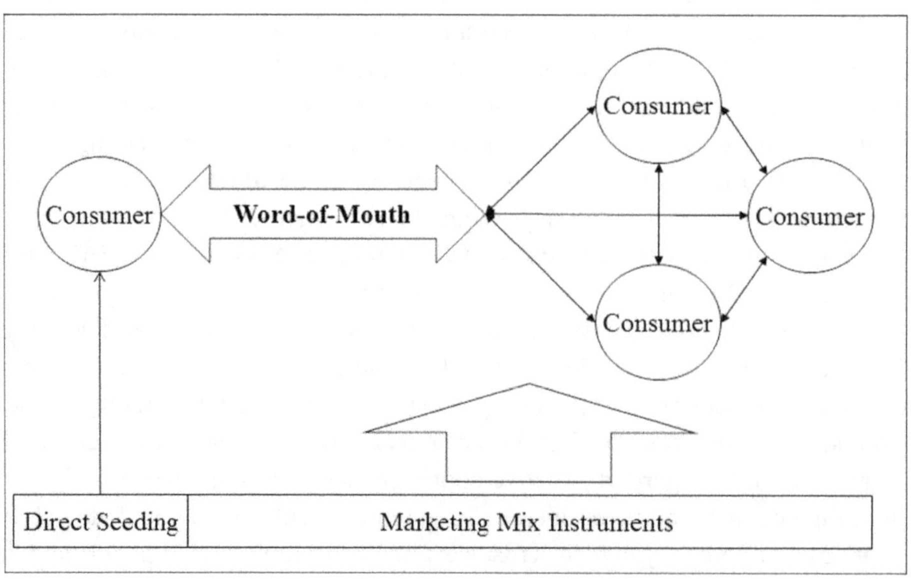

beyond transactions and may be defined as "a customer's behavioral manifestations that have a brand or firm focus, beyond purchase, resulting from motivational drivers". Brodie, Hollebeek, Juric, and Ilic (2011), suggest that within interactive, dynamic business environments, customer engagement today represents a strategic imperative for generating enhanced corporate performance, including sales growth, superior competitive advantage and profitability.

Customer engagement can take place online or offline. Offline engagement is the nature of engagement, but is qualitatively different from online engagement because online engagement offers ways to communicate and socialize which cannot be replaced by an offline medium. Offline engagement is mainly a one-way communication, such as word-of-mouth, reviews or referrals. In contrast to this, online media provides customers the opportunity not only to engage but also to discuss and interact in discussion forums, blogs or social media platforms as Facebook or Twitter. Thus, online customer engagement is "a cognitive and affective commitment to an active relationship with the brand as personified by the website or other computer mediated entities designed to communicate brand value" (Mollen & Wilson, 2010).

SOCIAL MEDIA PERFORMANCE MEASUREMENT

Understanding social media is a prerequisite for adequately managing social media channels. Thus, measuring performance outcomes of marketing activities in social media is an important task for today's companies. Social media performance measurement requires metrics that are theoretically grounded, complete, valid, and reliable. A metric is a measurement system that quantifies static or dynamic characteristics (Farris, Bendle, Pfeifer, & Reibstein, 2006). Due to the interactive nature of social networks, a single metric in the context of social media is not advisable (compare Amber & Roberts, 2006). Instead, a variety of metrics to capture the unique character of social media is suggested along the following dimensions: motives, content, networks structure, social roles and interactions (Peters et al., 2013) and sentiment.

Motives

Engagement in social media is grounded by the Motivation, Opportunity, and Ability (M-O-A) paradigm (MacInnis, Moorman, & Jaworski, 1991). The MOA paradigm highlights the importance of motivation as a driver of behavior (action).

Motivation refers to amplifying arousal so that inactive users are ready, willing, or interested to process and distribute a message. Functionally, amplified motivation represents a predisposition to allocate scarce cognitive resources to processing information. Motivation, represented in topic involvement, moderates the linkage between exposure, cognitive processing, and attitude formation. Ability refers to the need to maximize a user's skills in interpreting a message. In general, sapient users can process information more efficiently than can novices. Opportunity relates to the characteristics of the message that favor information processing. According to Batra and Ray (1985), opportunity refers to executional factors of a message that are beyond the control of the user, such as exposure time, message length, the number of arguments, and the absence of distractions that detract from message processing.

Conversations in social networks, e.g. Facebook or Twitter, are usually discontinuous in nature. Consumers post comments but do not expect an immediate response right away. And if a consumer decides to response, it could happen hours or even days later as breaks in conversations are not regarded as lack of interest in these conversations (Berger & Iyengar, 2011, pp. 6). Thus, as in online conversations normally people think through what they say, a threshold for discussion can be expected. People do not share everything they discover, yet it should be regarded as interesting for others. Hennig-Thurau et al. (2004) identify eight specific factors, which motivate consumers to make contributions to online communities:

- venting negative feelings,
- concern for other consumers,
- self-enhancement,
- advice-seeking,
- social benefits,
- economic benefits,
- platform assistance, and
- helping the company.

In contrary, continuous conversations, e. g. face-to-face communications, the threshold for discussion is much lower. People normally dislike if the conversation partner is not responding quickly to statements. Periods of quietness are regarded as uncomfortable situations in continuous conversations. To conclude, in online conversations, interesting brands, products or customer-related issues, e.g. service issues, should receive more WOM than less interesting counterparts.

From a company's perspective it is fundamental to analyze the motives or why people act or react as they do.

Content

Content drive social media action. People share information for different reasons, e.g. for self-enhancement purposes or altruistic reasons (Wojnicki & Godes, 2008). Vividness and interactivity are important attributes of brand posts for consumers to like, comment and share (De Vries, Gensler, & Leeflang, 2012). Thus, entertainment is an important motive for social media users to contribute and create content. In addition to this, positive content is more often shared than negative content (Berger & Milkman, 2012). Regarding the valence of content, they found that content that induces high-arousal positive (e.g., awe) or negative (e.g., anger, anxiety) emotions is more frequently shared and content that elicits low-arousal emotions (e.g., sadness) is less often shared. Based on Peters et al. (2013), content contains of:

- Content quality (e.g. interactivity, vividness),
- Content valence (e.g. emotions, tonality), and
- Content volume (e.g. counts, volumes).

Network Structure

The network structure of social media can be described by the following dimensions (e.g. Hannemann & Riddle, 2011; Kadushin, 2012; Scott, 2012): Centrality, tie strength, and homophily,

Centrality

The centrality of a node in a network is a measure of its structural importance (e.g., how important a person is within a social network. Bonacich (1987) argued that an actor's centrality is a function of how many connections the actor has, but also on how many connections the actor's neighbors have. There are three approaches to calculate the centrality of a node: Based on degree, on closeness, and on betweenness.

Degree approaches measure the number of other consumers directly related to one consumer. Highly connected consumers are considered to likely influence others consumers' behavior (Van den Bulte & Wuyts, 2007) and vice versa. Conventional wisdom is that the best seeds for facilitating WOM are consumers with high degrees of social connectivity (i.e. social hubs) because they have access to and can reach more people than others (Stephen & Lehmann, 2012). This logic is supported by prior research showing that diffusion processes speed up once higher-connectivity consumers transmit WOM (Goldenberg, Han, Lehmann, & Hong 2009) and that, for Social CRM, hub seeding often outperforms alternatives in field experiments (Hinz et al. 2011), simulations (Libai, Muller, & Peres, 2012), and analytical models (Zubcsek & Sarvary, 2011).

Closeness approaches go slightly further and they assume that actors who are able to reach other actors at shorter path lengths, or who are more reachable by others at shorter path lengths, are in favored positions (see figure 4).

Finally, betweenness is the extent to which a node lies between other nodes in the network. This measure takes into account the connectivity of the node's neighbors, giving a higher value for nodes which bridge clusters. The measure reflects the number of people who a person is connecting indirectly through their direct links (see figure 5).

Figure 4. Closeness centralities using geodesic distance in an undirected network (Node A is the most central node, whilst node B is the least central)

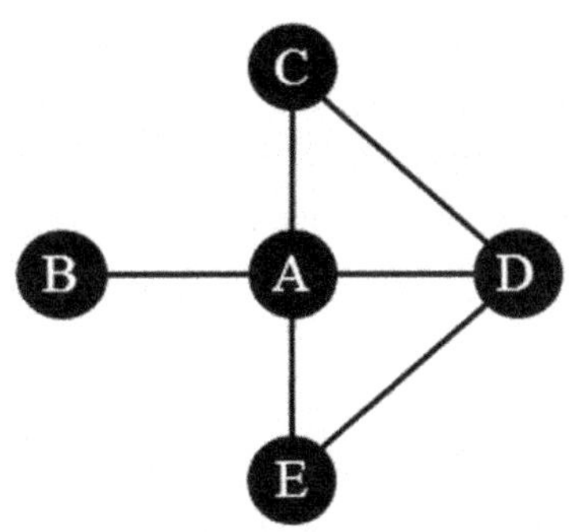

Closeness centralities:

Node A = 1 / 1+1+1+1 = 0.25
Node B = 1 / 1+2+2+2 = 0.14
Node C = 1 / 1+2+1+2 = 0.17
Node D = 1 / 1+2+1+1 = 0.20
Node E = 1 / 1+2+2+1 = 0.17

Figure 5. An undirected network. Nodes D and I have higher betweenness than the rest of the nodes.

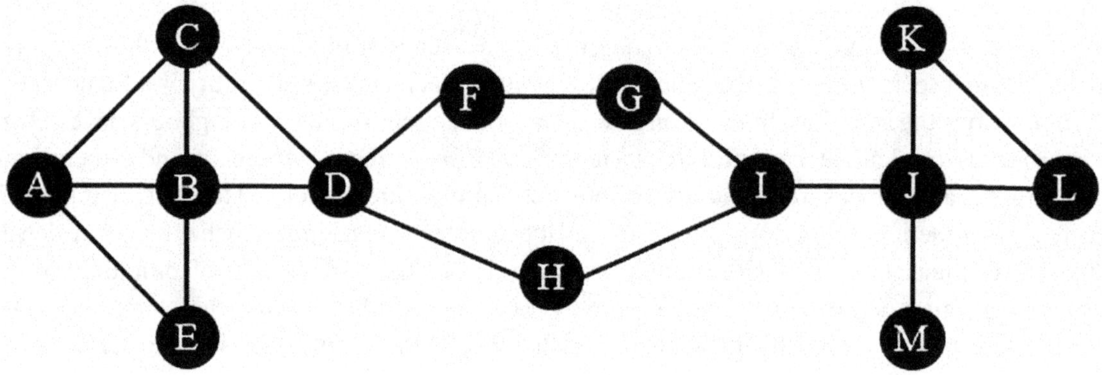

Tie Strength

All WOM communication occurs within a social relationship that may be categorized according to the closeness of the relationship between consumers, represented by the construct tie strength. Tie strength is "a multidimensional construct that represents the strength of the dyadic interpersonal relationships in the context of social networks" (Money, Gilly, & Graham, 1998, p. 79) and includes closeness, intimacy, support, and association (Frenzen & Davis, 1990).

Granovetter (1973) distinguishes between "strong ties" and "weak ties" for understanding interpersonal communication flows. Weak ties form bridges to otherwise isolated strong-tie networks. Thus, information spread via a weak tie results in a greater increase in the number of people informed (Goldenberg, Libai, & Muller, 2001) and people may be more affected by people with whom they have closer relationships (Brown & Reingen, 1987).

Tie strength may indicate the intensity of a social relationship (Van den Bulte & Wuyts, 2007). Research suggests that tie strength affects information flows. Consumers with a strong tie relationship tend to exchange more and more frequently information, compared to consumers in weak tie relationships (Brown & Reingen, 1987). From a social media performance measurement perspective, it is of particular interest that tie strength influences referral behavior among social contacts.

Homophily

Homophily explains group composition in terms of the similarity of members' characteristics:

the extent to which pairs of individuals are similar in terms of certain attributes, such as age, gender, education, or lifestyle (Rogers, 1983)."The measure of homophily reflects the level of similarity between two people who take part in a social tie, that is, how alike they are with respect to their personal attributes" (Nitzan & Libai, 2011, p. 26). Customers are more likely to trust people whose preferences they share and people are likely to feel more comfortable sharing experiences with people who are similar to them (Feick & Higie, 1992). Thus, the stronger the social tie between two consumers is, the more similar they tend to be (McPherson & Smith-Lovin, 1987; Granovetter, 1973). Tie strength, therefore, increases with homophily.

SOCIAL ROLES AND SOCIAL INTERACTIONS

A social role is continuously mediated between actors in a social network. Social roles are constantly shaped through social interactions. Social interactions are "dynamic, changing sequences of social actions and communication between social actors" (Peters et al., 2013, p. 288). The particular impact, modification, and sharing of content received by a user depends on its own as well as on the type of content and the sender's motivations and social influence in the network. Social influence occurs when a user adapts his or her behavior, attitudes, or beliefs to the behavior, attitudes, or beliefs of others in a social network (Leenders, 2002). Most of the links in a social network are "weak" in the sense that the relationships do not significantly influence behavior in the network; thus, identifying the "strong" links (i.e., the links corresponding to friends who affect a given user's behavior) is of interest. Based on an extensive literature review, Peters et al. (2013) derived four types of social interactions:

- sharing,
- gaming,
- expressing, and
- networking.

Social effects by influencers are unquestioned. Many researchers (e.g., Nitzan & Libai, 2011; Trusov, Bucklin, & Pauwels, 2009) have proved that social influence can impact CRM performance measures, i.e. acquisition and retention.

Social Effects on Customer Acquisition

Targeting opinion leaders and strongly connected members of a social network ensures rapid diffusion (Iyengar, Van den Bulte, & Valente, 2011) through WOM referrals that have a strong impact on new customer acquisition. The elasticity for WOM in social networking sites is "approximately 20 times higher than that for marketing events and 30 times that of traditional media appearances" (Trusov et al., 2009, p. 91). This aspect seems to be eminently attractive, as often WOM campaigns are relatively inexpensive: Customer's social networks take care of spreading the marketing message instead of expensive media exposure needs to be purchased. Stephen and Lehmann (2012) empirically showed that incentivizing consumers to spread the word to highly-connected friends result in a higher speed of information diffusion. Hinz et al. (2011) found, that seeding to well-connected people is the most successful approach as these people are more likely to take part in WOM, thus highlighting the importance of gathering social network data. Thus, using social network data may enable marketers to accurately target key influencers to make their marketing activities effective.

Nevertheless, using social networks for CRM requires a data integration approach that combines customer data and social network data as well as new modeling techniques to forecast how well a Social CRM activity will develop over time and how many responses will be received (van der Lans, van Bruggen, Eliashberg, & Wierenga, 2010, pp. 362).

Social Effects on Customer Retention

In social networks, a defecting customer may have a direct effect on its connected neighbors, thus, mere exposure to defecting customers has a relatively strong effect on the defection decision of its neighbors. Nitzan and Libai's (2011) results indicate that customers connected to a defecting customer show an increase of 80% in the defection probability. The level of social influence on retention declines exponentially over time, and the likelihood of customer churn is affected by tie strength and homophily with defecting neighbors and by these neighbors' average number of connections. On the one hand, highly connected customers are more affected. On the other hand, loyal customers are less affected by defections that take place in their social networks as social interaction between consumers can increase future purchase intention and willingness to pay a price premium (Srinivasan, Anderson, & Ponnavolu, 2002).

Therefore, when determining how much a firm should spend to retain a customer, the customer's social network should be taken into account (Trusov, Bodapati, & Bucklin, 2010, p. 655). Thus, the addition of network-related information to the commonly used geographic, demographic, and prior purchase data might substantially improve analysis and thus, social media performance measurement.

Sentiment

For marketers it is important to understand the individual behavior driving the decision to express an opinion in social media. Moe and Schweidel (2012) propose that the decision consists of two components: whether to post (incidence decision) and what to post (evaluation decision). Most researchers have focused so far on the incidence decision (e.g., Berger & Schwartz, 2011; Duan, Gu, & Whinston, 2008). However, Moe and Schweidel (2012) propose that incidence and evaluation decisions are inter-related and driven by post-purchase product evaluations and social interactions within the social network. Thus, the sentiment expressed can vary across different social media sites due to the fact that audiences and participants may vary across different social media sites. Another research finding shows that a user can show strategic posting behavior if its goal is to influence others (Chen & Kirmani, 2011).

SOCIAL MEDIA PERFORMANCE METRICS

To sum it up, researchers have little guidance as to how they should interpret the volumes of comments posted online. As a result, leading firms often rely on simplified measures such as the total volume of posted comments or the average sentiment expressed across all posted comments. Additionally, researchers have tracked aggregate measures of opinion expressed in the text of posted comments to assess reactions (Kinon, 2010). These aggregate metrics may offer some guidance for marketers to assess customer engagement. Nevertheless, there are several limitations that have prevented companies from integrating social media listening into their marketing information systems. First, as social media allow the posting of any content, social media raise the complexity of analysis. Second, simple metrics based on an aggregation across comments (e.g. average sentiment) ignore differences between product- or attribute-specific evaluations and general brand impressions (Dillon, Madden, Kirmani, & Mukherjee, 2001). Third, comments posted online are not always provided by users who have the requisite experience needed for an informed evaluation. Thus, firms should rely on metrics across social media and metrics within a social medium.

Metrics Across Social Media

Company's brand's metrics should cover all relevant social media due to the fact that consumers may use specific platforms for specific content, e.g. Twitter to complain, Facebook to comment brand experience and Instagram to post brand visuals. As Twitter is an asymmetric social medium and e.g. Facebook a symmetric one, these different characteristics require different metrics. In addition to this, social media users can regularly observe spillovers from e.g. Facebook to Twitter activity and vice versa. Thus, managers must account for both effects: General metrics at the meta level across social media (e.g., Klout Score), and specific metrics that reflect the particular nature of any social medium (e.g., EdgeRank), see also Peters et al., 2013, p. 294 for a detailed discussion).

Metrics Within a Social Medium

As network theory suggests, there are no metrics that cover all levels of a network. Neither does a metric capture the relational and positional view of a network simultaneously (Peters et al., 2013, p. 295). Thus, managers should account for different levels of important aspects like engagement. Engagement, which manifests itself in social interactions, can take different levels of intensity as the research on involvement (e.g., Arora, 1982) suggests. For instance, likes, comments and shares of brand-related posts should closely be monitored and individually captured to analyze the overall volume as well as the evolution (from likes to comments to shares) over time. In addition to this, a weighted engagement metric can be calculated. This detailed view is essential as brands need a vital distribution across these levels, i.e., "too many 'likes' without 'comments' and 'shares' are not sufficient to build reach, as is having too many 'shares' within a small community of 'likes'" (Peters et al., 2013, p. 295). In social media, higher engagement levels are crucial for generating sustained traffic and dialogue. Developing and employing adequate metrics to measure engagement levels of consumers will drive brand managers to more sincere and sustained modes of interaction, i.e., higher quality contacts. Such highly engaged fans, and not necessarily high numbers of them, are crucial in building sustained and authentic reach in social media.

Today social media performance measurement tools can only insufficiently depict the theoretical foundations of social network structures. Though, the large Social CRM software companies (e.g., Salesforce Radian6, Attensity, or Lithium) only offer tools for sentiment analysis based on data from blogs, community sites, micro-blogs or social media sites which is related to the company or product. Another field of analysis offer vendors, who identify so called key influencer within social networks. This guarantees for including the centrality dimensions of the underlying network structure into the social media performance measurement. E.g., the vendor Booshaka offers, Facebook user scores, based on posts, comments, likes and user activity. For Twitter, vendors like Twitalyzer or TweetRank base their scores on the number of follower and the tweet/re-tweet frequency. Vendors like e.g. PeerIndex, Klout or Proliphiq calculate a combined score based on different social networks.

For measuring performance outcomes of marketing actions in social media, this information only allows for an ex-post analysis. For a more detailed and future oriented analysis, the metrics depicted in table 1 must be included into a marketing information system.

Table 1. Social media metrics

Social Media Dimensions	Elements	Metrics	Data Sources
Motives	• venting negative feelings • concern for other consumers • self-enhancement • advice-seeking • social benefits • economic benefits • platform assistance • helping the company	Multi-attributive attitude measurement	• Online survey • Text-analytics software
Content	• content quality (e.g. interactivity, vividness) • content valence (e.g. emotions, tonality) • content volume (e.g. counts, volumes)	• Unique user • Page impressions • Visits • Unique page views • Growth rate active user • Growth rate returning user • Topics and theme analysis • # posts	• Social media monitoring • Social media analytics • Text-analytics software • Sentiment analysis
Network structure	• Centrality • Tie strength • Homophily	• # of fans / friends / circles • # of followers • # posts / re-posts • # tweets / re-tweets	• Social media monitoring • Social media analytics
Social roles & interactions	• sharing, • gaming, • expressing, and • networking. • Social influence	• # of likes • # of shares • # of user-generated videos • # of user-generated pictures	Influencer profiling (e.g. Klout, Kred, PeerIndex)
Sentiment	• valence • emotions • tonality • counts • volume	• total volume of posted comments • average sentiment expressed across all posted comments • aggregate measures of opinion expressed in the text of posted comments	• Text-analytics software • Sentiment analysis

SOCIAL MEDIA PERFORMANCE MEASUREMENT AS AN INTEGRAL PART OF A MARKETING INFORMATION SYSTEM

The term 'Marketing Information System' was introduced first by Cox and Good (1967) as a set of procedures and methods for the regular planned analysis and presentation of information for use in making marketing decisions. Following Boone and Kurtz (2007), a marketing information system is "a planned computer-based system designed to provide managers with continuous flow of information relevant to their specific decisions and areas of responsibility". Kotler and Keller (2012), define marketing information system as "an interacting structure of people, equipment and procedures to gather sort, analyze, evaluate and distribute, timely and accurate information for use by marketing decision makers to improve their marketing planning, implementation, and control". However, the rapid development of online marketing and the diffusion of social media are transforming the requirements for marketing information systems fast. According to Harmon (2003), the primary benefit of a marketing information system is to integrate, analyze and distribute monitoring data of market participants. Thus, the incorporation of social media data is a central issue of today's further development of marketing information systems.

However, the explosion of unstructured data volumes of social media requires new approaches to data consolidation and analytics applications. It results in four requirements of a company's hardware and software solutions: First, data access speeds of physical storage mechanisms have not kept up with improvements in network speeds. Second, traditional data storage techniques like relational database management systems (RDBMS) have limited scalability to manage growing data volumes. Third, today's data processing tasks increasingly need to access and combine data from many different unstructured sources, often online. Last, data volumes have phenomenal grown over the past years.

Thus, unstructured data integration and analytics face multiple challenges. Companies must capture and analyze multiple streams of data. Customers normally use multiple platforms (e.g. different social networking sites like Facebook, Youtube, and Twitter) to interact on, which results in added sources of data and complexity of integration from multiple platforms and devices (smartphones, tablets). Hence, companies face the challenge of integrating structured data with unstructured data from e.g. social media, blogs or micro-blogs. Also, interacting in social media means a never-ending, continuous stream of data.

To meet the challenges and gain the benefits of integrating web and enterprise data, multiple technology enhancements are needed:

- Upgrade infrastructure (e.g., Hadoop clusters, tag management systems) and processes to collect data from multiple online streams including social media, and smartphone applications
- Implement validation process and engines to ensure correct data capture
- Implement multiple Web tools (Google, Omniture, etc.) and enterprise analytics tools (SAS) to fill any gaps in data capture and enhance analytic capabilities

Especially, traditional technologies are optimized for processing structured data and presenting results for a narrow range of analytic applications. Substantial manipulations are required to process large volumes of unstructured data. New distributed technologies such as MapReduce (developed by Google) and Hadoop (open-source Apache platform) are created for the purpose of processing large volumes of unstructured data and importing the results for use by a broad range of analytic applications. MapReduce and Hadoop enable the execution of analytical procedures on the entire universe of data rather than on a sample, as done traditionally in an RDBMS (see figure 6). Hence, this provides better analytic output for higher-quality decision making in marketing (Zikopolous et al., 2013).

MANAGERIAL IMPLICATIONS

With respect to customer and social media user data companies have an abundance of structured and especially unstructured data available. For measuring performance outcomes of marketing actions in social media, unstructured data of blogs, micro-blogs, or social media sites are of special interest, because this data offers the possibility to analyze aspects of centrality, tie strength and homophily between users of social media sites. However, the abundance of available data requires companies to rethink their approach to data collection, data warehousing, and data analysis. Especially, unstructured data is not suited for being stored in relational data warehouse systems. Hence, the following special requirements must be taken into consideration:

Figure 6. Big-Data-integrated application framework (Adapted from Zikopolous et al., 2013, p. 87)

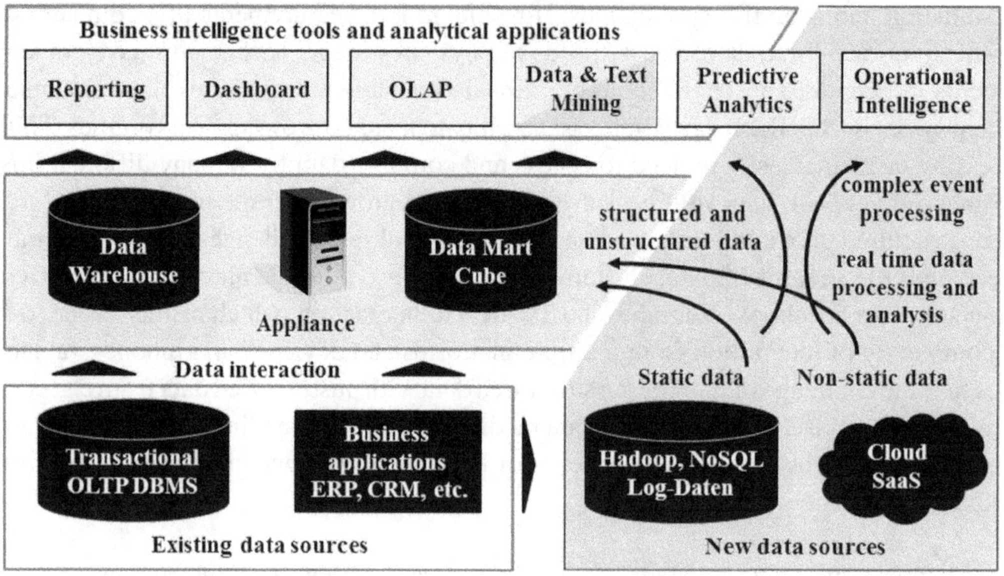

Data Collection

Because Social CRM Big Data is produced at high speed and heterogeneity, the IT infrastructure must be capable of processing large transaction volumes. Instead of relying on traditional relational database structures with entities and relationships, companies should implement NoSQL-databases, which are capable of storing data without predefined structures.

Data Integration

As a vast amount of unstructured data is being collected, a scalable and flexible IT infrastructure is a basis prerequisite. Data should be decentralized stored, disseminated, and analyzed to minimize time and cost of further data processing and relocating. A common development tool for highly distributed data processing offers e.g. the open source framework Hadoop, which is based on Google's Mapreduce Framework. Hadoop is capable of storing and analyzing large sets of unstructured data on loosely coupled clusters of cost efficient server, i.e. as a cloud solution.

Data Analysis

Future analysis tools will integrate statistical methods, predictive modeling, optimization methods, and data mining techniques. It will be inevitable to combine traditional structured data and Big Data. Data analysis capabilities should include In-Database Text Mining for sentiment analysis, In-Database Graph Analysis for analyzing tie strength and homophily, and In Database Spatial Analysis for revealing connectivity between users of social networks.

CONCLUSION

Social media performance measurement is still in its infancy. From a practical perspective, companies mainly use metrics provided by social network providers or obtained from singular social media monitoring software applications. These metrics may not necessarily be the most accurate metrics for guiding marketing decision making for Social CRM activities. The article has introduced a theoretically sound framework of social media performance measurement that incorporates different dimensions of social media performance measurement. However, incorporating such a performance measurement system into a marketing information system requires huge data integration efforts as well as implementing additional analytical capabilities.

As the field of social media is still emerging, no ultimate social media performance measurement can be applied that addresses all requirements for all companies alike. Thus, companies should focus on designing appropriate dashboards of social media performance measurement that incorporate the different dimension of social media performance measurement relevant for the respective marketing activities.

REFERENCES

Amber, T., & Roberts, J. (2006). *Beware the Silver Metric: Marketing Performance Measurement Has to Be Multidimensional* (Marketing Science Institute Working Paper Series No. 06-113). Cambridge, MA: Marketing Science Institute.

Arndt, J. (1967). Role of product-related conversations in the diffusion of a new product. *Journal of Marketing Research*, *4*(August), 291–295. doi:10.2307/3149462

Batra, R., & Ray, M. (1985). How Advertising Works at Contact. In L. F. Alwitt & A. A. Mitchell (Eds.), *Psychological Processes and Advertising Effects* (pp. 13–44). Hillsdale, NJ: Lawrence Erlbaum Associates.

Berger, J., & Iyengar, R. (2011). *How interests shapes word-of-mouth over different channels* (Marketing Science Institute Working Paper Series No. 11-110). Cambridge, MA: Marketing Science Institute.

Berger, J., & Milkman, K. L. (2012). What makes online content viral? *Journal of Marketing Research*, *49*(April), 192–205. doi:10.1509/jmr.10.0353

Berger, J., & Schwartz, E. (2011). What drives immediate and ongoing word-of-mouth? *JMR, Journal of Marketing Research*, *48*(October), 869–880. doi:10.1509/jmkr.48.5.869

Bonacich, P. (1987). Power and centrality: A family of measures. *American Journal of Sociology*, *92*(5), 1170–1182. doi:10.1086/228631

Boone, L. E., & Kurtz, D. L. (2007). *Contemporary Marketing*. New York, NY: Harcourt College Publisher.

Brodie, R. J., Hollebeek, L. D., Juric, B., & Ilic, A. (2011). Customer Engagement: Conceptual Domain, Fundamental Propositions, and Implications for Research. *Journal of Service Research*, *13*(3), 252–271. doi:10.1177/1094670511411703

Brown, B., & Sikes, J. (2012). Minding Your Digital Business: McKinsey Global Survey Results. *McKinsey and Company Research Report*.

Brown, J. J., & Reingen, P. H. (1987). Social ties and word-of-mouth referral behavior. *The Journal of Consumer Research, 14*(December), 350–362. doi:10.1086/209118

Chen, Y.-J., & Kirmani, A. (2011). *Persuading others online: The consumer as media planner* (University of Maryland working paper).

Chevalier, J. A., & Mayzlin, D. (2006). The effect of word-of-mouth on sales: Online book reviews. *JMR, Journal of Marketing Research, 43*(August), 345–354. doi:10.1509/jmkr.43.3.345

Cox, D., & Good, R. (1967). How to build a marketing information system. *Harvard Business Review, 45*(3), 145–154.

de Vries, L., Gensler, S., & Leeflang, P. S. H. (2012). Popularity of Brand Posts on Brand Fan Pages: An Investigation of the Effects of Social Media Marketing. *Journal of Interactive Marketing, 26*(2), 83–91. doi:10.1016/j.intmar.2012.01.003

Dillon, W. R., Madden, T. J., Kirmani, A., & Mukherjee, S. (2001). Understanding what's in a brand rating: A model for assessing brand and attribute effects. *JMR, Journal of Marketing Research, 28*(4), 415–429. doi:10.1509/jmkr.38.4.415.18910

Divol, R., Edelman, D., & Sarrazin, H. (2012). Demystifying Social Media. *The McKinsey Quarterly, 26*(2), 66–77.

Duan, W., Gu, B., & Whinston, A. B. (2008). The dynamics of online word-of-mouth and product sales: An empirical investigation of the movie industry. *Journal of Retailing, 84*(2), 233–242. doi:10.1016/j.jretai.2008.04.005

Farris, P. W., Bendle, N. T., Pfeifer, P. E., & Reibstein, D. J. (2006). *Marketing Metrics: 50+ Metrics Every Executive Should Master*. Upper Saddle River, NJ: Prentice Hall.

Feick, L., & Higie, R. A. (1992). The effects of preference heterogeneity and source characteristics on ad processing and judgments about endorsers. *Journal of Advertising, 21*(2), 9–24. doi:10.1080/00913367.1992.10673364

Frenzen, J. K., & Davis, H. L. (1990). Purchasing behavior in embedded markets. *The Journal of Consumer Research, 17*(1), 1–12. doi:10.1086/208532

Godes, D., & Mayzlin, D. (2009). Firm-created word-of-mouth communication: Evidence from a field test. *Marketing Science, 28*(4), 721–739. doi:10.1287/mksc.1080.0444

Goldenberg, J., Han, S., Lehmann, D. R., & Hong, W. J. (2009). The role of hubs in the adoption process. *Journal of Marketing, 73*(2), 1–13. doi:10.1509/jmkg.73.2.1

Goldenberg, J., Libai, B., & Muller, E. (2001). Talk of the network: A complex systems look at the underlying process of word-of-mouth. *Marketing Letters, 12*(3), 211–223. doi:10.1023/A:1011122126881

Granovetter, M. S. (1973). The strength of weak ties. *American Journal of Sociology, 78*(6), 1360–1380. doi:10.1086/225469

Greenberg, P. (2010). CRM at the speed of light: Social CRM strategies, tools, and techniques for engaging your customers (4th ed.). New York, NY: McGraw Hill.

Hanneman, R. A., & Riddle, M. (2011). Concepts and Measures for Basic Network Analysis. In J. Scott, & P. J. Carrington (Eds.), The SAGE Handbook of Social Network Analysis (pp. 364-367). Thousand Oaks, CA: Sage Ltd.

Harmon, R. R. (2003). Marketing Information Systems. In H. Bidgoli (Ed.), *Encyclopedia of Information Systems* (Vol. 3, pp. 137–151). New York, NY: Elsevier Science. doi:10.1016/B0-12-227240-4/00110-6

Hennig-Thurau, T., Gwinner, K. P., Walsh, G., & GremleR, D. D. (2004). Electronic word-of-mouth via consumer-opinion platforms: What motivates consumers to articulate themselves on the internet? *Journal of Interactive Marketing*, *18*(1), 38–52. doi:10.1002/dir.10073

Hinz, O., Skiera, B., Barrot, C., & Becker, J. U. (2011). Seeding strategies for viral marketing: An empirical comparison. *Journal of Marketing*, *75*(6), 55–71. doi:10.1509/jm.10.0088

Hollebeek, L. (2011). Demystifying Customer Brand Engagement: Exploring the Loyalty Nexus. *Journal of Marketing Management*, *27*(7-8), 785–807. doi:10.1080/0267257X.2010.500132

Iqbal, M. (2011, June 6). An inquiry into "customer engagement" – making the abstract concrete The Customer Blog. Retrieved from http://thecustomerblog.co.uk/2011/06/06/an-inquiry-into-customeren-gagement-making-the-abstract-concrete/

Iyengar, R., Van den Bulte, C., & Valente, T. W. (2011). Opinion Leadership and Social Contagion in New Product Diffusion. *Marketing Science*, *30*(2), 195–212. doi:10.1287/mksc.1100.0566

Jansen, B. J., Zhang, M., Sobel, K., & Chowdury, A. (2009). Twitter power: Tweets as electronic word-of-mouth. *Journal of the American Society for Information Science and Technology*, *60*(11), 2169–2188. doi:10.1002/asi.21149

Kadushin, C. (2012). *Understanding Social Networks: Theories, Concepts, and Findings*. Oxford, United Kingdom: Oxford University Press.

Kaplan, A. M., & Haenlein, M. (2010). Users of the world, unite! The challenges and opportunities of social media. *Business Horizons*, *53*(1), 59–68. doi:10.1016/j.bushor.2009.09.003

Kinon, C. (2010, February 3). Creators of Glee, Modern Family, track fan reaction via Twitter. Retrieved from http://www.nydailynews.com/entertainment/tv-movies/creators-glee-modern-family-track-fan-reaction-twitter-article-1.175907

Kotler, P., & Keller, K. L. (2011). *Marketing Management* (14th ed.). Upper Saddle River, NJ: Prentice Hall.

Kozinets, R. V., de Valck, K., Wojnicki, A. C., & Wilner, S. J. S. (2010). Networked narratives: Understanding word-of-mouth marketing in online communities. *Journal of Marketing*, *74*(2), 71–89. doi:10.1509/jmkg.74.2.71

Leenders, R. Th. A. J. (2002). Modeling Social Influence through Network Autocorrelation: Constructing the Weight Matrix. *Social Networks*, *24*(1), 21–47. doi:10.1016/S0378-8733(01)00049-1

Libai, B., Muller, E., & Peres, R. (2012). *Sources of social value in word-of-mouth programs* (Marketing Science Institute Working Paper Series No. 10-103). Cambridge, MA: Marketing Science Institute.

MacInnis, D. J., Moorman, C., & Jaworski, B. J. (1991). Enhancing and Measuring Consumers' Motivation, Opportunity, and Ability to Process Brand Information from Ads. *Journal of Marketing*, *55*(4), 32–53. doi:10.2307/1251955

McPherson, J. M., & Smith-Lovin, L. (1987). Homophily in voluntary organizations: Status, distance and the composition of face-to-face groups. *American Sociological Review*, *52*(3), 370–379. doi:10.2307/2095356

Moe, W. W., & Schweidel, D. A. (2012). Online Product Opinions: Incidence, Evaluation, and Evolution. *Marketing Science*, *31*(3), 372–386. doi:10.1287/mksc.1110.0662

Mollen, A., & Wilson, H. (2010). Engagement, Telepresence and Interactivity in Online Consumer Experience: Reconciling Scholastic and Managerial Perspectives. *Journal of Business Research. Special Issue on Internet Customer Behavior*, *6*(9-10), 919–925.

Money, R. B., Gilly, M. C., & Graham, J. L. (1998). Explorations of national culture and word-of-mouth referral behavior in the purchase of industrial services in the United States and Japan. *Journal of Marketing*, *62*(4), 76–87. doi:10.2307/1252288

Nitzan, I., & Libai, B. (2011). Social effects on customer retention. *Journal of Marketing*, *75*(November), 24–38. doi:10.1509/jm.10.0209

Peters, K., Chen, Y., Kaplan, A. M., Ognibeni, B., & Pauwels, K. (2013). Social media metrics – a framework and guidelines for managing social media. *Journal of Interactive Marketing*, *27*(4), 281–298. doi:10.1016/j.intmar.2013.09.007

Rainie, L., Purcell, K., & Smith, A. (2011). The Social Side of the Internet. *Pew Internet & American Life Project, Washington, DC*. Retrieved from http://www.pewinternet.org/files/old-media/Files/Reports/2011/PIP_Social_Side_of_the_Internet.pdf

Rogers, E. M. (1983). *Diffusion of innovations*. New York, NY: Free Press.

Scott, J. P. (2008). *Social Network Analysis* (3rd ed.). Thousand Oaks, CA: Sage Ltd.

Srinivasan, S. S., Anderson, R., & Ponnavolu, K. (2002). Customer loyalty in e-commerce: An exploration of its antecedents and consequences. *Journal of Retailing*, *78*(1), 41–50. doi:10.1016/S0022-4359(01)00065-3

Stephen, A. T., & Lehmann, D. R. (2012). Using incentives to encourage word-of-mouth transmissions that lead to fast information diffusion. *SSRN Electronic Journal, 07/2012*. doi:10.2139/ssrn.2102661

Trusov, M., Bodapati, A. V., & Bucklin, R. E. (2010). Determining influential users in internet social networks. *JMR, Journal of Marketing Research*, *47*(4), 643–658. doi:10.1509/jmkr.47.4.643

Trusov, M., Bucklin, R. E., & Pauwels, K. H. (2009). Effects of word-of-mouth versus traditional marketing: Findings from an internet social networking site. *Journal of Marketing*, *73*(5), 90–102. doi:10.1509/jmkg.73.5.90

Van den Bulte, C., & Wuyts, S. (2007). *Social networks and marketing*. Cambridge, MA: Marketing Science Institute.

van der Lans, R., van Bruggen, G., Eliashberg, J., & Wierenga, B. (2010). A viral branching model for predicting the spread of electronic word-of-mouth. *Marketing Science*, *29*(2), 348–365. doi:10.1287/mksc.1090.0520

van Doorn, J., Lemon, K. N., Mittal, V., Nass, S., Pick, D., Pirner, P., & Verhoef, P. C. (2010). Customer Engagement Behaviour: Theoretical Foundations and Research Directions. *Journal of Service Research*, *13*(3), 253–266. doi:10.1177/1094670510375599

Vivek, S. D., Beatty, S. E., & Morgan, R. M. (2012). Customer Engagement: Exploring customer relationships beyond purchase. *Journal of Marketing Theory and Practice*, *20*(2), 122–145. doi:10.2753/MTP1069-6679200201

Wasserman, S., & Faust, K. (1994). *Social Network Analysis: Methods and Applications*. Cambridge, MA: Cambridge University Press. doi:10.1017/CBO9780511815478

Wojnicki, A. C., & Godes, D. (2008). *Word-of-mouth as self-enhancement* (HBS Marketing Research Paper No. 06-01). Boston, MA: Harvard Business School Marketing Unit.

Zikopolous, P. C., de Roos, D., Parasuraman, K., Deutsch, T., Corrigan, D., & Giles, J. (2013). Harnessing the Power of Big Data. The IBM Big Data Platform. New York, NY: McGraw-Hill.

Zubcsek, P. P., & Sarvary, M. (2011). Advertising to a social network. *Quantitative Marketing and Economics*, *9*(1), 71–107. doi:10.1007/s11129-010-9093-9

ADDITIONAL READING

Aggarwal, C. C. (2011). An introduction to social network data analytics. In C. C. Aggarwal (Ed.), Social Network Data Analytics (pp. 1-15). New York, NY: Springer. doi:10.1007/978-1-4419-8462-3_1

Barbier, G., & Liu, H. (2011). Data mining in social media, in C. C. Aggarwal (Ed.). Social network data analytics (pp. 327-351). New York, NY: Springer.

Fuhrt, B. (2011). Handbook of social network technologies and applications. New York, NY: Springer.

Hoi, S. C. H., Luo, J., Boll, S., Xu, D., Jin, R., & King, I. (2011). Social media modeling and computing. London, United Kingdom: Springer. doi:10.1007/978-0-85729-436-4

Jaokar, A. V., Jacobs, B., & Moore, A. (2009). *Social media marketing: How data analytics helps to monetize the user base in telecoms, social networks, media and advertising in a converged ecosystem.* London, United Kingdom: Future Text.

Kaushik, A. (2010). *Web analytics 2.0. The art of online accountability & science of customer centricity*. Indianapolis, IL: Wiley.

Lo, B. (2008). *Social media analytics in business intelligence applications*. Massachusetts Institute of Technology, Department of Electrical Engineering and Computer Science.

Lovett, J. (2000). *Social media metrics secrets*. Indianapolis, IL: Wiley.

Metz, A. (2012). The social customer. How brands can use Social CRM to acquire, monetize, and retain fans, friends, and followers. New York, NY: McGraw Hill.

Mislove, A., Marcon, M., Gummadi, K. P., Druschel, P., & Bhattacharjee, B. (2007). Measurement and analysis of online social networks. *Proceedings of the 7th ACM SIGCOMM Conference on Internet Measurement*. New York, NY: ACM. doi:10.1145/1298306.1298311

Nazir, A., Raza, S., & Chuah, C.-N. (2008). Unveiling facebook. A measurement study of social network based applications. *Proceedings of the 9th ACM SIGCOMM Conference on Internet Measurement*. New York, NY: ACM.

Pauwels, K. H., Ambler, T., Clark, B., LaPointe, D., Reibstein, D., Skiera, B., & Wiesel, T. et al. (2009). Dashboards and marketing: Why, what, how and what research is needed? *Journal of Service Research*, *12*(2), 175–189. doi:10.1177/1094670509344213

Roebuck, K. (2011). *Social analytics: High-impact emerging technology - What you need to know: Definitions, adoptions, impact, benefits, maturity, vendors*. Newstead: Emereo Pty Limited.

Sponder, M. (2012). Social media analytics. Effective tools for building, interpreting, and using metrics. New York, NY: McGraw Hill.

Stern, J. (2010). *Social media metrics. How to measure and optimize your marketing investment*. Hoboken, NJ: Wiley.

KEY TERMS AND DEFINITIONS

Centrality: Represents the connectivity of a person in the network.

Data Integration: Ability to include additional data into an existing system.

Homophily: Extent to which pairs of individuals are similar in terms of certain attributes, such as age, gender, education, or lifestyle.

Marketing Information System: A set of procedures and methods for the regular planned analysis and presentation of information for use in making marketing decisions.

Metric: A measurement system that quantifies static or dynamic characteristics.

Network Coproduction Model: Approach, where consumers are regarded as active coproducers of value and meaning, whose word-of-mouth use of marketing communications can be idiosyncratic, creative, and even resistant.

Sentiment: Aggregate tonality of posts in social media.

Social CRM: Business strategy designed to engage customers in a collaborative conversation in order to provide mutually beneficial value for the company and the customers.

Social Effects: Influence of social interaction on e.g. customer acquisition and retention.

Social Interactions: Dynamic, changing sequences of social actions and communication between social actors.

Social Media: A group of Internet-based applications allowing the creation and exchange of user generated content.

Social Network: Online service, platform, or site that focuses on facilitating the building of social relations among people.

Tie Strength: Multidimensional construct that represents the strength of the dyadic interpersonal relationships in the context of social networks and includes closeness, intimacy, support, and association.

Virality: Social, cultural, emotional and affective contagions that spread through networks.

Word-of-Mouth: Statement made by potential, actual, or former customers about a product or company, which is made available to a multitude of people and institutions via the Internet.

Chapter 12
The Role of Online Social Networking in the Recruitment Context

Vanessa Ratten
La Trobe University, Australia

ABSTRACT

The usage of online social networking has increased as more people use digital technology to access and store information. In this chapter, the way recruiting services are being used by online social networks is discussed. This chapter utilizes the theoretical framework of social cognitive theory to understand the factors affecting intentions to adopt online social networking recruiting services. The chapter discusses the role of online behavioral advertising, ethical orientation, social influencers and online privacy concerns to see who they affect behavioral intentions. The results of the study reported in the chapter extend current understanding about online recruitment to see how social networks are an important part of the adoption process. The chapter provides practical and managerial insights into the role of online social networking in the recruitment context.

INTRODUCTION

The advances in internet technology have resulted in a transformation of employee recruitment to electronic recruitment (Kashi and Zheng, 2013). The internet has changed the way job seekers access information about recruiting opportunities (Howard & Behrend, 2014). In the past, most job seekers relied on conventional recruitment practices that utilized traditional print media for advertising new positions (Ratten, 2014a). This has altered so that more recruiters now place information on the internet to advertise potential employment positions (Lievens & Harris, 2003). The emerging technological advances on the internet have resulted in large numbers of job seekers searching for information online. Job seekers who are more internet savvy have a better chance of finding relevant information about employment positions (Capelli, 2001). Given that more information will be obtained by individuals effectively managing their online surfing behavior, it becomes important to understand how individuals

DOI: 10.4018/978-1-4666-8459-1.ch012

use their social networks to obtain better information about employment positions. One way individuals incorporate social networks into online searching behavior is by the use of interactive technologies that integrate user information (Villano, 2008).

Online social networks may help individuals engage with potential employers and generate interest in job opportunities. This is based on internet technology serving as a way to link individuals to the recruitment process (Howard & Behrend, 2014). Individuals can influence the attractiveness of their applications by engaging in online social networks as part of the recruitment process. Online social networks can also provide individuals with the ability to use their personal contacts (Boyd & Ellison, 2007).

Individuals can use self expression on online social networking sites to access beneficial relationships (Pena and Brody, 2014). There are a number of perceptual and linguistic factors that are part of online relationships (Walther, 2004). This means that the key to developing online social networks is self-disclosure, which reduces the uncertainty process in recruiting practices (Ratten, 2013). Online self-disclosure has been found to foster information access by individuals in online networks (Pena & Brody, 2014).

Most job seekers prefer online websites to search and apply for positions (Hooper, 2007). This is due to online recruiting changing the application process in employment positions (Viswesvaran, 2003). A wide range of job information can be found in the online environment (Kashi & Zheng, 2013). Although online recruitment has increased, little is known about how social networking sites such as Facebook, LinkedIn and GooglePlus affect individual intention to use online recruiting services. Past research on online recruitment has focused more on website features (e.g. Pfleffelman, Wagner & Libkuman, 2010; Kashi & Zheng, 2013) and less on social networking tools used by individuals. It is useful for organizations to know how individuals use social networking when applying for jobs online.

Previous research by Allen, Mahto and Otondo (2007) found that job information directly affects employment intentions. Including feedback tools on websites affects job applicants perceptions of future employment (Cober et al, 2003). Allen et al (2007) in a study of web-based recruitment found that organizations information in the form of culture and goals affects job applicants attitudes toward the website. This means that tt is important that online recruiters provide information about organization attitudes to help job seekers use their website (Kashi & Zheng, 2013). A recruiter's website that is easier to use is perceived by job seekers to be an indicator of the organizations procedures (Cober et al, 2004).

Recruitment websites can provide signals about the benefits of working for an organization (Sinar, Paquet & Reynolds, 2003). They can highlight aspects of the organizations culture and the nature of the working environment (Kashi & Zheng, 2013). The website design of recruitment agencies is important as it determines the time individuals spend on information reported on the website (De Goede et al, 2010). Recruitment websites should be designed to take into account aesthetic features (e.g. interactive links, audio files, graphic images) that shape job seekers employment decisions (Kashi & Zheng, 2013).

Social networking sites including Facebook, Twitter and LinkedIn have become very popular in recent years (Lepp et al, 2014). Most people use social networks to maintain existing relationships and to meet people with shared interests (Hew, 2011). Individual usage of social networking sites has changed since the internet was introduced as there are more web applications that enable individuals to share their interests with others on the internet (Kuo & Tang, 2014). Facebook is one of the most popular social networking sites that enable individuals to connect with people of similar interests and share job opportunities. The number of people using social networking sites has increased as more information is shared and communicated online (Smith and Caruso, 2010). Social network sites enable people to find out more about jobs and invite people to apply for positions (Ratten, 2012a).

People with a high level of openness like to be socialable on social networking sites (Ross et al, 2009). In addition, people who are extroverted tend to use social media more often that other types of people (Correa et al, 2010). Social networking can include talking to people online, instant messaging and blogging (Kuo & Tang, 2014). In addition, people are using the internet more as a substitution to face to face communication (Tosun & Lajunen, 2010). This enables the internet to be an extension of social connections and encourage the increase in online activities (Ratten, 2014b). The internet is used for improving the quality of life for individuals enabling people to participate in community activities (Leung & Lea, 2005).

Online social networks are a technology with the potential to improve recruiting efforts (Ratten, 2012b). In order to realize the potential of online social networking recruiting services, there is a need for research that can identify the factors influencing the adoption of the technology. In the context of online recruitment it is important to identify how individuals use social networks to support their job search. Individuals are influenced to apply for certain jobs based on their perceptions of internet recruitment technology (Cober et al, 2004). Job seekers who find it easy to acquire information via online recruitment will help them with the job application decisions (Allen et al, 2007). The usability perceptions of online recruiting are important in compiling job application information (Howardson & Behrend, 2014).

The aim of this paper is to gain more insight into an understanding of the reasons why consumers use online social networking recruiting services. The role of different factors influencing consumer behavior intentions is examined in terms of how technological innovations in the online environment affect consumers. To understand this aim, the following research question is addressed: How do consumers decide to adopt online social networking recruiting services? As online social networking is a technological innovation gaining ascendancy in the marketplace, more information is required on the role of ethics and privacy in adoption behavior. This leads to the other research issues being addressed: What role does ethics, online privacy concerns, social influence and online behavioral advertising have in the online social networking recruiting context? Answering these questions will help to determine how to influence consumers to use online social networking recruiting services. The next section will discuss the theoretical framework and research hypotheses before presenting the methodology and results of the survey.

BACKGROUND

In this study, social cognitive theory is the theoretical framework underpinning the research hypotheses. Social cognitive theory provides a theoretical foundation to examine the factors influencing an individual's intention to use online social networking recruiting services. This theory enables an approach that links technology innovation adoption behavior with relationships in an individual's social environment. Social cognitive theory is useful for examining learning in an online environment (Chen, 2014). In the online environment, there are five main factors influencing behavior: technology, content, interaction, learning model and learner control. These factors can be classified as either technological or social structures based on the system context functions and learning interaction (Wu et al, 2011).

Originally developed by psychologists, social cognitive theory incorporates individual's experiences to understand future behavior. An individual engages in behavior based on their expectations (Wu et al, 2011). These expectations are influenced by an individual's internal and external environment. Environmental influencers are shaped by the cognition processes that occur as a result of social contexts (Bandura, 1986). Often learning results from the interaction of dynamic learning environments, which influence behavior. Both social and physical environments can affect behavior as a result of cognitive processes by individuals. The next sections will explain each research hypothesis and how they contribute to an understanding of possible connections between online behavioral advertising, ethics, privacy and social influencers and social networking activities. This research is relevant as more individuals spend increasing amounts of time on social networking websites.

Ethical Orientation

Ethics in the online environment refers to the beliefs and standards shared by individuals about appropriate behavior (McMahon and Cohen, 2009). The attitudes individuals have towards ethics may depend on whether they perceive the online environment different to the physical (Woodward et al, 2007). Ethics is important as increased usage of online resources has resulted in a large digital repository of information. Digital technology has increased the amount of information stored and shared online, which has created a number of ethical issues related to the ownership and access of sensitive data.

Information stored electronically creates ethical issues around the appropriate usage of personal data (McMahon & Cohen, 2009). Some people recognize unethical behavior in the online environment but this has been hampered by the lack of existing standards of behavior. The rules and norms of digital information have presented an ethical issue perpetuated by the perception that different ethical standards exist in cyberspace (Wu et al, 2011). When individuals have a higher ethical orientation they are likely to trust online social networks to access job opportunities. Therefore, this leads to the first hypothesis:

Hypothesis 1: Ethical orientation positively affects intention to use online social networking recruiting services

Online Privacy Concerns

Online privacy involves the degree a consumer is worried about potential invasion of online personal information divulged to others (Beal and Morimoto, 2012). Privacy is an individual right that sensitive data is not disclosed to third parties (Smith et al, 2014). Some consumers concerned about privacy cope by installing technological software (Raman & Pashupati, 2004). By doing this individuals rely on the software to stop cookies giving personal information to e-marketers (Lepp et al, 2014).

Consumers are worried about identifying information being given without their consent (Fogel & Nehmad, 2009). Previous research by Hoofnagle et al (2010) indicated that consumers have little information about privacy issues due to the high-tech systems employed by many websites. Consumers are worried about online privacy as they cannot be certain about the purpose of information being collected (Turow et al, 2009). Privacy concerns are a key antecedent of behavior in the online context. Consumers that are more concerned about privacy have been found to refrain from using websites that ask for personal information (Youn, 2009).

Privacy is important in the online environment because individuals are concerned about information being accessed and stored by third parties (Gao et al, 2012). This means that individuals are worried about improper usage of information that leads them to be anxious about computer usage (Compeau & Higgins, 1995). When individuals perceive their privacy is secure and safe then they are more likely to use new technologies (Chen & Chang, 2013). Therefore, the next hypothesis is proposed:

Hypothesis 2: Online privacy positively affects intention to use online social networking recruiting services

Online Behavioral Advertising

Online behavioral advertising is when advertising is adjusted by previous online surfing behavior (Smit et al, 2014). Many marketers are using online behavioral advertising as a way of targeting communications to consumers. In these communications, data is collected by installing cookies that collect consumer profile information (Smit et al, 2014). Cookies are small text files on consumer's electronic devices that store data about online behavior. Many consumers misunderstand online behavioral advertising because they do not comprehend how cookies are used by online advertisers. As cookies contain information often of a personal nature some consumers are unaware of the information acquired.

Online behavioral advertising focuses on previous internet site visits. Advertising companies can use browsing history when it is tied to personal information to target marketing campaigns. Online tracking for the purposes of marketing is a sensitive issue for consumers because of confidentiality concerns. Some consumers avoid websites because of concerns about personal information being collected (Pena & Brody, 2014). As individuals give personal information on online recruiting websites they are likely to be sensitive to any cookies that are included on websites they visit. This means that when individuals have more faith in online behavioral advertising they will feel more comfortable answering job questions in an online environment. Therefore, the next hypothesis is proposed:

Hypothesis 3: Online behavioral advertising positively affects intention to use online social networking recruiting services

Social Influencers

Social influence is defined as a consumer's intention to use technology services based on the influence of other people (Chen & Chang, 2013). Consumers may rely on social influencers depending on whether they want to access their social networks to obtain information about jobs. Social trends are key factors that help determine the introduction of new technology into the marketplace. An individual's social circle is an important component of their decision making process as it influencers the decision a person takes about adopting a technological innovation.

Social influence can take a variety of different forms but all focus on factors that affect an individual's decision to adopt a behavior (Venkatesh et al, 2003). People are influenced by the suggestions of people around them when deciding on the course of action to take. In the case of technology innovations, individuals often listen to other people's perceptions about the value of a service (Pavon & Brown, 2010). An increased perception of value added services benefitting a person's lifestyle will influence how quickly technological innovations are adopted. This then leads to the next hypothesis:

Hypothesis 4: Social influencers positively affect intention to use online social networking recruiting services

RESEARCH METHODOLOGY

Participants and Procedure

The participants of the study were undergraduate college students from a large United States university. Participants were recruited during class time from business courses and the principal investigator visited classrooms to explain the survey to students present. The principal investigator answered questions and explained that the survey was voluntary and would be confidential. The survey was distributed over a month long period in 2010 and completed by students in the class. There were 218 undergraduate students who participated in the study. The respondents to the study were 52% male and 48% female and the majority was between 20-25 years old. Anonymity was ensured of completed surveys and it took approximately 20 minutes for each person to complete the survey.

Measurement of Variables

The survey questionnaire consisted of a number of variables the majority of which were measured by a 7-point likert scale (1= strongly disagree, 7= strongly agree) derived from the literature. All measurement items are stated in table 1. Online behavioral advertising was measured with six items (α=0.81) adopted from Turow et al (2009) and Smith et al (2014). Ethical orientation was assessed using the same scale used by Woodward et al (2007) being a seven item scale ($\alpha = 0.74$). The wording of both the online behavioral advertising attitudes and ethical orientation scales was changed to focus on website usage in

Table 1. Measurement item scales

Construct	Measurement Items
Social influence (adapted from Chen and Chang, 2013)	1. The people around me think I should use online social networking recruiting services. 2. I will discuss online social networking recruiting services with my family and friends. 3. I will use online social networking recruiting services because I am influenced by my family and friends.
Online behavioral advertising attitudes (adapted from Smith et al, 2014 and Turow et al, 2009)	1. I prefer that websites show advertisements targeted to my interests. 2. I prefer that websites offer discounts targeted to my interests. 3. No-one should use data about my website use because it is private. 4. I do not like the idea that advertisements that are adjusted to my website use. 5. I prefer advertisements that are adjusted to my preferences. 6. I think that someone monitoring my website is conducting a violation of my privacy.
Ethics orientation (adapted from Woodward et al, 2007)	1. A person creates a virus to force website users to register for a shareware program they created. 2. A website designer posts a seal on a website to increase sales without permission. 3. A manager tells a website programmer to write a program that will generate inaccurate information. 4. A person downloads items from a website and gives them free to their friends. 5. An employee of a website company gives the password of a registered technology to their friends. 6. An employee of a website company gives a technology product to their friends without getting permission. 7. A website maintenance programmer finds an error in a website and does not correct the error.
Adoption intention (adapted from Anton et al, 2013)	1. How likely are you to be willing to use online social networking recruiting sources? 2. If you had access to online social networking recruiting sources, would you be willing to use it to store and access job information?
Online privacy concerns (adapted from Gao et al, 2012)	1. Before revealing any personal information online, I like to find out how marketers are going to use it. 2. I look for and read privacy policies on the web. 3. I am careful not to give companies more information online than I have to.

order to be consistent throughout the survey questionnaire. Online privacy concerns was measured by three items (α= 0.78) used by Gao et al (2012). Social influence was measured by three items drawn from Chen and Chang (2013) but the wording was changed to focus on online social networking recruiting services (α =0.73). To assess for the behavioral intention of individuals to adopt online social networking services, a two item scale adapted from Anton et al (2013) was used (α=0.82). The wording from the original scale was altered to include online social networking recruiting services.

ANALYSIS METHODS AND RESULTS

Table 2 indicates the means, standard deviations and correlations amongst the variables in the study. A confirmatory factor analysis using AMOS 17.0 assessed the reliability, validity and overall fit of the measurement model was conducted. Convergent validity was analyzed from factor loadings of each variable item, composite reliabilities and variance extracted from latent constructs. The analysis shown in Table 2 found that factor loadings were above the 0.50 recommended level and composite reliabilities above the 0.70 recommended level (Gefen, Straub and Bourdreau, 2000). The analysis also found that the average variances extracted were above the 0.50 recommended level. As a result of this analysis, it indicated that there was convergent validity.

- 1=female, 0= male
- Values in the parentheses on the main diagonal are Cronbach's alpha reliabilities
- Significant at the $p<0.05$ level

The discriminate validity of the measurement model was tested by comparing the correlation between constructs and the square root of the average variance extracted for each construct (Byrne, 2009). Table 3 depicts that the correlation of each construct is lower than the square root of the average variance extracted so the constructs demonstrate discriminate validity. Therefore, the measurement model indicates adequate reliability, convergent and discriminate validity. The measurement model fits the data adequately (chi-square/degrees of freedom=2.78, root mean square error of approximation=0.08, normed fit index=0.91, composite fit index=0.83).

Table 2. Summary of means, standard deviations and correlations amongst variables in the study

Variable	Mean	SD	1	2	3	4	5
Gender*	.52	0.54					
Age	21.05	7.18					
1 Online behavioral advertising	5.59	0.92	(0.81)				
2 Ethical orientation	5.12	0.69	0.54	(0.74)			
3 Online privacy concerns	5.73	1.08	0.31	0.07	(0.78)		
4 Social influences	6.09	0.67	0.34	0.19	0.12	(0.73)	
5 Adoption intention	4.78	0.92	0.46	0.52	0.39	0.52	(0.82)

Table 3. The results of the confirmatory factor analysis of the measurement model

Construct	Item	Factor Loading	Composite Reliability	Variance Extracted
Online privacy concerns (OPC)	OPC1 OPC2 OPC3	0.71 0.84 0.72	0.82	0.69
Social influence (SI)	SI1 SI2 SI3	0.71 0.74 0.78	0.87	0.64
Adoption intention (AI)	AI1 AI2	0.81 0.71	0.78	0.64
Online behavioral advertising (OBA)	OBA1 OBA2 OBA3 OBA4 OBA5 OBA6	0.78 0.74 0.77 0.81 0.76 0.79	0.89	0.61
Ethical orientation (EO)	EO1 EO2 EO3 EO4 EO5 EO6 EO7	0.71 0.69 0.74 0.69 0.71 0.72 0.78	0.79	0.59

The hypothesized model was then compared to a set of competing models acting as alternative explanations to the proposed model (Byrne, 2009). This enabled a conclusion to be made that as no other competing model achieves the same level of fit the original hypothesized model is acceptable. In the alternative models proposed, one parameter was changed at a time then compared to the proposed theoretical model (Anderson and Gerbing, 1988). The final adjusted model fitted the data (chi-square/degrees of freedom=2.83, root mean square error of approximation=0.07, goodness of fit=0.93, normed fit index=0.90, Tucker Lewis index=0.91, adjusted goodness of fit index=0.83). Most of the paths in the hypothesized model were significant ($p<0.05$) in the hypothesized direction. Hypothesis 1, 3 and 4 were supported but 2 was not supported in the data analysis. Ethical orientation was positively related to adoption intention (path coefficient=0.16), online behavioral advertising was positively related to adoption intention (path coefficient=0.29) and social influences was positively related to adoption intention (path coefficient=0.39). Online privacy concerns was found to be insignificant and the proposed positive relationship not accepted.

There was also an additional new path that emerged from the final adjusted model, which was a positive relationship between ethical orientation and online behavioral advertising (path coefficient=0.18). This additional path improved the model fit (chi square=3.08, $p<0.05$). The data was also analyzed for common method bias using Harman's single factor test. All of the study variables were forced onto a single latent construct to see if a single factor accounted for all the variance in the data (Podsakoff et al, 2003). The results showed that common method variance did not seem to be an issue but it is addressed as a potential future research issue.

SOLUTIONS AND RECOMMENDATIONS

In the final model, ethical orientation was positively related to adoption intention of online social networking recruiting services. In the online recruiting context, ethical orientation is an important part of monitoring moral behavior (Woodward et al, 2007). Therefore, the results suggest that ethical behavior on the internet (e.g. illegal downloading, social engineering and online piracy) play an important role in the intention of individuals to use their social networks as part of online recruiting.

The results of the study found that the relationship between online privacy concerns and adoption intention of online social networking services to be insignificant. This is in contrast to the expected relationship and differs with previous research by Forester and Morison (1994) who found that privacy is an important part of the adoption process of technological innovations.

The results of the study found a positive relationship between online behavioral advertising and adoption intention of online social networking services. This finding is in line with Bagozzi et al's (1992) research that there is a high level of uncertainty about new technologies because of the lack of familiarity and behaviors can change as a result of advertising. This finding is also consistent with previous research by McMahon and Cohen (2009) who found that time and support is required when adopting new technologies and behavior can affect the adoption process.

The results of the study confirm a positive relationship between social influence and adoption intention of online social networking services. Job applicants using online recruiting services learn about positions in postings on organizations websites (Cable & Graham, 2010). When there is little information about organizations under consideration for job applicants, more decisions are based on the opinion of people within an individual's social circle. If an organizations recruitment website has good advertising about the benefits of working at the organization, applicants may be more likely to share this information with their online social networks.

Practical Implications

The findings of this paper provide implications for practitioners. To enhance the probability that a consumer will use online social networking recruiting services, employment agencies should pay attention to how their website is perceived by people. As online privacy concerns and behavioral advertising influence individual's intention to adopt online networking recruiting services, it is important that employment agencies develop appropriate strategies to ensure that job seekers are comfortable in using online resources. This will help people feel satisfied with online recruitment services and the information people share with their social networks. Employment agencies should carry out measures to improve online satisfaction with recruiting services. These may include displaying ethics statements to help people trust online recruiting services that encourage trust in the service encounter.

Practitioners could improve service quality by educating people about the value their social influence has in helping people adopt technological innovations. Online service providers should train recruiters to better deal with consumer concerns including how online advertising is done to increase trust of online recruitment. As the interaction between individual's social networks has an impact on their intention to adopt online social networking recruiting services it is important that recruitment companies build relationships. Recruitment companies should continually improve the cyber infrastructure of their websites and related mobile applications to encourage more people to adopt online recruitment services. These efforts will help to cultivate increase consumer satisfaction and loyalty over a long period of time.

Theoretical Implications

The theoretical implications of this paper include the development of a set of antecedent factors that impact the adoption of online social networking recruiting services. This is important as more employment opportunities are being incorporated into an individuals social networks. Technological advances have meant that individuals perceive online services as important ways to communicate. The current study has empirically demonstrated that individuals perceive ethical orientation and online behavioral advertising to be a concern before they are willing to adopt online social networking recruiting services. These findings indicate that it is essential for online recruiters to clarify the safeguards they have in place on their websites to maintain consumer confidentiality.

When organizations websites state their policies in an understandable way it is easier for job applicants to follow them. Organizations should develop easy to follow e-recruiting pages that can be used by individuals who are sensitive to privacy and advertising concerns. The results of this study confirm the role of ethics, advertising and social influence in influencing the intention of individuals to adopt online social networking recruiting services. Social cognitive theory was applied to explain why some individuals might use e-recruitment based on their social networks.

FUTURE RESEARCH DIRECTIONS

One limitation from this study is that it looked at intention to use online social networking recruiting services instead of actual usage. This may lead to potential recall bias as an individual's intention may be different to their real behavior (Pena & Brody, 2014). Although prior research in the technology innovation literature suggests that intentions are a reliable indicator of actual behavior (Ajzen, 1985) it may be hard to measure intentions when they change as technology evolves. Future studies should try to measure the process of online social networking recruiting service adoption in a longitudinal study in which individuals are observed in real time logging onto the internet and searching for job positions based on online social networks recommendations.

The second limitation is the sampling procedure used in this study. As a convenience sample of university students were utilized this may limit the generalizability of the results to a broader range of the population. Despite previous research by Howardson and Behrend (2014) suggesting that student participant pools can be generalizable to a wider range of individuals, there may be some differences in technology usage by individuals in different income and age segments. An individual's effectiveness in using technology may be related to their internet recruitment experience that depends on their personality characteristics (Agarwal & Prasad, 1998). This means that future research should explore the effect of personal innovativeness with technology to see how it impacts on an individual's online social networking activities.

The third limitation is the use of self-reported survey data. As all measures in the study were collected in the same survey this may lead to common method bias. When the observed relationships between constructs are measured at the same time common method variance may occur (Podsakoff et al, 2003). In the online recruitment context some individuals may already have had exposure to the familiarity of the advertising based on organizations involved (De Goede et al, 2011). This may lead to a bias both in terms of how the constructs were measured but also due to prior familiarity with online social networking recruiting services. Future studies should gather data from multiple sources at different time periods to overcome these limitations. More research should be conducted that include control variables such as prior technology usage and familiarity with online social networking to see how they might affect intentions to use online recruitment services. As this study used social cognitive theory, it could be further tested using other technology theories including the technology acceptance model to see if it applies in the online recruitment context.

CONCLUSION

Due to the increased usage of online social networks by individuals and organizations around the world there have not been many studies that have focused on the role of online social networks in developing recruiting services. This paper has examined the role of online social networking recruiting services by focusing on the antecedent factors affecting behavioral intentions. By doing so, social cognitive theory was utilized to address how ethics, online behavioral advertising, social influencers and online privacy concerns influence an individual's decision to adopt online social networking recruiting services. The findings lead to a number of managerial and theoretical implications being proposed that highlight the importance of emerging technological innovations in the online environment.

REFERENCES

Agarwal, R., & Prasad, J. (1998). A conceptual and operational definition of personal innovativeness in the domain of information technology. *Information Systems Research*, *9*(2), 204–215. doi:10.1287/isre.9.2.204

Ajzen, I. (1985). From intentions to actions: A theory of planned behavior. In J. Kuhl & J. Beckman (Eds.), *Action control: From cognition to behavior* (pp. 11–39). Heidelberg, Germany: Springer. doi:10.1007/978-3-642-69746-3_2

Allen, D. G., Mahto, R. V., & Otondo, R. F. (2007). Web-based recruitment: Effects of information, organizational brand and attitudes towards a website on applicant attraction. *The Journal of Applied Psychology*, *92*(6), 1696–1708. doi:10.1037/0021-9010.92.6.1696 PMID:18020806

Anderson, J. C., & Gerbing, D. W. (1988). Structural equation modeling in practice: A review and recommended two-step approach. *Psychological Bulletin*, *103*(3), 411–423. doi:10.1037/0033-2909.103.3.411

Antón, C., Camarero, C., & Rodríguez, J. (2013). Usefulness, enjoyment and self-image congruence: The adoption of e-book readers. *Psychology and Marketing*, *30*(4), 372–384. doi:10.1002/mar.20612

Bagozzi, R., & Yi, Y. (1988). On the evaluation of structural equation models. *Journal of the Academy of Marketing Science*, *16*(1), 74–94. doi:10.1007/BF02723327

Bandura, A. (1986). *Social foundations of thought and action: A social cognitive theory*. Englewood Cliffs, New Jersey: Prentice Hall.

Beak, T. H., & Morimoto, M. (2012). Stay away from me: Examining the determinants of consumer avoidance of personalized advertising. *Journal of Advertising*, *41*(1), 59–76. doi:10.2753/JOA0091-3367410105

Boyd, D., & Ellison, N. (2007). Social network sites: Definition, history and scholarship. *Journal of Computer-Mediated Communication*, *13*(1), 210–230. doi:10.1111/j.1083-6101.2007.00393.x

Byrne, B. M. (2009). *Structural equation modeling with AMOS: Basic concepts, applications and programming*. New York: Taylor and Francis Group.

Cable, D. M., & Graham, M. E. (2000). The determinants of job-seekers reputation perceptions. *Journal of Organizational Behavior*, *21*(8), 929–947. doi:10.1002/1099-1379(200012)21:8<929::AID-JOB63>3.0.CO;2-O

Cappelli, P. (2001). Making the most of on-line recruiting. *Harvard Business Review*, *79*, 139–146. PMID:11246921

Chen, K. Y., & Chang, M. L. (2013). User acceptance of 'near field communication' mobile phone service: An investigation based on the unified theory of acceptance and use of technology model. *Service Industries Journal*, *33*(6), 609–623. doi:10.1080/02642069.2011.622369

Cober, R. T., Brown, D. J., Levy, P. E., Cober, A. B., & Keeping, L. M. (2003). Organizational websites: Website content and style as determinants of organizational attractiveness. *International Journal of Selection and Assessment*, *11*(2/3), 158–169. doi:10.1111/1468-2389.00239

Compeau, D. R., & Higgins, C. A. (1995). Computer self-efficacy: Development of a measure and initial test. *Management Information Systems Quarterly*, *19*(2), 189–211. doi:10.2307/249688

Correa, T., Hinsley, A., & De-Zuniga, H. (2010). Who interacts on the web? The interaction of users personality and social media use. *Computers in Human Behavior*, *26*(2), 247–253. doi:10.1016/j.chb.2009.09.003

De Goede, M. E., Van Vianen, A.E.M., & Kiene, U.-C. (2011). Attracting applicants on the web: PO fit, industry culture stereotypes and website design. *International Journal of Selection and Assessment*, *19*(1), 51–61. doi:10.1111/j.1468-2389.2010.00534.x

Fogel, J., & Nehmad, E. (2009). Internet social network communities: Risk taking, trust and privacy concerns. *Computers in Human Behavior*, *25*(1), 153–160. doi:10.1016/j.chb.2008.08.006

Gao, T., Rohm, A. J., Sultan, F., & Huang, S. (2012). Antecedents of consumer attitudes toward mobile marketing: A comparative study of youth markets in the United States and China. *Thunderbird International Business Review*, *54*(2), 211–224. doi:10.1002/tie.21452

Gefen, D., Straub, D., & Bourdreau, M. (2000). Structural equation modeling and regression: Guidelines for research practice. *Communications of the Association for Information Systems*, *4*, 1–79.

Hew, K. (2011). Students and teachers use of Facebook. *Computers in Human Behavior*, *27*(2), 662–676. doi:10.1016/j.chb.2010.11.020

Hoofnagle, C.J., King, J., Li, S. & Turow, J. (2010). *How different are young adults from older adults when it comes to information privacy attitudes and policies?* Research Report, November.

Hooper, D. (2007). Getting better all the time. *HR Monthly*, May.

Howardson, G. M., & Behrend, T. S. (2014). Using the internet to recruit employees: Comparing the effects of usability expectations and objective technological characteristics on internet recruitment outcomes. *Computers in Human Behavior*, *31*, 334–342. doi:10.1016/j.chb.2013.10.057

Kashi, K., & Zheng, C. (2013). Extending technology acceptance model to the e-recruitment context in Iran. *International Journal of Selection and Assessment*, *23*(1), 122–129.

Kuo, T., & Tang, H. (2014). Relationships amongst personality traits, Facebook usages, and leisure activities- A case of Taiwanese college students. *Computers in Human Behavior*, *31*, 13–19. doi:10.1016/j.chb.2013.10.019

Lepp, A., Barkley, J. E., & Karpinski, A. C. (2014). The relationship between cell phone use, academic performance, anxiety and satisfaction with life in college students. *Computers in Human Behavior*, *31*, 343–350. doi:10.1016/j.chb.2013.10.049

Leung, L., & Lee, P. (2005). Multiple determinants of life quality: The roles of internet activities, use of new media, social support and leisure activities. *Telematics and Informatics*, *22*(3), 161–180. doi:10.1016/j.tele.2004.04.003

Lievens, F., & Harris, M. M. (2005). Research on internet recruiting and testing: Current status and future directions. In C. L. Cooper & L. T. Robertson (Eds.), *International review of industrial/organizational psychology* (pp. 131–165). Chichester, England: John Wiley & Sons. doi:10.1002/0470013346.ch4

McMahon, J. M., & Cohen, R. (2009). Lost in cyberspace: Ethical decision making in the online environment. *Ethics and Information Technology*, *11*(1), 1–17. doi:10.1007/s10676-008-9165-7

Pavon, F., & Brown, I. (2010). Factors influencing the adoption of the world wide web for jobseeking in South Africa. *Journal of International Management*, *12*(1), 443–452.

Peña, J., & Brody, N. (2014). Intentions to hide and unfriend Facebook connections based on perceptions of sender attractiveness and status updates. *Computers in Human Behavior*, *31*, 143–150. doi:10.1016/j.chb.2013.10.004

Pfieffelman, P. M., Wagner, S. H., & Libkuman, T. (2010). Recruiting on corporate web sites: Perceptions of fit and attraction. *International Journal of Selection and Assessment*, *18*(1), 40–47. doi:10.1111/j.1468-2389.2010.00487.x

Podsakoff, P. M., MacKenzie, S. B., Lee, J., & Podsakoff, N. F. (2003). Common method biases in behavioral research: A critical review of the literature and recommended remedies. *The Journal of Applied Psychology*, *88*(5), 879–903. doi:10.1037/0021-9010.88.5.879 PMID:14516251

Raman, P. & Pashupati, K. (2004). Online privacy: The impact of self-perceived technological competence. *American Marketing Association Educators Proceedings*, 5-6.

Ratten, V. (2012a). Does the Sky have to be the limit? Utilizing Cloud-Based Learning in the Workplace. *Development and Learning Organization*, *26*(5), 21–23. doi:10.1108/14777281211258662

Ratten, V. (2012b). Entrepreneurship, E-Finance and Mobile Banking. *International Journal of Electronic Finance*, *6*(1), 1–12. doi:10.1504/IJEF.2012.046590

Ratten, V. (2013). The evolution of mobile social networks through technological innovation. In A. Brem & E. Viardot (Eds.), *Evolution of Innovation Management* (pp. 132–150). London: Palgrave MacMillan. doi:10.1057/9781137299994.0013

Ratten, V. (2014a). Indian and US consumer purchase intentions of cloud computing services. *Journal of Indian Business Research*, *6*(2), 170–188. doi:10.1108/JIBR-07-2013-0068

Ratten, V. (2014b). Behavioral intentions to adopt technological innovations: The role of trust, innovation and performance. *International Journal of Enterprise Information Systems*, *10*(3), 1–12. doi:10.4018/ijeis.2014070101

Ross, C., Orr, E. S., Sisic, M., Arseneault, J. M., Simmering, M. G., & Orr, R. R. (2009). Personality and motivates associated with Facebook use. *Computers in Human Behavior*, *25*(2), 575–586. doi:10.1016/j.chb.2008.12.024

Sinar, E. F., Reynolds, D. H., & Paquet, S. L. (2003). Nothing but net corporate image and web-based testing. *International Journal of Selection and Assessment*, *11*(2-3), 150–157. doi:10.1111/1468-2389.00238

Smit, E. G., Van Noort, G., & Voorveld, H. (2014). Understanding online behavioral advertising: User knowledge, privacy concerns and online coping behavior in Europe. *Computers in Human Behavior*, *32*, 15–22. doi:10.1016/j.chb.2013.11.008

Smith, S., & Caruso, J. (2010). *The ECAR study of undergraduate students and information technology*. Boulder: Colorado Press.

Tosun, L., & Lajunen, T. (2010). Does internet use reflect your personality? Relationship between Eysenk's personality dimensions and internet use. *Computers in Human Behavior*, *26*(2), 162–167. doi:10.1016/j.chb.2009.10.010

Turow, J., King, J., Hoofnagle, C., Bleakley, A., & Hennesy, M. (2009). *Americans reject tailored advertising and three activities that enable it*. Annenberg School of Communication Department Papers.

Venkatesh, V., Morris, M. G., Davis, G. B., & Davis, F. D. (2003). User acceptance of information technology: Toward a unified view. *Management Information Systems Quarterly*, *27*(3), 425–478.

Villano, M. (2008). Technology acceptance model 3 and a research agenda on interventions. *Decision Sciences*, *39*(2), 272–315.

Viswesvaran, C. (2003). Introduction to special issue: Role of technology in shaping the future of staffing and assessment. *International Journal of Selection and Assessment*, *11*(2-3), 1078–1112. doi:10.1111/1468-2389.00233

Walther, J. B. (2004). Language and communication technology: Introduction to the special issue. *Journal of Language and Social Psychology*, *23*(4), 384–396. doi:10.1177/0261927X04269584

Woodward, B., Davis, D. C., & Hodis, F. A. (2007). The relationship between ethical decision making and ethical reasoning in information technology students. *Journal of Information Systems Education*, *18*(2), 193–202.

Wu, F., Hoon, L. S., & Yuzhu, Z. (2011). Dos and donts for Chinese companies investing in the United States: Lessons from Huawei and Haier. *Thunderbird International Business Review*, *53*(4), 501–515. doi:10.1002/tie.20426

Youn, S. (2009). Determinants of online privacy concern and its influence on privacy protection behaviors among young adolescents. *The Journal of Consumer Affairs*, *43*(3), 389–418. doi:10.1111/j.1745-6606.2009.01146.x

ADDITIONAL READING

Aungst, S. G., & Wilson, D. T. (2005). A primer for navigating the shoals of applying wireless technology to marketing problems. *Journal of Business and Industrial Marketing*, *20*(2/3), 59–69. doi:10.1108/08858620510583650

Bandura, A. (2001). Social cognitive theory: An agentic perspective. *Annual Review of Psychology*, *52*(1), 1–26. doi:10.1146/annurev.psych.52.1.1 PMID:11148297

Barnett, N., Hodges, S., & Wiltshire, M. (2000). M-commerce: An operators manual. *The McKinsey Quarterly*, *3*, 163–173.

Beckman, J. (Ed.), *Action-Control: From Cognition to Behavior* (pp. 11–39). Heidelberg: Springer.

Birkinshaw, J., & Mol, M. (2006). How management innovation happens. *MIT Sloan Management Review*, *47*(4), 81–89.

Cantisani, A. (2006). Technological innovation processes revisited. *Technovation*, *26*(11), 1294–1301. doi:10.1016/j.technovation.2005.10.003

Celsi, R., Rose, R., & Leigh, T. (1993). An exploration of high-risk leisure consumption through Skydiving. *The Journal of Consumer Research*, *20*(6), 1–23. doi:10.1086/209330

Guan, J. C., Mok, C. K., Yam, R. C. M., Chin, K. S., & Pun, K. F. (2006). Technology transfer and innovation performance: Evidence from Chinese firms. *Technological Forecasting and Social Change*, *73*(6), 666–678. doi:10.1016/j.techfore.2005.05.009

Harris, P., Rettie, R., & Kwan, C. C. (2005). Adoption and usage of m-commerce: A cross-cultural comparison of Hong Kong and the United Kingdom. *Journal of Electronic Commerce Research*, *6*(3), 210–224.

Li, Y., Liu, Y., & Ren, F. (2007). Product innovation and process innovation in SOEs: Evidence from the Chinese transition. *The Journal of Technology Transfer*, *32*(1-2), 63–85. doi:10.1007/s10961-006-9009-8

Lu, J., Yu, C., Liu, C., & Yao, J. (2003). Technology acceptance model for wireless Internet, Internet research. *Electronic Networking Applications and Policy*, *13*(3), 206–222. doi:10.1108/10662240310478222

McCoy, S., Galletta, D. F., & King, W. R. (2007). Applying TAM across cultures: The need for Caution. *European Journal of Information Systems*, *16*(1), 81–90. doi:10.1057/palgrave.ejis.3000659

Ratten, V. (2009). Adoption of technological innovations in the m-commerce industry. *International Journal of Technology Marketing*, *4*(4), 355–367. doi:10.1504/IJTMKT.2009.032181

Rogers, E. (1995). *Diffusion of Innovations* (4th ed.). New York: The Free Press of Glencoe.

Rycroft, R. W. (2006). Time and Technological Innovation. *Implications for Public Policy*, *28*, 281–301.

Salo, J., & Karjaluoto, H. (2007). Mobile games as an advertising medium: Towards a new research agenda. *Innovative Marketing*, *3*(1), 71–82.

Sheeshka, J., Woolcott, D., & MacKinnon, N. (1993). Social cognitive theory as a framework to explain intentions to practice healthy eating behaviors. *Journal of Applied Social Psychology*, *23*(19), 1547–1573. doi:10.1111/j.1559-1816.1993.tb01047.x

Sheth, J., Mittal, B., & Newman, B. (1999). *Consumer Behavior: Consumer Behavior and Beyond*. Texas: Dryden Press.

Smith, B., & Morse, E. (2005). *Entrepreneurial Competencies: Literature Review and Best Practices*. Ottawa: Small Business Policy Branch, Industry Canada.

Snowden, S., Spafford, J., Michaelides, R., & Hopkins, J. (2006). Technology acceptance and m-commerce in an operational environment. *Journal of Enterprise Information Management*, *19*(5), 525–539. doi:10.1108/17410390610703657

Steyaert, C. (2007). 'Entrepreneuring' as a conceptual attractor? A review of process theories in 20 years of entrepreneurship studies. *Entrepreneurship & Regional Development*, *19*(6), 453–477. doi:10.1080/08985620701671759

Steyaert, C., & Katz, J. (2004). Reclaiming the space of entrepreneurship in society: Geographical, discursive and social dimensions. *Entrepreneurship & Regional Development*, *16*(May), 179–196. doi:10.1080/0898562042000197135

Townsend, D. M., Busenitz, L. W., & Arthurs, J. D. (2010). To start or not to start: Outcome and ability expectations in the decision to start a new venture. *Journal of Business Venturing*, *25*(2), 192–202. doi:10.1016/j.jbusvent.2008.05.003

Werbel, J. D., & Danes, S. M. (2010). Work family conflict in new business ventures: The moderating effects of spousal commitment to the new business venture. *Journal of Small Business Management*, *48*(3), 421–440. doi:10.1111/j.1540-627X.2010.00301.x

KEY TERMS AND DEFINITIONS

Innovation: The creation of a new product or service.
Media: Any communication that is spoken or written, which acts as an information source.
Mobile Commerce: A mobile way in which business transactions are conducted.

Mobile Reading Devices: A portable device used to read electronic material.
Modeling: Imitating or copying another person's actions.
Technological Adoption: The process to explain how a person utilises a technology.
Technological Innovation: A new product or service involving knowledge change.

Section 4

Improving Market Performance through Marketing

Chapter 13
Online Pricing and Auctions

Kalender Özcan Atilgan
University of Mersin, Turkey

ABSTRACT

Recently, the role of information technology facilitating the exchange of information in markets has enabled new pricing mechanisms between buyers and sellers. Such electronic marketplaces, specifically Internet-based markets have supported customization of marketing mix elements efficiently. In response to supply and demand fluctuations, prices change more dynamically and quickly in the Internet than in physical markets. This chapter focuses on the revolution in pricing of businesses driven by the Internet. Within this context, primary characteristics of online pricing and auctions are reviewed systematically from the both view of buyers and sellers interacting. Furthermore, this chapter evaluates the effects of Internet as a new pricing mechanism and future trends of pricing rules within this attractive option.

INTRODUCTION

Markets (electronic or otherwise) have three main functions: matching buyers and sellers; facilitating the exchange of information, goods, services and payments associated with market transactions; and providing an institutional infrastructure, such as a legal and regulatory framework, that enables the efficient functioning of the market (Bakos, 1998). As the internet reaches every aspect of our lives, many traditional retailers find that the internet is a new channel for selling their goods (Tang & Gan, 2004). E-Business companies are currently grappling with the complex task of determining the right prices to charge a customer for a product or a service (Narahari, Raju, Ravikumar, & Shah, 2005).

Bakos (1998) suggested that a key function of markets in new economic system is price discovery, which is the process of determining the prices at which demand and supply "clear" and trade occurs. For financial markets, price discovery is their primary function. Similar to the financial markets, electronic businesses enable new types of price discovery to be employed in different markets. For instance, online reservation systems of hotels can provide price-sensitive customers to lock-in a price for future services, airlines auction last-minute unsold seats to the highest bidders, and ebay.com, predominantly characterized as a person-to-person auction site as it provides a market place for individual buyers and sellers to trade online may be given (Bakos, 1998; Brint, 2003).

DOI: 10.4018/978-1-4666-8459-1.ch013

The scope of this chapter is a review of literature related with online pricing and its effect on both consumers and businesses. Thus it highlights the contemporary internet pricing issues by providing a critique review of miscellaneous studies related with dynamic pricing such as online pricing and auctions.

PRICING AND TRADITIONAL PRICING STRATEGIES

Price can be defined as the total resources expanded by a buyer or lessee in acquiring a given good or service. Price in a transaction consists both of what the buyer explicitly pays the seller in exchange for a specified good or service and, in that for many people time and effort have a cost equivalent, also the resources expanded by the buyer in terms of purchase time, travel effort and other associated tasks and inconveniences (Narver & Savitt, 1971).

Kotler and Armstrong (2014, p. 312) define price in the narrowest sense as "the amount of money charged for a product or service", and in the more broadly, "price is the sum of all the values that customers give up to gain the benefits of having or using the product or service".

This essential role of price in commerce is sometimes disguised by the use of traditional terms. If the product in the commercial exchange is a good, then the product's price will most likely be called "price." (Schindler, 2012). The other terms used to mean price is listed in Table 1.

From the view of companies, pricing is one of the most important elements of the marketing mix that generates income, thus a key determinant of performance (Shipley & Jobber, 2001; Breidert, 2005; Rao & Kartono, 2009). Perhaps, the fastest and most effective way for a company to realize its maximum profit is to get its pricing right (Marn & Rosiello, 1992). The effects of price changes are more immediate and direct, and appeals based on price are the easiest to communicate to prospective buyers (Rao, 1984). Despite its high importance, price (or pricing) as the least researched and mastered areas of marketing, is the most neglected element of the marketing mix (Rao, 1984; Avlonitis & Indounas, 2006; Carricano, Trinquecoste, & Mondejar, 2010).

During the last decades, marketers have become aware of the importance of developing an appropriate pricing strategy, and of the complexity of such a task (Gijsbrechts, 1993). However, pricing can be seen

Table 1. Some Terms Used to Mean "Price"

Price	most goods
Tuition	college courses, education
Rent	use of a place to live or use of equipment for a period of time
Interest	use of money
Fee	professional services: for lawyers, doctors, consultants
Premium	insurance
Fare	transportation: air, taxi, bus
Toll	use of a road or bridge, or long-distance phone rate
Salary	work of managers
Wages	work of hourly workers
Commission	sales effort

Source: Schindler, 2012, p. 3

as a highly complex process that incorporates strategic role of price, pricing objectives, the plethora of internal and external pricing determinants, pricing strategy, the pricing technique, and the necessary implementation and control procedures (Shipley & Jobber, 2001). Oxenfeldt (1973) suggested a framework for pricing decisions as:

1. Recognize the need for a pricing decision,
2. Price determination,
3. Develop a model,
4. Identify and anticipate pricing problems,
5. Develop feasible course of action,
6. Forecast the outcomes of each alternative,
7. Monitor and review the outcome of each action.

The setting of any price involves (Oxenfeldt, 1973): 1. Values that particular segments of customers place on a firm's offering; 2. Consumer responses to price changes of the product; 3. Competitive responses to price changes of the product; and 4. Resellers' sensitivity to price changes. Thus, the price the company charges will fall somewhere between one that is too low to produce a profit and one that is too high to produce any demand (Kotler & Armstrong, 2014). To set price, there are major considerations as depicted in Figure 1 that compares value-based pricing with cost-based pricing.Whereas customer-value perceptions set tha price ceiling, costs set the floor for the price that the company can charge.

Cost-based pricing involves setting prices based on the costs of producing, distributing, and selling the products plus a fair rate of return for its effort and risk. In the value-based pricing, that company assesses customer needs and value perceptions, and then sets its target price based on customer perceptions of value (Kotler & Armstrong, 2014). One another pricing strategy is competition-based pricing which involves setting prices based on competitors' strategies, costs, prices, and market offerings.

Figure 1. Considerations in Setting Price and Related Pricing Strategies (Adapted from Kotler & Armstrong, 2014, p. 313)

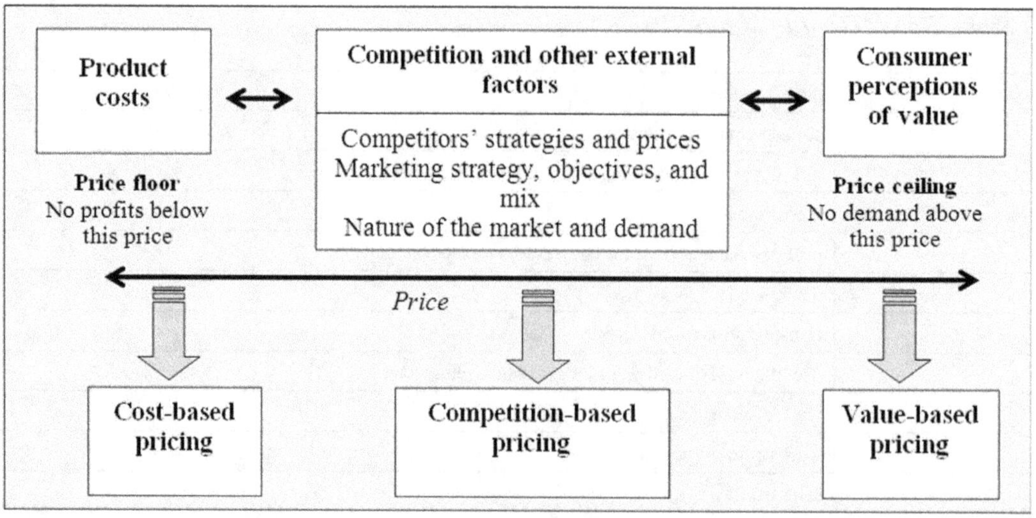

PRICES FROM THE VIEW OF CONSUMERS

Marketing and economics differ markedly in the manner in which they perceive and analyse buyers' response to prices (Skouras, Avlonitis, & Indounas, 2005). Traditionally, the economist explain price as a function of the interplay between demand and supply. The microeconomic theory of demand and supply describes and predicts price and quantity of goods and services sold in a perfectly competitive market, examining demand in terms of the customer and supply from a seller perspective (Parsa & Njite, 2008). Also, pricing remains largely the domain of economic theorists who discuss price primarily in relation to the analyses of specific market structures (Oxenfeldt, 1973). In the economical view, price is seen as an important constraint on purchase decision that a consumer maximizes utility by allocating a limited budget over alternative goods and services (Erickson & Johansson, 1985).

However, the goal of behavioral science pricing models is to explain the actual, sometimes limited rational behavior of consumers when they attend to and process price information (Herrmann & Wricke, 1998). Thus, the main difference concerns the treatment of rationality and the question of whether buyers are characterised or not by rational behavior (Skouras, Avlonitis, & Indounas, 2005).

Prices can mean more than just a monetary exchange of value for consumers and a consumer's psychological reaction to a price is an important determinant of the overall response to the price (Campbell, 1999). Also, a price can give some cues about the character of a product "attribute" such as operating as an indicator of quality (Erickson & Johansson, 1985).

In recent years there has been a growing awareness of the complex role of price as a determinant of a purchase decision (Monroe, 1973). The way prices are presented to consumers influences consumers' processing of price information and evaluation of the offer (Kim & Kachersky, 2006). Recent research in marketing also suggests that, price judgments, reference price, odd pricing, and the communication aspects of price are some key concepts relating to the psychological aspects of pricing (Ofir & Winer, 2002). The psychological aspects of pricing consider consumers' perception of offer value, perception of price saving or discounts, perceived sacrifice and perception of quality by the consumer (Parsa & Njite, 2008, Zeithaml, 1988). With the growth of the Internet, new dimensions are added and renewed studies are needed on how prices are set and perceived by means of psychology of pricing (Miyazaki, 2003).

EFFECT OF THE INTERNET ON PRICING

Internet is an electronic medium based on broadcasting and publishing that facilitates two-way communication. In exchanges, there are neither physically face-to-face nor time-bound, buyer and seller interact through networked computers (Pitt, Berthon, Watson, & Ewing, 2001). Thus, the Internet can be used to build up a community for buyers and sellers or electronic marketplaces where a group of buyers and sellers communicate directly to trade, consolidate sales, and set prices for transactions (Kung, Monroe, & Cox, 2002). The issue of online pricing is of particular importance in the online marketing research. This is because pure dotcoms tend to differentiate themselves from other types of retailer via flexibly pricing their products (Li & Tang, 2011). Schindler (2012) suggested that sites on the Internet could be used as locations to accomplish price segmentation. According to Schindler (2012), price segmentation is between a seller's branded site (the Internet location of a product's manufacturer such as Sony.com) and a shopping site (shopping agents show the prices of many sellers of an item in a format that facilitates price comparison such as Amazon.com). Unlike physical markets where change occurs slowly because of information delays, change occurs very rapidly on the Internet (Jayaraman & Baker, 2003). Online markets possess several characteristics described in the economic theory of perfect competition. For example, consumers can search prices at low cost, new firms enjoy low barriers to entry, and existing stores can change prices efficiently (Jap & Naik, 2004).

The advent of a new medium for buyer and seller interaction, the Internet, has changed the issue of price for both customers and suppliers (Pitt, Berthon, Watson, & Ewing, 2001). Smith, Bailey and Brynjolfsson (1999) identified four dimensions of efficiency internet market compared to brick and mortar markets:

- Price Levels: Are the prices charged on the Internet lower?
- Price Elasticity: Are consumers more sensitive to small price changes on the Internet?
- Menu Costs: Do retailers adjust their prices more finely or more frequently on the Internet?
- Price Dispersion: Is there a smaller spread between the highest and lowest prices on the Internet?

The effect of the Internet on the changing nature of pricing can be summarized as follows (Kung, Monroe, & Cox, 2002; Pitt, Berthon, Watson, & Ewing, 2001):

- Internet would lead to perfect competition, many online companies set prices below consumers' value-based prices.
- Compared to traditional shopping, searching online for the lowest prices of products can be convenient, quick, and costless.
- Search engines, or shopbots help to reduce asymmetric information between buyers and sellers. Thus, buyers have additional influence in the negotiating process, transaction costs are reduced, and buyers have increased ability to make informed decisions.
- The direct supplier-buyer relationship in Internet transactions reduces or eliminates the various intermediaries in traditional distribution systems.
- Shopbots have weakened the ability of online firms to charge higher prices by reducing the effects of imperfect information and by giving online buyers increased convenience through technology that searches a variety of sites for pricing and product information. So, the Internet homogenize products, resulting in price competition.
- The internet offers managers the opportunity to differentiate prices of the same product or service for different customers (having different values of this product or service).
- The internet allows sellers to collect detailed data about customers' buying habits, preferences, spending limits, etc., so they can tailor their products and prices to the individual buyer.
- Businesses have an opportunity to maximize revenue rather than price by use of some technics such as yield management.

PRICING MECHANISMS IN THE INTERNET: TOWARDS CONSUMERS AS PRICE SETTERS

Before the emergence of the Internet, buyers could evaluate prices by only comparing them either to other prices available for comparison in the market or to reference prices that are stored in memory (Monroe, 1990). The Internet has allowed for larger and richer data sets by which pricing can be investigated

(Miyazaki, 2003). In interactive environments, consumers can more easily participate in the process of setting the prices of goods and services than in off-line environments. For example, eBay and Priceline enable geographically dispersed consumers to transact with each other via computer-mediated interfaces (Jap & Naik, 2004). Alternative pricing strategies are being applied to goods and services sold over the Internet (Jayaraman & Baker, 2003).

Figure 2 captures the main pricing mechanisms. The internet enables customers to become both price takers and price makers, and for firms to gain buying advantages and earn commissions on customer trades by allowing and facilitating customers to trade with each other. Historically, fixed pricing has tended to dominate. However, there is a natural variation in buyer's demand over time. Thus, fixed pricing mechanisms are inefficient as they result in under-utilization of resources when demand is low and under-pricing when demand is high (Lee & Szymanski, 2006). On the other hand, in some e-markets like electronic catalogues prices are fixed, portals do not have a pricing mechanism (Grieger, 2003). By the development of IT -particularly the Internet-, many firms have got the opportunity to change and disseminate prices as often as desired (Pitt, Berthon, Watson, & Ewing, 2001). There are two trends in electronic business causing a paradigm shift from fixed pricing to dynamic pricing (Bichler, Lawrence, Kalagnanam, Lee, Katircioglu, Lin, King, & Lu, 2002):

1. The Internet has reduced transaction costs associated with dynamic pricing by
    - eliminating the need for people to be physically present in time and space, and
    - reducing the menu costs and costs of price changing.

Figure 2. Pricing Mechanisms (Pitt, Berthon, Watson, & Ewing, 2001: 50).

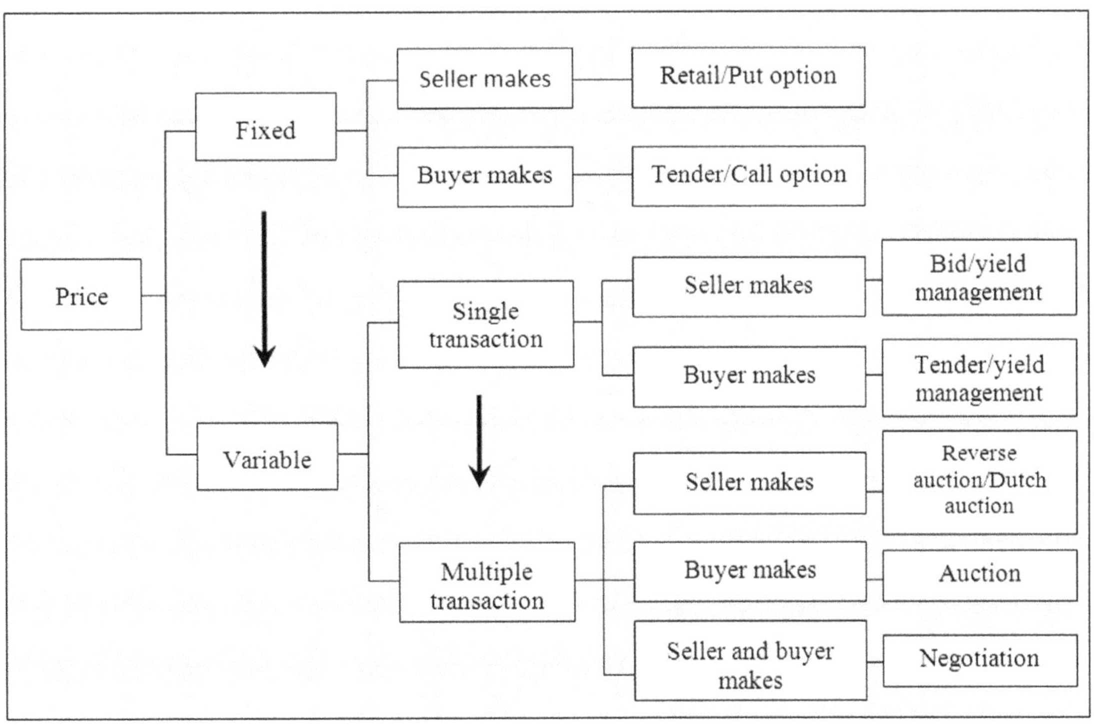

2. Price uncertainty and demand volatility has risen and the Internet has increased number of customers, competitors, and the amount and timeliness of information.

One another typology of pricing mechanisms on the Internet is discussed by Dolan and Moon (2000). According to Dolan and Moon (2000), the mechanisms are of three fundamentally different types as Type I (set price mechanism), Type II (negotiated price mechanism), and Type III (consisted of three cases as auction, reverse buying, and exchange).

Pricing power of buyers and sellers determines the pricing strategy as can be seen from Figure 3. It is known that, when buyers have more power than sellers, they force prices lower; when power swings in the other direction, prices move upward. When both parties (buyers and sellers) are weak, retailing (fixed prices), stock and commodity markets, and Dutch auctions can be seen as pricing system. When buyer and seller are both strong, both parties will try to find opportunities to increase their power and strengthen their hand in negotiations. Strong sellers will typically do better when they force buyers to make the price (with auctions) (Pitt, Berthon, Watson, & Ewing, 2001).

DYNAMIC PRICING

Advances in Internet technologies and e-commerce have dramatically increased the amount of information the sellers can gather about customers and have provided universal connectivity to customers making it easy to change the prices (Narahari, Raju, Ravikumar, & Shah, 2005). The Internet facilitates dynamic pricing, in which prices are adjusted instantly and frequently in line with what the market will bear (Etzel, Walker, & Stanton, 2001).

Figure 3. Pricing Strategy Circumplex (Pitt, Berthon, Watson, and Ewing, 2001: 51).

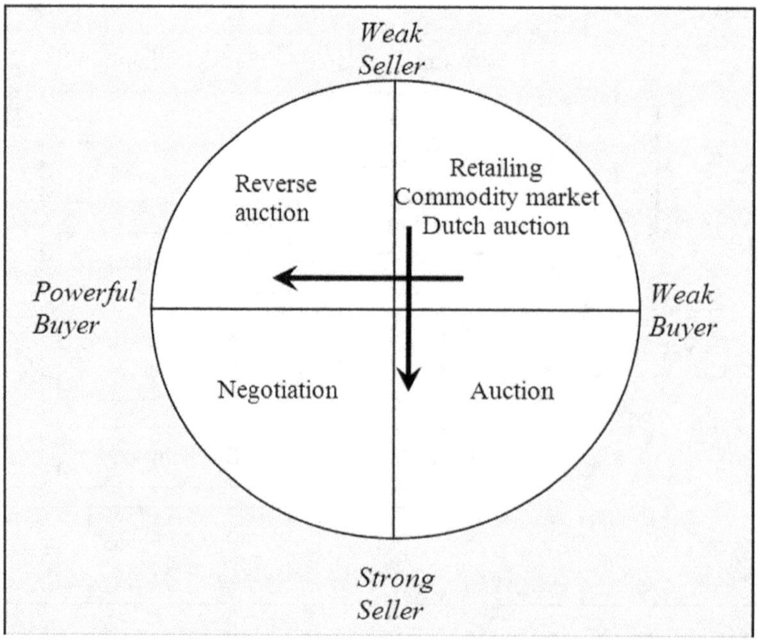

Dynamic pricing can be formally defined as the buying and selling of products and services in markets where prices change in response to imbalances in supply and demand. Dynamic pricing could also be defined as a pricing strategy in which prices change either over time, across consumers, or across product bundles (Jayaraman & Baker, 2003). Dynamic pricing can include a variety of auction models and name-your-own-price models, and most retailers have the ability to use newly available information to individually set prices based on a given customer's willingness to pay. In this sense, dynamic pricing is a variation of the traditional practice of price discrimination (Garbarino & Lee, 2003). The advantage of dynamic pricing is that it allows for the management of a firm to vary prices, thereby increasing the difference between price and cost in comparison to firms that use a static pricing model (Jayaraman & Baker, 2003). Thus, the main purpose of dynamic pricing is maximizing revenues. Matching capacity with demand to increase revenues with information systems (here, Internet) is named as yield management. Capacity-constrained service industries such as the airlines, hotels, car rentals, and cruise-lines practice yield management. Yield management success is effected by dynamic pricing (Gallego & van Ryzin, 1997; McGill & van Ryzin, 1999). Perhaps, airline industry is often cited as an illustrative case that implement dynamic pricing successfully (Bichler et al., 2002).

Whereas the airlines had to spend enormous sums to build proprietary networks to support reservations and related business processes, the Internet now places a comparable infrastructure at the disposal of almost any company (Geoffrion & Krishnan, 2003). By use of dynamic pricing, airline companies can sell their tickets both to attain the maximum possible revenue for each flight and to solve inventory control problem (You, 1999). The hotel industry is one another field of application for the revenue management that differentiate their prices according to the physical attributes concerning service provision (facilities and amenities), reputation (star classification and brand affiliation),or site-specific attributes (location, local attractions, climate, and beach) (Abrate, Fraquelli, & Viglia, 2012).

PRICE COMPARISON ENGINES (SHOPBOTS)

Price variation and the large number of vendors have made it difficult for a user to find the best price for an item or items (Garfinkel, Gopal, Tripathi, & Yin, 2006). Also, Internet shoppers who use multiple search engines may receive information that is not organized or may receive too much information, which can inhibit decisions (Vijayasarathy & Jones, 2001). Shopbots are Internet-based services that provide 'one-click' access to price and product information from numerous competing retailers. In so doing, they reduce buyer search costs for product and price information (Smith & Brynjolfsson, 2001). In 1995, Anderson Consulting developed BargainFinder, first shopbot service as an experimental intelligent agent for the World Wide Web. Designed initially as a shopbot for music CDs, BargainFinder's interface design looked rather primitive compared to the most shopbots have today (Wan & Peng, 2010).

As can be seen from Table 2, it is possible to categorize shopbot design into three generations (Smith, 2002):

- **Stand-alone shopbots (unbiased):** They only provide comparison information across retailer offerings, as opposed to providing information about the product itself. Thus, customers must come to stand-alone shopbot sites having already determined which product they are interested in purchasing.

Table 2. Shopbot Taxonomy

Category	Description	Examples
Stand alone (unbiased)	Price comparison separate from product information; offers sorted by price	PriceScan
Stand alone (biased)	Price comparison separate from information; offers sorted by retailer promotional spending	MySimon, Dealtime, BizRate
Contextual	Associate price comparison search with product information	CNET Shopper, EdgeGain, ClicktheButton, Books.com
Personalized	Personalize prices, product search, or display of results	Frictionless.com, ValueShopper, IBM Information Economies Project

Source: Smith, 2002, p. 448.

- **Stand-alone shopbots (biased):** Originally, stand-alone shopbots offered unbiased listings of products, typically sorted based on price. The revenue model of these shopbots was based on banner advertisements and retailer commissions (typically 3%-5%) for sales generated through the shopbot's site. However, in late 2000 and early 2001, most shopbots migrated to biased listings in which retailers could pay a fee for priority positioning in the shopbot's comparison tables.
- **Contextual shopbots:** Price comparison services initiated by retailers are a third example of contextual shopbots. For example, the now defunct retailer Books.corn had a service that allowed customers to compare Books.com's prices to the prices offered by other leading book retailers.
- **Personalized shopbots:** The third generation of shopbot services personalizes offers to the preferences of individual consumers. The ValueShopper service offered by Frictionless.com is one example of a personalized shopbot. ValueShopper compares differentiated products on the basis of a value score personalized to customers' preferences.

Despite shopbots may provide a cheaper price by giving a comparison list of retailers, a store's other potential competitive advantages such as customer service, delivery delay and payment methods may be totally ignored (Zahir, 2002). On the other hand, shopbots provide researchers with an opportunity to observe customer choice behavior as consumer evaluate the listed alternatives and click on a particular product offer (Smith & Brynjolfsson, 2001).

NEGOTIATIONS

In the last decade, electronic commerce supports alternative selling mechanisms, such as online negotiations, and auctions (Sierra, 2004; Caldentey & Vulcano, 2007). Negotiations are bargaining processes that not necessarily have to, but can be part of the coordination effort in markets (Ströbel, 2000a). On the other hand, negotiation can be stil supported because, having the opportunity to determine price through a one-on-one interaction with sellers offers buyers the ability to feel that they are paying the lowest possible price (Schindler, 2012). Since electronic markets provide low transaction costs and especially low search costs for negotiations that consumers enjoy perfect price information, this typically leads to price wars. In this situation, providers may make price comparisons more difficult, differentiate their products, or create markets that emphasise product information over price information (Ströbel, 2000b).

Traditional negotiation process requires time-consuming human engagement with complicated procedures; hence it is not practical for average online buyers and sellers (Lung, Phil, Wan-Cheng, Lian-Chen, & Cheng, 2007). While two or more parties bargain with one another to determine the price or other transaction terms in human negotiations, in an automated negotiation, software agents engage in broadly similar processes to achieve the same end (He, Jennings, & Leung, 2003).

Negotiations can be classified as integrative and distributive. Distributive negotiation (bidding) is the decision- making process of resolving a conflict involving two or more parties over a single

mutually exclusive goal (Guttman & Maes, 1999). In the distributive negotiations, the parties are competitive and they claim value thus characterised as 'win-lose' negotiations. On the other hand, integrative negotiation is based on the premise that solutions can be found, during and because of the process, which reconcile the parties' interests (Ströbel, 2000b).

ONLINE AUCTIONS

Perhaps the best-known of the emerging negotiation models is the auction, in which customers bid a price on a particular product or service (Hobson, 1999). Because prices fluctuate continually in dynamic pricing systems, supply and demand must be aggregated in the marketplace to effectively establish a price for a product or service. Auctions are the standard means of performing this aggregation (Wurman, 2001). An auction is defined as a selling mechanism where a plurality of goods or services are open to bids and then transferred to the winning bidder or bidders (Wenyan & Bolivar, 2008). A bid is a prospective buyer's indication or offer of a price he or she will pay to purchase an item at an auction (Menascé & Akula, 2004). The primary characteristic of auctions is that prices are determined dynamically by competitive bidding (Rainer & Cegielsk, 2011). Despite auctions have a long history that spans many different domains, recently, an auction is a kind of economic activity that has been brought into many people's everyday lives by the Internet, through sites such as eBay (Easley & Kleinberg, 2010). The Internet provides an infrastructure for executing auctions and bids much cheaper, with many more involved sellers and buyers. Individual consumers and corporations alike can participate in this rapidly growing and very convenient form of electronic commerce (Turban, 1997).

A vast number of auctions have been conducted over the Internet (Lee & Szymanski, 2006). The elimination of information asymmetry between sellers and buyers has been critical to the rapid growth in online auction markets (Shiu & Sun, 2014). OnSale (www.onsale.com) and eBay (www.ebay.com) are pioneers of the Internet auction websites which started operations in 1995 (Pinker, Seidmann, & Vakrat, 2003). Nowadays internet auctions have grown significantly and some of the most successful and active players in the sector include eBay, Yahoo, OnSale, Fairmarket, and Amazon (Aleem & Antwi-Boasiako, 2011). Most current Internet auctions, such as eBay and OnSale, use the English auction, since their primary goal is entertainment, delivered in the form of buyer speculation (Huhns & Vidal, 1999).

Online auction systems are classified base on different aspects such as: bid definition, specification of auction rules, and definition of transactions (Otair & Hattab, 2008). Auctions may be characterized by common features in both the online and offline world. Some of these features are (Wenyan & Bolivar, 2008):

- Public vs. Private: In public auctions, the bidders' identities are open and anyone is welcome to attend the auction. Private auctions hide the bidders' identities and whoever wins the auction remains anonymous.
- Open vs. Sealed: In open auctions, all bid amounts are exposed to the world, while in sealed auctions, on the other hand, bid amounts are concealed, additionally, all bidders ignore the number of bids or bid amounts during the duration of the auction.
- First-price vs. Second-price: This feature refers to the price to be paid at the end of auction. In first-price auctions, the winner pays exactly the highest bid. In second-price auctions, the second highest bid is paid.
- English vs. Dutch: This feature defines the price direction during the auction's lifespan. An auction may start with a low price and increase as new bids arrive until the end of the auction: English auction; or, start with a high price, which drops in some fashion until it reaches someone's bid or the auction ends at a minimum price: Dutch auction.
- Fixed End-time vs. Auto-extend End-time: The end time of auction could be fixed or auto-extended depending of the activity at the end of the auction. For example, an auction is ended until N minutes have passed without new bids.
- Hidden Reserve Price: A hidden reserve price is the minimum amount that a seller is willing to receive for an item. This price remains hidden until the reserve is reached.

E-markets can be characterized by the number of buyers and sellers and whether the participants are consumers or businesses (see Figure 4). Auctions are found when a single seller is selling to multiple buyers, or when multiple sellers are selling to single or multiple buyers (Pinker, Seidmann, & Vakrat, 2003). Bapna, Goes, and Gupta (2001) categorize online auctions into three main dimensions (see Table 3): business-to-consumer (B2C); consumer-to-consumer (C2C); and business-to-business (B2B).

In B2C and C2C market, English auction is the most popular auction type since it provides simple negotiation structure, and is particularly well suited for negotiation for short time period. On the other hand, B2B markets rely on a procurement process that requires Reverse Auction (Lee & Szymanski, 2006). In reverse auction, sellers bid instead of buyers, and prices are bid down instead of up as the auction continues (Jap, 2003). In this sense, reverse auctions are similar to the English auction, except with descending bids (Mithas & Jones, 2007).

Because Internet auction is automated, it is much less costly to the seller and brings access to far more potential bidders than a traditional auction. Nowadays, there are some new uses for price setting in the Internet auctions such as offering promotional discounts or end-of-season markdowns to dispose of excess inventory (Schindler, 2012).

Figure 4. Classification of Online Auction Type (Pinker, Seidmann, & Vakrat, 2003, p. 1462)

		BUYERS: ONE	BUYERS: MANY
SELLERS	ONE	Bilateral negotiations EDI/XML	Web-based sales auctions C2C and B2C
	MANY	Web-based (Reverse) procurement auctions C2B and B2B	Web-based exchanges

Table 3. Dimensions of Online Auctions.

Dimension	Characteristics
Business-to-Consumer (B2C)	• Early trend setters • Clear excess, aging, or perishable inventory • Goods subject to technological obsolescence • Onsale.com • Consumer-driven demand-price equilibrium • Opportunity for firms to dynamically reconfigure their supply curves to fit bids received from the market • Priceline.com • Currently omnipresent on the Web
Consumer-to-Consumer (C2C)	• Create vastly efficient secondary markets • 100,000 flea markets in one Web site • Community centric architecture • Primarily honor-based transactions • Cult-like following; many people stay on the Web site long after auctions close • Increasing sophistication • Third-party escrow services and credit card processing • eBay.com
Business-to-Business (B2B)	• Expected to grow rapidly • Significant impact on the supply chain • Facilitate efficient procurement • Require complex multi-criteria auctions, such as price and quality • Globally competitive liquidation of used equipment or unneeded parts • Used parts dealers known not to give market value • Can be done anonymously, if desired • Fastparts.com, Labx.com

Source: Bapna, Goes, & Gupta, 2001, p. 45

CONCLUSION

In this chapter, some concepts and mechanisms related with pricing on the Internet have been described and examined. For managers, pricing is the fastest and effective way to increase profits. Importance and dynamic structure of pricing has newly recognized by academics and managers with the growth of the Internet. Besides marketing communication and distribution channel benefits, the Internet has emerged as a huge potential for pricing strategy. While price elasticity is often expensive and time-consuming in the off-line world, the internet provides a transparent environment with dynamic and customer-sensitive pricing structure (Marn, 2000). Online pricing also affects the power of seller and buyer. Nowadays, prices are largely set through an interaction between buyers and sellers, thus prices are no longer fixed. Specifically, online auctions and negotiations are two broad categories that prices are determined interatively.

Web page design features, ease of use or usefulness differences may be some other factors that can be effective than the prices of online auction marketplaces. Buyers can share more than price information by online programs or facilities such as online chat, feedback forum, notes, and messages (Su & Hu, 2000). Another important issue is the impact of advances in the area of electronic commerce with computer technologies (specifically database, security, and networking) on pricing mechanism. In this sense, airline industry is one successful case using the online pricing mechanism for both controlling the capacity and optimum revenue.

All in all, further research is still needed to know much about online pricing, its mechanism, and price perception of consumers within this price-setting process. In this way, discussion on the effective management of online pricing and its reflections on consumers may open many opportunities for both academicians and managers.

Case: How eBay's Auction Mechanism Works?

Founded in 1995 by Pierre Omidyar, AuctionWeb and later renamed eBay, is one of the largest consumer-oriented auction site, where individual sellers register their items for sale, and individual consumers bid on the item. Initially, most of the items auctioned on eBay were collectibles such as antiques, coins, stamps, and memorabilia. eBay's success has attracted many online person-to-person auction competitors, including generalists such as Yahoo! Auctions, Amazon.com Auctions, and a host of smaller niche players. Most of these competitors follow a negotiation and business model similar to eBay's, with some minor deviations.

All eBay auctions use an ascending-bid (English) format, with the twist that there is a fixed end time and date set by the seller instead of a going- going-gone ending rule. A seller can choose a number of parameters to specify how the auction will run. The company simply provides a meeting place for buyers and sellers, thereby avoiding inventory risk and carrying costs. Online business model of eBay is significantly different from electronic retailers. Because individual sellers, rather than eBay, sell the items listed. The eBay auction process works as follows: A seller decides to list an item for sale on eBay. After registration, the seller pays a listing fee ranging from $0.25 to $2.00 per item and can choose to pay extra for pictures, bolded or italicized listings, or placement in the "Featured Auctions" section on eBay's front page. The seller then defines the auction type (usually a reserve price auction, but Dutch auction is also available); sets the duration of the auction (three, five, or seven days); and sets a reserve price and minimum bid. As potential customers make their bids, these bids are shown on the item's listing. When eBuy uses English auction mechanism, each bid must be higher than the previous one, and the person who makes the last bid before the bidding closes buys the item and pays the amount that he or she bid. The reserve price is kept confidential and, in the event that it is not met, the seller is under no obligation to sell the item.

Recently, it is noted that most of eBay's growth came from mobile retailing and its PayPal online payments division. As consumers embrace shopping on their smartphones, "mobile continues to be a game-changer," CEO of eBay, Mr. Donahoe said. "A woman's handbag is purchased on eBay mobile every 30 seconds," he said. "Mobile is revolutionizing how people shop and pay."

REFERENCES

Abrate, G., Fraquelli, G., & Viglia, G. (2012). Dynamic pricing strategies: Evidence from European hotels. *International Journal of Hospitality Management*, *31*(1), 160–168. doi:10.1016/j.ijhm.2011.06.003

Aleem, A., & Antwi-Boasiako, A. (2011). Internet auction fraud: The evolving nature of online auctions criminality and the mitigating framework to address the threat. *International Journal of Law, Crime and Justice*, *39*(3), 140–160. doi:10.1016/j.ijlcj.2011.05.003

Avlonitis, G. J., & Indounas, K. A. (2006). Pricing practices of service organizations. *Journal of Services Marketing*, *20*(5), 346–356. doi:10.1108/08876040610679954

Bakos, Y. (1998). The emerging role of electronic marketplaces on the internet. *Communications of the ACM*, *41*(8), 35–42. doi:10.1145/280324.280330

Bapna, R., Goes, P., & Gupta, A. (2001). Insights and analyses of online auctions. *Communications of the ACM*, *44*(11), 42–50. doi:10.1145/384150.384160

Bichler, M., Kalagnanam, J., Katircioglu, K., King, A. J., Lawrence, R. D., Lee, H. S., & Lu, Y. etal. (2002). Applications of flexible pricing in business-to-business electronic commerce. *IBM Systems Journal*, *41*(2), 287–302. doi:10.1147/sj.412.0287

Breidert, C. (2005). *Estimation of willingness-to-pay, Theory, measurement, and application* [Doctoral thesis]. Vienna University of Economics and Business. Retrieved from http://epub.wu.ac.at/1934/

Brint, A. T. (2003). Investigating buyer and seller strategies in online auctions. *The Journal of the Operational Research Society*, *54*(11), 1177–1188. doi:10.1057/palgrave.jors.2601629

Caldentey, R., & Vulcano, G. (2007). Online auction and list price revenue management. *Management Science*, *53*(5), 795–813. doi:10.1287/mnsc.1060.0646

Campbell, M. C. (1999). "Why did you do that?" The important role of inferred motive in perceptions of price fairness. *Journal of Product and Brand Management*, *8*(2), 145–152. doi:10.1108/10610429910266995

Carricano, M., Trinquecoste, J.-F., & Mondejar, J.-A. (2010). The rise of the pricing function: Origins and perspectives. *Journal of Product and Brand Management*, *19*(7), 468–476. doi:10.1108/10610421011086883

Dolan, R. J., & Moon, Y. (2000). Pricing and market making on the internet. *Journal of Interactive Marketing*, *14*(2), 56–69. doi:10.1002/(SICI)1520-6653(200021)14:2<56::AID-DIR5>3.0.CO;2-4

Easley, D., & Kleinberg, J. (2010). *From the book networks, crowds, and markets: reasoning about a highly connected world.* Cambridge University Press. doi:10.1017/CBO9780511761942

Erickson, G. M., & Johansson, J. K. (1985). The role of price in multi-attribute product evaluations. *The Journal of Consumer Research*, *12*(2), 195–199. doi:10.1086/208508

Etzel, M. J., Walker, B. J., & Stanton, W. J. (2001). *Marketing* (12th ed.). New York: McGraw Hill/Irwin.

Gallego, G., & Van Ryzin, G. (1997). A Multi-product dynamic pricing problem and its applications to network yield management. *Operations Research*, *45*(1), 24–41. doi:10.1287/opre.45.1.24

Garbarino, E., & Lee, O. F. (2003). Dynamic pricing in internet retail: Effects on consumer trust. *Psychology and Marketing*, *20*(6), 495–513. doi:10.1002/mar.10084

Garfinkel, R., Gopal, R., Tripathi, A., & Yin, F. (2006). Design of a shopbot and recommender system for bundle purchases. *Decision Support Systems*, *42*(3), 1974–1986. doi:10.1016/j.dss.2006.05.005

Geoffrion, A. M., & Krishnan, R. (2003). E-Business and management science: Mutual impacts (Part 1 of 2). *Management Science*, *49*(10), 1275–1286. doi:10.1287/mnsc.49.10.1275.17311

Gijsbrechts, E. (1993). Prices and pricing research in consumer marketing: Some recent developments. *International Journal of Research in Marketing*, *10*(2), 115–151. doi:10.1016/0167-8116(93)90001-F

Grieger, M. (2003). Electronic marketplaces: A literature review and a call for supply chain management research. *European Journal of Operational Research*, *144*(2), 280–294. doi:10.1016/S0377-2217(02)00394-6

Guttman, R. H., & Maes, P. (1999). Agent-mediated integrative negotiation for retail electronic commerce. *Agent Mediated Electronic Commerce. Lecture Notes in Computer Science*, *1571*, 70–90. doi:10.1007/3-540-48835-9_5

He, M., Jennings, N. R., & Leung, H.-F. (2003). On agent-mediated electronic commerce. *IEEE Transactions on Knowledge and Data Engineering*, *15*(4), 985–1003. doi:10.1109/TKDE.2003.1209014

Herrmann, A., & Wricke, M. (1998). Evaluating multidimensional prices. *Journal of Product and Brand Management*, *7*(2), 161–169. doi:10.1108/10610429810216973

Hobson, C. A. (1999). E-negotiations: Creating a framework for online commercial negotiations. *Negotiation Journal*, *15*(3), 201–218. doi:10.1111/j.1571-9979.1999.tb00192.x

Huhns, M. N., & Vidal, J. M. (1999). Online auctions. *IEEE Internet Computing*, *3*(3), 103–105. doi:10.1109/4236.769429

Jap, S. D. (2003). An exploratory study of the introduction of online reverse auctions. *Journal of Marketing*, *67*(3), 96–107. doi:10.1509/jmkg.67.3.96.18651

Jap, S. D., & Naik, P. A. (2004). Introduction to the special issue on online pricing. *Journal of Interactive Marketing*, *18*(4), 4–6. doi:10.1002/dir.20026

Jayaraman, V., & Baker, T. (2003). The internet as an enabler for dynamic pricing of goods. *IEEE Transactions on Engineering Management*, *50*(4), 470–477. doi:10.1109/TEM.2003.820134

Kim, H. M., & Kachersky, L. (2006). Dimensions of price salience: A conceptual framework for perceptions of multi-dimensional prices. *Journal of Product and Brand Management*, *15*(2), 139–147. doi:10.1108/10610420610658974

Kotler, P., & Armstrong, G. (2014). Principles of marketing (15th global ed.). Essex: Pearson Education Limited.

Kung, M., Monroe, K. B., & Cox, J. L. (2002). Pricing on the internet. *Journal of Product and Brand Management*, *11*(5), 274–287. doi:10.1108/10610420210442201

Lee, J.-S., & Szymanski, B. K. (2006). Auctions as a dynamic pricing mechanism for e-services. In C. Hsu (Ed.), *Service Enterprise Integration* (pp. 131–156). New York: Kluwer.

Levy, M., & Weitz, B. A. (2004). *Retailing management* (5th ed.). New York: McGraw-Hill/Irwin.

Li, B., & Tang, F.-F. (2011). Online pricing dynamics in internet retailing: The case of the DVD market. *Electronic Commerce Research and Applications*, *10*(2), 227–236. doi:10.1016/j.elerap.2010.06.004

Lucking-Reiley, D., Bryan, D., Prasad, N., & Reeves, D. (2007). Pennies from eBay: The Determinants of price in online auctions. *The Journal of Industrial Economics*, *55*(2), 223–233. doi:10.1111/j.1467-6451.2007.00309.x

Lung, N., Mak, P., Wan-Cheng, N., Lian-Chen, L., & Cheng, W. (2007). A Semi-automated negotiation process to improve the usability for online marketplaces. *Proceeding of 7th IEEE International Conference on Computer and Information Technology (CIT 2007)* (pp. 253–258). Fukushima, Japan.

Marn, M. V., & Rosiello, R. L. (1992). Managing price, gaining profits. *Harvard Business Review*, *70*(5), 84–93. PMID:10121318

McGill, J. I., & van Ryzin, G. J. (1999). Revenue management: Research overview and prospects. *Transportation Science*, *33*(2), 233–256. doi:10.1287/trsc.33.2.233

Menascé, D. A., & Akula, V. (2004). Improving the performance of online auction sites through closing time rescheduling. *Proceedings of the First International Conference on the Quantitative Evaluation of Systems (QEST'04)*, Twente, Netherlands. doi:10.1109/QEST.2004.1348033

Mithas, S., & Jones, J. L. (2007). Do auction parameters affect buyer surplus in e-auctions for procurement? *Production and Operations Management POMS*, *16*(4), 455–470. doi:10.1111/j.1937-5956.2007.tb00272.x

Miyazaki, A. D. (2003). Guest editorial: The psychology of pricing on the internet. *Psychology and Marketing*, *20*(6), 471–476. doi:10.1002/mar.10082

Monroe, K. B. (1973). Buyers' subjective perceptions of price. *JMR, Journal of Marketing Research*, *10*(1), 70–80. doi:10.2307/3149411

Monroe, K. B. (1990). *Pricing: Making profitable decisions* (2nd ed.). New York: McGraw-Hill.

Narahari, Y., Raju, C. V. L., Ravikumar, K., & Shah, S. (2005). Dynamic pricing models for electronic business. *Sadhana*, *30*(2-3), 231–256. doi:10.1007/BF02706246

Narver, J. C., & Savitt, R. (1971). *The marketing economy: An analytical approach*. New York: Holt, Rinehart and Winston.

Ofir, C., & Winer, R. S. (2002). Pricing: economic and behavioral models. In B. A. Weitz & R. Wensley (Eds.), *Handbook of Marketing* (pp. 267–281). London: Sage Publications. doi:10.4135/9781848608283.n12

Otair, M., & Hattab, E. (2008). An implementation of a new type of online auction. *International Journal of E-Business Research*, *4*(2), 88–102. doi:10.4018/jebr.2008040106

Oxenfeldt, A. R. (1973). A Decision-making structure for price decisions. *Journal of Marketing*, *37*(1), 48–53. doi:10.2307/1250774

Parsa, H. G., & Njite, D. (2008). Psychology of pricing: A review and suggestions. In H. Oh & A. Pizam (Eds.), *Handbook of Hospitality Marketing Management* (pp. 353–380). Oxford, UK: Butterworth-Heinemann. doi:10.1016/B978-0-08-045080-3.50016-0

Pinker, E.J., Seidmann, A., & Vakrat, Y. (2003). Managing online auctions: Current business and research issues. *Management Science, 49*(11), 1457-1484.

Pitt, L. F., Berthon, P., Watson, R. T., & Ewing, M. (2001). Pricing strategy and the net. *Business Horizons*, *44*(2), 45–54. doi:10.1016/S0007-6813(01)80022-7

Rainer, R. K., & Cegielsk, C. G. (2011). *Introduction to information systems: Enabling and transforming business* (3rd ed.). Hoboken, NJ: John Wiley & Sons.

Rao, V.R. (1984). Pricing research in marketing: the state of the art. *The Journal of Business, 57*(1), *Part 2: Pricing Strategy*, S39-S60.

Rao, V. R., & Kartono, B. (2009). Pricing objectives and strategies: a cross-country survey. In V. R. Rao (Ed.), *Handbook of Pricing Research in Marketing* (pp. 9–36). Massachusetts: Edward Elgar Publishing Limited. doi:10.4337/9781848447448.00009

Schindler, R. M. (2012). *Pricing strategies: A marketing approach*. Thousand Oaks, CA: Sage Publications.

Shipley, D., & Jobber, D. (2001). Integrative pricing via the pricing wheel. *Industrial Marketing Management, 30*(3), 301–314. doi:10.1016/S0019-8501(99)00098-X

Shiu, J.-L., & Sun, C.-H. D. (2014). The determinants of price in online auctions: More evidence from unbalanced panel data. *Journal of Applied Statistics, 41*(2), 382–392. doi:10.1080/02664763.2013.839639

Sierra, C. (2004). Agent-mediated electronic commerce. *Autonomous Agents and Multi-Agent Systems, 9*(3), 285–301. doi:10.1023/B:AGNT.0000038029.82331.c0

Skouras, T., Avlonitis, G. J., & Indounas, K. A. (2005). Economics and marketing on pricing: How and why do they differ? *Journal of Product and Brand Management, 14*(6), 362–374. doi:10.1108/10610420510624512

Smith, M. D. (2002). The impact of shopbots on electronic markets. *Journal of the Academy of Marketing Science, 30*(4), 446–454. doi:10.1177/009207002236916

Smith, M. D., Bailey, J., & Brynjolfsson, E. (1999). Understanding digital markets: Review and assessment. In E. Brynjolfsson & B. Kahin (Eds.), *Understanding the digital economy* (pp. 99–136). Cambridge, MA: MIT Press.

Smith, M. D., & Brynjolfsson, E. (2001). Consumer decision-making at an internet shopbot: Brand stil matters. *The Journal of Industrial Economics, 49*(4), 541–558. doi:10.1111/1467-6451.00162

Stewart, J. B. (2012, July 27). Behind eBay's comeback. *New York Times*. Retrieved from http://www.nytimes.com/2012/07/28/business/ebays-turnaround-defies-convention-for-internet-companies.html?pagewanted=all&_r=0

Ströbel, M. (2000a). On auctions as the negotiation paradigm of electronic markets: Success factors, limitations and research directions. *Journal of Electronic Markets, 10*(1), 39–44. doi:10.1080/10196780050033962

Ströbel, M. (2000b). Effects of electronic markets on negotiation processes. *Proceedings of 8th European Conference on Information Systems, Trends in Information and Communication Systems for the 21st Century, ECIS 2000*, Vienna, Austria.

Su, M., & Hu, Q. (2000). An exploratory study of internet auction business models. *Proceedings of IRMA Conference,* Anchorage, Alaska. (pp. 561-565).

Tang, F.-F., & Gan, L. (2004). Pricing convergence between dot.coms and hybrids: Empirical evidence from the online toy market. *Journal of Targeting. Measurement and Analysis for Marketing, 12*(4), 340–352. doi:10.1057/palgrave.jt.5740121

Turban, E. (1997). Auctions and bidding on the internet: An assessment. *Focus Theme, 7*(4), 7–11.

Vijayasarathy, L. R., & Jones, J. M. (2001). Do internet shopping aids make a difference? An empirical investigation. *Electronic Markets*, *11*(1), 75–83. doi:10.1080/10196780151105483

Wan, Y., & Peng, Gang (2010). What's next for shopbots? *IEEE Computer Society*, 43(5), 20-26.

Wenyan, H., & Bolivar, A. (2008). Online auctions efficiency: A survey of eBay auctions. *WWW*, *2008*, 925–933.

Wurman, P. R. (2001). Dynamic pricing in the virtual marketplace. *IEEE Internet Computing*, *5*(2), 36–42. doi:10.1109/4236.914646

You, P.-S. (1999). Dynamic pricing in airline seat management for flights with multiple flight legs. *Transportation Science*, *33*(2), 192–206. doi:10.1287/trsc.33.2.192

Zahir, S. (2002). Designing a knowledge-based interface for intelligent shopping agents. *Journal of Computer Information Systems*, *43*(1), 31–41.

Zeithaml, V. A. (1988). Consumer perceptions of price, quality, and value: A means-end model and synthesis of evidence. *Journal of Marketing*, *52*(3), 2–22. doi:10.2307/1251446

ADDITIONAL READING

Andrews, W. (1999). The new laws of dynamic pricing. *Internet World*, *5*(35), 27–34.

Bapna, R., Goes, P., & Gupta, A. (2000). A theoretical and empirical investigation of multi-item on-line auctions. *Information Technology Management*, *1*(1-2), 1–23. doi:10.1023/A:1019100419867

Becherer, R. C., Halstead, D., & Taylor, A. J. (2008). Auction characteristics and outcomes: An empirical examination of eBay. *Journal of Internet Commerce*, *7*(3), 403–424. doi:10.1080/15332860802250542

Chevalier, J., & Goolsbee, A. (2003). Measuring prices and price competition online: Amazon.com and BarnesandNoble.com. *Quantitative Marketing and Economics*, *1*(2), 203–222. doi:10.1023/A:1024634613982

Etzion, H., & Moore, S. (2013). Managing online sales with posted price and open-bid auctions. *Decision Support Systems*, *54*(3), 1327–1339. doi:10.1016/j.dss.2012.12.005

Gilkeson, J. H., & Reynolds, K. (2003). Determinants of Internet Auction Success and Closing Price: An Exploratory Study. *Psychology and Marketing*, *20*(6), 537–566. doi:10.1002/mar.10086

Hamer, L. O. (2011). Reducing online buyers' perceptions of risk: A study of online auctions. *Services Marketing Quarterly*, *32*(2), 83–95. doi:10.1080/15332969.2011.557594

Harmon, R. R., Demirkan, H., Hefley, B., & Auseklis, N. (2009). Pricing Strategies for Information Technology Services: A Value-Based Approach. *Proceedings of the 42nd Hawaii International Conference on System Sciences (HICSS/IEEE),* Waikoloa, Big Island, HI, USA.

Haws, K. L., & Bearden, W. O. (2006). Dynamic pricing and consumer fairness perceptions. *The Journal of Consumer Research*, *33*(3), 304–311. doi:10.1086/508435

Kasavana, M. L., & Singh, A. J. (2001). Online auctions. *Journal of Hospitality & Leisure Marketing*, *9*(3-4), 127–140. doi:10.1300/J150v09n03_09

Kauffman, R. J., & Wang, B. (2001). New buyers' arrival under dynamic pricing market microstructure: The case of group-buying discounts on the internet. *Proceedings of the 34th Hawaii Conference on Systems Science*, Maui, HI. doi:10.1109/HICSS.2001.927065

Kim, J.-Y., Natter, M., & Spann, M. (2009). Pay-what-you-want: A new participative pricing mechanism. *Journal of Marketing*, *73*(1), 44–58. doi:10.1509/jmkg.73.1.44

Lucking-Reiley, D. (2000). Auctions on the internet: What's being auctioned, and how? *The Journal of Industrial Economics*, *48*(3), 227–252. doi:10.1111/1467-6451.00122

Parsons, S., Rodriguez-Aguilar, J. A., & Klein, M. (2011). Auctions and bidding: A guide for computer scientists. *ACM Computing Surveys*, *43*(2), 1–59. doi:10.1145/1883612.1883617

Vakrat, Y., & Seidmann, A. (2000). Implications of the bidders' arrival process on the design of online auctions, In R.H. Sprague Jr. (Ed.), *Proceedings of the 33rd Hawaii International Conference on System Sciences*. Maui, HI: IEEE Computer Society Press. doi:10.1109/HICSS.2000.926822

Wolk, A., & Spann, M. (2008). The effects of reference prices on bidding behavior in interactive pricing mechanisms. *Journal of Interactive Marketing*, *22*(4), 2–18. doi:10.1002/dir.20118

Zettelmeyer, F. (2000). Expanding to the internet: Pricing and communications strategies when firms compete on multiple channels. *JMR, Journal of Marketing Research*, *37*(3), 292–308. doi:10.1509/jmkr.37.3.292.18777

Zhongcheng, L., & Hongyu, L. (2013). Research on pricing strategy of online reverse auction based on complete ınformation. *International Business and Management*, *6*(2), 71–76.

KEY TERMS AND DEFINITIONS

An Online Auction: A service method of selling products or services via the Internet by participation of multiple bidder.

Dynamic Pricing: Determining the prices based on changing circumstances such as demand level or type of customer.

Fixed Pricing (or Menu Pricing): Same price that sellers set for everyone.

Negotiation: A price determination mechanism by an interaction between a buyer and a seller.

Reverse Auctions: Allow buyers to put up their price and have sellers bid for the prices.

Shopbot (Shopping Robot): Automated tools that allow customers to search for and compare prices and product characteristics from different online retailers effectively.

Chapter 14
Risk Management, Trust and Repeat Online Shopping Intentions:
A South African Perspective

Mercy Mpinganjira
University of Johannesburg, South Africa

ABSTRACT

E-commerce is a growing phenomenon in Africa. One area of e-commerce that is growing at a very fast rate is online retailing. This is despite concerns that individuals often have in relation to online shopping being associated with more risk than traditional retailing. This chapter looks at practices of online retailers that help in mitigating online shopping risk and the influence of these on customers' levels of trust as well as on their intentions to re-purchase from specific online stores. The findings show that provision of adequate online product information and online store security has positive influence on customers' level of trust in an online store. The findings also show that trust in an online store has significant influence on customers' intentions to repurchase from a store. The findings have wide implications on successful management of online store outlets and these have been highlighted in the chapter.

INTRODUCTION

The Internet has revolutionalised the business and communications worlds like no other innovations before it. It is the force behind the current information age which is characterised by ability of individuals and business to freely share information and have ready access to knowledge. According to Sernau (2014) the information age signalled a shift from traditional industry that was brought by the industrial revolution, to an economy based on information manipulation. Hanson and Kalyanam (2012) pointed out that the internet provides great potential for productivity increases in business. It is for this reason that countries in Africa just as many others in the around the world are investing in efforts aimed at bringing their nations to the forefront of the information era.

DOI: 10.4018/978-1-4666-8459-1.ch014

Among other impacts, the internet has made it possible for companies to conduct their commercial transactions electronically, a concept that is widely referred to as e-commerce. E-commerce encompasses electronic buying and selling of products as well as facilitation of the same (Zaker & Ansari, 2013). According to E-marketer (2014) global business-to-consumer e-commerce sales were estimated at US$1.25 trillion. While over half (59.4 percent) of e-commerce sales in 2013 were attributable to countries in Western Europe and North America with the Middle East and Africa region contributing only 2.16 percent, e-commerce sales are noted to be growing at a very fast pace in all the regions of the world. Forecast show that total sales in the Middle East and Africa region are expected to grow from US$27 billion in 2013 to US$51.4 billion in 2017, a jump of around 90 percent over a five year period (E-marketer (2014). On the African continent, South Africa is considered the biggest e-commerce market (BizCommunty, 2013). Compounding the increase in online sales globally is the influence of the internet on offline sales. Results of a global survey by the marketing and technology agency DigitasLBi (2014) showed that as many as 88 percent of consumers with internet access use it to ROPO which stands for research online, purchase offline. Clearly, there are benefits associated with having an online retail presence.

While there has been a continuous rise in retail online sales worldwide and in many individual countries, the fact that many online retailers fail to meet their sales and profit goals is widely acknowledged in literature (Shaker, 2013; Hausman & Siekpe, 2009). This problem is of interest to researchers and online retailers as they aim to understand factors that may explain customers' reluctance to shop at some online stores and not others. This chapter aims at contributing to this understanding by looking at issues of risk and trust in online shopping.

Researchers including D'Alessandro, Girardi, and Tiangsoongnern, (2012) as well as Jøsang and Presti (2004) identify risk and trust as two important facets of decision making through which individuals view things and choose to act. In the context of online shopping, Ko et al. (2004) defined risk as "the potential for loss in pursuing a desired outcome while engaged in online shopping" p. 20. Trust in an online store can on other hand be defined as "an attitude of confident expectation in an online situation of risk that one's vulnerabilities will not be exploited" (Corritore, Kracher, & Wiedenbeck, 2003, p. 740). A review of literature shows that studies that look at risk and trust issues at individual customer and online business level often focus on the influence of these on adoption of online shopping. This chapter takes a different perspective in that the focus is on online shoppers only. The objectives of the chapter are to (i) examine global, regional and country trends in online sales (ii) understand some environmental conditions that have an influence on a country's level of online retail business (iii) examine online customers' levels of perceived risk associated with online shopping (iv) identify risk management practices that influence trust in online stores and (v) examine the influence of trust in online store on repeat shopping intentions.

The chapter has been organised such that the next section provides an analysis of international and local trends in online sales. This is followed by the section looking at the state of facilitating environmental conditions to online shopping in South Africa and beyond. Thereafter the chapter provides a review of literature on trust and risk in relation to online shopping followed by presentation of details relating to an investigation done in order to empirically examine levels of perceived online shopping risk as well as relationships between online stores risk mitigating practices, trust in online stores and customers' online store repeat purchase intentions. The chapter ends by providing directions for future research before concluding.

TRENDS IN ONLINE SALES

Global Trends

The retail industry is one of the biggest sectors in many economies. According to the global report by Luce (2013) the industry accounts for over US$15 trillion in revenue. This shows that the industry has more than doubled since 2003 when its revenues were estimated at US$7 trillion (IMAP, 2010). Table 1 provides statistics on the industry's past and forecasted growth rates covering the period from 2012 to 2016. The statistics show that, at global level the industry has been and is expected to continue experiencing positive growth. Also provided in table 1 are statistics on past and forecasted online retail sales covering the period 2012 to 2017. These statistics clearly show that one of the leading factors to strong growth in global retail sales has been high growth rates experienced in online retailing.

Regional and Country Trends

While online retaining is a global phenomenon, statistics at regional and country level show the dominance of a few in the trade. Statistics in table 1 make it evident that global sales are heavily dominated by North America, Western Europe and the Asia- Pacific region. Together these regions contributed 90.6 percent of total online sales in 2012 and are expected to contribute 91.6 percent of total online sales in 2017. The statistics further show that by the end of 2014, the Asia-Pacific region will overtake North America and be the number 1 contributor to global online sales. Online retail sales for the Asia Pacific region for 2014 are estimated at US$525.2 billion which is 34.9 percent of global sales compared to US$482.6 for North America which is 32.1 percent of global sales (E-Marketer, 2014). Rapid growth in online sales experienced by the Asia Pacific region is mainly attributable to growth in China which was at over 70 percent in 2012 and 2013.

Table 1. Global retail sales

	2012	2013	2014*	2015*	2016*	2017*
Global Retail Sales growth	2.9	3.4	4.1	4.1	4.2	-
Global Online retail sales growth	22.3	18.3	20.2	17.7	15.9	14.8
Online retail sales US$ (Trillion)	1.058	1.251	1.505	1.771	2.053	2.357
Percentage contribution						
Asia Pacific	28.5	30.7	34.9	38.5	41.7	44.7
North America	35.9	34.4	32.1	30.4	29.1	28.0
Western Europe	26.2	24.9	23.1	21.6	20.2	18.9
Central and Eastern Europe	3.9	4.0	3.9	3.6	3.4	3.1
Latin America	3.6	3.8	3.8	3.7	3.4	3.2
Middle East and Africa	1.9	2.2	2.2	2.2	2.2	2.2

* Based on forecasts
Sources: Statista (2014) and E-Marketer (2014)

Statistics in table 1 show that the Middle East and Africa region makes the lowest contribution to global online sales. While this is so, the region is experiencing one of the fastest growth rates of all regions in the world. Total online retail sales in the region were estimated at US$20.6 billion in 2012 and the figure is expected to more than double and reach 51.4 billion in 2017 (E-Marketer, 2014). Except for the Asia Pacific region, no other region is expected to more than double its 2012 online retails sales by 2017.

Country level statistics also show the dominance of some countries in regional online retail sales figures. The USA for example is the main driver of online retail sales in the North America. Sales in the whole of Europe are dominated by three countries namely Germany, the UK and France. The dominant players in the Asia Pacific region are China and Japan. Other prominent players in the market include India, South Korea and Australia. Brazil dominates online retail sales in Latin America. Other important players in the region are Mexico, Chile and Argentina. The United Arab Emirates and South Africa are considered the dominant players in the Middle East and Africa region. Cushman and Wakefield (2013) rankings of countries of the world based on 2012 online sales had of all countries in the Middle Eastern and Africa region, only South Africa and United Arab Emirates feature in the top 50. South Africa was at number 41 while the United Arab Emirates was ranked at number 45. The top five countries on the list included in order of size, the USA, China, United Kingdom, Japan, and Germany.

While South Africa is the biggest online retail market in Africa based on sales, other countries are known to have very high potential of catching up. A report by Ystats (2013) on Africa business-to-consumer e-commerce shows that other high potential markets on the African continent include Egypt, Morocco, Nigeria and Kenya. The report forecasts annual growth rates of around 40 percent for the African continent over the next 10 years.

FACILITATING CONDITIONS TO ONLINE RETAILING: A FOCUS ON INFRASTURAL AND LEGAL ISSUES IN AFRICA

The success of e-commerce in any country depends on the presence of facilitating conditions such as technological infrastructure to support e-commerce as well as legal and regulatory frameworks to provide much needed certainty and protection to online businesses and customers.

Technological Infrastructure

Low levels of availability and access to internet in general and broadband internet in particular is regarded as one of the factors that work against e-commerce development in many African countries. Governments on the continent have a critical responsibility to make sure that investments are made in efforts aimed at improving provision of modern ICT infrastructure capable of handling varied services and applications. Governments need to also take a keen interest in promoting access by all to available infrastructure.

Statistics in table 2 show that while Africa has made significant progress in terms of growing access to ICT infrastructure including internet in general, mobile broadband in particular the continents performance is below both the world average and the average for developing countries.

One area where significant progress has been made worldwide is in the area of mobile cellular penetration. Statistics in table 2 show that by the end of 2014 the total number of mobile subscriptions worldwide will be at almost 96 percent. While at 69.3 percent Africa lags behind the world average, the

Table 2. ICT Infrastructure

	2005	2010	2014*
Mobile-cellular subscription (%)			
Africa	**12.4**	**45.4**	**69.3**
South Africa	70.4	97.90	130^{-2}
World	**33.9**	**76.6**	**95.5**
Developing countries	22.9	113.3	90.2
Developed Countries	82.1	68.5	120.8
Individuals using the internet (%)			
Africa	**2.4**	**9.8**	**19.0**
South Africa	7.5	24.0	41.0^{-2}
World	**15.8**	**29.4**	**40.4**
Developing countries	50.9	62.9	32.4
Developed Countries	15.8	29.4	78.3
Active mobile-broadband subscriptions (%)			
Africa	-	**1.8**	**19.0**
South Africa	-		26.0^{-2}
World	-	**11.5**	**32.0**
Developing countries	-	4.5	21.1
Developed Countries		44.7	83.7

Note: * = 2014 forecasted figures
$^{-2}$= 2012 statistics
Sources: Broadband Commission (2013); International Telecommunication Union [ITU] (2014),

continent has over the years significantly grown the number of people with access to mobile cellular technology. South Africa has done particularly well in this area with estimates showing that by 2012 the country had reached 130.6 percent in mobile-cellular subscription (ITU, 2014). Growth in number of people with access to mobile cellular technology has also resulted in significant growth in number of people with access to internet, more so in Africa. This is due to the fact that Africa has very limited fixed telephone network with 2014 statistical estimates showing fixed telephone subscriptions at 1.3 percent against a global average of 15.8 percent (ITU, 2014). Mobile broadband subscriptions in Africa were estimated at 19 percent in 2014 up from 1.8 percent in 2010. Thus while below the global average of 32.0 percent, Africa is leading the world in mobile broadband growth. South Africa's fixed broad band subscriptions were in 2012 estimated at 26 percent while fixed broadband subscriptions were at 2.2 percent (Broadband Commission, 2013).

The fact that Africa's ICT infrastructure is not accessible to many means that many Africans are not in a position where they can buy products online. While this is so, the rapid growth in internet penetration including mobile broadband on the continent may explain why businesses on the continent are taking the online retail channel seriously. It is important to note that while the percentages of people accessing ICT infrastructure may be low, in absolute terms the numbers are quite significant. This is because Africa is the second largest continent after Asia in terms of population. 19 percent in mobile broadband penetration translates to around 200 million individuals which is a significant market segment for business to target.

Legal and Regulatory Framework

A well-developed legal and regulatory framework is critical to the development of e-commerce (Farrokhnia & Richards, 2013). A well-developed e-commerce related legal framework is one that addresses all the different factors and challenges associated with using information technology to conduct transactions that are legally acceptable. Many African countries are however known to have laws lacking these. This does not mean that e-commerce in such countries is taking place in a legal vacuum. Often the problem is to do with existing commercial laws being geared more towards traditional paper based transactions. What is needed in most cases is adaptation of existing laws so as to ensure that they accommodate electronic transactions. Gibbs and Kraemer (2004) in their study which among other things looked at institutional theory and development of e-commerce noted that the institutional environment in a country in particular with respect to the rule of law contributes significantly to promoting or undermining confidence in markets.

South Africa is among the first countries in Africa to have seen the need to have in place laws that would help promote electronic transactions including e-commerce. As far back as in 2002 the country come up with what is known as the Electronic Communications and Transactions Act No 25 of 2002. The purpose of the Act as stipulated in section 2 is to 'promote the acceptance and growth of electronic transactions; remove and prevent of barriers to electronic transactions; ensure that electronic transactions in the country conform to the highest international standards; develop a safe, secure and effective environment for the consumer, business and government to use electronic transactions'. Under the Act, providers of goods and services for sale are obliged to make available certain information on their websites. The information required includes the suppliers' full name and legal status; their physical and e-mail address as well as telephone number; details of membership to any self-regulatory or accredited bodies to which the supplier belongs or subscribes and the contact details of that body; code of conduct to which the supplier subscribes; the manner of payment and any terms of agreement that will apply to the transaction. The Act also provides for a cooling off period for electronic transactions during which a customer may cancel a purchase agreement without penalty. The customer may however be levied the cost of returning goods bought.

Consumer protection is widely acknowledged to be very critical if efforts to build a certain and stable environment for conducting e-commerce are to be realized in any country or globally. This is because while e-commerce provides many opportunities for business, it also bring with it new threats in the form of cybercrimes including threats to privacy. The ease with which e-commerce enables business to operate across borders makes it imperative for e-commerce related laws and regulations to have an international perspective and be in line with international agreements. In order to facilitate the meeting of this need, the United Nations through the UN Commission on International Trade (UNCITRAL) came up with the Model Law on Electronic Commerce (MLEC) to help in the harmonisation of member countries' e-commerce related laws. The law purports to offer national legislators a set of internationally acceptable rules aimed at removing legal obstacles, and creating a more secure legal environment for e-commerce (United Nations Commission of International Trade Law, 1999).

While the importance of laws cannot be underestimated, it is also important to note that the presence of laws alone may not be effective in ensuring business and customer protection unless it is accompanied by effective law enforcement. People need to have confidence that if things go wrong, the law will be enforced without too many hassles. Unfortunately this is rarely the case in many countries and that is why litigation is often recommended as one of the last resorts in dispute resolution. In terms of customer management, this is where retailers need to come in and find ways of building trust and managing perceived risk associated with shopping at their specific online store. The next section looks at issues of risk and trust associated with online shipping in more detail. This section culminates in an empirical investigation conducted to investigate relationships between online shopping risk, trust in an online store and re-purchase intentions.

ONLINE SHOPPING RISK AND TRUST

Online Shopping Risk

Shopping, irrespective of whether it is done online or offline is associated with some level of risk. According to Dowling and Staelin (1994) shopping risk can be defined as "the consumer's perceptions of the uncertainty and adverse consequences of buying a product or service" (p.119). Sources of uncertainty are many and varied in nature. For example a customer may feel uncertain as to whether friends or family members may approve of what is bought. While risk is associated with both online and offline shopping, it is widely acknowledged that shopping online is more risky than offline (Belanche, Casaló, & Guinalíu, 2012; Van Noort, Kerkhof, & Fennis, 2007).

Bhatnagar and Ghose (2004) identified two main factors that make online shopping more risky than offline. These relate to the fact that online shoppers cannot physically inspect products and uncertainties relating to privacy of personal information. These two main sources of online shopping risk are in this study referred to as product risk and privacy risk.

Product risk: Dimoka, Hon and Pavlou (2012) noted that difficulties associated with evaluating products online results in uncertainty regarding performance. This is because limitations to ones' ability to assess products make it difficult if not impossible to be sure if expectations will be met. Pavlou, Benbasat, Krishnan, and Dellarocas (2008) observed that buyers' difficulties in evaluating product offers online are often a problem of product information. Buyers rely on information available online in order to make informed choices. Individual online retailers may thus help reduce their customers' levels of uncertainty relating to product quality by ensuring that customers are provided with detailed information about products on offer. Chiou and Ting (2011) pointed out that availability of detailed product information helps enhance online shopping efficiency. It can also help reduce product returns.

Privacy risk: Shopping online requires that customers provide accurate personal information online (Liao, Liu, & Chen, 2011). Such information often includes their name and address and credit card details. Research shows that customers are sometimes hesitant to shop online because they fear that their personal information may not be secure. Customers are often wary that their personal information may be accessed by unauthorised users or may be used in ways that seriously compromises their privacy (D'Alessandro et al., 2012). Such concerns can exist irrespective of customer privacy protection laws being in place or not. It is important to note that customers always surrender some degree of privacy when they provide personal information to third parties including online retailers. While this is so, they want some assurance that their information will be handled securely so as not to compromise their privacy. Tsai and Yeh (2010) found that high levels of perceived privacy risk have negative influence online shopping intentions. Fujinoki, Chelmecki, and Henry (2014) noted that privacy concerns are heightened when customers are uncertain about access and use of their information. It can therefore be said that measured aimed at managing this risk need to look at issues relating to access and use of customers personal information. On access Shah, Peikari, and Yasin (2014) pointed out that curtailing unauthorised access to data requires that businesses invest in enhancing the technical security features of their sites including authentication requirements. Wu, Huang, Yen, and Popova (2012) pointed out the need for organisations to have clear policies that can help enhance the security of customers private information including policies on who is allowed access to customers data within the organisation and for what purposes. Kurt and Hacioglu (2010) remarked that online security issues are perceived by customers as an ethical matter and thus expect online businesses to act accordingly.

Trust in Online Store

Trust is one of the key constructs in relationship marketing theory. Researchers note that trust is one of the main issues that buyers consider when making purchase decisions online (Bartikowski & Singh 2014). While there is no single agreed definition of what trust is, most of them point out that trust is evidenced by confidence in another party that one will not be taken advantage of. Mayer, Davis, and Schoorman (1995) specifically defined trust as "the willingness of a party to be vulnerable to the actions of another party based on the expectation that the other will perform a particular action important to the trustor, irrespective of the ability to monitor or control that other party" p. 712.

Studies including Segarra-Moliner, Moliner-Tena and Sánchez-Garcia (2013) as well as Chang, Wang, Chih, and Tsai (2012) acknowledge the positive influence trust has on commitment in buyer seller relations as evidenced by willingness to continue the relationship. While this is so, it should be noted that the fact that one is in a continual relationship with another party does not necessarily mean that high levels of trust exist. Lack of choice in case of markets that may not be very competitive for example, may result in buyers sticking with a supplier who may not be highly trusted. While such cases are possible, where the buyer has a lot of choice as is often the case with online shopping, trust is likely to have an influence on customer's buying decision. Aren, Güzel, Kabadayı, and Alpkan (2013) and Wen, Prybutok, and Xu (2011) found that trust influences customers' willingness to patronise some retail outlets. This study thus proposed that trust in an online store is positively related to customers re-purchase intentions.

H1: There is a positive relationship between trust in an online store and re-purchase intentions.

On the relationship between trust and risk, D'Alessandro et al. (2012) noted that the relationship is normally depicted in literature as being a negative one. In their study they found that perceived risk associated with buying products online has a negative impact on trust of online buyers. Eastlick, Lotz, and Warrington (2006) found that risk concerns negatively affect trust in a services e-retailer. This study thus hypothesised that customers who associate online shopping with higher levels of risk are less likely to have high levels of trust in online stores. Of concern are levels of perceived product and privacy risk. Hypothesis 2 and 3 are thus that:

H2: There is a significant relationship between perceived product risk and customer trust an online store.
H3: There is a significant relationship between perceived privavcy risk and customer trust in an online store.

Risk Management and Trust in Online Store

Risk and trust are known to be two important tools for making decisions in uncertain environments (Josang and Presti, 2004). High levels of trust propel individuals towards task while high levels of risk push them towards task avoidance. Bianchi and Andrews (2012) noted that online customers rely on cues provided by retailers in assessing levels of risk and ultimately deciding on whether to trust an online retailer or not. Research show that that there are varied cues or signals that customers use in assessing risk including information provided about products, web store features, warranties as well as retailer reputation (Kesharwani & Bisht, 2012; Ranganathan, 2012). Depending on the nature of risk in question, the cues that may be effective in providing evidence of risk or lack thereof may differ.

Taking cognisant of the importance of information in assisting customers to make informed choices and of security features and policies in managing security risk, this study posits that perceptions regarding availability of adequate product information i.e perceived product informativeness and perceptions relating to online store security respectively is positively related to trust in online retailer. It is thus hypothesised that:

H4: There is a positive relationship between product informativeness and trust in online retail store.
H5: There is a positive relationship between perceived online store security and trust in online store.

EMPIRICAL INVESTIGATIONS

Methodology

Research Approach, Target Population and Sampling

The research study followed a quantitative research approach. This approach entails collection of statistical data that is used to quantify perceptions and opinions in a study. The target population was online shoppers from Gauteng South Africa who were aged 18 years and above. Due to lack of readily available comprehensive list of online customers, non-probability sampling in the form of quota sampling was used to select respondents. Quota sampling entails segmenting the target population into mutually exclusive groups and using judgment to select the subjects from each segment based on specified proportion (Burns & Bush, 2014; Malhotra, Birks & Wills, 2012). Of interest in the study was the need to ensure that both male and female shoppers were adequately represented with no group making up less than 45 percent of the respondents.

Measures

A structured questionnaire was used to collect the required data. Constructs of interest in the study were product risk, privacy risk, product informativeness, perceived online store security, trust is online store and store re-purchase intentions. Items used to measure these constructs were sourced from literature. This helped to enhance the validity of the constructs. Items used to measure product risk were specifically adapted from Suresh and Shashikala (2011) as well as Masoud (2013) while privacy risk was measured using items adapted from Zhang, Tan, Xu and Tan (2012). Items used to measure informativeness were sourced and adapted from Gao and Wu (2010) while items used to measure perceived online store security were sourced and adapted from Chang and Chen (2009) as well as Yen and Lu (2008). Items used to measure trust in online store were sourced and adapted from Qureshi et al. (2009) while those used to measure online store re-purchase intention were sourced and adapted from Hausman and Siekpe (2009). For each item, respondents were asked to indicate on a five point Lickert scale that ranged from 1 = strongly disagree to 5 = strongly agree, the extent to which they agreed with the statement.

Data Collection

Data was collected with the help of trained research assistants. The assistants were trained on a variety of topics relating to research data collection including how to screen respondents for eligibility and issues of ethics in data collection. Respondents were personally approached by the data collectors and asked to participate in the study by filling in the questionnaires. The research assistants were present during the questionnaire filling time ready to attend to any questions that the respondents may have and to ensure that the questionnaire was fully completed. At the end of the data collection period a total of 201 usable responses were received, 98 from male online customers representing 49 percent of the sample and 103 from female online customers representing 51 percent of the sample. In terms of age distribution 24.9 percent were between the ages of 18 and 29, 44.3 percent were aged between 30 and 40; 19.4 percent were between 41 and 49 while 11.4 percent were above 50.

Data Analysis

Version 21 of SPSS/AMOS statistical data analysis software was used to analyse the data collected. The statistical technique used for the analysis was structural equation modelling. A two stage approach was used in the analysis. The first step involved assessment of the measurement model for goodness of fit, construct reliability and validity. The second stage involved assessment of the structural model for goodness of fit and testing of hypothesis. Multiple indices were used to test the goodness of fit of both the measurement and structural model. These included the normed Chi-Square (X^2/df), the Goodness of Fit Index (GFI), the Normed Fit Index (NFI), The Comparative Fit Index (CFI), the Tucker Lewis Index (TLI) and the Root Mean Square Error of Approximation (RMSEA).

Composite reliability coefficients were used to determine the reliability of each construct. Validity tests involved assessment of convergent and discriminant validity. Convergent validity was determined using Average Variance Extracted (AVE) value. Discriminant validity was determined by comparing the AVE with the Maximum Shared Variance (MSV) values.

Results

Assessment of the Measurement Model

Findings on goodness of fit measures showed satisfactory fit of the measurement model. According to Hair, Black, Babin, and Anderson (2010) as well as Gaskin (2013), recommended fit values are a maximum of 3 for normed chi-square; maximum of .6 for RMSEA and minimum value of .9 for GFI, NFI, CFI and TLI. The results in this study showed that the Chi-square value (χ^2) was 188.36 with 119 degrees of freedom (df) and a significant p value of .000. The normed Chi-square (χ^2/df) was thus found to be 1.583. The GFI was .905; the NFI was .923, the CFI was .970; the TLI was .961 while the RMSEA was .054.

Results on construct reliability test, presented in table 3 show that all constructs were highly reliable. According to Hair et al. (2010), composite reliability coefficients of .7 and above are indicative of high construct reliability. The composite reliability coefficients of the constructs in the study ranged from .815 to .948 with the lowest being for online store re-purchase intention and the lowest being for trust in online store.

Table 3. Measurement Scales, Reliability and Factor Loadings

Constructs and items	Composite Reliability Coefficient	Factor Loadings
Product Risk		
When I shop online I am concerned with/that		
- quality of the delivered product may not live up to expectations	.828	.875
- product delivered may not be exactly as it appeared online		.891
- difficulties in feeling and experiencing the product prior to purchase		.796
Privacy Risk		
When I shop online I am concerned with/that		
Personal information may be passed on to others without my consent	.948	.884
Personal Information may be used for other unintended purposes		.932
Personal information could be accessed by unauthorised users		.898
PInf – Product Informativeness		
The store website provides		
PInf 1 - detailed information about the products featured	.814	.844
PInf 2 - enough information to assess the products		.870
PInf 2 - enough information to compare alternatives		.731
PInf 3 - enough information for me to make a well informed purchase decision		.767
OSSec – Online Store Security		
OSSec 1 - I feel this site keeps secret information about my transactions	.833	.647
OSSec 2 - This site will protect my personal information from unauthorised access		.826
OSSec 3 - I believe this online retailer has adequate security features		.884
OSSec 4 - This website seems security conscious		.861
TrOS – Trust in online store		
TrOS 1 - I feel that I can trust this online retailer	.890	.821
TrOS 2 - I believe that this online retailer is dependable		.783
TrOS 3 - I believe that this online retailer has high integrity		.853
OSRepI – Online store repurchase intention		
OSRepI 1 - I intend to purchase through this site in near future	.815	.775
OSRepI 2 - It is likely that I will purchase through this site in the near future		.688
OSRepI 3 - I will definitely buy products from this site again in the near future		.718

In terms of convergent validity, the results presented in table 4 show that the AVE coefficients of all constructs in the proposed model were greater than .5. According to Hair et al. (2010) AVE values of .5 or higher are proof of convergent validity. They also note that factor loadings of .5 and above provide additional evidence of convergent validity. Results in table 3 show that all the items used to measure each construct in the study had loadings of greater than .5.

Results of correlation analysis, presented in table 4 show that there are significant relationships between constructs hypothesised in the proposed model to be related. These include correlation between product risk, privacy risk, product informativeness, online store security respectively and trust in online store as well as the relationship between trust in online store and online store repurchase intentions. The results in table 4 also provide evidence of discriminant validity. As per Gaskin (2013) discriminant validity is evident when the MSV is less than the AVE. This condition was met in the case of all constructs used in the study, thereby providing evidence that each construct was distinctively different from the others.

Assessment of the Structural Model

Results on tests of the structural model showed acceptable fit. The Chi-square value (χ^2) was 192.317 with 123 degrees of freedom (df) and a significant p value of .000. The normed Chi-square (χ^2/df) was thus 1.564. The GFI was .903; the NFI was .922, the CFI was .970; the TLI was .963 while the RMSEA was .054. Examination of results on the structural paths, refer table 5, showed that all the three hypothesised relationships were supported.

Discussion and Implications

The findings in the study show that the fact that one shops online does not mean that they do not associate online shopping with risk. This is evidenced by the mean values of product risk and privacy risk which are both in the 'agree' range. The findings also show that while customers may perceive online shopping in general to be associated with risk, this does not mean that they will have less levels

Table 4. Descriptives and validity tests

Construct	Mean	Standard Deviation	PRk	PRk	PInf	OSSec	Trust	RInt
PRk	3.52	.940	0.787					
PRk	3.67	.989	0.705	0.927				
PInf	4.18	.687	0.014	-0.097	0.781			
OSSec	4.08	.747	-0.158	-0.172	0.530	0.827		
Trust	4.30	.710	-0.037	-0.021	0.626	0.687	0.854	
RInt	4.23	.651	0.050	0.050	0.478	0.516	0.651	0.753
AVE			**0.619**	**0.859**	**0.609**	**0.683**	**0.730**	**0.568**
MSV			**0.497**	**0.497**	**0.392**	**0.472**	**0.472**	**0.424**

Note: Diagonal values in bold are the square root of the AVE. Off diagonal values are construct correlations

Table 5. Results of the Hypothesis Testing

		Standardised Regression Coefficient	SE	P	Conclusion
Online store repurchase intention	Trust in online store	.665	.070	.000	H1 Supported
Trust in online store	Product risk	-.067	.082	.464	H2 Supported
Trust in online store	Privacy risk	.155	.060	.071	H3 Supported
Trust in online store	Product informativeness	.379	.111	.000	H4 Supported
Trust in online store	Online store security	.509	.082	.000	H5 Supported

of trust in all online stores. Thus while empirical evidence abound that shows the negative influence of perceived risk on trust (D'Alessandro et al., 2012), online stores can take measures aimed at effectively reducing risk and enhancing trust that customers associate with shopping at their specific online stores. The findings affirm the importance of trust in influencing customers' repurchase intentions. The importance of repeat customers is widely underscored in marketing mainly because it costs significantly more to recruit new customers than to retain existing ones (Beitelspacher, Richey, & Reynolds, 2011). In countries where online retailing is still a new phenomenon as is the case in most African countries including South Africa, online stores that are able to win the trust of customers are also likely to gain more new customers through referrals from existing customers.

In terms of management of risk the findings show that provision of adequate information and enhancement of store security can have significant influence on customers' trust in an online store. The findings on product information are in line with assertions by Dimoka et al. (2012) who noted that lack of adequate product information creates uncertainty on the part of the customer as to what to expect and whether to order a product from an online store or not. This is more so when one bears in mind that there are in existence many unscrupulous online stores which will deliberately misinform customers for the purpose of making a sale. While such practices are unlikely to result in repeat purchase, they heighten customer's suspicions and sensitivity to online product offers in general. Managers of online stores need to find ways of managing product uncertainty by providing information that will be helpful to making of informed buying decision. To this end, managers need to look at possible factors that can result in customers not perceiving the product information that they provide on their online stores not to be very helpful in their purchase decision making.

One of the possible contributing factors could be lack of skills on the part of their staff on how best to describe products. While research often focuses on seller unwillingness to truthfully describe products, managers need to be aware that even where good intentions may exist, not all staff may be in a position to adequately and properly describe a product. Two staff members may actually end up describing the same product differently. Keeping in mind the importance of online product information, managers thus need to ensure that their staff are skilled enough to fulfil the task. Where necessary, training needs to be provided so as enhance their skills in this area. Managers can also deal with difficulties of adequately describing products online by making use of IT enabled solutions such as provision of clear product pictures and making it possible for customers to view products from different angles. Another possible solution to the problem lies in providing customers with an opportunity to provide product reviews on the store site so that other customers who may want to buy the same product may get information from a third party on what they think about the product having bought it.

On privacy, the findings showing high mean value for online shopping privacy risk concerns compared to product risk highlights the serious concerns that customers often have relating to privacy of personal information when they shop online. It is thus important that managers of online stores look for ways in which they can reduce privacy risk concerns for customers shopping at their stores. Effective management of this risk requires that managers be conversant with available security features that they can use to protect customers from cyber criminals (Shah et al., (2014). Focus needs to be paid to not only preventing outsiders from accessing customers' personal information but also on how customers' information is handled by the retailer's staff. Clear policies need to be in place on how customers' personal information is to be handled by insiders so as to protect their privacy. In order to make sure that such security efforts are accorded the seriousness in approach that they deserve online retailers need to make sure that their staff are conversant with laws relating to the same including the consequences of not being compliant with the laws.

FUTURE RESEARCH DIRECTIONS

Online retailing is a new phenomenon in Africa. While its rate of growth is very high, not much research has been done to understand the different factors that are influencing this growth and more so factors influencing success or failure of retailers who have decided to take up the new mode of retailing by targeting customers from the region. While this chapter helps in contributing to understanding of some of the factors that may help these issues more research is needed to help validate and establish new insights into what it takes to successfully appeal to online customers in the region. Future research can specifically examine issues of risk and trust in online retailing from different facets including the relationship between customer background characteristics and risk perceptions as well as trust in online retailers. Other areas that need future research attention include customer management practices of online retailers so as to help identify good practices that are more appealing to customers from those that are not.

CONCLUSION

The future of online retailing in Africa looks bright. Projections show that sales in the short to medium term are likely to continue to grow at a much faster rate than growth in traditional retailing. These projections are however not a guarantee to any individual retailer that they stand to reap the benefits and provide good returns to investors. The ability of any online retailer to benefit from the positive outlook of online retailing in Africa and South Africa in particular will depend on their ability to come up with effective strategies aimed at attracting and retaining customers to their stores. Risk and trust are two factors that online retailers need to pay serious attention to if they are to succeed in ensuring that customers keep on patronising their stores. While there are many possible sources of risk in online retailing, empirical findings in this study show that product risk and privacy risk are of concern even among customers who have adopted online shopping. The findings show that by having in place effective ways of managing these risks mangers of online stores can influence customers' levels of trust in their online stores. Specifically the findings point to the need for managers to ensure that they provide adequate information that can help customers make informed purchase decisions as well as ensuring that security levels associated with their online stores are high enough to draw the confidence of customers.

REFERENCES

Aren, S., Güzel, M., Kabadayı, E., & Alpkan, L. (2013). Factors affecting repurchase intention to shop at the same website. *Procedia: Social and Behavioral Sciences*, *99*, 536–544. doi:10.1016/j.sbspro.2013.10.523

Bartikowski, B., & Singh, N. (2014). Doing e-business in France: Drivers of online trust in business-to-consumer websites. *Global Business and Organizational Excellence*, *33*(4), 28–36. doi:10.1002/joe.21551

Beitelspacher, L. S., Richey, R. G., & Reynolds, K. E. (2011). Exploring a new perspective on service efficiency: Service culture in retail organizations. *Journal of Services Marketing*, *25*(3), 215–228. doi:10.1108/08876041111129191

Belanche, D., Casaló, L. V., & Guinalíu, M. (2012). Website usability, consumer satisfaction and the intention to use a website: The moderating effect of perceived risk. *Journal of Retailing and Consumer Services*, *19*(1), 124–132. doi:10.1016/j.jretconser.2011.11.001

Bhatnagar, A., & Ghose, S. (2004). Segmenting consumers based on the benefits and risks of Internet shopping. *Journal of Business Research*, *57*(12), 1352–1360. doi:10.1016/S0148-2963(03)00067-5

Bianchi, C., & Andrews, L. (2012). Risk, trust, and consumer online purchasing behaviour: A Chilean perspective. *International Marketing Review*, *29*(3), 253–275. doi:10.1108/02651331211229750

Bizcommunity. (2013). South Africa leads in African e-commerce. Retrieved from http://www.bizcommunity.com/Article/196/394/96986.html

Broadband Commission. (2013). *The state of broadband 2013: Universalizing broadband*. Geneva, Switzerland: The Broadband Commission.

Burns, A., & Bush, R. (2014). *Marketing research*. Boston: Pearson Education.

Chang, H. H., & Chen, S. W. (2009). Consumer perception of interface quality, security, and loyalty in electronic commerce. *Information & Management*, *46*(7), 411–417. doi:10.1016/j.im.2009.08.002

Chang, S. H., Wang, K. Y., Chih, W. H., & Tsai, W. H. (2012). Building customer commitment in business-to-business markets. *Industrial Marketing Management*, *41*(6), 940–950. doi:10.1016/j.indmarman.2011.11.026

Chiou, J. S., & Ting, C. C. (2011). Will you spend more money and time on internet shopping when the product and situation are right? *Computers in Human Behavior*, *27*(1), 203–208. doi:10.1016/j.chb.2010.07.037

Corritore, C. L., Kracher, B., & Wiedenbeck, S. (2003). On-line trust: Concepts, evolving themes, a model. *International Journal of Human-Computer Studies*, *58*(6), 737–758. doi:10.1016/S1071-5819(03)00041-7

Cushman & Wakefield. (2013). Global perspective on retail: Online retailing. Retrieved from http://www.cushmanwakefield.com/~/media/global-reports/Global%20Perspective%20on%20Retail%201st%20July%202013.ashx

D'Alessandro, S., Girardi, A., & Tiangsoongnern, L. (2012). Perceived risk and trust as antecedents of online purchasing behavior in the USA gemstone industry. *Asia Pacific Journal of Marketing and Logistics*, *24*(3), 433–460. doi:10.1108/13555851211237902

DigitasLBi. (2014). M-commerce, social media and ROPO (research online, purchase offline) lead retail trends, according to DigitasLBi's Global Survey. Retrieved from http://www.digitaslbi.com/news/global/m-commerce-social-media-and-ropo-research-online-purchase-offline-lead-retail-trends-according-to-digitaslbis-global-survey/

Dimoka, A., Hong, Y., & Pavlou, P. A. (2012). On product uncertainty in online markets: Theory and evidence. *Management Information Systems Quarterly*, *36*(2), 395–426.

Dowling, G. R., & Staelin, R. (1994). A model of perceived risk and intended risk-handling activity. *The Journal of Consumer Research*, *21*(1), 119–134. doi:10.1086/209386

E-marketer. (2014). Global B2C ecommerce sales to hit $1.5 trillion this year driven by growth in emerging markets. Retrieved from http://www.emarketer.com/Articles/Print.aspx?R=1010575

Eastlick, M. A., Lotz, S. L., & Warrington, P. (2006). Understanding online B-to-C relationships: An integrated model of privacy concerns, trust, and commitment. *Journal of Business Research*, *59*(8), 877–886. doi:10.1016/j.jbusres.2006.02.006

Farrokhnia, F., & Richards, C. K. (2013). The accountability challenge to global e-commerce: The need to overcome the developed-developing country divide in WTO e-commerce policies. *Advances in Sustainability and Environmental Justice*, *12*, 161–181. doi:10.1108/S2051-5030(2013)0000012012

Fujinoki, H., Chelmecki, C. A., & Henry, D. M. (2014). Fail-safe security architecture to prevent privacy leaks from e-commerce servers. *Journal of Internet Services and Information Security*, *4*(2), 38–54.

Gao, Y., & Wu, X. (2010). A cognitive model of trust in e-commerce: Evidence from a field study in China. *Journal of Applied Business Research*, *26*(1), 37–44.

Gaskins, J. (2013). Confirmatory factor. Retrieved from http://statwiki.kolobkreations.com/wiki/Confirmatory_Factor_Analysis

Gibbs, J. L., & Kraemer, K. L. (2004). A cross-country investigation of the determinants of scope of e-commerce use: An institutional approach. *Electronic Markets*, *14*(2), 124–137. doi:10.1080/10196780410001675077

Hair, J., Black, W., Babin, B., & Anderson, R. (2010). *Multivariate data analysis: A global perspective*. New Jersey: Pearson Education.

Hanson, W. A., & Kalyanam, K. (2007). *Internet marketing & e-commerce*. Mason, OH: Thomson/South-Western.

Hausman, A. V., & Siekpe, J. S. (2009). The effect of web interface features on consumer online purchase intentions. *Journal of Business Research*, *62*(1), 5–13. doi:10.1016/j.jbusres.2008.01.018

IMAP. (2010). Retail industry global report. Retrieved from http://www.imap.com/imap/media/article_documents/IMAP_Global_Retail_Industry_Report__BEDF5F30C7201.pdf

International Telecommunication Union [ITU] (2014). ICT statistics. Retrieved from http://www.itu.int/en/ITU-D/Statistics/Pages/default.aspx

Jøsang, A., & Presti, S. L. (2004). Analysing the relationship between risk and trust. In T. Dimitrakos (Ed.), *Trust Management* (pp. 135–145). Berlin, Heidelberg: Springer. doi:10.1007/978-3-540-24747-0_11

Kesharwani, A., & Singh Bisht, S. (2012). The impact of trust and perceived risk on internet banking adoption in India: An extension of technology acceptance model. *International Journal of Bank Marketing*, *30*(4), 303–322. doi:10.1108/02652321211236923

Ko, H., Jung, J., Kim, J., & Shim, S. W. (2004). Cross-cultural differences in perceived risk of online shopping. *Journal of Interactive Advertising*, *4*(2), 20–29. doi:10.1080/15252019.2004.10722084

Kurt, G., & Hacioglu, G. (2010). Ethics as a customer perceived value driver in the context of online retailing. *African Journal of Business Management*, *4*(5), 672–677.

Luce, S. (2013). *Global retail report*. Nyon, Switzerland: UNI Global Union.

Malhotra, N. K., Birks, D. F., & Wills, P. (2012). *Essentials of marketing research*. Harlow: Pearson Education.

Mayer, R. C., Davis, J. H., & Schoorman, F. D. (1995). An integrative model of organizational trust. *Academy of Management Review*, *20*(3), 709–734.

Pavlou, P. A., Benbasat, I., Krishnan, R., & Dellarocas, C. 2008. *Mitigating product uncertainty in online markets: it and business solutions and research implications*. Paper presented at the 29th International Conference on Information Systems, Paris, France.

Qureshi, I., Fang, Y., Ramsey, E., McCole, P., Ibbotson, P., & Compeau, D. (2009). Understanding online customer repurchasing intention and the mediating role of trust–an empirical investigation in two developed countries. *European Journal of Information Systems*, *18*(3), 205–222. doi:10.1057/ejis.2009.15

Ranganathan, C. (2012). The role of extrinsic cues in consumer decision process in online shopping environments. *Journal of Electronic Commerce in Organizations*, *10*(1), 52–71. doi:10.4018/jeco.2012010104

Segarra-Moliner, J. R., Moliner-Tena, M. A., & Sánchez-Garcia, J. (2013). Relationship quality in business to business: A cross-cultural perspective from universities. *Marketing Intelligence & Planning*, *31*(3), 196–215. doi:10.1108/02634501311324573

Sernau, S. (2014). Social inequality in a global age. Thousand Oaks, California: Sage Publications.

Shah, M. H., Peikari, H. R., & Yasin, N. M. (2014). The determinants of individuals' perceived e-security: Evidence from Malaysia. *International Journal of Information Management*, *34*(1), 48–57. doi:10.1016/j.ijinfomgt.2013.10.001

Shaker, W. (2013). EP016: How to avoid failure & succeed as an online entrepreneur. Retrieved from http://www.williamshaker.com/how-to-avoid-failure-succeed-as-an-online-entrepreneur/

South African Goverment. (2002). Electronic Communications and Transactions Act No 25.

Statista. (2014). Forecast for global retail sales growth from 2008 to 2016. Retrieved from http://www.statista.com/statistics/232347/forecast-of-global-retail-sales-growth/

Tsai, Y. C., & Yeh, J. C. (2010). Perceived risk of information security and privacy in online shopping: A study of environmentally sustainable products. *African Journal of Business Management*, *4*(18), 4057–4066.

United Nations Commission on International Trade Law. (1998). *UNCITRAL model law on electronic commerce guide to enactment*. Vienna, Austria: United Nations.

Van Noort, G., Kerkhof, P., & Fennis, B. M. (2007). Online versus conventional shopping: Consumers' risk perception and regulatory focus. *Cyberpsychology & Behavior*, *10*(5), 731–733. doi:10.1089/cpb.2007.9959 PMID:17927547

Wen, C., Prybutok, V. R., & Xu, C. (2011). An integrated model for customer online repurchase intention. *Journal of Computer Information Systems*, *52*(1), 14–23.

Wu, K. W., Huang, S. Y., Yen, D. C., & Popova, I. (2012). The effect of online privacy policy on consumer privacy concern and trust. *Computers in Human Behavior*, *28*(3), 889–897. doi:10.1016/j.chb.2011.12.008

Yen, C. H., & Lu, H. P. (2008). Effects of e-service quality on loyalty intention: An empirical study in online auction. *Managing Service Quality*, *18*(2), 127–146. doi:10.1108/09604520810859193

Ystats. (2013). Africa B2C ecommerce report. Retrieved from http://www.ystats.com/uploads/report_abstracts/1058.pdf?PHPSESSID=2a2ba9548054959d1dfc4668b2754844

Zaker, R. A., & Ansari, A. A. (2013). Towards improving quality of e-commerce websites in hospitals. Paper presented at the knowledge globalisation conference, Istanbul, Turkey.

Zhang, L., Tan, W., Xu, Y., & Tan, G. (2012). Dimensions of consumers' perceived risk and their influences on online consumers' purchasing behaviour. *Communications in Information Science and Management Engineering*, *2*(7), 8–14.

ADDITIONAL READING

Akintola, K. G., Akinyede, R. O., & Agbonifo, C. O. (2011). Appraising Nigeria readiness for ecommerce towards: Achieving vision 20: 2020. *International Journal of Research and Reviews in Applied Sciences*, *9*(2), 330–340.

Bowman, W., Mensah, M., & Urama, K. (2014). Information and telecommunication technologies in Africa: a potential Revolution? In J. Y. Grosclaude, R. K. Pachauri, & L. Tubiana (Eds.), Innovation for sustainable development (p. 45-50). New Delhi, India: TERI Press.

Cook, M. T. (2014). Africa leapfrogs into the world economy. In J. O'Neill, E. M. Noam, & D. Gerbarg (Eds.), *Broadband as a Video Platform* (pp. 151–165). New York, NY: Springer. doi:10.1007/978-3-319-03617-5_12

Datta, P. (2011). A preliminary study of ecommerce adoption in developing countries. *Information Systems Journal*, *21*(1), 3–32. doi:10.1111/j.1365-2575.2009.00344.x

Eid, M. I. (2011). Determinants of e-commerce customer satisfaction, trust, and loyalty in Saudi Arabia. *Journal of Electronic Commerce Research*, *12*(1), 78–93.

Ewelukwa, N. (2011). Is Africa ready for electronic commerce-a critical appraisal of the legal framework for ecommerce in Africa. *European Journal of Law Reform*, *13*(3/4), 550–576.

Hasan, L., Morris, A., & Probets, S. (2013). E-commerce websites for developing countries–a usability evaluation framework. *Online Information Review*, *37*(2), 231–251. doi:10.1108/OIR-10-2011-0166

Jobodwana, Z. N. (2009). E-commerce and mobile commerce in South Africa: Regulatory challenges. *Journal of International Commercial Law and technology, 4(4)*, 287-298.

Joseph, B. K. (2010). E-commerce penetration in the SADC region: Consolidating and moving forward. In M. M. Cruz-Cunha, & J. Varajao (Eds.), E-business managerial aspects, solutions and case studies (pp. 235 -253). IGI Global.

Kinuthia, J. N., & Akinnusi, D. M. (2014). The magnitude of barriers facing e-commerce businesses in Kenya. *Journal of Internet and Information Systems*, *4*(1), 12–27. doi:10.5897/JIIS2013.0074

KPMG. (2013).Retail industry outlook survey: Tech innovations leads to brighter future. Retrieved from https://www.kpmg.com/US/en/IssuesAndInsights/ArticlesPublications/Documents/retail-outlook-survey.pdf

Lawal, L. S., Ahmed-Rufai, T., Chatwin, C. R., & Young, R. C. D. (2013). Delivery of broadband services to sub-Saharan Africa via Nigerian communications satellite. *International Journal of Information and Computer Science*, *2*(5), 77–88.

Lawrence, J. E. (2011). The growth of e-commerce in developing countries: An exploratory study of opportunities and challenges for SMEs. *International Journal of ICT Research and Development in Africa*, *2*(1), 15–28. doi:10.4018/jictrda.2011010102

Liao, C., Liu, C. C., & Chen, K. (2011). Examining the impact of privacy, trust and risk perceptions beyond monetary transactions: An integrated model. *Electronic Commerce Research and Applications*, *10*(6), 702–715. doi:10.1016/j.elerap.2011.07.003

Makulilo, A. B. (2013). Cyber law in Kenya. *Information & Communications Technology Law*, *22*(1), 86–87. doi:10.1080/13600834.2013.774519

Mayayise, T., & Olusegun Osunmakinde, I. (2014). E-commerce assurance models and trustworthiness issues: An empirical study. *Information Management & Computer Security*, *22*(1), 76–96. doi:10.1108/IMCS-01-2013-0001

Mbatha, B. (2013). Exploring the potential of electronic commerce tools in South African SME tourism service providers. *Information Development*, *29*(1), 10–23. doi:10.1177/0266666912452270

Molla, A., & Licker, P. S. (2005). E-commerce adoption in developing countries: A model and instrument. *Information & Management*, *42*(6), 877–899. doi:10.1016/j.im.2004.09.002

Murungi, M. (2011). *Cyber Law in Kenya*. Netherlands: Kluwer Law International.

Nabareseh, S., & Osakwe, C. N. (2014). Can business-to-consumer electronic commerce be a game-changer in Anglophone West African countries? Insights from secondary data and consumers' perspectives. *World Applied Sciences Journal*, *30*(11), 1515–1525.

Ndonga, D. (2012). E-commerce in Africa: Challenges and solutions. *African Journal of Legal Studies*, *5*(3), 243–268. doi:10.1163/17087384-12342009

Nwaobi, G. (2012). Global e-commerce and African participation: a critical assessment. Retrieved from http://mpra.ub.uni-muenchen.de/39237/1/MPRA_paper_39237.pdf

Oluyinka, S., Shamsuddin, A., Ajabe, M. A., & Enegbuma, W. I. (2013). A study of electronic commerce adoption factors in Nigeria. *International Journal of Information Systems and Change Management*, *6*(4), 293–315. doi:10.1504/IJISCM.2013.060974

Srivastava, A., & Koekemoer, M. (2013). The legal recognition of electronic signatures in South Africa: A critical overview. *African Journal of International and Comparative Law*, *21*(3), 427–446. doi:10.3366/ajicl.2013.0071

Zhou, Q. S., Yang, M. X., Zhang, P. F., & Qiu, Y. (2013). Study on the innovative jewelry B2C business Model in China and Africa. *International Journal of Engineering Research in Africa*, *10*, 65–77. doi:10.4028/www.scientific.net/JERA.10.65

KEY TERMS AND DEFINITIONS

E-Commerce: The conduct of business activities over electronic networks, commonly the internet.

Online Product Informativeness: The quality of product related information provided online in terms of ability to aid users make informed purchase decisions.

Online Retailing: The sale of goods and services to end users over the internet.

Online Shopping Risk Management: Activities associate with identification, analysis and mitigation of uncertainties associated with online shopping.

Perceived Online Privacy Risk: Subjective assessment of potential problems involving access, use and disclosure of personal information collected online.

Perceived Online Shopping Risk: Subjective assessment of vulnerability associated with buying products online.

Trust in Online Store: A firm belief in the reliability of an online store.

Chapter 15
Confronting the Challenges of Asymmetry of Information and Competition:
The Rise of eBay

Mikhail Ion Melnik
Kennesaw State University, USA

ABSTRACT

During its history, the largest U.S. consumer-to-consumer online platform, eBay, had to overcome two major obstacles: Asymmetry of information and competition from Yahoo Auctions. This chapter examines two of the mechanisms used by eBay that may account for the company's success story: the seller's rating mechanism and the insertion fee structure. The first of these mechanisms seems to have played an important role in addressing the problem of asymmetry of information in consumer-to-consumer online commerce. In addition, the eBay rating may have served as a barrier to entry for competing platforms in the consumer-to-consumer online commerce. The second mechanism appears to have aided eBay in its competition with Yahoo Auctions in the U.S. online auction market.

INTRODUCTION

Online Auctions and Importance of eBay

Online commerce (often referred to as ecommerce) is a relatively young phenomenon that developed in the 1990's and fortified its position in the first decade of the XXI century. Despite its short history, ecommerce has already produced its own well-known brand names. One such widely recognized name is eBay. In the U.S., online auctions have effectively become synonymous with the eBay brand. The ease of adaptability of auctions to online commerce further contributed to the growing popularity of eBay. However, the history of online auctions has not been free of competition, and serious competitive battles indeed took place before eBay became synonymous with online auctions in the U.S. market. In fact, it was following the closing of Yahoo Auctions in the summer of 2007, that eBay's hegemony over the

DOI: 10.4018/978-1-4666-8459-1.ch015

U.S. online auction market was finally sealed. In addition to competition, online businesses operating in the consumer-to-consumer space also faced other challenges that included asymmetry of information. The industry and particularly eBay were successfully able to overcome this challenge and turn it into a shield against potential competitors.

Much like all online commerce, eBay is a relatively young firm, making its success story even more exciting. Indeed, eBay has come a long way since its debut on Labor Day of 1995. In 2013, eBay reported that the total volume of merchandize sales on its U.S. website (excluding vehicles) reached $30.403 billion a year (eBay, 2014). For comparison, according to the most recent estimates by the U.S. Census, the size of the U.S. online retail sales in 2011, the last year for which the data is currently available, was around $193.904 billion (U.S. Census, 2013). A mere comparison between these numbers highlights the relative importance of eBay.

Although eBay is associated with online auctions, the company does not act as the seller in any auctions listed on its website, but merely serves as a platform for its users. Its customers are the individuals and businesses who wish to sell their items on eBay. In turn, eBay serves as a platform in consumer-to-consumer and business-to-consumer ecommerce.

In its short history, eBay has had to overcome two important obstacles: asymmetry of information and competition with Yahoo. These two obstacles received significant attention in economic literature. The proceeding discussion examines each of these two aspects of eBay's experience and highlights the unique and creative ways in which eBay has met these challenges.

BACKGROUND

Asymmetry of Information

Online commerce differs from the traditional brick and mortar setting in the way the interaction between buyers and sellers is conducted. In online commerce, this interaction does not need to take place in person. Transactions may involve participants who not only never meet face to face, but may even reside in different countries. In such a setting, trust inevitably becomes an integral part of any transaction, making asymmetry of information a serious challenge for any online business. In the context of eBay, where sellers are individuals or businesses, the asymmetry of information problem has two characteristics: the accuracy of the description of the item being offered for sale and the reliability of the seller in complying with the terms of the transaction.[1]

Over time, ecommerce developed a number of mechanisms aimed at reducing the risks arising from asymmetry of information. Online payment methods, buyer protection, insurance, escrow accounts, etc. all constitute examples of the mechanisms that help facilitate online transactions and reduce the problem of asymmetry of information today. However, in the 1990s, during the rise of eBay, such mechanisms did not exist.

From the start, eBay came up with a simple mechanism to address the problem of asymmetry of information – rating. The eBay rating mechanism is an ingenious solution to a complex issue. It is simple to understand and interpret, making it an easily adaptable tool for all users. It represents a measure of reputation a user has on eBay, and as such, it can serve as a signal about the reliability of that user. This signaling property helps reduce the problem of asymmetry of information. In the design of the rating mechanism, eBay limited the possibility of manipulating one's rating value by creating multiple accounts. In addition to all of these properties, eBay rating can also act as a barrier to entry for competing with eBay platforms. We will focus on each of these characteristics of the rating mechanism in the proceeding discussion.

The Rating Mechanism

A user's eBay rating is a result of that user's transactional experience on eBay. After completing a transaction, the participants are given an opportunity to rate each other. The rating choices are: positive, negative, and neutral. Only one rating comment can be made per transaction. The rating is simply the difference between the number of unique positive and unique negative comments. Furthermore, the value of the rating is not based on the number of transactions a user had, but rather on the number of unique individual eBay users the user conducted transactions with. For instance, if two users complete ten transactions between them, they can leave ten positive comments about each other, but only one of these comments will count in the rating. This last characteristic of the rating mechanism reduces the possibility of fraudulent activity because the rating cannot be generated by a large number of transactions between few individual eBay accounts.[2]

It is important to note that the eBay rating mechanism is not completely free of manipulation. Sellers can accumulate positive feedback by engaging in buying activities. Furthermore, the cost of creating additional eBay IDs is relatively low. For an illustration of issues associated with the eBay rating mechanism see Dini and Spagnolo (2009).

Over the years, eBay has continued to evolve its rating mechanism, but its fundamental structure has remained the same. In May of 2007, the eBay rating mechanism was significantly revised. In addition to the overall rating, buyers have been given an opportunity to rate sellers based on a number of different categories: accuracy of item description, communications, shipping time, and shipping charges. In each category, a seller can be rated on a scale from one to five. The addition of the individual categories increased the information conveyed by the rating. However, the computation of the overall rating was left unaffected.

It is important to note that the rating plays a much more important role in the evaluation of the seller than the buyer. In an eBay transaction, the buyer is required to submit their payment before the seller completes their part of the transaction and ships the item to the buyer. This sequence of events requires the buyer to trust the seller, whereas the seller does not have the same risk. Furthermore, it is the buyer who ultimately makes the decision to enter into a transaction. Hence, the information signaling property of the rating of a buyer is not as important as that of a seller. However, the information signaled by the seller's rating to a perspective buyer can influence the buyer's decision. If a seller's eBay rating indeed has signaling properties, and the signaled information impacts the buyer's decision, then such an instrument has a value to the market participants. In fact, there is plenty of empirical and anecdotal evidence that eBay participants value this mechanism and its role in signaling information. One possible illustration of this is a recently filed lawsuit in which an eBay seller is suing a buyer for leaving a negative feedback comment about them on eBay (Wolford, 2013).

Cabral and Hortacsu (2010) developed a very insightful and intuitive theoretical model of the role the seller's rating plays on eBay. However, investigating the effects of the eBay rating is very much an empirical issue. Any empirical findings demonstrating statistically significant effects of the seller's rating on the auction outcome would highlight the signaling property of the eBay rating mechanism. If eBay bidders were to reward sellers with high ratings and penalize sellers with low overall ratings or high negative ratings, then that would imply that they value the eBay rating as a signaling mechanism. In such a case, the eBay rating would fulfill an important function of addressing the asymmetry of information problem in consumer to consumer online commerce. For further discussion of online feedback mechanisms see Dellarocas (2003).

Empirical Literature

The continuous numerical nature of the rating has enabled researchers to investigate the impact the seller's rating has on the outcome of an auction on eBay. For empirical economists, the emergence of eBay, and its subsequent popularity, served as a goldmine of data. As a result, numerous empirical studies emerged using eBay data. The seller's reputation and its role in price determination quickly became a popular topic of empirical research (Bolton et al., 2004; Bruce et al., 2004; Standifird, 2001). Several early studies into the role the seller's rating plays on eBay demonstrated that the seller's rating has a positive and statistically significant impact on the closing price, thereby underscoring the importance of the price-rating relationship (Livingston, 2005; Kalyanam & McIntyre, 2001; Houser & Wooders, 2006; Dewan & Hsu, 2004; Melnik & Alm, 2002; Bajari & Hortacsu, 2004). For a detailed overview of the early literature in this area of research, see Dellarocas (2003) and Bajari and Hortacsu (2004). For a general overview of auction theory, see Klemperer (1999). Although the bulk of the literature focused merely on the rating score, some researchers centered their investigation on the content of the actual feedback comments, see Pavlou and Dimoka (2006). Recall that the eBay rating system allows users to not only rate each other but also post comments about their transaction experience.

The topic became popular not only with academic researchers but with online businesses as well. In 2003, MIT hosted its First Interdisciplinary Symposium on Online Reputation Mechanisms. The symposium received wide support from online business community as representatives of companies such as Microsoft and Epinions were in attendance. For a detailed discussion of the Symposium, please see Resnick and Dellarocas (2003).

Empirically, an auction can be considered as a two-stage process. First, an auction may or may not result in a sale; therefore, the first criterion of investigation focuses on the impact the seller's rating has on the probability of sale. Second, an English auction is a setting where the closing price is determined by the market and represents the valuation placed on the item by the bidder with the second highest willingness to pay.[3] Because of this two-stage nature of an auction outcome, the empirical literature took different approaches to investigating the impact a seller's reputation played in eBay auctions. These methods are discussed later.

Heterogeneity vs. Homogeneity

One of the main challenges faced by anyone who wishes to conduct an empirical investigation using eBay generated data is the choice of the product for data collection. Some products might exhibit significant variability in item-specific characteristics, presenting challenges for empirical investigations. For example, in the market for used textbooks, some books might be more worn out than others. If one does not control for the quality of each individual textbook, one omits an important regressor.

This induced many researches to focus on items with controlled item-specific characteristics. Such controls can come in a variety of ways. For some items, the mere presence of a photo of the actual item may be sufficient. Although, a photo does convey a lot of information to the perspective bidders, such information is not easily quantifiable into a continuous numerical variable. As a consequence, a frequently favored approach by empirical researchers was to focus on a product that had easily measurable item-specific characteristics, had a third party evaluation (certification), or was simply one that exhibited no heterogeneity.

Houser and Wooders (2006) selected Pentium processor chips in their study. Since Pentium processors are unlikely to exhibit significant item-specific variability (for each particular processor model), this practically ruled out heterogeneity. Many investigators decided to focus on items with easily measurable quality and third party certifications, e.g. collectible coins. Examples of such studies include Lucking-Reiley et al. (2007), Bajari and Hortacsu (2003), and Melnik and Alm (2002, 2005).

Another approach to address the issue of item-specific heterogeneity is to conduct a controlled experiment. This approach allows not only to control for the item-specific characteristics, but also for the behavior of the seller. One such study was done by Resnick et al. (2006) in which the same established eBay seller sold identical items using two different eBay accounts: their own established account and a new account with a zero rating (established for the purpose of the experiment). The results demonstrated that the difference in willingness to pay was about 8.1% of the selling price (Resnick et al., 2006). This study suggested a rather large penalty being placed on a new seller and highlighted the importance of the eBay rating for sellers. As discussed later, such penalties can play an important role because they increase the costs eBay sellers face when switching to a competing platform, thereby potentially reducing the competitive pressure on the platform itself.

However, item-specific heterogeneity is a double-edged sword as it also presents a unique opportunity to differentiate between the various roles the reputational mechanism plays. In the case of a product with unobserved item-specific characteristics, the seller's reputation signals two important pieces of information: the reliability of the seller in complying with the transaction's terms, and the reliability of the seller in accurately describing the item. In the case of a homogeneous good, the signaling role of the mechanism is reduced to the first of these properties only.

Melnik and Alm (2005) attempted to analyze these different signaling properties of the seller's reputation on eBay by contrasting uncertified, high quality (AU – almost uncirculated) collectible U.S. Morgan silver dollar coins with the same category coins that were certified by an independent coin grading agency. Their results indicated that the overall seller's rating played an important role in the case of the non-certified coins. However, in the case of the certified coins, the overall rating was insignificant while the negative rating had a statistically significant negative impact on the willingness to pay. It is important to note that the average prices differed sizably between these two groups of coins, with the certified coins being significantly more expensive on average ($327 versus $58). The results suggested that the negative rating conveyed the signal of the reliability of the seller when it came to complying with the terms of the transaction. This is because in the case of a more expensive item, the consequences to the buyer of the seller's failure to comply with the terms of the transaction were more severe.

eBAY RATING AND FEE MECHANISMS

Empirical Approach

We previously mentioned that an auction can be perceived as a two stage process. An auction may or may not result in a sale. And, contingent on receiving bids, the closing price is determined by the willingness to pay of the bidder with the second highest valuation. As a result of this two stage issue, a number of techniques can be used in the empirical investigation.

Estimating Willingness to Pay

One popular empirical approach has been to estimate the willingness to pay. Since willingness to pay is censored for those listings where no bids were received, i.e. the listings resulting in no sale, a censored regression technique, such as the Tobit maximum likelihood estimation method, became a popular approach. In an eBay auction, the seller has the choice of the starting (opening) price. Since opening prices can vary from listing to listing, the proposed variation of the estimation technique by Amemiya (1984) has become frequently used in studies using eBay data. Amemiya (1984) modified the Tobit model to allow for variability in the censoring point across observations. The use of this variation of the Tobit model allowed for grouping of all observations (censored, i.e. with no bids, and uncensored, i.e. with bids) into one dataset. This simplified the estimation technique to the following setup:

$$Y_i^* = X_i\beta + \varepsilon_i, \tag{1}$$

where Y^* represents the willingness to pay and is only observed for those listings that resulted in a sale. For listings with no bids, Y^* is not observed and hence is assumed to be below the opening price (P_0):

$$Y_i = Y_i^* \text{ if } Y_i^* > P_0, \text{ otherwise: } Y_i = P_0. \tag{2}$$

This allows one to construct the following log-likelihood function (for a further discussion of the use of this method in eBay data, please see Melnik & Alm, 2002):

$$l = -\frac{1}{2}\sum_{Y_i > P_0^i}\left[\left(\frac{Y_i - X_i\beta}{\sigma}\right) + \log(2\pi\sigma^2)\right] + \sum_{Y_i < P_0^i}\log\Phi\left(\frac{P_0^i - X_i\beta}{\sigma}\right), \tag{3}$$

where Φ represents the cumulative standard normal distribution and σ is the standard deviation. For empirical illustrations of this approach see Dewally and Ederington (2006), Melnik and Alm (2002, 2005), and Reiley et al. (2007).

These studies generally find that reputation has an impact on the buyer's willingness to pay in online auctions. Dewally and Ederington (2006) use data on collectible comic books and show that a higher reputation increases willingness to pay. Furthermore, they demonstrate that the effect is larger for those items that are not professionally graded (i.e. items with third-party certified product characteristics). Melnik and Alm (2002) focus on a homogeneous product, a 5 dollar U.S. gold coin which derives virtually all of its value from its gold content. They demonstrate that the seller's overall rating has a positive effect on willingness to pay and their negative reputation has a significant penalty (Melnik & Alm, 2002). Reiley et al. (2007) find that the overall reputation has no statistically significant effect, while the negative reputation significantly reduces the buyer's willingness to pay.

Probability of Sale

Another approach has been to investigate the probability of sale. Here, a simple probit or logit model is employed to investigate how the various characteristics of an auction, including the seller's rating, impact the probability of sale.

Using a logit model, Eaton (2002) demonstrated that negative feedback reduced the probability of sale. The results also showed that the seller's positive rating had no significant impact on the probability of sale (Eaton, 2002). Employing a probit model, Jin and Kato (2008) showed that the seller's positive reputation (feedback) increased the probability of sale while the negative reputation (feedback) decreased it.

Jin and Kato (2008) used collectible sports trading cards in their study and the results showed that a certification by a third party reduced the effect of the seller's negative reputation. Their findings demonstrated that the presence of certification by a credible third party reduces the uncertainty about the item. This reduces the signaling property of the seller's rating, thereby reducing its importance in the buyer's decision.

Sold Items Only

A number of studies focused on sold items only. This approach enables the researcher to directly estimate the willingness to pay of the second highest bidder using the OLS technique. However, the downside of this approach is that it ignores all observations with no bids (or in the case of the more restricted studies, one bid listings as well). It is important to note that in an English auction, the winning bid represents the willingness to pay of the bidder with the second highest valuation. This implies that listings with a single bid become censored as the second highest valuation is unobserved and lies below the observed bid. As a result, some of the studies focused on successfully completed listings only restricted their data to observations with two or more bids. For example, Houser and Wooders (2006) restricted their estimation to observations with at least two bids and showed that positive rating increased the winning bid while negative rating decreased it. Another illustration of an earlier work using sold only auctions was a study by McDonald and Slawson Jr. (2002). This study also found that a higher seller's rating resulted in a higher closing price and an increased number of bids.

eBay Seller's Rating as a Barrier to Entry

As the preceding discussion illustrates, the eBay rating mechanism has played an important role as a signal of information about the quality and reliability of the seller in an online auction. The rating mechanism enabled eBay to overcome the asymmetry of information problem in online commerce prior to the development of various forms of buyer protection. In this sense, the rating has played an important historical role in the growth and popularity of the eBay website (Brown and Morgan, 2006). However, the implications of the rating mechanism did not stop there.

The eBay rating mechanism has also created a sizable barrier to entry for competing to eBay consumer-to-consumer online platforms. Resnick et al. (2006) demonstrated that the difference between an established seller and a newcomer can be around 8.1% of the sales price. Melnik and Alm (2002) show a much smaller but still sizable impact of the seller's reputation on the realized auction price. They find the difference in the willingness to pay to be about 4.8% between an established seller and a new one. Such empirical results indicate that an established eBay seller would potentially incur a sizable price penalty if they were to shift from eBay to a competing online auction platform and start there anew. Indeed, this characteristic of eBay rating was tested in the competition with Yahoo Auctions in the U.S. market.

Fees as Incentives and Competition with Yahoo Auctions in the U.S.

Just like any for-profit business, eBay charges its customers for the services it provides. It is important to note that eBay's customers are the sellers who utilize the services of the eBay platform. The use of the eBay website has been completely fee-free to buyers since the launch of the website in 1995. Since sellers are responsible for a number of decisions, including the choice of the opening or reserve price, etc., eBay fees may be used to create incentives and influence the choices made by sellers. One such fee, the opening price fee, potentially may have played a very important role in turning eBay into the popular platform it has become.

Opening or reserve prices play an important role in auctions.[4] One objective of the opening price is to protect the seller from being forced to sell their item at too low a price, a price below the opening price. However, a higher opening price may discourage potential bidders and reduce the probability of an auction resulting in a sale. This nature of the opening price enabled eBay to potentially influence the auction outcome by creating a fee that was structured as a function of the declared opening price. A fee that rises with the opening price could effectively be used to induce sellers to lower their opening prices. In turn, lower opening prices would make listings more attractive to potential bidders and increase the probability of a sale. In the case of a fixed price listing, the price serves as the reserve price. In this case, no transaction is possible below the reserve price. Just as in the case of the opening price fee, a fee that is a function of the reserve price can also be used to induce lower reserve prices.

These characteristics of opening or reserve prices have received significant attention in economic literature. For example, Myerson (1981) showed that the choice of the reserve price can significantly impact the seller's revenue, thereby making it an important consideration factor in the seller's decision. Theoretical formulations of optimal reserve price strategies in auctions of goods with private values were constructed by Laffont and Maskin (1980) and Riley and Samuelson (1981). Levin and Smith (1996) extended the theoretical formulation to common value goods.

The emergence of eBay data enabled further empirical investigations into the effects of reserve prices in auctions. Katkar and Reiley (2006) conducted a controlled experiment on eBay to investigate the differences in the impact on the seller's revenue between hidden (eBay reserve price) and open reserve prices (eBay opening price). Similarly, Bajari and Hortacsu (2003), investigated the relationship between the reserve price and the seller's revenue on eBay. They demonstrated that lower opening values encourage bidder participation in eBay auctions. Another important theoretical extension of this literature was developed by Caillaud and Mezzetti (2004) when they expanded the analysis of auctions with reserve prices to more than one period by introducing two sequential auctions of the identical items. Another illustration of expanding the analysis into a multi-period framework is provided by Zeithammer (2007). Zeithammer (2007) develops a game model to understand the interaction between the seller and the bidders.

The relationship between the opening price, the level of bidding activity, and the auction outcome has also been investigated empirically using eBay data. For instance, Reiley demonstrated that lower reserve prices not only increase the number of bids but also increase the probability of an auction resulting in a sale (Reiley, 2006).

These studies tend to focus their attention on the strategic problem faced by the auction participants (bidders and sellers) and yet there is one more auction participant - the auctioneer. The auctioneer is capable of imposing fees on the auction participants and therefore is able to impact their behavior. The findings of the above listed studies underscore the importance of investigating the connection between the opening price (and the reserve price) and the auctioneer's fee structure. However, the volume of literature examining the effect of auction fees on the choice of opening and reserve prices is rather limited. In one such study, Melnik et al. (2009) connected the choice of the opening price on eBay to the eBay fee structure. The empirical section of their study found that a fee structure that rises with the opening price induces eBay sellers to reduce their opening prices. This connection is rather important because lower opening prices may induce higher bidder participation and increase the probability an auction results in a sale (Reiley, 2006).

The eBay Fee Structure and Its Incentive Effect

Historically, eBay employed a rising opening fee structure, referred to on eBay as the "insertion fee". An important characteristic of these fees was that they were not a function of the auction outcome and were charged at the time the item was listed. This meant that even in those cases where the listing resulted in no sales, these fees were still applied. However, these fees were structured as a function of the reserve or opening price, see Table 1. More importantly, they were structured as a rising function of the opening price, meaning that higher opening prices resulted in higher insertion fees. Table 1 reports the insertion fee schedule of eBay for 2001 (and the prior years), 2002, and 2007. These fee schedules were used during the period of competition between Yahoo Auctions and eBay for the U.S. online consumer-to-consumer auction market.

The two previously listed important characteristics of the eBay insertion fee structure converted these fees into an important incentives mechanism. Melnik et al. (2009) setup an intuitive expected revenue (E[R]) maximization problem of the seller who faces insertion fees:

$$\max_{P_0} E[R] = \int_0^{P_0} v\varphi(P)dP + \int_{P_0}^{P_m} P\varphi(P)dP - C(P_0), \quad (4)$$

Table 1. Insertion fee schedule

Opening Price ($)	Insertion Fee ($)		
	2001	2002	2007
0.01 - 0.99	0.30	0.30	0.20
1.00 - 9.99	0.30	0.35	0.40
10.00 - 24.99	0.55	0.60	0.60
24.99 - 49.99	1.10	1.20	1.20
50.00 -199.99	2.20	2.40	2.40
200.00 - 500.00	3.30	3.60	3.60
500 and up	3.30	4.80	4.80

Source: Melnik et al., 2009 and Melnik, 2011

where v represents the valuation of the item to the seller, $\phi(P)$ represents the point density function of the price distribution, P_0 is the opening price, and $C(P_0)$ is the fee structured as a function of the opening price. They derive a number of propositions, two of which are important here.

Their first proposition is that the presence of a non-refundable fee induces the seller to select an opening price below their own internal valuation, i.e. $P_0<v$.

And the second proposition is that the choice of the optimal opening price is a function of the insertion fee. Furthermore, it is a decreasing function of the fee. Melnik et al. (2009) structure the fee term as:

$$C=C_0+rP_0, \quad (5)$$

where C_0 represents all other fees and the rP_0 term represents the insertion fee. Here, the insertion fee is simply structured as a percentage of the opening price (assuming that r is restricted to be between zero and one, but less than one). This formulation allows them to construct the following proposition:

$$\partial P_0/\partial r<0. \quad (6)$$

This second proposition is an important theoretical result as it demonstrates that the optimal opening price decreases with a higher insertion fee. For further details of this model, see Melnik et al. (2009).

Melnik et al. (2009) also demonstrated empirically that eBay sellers respond to a rising insertion fee structure by lowering their opening prices. In their data, the opening price observations also appeared to cluster near the upper point of each of the steps of the fee structure. This behavior is rational as the marginal cost increases with moving into the range of the next step. Melnik et al. (2009) collected the data on a number of different items which enabled them to investigate the relationship between the opening price and the characteristics of the price distribution. They empirically demonstrated that the selection of opening prices was a function of the characteristics of the distribution of prices on eBay. Opening or reserve prices serve as a protection against low winning bids (bids below the opening price). In essence, much like any other form of insurance, the optimal opening price in an auction is a function of the degree of risk associated with receiving a low winning bid. Please note that since opening and reserve prices fulfill the same role, our discussion uses these terms synonymously. For further discussion of opening versus hidden reserve prices in eBay auctions, see Katkar and Reiley (2006).

If a rising insertion fee structure induces sellers to select lower opening or reserve prices, then it might have played a role during the competition with Yahoo Auctions. Yahoo entered the U.S. online auction market on September 14 of 1998. At that point, the hegemony of eBay was not yet established. At the time of Yahoo's entry into the online auction market in 1998, its popularity as a search engine was widespread. In 1999, Yahoo estimated that its user base (for all aspects of their business, not just auctions), was above 100 million, making it 13 times the multiple of the eBay user base at the time (Melnik, 2011).

In an attempt to lure sellers, Yahoo made its auction platform appealing to sellers. In an attempt to make its platform attractive to sellers, Yahoo did not charge any insertion fees, making listing an item on Yahoo free. Only in the case of a sale would a closing fee based on the realized price (the winning bid) be applied. This strategy achieved its objective as the number of listings on Yahoo Auctions increased quickly, but the average opening price on these listings ended up being above the average opening price on eBay (see Melnik, 2011). These differences in opening values may have played an important role in creating the differences in the rates of successful completion of listings across these two platforms. A listing can be considered as successful if it results in a sale. In essence, sellers used the Yahoo platform to advertise their items while asking higher and more attractive (for sellers) prices. However, higher opening prices reduced bidder participation, resulting in a lower success rate. On eBay, where the insertion fee structure induced lower opening prices, the successful completion rates were higher.

In essence, the eBay platform focused on attracting buyers, while the Yahoo Auctions platform focused its attention on sellers. Although no transaction can be possible without either one of these participants, ultimately, it is the buyer who makes the transaction possible. Higher participation by buyers also makes the platform more attractive to sellers, since their objective is to have their items sold.

The competition from Yahoo Auctions failed to derail the expansion of eBay, and by 2001, the number of eBay users approached 30 million, increasing rapidly between 1998 - 2001 (Melnik, 2011). In January of 2001, Yahoo Auctions introduced a small insertion fee. However, this step seemed to be too little too late in its competitive battle with eBay. Furthermore, even when the insertion fee was introduced, it came with a number of different provisions allowing sellers to waive the fee. For further discussion of the role eBay fees may have played in the eBay-Yahoo competition see Melnik et al., (2009) and Melnik, (2011).

Ultimately, the Yahoo Auctions platform in the U.S. ceased its operations in June of 2007. This sealed the hegemony of eBay in the U.S. online consumer-to-consumer auction space. Today, eBay is practically synonymous with online consumer-to-consumer auctions in the U.S.

In the last several years, perhaps in an attempt to attract more sellers, or maybe due to a reduced competitive pressure, eBay has diminished its use of insertion fees (fees based on the reserve or opening prices). Presently, eBay sellers may be eligible for a number of insertion-fee free listings each month. Depending on the category in which the item is listed, a seller can get 50 or even 100 insertion-fee free listings a month. For additional listings, the insertion fee is a flat amount of either \$0.05, or \$0.30 depending on the category and listing format.[5]

This shift in fees changed the very nature of the eBay business. Historically, eBay was established as an online auction website in the consumer-to-consumer online space. This status has evolved over time and today, most listings on eBay are fixed price listings. According to eBay Inc., in the fourth quarter of 2013, 73% of all gross merchandize volume traded on eBay was conducted at fixed prices (eBay, 2014). For comparison, the contribution of fixed price listings to the total gross merchandize volume in the last quarter of 2001 was a mere 19% (eBay, 2002). In part, this shift to fixed prices may have been stimulated by a gradual decline in the use of fees based on opening or reserve prices.

Other Empirical Research Areas Based on eBay Data

In addition to the topics covered in this chapter, the emergence of eBay facilitated a volume of research in other areas of economics and marketing. eBay is a well-developed platform that includes a number of different marketing features. This enables researchers to examine the signaling properties of these features (see Melnik & Richardson, 2011). The cross-border nature of online commerce also attracted the attention of public finance literature; see Alm and Melnik (2010).

CONCLUSION

The eBay story illustrates the evolution of consumer-to-consumer online commerce during its early development. The story shows how simple and intuitive solutions were developed to address complex problems of trust and asymmetry of information in online consumer-to-consumer commerce. One of such solutions was the eBay rating mechanism. The eBay rating mechanism was an intuitive and simple instrument designed to be easily interpreted by online users. Its ability to successfully signal the information about the past behavior of an eBay seller, helped reduce the effects of asymmetry of information in consumer-to-consumer online commerce. However, such a solution can also serve as a double-edged sword because it is capable of providing a barrier to entry for competing online consumer-to-consumer platforms. In turn, this is capable of reducing the level of competition between the online platforms.

This barrier to entry could be overcome if the seller's rating were transferable from one platform to another. A transferable measure of reputation or a measure of reputation that is independently established (outside of any particular commercial platform) would remove this barrier to entry. In fact, recent industry developments point in this direction. For instance, the creation of independent payment platforms that can establish and maintain their own ratings for their users can circumvent the barrier to entry property of the rating.

The eBay experience also underscores the importance of incentives in markets. The eBay insertion fee structure induced its sellers to lower opening prices, making their listings more attractive to bidders. This attracted more bidders leading to more auctions resulting in sales. In turn, this created an incentive for sellers to list on eBay. This simple incentive mechanism may have played an important role in ensuring eBay's success in its competition with Yahoo Auctions for the U.S. online consumer-to-consumer auction market. This also highlights the need of expanding the analysis of auctions to include another participant - the auctioneer.

The story of eBay illustrates how the basic and old economic principles of incentives can be successfully applied in a modern online environment.

REFERENCES

Akerlof, G. (1970). The market for "lemons": Quality uncertainty and the market mechanism. *The Quarterly Journal of Economics*, *84*(3), 488–500. doi:10.2307/1879431

Alm, J., & Melnik, M. (2010). Do eBay sellers comply with state sales taxes? *National Tax Journal*, *63*(2), 215–236. doi:10.17310/ntj.2010.2.02

Amemiya, T. (1984). Tobit models: A survey. *Journal of Econometrics*, *24*(1-2), 3–61. doi:10.1016/0304-4076(84)90074-5

Bajari, P., & Hortacsu, A. (2003). The winner's curse, reserve prices, and endogenous entry: Empirical insights from eBay auctions. *The Rand Journal of Economics*, *34*(2), 329–355. doi:10.2307/1593721

Bajari, P., & Hortacsu, A. (2004). Economic insights from internet auctions. *Journal of Economic Literature*, *42*(2), 457–486. doi:10.1257/0022051041409075

Bolton, G., Katok, E., & Ockenfels, A. (2004). How Effective Are Electronic Reputation Mechanisms? An Experimental Investigation. *Management Science*, *50*(11), 1587–1602. doi:10.1287/mnsc.1030.0199

Brown, J., & Morgan, J. (2006). Reputation in online markets: The market for trust. *California Management Review*, *49*(1), 61–81. doi:10.2307/41166371

Bruce, N., Haruvy, E., & Rao, R. (2004). Seller rating, price and default in online auctions. *Journal of Interactive Marketing*, *18*(4), 37–50. doi:10.1002/dir.20021

Cabral, L., & Hortacsu, A. (2010). The dynamics of seller reputation: Evidence from eBay. *The Journal of Industrial Economics*, *58*(1), 54–78. doi:10.1111/j.1467-6451.2010.00405.x

Caillaud, B., & Mezzetti, C. (2004). Equilibrium reserve prices in sequential ascending auctions. *Journal of Economic Theory*, *117*(1), 78–95. doi:10.1016/j.jet.2003.11.002

Dellarocas, C. (2003). The digitalization of word-of-mouth: Promise and challenges of online reputation measures. *Management Science*, *49*, 1407–1424. doi:10.1287/mnsc.49.10.1407.17308

Dewally, M., & Ederington, L. (2006). Reputation, certification, warranties, and information asymmetries: Lessons from the online comic book market. *The Journal of Business*, *79*(2), 693–730. doi:10.1086/499169

Dewan, S., & Hsu, V. (2004). Adverse selection in electronic markets: Evidence from online stamp auctions. *The Journal of Industrial Economics*, *52*(4), 497–516. doi:10.1111/j.0022-1821.2004.00237.x

Dini, F., & Spagnolo, G. (2009). Buying reputation on eBay: Do recent changes help? *International Journal of Electronic Business*, *7*(6), 581–598. doi:10.1504/IJEB.2009.029048

Eaton, D. H. (2002). Valuing information: Evidence from guitar auctions on eBay. Working Paper. Murray, KY: Murray State University.

eBay Inc., (2002). *eBay Announces Fourth Quarter and Year End 2001 Financial Results.* Retrieved from http://investor.ebayinc.com/financial_releases.cfm

eBay Inc., (2014). *eBay Reports Fourth Quarter and Full Year 2013 Results.* Retrieved from http://investor.ebayinc.com/financial_releases.cfm

Houser, D., & Wooders, J. (2006). Reputation in auctions: Theory, and Evidence from eBay. *Journal of Economics & Management Strategy*, *15*(2), 353–369. doi:10.1111/j.1530-9134.2006.00103.x

Jin, G. Z., & Kato, A. (2008). Price, quality, and reputation: Evidence from an online field experiment. *The Rand Journal of Economics*, *37*(4), 983–1005. doi:10.1111/j.1756-2171.2006.tb00067.x

Katkar, R., & Reiley, D. (2006). Public versus secret reserve prices in eBay auctions: Results from a pokémon field experiment. *Advances in Economic Analysis & Policy*, *6*(2), 1–23.

Klemperer, P. D. (1999). Auction theory: A guide to the literature. *Journal of Economic Surveys*, *13*(3), 227–286. doi:10.1111/1467-6419.00083

Laffont, J., & Maskin, E. (1980). Optimal reservation price. *Economics Letters*, *6*(4), 309–313. doi:10.1016/0165-1765(80)90002-6

Levin, D., & Smith, J. (1996). Optimal reservation prices in auctions. *The Economic Journal*, *106*(438), 1271–1283. doi:10.2307/2235520

Livingston, J. A. (2005). How valuable is a good reputation? A sample selection model of internet auctions. *The Review of Economics and Statistics*, *87*(3), 453–465. doi:10.1162/0034653054638391

McDonald, C. G., & Slawson, V. C. Jr. (2002). Reputation in an internet auction market. *Economic Inquiry*, *40*(4), 533–650. doi:10.1093/ei/40.4.633

Melnik, M. I. (2011). Listing fees and their role on eBay: Evidence from a natural experiment. *Journal of Internet Commerce*, *10*(4), 1–21. doi:10.1080/15332861.2011.622695

Melnik, M. I., & Alm, J. (2002). Does a seller's reputation matter? Evidence from eBay auctions. *The Journal of Industrial Economics*, *50*(3), 337–349. doi:10.1111/1467-6451.00180

Melnik, M. I., & Alm, J. (2005). Seller reputation, information signals, and prices for heterogeneous coins on eBay. *Southern Economic Journal*, *72*(2), 305–328. doi:10.2307/20062113

Melnik, M. I., Richardson, P., & Tompkins, D. (2011). How seller and product characteristics impact promotion on eBay. *Journal of Promotion Management*, *17*(4), 426–437. doi:10.1080/10496491.2011.597317

Melnik, M. I., Xu, Y., & Alm, J. (2009). The choice of opening prices on eBay. *The Manchester School Journal*, *77*(4), 411–429. doi:10.1111/j.1467-9957.2009.02105.x

Myerson, R. (1981). Optimal auction design. *Mathematics of Operations Research*, *6*(1), 58–73. doi:10.1287/moor.6.1.58

Pavlou, P., & Dimoka, A. (2006). The nature and role of feedback text comments in online marketplaces: Implications for trust building, price premiums, and seller differentiation. *Information Systems Research*, *17*(4), 392–414. doi:10.1287/isre.1060.0106

Reiley, D. H. (2000). Auctions on the internet: What's being auctioned and how? *The Journal of Industrial Economics*, *48*(3), 227–252. doi:10.1111/1467-6451.00122

Reiley, D. H. (2006). Field experiments on the effects of reserve prices in auctions: More Magic on the Internet. *The Rand Journal of Economics*, *37*(1), 195–211. doi:10.1111/j.1756-2171.2006.tb00012.x

Reiley, D. H., Bryan, D., Prasad, N., & Reeves, D. (2007). Pennies from eBay: The determinants of price in online auctions. *The Journal of Industrial Economics*, *55*(2), 223–233. doi:10.1111/j.1467-6451.2007.00309.x

Resnick, P., & Dellarocas, C. (2003). Online Reputation Mechanisms: A Roadmap for Future Research. *Technical report, First Interdisciplinary Symposium on Online Reputation Mechanisms*. Retrieved from http://ccs.mit.edu/dell/symposium.html#publications

Resnick, P., Zeckhauser, R., Swanson, J., & Lockwood, K. (2006). The value of reputation on eBay: A controlled experiment. *Experimental Economics*, *9*(2), 79–101. doi:10.1007/s10683-006-4309-2

Riley, J., & Samuelson, W. (1981). Optimal auctions. *The American Economic Review*, *71*, 381–392.

Standifird, S. (2001). Reputation and e-commerce: eBay auctions and the asymmetrical impact of positive and negative ratings. *Journal of Management*, *27*(3), 279–295. doi:10.1177/014920630102700304

U.S. Department of the Census. (2013). The 2011 E-commerce multi-sector E-Stats report. Retrieved from http://www.census.gov/econ/estats/

Wolford, J. (2013). eBay Seller Sues Buyer Over Negative Feedback. *WebProNews*. Retrieved from http://www.webpronews.com/ebay-seller-sues-buyer-over-negative-feedback-2013-04

Zeithammer, R. (2007). Optimal Selling in Dynamic Auctions: Adaptation versus Commitment. *Marketing Science*, *26*(6), 859–867. doi:10.1287/mksc.1070.0269

KEY TERMS AND DEFINITIONS

Asymmetry of Information: Transaction participants have access to different information relevant to the transaction.

eBay Rating: A numerical representation of the user's past-transaction based feedback on eBay.

Hidden Reserve Price: A reserve price that is unknown to the auction bidders.

Insertion Fee: An eBay term used for fees applied at the time the listing/auction on eBay is launched.

Opening Price: The starting price in an auction.

Reserve Price: For a seller, this is the lowest price in an auction at which the seller agrees to sell the item.

Willingness to Pay: The maximum amount a buyer is willing to pay for an item.

ENDNOTES

1 For further discussion on asymmetry of information, please see Akerlof (1970).

2 Note that this does not remove the possibility of fraud. Since the cost of establishing an eBay account is low, multiple accounts can be generated by a single user and then used to generate the rating.

3 eBay uses fixed price listings and auctions of English design only (rising price).

4 The use of the terms opening price and reserve price requires a clarification. EBay labels the price at which an auction is listed as the opening price, while the term reserve price is used to describe a hidden reserve price, the lowest price at which the seller agrees to sell their item on eBay. In the context of the existing auction literature, the role of the opening price on eBay is similar to that of the reservation price.

5 Current eBay fee policies can be accessed online at: http://pages.ebay.com/help/sell/fees.html

Chapter 16
Successful New Product Planning

Nicholas Grigoriou
Monash University, Malaysia

ABSTRACT

Successful organizations continually operate in a state of innovation in terms of the offerings they produce, frequently introducing new products or modifying and improving existing products as needed and by the market. The means of conceptualizing, designing, and marketing new products is known as new product development. Successful new product development is a considerable challenge for any market oriented organization. The cost of designing and developing new products is increasing while the rate of success of new products is not. Marketing managers are constantly looking for ways to improve their new product development process. This necessitates, among other things, linking an organization's capabilities and resources with the new product demands of the markets they serve. This chapter considers some of the internal process any market driven organization should focus on to improve the likelihood that their new products will enjoy market success.

INTRODUCTION

The continuous development and introduction of new product offerings is considered an important strategy for a firm's continued success. New products can enhance a firm's overall performance by satisfying customer needs more effectively than existing products or competitors' offerings. As such, a firm's success is partially contingent on the success of new product development (Salomo et al. 2007; 2008). This implies that firms are oriented towards the markets they serve, a managerial paradigm known as *market orientation*. Shapiro (1988) suggest that a firm is *market oriented* if information on all important customers and buying influences permeates every corporate function, so that strategic and tactical decisions are made inter-functionally and inter-divisionally, and these well-coordinated decisions are executed with a sense of commitment. A customer orientation is posited to improve overall firm performance (Deshpande et al. 1993).

DOI: 10.4018/978-1-4666-8459-1.ch016

An alternative definition of *market orientation* favored by marketing scholars comes from the work of Narver and Slater (1990: 21) who define it as '*the organization culture that most effectively and efficiently creates the necessary behaviors for the creation of superior value for buyers and, thus, continuous superior performance for the business.*' Customer orientation, according to Narver and Slater (1990), requires a sufficient understanding of consumer needs to create goods and services of superior value. As such, their definition of *market orientation* confirms to the central notion of the marketing concept (Deshpande & Farley, 1999), a notion that the entire purpose of any business is to '*create a customer*' (Drucker, 1954, p. 39) such that '*the whole business is seen from the point of view of its final result, that is, from the customer's point of view*' (ibid).

Some scholars have recognized the existence between market orientation and new product development and an organization's market orientation. The role of market orientation as an antecedent of organizational performance has been extensively studied in various contexts (Deshpande & Farley, 2004; Narver & Slater, 1990; Voss & Voss, 2000). Previous new product performance-market orientation research has yielded mixed results. For example, Langerak, Hultink, and Robben (2004) found no significant link between the two variables, whereas Subramanian and Gopalakrishna (2001) found a significant impact on new product performance, as a result of an organization's market orientation.

Whilst a market oriented/customer focused approach to new product development makes sense from a marketing perspective, scholars have raised concerns about the positive impact market orientation has on new product development, and in particular product innovation (Zhang & Duan, 2010). For instance, Bennett and Cooper (1979) posit that a strong market orientation may lead to imitations and marginally new products, whilst Leonard-Barton and Doyle (1996) find that listening too closely to current markets can constitute a barrier to launching new technology and leads to reduced competitiveness. In an earlier work, Lawton and Parasuraman (1980) found no significant relationship between implementation of the marketing concept (that is, market orientation) and product innovation.

Two specific concerns of having too much managerial focus on market orientation are prevalent in the literature. The first is posited by Berthon, et al. (1999) who suggest a market orientation may detract from product innovation. The second, proposed by Frosch (1996) suggests that it may lead to myopic research and development (a cornerstone in new product development and product innovation). It is these two positions that form the underpinning work of this chapter. That is not to say that I don't believe market orientation-product development (and subsequent market performance) relationship is not important. The work of Atuahene-Gima (1995) provides evidence of this causal relationship. Indeed, there has been sufficient empirical evidence to suggest that market orientation has influenced many aspects of marketing practice such as *advertising expenditure* (Ozturan et al. 2014), *distribution channel management* (Langerak, 2001), *pricing strategies* (Jobber & Ellis-Chadwick, 2005), *customer relationship management* (Tuominan et al. 2004), *innovation* (Atuahene-Gima, 1996), and *service quality* (Chang & Chen, 1998). Rather, I adopt the view that market orientation is only useful to successful new product development, if the insights gathered from such a managerial outlook are used to improve internal new product development practices. As such, the stance taken in this chapter takes an internal (e.g. successful managerial practices in new product development) rather than an external approach (e.g. market factors) to new product development.

BACKGROUND

Research has shown that there is a great need for more systematic research to advance the understanding of new product development and the strategic decisions associated with developing new products (Leonidou, 1996; 1998).

The prevailing view of products from a marketing viewpoint is that products are a bundle of attributes and that customer utility is a function of those product attributes (Ailawadi, Neslin & Gedenk, 2001; Krishnan and Ulrich, 2001). As such, managerial decision makers are charged with the responsibility of developing new products that are sought by targeted consumers, and these products form part of the new product development (Landwehr et al. 2012). Scholars have considered new product development from various perspectives. These include *process performance and product attractiveness* (Brown & Eisenhardt, 1995; Landwehr et al. 2012), *market conditions* (Cooper & Kleinschmidt, 1994), *research and development execution* (Maidique & Zirger, 1984), competitive advantage (Frambach, Prahbu, & Verhallen, 2003), *information sharing among new product development team members* (Song & Parry, 1994; 1997), *resource commitment* (Lages & Montgomery, 2004; Maidique & Zirger, 1984), *research and development* (Atuahene-Gima & Evangelista, 2000), *decision making* (Krishnan and Ulrich, 2001), and *timeliness of international product rollout* (Chryssochoidis & Wong, 1998). Given this diversity, Krishnan and Ulrich (2001, p.1) provide a useful operational definition of product development as *'transformation of a market opportunity into a product available for sale.'*

Another stream of new product development research explores the factors that lead to success (or failure) of new products. Notably, Brown and Eisenhardt (1995) developed a model that highlights the distinction between process performance and product effectiveness and the importance of agents, including team members, project leaders, senior management, customers and suppliers, whose behaviour affects the successful (or otherwise) outcomes of new product development. They found that new product development is a critical means by which members of organizations diversify, adapt, and re-invent their firms to match the evolving market conditions. They conclude product development is among the essential processes of success, survival, and renewal of firms, particularly for firms in either fast paced or highly competitive markets. That is, products are more likely to be success when the product has marketplace advantages, is targeted at an attractive market, and is well executed through excellent internal organization (Sheremata, 2000).

The underlying rationale of the Brown and Eisenhardt model appears to be that although technical and market changes can never be fully controlled, proactive product development can influence the competitive success. Another important issue stemming from the Brown and Eisenhardt (1995) study is that successful new product development is the result of:

- Careful planning of a superior product for an attractive market;
- The execution of that plan by competent and well-coordinated cross-functional teams (Durmusoglu, Calantone & McNally, 2013) that operate with
- The blessings of senior management.

This chapter examines the role that agents, new product development teams, project leaders, and senior management play in successful, market driven new product development.

NEW PRODUCT DEVELOPMENT BEST PRACTICE

Issues/Controversies/Problems

New product development has a significant role in building competitive advantage and can contribute significantly to a firm's growth and profitability. Although product development is widely recognized as a potentially vital source of competitive advantage, firms still struggle to find effective processes and management activities for new product development (Salomo et al. 2007). Specifically, the need to engage in product innovation has become increasingly important as firms face the threat of loss of growth and profit if they are not able to keep pace with changes in consumer demand for products in their industries (Christensen & Overdorf, 2000). Cooper and Kleinschmidt (1994) indicated that getting products to market on or before routine has a positive connection with financial efficiency of a new item venture. Ali et al. (1995) revealed that quicker new product development results in firms reaching their break-even status in shorter time. Gupta and Souder's (1998) analysis revealed that shorter new product development cycle-time firms display greater sales, benefit and come back on value than those with longer cycle-times.

Any firm that undertakes new product development will develop internal resources over time that make repetition easier (Wernerfelt, 2005). This chapter examines these resources from the standpoint of internal planning and process activities as central practices of new product development. Different organizations will make different choices and may use different methods, but all of them make decisions about a range of issues such as the product concept, product architecture, configuration, team member selection, and project schedules (Krishnan & Ulrich, 2001). Each of these decisions affects, to some extent, organizational performance.

What Makes New Products 'Successful?'

Firms must development and market new products for ongoing survival. Given the commercial imperative that new products represent to their owners, knowledge of what makes new products successful is of great importance to marketing managers. One such ingredient *is differentiation.* Such uniqueness separates one product from a competing offering. Components of differentiation include: visual benefits, value for money, and superior (product) quality (Cooper, 1996; Montoya-Weiss & Calantone, 1994). Whilst designing and developing different products is a known component of the new product development process, knowing the *right* differences (that is, product attributes) to embed in a new product and the right *amount* of differences (not too many, not too few) is a significant managerial challenge. Whilst marketing research is useful in determining the level of product differentiation, recruiting and training new product development teams who can design the differences and embed them into new products is a significant managerial challenge.

A second factor for new product success is *time to market*, or commercializing a product in time to embrace market opportunities (Cohen et al. 1996). This is an issue of timing. Products that are late in being launched onto the market often miss out on sales, profit, or market share advantages which are lost to more agile competitors. Faster new product development has been associated with better initial market performance (Ali et al. 1995). The focal challenge here is not so much the timeliness of the product launch, rather the development and timely launch of a new product without compromising product quality or safety. Such compromises can be avoided when:

- The product development scope and scale has been carefully mapped out, approved by senior management, and explained in detail to the new product development team members;
- New product development activities are performed, wherever possible, concurrently.

Both the mapping and the concurrent activities must form part of management's thinking of new product development. This thinking and subsequent practice needs to occur at the start of the new product development cycle.

A third ingredient in new product development success is to have a defined *new product development system*. These internal new product development systems center on processes that move product from the initial idea/concept through to commercialization/launch. The marketing literature refers to such processes as stage-gate approaches. A stage-gate process is a conceptual and operational blueprint for moving new product projects from idea to launch and beyond. It serves as a map for managing the new product development (NPD) process to improve effectiveness and efficiency. It maps out what needs to be done, how it should be done, and who needs to do it (Cooper, 2008). Unfortunately, whilst many organizations have developed their own stage-gate models, too often these approaches to new product development fail. Suggested reasons for such failure include: missed timelines, missing steps and activities, poor organizational design and leadership, inadequate quality of execution, and the reliance unreliable data (Cooper, 2008). Figure 1 illustrates a basic stage-gate model.

The stage-gate approach to new product development depicted in Figure 1 is potentially misleading. Whilst the model looks linear, there is in fact much looping, iterations, and back-and-forth play as the project proceeds; some activities are undertaken sequentially, others in parallel, and others overlapping. It should also be noted that the model is not as rigid as it looks. For instance, not all new product development projects pass through every stage of the model. As such, the model is not a set of mandatory procedures that must be adhered to in every new product development circumstance. The challenge for new product development managers is to establish a flexible product development system that incorporates the multiple facets of the stage-gate model. Such flexibility is often compromised (usually, for a more rigid, linear approach) under related product development pressures (for example, time to market-product release).

A fourth ingredient in new product development success is the necessity to *design innovative products*. There is agreement on the significance of a number of specific actions for successful new product development. They can be grouped in actions that aim at the recognition of possibilities and other basic actions in the advance stage of the new product development and organisational routines that aim at

Figure 1. A Basic Stage-Gate Model for New Product Development (Cooper, 2008).
Activities: *Information gathering activities by the project team*
Integrated Analysis: *An integrated analysis of the results of the activities by the project team*
Deliverables: *The result of integrated analysis, that is, input to the Gate*
Go/Kill: *A Go/Kill decision point, that is, results are assessed and a decision to invest more is made*

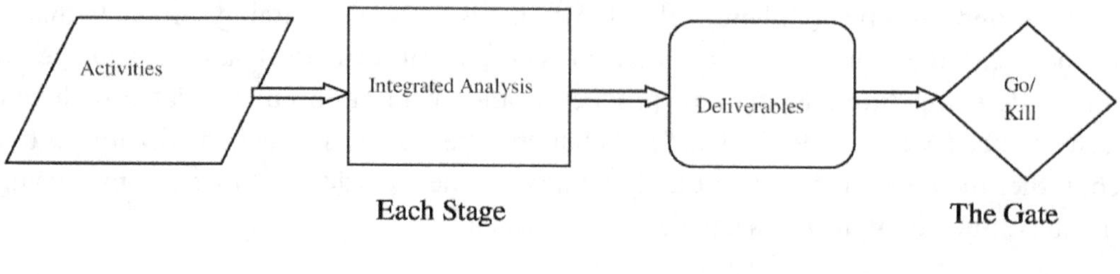

structuring and planning the product development process. These actions and organisational routines are the noticeable artifacts of what can be known as the firm's product innovation culture (Enzing et al. 2011). Success in product innovation relies on two key ingredients: the technological sources and the abilities in the firm to oversee them. The firm's ability to manage the resources pertains to its organisational process, also generally known as "routines" or styles of present exercise and learning. These processes are the nature of the firm's powerful capabilities and are the foundation for its competitive advantage (Teece et al. 1997, p. 518). Within these routines the particular behavior of firm has developed as a result of doing things over a period of time; the present exercise is what has showed up to perform well. A firm's routines consist of how innovative processes are handled, how new product development teams are formed, and their product development tasks are organized and supervised. They can be described as including recognized series of activities for challenge projects including an assortment of technological innovation and methods, official techniques but also casual routines (Levitt & March, 1988). These routines are constantly changing when new methods turn out to perform better than the old ones. Therefore, managing the transition from existing to new routines is a significant managerial challenge within new product development. Forecasting when these routine changes are likely to occur is imperative.

A fifth and final imperative of new product success involves the notion that firms should involve both suppliers and consumers in the new product development process. Such *supplier and customer involvement* is often neglected because firms see the new product development process as something that is confidential and cannot be shared with external stakeholders. They believe the commercial viability of the new product development project is potentially threatened if information about the new product makes its way onto the market, from which more agile competitors could benefit and thus potentially gain a competitive advantage. Despite this, there is a growing body of literature (e.g. Koh et al. 2007; Lin et al. 2010; Zhao et al. 2011) suggesting organizations enjoy better product related market-based performance if customers and suppliers are involved in the new product development project. Such thinking makes sense since customers and suppliers form the external knowledge sources upon which new product development projects are based (Lau et al. 2010). Indeed, research has found that customer and supplier involvement helps identify the appropriate market opportunities, leads to better new product idea generation and reduces the likelihood of poor product design (Lin et al. 2010). Further, Monckza et al. (2000) found that customer and supplier involvement lead to higher quality (fewer defect) products, reduced product development costs, shorter development lead times, and fewer engineering changes. This suggests that an organization's ability to manage external sources within its supply chain is considered key component in achieving the role of product innovator within a new product development framework (Fossas-Alalla et al. 2010). In other words, product development and product innovation are no longer imperatives that happen solely within the firm, but rather they involve the organization's total supply chain, notable within this being the crucial role played by the supplier (Schiele, 2006).

In light of the customer and supplier integration in the new product development process, the challenge facing marketing managers is: how do we do this? One approach is to consider leverage lead users of the new product. Empirical evidence supports such an initiative (Schreier & Prügl, 2008). Lead users are those consumers who are ahead of important market trends and who experience benefits from product innovations. The provide firms with useful information about future trends in product demand and product use. They also act as agents to communicate the benefits of new product innovations to the rest of the market. The use of lead users is common in both consumer product and industrial product markets. Firms typically identify lead users through marketing research.

The Role of a Supply Chain in New Product Development

Since supply chain management is the systematic and strategic coordination of traditional business functions, new product development managers should pay significant attention to their supply chains to develop products that gain competitive advantage in the market. Merely having a supply chain does not guarantee new product development success. Supply chain *integration* is a mandatory ingredient in the new product development process, and is one of the most important aspects of supply chain management as it highlights the integrated nature of supply chain partners which is essential for the efficiency and effectiveness of managing information and capital flows along the supply chain (Lau, 2011). This involvement may range from basic ongoing consultation with suppliers on design ideas, to making suppliers fully responsible for the design of components or systems they will supply. Suppliers may even be involved at different stages of the new product development process (Petersen et al. 2005). For instance, early supplier involvement is a key coordinating process in supply chain design, product design and process design. As such, an integrated supply chain also represents the strategic integration of internal resources across different departments into the product development process (Mishra and Shah, 2009). Despite the benefits of supply chain integration into the new product development process, there are questions marketing managers need to address. For example, what mechanisms allow product design, manufacturing process design, and supply chain design decisions to be coordinated. Who is responsible for this coordination? When should the coordination commence? The answers to these questions will undoubtedly lead to trade-offs within the firm (Forza et al. 2005). How should these trade-offs be managed in a manner that minimizes the disruption to the new product development process and achieves the desired organizational outcomes?

Linking New Product Development with R&D

Integrating the marketing and research and development (R&D) functions has been widely acknowledged as an important factor in new product development (Ernst et al. 2010; Troy et al. 2008). Much conceptual and scientific research has been dedicated to the collaboration between marketing and R&D because both functional areas are necessary for successful new product development. Whilst marketing is responsible for a variety of actions that provide appropriate details for the entire new product development project, research and development is mainly concerned with the generation of new technical details and applying these details to design new products. Both marketing and R&D need to be synchronized in a manner where both functions share information to develop a new product that fit the industry requirements and produces acceptable financial profits to the firm. This is improved through an advanced level of cross-functional collaboration between R&D and marketing during the new product development process (Griffin & Hauser, 1996).

Since new product development is a process, where each stage is dependent upon the stages before and after it, getting the early stage of the new product development process correct influences how later stages in the process are undertaken by the marketing and R&D teams. Getting the early stages of the new product development process is critical given that 75 per cent of all costs within the new product development process are consumed in the idea generation to idea conception (i.e. early) stage (Gebhard, 2003). To underscore this point further, 85 per cent of product development time is invested in products that never reach the market (Bauer, 2004).

The initial phase or the *fuzzy front end* is one primary factor for the success of new product development. Cooper (2008) and Cooper and Kleinscmidt (1994) posit that the initial phase in product development as the stages which distinguishes the winners from the losers. The *fuzzy front end*, a term coined by Smith and Reinertsen (1991), is considered the first stage of the New Product Development process and covers the period from the generation of an idea to its approval for development or its termination (Murphy and Kumar, 1997). As products are described in the concept creation and concept development stages, the *fuzzy front end of innovation* shifts its focus to product designers. Tasks that designers face during this stage include: idea creation, the assessment of ideas, and their concretion in form of product specifications. The *fuzzy front end* is defined by his risk and the constant creation of new and relevant knowledge (Klunder, 2006). The information is produced and instantly used in non-linear line work steps. Information from several stakeholders in product development is needed to guarantee the project will meet the market and user specifications. To create effective new products firms use several methods to figure out the customers' specifications. The incorporation of end-users and other stakeholders into new product development processes leads to decreased risk, such as the innovation and market acceptance of new products.

The Role of Product Development in Organizational Performance

Moving closer to the heart of the current research concern, the product or service offering - organizational performance link has been given considerable attention in the literature (Qian, 2002). For example, Ulrich (1995) argues that a product's 'architecture', defined as the scheme by which the function of a product is allocated physical components, can be a key driver of the performance of an organization. The functionality of a product is the basic purpose it serves (Guo, Hao & Shang, 2011). Ulrich (1995) posits that an organization has substantial latitude in choosing a product's architecture and that the architecture of the product is important to managerial decision making, since a product's function is often linked with the country in which it is made, or the country to which it is being sold (Keller & Moorthi, 2003). Product development then, should offer the greatest opportunities for a firm to generate sufficient revenue to meet its profit objectives (Qian, 2002). From a new product development perspective, Prahalad (1990) posits that the long term performance of firms is based on their ability to develop product and process innovations.

An organization's tangible or intangible offering is its most visible source of profit. Not surprisingly then, the innovation of such offering is a key managerial decision that directly affects organizational performance (Audretsch, 1995). An 'innovation' is defined as the commercial introduction of a new product, process or service, and organizations have used technology as a means by which to develop their innovative product or service offering (Scherer and Ross, 1990).

Extending the notion of 'product as a profit generator', having appropriate product diversity among an organization's offerings was found to have a positive effect on organizational performance (Gruca and Rego, 2005). Product diversity refers to the degree of relatedness among various product segments (Abernethy et al., 2005). Marketing and product diversification are two important directions for corporate expansion (Qian, 2002). To better understand the effect that product diversity can have on an organization's profit, Rumelt (1982) suggests that there are two types of product diversity. Related product diversification refers to a situation organizations diversify within industries, while unrelated diversification occurs when organizations diversify across industries. The relative costs and profits of such product diversification are likely to depend on the interrelationships between the different business activities of the organization (Qian, 1997). Organizations with related businesses can avoid duplicate facilities and individual business units can provide for themselves and related businesses. This should result in lower fixed costs and a decrease in average costs, assisting the organization to become profitable (Qian, 2002).

Whilst product diversity takes a macro view of product management, product variety is its micro equivalent. Product variety refers to the number of different products offered by an organization at a single point in time (Randall and Ulrich, 2001). Generally, the greater the variety of product offering, the greater the inventory and production costs an organization incurs. Product variety costs usually have a flow on effect to the cost of employing intermediaries who carry the organization's products to the chosen markets. These costs need to be covered to achieve organizational profit. An important challenge for marketing managers is to find the right balance of macro/micro product diversity in a manner that maximizes organizational performance.

Formation of New Product Development Teams

The value of teams in new product development is indisputable. Understanding the conditions that facilitate teamwork has long been a pursuit of scholarly and practitioner interest. Composed of members drawn from different functions, new product development teams must integrate their expertise in multiple areas to conceptualize, develop, and commercialize new products (Edmondson & Nembhard, 2009). A diverse team will increase the team's overall effectiveness. When people are blended together with different backgrounds, different knowledge bases, and different preferences, a more productive new product development team emerges. For example, teams having all members who are detail-oriented will surely miss the big picture. Conversely, a team of only analytical people might miss the true product value because the data tell them differently (Brethauer, 2002).

Mital et al. (2001) suggest that for product development teams to succeed, they must be multifunctional *and* empowered. This means that -:

- Teams comprise members from all basic functions: research and development, engineering design, production, quality, and sales and marketing.
- Each member of the team represents the team and his or her "function," not the department and its "territory."
- Teams devote most of their time to project planning and product development.
- The team members share excellent communication and are in constant contact with each other.
- The entire team is accountable for the entire project.
- The team is led by a strong and motivating leader.
- The firm's management strongly supports the project, the team, and the team leader.

The development of new products is a very complex process that requires the participation of different functional areas of the firm (Vales and Avella, 2003). The more complex the product, the larger the number and arguably the heterogeneity of the people involved in the development effort. In the firm, people, working on one or a small number of projects each, are arranged according to their technological skills. Thus, people with similar technological qualifications type the primary building blocks of the official confirming collections. The extent of the expertise depends on the level of skills that the individual team member needs to accomplish. Team members with varied expertise (e.g. marketing, engineering, finance) have competing interests in seeing new products developed and launched. This fact is exacerbated by tight time-to-market deadlines, shorter product life cycles, increasing rates of technical obsolescence, changing market needs, and the interdisciplinary nature of new product development team work. Indeed, the mere formation of teams, specifically team member selection poses great challenges for senior management. Thus, greater cooperation among functional areas is essential for successful new product development. Despite these process challenges, teams are increasingly popular in business organizations for new product development (McDonough, 2000).

The use of new product development teams has beneficial effects that are both internal and external to the firm. Internally, successful teams have accelerated the product development cycle, reduced development costs, and increased the quality of new products (Sarin & Mahajan, 2001), whilst externally new product development teams are associated with increased product success in the market (Valle and Avella, 2003). The new product team, whether temporary or permanent, is the epicenter of innovation work. As such, the success of a new product development project relies on the capabilities of the team that is accountable for its conceptualization, ingredients, growth, and commercialization. The new product development team needs to be experienced in a variety of projects, such as effectively establishing a product and perfectly predicting sales. How well the team's technical and marketing proficiencies are used in NPD decides a venture's failing or achievements (Song & Parry 1997).

Much of the success of new products stems from their perceived quality by consumers. As such, a focal aspect of any new product development team is to determine the requisite quality of any product as demanded by the targeted consumer and in line with the firm's overall product strategy. Whilst the role of product quality is widely acknowledged as a recipe for market competitiveness and firm success, little is known about how new product development teams affect product quality. The mere cross disciplinary and cross functionality of new product teams does not guarantee the development of quality products (Bounds et al. 1994). The ability of a team to produce a high-quality outcome can be helped or harmed by contextual influences on the team (Bounds et al. 1994). Therefore, in, it is necessary to understand how various contextual influences affect new product quality. One such factor is time pressure.

Time Related Pressures in New Product Development

Time related factors in decision making have been of interest to scholars. For instance Payne et al. (1996) posit that decision making errors may result from deciding too soon, or from delaying decisions too long. Delays can result in lost market opportunities or reductions in payoffs from the most accurate decision. Their study subjects were generally adaptive to opportunity cost time pressure. However failures in new product development were identified when choice environment properties with conflicting implications for customisation were present simultaneously. In particular, the Payne et al. (1996) study demonstrates that under opportunity cost time pressure, subjects received a lower expected payoff when the goal was to emphasize choice accuracy than when the goal was to emphasize savings in costs. Payne et al. (1996) posit that the longer the delays in making new product development related decisions, the lower the expected return (value) from even the most accurate decision. An implication for marketing managers is that if the firm delays of the introduction of a new product into a market to conduct test marketing, competitors may become aware of the test marketing, develop their own offer for the same market, and introduce their offer before the test marketing has been completed.

Research suggests three major ways in which people respond to decision problems under time pressure. First, processing tends to be more selective under time pressure, focusing more on the important and/or negative information (Maule et al. 2000). Second, decision strategies may shift as a function of increased time pressure (Kocher & Sutter, 2006) and finally, new product development team members accelerate their processing, that is, they spend less time processing each item of information, under time pressure (Maule et al. 2000).

These findings alert marketing manager to the possible compromises associated with their decision making process. They suggest executives need to plan decisions such as which markets to target the new product into, or how best to develop the product for a given market, in such a way as to reduce the amount of time pressure.

As noted, decision makers tend to speed up the execution of their decision strategies or switch to simpler decisions under time pressure (Lin at al., 2008). When faced with high levels of time constraint, decision makers tend to rely most heavily on negative information (Greitmeyer et al., 2006). Under time constraint, decision makers either filter information that is used, or omit certain information from consideration altogether (Farhoom & Drury, 2002). Marketing managers are often charged with making timely decisions so as to embrace a particular marketing opportunity, and such opportunities are usually time bound.

Cognitive Consensus and Teams in Group Decision Making

Larson and LaFasto (1989) developed an instrument to measure teamwork, based on in-depth interviews with nationally recognized leaders from varying organization types and industries. The items are clustered into a set of factors which could be expected as characteristics of high performing teams making product development decisions. Clear organizational goals, from which clear product goals can be derived is an expectation that most team members would have of a decision making group and its leaders. Having a result driven structure implies that marketing organizations would be expected to establish an organizational structure that supports the manufacture and marketing of products. Unified commitment and collaborative climate suggest that marketing managers will require commitment not only from the organization's senior management, but also commitment from other business units within the organization. For instance, the marketing department may require the research and development department to assist in developing appropriate designs the new product. Clear and appropriate standards of excellence and competent team members are crucial, as is a carefully considered composition of the decision making group. Finally, external support and recognition and principled leadership suggest the key roles of leadership in the new product development team.

Groups are frequently employed to provide different types of expertise and to ensure cognitive quality (having properly thought the issue through) and also the acceptability of decisions within the organization. The quality of strategic decisions by top management influences organizational performance (Miles et al., 1978). The cognitive quality of the decisions reached has long been of interest to researchers for example, Mohammed and Ringseis (2001) investigated antecedents and correlates of cognitive consensus, finding that unanimity decision rule groups achieved more cognitive consensus than majority rule groups. The notion of cognitive consensus is also central to a study by Mohammed and Ringseis (2001). Further, they define *cognitive consensus* as the similarity among group members regarding how key decision issues are defined and conceptualized. Therefore, cognitive consensus assists the group in operating as a unified structure. Mohammed and Ringseis sought an understanding of factors that facilitate groups in achieving consensus, processes related to shared assumptions, and consequences of arriving at more of a group representation of the issues.

These findings suggested that cognitive consensus was positively influenced by expectations regarding decision implementation and satisfaction. Achieving greater cognitive consensus may be necessary for the medium and long-term productivity of the new product development group. There is no reason to expect that marketers making product related decisions would not reap these benefits from the use of consensus based team approaches. The findings may have implications for consideration of where the new product development product decisions are made (that is, head office or subsidiary locations or both).

Van Kippenberg and Schippers (2007) support the view that top management teams with diverse capabilities made more innovative, higher quality decisions than teams with less diverse capabilities. Does the size and resource base of marketing organization influence the quality of the new product development decisions? This important question has been given little attention in the product development literature, yet has significant managerial implications for new product development.

The effective implementation of a strategic decision requires the active cooperation of the group members (West, 2002) with senior management (Chen et al. 2005). Such active cooperation is important because strategic decisions are rarely articulated in full detail (Love et al. 2002). New product development team members need confidence in the group's procedures and decisions, rather mere grudging acceptance. Group members who merely comply with decisions may begin to distance themselves from the group during the decision implementation phase (Verzberger, 1994).

The Use of Virtual Teams in New Product Development

Virtual teams, in which members use technology to interact with one another across geographic, organizational, and other boundaries, are becoming common in organizations (Gibson &Cohen, 2003). Contrasted with face to face teams, members of virtual teams are not constrained to one physical location and can be located throughout the world (Montoya-Weiss et al. 2001). These teams are conceptualized as having a more fluid membership such that specific expertise can be added or removed as tasks change (Alge et al. 2003). Additionally, researchers have noted the tendency for virtual teams to possess a shorter lifecycle as compared to face-to-face teams (Jarvenpaa & Leidner, 1999). A benefit of virtual teams is that they can bring together individuals with the needed key success factors regardless of their location (Blackburn et al. 2003).

To date, the foundation for the majority of definitions of virtual teams centers around the idea that virtual teams are functioning teams that rely on technology-mediated communication while crossing several different boundaries (Lipnack & Stamps, 1999). Martins et al. (2004) offer the following definition of virtual teams: teams whose members use technology to varying degrees in working across locational, temporal, and relational boundaries to accomplish an interdependent task. The locational boundary refers to any physical dispersion of team members, such as different geographic locations or different workplaces at the same geographic location. The temporal boundary encompasses lifestyle and synchronicity, whilst relational boundary refers to the differences in relational networks of virtual team members, that is, their affiliations with other teams, departments, organizations, and cultural sub-groups.

A key aspect of the Martins et al. (2004) definition focuses on 'teamness' in conjunction with 'virtualness' and moves away from simply describing input factors. As firms increase the number of markets they access, virtual teams may assist the firm to improve the quality of the decisions they make by drawing on knowledge and experience from team members located in the nations in which the products are designed or manufactured.

Though they differ in their levels of complexness, almost all new product development procedures have two primary features, namely activities and decisions (Schmidt et al. 2001). Specifically, actions include various marketing, technological, and business/financial research projects required to produce details and take an idea from an idea to a concrete market providing. Distributed throughout these actions are venture evaluation factors, frequently called gateways or go/stop factors, where the various venture details is analyzed and choices are made to either continue the venture onto the next level or quit it (permanently or temporarily). Typically, people from various organizational areas perform the new product development actions while a different set of people act as decision creators by performing venture opinions, creating extension choices, showing priority for new product development projects, and creating crucial source responsibilities (Cooper, 1993).

Compromise and Group Decision Making

A key ingredient in new product development decision-making is the degree of compromise associated with the decision being made. Hinsz (1999) proposes that group decision processes related to quantities involve compromise, and are characteristically different from the consensus processes that occur for discrete choices. Deadline, rising product development costs, and time to market pressures often cause new product development teams to cut corner and compromise on quality (Menon & Lukas, 2004; Wheelwright & Clark, 1992), Thus, the decision process associated with group outcomes varies as a function of the context in which the decision is made.

Hinsz (1999) posits that the consensus processes that have been used to describe group decision processes with categorical responses may be inadequate or inappropriate for predicting group decision processes of a quantitative nature – such as is often the case in making new product development decisions. Since quantitative judgments will rarely have more than one member favoring a single value, majority and plurality decision process are not as likely to exist for quantities as they are for nominal decision categories. More importantly, from a managerial perspective, Hinsz (1999) also argues that the more influential members of within a decision making group depends on the group's context and tasks. He has formulated a variety of models that differ as a function of the weights given to members based on their position along a judgmental continuum. In doing so, he provides new product development managers with the responsibility of allocating importance to each team member based on the importance of the function they provide and the skill they bring into the group. This may, unfortunately, give rise to the possibility of group conflict and therefore potential compromise aspects of the new product development process.

Traditional New Product Development Decision Making

The high failure rate of new products has resulted in decisions related to the conceptualization, design, development, and marketing of new products posing a significant organizational challenge (Yahaya & Abu-Bakar, 2007). The failure rates of new products vary from 33 per cent to 60 per cent (Cooper, 2005), 40 percent to 75 percent (Stevens and Burley, 2003), and even up to 90 per cent (Balanchandra & Friar, 1997). Such risk creates uncertainty in the new product development process. Marketing managers may be less willing to commit research and development funds to product ideas that may never reach the commercialization (launch) stage, and if they do, there is a relatively high risk of failure following their release (Martin and Scott, 2000).

Considering the level of organizational resource commitment required to develop new products and new product failure rates (Lages & Montgomery, 2004), it is imperative that managerial decision making for new product development be given additional attention and frameworks be developed to assist in such decision making.

Traditional product decision making focused on stage-gate models (Krishnan & Ulrich, 2001). These product development decisions focus on various criteria associated with new product development projects, such as *project selection* and *start decisions* (Bhattacharya et al. 2003), *product launch decisions* (Calantone et al. 2011) and *product termination decisions* (Calantone et al. 2003). These studies identify criteria to address different product development issues such as organizational performance factors, technology potential, long term market based opportunities and resource allocation (Steffens et al. 2007).

New product development decisions are by their very nature, characterized by uncertainty (Davila, 2000). Managing uncertainty is a fundamental decision in the new product development and so it can be observed that different techniques are available to determine and evaluate and reduce uncertainty in new product development. Such methods include: *behavioral approaches* which are methods designed to bring managers to a decision making consensus in terms of which projects to undertake; *probabilistic approaches* are usually computer simulation based and are designed to achieve a range of solutions to a new product development problem; *scoring models* and checklists where projects are rated and scored on a variety of qualitative questions; and *Sensitivity analysis* which tests how the optimal solution and the optimal objective value are affected from the changes of the pre-determined uncertainty parameters (see Buyukozkan & Feyzioglu, 2004). Marketing managers should consider the use of combinations of these approaches to improve their decision making. Selecting the right combination poses a challenge for marketing managers. An additional challenges stems from ongoing refinement of the combination(s) chosen.

Traditionally, organizations make two types of erroneous decisions when evaluating their new product ideas. First, they pursue a potentially unsuccessful new product idea, or they decide not to develop a potentially successful new product. In either case, the product developing organization incurs big losses. While the former leads to investment loses the latter leads to missed investment opportunities (Ozer, 2005). To better understand some of the decision making challenges facing managers of new product development, researchers have moved away from linear stage-gate approaches to new product decision making, to a more comprehensive, adaptive and flexible approaches collectively referred to as Complex Adaptive Systems (CAS). Whereas linear systems are highly structured and tightly coupled, leading to relatively high levels of predictability and efficiency but with low levels of adaptability (Eisenhardt & Bhatia, 2002), CAS systems are underpinned by non-linearity and self-organization (McCarthy et al. 2006). As such, the CAS framework asserts that new product development process behaviors, configurations and decisions are not necessarily fixed. Individual processes within the new product development process have the ability to adapt and to produce a range of process behaviors, namely linear to chaotic; with corresponding types of innovation output, that is, incremental to radical. A CAS framework of new product development extends the linear, perspective by recognizing that nonlinearity and feedback can occur at multiple levels between individual agents and between groups of agents (McCarthy et al. 2006). Agents can be individuals, teams, or organizations (Harkema, 2003).

Whilst CAS offers an alternative look at managerial decision making within a new product development process, CAS are not without their problems. For instance, research has shown that it is difficult for people to understand complex adaptive systems that incorporate delays between actions and outcomes

(Van Oorschot et al. 2010) and the associated decisions that come from these delays. Thus, close managerial supervision of the new product development process, and its members is necessary to ensure that a CAS approach to decision making is effective.

Knowledge Based Systems for New Product Development

Since the invention of computers, managerial decision makers have relied on knowledge based systems to assist them with their new product development decisions (Marin & Scott, 2000). Typically, this involves the use of artificial intelligence in decision making processes. Knowledge based systems incorporate a database of expert knowledge, often gained through market based research, and are designed to facilitate its retrieval in response to specific queries.

Historically, product development was conducted within a single firm by co-located design teams. Recently, there has been a shift in product development paradigms. The complexity of modern products means that a single designer or design team can no longer manage the complete product development effort (Szykman et al. 2001). Knowledge based systems helps overcome some of these new product development concerns using a heterogeneous set of software tools, and still meaningfully exchange information and pass knowledge between various phases in the process. Yet, many organizations are still using outdated, 'monolithic' knowledge based systems in their new product development (Szykman et al. 2001).

Given the importance of making accurate new product managerial decisions, research on knowledge based decisions has attracted much scholarly interest. For instance, Wilkinson (1991) suggested a three stage system for new product evaluation. The first stage relates to normal or probable time of completion. This notion is linked to the marketing idea of a having a new product ready for timely entry into a chosen market. Second, corporate urgency to have the project completed relates to having initial and ongoing corporate commitment to the new product develop. Finally, Wilkinson (1991) suggests the ongoing need for technological innovation (such as knowledge based decision systems) to assist with the managerial decision making in new product development. Despite Wilkinson's (1991) call, research in this area is still in its infancy (Kohlbacher, 2008). One explanation for this, is that knowledge based systems are typically computer and software based. With the rapid progress in new software and hardware technology, it is difficult for marketing managers to keep abreast of the appropriate knowledge based systems to adopt.

Packaging: The Forgotten Element of New Product Development

A product's packaging presents an important opportunity for firms to develop a product that communicates with the consumer, both at the point of sale (Simms & Trott, 2010) and through experience of a product from usage over time (Underwood, 2003). Packaging design provides firms with several marketing related opportunities that must be embraced during the new product development stage. These opportunities include: *positioning a product* within a category (Ampuero & Vila, 2006), *attracting attention* to a product (Creusen & Schoormans, 2005), and *communicating information* regarding brand identity (Underwood, 2003). Unfortunately, packaging is often treated as a cost in the new product development process rather than a value added activity (Simms & Trott, 2010). As a result, packaging is as an afterthought in the design and development of new products (Pilchick, 2000). Given the importance consumers place on a product's packaging (Rundh, 2005), packaging is now critical component of the marketing mix (Pilchick, 2000).

Customers often make their product selection choices when standing at the retail shelf. This is first place they regularly form an opinion on the product. The product's packaging at this stage attempts to capture the attention of the consumer (Löfgren, 2006). Also at this stage, consumers evaluate the product's packaging and the product itself simultaneously (Rundh, 2009). Until the product is consumed, the product and the packaging are considered as one. The sole judgment on the product's packaging is made at after the product is consumed for first time, which indicates that the packaging must functional (Rundh, 2005). Therefore, a product's packaging must be more than a simple promotion of the product and integrate the more technological facets as well. By identifying the important packaging functionalities during these interactions, a better understanding of consumer packaging preferences is created.

The idea development stage is the aspect in the new product development process where concepts are designed into one or more product concepts. Ulrich and Eppinger (1995) determine these product concepts as a depiction of the type, function, and features of the new product. An important issue for product development teams is to determine the extent to which consumers' preferences for specific design features interact with product type. This could arise as a result of associations between the packaging design and the characteristics of the product contained within the packaging (Westerman et al. 2013).

SOLUTIONS AND RECOMMENDATIONS

A holistic approach to new product development is a mandatory requirement for success. From team member selection, to task allocation within the team, to selecting the correct design and decision making paradigms, new products can only succeed when management can see the 'big picture'. This is not as simple as it seems. Too often, new product development managers are bogged down with minutiae. This is hardly surprising given the level of detail associated with the conception, design, launch, and marketing of any new product. However, failing to see 'the bigger picture', namely, considering each of the relevant elements in new product development as a whole rather than the sum of its individual parts, severely reduces a new product's likelihood of market success.

Most organizations who market new products have some degree of market orientation and, through processes such as marketing research, have sufficient market-based information to ensure that new products meet the market's needs. New product success goes beyond having a clear, concise understanding of market needs. Project synergies (the degree of fit between the project and the organization's existing product lines and skills) and the levels of technical, marketing, and management skills applied have been found to correlate with new product development success and failure (Yap & Sounder, 1994).

In trying to deal with the challenges of successfully developing new products, market driven organizations first look at their markets to find unmet demand which they then consider fulfilling with new (or existing) products through their internal processes capabilities. Whilst this is a conventional approach to new product development, I advocate a different approach. Many new products are never developed because new product ideas, based on unmet market needs, are unable to be developed because of a lack of organizational resources (for example, time, money, people, and machinery). These unmet product needs are often developed by competing organizations.

I advocate that organizations should continually remain internally agile when it comes to new product development. Too often, this is not the case. Organizations will spend thousands of dollars on marketing research (to uncover market needs) and very little on new product development systems, capabilities and processes (to meet those needs). There is little point in an organization's marketing researching revealing a market need which does not result in a successful new product being developed to meet that need. I therefore recommend that organizations keep their new product development processes and competencies current. Static, outdated process, and unskilled product development team members severely hampers the new product development process.

How do organizations achieve such internal agility? The answer involves shifting managerial thinking from a dominant focus on market driven imperatives (for example product demand and competition) to a more balanced approach to new product development where the ongoing development and improvement of internal systems for new product success takes equal priority to market focused approaches. For many organizations, this is a considerable paradigm shift. Yet, too often, organizations embrace a 'square peg in a round hole' approach to new product development, where they attempt to adjust their internal capabilities, systems, and processes (often on very short notice) to meet the needs of the market. This compromised approach often results in under-developed products that don't always meet their full market potential. Nor do they necessarily contribute to organizational success.

FUTURE RESEARCH DIRECTIONS

Given the global nature of business today, future work on improving new product development should consider how new product development teams work together across international borders. For instance an organization developing a new product could have its product design team in Italy, its research and development team in Canada, and its prototype development team in Mexico. What might be the cross cultural decision making implications of having new product development team members be scattered around the world?

Future new product development research should focus on time efficiency. Whilst time to market is widely accepted as a critical new product development metric, and there have been numerous empirical works addressing this imperative, there is little synthesis bringing such diverse time to market studies together. Thus, we currently have a fragmented understanding of this imperative. Future studies should also address the involvement of suppliers in the new product development process. Whilst supplier involvement in new product development is not a new idea (see for instance, Handfield et al. 1999) empirical works thus far have provided mixed results. What is needed is a synthesis of previous research into one or several frameworks and strategies for not engaging suppliers in the new product development process, but also a clearer understanding on how best to engage suppliers, and the role that suppliers play in new product development.

CONCLUSION

For many industry sectors, new products are a critical aspect driving an organization's success or failure. The focus on new products has been of interest to academics from a range of research disciplines including: management, technological innovation, research and development and marketing. Research suggests that in order to be effective at new product development an organization must develop internal process that meet the needs of markets. Successful organizations are those that communicate their ideal purpose and map their research and development profile to find a fit between their new product development objectives and their current sources and capabilities. Their achievements also sets on how well the technology areas they enter promote the long run direction of the organization by helping them build new core capabilities crucial to the organization's long-term survival. The end game is to develop market relevant innovative products. This can only be achieved by the careful identification, selection, and training of new product development teams. Development teams should consist of people from a different range of functions and should consist of suppliers and customers to improve the new product's chances of success.

REFERENCES

Abernethy, M. A., Lillis, A. M., Brownell, P., & Carter, P. (2001). Product Diversity and Costing System Design Choice: Field Study Evidence. *Management Accounting Research*, *12*(3), 261–267. doi:10.1006/mare.2001.0168

Ailawadi, K. L., Neslin, S. A., & Gedenk, K. (2001). Pursuing the value-conscious consumer: Store brands versus national brand promotions. *Journal of Marketing*, *65*(1), 71–89. doi:10.1509/jmkg.65.1.71.18132

Alge, B. J., Wiethoff, C., & Klein, H. J. (2003). When does the medium matter? Knowledge building experiences and opportunities in decision-making teams. *Organizational Behavior and Human Decision Processes*, *9*(1), 26–37. doi:10.1016/S0749-5978(02)00524-1

Ali, A., Krapfel, R., & LaBahn, D. (1995). Product innovativeness and entry strategy: Impact cycle time and break-even time. *Journal of Product Innovation Management*, *12*(1), 54–70. doi:10.1016/0737-6782(94)00027-D

Ampuero, O., & Vila, N. (2006). Consumer perceptions of product packaging. *Journal of Consumer Marketing*, *23*(2), 102–114. doi:10.1108/07363760610655032

Atuahene-Gima, K. (1995). An exploratory analysis of the impact of market orientation on new product performance. *Journal of Product Innovation Management*, *12*(4), 275–293. doi:10.1016/0737-6782(95)00027-Q

Atuahene-Gima, K. (1996). Market orientation and innovation. *Journal of Business Research*, *35*(2), 93–103. doi:10.1016/0148-2963(95)00051-8

Atuahene-Gima, K., & Evangelista, F. U. (2000). Cross-Functional Influence in New Product Development: An Exploratory Study of Marketing and R&D Perspectives. *Management Science*, *46*(10), 1269–1284. doi:10.1287/mnsc.46.10.1269.12273

Audretsch, D. B. (1995). Firm Profitability, Growth and Innovation. *Review of Industrial Organization*, *10*(5), 579–588. doi:10.1007/BF01026883

Balachandra, R., & Friar, J. H. (1997). Factors for Success in R&D Projects and New Product Innovation: A Conceptual Framework. *IEEE Transactions on Engineering Management*, *44*(3), 267–287. doi:10.1109/17.618169

Bauer, R. (2004) Kein Bedarf für Plastikräder. *Freitag*. Retrieved from http:// www.freitag.de/2004/43/04431801.php

Bennett, R. C., & Cooper, R. G. (1979). Beyond the Marketing Concept. *Business Horizons*, *22*(June), 76–83. doi:10.1016/0007-6813(79)90088-0

Berthon, P., Hulbert, J., & Pitt, L. (1999). To serve or to create? Strategic orientations towards customers & innovation. *California Management Review*, *42*(1), 37–58. doi:10.2307/41166018

Bethauer, D. M. (2002). *New Product Development and Delivery Ensuring Successful Products Through Integrated Process Management*. New York, NY: Amacom.

Bhattacharya, S., Krishnan, V., & Mahajan, V. (2003). Operationalizing Technology Improvements in Product Development Decison Making. *European Journal of Operational Research*, *149*(1), 102–130. doi:10.1016/S0377-2217(02)00428-9

Blackburn, R., Furst, S. A., & Rosen, B. (2003). Building a winning virtual team: KSA's, selections, training, and evaluation. In C. B. Gibson & S. G. Cohen (Eds.), *Virtual teams that work: Creating conditions for virtual team effectiveness*. San Francisco: Jossey-Bass.

Bounds, G., Yorks, L., Adams, M., & Ranney, G. (1994). *Beyond Total Quality Management*. New York: McGraw-Hill.

Brown, S. L., & Eisenhardt, K. M. (1995). Product development: Past research, present findings, and future directions. Academy of Management Review, 20(2), 343–378.

Büyüközkan, G., & Feyzıoğlu, O. (2004). A fuzzy-logic-based decision-making approach for new product development. International Journal of Production Economics, 90(1), 27–45. doi:10.1016/S0925-5273(02)00330-4 doi:10.1016/S0925-5273(02)00330-4

Calantone, R. J., Di Benedetto, A., & Song, M. (2011). Expecting Marketing Activities and New Product Launch Execution to Be Different in the U.S. and China: An Empirical Study. International Journal of China Marketing, 2(1), 14–44.

Calantone, R. J., Garcia, R., & Droge, C. (2003). The Effects of Environmental Turbulence on New Product Development Strategy Planning. *Journal of Product Innovation Management*, *20*(2), 90–103. doi:10.1111/1540-5885.2002003

Chang, T. Z., & Chen, S. J. (1998). Market orientation, service quality & business profitability: A conceptual model & empirical evidence. *Journal of Services Marketing*, *12*(4), 246–264. doi:10.1108/08876049810226937

Chen, G., Liu, C., & Tjosvold, D. (2005). Conflict management for effective top management teams & innovation in China. *Journal of Management Studies*, *42*(2), 277–300. doi:10.1111/j.1467-6486.2005.00497.x

Christensen, C. M., & Overdorf, M. (2000). Meeting the Challenge of Disruptive Change. *Harvard Business Review*, *78*, 67–76.

Chryssochoidis, G., & Wong, V. (1998). Rolling Out New Products across Country Markets: An Empirical Study of Causes & Delays. *Journal of Product Innovation Management*, *15*(1), 16–41. doi:10.1016/S0737-6782(97)00065-9

Cohen, M. A., Eliasberg, J., & Ho, T. H. (1996). New product development: The performance & time-to-market tradeoff. *Management Science*, *42*(2), 173–186. doi:10.1287/mnsc.42.2.173

Cooper, R. (1988). Pre-development activities determined new product success. *Industrial Marketing Management*, *17*(3), 237–247. doi:10.1016/0019-8501(88)90007-7

Cooper, R. G. (1996). New Products: What Separates the Winners from the Losers. In *The PDMA Handbook of New Product Development*. New York: John Wiley.

Cooper, R. G., & Kleinschmidt, E. J. (1994). Determinants of timeliness in product development. *Journal of Product Innovation Management*, *11*(5), 381–396. doi:10.1016/0737-6782(94)90028-0

Creusen, M. E. H., & Schoormans, J. P. L. (2005). The different roles of product appearance in consumer choice. *Journal of Product Innovation Management*, *22*(1), 63–81. doi:10.1111/j.0737-6782.2005.00103.x

Davila, T. (2000). An empirical study on the drivers of management control systems' design in new product development. *Accounting, Organizations and Society*, *25*(4-5), 383–409. doi:10.1016/S0361-3682(99)00034-3

Deshpande, R., & Farley, J. (2000). Market-Focused Organisational Transformation in China. *Journal of Global Marketing*, *14*(1-2), 7–35. doi:10.1300/J042v14n01_02

Deshpande, R., & Farley, J. U. (1999). Corporate Culture & Market Orientation: Comparing Indian & Japanese Firm. *Journal of International Marketing*, *7*(4), 111–127.

Deshpande, R., Farley, J. U., & Webster, F. (1993). Corporate Culture, Customer Orientation, & Innovativeness in Japanese Firms: A Quadrad Analysis. *Journal of Marketing*, *57*(1), 23–37. doi:10.2307/1252055

Durmuşoğlu, S. S., Calantone, R. J., & McNally, R. C. (2013). Ordered to Innovate: A Longitudinal Examination of the Early Periods of a New Product Development Process Implementation in a Manufacturing Firm. *Journal of Product Innovation Management*, *30*(4), 712–731. doi:10.1111/jpim.12016

Edmondson, A. C., & Nembhard, I. M. (2009). Product development & learning in project teams: The challenges are the benefits. *Journal of Product Innovation Management*, *26*(2), 123–138. doi:10.1111/j.1540-5885.2009.00341.x

Eisenhardt, K. M., & Bhatia, M. M. (2002). Organizational Complexity & Computation. In J. A. C. Baum (Ed.), *Companion to Organizations* (pp. 442–466). Oxford: Blackwell.

Enzing, C. M., Batterink, M. H., Janszen, F. H., & Omta, S. O. (2011). Where innovation processes make a difference in products' short-& long-term market success. *British Food Journal*, *113*(7), 812–837. doi:10.1108/00070701111148379

Ernst, H., Hoyer, W. D., & Rübsaamen, C. (2010). Sales, marketing, & research-and-development cooperation across new product development stages: Implications for success. *Journal of Marketing*, *74*(5), 80–92. doi:10.1509/jmkg.74.5.80

Farhoomand, A. F., & Drury, D. H. (2002). Overload. *Communications of the ACM*, *45*(10), 127–131. doi:10.1145/570907.570909

Filipe Lages, L., & Montgomery, D. B. (2004). Export performance as an antecedent of export commitment & marketing strategy adaptation. *European Journal of Marketing*, *38*(9/10), 1186–1214. doi:10.1108/03090560410548933

Forza, C., Salvador, F., & Rungtusanatham, M. (2005). Coordinating product design, process design, & supply chain design decisions: Part B. Coordinating approaches, tradeoffs, & future research directions. *Journal of Operations Management*, *23*(3), 319–324. doi:10.1016/j.jom.2004.10.001

Fossas-Olalla, M., Lopez-Sanchez, J. I., & Minguela-Rata, B. (2010). Cooperation with suppliers as a source of innovation. *African Journal of Business Management*, *4*(6), 3491–3499.

Frambach, R. T., Prabhu, J., & Verhallen, T. M. M. (2003). The influence of business strategy on new product activity: The role of marketing orientation. *International Journal of Research in Marketing*, *20*(4), 377–397. doi:10.1016/j.ijresmar.2003.03.003

Frosch, R. (1996). The customer for R&D is always wrong! *Research-Technology Management*, *39*(6), 22–27.

Gebhard, A. (2003). *Rapid Prototyping*. Munich, Germany: Hanser-Gardner Publication. doi:10.3139/9783446402690

Gibson, C. B., & Cohen, S. G. (2003). *Virtual teams that work: Creating conditions for virtual team effectiveness. San Fransisco*. Jossey-Bass.

Greitemeyer, T., Schulz-Hardt, S., Brodbeck, F. C., & Frey, D. (2006). Information Sampling & Group Decision Making: The Effects of an Advocacy Decision Procedure & Task Experience. *Journal of Experimental Psychology*, *12*(1), 31–42. PMID:16536657

Griffin, A., & Hauser, J. R. (1996). Integrating R&D & Marketing: A Review & Analysis of the Literature. *Journal of Product Innovation Management*, *13*(3), 191–215. doi:10.1111/1540-5885.1330191

Gruca, T. S., & Rego, L. L. (2005). Customer Satisfaction, Cash Flow, & Shareholder Value. *Journal of Marketing*, *69*(3), 115–130. doi:10.1509/jmkg.69.3.115.66364

Gupta, A. K., & Souder, W. E. (1998). Key drivers of reduced cycle time. *Research Technology Management*, *41*(4), 38–43.

Harkema, S. (2003). A complex adaptive perspective on learning within innovation projects. *The Learning Organization*, *10*(6), 340–346. doi:10.1108/09696470310497177

Hinsz, V. B. (1999). Group decision-making with responses of a quantitative nature: The theory of social decisions schemes for quantities. *Organizational Behavior and Human Decision Processes*, *80*(1), 28–49. doi:10.1006/obhd.1999.2853 PMID:10508567

Jobber, D., & Ellis-Chadwick, F. (1995). *Principles & Practice of Marketing*. Maidenhead: McGraw-Hill, Inc.

Klünder, P. (2006). Planbarer Brückenschlag. *Design Report*, *11*, 26–27.

Kocher, M. G., & Sutter, M. (2006). Time is Money—Time Pressure, Incentives, & the Quality of Decision-Making. *Journal of Economic Behavior & Organization*, *61*(3), 375–392. doi:10.1016/j.jebo.2004.11.013

Kohlbacher, F. (2008). Knowledge-based New Product Development fostering innovation through knowledge co-creation. *International Journal of Technology Intelligence & Planning*, *4*(3), 326–346. doi:10.1504/IJTIP.2008.020100

Krishnan, V., & Ulrich, K. T. (2001). Product Development Decisions: A Review of the Literature. *Management Science*, *47*(1), 1–21. doi:10.1287/mnsc.47.1.1.10668

Landwehr, J. R., Wentzel, D., & Herrmann, A. (2012). The Tipping Point of Design: How Product Design & Brands Interact to Affect Consumers' Preferences. *Psychology and Marketing*, *29*(6), 422–433. doi:10.1002/mar.20531

Lane Keller, K., & Moorthi, Y. L. R. (2003). Branding in Developing Markets. *Business Horizons*, *46*(3), 49–59. doi:10.1016/S0007-6813(03)00029-6

Langerak, F. (2001). Effects of market orientation on the behaviors of salespersons & purchasers, channel relationships, & performance of manufacturers. *International Journal of Research in Marketing*, *18*(3), 221–234. doi:10.1016/S0167-8116(01)00040-4

Langerak, F., Hultink, E. J., & Robben, H. S. (2004). The impact of market orientation, product advantage, & launch proficiency on new product performance & organizational performance. *Journal of Product Innovation Management*, *21*(2), 79–94. doi:10.1111/j.0737-6782.2004.00059.x

Larson, C., & LaFasto, F. (1989). *Teamwork: What must go right/What can go wrong. Newberry Park.* Sage.

Lau, A. K. W. (2011). Supplier & customer involvement on new product performance: Contextual factors & an empirical test from manufacturer perspective. *Industrial Management & Data Systems*, *111*(6), 910–942. doi:10.1108/02635571111144973

Lawton, L., & Parasuraman, A. (1980). The Impact of the Marketing Concept on New Product Planning. *Journal of Marketing*, *44*(January), 19–25. doi:10.2307/1250030

Lenny Koh, S. C., Demirbag, M., Bayraktar, E., Tatoglu, E., & Zaim, S. (2007). The impact of supply chain management practices on performance of SMEs. *Industrial Management & Data Systems*, *107*(1), 103–124. doi:10.1108/02635570710719089

Leonard-Barton, L., & Doyle, J. L. (1996). Commercializing Technology: Imaginative Understanding of User Needs. In R. S. Rosenbloom & W. J. Spencer (Eds.), *Engines of Innovation* (pp. 177–207). Boston: Harvard Business School Press.

Leonidou, L. C. (1996). Product standardization or adaptation: The Japanese approach. *Journal of Marketing Practice*, *2*(4), 53–71. doi:10.1108/EUM0000000004136

Leonidou, L. C. (1998). Organisational determinants of exporting: Conceptual, methodological, & empirical insights. *Management International Review*, *38*(1), 7–52.

Levitt, B., & March, J. (1988). Organisational learning. *Annual Review of Sociology*, *14*(1), 319–338. doi:10.1146/annurev.so.14.080188.001535

Lin, R.-J., Chen, R.-H., & Kuan-Shun Chiu, K. (2010). Customer relationship management & innovation capability: An empirical study. *Industrial Management & Data Systems*, *110*(1), 111–133. doi:10.1108/02635571011008434

Lipnack, J., & Stamps, J. (1999). Virtual teams: The new way to work. *Strategy and Leadership*, *27*(1), 14–19. doi:10.1108/eb054625

Löfgren, M. (2006). *The Leader of the Pack: A Service Perspective on Packaging & Customer Satisfaction* [Dissertation]. Karlstad University.

Love, L. G., Priem, R. L., & Lumpkin, G. T. (2002). Explicitly articulated strategy & firm performance under alternative levels of centralization. *Journal of Management*, *28*(5), 611–627. doi:10.1177/014920630202800503

Maidique, M. A., & Zirger, B. J. (1984). A study of success & failure in product innovation: The case of U.S. electronics industry. *IEEE Transactions on Engineering Management*, *EM-31*(4), 192–203. doi:10.1109/TEM.1984.6447537

Martin, J. H., & Grbac, B. (2003). Using supply chain management to leverage a firm's market orientation. *Industrial Marketing Management*, *32*(1), 25–38. doi:10.1016/S0019-8501(01)00192-4

Martin, S., & Scott, J. T. (2000). The nature of innovation market failure & the design of public support for private innovation. *Research Policy*, *29*(4), 437–447. doi:10.1016/S0048-7333(99)00084-0

Martins, L. L., Gilson, L. L., & Maynard, M. T. (2004). Virtual teams: Where do we go from here? *Journal of Management*, *30*(6), 805–835. doi:10.1016/j.jm.2004.05.002

Maule, A. J., Hockey, G. R. J., & Bdzola, L. (2000). Effects of time-Pressure on Decision-Making Under Uncertainty: Changes in Affective State & Information Processing Strategy. *Acta Psychologica*, *104*(3), 283–301. doi:10.1016/S0001-6918(00)00033-0 PMID:10900697

McCarthy, I. P., Tsinopoulos, C., Allen, P., & Rose-Anderssen, C. (2006). New product development as a complex adaptive system of decisions. *Journal of Product Innovation Management*, *23*(5), 437–456. doi:10.1111/j.1540-5885.2006.00215.x

McDonough, E. F. III. (2000). Investigation of Factors Contributing to the Success of Cross-Functional Teams. *Journal of Product Innovation Management*, *17*(3), 221–235. doi:10.1016/S0737-6782(00)00041-2

Menon, A., & Lukas, B. A. (2004). Antecedents & outcomes of new product development speed: A propositional inventory germane to marketing. *European Journal of Marketing*, *38*(1/2), 209–223. doi:10.1108/03090560410511195

Mishra, A. A., & Shah, R. R. (2009). In union lies strength: Collaborative competence in new product development & its performance effects. *Journal of Operations Management*, *27*(4), 324–338. doi:10.1016/j.jom.2008.10.001

Mital, A., Desai, A., Subramanian, A., & Mital, A. (2011). *Product Development: A Structured Approach to Design & Manufacture*. Butterworth-Heinemann.

Mohammed, S., & Ringseis, E. (2001). Cognitive diversity & consensus in group decision making: The role of inputs, processes & outcomes. *Organizational Behavior and Human Decision Processes*, *85*(2), 310–335. doi:10.1006/obhd.2000.2943 PMID:11461204

Monczka, R. M., Handfield, R. B., Scannell, T. V., Ragatz, G. L., & Frayer, D. L. (2000). *New Product Development Strategies for Supplier Integration*. Milwaukee, WI: ASQ Quality Press.

Montoya-Weiss, M., Massey, A., & Song, M. (2001). Getting it together: Temporal coordination & conflict management in global virtual teams. *Academy of Management Journal*, *44*(6), 1251–1262. doi:10.2307/3069399

Montoya-Weiss, M. M., & Calantone, R. (1994). Determinants of New Product Performance: A Review & Meta-Analysis. *Journal of Product Innovation Management*, *11*(5), 397–417. doi:10.1016/0737-6782(94)90029-9

Murphy, S. A., & Kumar, V. (1997). The front end of new product development: A Canadian survey. *R & D Management*, *27*(1), 5–15. doi:10.1111/1467-9310.00038

Narver, J. C., & Slater, S. F. (1990). The Effect of a Market Orientation on Business Profitability. *Journal of Marketing*, *54*(4), 20–35. doi:10.2307/1251757

Ozer, M. (2005). Factors which influence decision making in new product evaluation. *European Journal of Operational Research*, *163*(3), 784–801. doi:10.1016/j.ejor.2003.11.002

Payne, J. W., Bettman, J. R., & Luce, M. F. (1996). When time is money: Decision behaviour under opportunity-cost time pressure. *Organizational Behavior and Human Decision Processes*, *66*(2), 131–152. doi:10.1006/obhd.1996.0044

Petersen, K. J., Handfield, R. B., & Ragatz, G. L. (2005). Supplier integration into new product development: Coordinating product, process & supply chain design. *Journal of Operations Management*, *23*(3-4), 371–388. doi:10.1016/j.jom.2004.07.009

Pilchik, R. (2000). Pharmaceutical blister packaging, Part I. *Pharmaceutical technology*, 24(11), 68.

Prahalad, C. K. (1990). The Changing Nature of Worldwide Competition. *Vital Speeches of the Day*, *56*, 354–357.

Qian, G. (1997). Assessing Product-Market Diversification in US Firms. *Management International Review*, *27*(2), 127–149.

Qian, G. (2002). Multinationality, Product Diversification, & Profitability of Emerging US Small & Medium Sized Enterprises. *Journal of Business Venturing*, *17*(6), 611–633. doi:10.1016/S0883-9026(01)00080-5

Randall, T., & Ulrich, K. (2001). Product Variety, Supply Chain Structure, & Firm Performance: Analysis of the U.S. Bicycle Industry. *Management Science*, *47*(12), 1588–1604. doi:10.1287/mnsc.47.12.1588.10237

Rumelt, R. P. (1982). Diversification Strategy & Profitability. *Strategic Management Journal*, *3*(4), 359–369. doi:10.1002/smj.4250030407

Rundh, B. (2005). The Multi-Faceted Dimension of Packaging: Marketing Logistic or Marketing Tool? *British Food Journal, 107*(9), 670–684. doi:10.1108/00070700510615053

Rundh, B. (2009). Packaging Design: Creating Competitive Advantage with Product Packaging. *British Food Journal, 111*(9), 988–1002. doi:10.1108/00070700910992880

Salomo, S., Talke, K., & Strecker, N. (2008). Innovation field orientation & its effect on innovativeness & firm performance. *Journal of Product Innovation Management, 25*(6), 560–576. doi:10.1111/j.1540-5885.2008.00322.x

Salomo, S., Weise, J., & Gemünden, H. G. (2007). NPD planning activities & innovation performance: The mediating role of process management & the moderating effect of product innovativeness. *Journal of Product Innovation Management, 24*(4), 285–302. doi:10.1111/j.1540-5885.2007.00252.x

Sarin, S., & Mahajan, V. (2001). The Effect of Reward Structures on the Performance of Cross-Functional Product Development Teams. *Journal of Marketing, 62*(2), 35–53. doi:10.1509/jmkg.65.2.35.18252

Scherer, F. M., & Ross, D. (1990). *Industrial Market Structure & Economic Performance*. Boston, Mass: Harvard Business School Press.

Schiele, H. (2006). How to Distinguish Innovative Suppliers? Identifying Innovative Suppliers as New Task for Purchasing. *Industrial Marketing Management, 35*(2), 925–935. doi:10.1016/j.indmarman.2006.05.003

Schmidt, J. B., Montoya-Weiss, M. M., & Massey, A. P. (2001). New Product Development Decision-Making Effectiveness: Comparing Individuals, Face-To-Face Teams, & Virtual Teams. *Decision Sciences, 32*(4), 575–600. doi:10.1111/j.1540-5915.2001.tb00973.x

Schreier, M., & Prügl, R. (2008). Extending Lead-User Theory: Antecedents & Consequences of Consumers' Lead Userness*. *Journal of Product Innovation Management, 25*(4), 331–346. doi:10.1111/j.1540-5885.2008.00305.x

Shapiro, B. P. (1988). What the Hell is 'Market Oriented'? *Harvard Business Review, 66*, 119–125.

Sheremata, W. A. (2000). Centrifugal & Centripetal Forcess in Radical New Product Development Under Time Pressure. *Academy of Management Review, 25*(2), 389–408.

Simms, C., & Trott, P. (2010). Packaging development: A conceptual framework for identifying new product opportunities. *Marketing Theory, 10*(4), 397–415. doi:10.1177/1470593110382826

Smith, P. G., & Reinertsen, D. G. (1991). *Developing Products in Half the Time*. New York: Van Nostr & Reinhold.

Song, X. M., & Parry, M. E. (1994). The dimension of industrial new product success & failure in state enterprises in the People's Republic of China. *Journal of Product Innovation Management, 11*(2), 105–118. doi:10.1111/1540-5885.1120105

Song, X. M., & Parry, M. E. (1997). The determinants of Japanese new product success. *JMR, Journal of Marketing Research, 34*(1), 64–76. doi:10.2307/3152065

Stevens, G. A., & Burley, J. (2003). Piloting the Rocket of Radical Innovation. *Research Technology Management, 46*(2), 16–26.

Subramanian, R., & Gopalakrishna, P. (2001). The market orientation–performance relationship in the context of a developing economy: An empirical analysis. *Journal of Business Research*, *53*(1), 1–13. doi:10.1016/S0148-2963(99)00109-5

Szykman, S., Sriram, R. D., & Regli, W. C. (2001). The role of knowledge in next-generation product development systems. *Journal of Computing and Information Science in Engineering*, *1*(1), 3–11. doi:10.1115/1.1344238

Teece, D. J., Pisano, G., & Shuen, A. (1997). Dynamic capabilities & strategic management. *Strategic Management Journal*, *18*(7), 509–533. doi:10.1002/(SICI)1097-0266(199708)18:7<509::AID-SMJ882>3.0.CO;2-Z

Troy, L. C., Hirunyawipada, T., & Paswan, A. K. (2008). Cross-Functional Integration & New Product Success: An Empirical Investigation of the Findings. *Journal of Marketing*, *72*(6), 132–146. doi:10.1509/jmkg.72.6.132

Tuominen, M., Rajala, A., & Möller, K. (2004). Market-driving versus market-driven: Divergent roles of market orientation in business relationships. *Industrial Marketing Management*, *33*(3), 207–217. doi:10.1016/j.indmarman.2003.10.010

Ulrich, K. T. (1995). The Role of Product Architecture in the Manufacturing Firm. *Research Policy*, *24*(3), 419–440. doi:10.1016/0048-7333(94)00775-3

Ulrich, K. T., & Eppinger, S. D. (1995). *Product Design & Development* (5th ed.). McGraw-Hill, Inc.

Underwood, R. L. (2003). The communicative power of product packaging: Creating brand identity via lived & mediated experience. *Journal of Marketing Theory and Practice*, *10*(4), 58–69.

Valle, S., & Avella, L. (2003). Cross-Functionality & Leadership of New Product Development Teams. *European Journal of Innovation Management*, *6*(1), 32–47. doi:10.1108/14601060310456319

van Knippenberg, D., & Schippers, M. C. (2007). Work group diversity. *Annual Review of Psychology*, *58*(1), 515–541. doi:10.1146/annurev.psych.58.110405.085546 PMID:16903805

Van Oorschot, K., Sengupta, K., Akkermans, H., & Van Wassenhove, L. (2010). Get Fat Fast: Surviving Stage-Gate® in NPD. *Journal of Product Innovation Management*, *27*(6), 828–839. doi:10.1111/j.1540-5885.2010.00754.x

Verzberger, Y. Y. I. (1994). Collective risk taking: The decision making group & organization. Paper presented at the 35th Annual Convention of the International Studies Association, Washington D.C.

Voss, G. B., & Voss, Z. G. (2000). Strategic Orientation & Firm Performance in an Artistic Environment. *Journal of Marketing*, *64*(1), 67–83. doi:10.1509/jmkg.64.1.67.17993

Wernerfelt, B. (2005). Product development resources & the scope of the firm. *Journal of Marketing*, *69*(2), 15–23. doi:10.1509/jmkg.69.2.15.60763

Westerman, S. J., Sutherland, E. J., Gardner, P. H., Baig, N., Critchley, C., Hickey, C., & Zervos, Z. et al. (2013). The design of consumer packaging: Effects of manipulations of shape, orientation, & alignment of graphical forms on consumers' assessments. *Food Quality and Preference*, *27*(1), 8–17. doi:10.1016/j.foodqual.2012.05.007

Wheelwright, S. C., & Clark, K. B. (1992). *Creating project plans to focus product development*. Harvard Business School Publishing.

Wilkinson, A. (1991). Developing an Expert System on Project Evaluation. *R & D Management*, *21*(1), 19–29. doi:10.1111/j.1467-9310.1991.tb00726.x

Yahaya, S. Y., & Abu-Bakar, N. (2007). New Product Development Management Issues & Decision Making Approaches. *Management Decision*, *45*(7), 1123–1142. doi:10.1108/00251740710773943

Yap, C. M., & Souder, W. E. (1994). Factors Influencing New Product Success & Failure in Small Entrepreneurial High-Technology Electronics Firms. *Journal of Product Innovation Management*, *11*(5), 418–432. doi:10.1016/0737-6782(94)90030-2

Zhang, J., & Duan, Y. (2010). The Impact of Different Types of Market Orientation on Product Innovation Performance. *Management Decision*, *48*(6), 849–867. doi:10.1108/00251741011053433

Zhao, X., Huo, B., Selen, W., & Yeung, J. H. Y. (2011). The impact of internal integration and relationship commitment on external integration. *Journal of Operations Management*, *29*(1/2), 17–32. doi:10.1016/j.jom.2010.04.004

Özturan, P., Ozsomer, A., & Pieters, R. (2014). The Role of Market Orientation in Advertising Spending During Economic Collapse: The Case of Turkey in 2001. *JMR, Journal of Marketing Research*, *51*(2), 139–152. doi:10.1509/jmr.11.0528

ADDITIONAL READING

Adams, J. L. (2012). *Good Products, Bad Products: Essential Elements to Achieving Superior Quality*. New York, NY: McGraw Hill.

Cooper, R.G. (0000). Winning at New Products: Accelerating the Process from Idea to Launch. (3rd ed.). Perseus Publishing. Cambridge, Massachusetts.

Daniels, A. C., & Daniels, J. E. (2004). *Performance Management: Changing Behavior that Drives Organizational Performance* (4th ed.). Atlanta, USA: Performance Management Publications.

Dent, A., Sherr, L., Caniato, M., & Chochinov, A. (2014). *Material Innovation: Product Design*. London, UK: Thames & Hudson Publishing.

DuPuis, S. (2008). *Package Design Workbook. The Art & Science of Successful Packaging*. Beverly, Massachusetts: Rockport Publishers.

Franz, T. M. (2012). Group Dynamics & Team Interventions: Understanding & Improving Team Performance. Wiley-Blackwell. Chichester, UK.

Geracie, G. (2010). *Take Charge Product Management: Take Charge of Your Product Management Development; Tips, Tactics, & Tools to Increase Your Effectiveness as a Product Manager*. Actuation Press.

Gibson, C. B., & Cohen, S. G. (Eds.). (2003). *Virtual Teams That Work: Creating Conditions for virtual Team Effectiveness*. San Francisco, USA: Jossey-Bass Publishing.

Gorchels, L. (2012). *The Product Manager's Handbook* (4th ed.). McGraw Hill, Inc.

Hackman, J. R. (2002). *Leading Teams: Setting The Stage for Great Performances*. Boston, USA: Harvard Business School Publishing Corporation.

Haines, S. (2013). *A Product Manager's Survival Guide: Everything You Need to Know to Succeed as a Product Manager*. New York, NY: McGraw Hill Education.

Hallgrimsson, B. (2012). *Prototyping & Modelmaking for Product Design*. London, UK: Laurence King Publishing Limited.

Hammond, J. S., Keeney, R. L., & Raiffa, H. (2002). *Smart Choices: A Practical Guide to Making Better Decisions. Broadway Books*. New York, NY: Random House.

Harvey, T. R., & Drolet, B. (2004). *Building Teams, Building People* (2nd ed.). Scarecrow Education.

Hitchcock, D. E., & Willard, M. L. (1995). *Why Teams Can Fail & What to Do About It. The Times Mirror Higher Education Group*. Chicago, USA: Irwin Publishing.

Kurtzberg, T. R. (2014). *Virtual Teams: Mastering Communication & Collaboration in the Digital Age. Praeger*. Santa Barbara, California, USA: ABC-CLIO.

Langley, G., Moen, R. D., Nolan, K. M., Nolan, T. W., Norman, C. L., & Provost, L. P. (2009). *The Improvement Guide: A Practical Approach to Enhancing Organizational Performance*. Sanfrancisco, USA: Jossey-Bass Inc.

Lipnack, J., & Stamps, J. (2000). *Virtual Teams. People Working Across Boundaries With Technology* (2nd ed.). New York, NY: John Wiley & Sons.

Mascitelli, R. (2007). *The Lean Product Development Guidebook. Everything Your Design Team needs To Improve Efficiency & Slash Time To Market*. Northridge, California, USA: Technology Perspectives.

Maxwell, J. C. (2001). *The 17 Indisputable Laws of Teamwork: Enbrace Them & Enpower Your Team*. Nashville, USA: Thomas Nelson, Inc.

Milton, A., & Rodgers, P. (2011). *Product Design*. London, UK: Laurence King Publishing.

Morris, R. (2009). *The Fundamentals of Product Design*. Lausanne, Switzerland: AVA Publishing SA.

Pichler, R. (2010). *Agile Product Management with Scrum: Creating Products that Customers Love*. Boston, Massachusetts: Pearson Education Inc.

Savage, S. L. (2003). *Decision Making With Insight*. Nashville, USA: South Western Educational Publishing.

Ulrich, K. T., & Eppinger, S. D. (2011). *Product Design & Development* (5th ed.). Boston, Massachusetts: McGraw Hill Inc.

Wethey, D. (2013). *Decide*. London, UK: Better Ways of Making Decisions. Kogan Page Limited.

KEY TERMS AND DEFINITIONS

Cognition: The act of knowing.

Compromise: A settlement of differences by mutual concessions; an agreement reached by adjustment of conflicting or opposing claims, and principles.

Decision Making: The cognitive process resulting in the selection of a belief or a course of action among several alternative possibilities.

Fuzzy Front End: The creation of a new product concept to address an unmet market need & that it happens sometime before a formal project is created to build it.

Knowledge Based System: A computer program that reasons and uses a knowledge base to solve complex problems.

New Product Development: New product development is the complete process of bringing a new product to market.

Organizational Performance: Organizational performance comprises the actual output or results of an organization as measured against its intended outputs (or goals and objectives)

Product: A product is a set of benefits offered for exchange and can be tangible or intangible.

Packaging: Packaging is the technology of enclosing or protecting products for distribution, storage, sale, and use.

Research and Development (R&D): The research and development is a specific group of activities within a business, the primary function of which is to develop new products; or to discover and create new knowledge about scientific & technological topics for the purpose of uncovering and enabling development of valuable new products, processes, and services.

Virtual Teams: A virtual team (also known as a geographically dispersed team, distributed team, or remote team) is a group of individuals who work across time, space and organizational boundaries with links strengthened by webs of communication technology.

Chapter 17
Upgrading Marketing Research:
Neuromarketing Tools for Understanding Consumers

Anka Gorgiev
The University of Sheffield International Faculty, City College, Greece

Nikolaos Dimitriadis
The University of Sheffield International Faculty, City College, Greece

ABSTRACT

The following chapter focuses on the recent developments in the marketing industry resulting from the rise of neuromarketing. It offers analysis of the problems initiated by the traditional marketing research approaches and how these problems are being resolved by implementation of neuromarketing techniques. Moreover, both physiological and neurological measures are explained, providing advantages and disadvantages of all available neuromarketing tools that may be used in overcoming previously mentioned problems. Finally, the authors provide initial insights from a small scale qualitative research conducted among representatives from all segments of marketing industry.

INTRODUCTION

Since the first recognitions of marketing as an independent field, it has always had the reputation of a dynamic area. The reason for such perception lays in its core function - to satisfy the needs of customers. The entire marketing field is designed in such manner to adapt to the changing needs and habits of the customers, regardless if the changes come from within the field or from neighboring disciplines. It is within the duty of marketing to satisfy the most recent needs, wants and desires of consumers by uncovering their emerging preferences, attitudes, interests and opinions.

The most recent trends in this respect are coming from the developments in behavioral economics, social psychology and neuroscience (Genco, Pohlmann & Steidl, 2013). These fields enable marketers to comprehend consumer behavior not as an action, but as a reaction to certain underlining processes.

DOI: 10.4018/978-1-4666-8459-1.ch017

They also take into consideration the individual as a member of a complex social system, rather than just considering one of the two constructs. And finally, it is becoming clear to scientists that consumers are not as conscious of their decisions as it was previously considered.

BACKGROUND

Generally speaking, behavioral science promises to provide the knowledge necessary to predict future behaviors. In the realm of economics, the entire system of economic theories has been based on the *Homo Economicus* assumption, which implies that people make rational and conscious decisions (Rubinson, 2010; De Vroey, 2009; Morgan, 2006). However, for some time now, it has been clear that people do not follow the rational economic postulates; rather, important ingredients in human decision making are emotions (DellaVigna, 2009; Lee, Amir & Ariely, 2009; Damasio, 2005). Empirical findings in this area are challenging many rules-of-thumb and establishing new confidence in the knowledge of human behavior.

Social psychology complements this knowledge by adding the social influencers into the equation. It has been a common understanding that people's answers, thoughts, choices, preferences and even attitudes and beliefs change depending on the fact if they are alone or in presence of others. Apart from the fact that acknowledging this phenomenon can have significant value to the marketing professional, understanding of such observation contributes vastly to the holistic construct of human behavior.

If behavioral economics and social psychology represent the front office of the behavioral studies, then neuroscience dominates the back office, by supplying the knowledge about the neural activities involved in particular behaviors. Brain science has received significant popularity in the recent years, mainly due to the two high profile projects that have budget of $2.3 billion since they joined forces (Reardon, 2014). The BRAIN (Brain Research through Advancing Innovative Neurotechnologies) Initiative in USA and the Human Brain Project in Europe are expected to provide detailed map of the brain and its neural network in a computerized simulation (Blau, 2013; Wolf & Morrissey, 2013).

While all these findings impose new perception of the world, they also call for new methodologies and tools to be used in order to investigate this new world. Put together, at the intersection of these fields is the newly formed neuromerketing area that can help marketing academics, researchers and practitioners to overcome the problems and get closer to reaching the ultimate goal in marketing - delighting the consumers - and have more effective approach towards issues of societal significance.

MAIN FOCUS OF THE CHAPTER

Problems with Traditional Marketing Research Tools

It is widely known that the holy trinity of research tools in traditional marketing consists of surveys, interviews and focus groups. Majority of the marketing knowledge that exists at this point is result of one of the three tools, or their combination. And it seems that they have shown to be quite useful for the purpose intended. In the previous marketing paradigms, with focus on products or sales, they were appropriately designed to achieve the necessary goals. However, as consumers and their needs become more sophisticated and more informed, new tools need to be employed in order to achieve more complex goals.

The three traditional marketing research methods are solely based on the self-reporting measures. This involves consumer to provide the necessary information based on which marketing theory or marketing strategy will be based upon. As a consequence, all the trust and confidence in the correctness of the information is leveraged towards the consumer. Nevertheless, there have been instances when inconsistencies appeared between consumer indications and implementation results. Numerous such examples exist within the 80% failure rate in new products. In order to demystify this, recent findings from behavioral economics, social psychology and neuroscience have brought to light activities that take place within a person and filter the inputs considered on both conscious and subconscious level, until this person provides information when asked a question (Ohme, 2009). These findings can explain why previously mentioned inconsistencies happen in the first place, but they also bring into questioning any result of traditional marketing research (Fugate, 2007).

The biggest concern regarding the three research instruments usually employed in marketing research is the response bias, when participants misrepresent the true answers (Martin, Engelland & Collier, 2011). Sometimes the failure to tell the truth can be deliberate, while sometimes people are simply not aware of the truth behind the questions asked. Genco, Pohlmann & Steidl (2013) have provided a list of all response biases previously studied by psychologists that affect marketing research, including both intentional and unintentional ones.

Agreeableness Bias - It is in human nature to try to find ways to be likable to those a person is interacting with. And in order to be likable to the person asking the question, people tend to provide answers they believe will satisfy the others (Detric, 2010). In trying to be agreeable with the person asking the questions, people provide incorrect answers, which distort the results of the study. However, traditional marketing research tools are designed in a way that makes it difficult to distance the researcher from the respondents, especially when interviews and focus groups are employed.

Social Desirability Bias - The phenomenon of socially desirable answers has been known to marketers for a long time (Nancarrow, Brace & Wright, 2001). It reflects the tendency of people to provide answers that are considered socially acceptable. This is especially the case with brands that are associated with particular target group characteristics that some might consider negative, but still buy the brand; for example, people are sometimes ashamed to admit that they consume brand that is believed to be associated with low income target group, as this might imply they have financial problems. Due to such beliefs, respondents sometimes give false answers which result in incorrect assumptions for the topic in question.

Knowledge Exposure Bias - Nobody wants to be caught not knowing the answer to the question they have been given. People would rather make something up to conceal the fact that they are not informed on particular topic or simply never even thought of it. In this way, they are not exposed in a negative way in front of the researcher. For example, this bias can be found in research investigating characteristics of a product or service, where participants would rather name some attributes than admit they are ignorant about it.

Misinformation Bias - Opposite from knowledge exposure bias is the misinformation bias. It can occur when participants in a research do not feel comfortable taking part and are deliberately giving incorrect answers. This can happen with people that are overwhelmed with inquiries to participate in studies and as a sign of protest provide answers that are opposite from their beliefs or attitudes. Such bias has been noticed among political voters in the United States.

Memory Bias - While previous biases involve providing incorrect answers consciously, memory bias represents involuntary misrepresentation of the respondent's beliefs and attitudes. Memory bias occurs when a participant is asked to recall some previous experiences (Singh & Churchill, 1986). Scientific findings reveal that creation of memories is a complex process that can be easily distorted in the process of retrieval, either by the researcher or other immediate factors. For example, memories that are emotionally relevant to the respondent are found to be carefully stored and easily retrieved, compared to memories lacking such component.

Emotion (and Preference) Access Bias - Since it has become clear that emotions play important part in building relationships between brand and consumers, researchers have included evaluation of emotional states in their studies. However, people do not always have clear understanding of their emotional state. Rather, in order to provide adequate answer to such questions, they start analyzing relevant situation. And by analyzing and rationalizing emotional state, the 'emotional' part gets distorted. For example, such bias can occur in projects studying how much consumers like or love a product or a brand. As it is the case with memory bias, regardless of the answer given at the time, the respondent will believe he/she answered truthfully.

Prediction Bias - Many research studies are conducted in order to develop estimations for the future as precise as possible. In such cases, consumers are asked to predict their future behavior in particular conditions. And even though they provide honest answer regarding how they expect to behave in future, this cannot be accurate. In order to predict their own future behavior, research shows that people analyze their past behavior and emotional experience in such behavior, and based on this data they predict how they will feel in the future and, thus, how they will behave (Genco, Pohlmann & Steidl, 2013). Like any prediction based on many unknown factors, answers provided by consumers represent an educated guess. And as such, can have significant consequences on research results and actions that are based on those results. For example, in market research studies consumers might be asked whether they would buy a particular product at a particular price; they analyze the feasibility of the price based on their previous purchases, disposable income, comparison with other products, and similar factors. However, they cannot predict the circumstances of their future purchase when exposed to this product, such as unforeseen costs or lifestyle changes.

Design-wise, self-reporting measures provide a lot of loose space where response biases can appear and distort the results of the research in question. Even though this is the case, there are ways to either eliminate or reduce the opportunity for the bias occurrence. This primarily involves the acknowledgement and understanding of these biases, and extensive training and experience with techniques designed to avoid them. And even then a researcher cannot be completely confident that all the loose ends have been tied.

Neuromarketing Tools and Measures as a Potential Solution

Based on previous discussion, traditional marketing research tools seem to be unreliable source of information due to the response biases, especially when used in market research as a base for formulation of consumer strategies and tactics. Therefore, in order to preserve the core function of the practice, marketers are in need of the tools that would allow access to true underlining needs, preferences, attitudes, interests and opinions of their customers, which new technologies are promising to deliver.

Advances in science have revealed tools that can be used in indentifying, monitoring and interpreting physiological and neurological signals from human body (Narvainen et al, 2013; Ohme et al, 2007). Human body is designed in such a way that brain controls all body movements, regardless if these movements are conscious or unconscious. Nevertheless, unconscious signals from the body represent a reliable source of information as they are unbiased and cognitively unfiltered response from the body, and thus not manipulated. They allow marketers to interpret messages from consumers beyond their cognitive comprehension. And as a result, marketers can use these signals in an effort to understand the effect stimuli has on a person.

Physiological body signals represent unconscious body movements that result from exposure to a particular stimuli. Physiological measures that are being used in marketing research involve study of facial expressions, tracking of eye movement, interpretation of heart rate and respiration, electrodermal activity, as well as the behavioral response times. Apart from interpreting signals from the body, marketers can use signals from the brain to understand reactions to a stimuli. These signals can either be of electrical, which is measured with EEG, or represent changes in blood flow in the brain, which is measured with fMRI.

Regardless of their nature, both physiological and neurological signals provide valuable resource in understanding human behavior and underlying processes influencing resulting actions (Bercea, 2012). In that respect, marketing is just one of the fields where these novel technologies have found its purpose.

Facial Expressions

Emotions experienced by a person are usually represented on one's face and they are difficult to conceal. They represent response to one's emotional state, which is why the interpretation of facial expressions in considered a very useful tool in understanding human emotions. The most prominent person in the area of facial expression research is certainly Dr. Paul Ekman. In late 1960s, Dr. Ekman studied the nonverbal behavior of the Fore tribe in Papua New Guinea (www.paulekman.com). As the result of this research, Dr. Ekman, together with his colleagues, identified six universal emotions, each represented in the distinctive form of universal facial expressions: happiness, sadness, surprise, fear, anger and disgust. Remarkable discovery is that these emotions appear to be manifested in the same way in people from different cultural backgrounds (Ekman, 1992). The research has identified patterns in certain muscle movements, such as frown or smile that points towards specific emotions.

Dr. Ekman and his colleagues observed movements of facial muscles for each of the emotion and were able to code each expression based on muscles involved in its making. Each muscle movement represents one action unit (AU). Under these assumptions, the researchers have developed Facial Action Coding System (FACS) (Ekman & Friesen, 1978). FACS keeps track of facial expressions by interpreting the micro-movements of facial muscles (Bove, 2008; Craig et al, 2008). According to Cohn, Ambadar & Ekman (2006), FACS distinguishes between 9 AUs in upper and 18 AUs in lower face and 5 miscellaneous AUs, that can be combined with 14 head and 9 eye movements, as well as "*9 action descriptors, 9 gross behaviors, and 5 visibility codes*" (p. 205). When analyzing facial expressions, experts view the video containing person(s) in question and carefully record the micro-movements of facial muscles. Combining the activation of different action units, experts gain insight into which emotion is being experienced by the person.

Facial action coding system represents important tool for interpreting human emotions as it is completely based on the knowledge of human face anatomy and understanding of the nervous system. Due to this, there is strong support towards the premise that facial expressions provide reliable representation of emotions experienced. Put in marketing context, facial expressions have be very insightful indication of consumer emotions, especially in real-life circumstances. Nevertheless, since facial expressions are partly consciously controlled, sometimes consumers might experience emotions that do not surface, and thus fail to be captured in the form of facial expressions. In addition, interpretation of facial expressions requires expertly trained professional who performs these analysis manually. Apart from low availability of such experts, it implies the difficulty for conducting analysis in real-time, significant time consumption, and costly set-up. There are some softwares available to marketers that can speed up the analysis of facial expressions and can cost less, but they seem to be less reliable.

Facial coding is very useful in analyzing advertisements prior to their broadcasting, as it can help companies identify emotional responses to their messages. It can also interpret consumer experience in whichever situation that is being recorded. In addition, there are softwares used today that can connect to customers' webcams and record their online experience. Of course, such analysis are conducted after the fact and can be used for improving marketing activities in future.

In an effort to overcome some of the limitations imposed by FACS, marketers use Facial Electromyography (EMG). EMG also interprets facial expressions, but it does so by measuring the electrical activity of facial muscles that are being active (Rasch & Teichert, 2013). This tools enables the researchers to identify even the smallest muscle movement that otherwise can be invisible to the naked eye in FACS technique. This applies especially to the unconscious movements that occur when specific emotions are experienced, even prior to their manifestation of the face. Electromyography can record muscle movements in real time and with high precision. However, it requires the participant to wear specially designed sensors on his face during the research, which makes it very difficult for usage in consumers' natural environment.

Due to its technical requirements, EMG is suitable only for laboratory settings. Similarly to FACS, it can provide significant insights when used in the analysis of marketing messages.

Eye Tracking

Human brain heavily relies on sight as the primary source of information and stimuli from the external environment. Research shows that visual inputs represent the most reliable source of information about our external environment. The evolutionary response to this phenomenon manifests in the existence of an entire brain area solely dedicated to receiving, interpreting and storing visual stimuli. Having in mind its importance to any individual, it is natural to consider it in trying to gather insight behind the human behavior.

First and foremost, tracking eye movements has provided useful way in identifying focus of attention (Becker, 2013; Casarotti, 2012). It is in human nature, or rather it is an involuntary reflex, to direct sight towards the source that grabs human attention. When a person is looking at something, it can be concluded that this stimulus in of his interest. The longer the fixation on a stimulus, the greater the interest for this stimulus; the reason behind it can be either the difficulty of processing the input or simply the high interest. Apart from fixations, the movement in-between fixations can have a significance to a researcher. If viewer is showing rapid shifts in fixations, it may indicate that the viewer has lost interest in the material viewed or that he is having difficulty following and comprehending the material. Moreover, the shifts that are inconsistent with the intended flow of the material may indicate the necessity to adapt it accordingly.

The pattern of eye movement has shown to be very useful in the analysis of websites. The fixations indicate the content that is considered more interesting to the viewer. For example, some research has shown that in an online behavior the majority of attention is given to the photos and titles compared to the textual content (Djamasbi, Siegel, Skorinko & Tullis, 2011). These findings can help website editors in managing their online content in order to make it more attractive for the target group.

Secondly, eye tracking can be used in identifying the occurrence of blinking, which has shown to be correlated with the attention and engagement (Mauri, 2011). More precisely, suppressed levels of blinking indicate higher level of attention and engagement, as in situations requiring higher concentration people tend to gather as much input as possible; in contrast, blinking at higher rate is present in tasks that require less attention. Similarly, blinking rate can indicate emotional state of the viewer. As blinking represent's our defense mechanism, its frequent occurrence can indicate negative emotions (Genco, Pohlmann & Steidl, 2013).

The blinking rate can be used as complementary analysis of eye movements to indicate sources of attention in exposure to marketing content. They can also be employed over longer periods of time in order to observe consumers' adaptation to a message or the effectiveness of pre-exposure (priming).

Finally, the most interesting and insightful information in eye movement analysis can be gained from the pupils. The changes in size of pupils represent unconscious actions, usually as a response to emotional reaction (Mauri, 2011). More precisely, increase in pupil size happens when a person experiences emotional arousal. However, analysis of pupil dilation cannot indicate whether the change is size is due to negative or positive emotions; it can only indicate an emotional response. Apart from emotional arousal, pupil dilation has been recorded in instances when participants in research have been involved in performing difficult tasks or tasks that required higher attention (Steinhauer, Siegle Condray & Pless, 2004). Having in mind its sensitivity to emotional and cognitive stimuli, pupil dilation represents very reliable measure for stimuli of such nature. And the best part is - the analysis can be performed in real time. Based on the dilation changes, marketers can instantly adapt content in question.

As one of the most reliable indicators of emotional state, analysis of eye movements, including the fixations, blinking rates and pupil dilations, have become very popular among marketers nowadays. With increasing spread, its cost becomes lower, which makes this tool more and more accessible for market research purposes. Nevertheless, due to the eye sensitivity to changes in brightness (especially pupils), this tool should be used primarily in evaluating print or web content rather than videos.

Respiration, Heart Rate and Blood Pressure

Everyone is familiar with what lie detector is, at least from the commercial movies involving government agencies. Lie detector or polygraph is a machine designed to monitor body functions throughout the sessions of questioning. The entire technique is based on establishing the referent point for physiological impulses, such as blood pressure, heart rate and respiration, and observe their change when a particular question is attended. For many years this technique has been used by governments throughout the world in pursue of truth. Neuromarketers nowadays use the same principle when conducting research of their own.

Going deeper into the brain, there are certain primary body functions, such as breathing and heart activity, which are controlled by the brain without any conscious effort (Afifi & Bergman, 2005). This implies that signals received through these functions represent true body responses, as they cannot be controlled or managed consciously. Given the situation, brain manages these activities based on the assessment of external environment, thus suppressing or increasing the rate of these actions.

According to De Melo, Kenny & Gratch (2010), there are specific patterns of respirations that are associated to specific emotional states. For example, extensive research has shown that deeper breathing at faster pace reflects excitement, but also anger and fear. Such pattern is present when brain is experiencing fight-or-flight effect. On the other hand, fast and shallow breathing reflects either anxiety or a situation when higher attention is needed. When a person is breathing slowly with deep intakes of air, it can mean that he is very relaxed or sad. Interestingly, the same slow and deep respiration pattern has been identified when a person is experiencing positive emotions, such as joy. There have been numerous studies conducted in an effort to identify emotional states through the respiratory patterns and the findings can be very useful to neuromarketers trying to understand the audience's feelings (Philippot, Chapelle & Blairy, 2002). Before new research findings are available, respiration *per se* might not be the best tool to use to identify particular emotions. Rather, at this point it should be used primarily as a measure of arousal, as it can be especially insightful when employed in pre-screening of marketing messages.

Hearth function is controlled by the brain in the same way as respiration, which is through the autonomic nervous system. Based on the inputs received from the external environment and brain's interpretation of these inputs, both hearth rate and blood pressure can show oscillations.

There are a lot of research studies investigating heart function and its relationship with emotional experiences, but there are many inconsistent results. In a study exploring the relationship between emotions and music, participants had lower heart rate when exposed to unpleasant music, while their heart rate increased when listening to music they liked (Sammler, 2007). On the other hand, there are studies that report increased heart rate when a person is experiencing positive emotions and decreased heart rate during negative emotions. Having this in mind, heart rate might not be the most reliable tool in interpreting emotional valance, but with high assurance it can identify the presence of emotional response. There are even indications that heart rate can be used in indicating attention or cognition levels, with heart rate decreasing at times of higher attention efforts.

In addition to heart rate, numerous clinical studies had blood pressure in focus, reporting increased activity when participants are experiencing negative emotions, while positive emotions are usually accompanied by decrease in blood pressure (Sundararajan, 2010). Apart from emotions, blood pressure seems to be highly sensitive to memory, as well. However, the results from this tool are considered unreliable, since they can differentiate based on the placement of the measurement object on participant's arm. As such, they are only used in combination with other techniques identifying the presence of emotion, but not its valance.

There is no question whether measures of heart rate, blood pressure and respiration can be useful in marketing research. Nevertheless, the interpretations of body responses using previously mentioned tools are still unreliable. As future research demystifies further these autonomic inputs, they will be more and more applicable when trying to understand emotional states of target group, especially in pre-launch market testing research.

Electrodermal Activity

Similarly to previously discussed body functions, perspiration is also controlled by the autonomic nervous system, and as such cannot be consciously manipulated (Lajante et al, 2012). As brain controls the glands producing the sweat, some of the emotional responses of human body result in the production of sweat on the skin surface, causing sweaty palms. In essence, electrodermal activity represents measure of electrical characteristics of the skin as the response to the presence or absence of sweat (Lajante, Droulers, Dondaine & Amarantini, 2012).

On the contrary to heart rate and respiration, though, significance of perspiration in marketing research has been acknowledged for thirty years now, while this tool has been used in marketing research since 1960s. In one of the first studies of such kind, the researchers were investigating correlation between the skin response and the feeling of warmth among participants exposed to advertising stimuli (Aaker,

Stayman & Hagerty, 1986). Accompanied with numerous other similar studies, measuring electrodermal activity became reliable tool for marketers due to its sensitivity to stimuli originating from advertising messages (Kroeber-Riel, 1979).

Reactions like this enable marketers to identify emotions experienced by consumers, even if they fail to report it. Electrodermal activity is measured using galvanic skin response (GSR) or skin conductance response (SCR). Sensors that are connected with the galvanometer are placed on participant's palms and fingers; these sensors report changes in electrical conductance of the skin, which can be monitored on the galvanometer. Studies conducted so far have found the connection between perspiration and arousal and stimulation (Kreibig, 2007). This means that when GSR is higher, it is safe to conclude that the participant is experiencing emotional arousal due to the exposure to presented stimuli (Gakhal & Senior, 2008). In addition, Caffyn (1964) found that results captured by GSR can even differentiate between print and TV ads.

Electrodermal activity represents a highly sensitive measure to changes in affective states. Some even consider it to be among the most reliable in capturing unconscious bodily signals (LaBarbera & Tucciarone, 1995). As such, they are considered a good measure of arousal. However, the studies conducted using GSR only managed to conclude whether there is an emotional reaction to stimuli, but not its directionality. EDA measures cannot be used to determine whether the consumer likes or dislikes the stimuli; it can be only used to see whether there is a reaction of some kind and how strong this reaction is. Moreover, marketers wanting to employ this measure in their research need to find experts and highly trained personnel who know how to handle galvanometer and read the galvanic skin responses. Even though more than twenty studies have been conducted in the past thirty years, still there is no standardized methodology or analysis of the signals used in interpreting result (Lajante, Droulers, Dondaine & Amarantini, 2012).

This tool still provides better indication of consumer emotional stimulation than any self-reporting method. But, the complexity involved with interpreting results prevents it from being primary source of market inputs. Nevertheless, when coupled with other tools, electrodermal activity can provide very insightful information to marketers. In a study conducted by Hensel (1970), it was found that high GSR and pupil dilation indicate higher receptiveness of the message, which ultimately leads to higher retention. Following this example, marketers can use galvanic skin response or skin conductance response measures to validate results gathered otherwise and support findings of other neuromarketing tools.

Behavioral Response Time

Human memory is one of the most complex cognitive functions by itself. However, it also represents a foundation for higher level cognitive functions, such as learning, decision making, language, etc (Del Missier et al, 2013; Flight, 2011; Ratnayake, Broderick & Mitchell, 2010; Jefferies, Frankish & Noble, 2009). People receive inputs from external environment through their senses. These inputs are then processed and stored in human memory. Brain creates mental representations as a way of storing all this information. This means that there are specific mental representations for each attitude, emotion, person, etc. When trying to retrieve some information, human brain searches a database of mental representations trying to find the correct one. As a way to facilitate this process, human brain creates associations among specific objects, words, pictures or sounds and attitudes, situations or emotions. Stronger the association, faster the retrieval or recall. Due to such diligent mechanism, these associations are of crucial importance to marketing professionals.

Attitudes represent one of the most intriguing concepts to contemporary marketers, since attitudes play an important role in the formation of opinions and preferences, which are crucial for brand and product consumption, and significantly affect human behavior. Explicit attitudes represent those attitudes that are created consciously and on purpose. For example, after watching a documentary on fast food, a person develops a strong opinion that fast food is not healthy. As such, explicit attitudes are controlled by a person and can easily self-reported during a research. Implicit attitudes, on the other hand, represent opinions, preferences and feeling that are developed based on previous experiences. Due to their nature, they cannot be consciously controlled, and thus cannot be correctly self-reported, but still significantly influence behavior (Dimofte, 2010). In the case of fast food, a person might believe that such food is not healthy, but he might go and eat it, regardless. For example, after many years of consuming Coca-Cola, a person might read about negative effects of this beverage and decided to stop drinking it; however, this would not stop him to feel excited and smile while watching Coca-Cola's Christmas commercial with polar bears or Santa Claus.

People are exposed to a large number of stimuli on daily basis. Some of these stimuli do not affect us at all, some are accommodated consciously and a person purposely redirects his behavior, and there are stimuli that affect behavior of a person without him even realizing it. Such phenomenon happens throughout the process of priming. Priming can be described as a process of influencing behavior by introducing a stimuli that will subconsciously trigger an idea associated with this stimuli; this can further activate a physical response and even behavior. In recent years, there have been numerous studies investigating priming and the effects of influence without awareness, providing very interesting results. For example, handing a warm cup of coffee to a business partner may make him friendlier and less aggressive during negotiations or exposing a person to Apple logo might trigger him to perform better on creative tasks. Research has revealed two types of priming: semantic and affective. Semantic priming reflects triggering a certain mental representation by using words, while affective priming involves triggering a feeling by using a prime of the same valance as the target feeling (Davis & Herr, 2014; Yi, 1990).

In order to be able to implement priming in marketing campaigns, marketers need to evaluate the strengths of associations between the stimuli with desired response or behavior. This can be achieved with measuring time needed to respond to particular concept. Depending on the research requirement, there are three techniques available: semantic priming, affective priming and implicit associations test. All three have the same research mechanism. The participant is exposed to paired concepts, either words or pictures, one after another only fraction of seconds apart. Based on the previously predetermined criteria, participant needs to make a decision of choosing one of the two concepts, usually by clicking on the corresponding button. Response latency, or time needed to respond can reveal whether and to what extend the stimuli has activated mechanisms necessary for desired behavior (Mast & Zaltman, 2005). Shorter time needed to respond indicates stronger association between the stimuli and the target concept.

The most common behavioral response method used among marketers is implicit associations test (IAT), which evaluates implicit attitudes towards brands. More importantly, IAT can provide comparative information when used to study two brands. However, IAT seems to be more complex that semantic and affective priming describe previously, as it can employ both techniques as part of the methodology (Genco, Pohlmann & Steidl, 2013; Gregg & Klymowsky, 2013; Gregg et al, 2013; Berger & Fitzsimons, 2008).

Behavioral time response studies represent very useful tool, since they allow marketers to observe behavioral responses that are not controlled by the participant. As discussed on several occasions previously, this is very important in evaluating marketing outputs. Priming and IAT are one of the most available neuromarketing tools, as they can be performed by the researcher alone. And most importantly, these studies can be conducted with minimal costs, which is usually not the case with neuromarketing tools. However, not all research questions can be answered through time response studies. The researcher needs to consider carefully all the aspect of this approach before conducting the experiment. Otherwise, the researcher might have serious problems with the validity of the results.

Blood Flow in Brain

All the tools discussed previously are designed to study the autonomic signals coming from the brain and influencing behavior subconsciously. The reason why there are tools interpreting every such signal is because scientists have always been interested in uncovering what is happening in the so-called 'black box'. For the past 22 years, there is the opportunity to look directly into the brain and observe how it functions using magnetic resonance imaging (Bandettini, 2012).

Magnetic resonance imaging (MRI) is a tool designed to develop images of the brain activity by measuring the blood flow. This approach is very often used in medicine to analyze the irregularities in the brain functioning and structure. Neuroimaging tools work on the principle of identifying blood oxygenation level dependent (BOLD) signal changes in brain as an indication of a neural activity (Parens & Johnston, 2014). The oxygenated parts are then identified by the magnetic field developed by the fMRI machine. Activation of a particular part of the brain requires higher supply of oxygen compared to other brain parts, and thanks to the increased level of oxygen, blood develops stronger magnetic field that is depicted on fMRI images.

Scientists from other disciplines that require brain activity analysis use functional magnetic resonance imaging (fMRI), as it allow them to see the brain activity while engaging participants in different tasks, such as watching videos, pictures or listening to music. The function of fMRI is based on the same principles as the regular MRI, but it provides the opportunity to the researcher to expose the participant to the wide range of stimuli. As a consequence, analysis of the fMRI images can provide more reliable results that are specific to the particular circumstances studied. For example, fMRI can show brain activity of a participant watching TV commercial or listening to a song.

Advances in studying the anatomy of human brain have indicated patterns in the activation of specific brain areas when performing specific tasks. As a result, there are indicative results that certain brain parts are activated when a person is experiencing pain, or love, or fear, or when a person is retrieving memories or talking. This properties of fMRI are very attractive to marketing researchers trying to uncover the significance of stimuli by identifying which part of the brain is engaged in such situation (Craig et al, 2012; Kenning, Plassmann & Ahlert, 2007).

fMRI has become very popular among neuromarketing researchers due to its ability to provide clearer understanding of the brain mechanisms behind certain behaviors, opinions and preferences. However, its usages cannot be widespread yet, because such studies involve very high costs. There is a small number of fMRI machines, since they cost several million dollars per unit, and only expertly trained personnel can operate them. This has resulted in limited availability of this research tool to neuromarketers.

Apart from the logistics problems, fMRI has its own technical shortcomings. fMRI creates images of the brain and it is very successful in depicting spatial resolution of brain activity. However, the images are not available instantly as the stimuli is introduced; rather, there is a time lapse between the capturing and producing the image of approximately six seconds (Genco, Pohlmann & Steidl, 2013). And even capturing a change in neural activity, researchers cannot still be sure why it happened. With future research, it is expected that this limitation will be eliminated. Also, in order to be able to receive a clear image, the participants are not supposed to move while in fMRI scan. This forbids neuromarketers the access to brain activity of participants in more natural consumption environment.

In addition to fMRI scans, positron emission tomography (PET) scans also measure brain activity based on the blood flow changes. Before the measurement, participants are being injected with radioactive isotopes. The levels of these isotopes increase in the parts of the brain that are being activated and they can be captured on an image. PET scan has technical advantages and disadvantages over an fMRI scan. Nevertheless, due to its invasive nature, it is not expected to become a tool neuromarketers would consider for their consumer research purposes.

Electrical Activity in Brain

While fMRI measures changes in the blood flow in the brain, Electroencephalography (EEG) measures the electrical activity of the brain (Morin, 2011). Brain is designed as a network of neurons that communicate among each other constantly. Individual brain cell, neuron, transmits information to its neighboring cell by "firing", or rather releasing electrical potential. EEG can capture whenever a brain cell fires. Participants being monitored under the EEG have electrodes placed on the top of their scalp in the form of a cap or a headset. The headset is connected to a computer operating a specific program designed to interpret input coming from the participant. The electrodes in headset can measure any change in the electrical potential within the brain. Scientists believe that whenever there is increased frequency of neuron firing, the brain has been engaged.

EEG has a wide spectra of inputs it can measure. Apart from just measuring signals from the brain, it can identify which signals are caused by which stimuli. Due to its very high temporal resolution, EEG can provide analysis of the event-related potentials, brain signals that happen as a response to particular event (Ohme, Matukin & Pacula-Lesniak, 2011). In addition, as different brain signals emit different frequency corresponding to different brain states, scientists have found a way to interpret this frequency inputs. EEG studies can reveal the strength of signals involved in performing certain mental activity and the parts of brain that are used in performing this activity.

Researchers have also found the way to apply the knowledge of frontal asymmetry paradigm in EEG frequency analysis. As the theory suggests, when people are motivated by desirable outcomes (approach motivation), there seems to be higher activation of the right brain hemisphere; on the contrary to that, behavior evoked by aversive outcomes (avoidance motivation), shows correlation with the activation of the left brain hemisphere (Pizzagalli, Sherwood, Henriques & Davidson, 2005). Now, neuromarketers can use EEG to determine consumer motivation for their brand or product and use this information in developing more effective marketing strategies (Ravaja, Somervuori & Salminen, 2013; Ohme, Reykowska, Wiener & Choromanska, 2010).

EEG represent highly valuable tool to marketers and neuromarketers. As a research tool, EEG can provide information whether and which part of the stimuli causes increased brain activity, thus indicating increased attention, arousal or even surprise (Silberstein & Nield, 2008). More importantly, all this information can be available almost instantly, which makes EEG highly reliable. Nevertheless, EEG has very limited spatial resolution. Since electrodes are placed on the surface of the scalp, it can only measure signals that originate closely to the electrodes and not the signals that occur deep within the brain. This permits researchers from identifying the involvement of the precise parts of the brain as a response to stimuli. Moreover, the electrodes used to measure electrical signals are very sensitive to body movements, which means that if a participant is not still during research, the results might be corrupted. There are efforts nowadays to develop wireless set that can monitor brain activity in natural consumption setting, but their reliability is still to be scientifically and empirically proven.

Impact and Challenges

It has been shown that at certain times consumers do not understand their needs or are not comfortable at expressing them (Nancarrow, Brace & Wright, 2001). In such cases, neuromarketing tools can provide valuable resource in interpreting body and brain signals, which are so strong that they cannot be consciously controlled, but they still influence human behavior. These tools enable marketing professionals the access to the underlining truth behind people's thoughts, feelings, attitudes and preferences.

Neuromarketing is sometimes disputed due to potential ethical issues of taking advantage of the "black box" and manipulating people into doing things beyond their free will. Nevertheless, such accusations have not been proven to this point. Even though people are not purely rational human beings, they are not slaves of consumerism either. The fact that sometimes consumers are not consciously aware of their needs does not mean they can be forced into choices. The subconscious mind, impulses and instincts are there to protect them from such instances.

Actually, neuromarketing research potential and the principles behind it, provide a great hope for solving serious societal issues. Understanding the brain mechanisms behind receiving, processing, memorizing, recalling and learning messages can be very useful in constructing the messages that need to reach great masses. Public campaigns can benefit greatly from neuromarketing, from constructing to testing and broadcasting campaigns. In addition, neuromarketing can contribute to better understanding of the consumerism as a behavioral aspect. There is a large set of data collected in commercial purposes mainly that points towards behavioral patterns observed over many years. This input can complement many studies in the areas of neuroscience and neurology, as well as psychology and other behavioral sciences (Javor, Koller, Lee, Chamberlain & Ransmayr, 2013).

Nevertheless, neuromarketing tools still represent novel technologies, which implies that there is not sufficient empirical evidence in order to make strong conclusion about the findings (Ariely & Berns, 2010). More so, it is believed that neuromarketing tools are very costly to obtain and require personnel with specialized training to handle them correctly. And this is true for some of the specialized tools, like fMRIs, EEGs and FACS. However, there are those tools that can deliver information about the subconscious signals, but do not require a fortune; these include time-response studies or even behavioral experiments.

Whatever the research budget available, the choice on the tools to use should depends on the research question and what is being investigated. Sometimes traditional tools are enough and neuromarketing tools simply do not justify the costs; but there are also times that require more advanced techniques and technologies to be used in solving the problem, which is when neuromarketing tools are irreplaceable. As a result, many scientists and marketing professionals still believe that neuromarketing tools are most effectively used in combination with the traditional marketing research techniques (Bercea, 2012; Fugate, 2007).

FUTURE RESEARCH DIRECTIONS

Small Scale Primary Research

Neuromarketing as a sub-discipline has been thriving for more than 10 years now (McClure, Li, Tomlin, Cypert, Montague & Montague, 2004). However, it seems that that the proliferation it experienced so far is nothing compared to what is expected of neuromarketing in the future.

In order to gain initial insights regarding neuromarketing in South East European region, the authors have conducted a small scale qualitative research. The data was collected using in-depth unstructured interviews, as such approach allows the identification of major topics and important themes (Arskey & Knight, 1999). In total, the authors conducted interviews with representatives from three companies operating in marketing industry. One company in the sample represents a neuromarketing consulting agency from Greece. Two participants from this company were interviewed, the director of neuromarketing and strategic communication and the market research and neuromarketing consultant. The second company provides market research services at the global level. The participant from this company holds the position of the regional managing director responsible for Adriatic region. The third company represents a big advertiser operating in the sector of financial services in Serbia, as a member of a regional group. The interviewee is the marketing and communications director in the company. The maximum variation sampling method was used to choose these individuals. This approach allowed the researchers to investigate the variations in the major topics depending on the industry segment (Patton, 1990).

The aim of this research was to start a conversation about neuromarketing that will include all players in marketing industry and acquire opinions and personal observations to complement the existing knowledge. Based on the qualitative data collected, several conclusions have been made.

Neuromarketing has low awareness, but high persuasive effect - As representatives from neuromarketing agency have argued, neuromarketing as a discipline is still experiencing low awareness among the marketing professionals. However, they claim that after marketers are being presented with the benefits and characteristics of neuromarketing, they realize the opportunities it can offer. As all the participants were aware of neuromarketing prior to this discussion, their opinions did not differ; they all believe neuromarketing is providing valuable insights into human behavior, and as such, can bring the consumer and the company closer.

Neuromarketing as a way of thinking and new research technique – The most interesting discussion was held regarding the ultimate impact of neuromarketing. On one hand, there are those who believe that neuromarketing will enrich the pool of market research tools and complement the traditional techniques. On the other hand, there are those who believe that neuromarketing represents a way of thinking that can be implemented even when neuromarketing research tools are not present. Regardless of how marketing professionals look at neuromarketing, they all seem to agree that neuromarketing input, primary or secondary, does make significant difference on the end result.

The most effective way to promote neuromarketing is through case studies – As the participants indicate, there are examples of neuromarketing studies being conducted in the South East European region. The most common ones involve using EEG and eye tracking systems, as well as the analysis of emotions. Even though there are not many, these studies represent the strongest persuasion tactic available at this stage. Nevertheless, all the studies need to be carried out according to strict protocol and thoroughly documented, so that science behind them cannot be disputed.

This small scale qualitative research represents only the first step towards realizing the true significance of neuromarketing among industry professionals in South East European region. Future investigation in this area is necessary and highly anticipated; there are still many questions to be answered. But there is a hope that neuromarketing will upgrade the entire marketing knowledge and will close the gap between the consumers and the companies.

CONCLUSION

This is the age of the brain. Many resources are being dedicated to uncovering the power behind the brain mechanisms and its impact on the world. It can be argued that the twenty first century is the period of brain paradigm. The knowledge from neuroscience is entering all aspects of business and science, from medicine and psychology to urbanism, economics and law. Luckily enough, marketing is not an exception.

Marketing research is changing and marketing professionals can no longer ignore it. Neuroscience tools have already found its application in marketing research and neuroscience knowledge is changing the perception and mechanisms of marketing. However, it is only the transition period right now. This means that the innovative techniques have not reached full confidence and mature usage levels. As such, they should be used in combination with traditional marketing techniques; in doing so, marketing professionals will be able to enrich their data and incrementally accept neuromarketing inputs.

REFERENCES

Aaker, D. A., Stayman, D. M., & Hagerty, M. R. (1986). Warmth in Advertising: Measurement, Impact, and Sequence Effects. *The Journal of Consumer Research*, *12*(4), 365–381. doi:10.1086/208524

Afifi, A., & Bergman, R. (2005). *Functional Neuroanatomy: Text and Atlas*. New York, NY: McGraw-Hill Medical.

Ariely, D., & Berns, G. S. (2010). Neuromarketing: The Hope and Hype of Neuroimaging in Business. *Nature Reviews. Neuroscience*, *11*(4), 284–292. doi:10.1038/nrn2795 PMID:20197790

Arksey, H., & Knight, P. (1999). *Interviewing for Social Scientists*. London, UK: Sage.

Bandettini, P. A. (2012). Twenty Years of Functional MRI: The Science and the Stories. *NeuroImage*, *62*(2), 575–588. doi:10.1016/j.neuroimage.2012.04.026 PMID:22542637

Becker, S. (2013). Why You Cannot Map Attention: A Relational Theory of Attention and Eye Movements. *Australian Psychologist*, *48*(6), 389–398. doi:10.1111/ap.12028

Bercea, M. D. (2012). Taking the Pulse of the Market: A Consumer's Decision-Making Algorithm Using Insights from Neuromarketing Research. *Proceedings of the Neuropsychoeconomics Conference* (pp. *42*).

Berger, J., & Fitzsimons, G. (2008). Dogs on the Street, Pumas on Your Feet: How Cues in the Environment Influence Product Evaluation and Choice. *Journal of Marketing Research*, *45*(1), 1–14. doi:10.1509/jmkr.45.1.1

Blau, J. (2013). Europe's Billion-Euro Brain Research. *Research Technology Management, 56*(3), 8–10.

Bove, J. (2008). What Makes Shoppers Tick? *Display & Design Ideas, 20*(3), 76–78.

Caffyn, J. (1964). Psychological Laboratory Techniques in Copy Research. *Journal of Advertising Research, 4*(4), 45–50.

Casarotti, M., Lisi, M., Umiltà, C., & Zorzi, M. (2012). Paying Attention through Eye Movements: A Computational Investigation of the Premotor Theory of Spatial Attention. *Journal of Cognitive Neuroscience, 24*(7), 1519–1531. doi:10.1162/jocn_a_00231 PMID:22452561

Cohn, J., Ambadar, Z., & Ekman, P. (2006). In J.A. Coan, & J.B. Allen (Eds.), *The Handbook of Emotion Elicitation and Assessment*. New York, NY: Oxford University Press.

Craig, A. W., Loureiro, Y. K., Wood, S., & Vendemia, J. M. (2012). Suspicious Minds: Exploring Neural Processes during Exposure to Deceptive Advertising. *Journal of Marketing Research, 49*(3), 361–372. doi:10.1509/jmr.09.0007

Craig, S. D., D'Mello, S., Witherspoon, A., & Graesser, A. (2008). Emote Aloud during Learning with Autotutor: Applying The Facial Action Coding System to Cognitive-Affective States During Learning. *Cognition and Emotion, 22*(5), 777–788. doi:10.1080/02699930701516759

Damasio, A. R. (2005). *Descartes' Error: Emotion, Reason, and the Human Brain*. New York, NY: Penguin Books.

Davis, D. F., & Herr, P. M. (2014). From Bye to Buy: Homophones as a Phonological Route to Priming. *The Journal of Consumer Research, 40*(6), 1063–1077. doi:10.1086/673960

De Melo, C. M., Kenny, P., & Gratch, J. (2010). Influence of Autonomic Signals on Perception of Emotions in Embodied Agents. *Applied Artificial Intelligence, 24*(6), 494–509. doi:10.1080/08839514.2010.492159

De Vroey, M. (2009). A Marshall-Walras Divide? A Critical Review of the Prevailing Viewpoints. *History of Political Economy, 41*(4), 709–736. doi:10.1215/00182702-2009-038

Del Missier, F., Mäntylä, T., Hansson, P., Bruine de Bruin, W., Parker, A. M., & Nilsson, L.-G. (2013). The Multifold Relationship between Memory and Decision Making: An Individual-Differences Study. *Journal of Experimental Psychology. Learning, Memory, and Cognition, 39*(5), 1344–1364. doi:10.1037/a0032379 PMID:23565790

DellaVigna, S. (2009). Psychology and Economics: Evidence from the Field. *Journal of Economic Literature, 47*(2), 315–372. doi:10.1257/jel.47.2.315

Detric, P. (2010). Demand Effects on Positive Response Distortion by Police Officer Applicants on the Revised NEO Personality Inventory. *Journal of Personality Assessment, 92*(5), 410–415. doi:10.1080/00223891.2010.497401 PMID:20706927

Dimofte, C. V. (2010). Implicit Measures of Consumer Cognition: A Review. *Psychology and Marketing, 27*(10), 921–937. doi:10.1002/mar.20366

Djamasbi, S., Siegel, M., Skorinko, J., & Tullis, T. (2011). Online Viewing and Aesthetic Preferences of Generation Y and the Baby Boom Generation: Testing User Web Site Experience through Eye Tracking. *International Journal of Electronic Commerce*, *15*(4), 121–158. doi:10.2753/JEC1086-4415150404

Ekman, P. (1992). An Argument for Basic Emotions. *Cognition and Emotion*, *6*(3), 169–200. doi:10.1080/02699939208411068

Ekman, P., & Friesen, W. V. (1978). *Facial Action Coding System*. Palo Alto, CA: Consulting Psychologists Press.

Flight, M.H. (2011). Memory: The Foundations of Accurate Recall. *Nature Reviews. Neuroscience*, *12*(7), 372–373. doi:10.1038/nrn3055 PMID:21610731

Fugate, D. L. (2007). Neuromarketing: A Layman's Look at Neuroscience and Its Potential Application to Marketing Practice. *Journal of Consumer Marketing*, *24*(7), 385–394. doi:10.1108/07363760710834807

Gakhal, B., & Senior, C. (2008). Examining the Influence of Fame in the Presence of Beauty: An Electrodermal 'Neuromarketing' Study. *Journal of Consumer Behaviour*, *7*(4/5), 331–341. doi:10.1002/cb.255

Genco, S., Pohlmann, A., & Steidl, P. (2013). *Neuromarketing for Dummies*. Mississauga, ON: John Wiley & Sons Canada.

Gregg, A. P., & Klymowsky, J. (2013). The Implicit Association Test in Market Research: Potentials and Pitfalls. *Psychology and Marketing*, *30*(7), 588–601. doi:10.1002/mar.20630

Gregg, A. P., Klymowsky, J., Owens, D., & Perryman, A. (2013). Let Their Fingers Do The Talking? Using The Implicit Association Test in Market Research. *International Journal of Market Research*, *55*(4), 2–14. doi:10.2501/IJMR-2013-013

Hensel, J. (1970). *Physiological Measures of Advertising Effectiveness: A Theoretical and Empirical Investigation* [Doctoral Dissertation]. Ohio State University, School of Business. Retrieved from https://etd.ohiolink.edu/

Javor, A., Koller, M., Lee, N., Chamberlain, L., & Ransmayr, G. (2013). Neuromarketing and Consumer Neuroscience: Contributions To Neurology. *BMC Neurology*, *13*(13), 1–12. PMID:23383650

Jefferies, E., Frankish, C., & Noble, K. (2009). Lexical Coherence in Short-Term Memory: Strategic Reconstruction or "Semantic Glue"? *Quarterly Journal of Experimental Psychology*, *62*(10), 1967–1982. doi:10.1080/17470210802697672 PMID:19255945

Kenning, P., Plassmann, H., & Ahlert, D. (2007). Applications of Functional Magnetic Resonance Imaging for Market Research. *Qualitative Market Research*, *2*(2), 135–152. doi:10.1108/13522750710740817

Kroeber-Riel, W. (1979). Activation Research: Psychobiological Approaches in Consumer Research. *The Journal of Consumer Research*, *5*(4), 240–250. doi:10.1086/208736

LaBarbera, P. A., & Tucciarone, J. D. (1995). GSR Reconsidered: A Behavior-Based Approach to Evaluating and Improving the Sales Potency of Advertising. *Journal of Advertising Research*, *35*(5), 33–53.

Lajante, M., Droulers, O., Dondaine, T., & Amarantini, D. (2012). Opening the "Black Box" of Electrodermal Activity in Consumer Neuroscience Research. *Journal of Neuroscience, Psychology, and Economics*, *5*(4), 238–249. doi:10.1037/a0030680

Lee, L., Amir, O., & Ariely, D. (2009). In Search of Homo Economicus: Cognitive Noise and the Role Of Emotion In Preference Consistency. *The Journal of Consumer Research*, *36*(2), 173–187. doi:10.1086/597160

Martin, W. C., Engelland, B. T., & Collier, J. E. (2011). Assessing the Impact of Acquiescence Response Bias on Marketing Data. *Marketing Management Journal*, *21*(1), 31–46.

Mast, F. W., & Zaltman, G. (2005). A Behavioral Window on the Mind of the Market: An Application of the Response Time Paradigm. *Brain Research Bulletin*, *67*(5), 422–427. doi:10.1016/j.brainresbull.2005.06.004 PMID:16216689

Mauri, M., Cipresso, P., Balgera, A., Villamira, M., & Riva, G. (2011). Why is Facebook so successful? Psychophysiological Measures Describe A Core Flow State While Using Facebook. *Cyberpsychology, Behavior, and Social Networking*, *14*(12), 723–731. doi:10.1089/cyber.2010.0377 PMID:21879884

McClure, S. M., Li, J., Tomlin, D., Cypert, K. S., Montague, L. M., & Montague, R. P. (2004). Neural Correlates Of Behavioral Preference For Culturally Familiar Drinks. *Neuron*, *44*(2), 379–387. doi:10.1016/j.neuron.2004.09.019 PMID:15473974

Morgan, M. S. (2006). Economic Man as Model Man: Ideal Types, Idealization And Caricatures. *Journal of the History of Economic Thought*, *28*(1), 1–27. doi:10.1080/10427710500509763

Morin, C. (2011). Neuromarketing: The New Science of Consumer Behavior. *Symposium: Consumer Culture in Global Perspective.*

Nancarrow, C., Brace, I., & Wright, L. (2001). Tell Me Lies, Tell Me Sweet Little Lies: Dealing With Socially Desirable Responses In Market Research. *Marketing Review*, *2*(1), 55–55. doi:10.1362/1469347012569427

Narvainen, J., Pulkkinen, K., Kuoppa, P., Tarvainen, M., Lankinen, M., & Lapveteläinen, A., & ... Karhune, L. (2013). Probing Psychophysiology by Pictorial Stimuli of Emotional Content: General Patterns and Personality Effects. *Neuropsychoeconomics Conference Proceedings* (p. *25).*

Ohme, R. (2009). Special Topics Session: How Neurophysiological Research Contributes to Advertising Research. *American Academy Of Advertising Conference Proceedings* (pp. 55-57).

Ohme, R., Kowalski, J., & Reykowska, D. (2007). Exploring Consumers' Mind Via EEG And EMG Activity. *Neuropsychoeconomics Conference Proceedings* (p. 26).

Ohme, R., Matukin, M., & Pacula-Lesniak, B. (2011). Biometric Measures For Interactive Advertising Research. *Journal of Interactive Advertising*, *11*(2), 60–72. doi:10.1080/15252019.2011.10722185

Ohme, R., Reykowska, D., Wiener, D., & Choromanska, A. (2010). Application of Frontal EEG Asymmetry To Advertising Research. *Journal of Economic Psychology*, *31*(5), 785–793. doi:10.1016/j.joep.2010.03.008

Parens, E., & Johnston, J. (2014). Neuroimaging: Beginning to Appreciate its Complexities. *The Hastings Center Report*, *45*(2), s2–s7. doi:10.1002/hast.293 PMID:24634082

Patton, M. (1990). *Qualitative Evaluation and Research Methods*. London, UK: Sage.

Philippot, P., Chapelle, G., & Blairy, S. (2002). Respiratory Feedback in the Generation of Emotion. *Cognition and Emotion*, *16*(5), 605–627. doi:10.1080/02699930143000392

Pizzagalli, D. A., Sherwood, R. J., Henriques, J. B. & Davidson, R. J. (2005). Frontal Brain Asymmetry and Reward Responsiveness. *Psychological Science (Wiley-Blackwell), 16*(10), 805-813.

Rasch, C., & Teichert, T. (2013). Assessing Consumers' Preferences with Facial Electromyography - Insights from a Discrete Choice Experiment. *Neuropsychoeconomics Conference Proceedings*, 54.

Ratnayake, N., Broderick, A. J., & Mitchell, R. C. (2010). A Neurocognitive Approach to Brand Memory. *Journal of Marketing Management*, *26*(13-14), 1295–1318. doi:10.1080/0267257X.2010.522531

Ravaja, N., Somervuori, O., & Salminen, M. (2013). Predicting Purchase Decision: The Role of Hemispheric Asymmetry over the Frontal Cortex. *Journal of Neuroscience, Psychology, and Economics*, *6*(1), 1–13. doi:10.1037/a0029949

Reardon, S. (2014). Brain-Mapping Projects to Join Forces. *Scientific American*. Retrieved from http://www.scientificamerican.com/article/brain-mapping-projects-to-join-forces/

Rubinson, J. (2010). What Behavioral Economics Can Teach Marketing Research. *Journal of Advertising Research*, *50*(2), 114–117. doi:10.2501/S0021849910091269

Sammler, D., Grigutsch, M., Fritz, T., & Koelsch, S. (2007). Music and Emotion: Electrophysiological Correlates of the Processing of Pleasant and Unpleasant Music. *Psychophysiology*, *44*(2), 293–304. doi:10.1111/j.1469-8986.2007.00497.x PMID:17343712

Silberstein, R. B., & Nield, G. E. (2008). Brain Activity Correlates of Consumer Brand Choice Shift Associated with Television Advertising. *International Journal of Advertising*, *27*(3), 359–380. doi:10.2501/S0265048708080025

Singh, S. N., & Churchill, G. A. Jr. (1986). Using the Theory of Signal Detection to Improve Ad Recognition Testing. *JMR, Journal of Marketing Research*, *23*(4), 327–336. doi:10.2307/3151808

Steinhauer, S. R., Siegle, G. J., Condray, R., & Pless, M. (2004). Sympathetic and Parasympathetic Innervation of Pupillary Dilation during Sustained Processing. *International Journal of Psychophysiology*, *52*(1), 77–86. doi:10.1016/j.ijpsycho.2003.12.005 PMID:15003374

Sundararajan, M. (2010). Physiological Emotions and Entrepreneurial Decisions. *Global Business and Management Research*, *2*(4), 310–322.

Wolf, L., & Morrissey, S. (2013). Brain Initiative Unveiled. *Chemical and Engineering News*, *91*(14), 9–9.

Yi, Y. (1990). Cognitive and Affective Priming Effects of the Context for Print Advertisements. *Journal of Advertising*, *19*(2), 40–48. doi:10.1080/00913367.1990.10673186

ADDITIONAL READING

Achrol, R., & Kotler, P. (2012). Frontiers of the Marketing Paradigm in the Third Millennium. *Journal of the Academy of Marketing Science*, *40*(1), 35–52. doi:10.1007/s11747-011-0255-4

Ariely, D. (2008). *Predictably Irrational: The Hidden Forces That Shape Our Decisions*. New York, NY: HarperCollins.

Ariely, D. (2009). The End of Rational Economics. *Harvard Business Review*, *87*(7/8), 78–84. PMID:19968059

Bargh, J. A. (2005). Bypassing the Will: Toward Demystifying the Nonconscious Control of Social Behavior. In R. R. Hassin, J. S. Uleman, & J. A. Bargh (Eds.), *The New Unconscious* (pp. 37–61). New York, NY: Oxford University Press.

Berkman, E. T., & Lieberman, M. D. (2011). What's Outside the Black Box?: The Status of Behavioral Outcomes in Neuroscience Research. *Psychological Inquiry*, *22*(2), 100–107. doi:10.1080/1047840X.2011.550182 PMID:21984865

Causse, M., Sénard, J.-M., Démonet, J. F., & Pastor, J. (2010). Monitoring Cognitive and Emotional Processes through Pupil and Cardiac Response during Dynamic versus Logical Task. *Applied Psychophysiology and Biofeedback*, *35*(2), 115–123. doi:10.1007/s10484-009-9115-0 PMID:19816770

Du Plessis, E. (2011). *The Branded Mind: What Neuroscience Really Tells Us about the Puzzle of the Brain and the Brand*. London, UK: Kogan Page Limited.

Eser, Z., Isin, F., & Tolon, M. (2011). Perceptions of Marketing Academics, Neurologists, and Marketing Professionals about Neuromarketing. *Journal of Marketing Management*, *27*(7/8), 854–868. doi:10.1080/02672571003719070

Fitzsimons, G. M., Chartrand, T. L., & Fitzsimons, G. J. (2008). Automatic Effects of Brand Exposure on Motivated Behavior: How Apple Makes You "Think Different". *The Journal of Consumer Research*, *35*(1), 21–35. doi:10.1086/527269

Fortunato, V. C. R., Giraldi, J. D. M. E., & De Oliveira, J. H. C. (2014). A Review of Studies on Neuromarketing: Practical Results, Techniques and Limitations. *Journal of Management Research*, *6*(2), 201–220. doi:10.5296/jmr.v6i2.5446

Genco, S., Pohlmann, A., & Steidl, P. (2013). *Neuromarketing for Dummies*. Mississauga, ON: John Wiley & Sons Canada.

Gladwell, M. (2007). *Blink: The Power of Thinking without Thinking*. New York, NY: Little, Brown and Company.

Kahneman, D. (2011). *Thinking, Fast and Slow*. New York, NY: Farrar, Straus, and Giroux.

Kim, K., Hayes, J. L., Avant, J., & Reid, L. N. (2014). Trends in Advertising Research: A Longitudinal Analysis of Leading Advertising, Marketing, and Communication Journals, 1980 to 2010. *Journal of Advertising*, *43*(3), 296–316. doi:10.1080/00913367.2013.857620

Lindstrom, M. (2008). *Buy-ology*. New York, NY: Doubleday.

Maison, D., Greenwald, A. G., & Bruin, R. H. (2004). Predictive Validity of the Implicit Association Test in Studies of Brands, Consumer Attitudes, and Behavior. *Journal of Consumer Psychology*, *14*(4), 405–415. doi:10.1207/s15327663jcp1404_9

Micu, A., & Plummer, J. T. (2010). Measurable Emotions: How Television Ads Really Work. *Journal of Advertising Research*, *50*(2), 137–153. doi:10.2501/S0021849910091300

Plassmann, H., Ramsoy, T. Z., & Milosavljevic, M. (2011). Branding the Brain: A Critical Review and Outlook. *Journal of Consumer Psychology*, 1–19.

Pradeer, A. K. (2010). *The Buying Brain: Secrets for Selling to the Subconscious Mind*. Hoboken, NJ: John Wiley & Sons.

Sinha, P., Sharma, A., & Singh, H. (2012). Prediction for the 2012 United States Presidential Election Using Multiple Regression Model. *Journal of Prediction Markets*, *6*(2), 77–97.

Stoll, M., Baecke, S., & Kenning, P. (2008). What They See is What They Get? An fMRI Study on Neural Correlates of Attractive Packaging. *Journal of Consumer Behaviour*, *7*(4-5), 342–359. doi:10.1002/cb.256

KEY TERMS AND DEFINITIONS

Attitude: Evaluation of objects, people, situation, etc., that has significant influence on one's behavior. Attitudes can be either positive or negative, present for a long time or changeable by present circumstances and experiences.

Behavioral Economics: Interdisciplinary field that studies how emotions, social environment, and psychological factors influence economic decisions.

Bias: Strong opinion about certain people or objects, even when contrary evidence is present. They are formed as a result of judgment heuristics, the shortcuts created by brain in making decisions.

Neuromarketing: Emerging independent discipline that studies actual behavior of consumers.

Social Psychology: Scientific field that studies how social environment influences individual's behavior and vice versa.

Chapter 18
Examining the Brand Communication Tools that Impact Brand Preferences of Women Consumer buying intentions–Empirical Investigation of Middle East

A. M. Sakkthivel
Sur University College, Oman

B. Sriram
Sur University College Oman

ABSTRACT

The chapter aims to design a model of constructs of brand communication tools (direct and indirect) and test the impact of the same on brand preferences of women consumer buying intentions from Middle Eastern countries with specific evidences from Sultanate of Oman. The survey was conducted among 200 women consumers with reference to identifying the influence of brand communication tools on their buying intentions. The results revealed that both the communication tools found to have a significant impact. It is found that the direct brand communication tools have a higher impact over women buying intentions.

INTRODUCTION

The role of communication tools is becoming very prominent in today's competitive business world, as the companies spend billions to build brands, identify, target, reach and influence target consumers to buy products/services. The availability of huge array of communications tools to communicate and reach to target consumers leave the companies in a deep dilemma, to identifying the appropriate communication tools that would influence and impact the brand preferences of target consumers buying intentions (Keller

DOI: 10.4018/978-1-4666-8459-1.ch018

2005; Dolekoglu et al, 2008; Choi et al, 2010) . Moreover, the companies depend on these communication tools, to build brand in order to ensure the mind share among the target consumers, to get the money (wallet) share. In this scenario, a serious research is called for to identify the appropriate communication tools that would build brand, and communicate the same to the target consumers, in order to create a brand preference in their minds while choosing products/services to make purchase. The increasing role of women consumers to involve in family decision-making made them an attractive target to corporate world (Venkatesh, 1980; Firat, 1991). Hence, the companies intend to identify and use the appropriate communication tools that would build brand and attract the women consumers towards products/services. So, it is imperative to do a serious study to identify the brand communication tools (direct and in direct) that would influence brand preferences among women consumers (Nedungadi and Hutchinson, 1985; Balabanis and Craven, 1997; Jamal and Goode, 2001). Therefore, the researcher identified a problem definition to identify the brand communication tools that would have significant impact on brand preferences of women consumer buying intentions. The reason behind the selection of women consumers to investigate is to provide a much needed direction to the companies that would primarily target women consumers, to sell the products/services. Moreover, the women are increasingly involved in family decision making of buying different products/services (Sakkthivel, 2013). Therefore, the researcher chose two major constructs viz. direct brand communication tools (tools which are used by the company) such as (advertising, public relations, sales promotion, events, shop decoration, celebrity, personal selling, direct marketing, internet etc (Sakkthivel, 2011a, 2011b; Sakkthivel and Babawale, 2011; Abideen and Saleem, 2011; Sakkthivel, 2012) and indirect brand communication tools (tools used by outsiders) such as influence of peer groups, opinion/reference groups, society, social network websites, blogs etc. (Rapp et al, 2013; Goh et al, 2013), in order to test and identify the impact of the same on influencing brand preferences of women consumers. With reference to finding the role of different communications tools in conveying brand message to target consumers, we found several studies were conducted with respect to interpersonal communications (Peres et al, 2010), impact of social networking websites, online interaction, integrated marketing communication strategy (Sreedhar et al, 2005; Jothi et al, 2011; Brodie et al,2011; Mihart, 2012; Onditi 2012; Karunanithy and Sivesan,2013; Saeed et al, 2013; Adetunji et al, 2014), celebrity endorsements and sales promotion (Vitor et al, 2013; Buil et al, 2013; Johnmark et al, 2014). Such studies have provided a vital direction to develop a theme for the study. With reference to studies related to Arab world and women consumers, several studies were attempted to examine the role of women consumers, brand and advertising aspects including shopping motivations. (Al-Olayan & Karande, 2000; Jamal et al, 2006; Khraim, 2011). Such studies were not directly pertinent to brand communications, however, focused on the areas related to brand loyalty, advertisements, and role of brands in influencing the consumer behavior. Therefore, it is imperative to state that the research works towards the women consumers from the Arab world has begun and elicited interest among the researchers. Al-Olayan & Karande (2000) found the gap in the literature related to Arab world, and embarked on a study in 2000s to fill such gap. The aforesaid studies have provided a vital direction to us to build a theme which led to this study. Albeit, few studies have been attempted in Arab world with related to brand communications, such studies were vital to give us the direction to conduct a comprehensive study with reference to brand communication tools. Whilst choosing brand communication tools, it is imperative to acknowledge the role of social media and external influence over consumers towards choose preferred brands. Therefore, we have included the in direct brand communication tools primarily consist of social media and related aspects. Having build such a vital theme intends to fill the gaps found from the above studies which make the study to be considered very important as it would unearth the women behavior and response towards brand communication tools (direct and in direct) in influencing the brand preferences in Oman. Albeit, the study is proposed to be conducted in Oman, the results could be generalized and used across the different parts of the world.

Research Objectives and Hypothesis Formulation

To identify the impact of direct brand communication tools (advertising, public relations, sales promotion, events, shop decoration, celebrity, personal selling, direct marketing, internet etc.) to influence brand preferences of women consumer buying intentions.

H1: *There is a positive impact of direct brand communication tools (advertising, public relations, sales promotion, events, In store advertisements, celebrity, personal selling, direct marketing, internet etc.) to influence brand preferences of women consumer buying intentions*

To identify the impact of indirect brand communication tools (influence of peer groups, opinion/reference groups, society, social network websites, blogs etc) to influence brand preferences of women consumer buying intentions

H2: *There is a positive impact of indirect brand communication tools (influence of peer groups, opinion/reference groups, society, social network websites, blogs etc) to influence brand preferences of women consumer buying intentions*

BACKGROUND

Venkatesh (1980) conducted one of the earlier studies to know the changing roles of women consumers. He focused on three major types of women consumers' viz. feminists, moderates, and traditionalists, in order to find the roles in the changing life style and buying behaviour towards different products. Firat (1991) stated that since gender is culturally derived, gender identity is similarly rooted in cultural understandings of what it means to be masculine or feminine. The aforesaid reviews portrayed the changing face and influence of women consumers. There were studies conducted to address the issues related brand communication aspects. As Shocker et al (1994) said the brand managers need to address the exigencies of evolving needs of buyers. They need to deal with product – market boundaries such as technological changes, power and independence of the channels of distributions, pressure from investors and the globalization of competition. Al-Olayan and Karande (2000) conducted a study among selected Arab and African countries with reference to fill the gap found in the literature with related to advertisements, in comparison with advertisements from United States. The study revealed that there was no difference of portrayal of women and men in advertisements from the selected Arab and African countries; however, there were several differences in different aspects among the advertisements from United States. The study offered the cue to the brand managers who intend to advertise in Arab and Middle Eastern countries and implications were discussed. As Kotler (2000) said, cultural, social personal and psychological factors are the important factors that have major influences on buyer behavior.

According to him, groups have direct influences on the buyer behavior. Consumers are also influenced even by the groups which they do not belong to. Buyer choices are influenced by psychological factors such as motivation, perception, learning, beliefs and attitudes. These psychological factors are mostly influenced by the direct brand communication tools.

As per Hanzaee and Farsani (2001) views, people seek cues in their relationships to guide them toward behavior that gains social acceptance. The brand image and perceived public relation are important variables that help customers to process, recall and recognize the information. The study proved that perceived public relation has a positive influence on the customer loyalty. Sreedhar et al (2005) studied the importance of integrated marketing communication and brand identity in brand equity strategy. Brand image is one of the important factors in brand communication. In the current emerging interaction based brand communication focuses on brand contacts. In their paper, they have identified that the brand communication shall be planned or unplanned, but it is transmitted through a combination of vehicles rather than advertising alone. Grace and O'Cass (2005) identified that the controlled communications and brand name have a significant effect on customer satisfaction, brand attitudes and brand reuse intentions. They also identified that WOM has only influence on brand reuse intentions. As they have suggested that the advertising should be utilized to communicate the realistic service experiences.

Jamal et al (2006) conducted a study among Qatari consumers to identify the shopping motivations. Peres et al (2010) discussed about the diffusion network which focuses on the interpersonal communications in paradigm for market evaluation. They discussed about the impacts of social networks in this diffusion. They identified that the new adopters join the market as a result of two types of influences such as advertising and the other communications initiated by the firm and the interactions among the adopters and the potential adopters in the social system. As Shimp (2010, p7) said, marketing communications are the critical tools to achieve overall marketing mission. They are the determinants of companies' success and failure. These marketing communication tools help to achieve financial and nonfinancial goals. This communication includes various collateral forms of communication devices.

According to Yakup et al (2011), learning of cultural properties in the analysis of consumer behavior is an important variable in marketing. As social classes and its subclasses have significant impacts on consumer buying behavior, the communication channels and communication styles should be determined with respect to social classes and subclasses. As Smith and Zook (2011) said, the firms need to find creative partnerships that take the brand's message and products to the target audiences. The brand communication tools should give relevant and useful information to the customers at right time to strengthen the brand relationship. The creativity and marketing should help to break the clutter of noise and the hyper competition. The firms need to think hard about what would make someone to buy a brand and convert it into stunningly creative message. Co-creation can go way beyond ads and promotions to generate brand names.

Abideen and Saleem (2011) studied the relationship between the environmental responses and emotional responses with attitudinal and behavioral aspects of consumer buying behavior with respect to advertisements. Advertisement has become one of the important sources of brand communication tool which motivates the consumer in product liking and attitude toward purchase. Their study identified that the environmental response of purchasing associated to unplanned or impulse buying. Jothi et al (2011) said that people get attached to brand communication in social networking sites that usual banners and pop ups. Their study on the effectiveness of brand communication strategy revealed that the audiences respond to the interactive marketing than the traditional ads. The firms have made to create interesting and interactive brand communication messages which make the users to develop closeness with brand communication strategy. Brodie et al (2011) identified that the consumer engagement process comprises various sub processes that depend on the consumer's online interactive experiences with respect to brand communities. Their study revealed that the consumer's engagement in brand communications should be listen by the businesses. These engagements enhance the loyalty, satisfaction, empowerment, connection, emotional bonding and trust and commitments. Ballester et al (2012) studied the impact of brand knowledge structure and brand familiarity on brand message which may be either through direct or indirect brand communication tools. Their study revealed that there were direct relationship between brand familiarity and brand messages. Moderately consistent messages increased the awareness, associations, favourable responses and brand attitudes for the familiar brands.

According Mihart (2012), integrated marketing communication is a constant progress of developing complex strategy process from simple brand promotional tools. The primary purpose of marketing communication is to build and strengthen the brand and hence the marketing communication will create and sustain competitive advantages. Onditi (2012) studied the influence of promotional mix elements on sales. According to the author, promotion brings an interactive dialogue between an organization and its customers during the various stages of selling such as pre-selling, selling, consuming and post-consuming stage. As Vitor et al (2013) said, sales promotion is collection of incentive tools that are designed to motivate the sales of a product or service in short duration. Their study shows that the companies need to organize sales promotion in regular intervals to improve the sales. They suggested that the sales promotions should stimulate short term demand and create loyal customers. This sales promotion should also encourage the customers to switch from the competitors. The intense competition between the firms national and international levels call for the use of sales promotions.

According to Karunanithy and Sivesan (2013), promotion mix is a blend of communication tools used by the firms to communicate with the customer directly. The purpose of promotion is to influence the customer to buy the product. The firms need to select right mix of promotional activities that suit to the particular business at particular time to reach the customers correctly. According to Saeed et al (2013), marketing communications consist of all components in a brand communication mix. They promote and build shared meanings with the stakeholders of brand. The objectives of these brand communication tools are to provide information to the target audiences and boost the sales. Goh et al (2013) identified that the engagement of social media brand communities increases positive increase in purchase expenditures. They also identified that user generated contents in social media had more impacts on consumer purchase behavior than the marketer generated contents through embedded information and persuasion. Buil et al (2013) studied the relationships between advertising and sales promotions and their impact on brand equity creation. They identified that the individuals' attitudes towards the advertisements plays a vital role in influencing brand equity dimensions. Apart from that, the advertisements spend on the brands under investigation improved brand awareness.

Rapp et al (2013) had identified that the social media usages positively contributes to brand performance, retailer performance and consumer – retailer loyalty. Also, they identified that the social media usage was moderated by brand reputation and service ambidexterity. As Adetunji et al (2014) said, it is logically impossible to implement the facets of integrated marketing communication through single marketing communication tool advertisement. Thus, the advertising agents must use different message strategies, communication techniques and communication channels to create positive attitudes and successful brand image and awareness. Johnmark et al (2014) studied the impact of celebrity endorsement of the product and the impact on the buyer behavior. As they said, celebrity endorsement has been established as one of the popular brand communication tools of advertising. This has gain acceptance by most organizations in creating brand awareness. They identified that the physical attractiveness, credibility and congruence of celebrity with reference to the endorsed advertisement all have the impact on the customer's perception about the advertised product.

The aforesaid reviews provided a direction to fill the gaps found and the need of a comprehensive study to identify the influence direct and in direct communication tools on the brand preferences of women consumers. However, Not much of studies have been conducted to assess the impact of brand communications tools (direct and indirect) that impact the brand preferences on consumer, especially on women consumer buying intentions. There were studies attempted to identify the influence of brand preferences on consumer behavior (Nedungadi and Hutchinson, 1985; Balabanis and Craven, 1997; Jamal and Goode, 2001). Lynch and de Chernatony (2004) conducted a study to identify the power of emotion in brand communication among business to business markets. The study explored the balance between functional and emotional values. There were studies conducted to find the influence of brand, brand awareness and brand preferences on brand development and extensions (Keller 2005; Dolekoglu et al (2008; Choi et al, 2010). The study revealed the different homogeneous groups with several focus on specific shopping preferences. The results and implications were meant for brand managers. Khraim (2011) conducted a study among the women consumers from UAE to identify the aspects influence brand loyalty towards cosmetics. The study revealed that brand name and promotion found to have significant impact over brand loyalty among other factors. The study did not reveal the type of promotion selected to test among the respondents.There were studies attempted to investigate the influence of brand on consumer behavior (Sakkthivel, 2011a, 2011b; Sakkthivel and Babawale, 2011; Sakkthivel, 2012). However, the studies did not include all the variables that have been selected for the study, in order to identify and build a model of direct and indirect brand communications tools that would have impact on brand preferences of women consumer buying intentions. Hence, the researcher had selected the constructs in order to define a problem for the study to bridge those gaps from the earlier studies, in order to provide a comprehensive model of the variables that would have impact on brand preferences of target consumers selected for the study.

METHODOLOGY

The study used the descriptive research design as it order to study the variables impact of brand preferences of women consumers buying intentions. The study was conducted in selected places (Muscat, Sohar, Sur, Nizwa etc.) in Sultanate of Oman which represents the target population (women consumers) selected for the study. The quota sampling technique has been used to collect primary data from the target respondents (N=200). 217 respondents have been contacted and used for the study. However, 17 respondents have been left out due to incomplete responses. Structured questionnaire has been used (in both *English* and *Arabic* language) to collect the data. The collection tool has been designed to obtain the requisite information from the target respondents. The tool has two parts such as part 1 focused on demographic profile of the respondents, and the part 2 focused on the influence of selected variables selected for the study i.e. direct and indirect brand communications, over brand preferences of women consumers. The respondents have been selected based on the different demographic profiles such as age, occupation, literacy, marital status, income, and place of living. The respondents have been briefed about the study, and only the willing participants have been asked to participate the study. Trained women investigators have been used to approach the respondents (women consumers) due to the prevailing cultural and societal restrictions to access such participants. One sample T-test has been administered to test the hypotheses and construct analysis (Manickam and Sriram, 2013) used to identify the high to low impact of the selected variables on brand preferences of women consumer buying intentions. Cronbach's Alpa Reliability Analysis has been conducted to test the validity of collection instrument which produced 0.815 which proved highly reliable. Constructs have been tested through Cornbach's Alpa reliability test and found direct brand communications tools (0.759) and indirect brand communication tools (0.733) which are highly reliable

Demographic Analysis

Table 1 shows the demographic analysis of the sample data collected for the study.

MAIN FOCUS OF THE CHAPTER

One-Sample T Test Analysis to Identify the Impact of Direct and Indirect Brand Communication Tools on Brand Preferences of Women Consumer Buying and Decision Making Behaviour (Testing of Hypothesis)

One sample T-Test (2- tailed, 99% confidence interval at 199df) has been conducted to identify the impact of direct and indirect brand communication tools on brand preferences of women consumer buying intentions. The results revealed the positive influence of direct brand communications tools selected for the study such as advertising $t=15.111$, $p<0.01$; public relations activities $t=12.051$, $p<0.01$; sales promotion activities $t=10.375$, $p<0.01$; promotional events (road shows) $t=10.561$, $p<0.01$; store advertisements $t=9.820$, $p<0.01$; celebrities (famous actors/singers/sport personalities) $t=6.343$,$p<0.01$; personal selling initiatives $t=10.231$, $p<0.01$; direct marketing initiatives $t=12.104$, $p<0.01$; internet initiatives $t=8.432$, $p<0.01$, over the brand preferences of women consumer buying intentions. With regard to finding the influence indirect brand communication tools, the results revealed the positive influence of the selected variables such as information from peer groups $t=10.023$, $p<0.01$; information from reference groups $t=7.305$, $p<0.01$; information from social circle/society $t=8.855$, $p<0.01$; information from social network websites $t=11.428$, $p<0.01$; information from independent blogs (websites give information about brands) $t=12.202$, $p<0.01$, on the brand preferences of women consumer

Table 1. Demographic Analysis

S No	Demographic Variables	No. of Respondents
1.	Age	<20 (N=52); 21-30 (N=113); 31-40 (N=27); 40 - 50 (N=4); >50 (N = 4)
2.	Occupation	Student (N=105); Ministry (N=31); Banks (N=25); Company (N=25); Teachers (N=8); Doctors (N=5); Housewife (N=1)
3	Literacy	Primary School (N=6); High School (N=20); Diploma (N=49); Bachelor (N=74); Masters (N=37); PhD (N=8)
4	Marital Status	Single (N=122); Married (N=78)
5	Income (RO) (1 RO = 2.6 US$ Approx.)	<500 (N=125); 501-1000 (N=57); 1001-1500 (N=11); >1501 (N=7)
6	Place of Living	City (N=99); Town (N=99); Village (N=2)

buying intentions. It is evident from the results that the hypothesis H1 and H2 found to have a positive influence over brand preference of women consumer buying intentions. The aforesaid results revealed the positive influence of the selected variables (direct and in direct brand communication tools) over brand preferences of women consumers. However, in order to identify the degree of influence of such variables, construct analysis modeling (Manickam and Sriram, 2013) has been administered. The results would reveal the high and low impact variables, thus enabling the practicing managers to focus on the impacting variables and incorporate the same into designing effective brand communication strategies.

Construct Analysis Modelling

$$f(IEi) = \left[\sum Cj \,/\, Cn\right]\left[\sum_{i=1}^{n} Si \,/\, n\right]$$

f(IEi) = Impact of Direct Communication and Indirect Communication tools on brand preferences of women consumer behaviour

Si = Agreement level score of the respondents towards the influence of direct and indirect communication tools

Cj = Sum of Constructs score

Cn = No. of constructs taken

The above modelling produced the following results of the constructs have high to low impact on brand preferences on women consumer buying and decision making behaviour (high to low value). 'i' denotes the agreement level score, 'j' denotes the sum of constructs score, and 'n' denotes the number of respondents and number of constructs taken for the study and analysis. The construct analysis has been developed to identify the influence of the selected constructs/variables on the respondents. The no. of questions asked has been grouped into constructs such as direct communication tools and indirect communication tools. Those scores arrived from the constructs in terms of mean value would be interpreted according the highest to the lowest value. The values would be provided ranks as 1,2,3…n. The highest score denotes the highest impact on brand preferences of women consumers and so on. The sum of the mean values of constructs has been divided by the no. of constructs selected for the study, and the mean value arrived will be considered midpoint. The mean value of the constructs above the midpoint will be considered high impact variables and vice versa.

The above modelling reveals that the direct communication tools secured (3.869) 1st Rank and indirect communication tools secured (3.825) 2nd rank with regard to influencing brand preferences of women consumers buying intentions. It is identified that direct communication tools have more impact over brand preferences of women consumer buying and decision behaviour rather indirect communication tools. Further analysis identified the high to low impact variables with in direct and indirect communication tools. The results revealed that advertising, public relations, personal selling and direct marketing have high impact direct communication tools, whereas, it is identified that sales promotion, promotional events, store advertisements, celebrities, and internet initiatives have low impact over brand preferences of women consumer behaviour. With reference to analysing the high to low impact indirect communications tools, it is found that society, social network websites, and independent blogs have high impact over brand preferences, whereas, information from peer groups and reference groups have low impact. Hence, it is inferred that direct communication tools have more influence over creating brand preferences of women consumers rather indirect communication tools elicit low impact. It is imperative to understand the direct communications elicit a higher influence over brand preferences of women consumers, thus enabling practicing managers to effectively control the brand preferences of consumers though effective use of the direct brand communication tools. Therefore, it is evident that the companies could control the brand preferences of consumers. While assessing the high and low impact direct brand communication tools, it is found advertising, public relations, personal selling (in store selling) and direct marketing (SMS promotions) to elicit a higher influence. While assessing the impact of in direct brand communication tools, it is identified that society, social network websites, and independent blogs to elicit a higher influence over brand preferences of women consumers. Therefore, the practicing managers ought to focus on such brand communication tools to identify, reach, target and influence the target consumers to buy and remain loyal to the brands.

Discussions and Implications

The study attempted and identified the impact of direct brand communication tools and indirect brand communication tools on brand preferences of women consumers. The study found the selected variables viz. direct brand communication tools and indirect brand communication tools have significant impact over brand preferences of women consumer buying intentions. However, in order to identify the clarity in impact, the researcher used construct analysis modeling to identify the high to low impact variables. The results revealed that direct brand communication tools have more impact and indirect brand communication tools have lesser impact over brand preferences of women consumer buying intentions. The study also further analyzed to identify the high to low impact variables from direct and indirect brand communication tools and found that advertising, public relations, personal selling and direct marketing have high impact direct communication tools, whereas, it is identified that sales promotion, promotional events, store advertisements, celebrities, and internet initiatives have low impact over brand preferences of women consumers. With reference to analyzing the high to low impact indirect communications tools, it is found that society, social network websites, and independent blogs have high impact over brand preferences, whereas, information from peer groups and reference groups have low impact (Figure 1). Hence, it is inferred that direct brand communication tools have more influence over brand preferences of women consumer buying intentions. It is imperative to understand the direct communications elicit a higher influence over brand preferences of women consumers, thus enabling practicing managers to effectively control the brand preferences of consumers though effective use of the direct brand communication tools. Therefore, it is evident that the companies could control the brand preferences of consumers.

While assessing the high and low impact direct brand communication tools, it is found advertising, public relations, personal selling (in store selling) and direct marketing (SMS promotions) to elicit a higher influence studies (Sreedhar et al, 2005; Jothi et al, 2011; Brodie et al,2011; Mihart, 2012; Onditi 2012; Karunanithy and Sivesan,2013; Saeed et al, 2013; Adetunji et al, 2014). While assessing the impact of in direct brand communication tools, it is identified that society, social network websites, and independent blogs to elicit a higher influence over brand preferences of women consumers. The results are consistent

Figure 1. Modeling of high to low impact variables that influence brand preferences of women consumer buying intentions

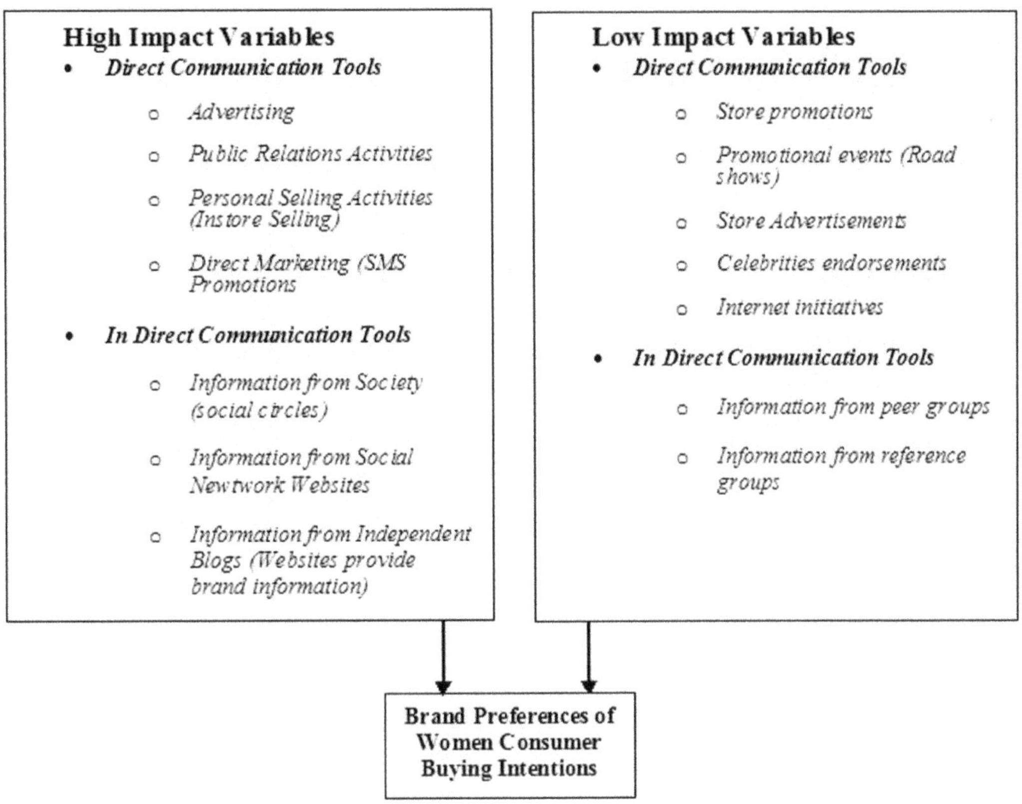

with the following studies (Rapp et al, 2013; Goh et al, 2013. Therefore, the practicing managers ought to focus on such brand communication tools to identify, reach, target and influence the target consumers to buy and remain loyal to the brands. Hence, the practicing managers must understand that the brand communication tools could be controlled by the companies in order to influence the brand preferences of women consumers. The outcomes of the study would provide much needed cue to industry and academia and make a significant contribution to the existing literature. Given the results, the practicing managers may work an effective strategic plan to suit to the target consumers, in order to reach, influence them to buy different products that are acceptable to culture, society and family.

RECOMMENDATIONS

Based on the above analyses and findings, the managers and the decision makers may use the following recommendations

1. It is found from the outcomes of the study, the direct brand communication tools found to have a higher influence over brand preferences of women consumers than that of in direct brand communication tools. It is evident that the companies could control the brand preferences of consumers

through effectively using the direct brand communication tools available at their disposal. Therefore, it is imperative for the companies to effectively such brand communication tools in order to effectively manage the brand preferences of consumers, make them remain loyal to the companies, thus increasing the customer life time value.

2. It is identified from the study about the high impact brand communication tools (direct and indirect). It is found, advertising, public relations activities, personal selling (instore selling) and direct marketing (SMS promotions) are the high impact direct brand communications tools, whereas, information from society, information from social network websites, and information form independent blogs (websites provide information about brands) have found to be high impact in direct communication tools. It is imperative the practicing managers use the above tools effectively to design an effective brand communication strategy to reach target consumers.
3. It is found from the study about the host of low impact brand communication tools (direct and in direct). The practicing managers ought to investigate the reasons behind in effectiveness, thus, enabling the low impact tools into high impact tools o left out from incorporating into the brand communication strategy.

FURTHER RESEARCH DIRECTIONS

The study attempted to design direct and in direct brand communications tools and test the influence of the same over brand preferences of women consumers from Middle Eastern Region. The study did not focus on the reasons behind such influence and why the women consumers sought such brand communication tools to understand certain brands, and use. The further research may focus on such aspects. The study attempted to Middle Eastern Region which is one of the restricted societies of the world, and the further studies could be conducted different parts of the world.

CONCLUSION

The study had been attempted to unveil the impact of direct and indirect brand communication tools on brand preferences of women consumer buying intentions. The study selected the two major constructs viz. direct brand communication tools (advertising, sales promotion, public relations, promotional events, store advertisements, personal selling, direct marketing, celebrities, internet initiatives) i.e. information provided by company and indirect brand communication tools (influence of peer groups, reference groups, society, social network websites, independent blogs) i.e. information provided by external sources and tested the impact of the same in influencing brand preferences of women consumers. The study revealed that the selected variables have significant impact over brand preferences of women consumer buying intentions and further attempted to identify the high to low impact variables. It found that direct brand communication tools have more impact, whereas indirect brand communication tools have lesser impact in influencing brand preferences (khraim, 2011). The study revealed the high to low impact variables over brand preferences of women consumers. With reference to direct brand communications tools found to have high impact over brand preferences, it is identified that advertising, public relations activities, personal selling activities (Inside the store selling), and direct marketing communications (SMS messages). The results are consistent with the following studies (Sreedhar et al, 2005; Jothi et al,

2011; Brodie et al,2011; Mihart, 2012; Onditi 2012; Karunanithy and Sivesan,2013; Saeed et al, 2013; Adetunji et al, 2014). Therefore, it is evident from the study that the direct brand communication tools used by the companies have more impact over influencing brand preferences of women consumers rather that of the indirect brand communication tools, provided by external sources. Therefore, the practicing managers ought to focus on such brand communication tools to identify, reach, target and influence the target consumers to buy and remain loyal to the brands. Hence, the practicing managers must understand that the brand communication tools could be controlled by the companies in order to influence the brand preferences of women consumers.

ACKNOWLEDGMENT

We acknowledge the moral and monetary support by Chairman and Management of Sur University College, Sur, Sultanate of Oman.

REFERENCES

Abideen, Z. U., & Saleem, S. (2011). Effective Advertising and Its Influence on Consumer Buying Behavior. *European Journal of Business and Management*, *3*(3), 55–65.

Adetunji. R.R., Nordin, S.M., & Noor, S.M. (2014). The Implementation of Integrated Marketing Communication Principles in Branding and Advertising: A Conceptual Exploration. *New Media and Mass Communication*, 24.

Al-Olayan, F., & Karande, K. (2000). A Content Analysis of Magazine Advertisements from the United States and the Arab World. *Journal of Advertising*, *29*(3), 69–82. doi:10.1080/00913367.2000.10673618

Balabanis, G., & Craven, S. (1997). Consumer Confusion from Own Brand Lookalikes: An Exploratory Investigation. *Journal of Marketing Management*, *13*(4), 299–313. doi:10.1080/0267257X.1997.9964474

Brodie, R. J., Llic, A., Juric, B., & Hollebeek, L. (2011). Consumer Engagement in Virtual Brand Communities: An Exploratory Analysis. *Journal of Business Research*. doi:10.1016/j.jbusres.2011.07.029

Buil, I., deChernatony, L., & Martinez, E. (2013). Examining the Role of Advertising and Sales Promotions in Brand Equity Creation. *Journal of Business Research*, *66*(1), 115–122. doi:10.1016/j.jbusres.2011.07.030

Choi, T.-M., Liu, N., Liu, S.-C., Mak, J., & To, Y.-T. (2010). Fast Fashion Brand Extensions: An Empirical Study of Consumer Preferences. *Journal of Brand Management*, *17*(7), 472–487. doi:10.1057/bm.2010.8

Delgado-Ballester, E., Navarro, A., & Sicilia, M. (2012). Revitalising brands through communication messages: The role of brand familiarity. *European Journal of Marketing*, *46*(1/2), 31–51. doi:10.1108/03090561211189220

Dolekoglu, C., Albayrak, M., Kara, A., & Keskin, G. (2008). Analysis of Consumer Perceptions and Preferences towards Store Brands Versus National Brands: An Exploratory Study in an Emerging Market. *Journal of Euromarketing*, *17*(2), 109–125. doi:10.1080/10496480802134787

Firat, A. Fuat. (1991). Consumption and Gender: A Common History. Gender and Consumer Behavior. First Conference Proceedings (pp. 378-386). Salt Lake City, UT: University of Utah Printing Service

Goh, K. M., Heng, C. S., & Lin, Z. (2013). Social Media Brand Community and Consumer Behavior: Qualifying the Relative Impact of User and Marketer Generated Contents. *Information Systems Research*, *24*(1), 88–107. doi:10.1287/isre.1120.0469

Grace, D., & O'Cass, A. (2005). Examining the Effects of Service Brand Communications on Brand Evaluation. *Journal of Product and Brand Management*, *14*(2), 106–116. doi:10.1108/10610420510592581

Hanzaee, K. H., & Farsani, F. T. (2011). The Effects of Brand Image and Perceived Public Relation on Customer Loyalty. *World Applied Sciences Journal*, *13*(2), 277–286.

Jamal, A., Davies, F., Chudry, F., & Al-Marri, M. (2006). Profiling Consumers: A Study of Qatari Consumers' Shopping Motivations. *Journal of Retailing and Consumer Services*, *13*(1), 67–80. doi:10.1016/j.jretconser.2005.08.002

Jamal, A., & Goode, M. H. (2001). Consumers and Brands: A study of the Impact of Self Image Congruence on Brand Preference and Satisfaction. *Marketing Intelligence & Planning*, *19*(7), 482–492. doi:10.1108/02634500110408286

Johnmark, D. R., Israel, K. J., & Zumbung, D. M. (2014). Celebrity Advertising and the Performance of New Products in Globacom Nigeria Limited. *Interdisciplinary Journal of Contemporary Research in Business*, *6*(4), 1–18.

Jothi, P. S., Neelamalar, M., & Prasad, R. S. (2011). Analysis of social networking sites: A study on effective communication strategy in developing brand communication. *Journal of Media and Communication Studies*, *3*(7), 234–242.

Karunanithy, M., & Sivesan, S. (2013). An Empirical Study on the Promotional Mix and Brand Equity: Mobile Service Providers. *Industrial Engineering Letters*, *3*(3), 1–9.

Keller, K. L. (2005). *Strategic Brand Management: Building*. Measuring and Managing Brand Equity.

Khraim, H. S. (2011). The Influence of Brand Loyalty on Cosmetics Buying Behavior of UAE Female Consumers. *International Journal of Marketing Studies*, *3*(2), 123–133.

Kotler, P. (2000). *Marketing Management Millennium Edition. 10e*. Prentice Hall.

Lynch, J., & De Chernatony, L. (2004). The Power of Emotion: Brand Communication in Business –to-Business Markets. *Journal of Brand Management*, *11*(5), 403–419. doi:10.1057/palgrave.bm.2540185

Manickam, S. A., & Sriram, B. (2013). Modeling the Impact of Marketing Information on Consumer Buying Behavior in a Matured Marketing Environment: An Exploratory of the Middle East Consumers. *Journal of Promotion Management*, *19*(1), 1–16. doi:10.1080/10496491.2012.715127

Mihart, C. (2012). Impact of Integrated Marketing Communication On Consumer Behavior: Effects on Consumer Decision Making Process. *International Journal of Marketing Studies*, *4*(2), 121–129. doi:10.5539/ijms.v4n2p121

Nedungadi, P., & Hutchinson, W. J. (1985). In C. H. Elizabeth & B. H. Moris (Eds.), *Prototypicality of Brands: Relationships with Brand Awareness, Preference and Usage Advances in Consumer Research (Vol. 12,* pp. 498–503). Provo, UT: Association of Consumer Research.

Onditi, A. A. (2012). An Evaluation of Promotional Elements Influencing Sales of an Organization: A Case Study of Sales of Agricultural and Non-Agricultural Products among Women Groups, Homa Bay District, Kenya. *International Journal of Business and Social Science*, *3*(5), 296–313.

Peres, R., Muller, E., & Mahajan, V. (2010). Innovation Diffusion and New Product Growth Models: A Critical Review and Research Directions. *International Journal of Research in Marketing*, *27*(2), 91–103. doi:10.1016/j.ijresmar.2009.12.012

Rapp, A., Beitelspacher, L. S., Grewal, D., & Hughes, D. E. (2013). Understanding Social Media Effects across Seller, Retailer and Consumer Interaction. *Journal of the Academy of Marketing Science*, *41*(5), 547–566. doi:10.1007/s11747-013-0326-9

Saeed, R., Naeem, B., & Naz, U. (2013). Integrated Marketing Communication: A Review Paper. *Interdisciplinary Journal of Contemporary Research in Business*, *5*(5), 124–133.

Sakkthivel, A M. & Babawale, Tinuki. (2011). Are the Same Determinants Influence Customer Satisfaction and Brand Loyalty – An Exploratory Study. *International Journal of Management. Entrepreneurship and Technology*, *1*(1), 93–102.

Sakkthivel, A. M. (2011a). Modeling of Determinants Influence Consumer Behavior towards Different Technology Products. *International Journal of Electronic Finance*, *5*(1), 84–103. doi:10.1504/IJEF.2011.038224

Sakkthivel, A. M. (2011b). Modeling the Impact of Internal and External Variables on Consumer Durables in a Matured Marketing Environment. *International Journal of Electronic Finance*, *5*(4), 316–332. doi:10.1504/IJEF.2011.043346

Sakkthivel, A. M. (2012). Modeling Consumer Choice (Buying) and Switching Behavior in a Restricted Marketing Environment. *International Journal of Electronic Finance*, *6*(1), 35–48. doi:10.1504/IJEF.2012.046592

Sakkthivel, A. M. (2013). Examining the impact of socio-cultural and psychographic/demographic variables on women consumer behaviour: An exploratory study from Arab League countries. *Int. J. Electronic Finance*, *7*(2), 161–175. doi:10.1504/IJEF.2013.057268

Shimp, T. A. (2010). *Integrated Marketing Communications in Advertising and Promotion. 8e*. Cengage Learning.

Shocker, A. D., Srivatsava, R. K., & Ruekert, R. W. (1994). Challenges and Opportunities Facing Brand Management: An Introduction to the Special Issue. *JMR, Journal of Marketing Research*, *31*(2), 149–158. doi:10.2307/3152190

Smith, P. R., & Zook, Z. (2011). *Marketing Communications: Integrating offline and online with Social Media. 5e*. KoganPage.

Sreedhar, M., Vishag, B., & McDonald, R. E. (2005). Integrated Marketing Communication (IMC) and Brand Identity As Critical Components of Brand Equity Strategy. *Journal of Advertising*, *34*(4), 69–80. doi:10.1080/00913367.2005.10639213

Venkatesh, A. (1980). Changing Roles of Women – A Life Style Analysis. *The Journal of Consumer Research*, *7*(2), 189–197. doi:10.1086/208806

Vitor, D. A., Ayimey, E. K., & Gayibor, R. A. (2013). Does Sales Promotion Influence Buyer Behavior? A Study of PZ Cussons Limited. *British Journal of Economics. Management & Trade*, *3*(2), 141–152.

Yakup, D., Mucahit, C., & Reyhan, O. (2011). The Impact of Cultural Factors on Consumer Buying Behaviors Examined through an Empirical Study. *International Journal of Business and Social Science*, *2*(5), 109–114.

KEY TERMS AND DEFINITIONS

Brand: The name of a product/service which distinct itself from other similar products.

Brand Preferences: The consumer's choice of buying a particular brand of product/service.

Brand Communication: An information which is aimed to reach the selected target audience with regard to specific brand/brands.

Brand Communication Tool: A communication tool which is primarily used to convey information about specific brand/brands to selected target audience.

Construct Analysis Modeling: A statistical method that portrays a degree of influence of the selected variables i.e. high to low.

Direct Brand Communication Tools: The brand communication tools which are used by a company to convey information about specific brand/brands to selected targeted audience. Such communications tools could be controlled by the company. The tools are Advertising, Sales Promotion, In Store Advertisements, Public Relation Activities, Personal Selling Activities, Direct Marketing Activities, Using Celebrities to endorse brands, Internet Initiatives etc.

In Direct Brand Communication Tools: The brand communication tools which are used by external body other than a company in order to convey information about specific brand/brands to selected targeted audience. Such communications tools could not be controlled by the company. The tools are Information obtained from peer groups, Information obtained from reference groups, Information obtained from society/social circles, Information obtained though social network websites, Information obtained through independent blogs (websites provide information about brands) etc.

Middle East Region: The region that covers major western part of Asia primarily Arabic speaking countries such as Saudi Arabia, Oman, UAE, Bahrain, Kuwait, Qatar, Yemen, Jordon, Syria, Iraq etc.

Women Consumer: A feminine gender who buys a product/service for her own consumption.

Compilation of References

Aaker, D. A., Stayman, D. M., & Hagerty, M. R. (1986). Warmth in Advertising: Measurement, Impact, and Sequence Effects. *The Journal of Consumer Research*, *12*(4), 365–381. doi:10.1086/208524

Abbott, J., Stone, M., & Buttle, F. (2001). Customer relationship management in practice: A qualitative study. *Journal of Database Marketing*, *9*(1), 24–34. doi:10.1057/palgrave.jdm.3240055

Abernethy, M. A., Lillis, A. M., Brownell, P., & Carter, P. (2001). Product Diversity and Costing System Design Choice: Field Study Evidence. *Management Accounting Research*, *12*(3), 261–267. doi:10.1006/mare.2001.0168

Abideen, Z. U., & Saleem, S. (2011). Effective Advertising and Its Influence on Consumer Buying Behavior. *European Journal of Business and Management*, *3*(3), 55–65.

Abrate, G., Fraquelli, G., & Viglia, G. (2012). Dynamic pricing strategies: Evidence from European hotels. *International Journal of Hospitality Management*, *31*(1), 160–168. doi:10.1016/j.ijhm.2011.06.003

Accenture. (2003).*CRM in Government: Bridging the Gap*. The Government Executives Series.

Accenture. (2004).*e-Government Leadership: High Performance, Maximum Value*. The Government Executives Series

Accenture. (2006). *Leadership in Customer Service: Building the Trust*. The Government Executives Series.

Adetunji. R.R., Nordin, S.M., & Noor, S.M. (2014). The Implementation of Integrated Marketing Communication Principles in Branding and Advertising: A Conceptual Exploration. *New Media and Mass Communication*, 24.

Adjei, M. T., Griffith, D. A., & Noble, S. M. (2009). When do relationships pay off for small retailers? Exploring targets and contexts to understand the value of relationship marketing. *Journal of Retailing*, *85*(4), 493–501. doi:10.1016/j.jretai.2009.09.001

Afifi, A., & Bergman, R. (2005). *Functional Neuroanatomy: Text and Atlas*. New York, NY: McGraw-Hill Medical.

Agariya, A., & Singh, D. (2011). What really defines relationship marketing? A review of definitions and general and sector-specific defining constructs. *Journal of Relationship Marketing*, *10*(4), 203–237. doi:10.1080/15332667.2011.624905

Agarwal, A., Harding, D. P., & Schumacher, J. R. (2004). Organizing for CRM. *The McKinsey Quarterly*, *3*, 80–91.

Agarwal, R., & Prasad, J. (1998). A conceptual and operational definition of personal innovativeness in the domain of information technology. *Information Systems Research*, *9*(2), 204–215. doi:10.1287/isre.9.2.204

Ahlqvist, T., Back, A., Halonen, M., & Heinonen, S. (2008). Social Media Roadmaps: Exploring the futures triggered by social media. VTT Research Notes 2454, Espoo, Finland.

Ahn, H., Moon, H., Fazzari, M. J., Lim, N., Chen, J. J., & Kodell, R. L. (2007). Classification by ensembles from random partitions of high-dimensional data. *Computational Statistics & Data Analysis*, *51*(12), 6166–6179. doi:10.1016/j.csda.2006.12.043

Ailawadi, K. L., Neslin, S. A., & Gedenk, K. (2001). Pursuing the value-conscious consumer: Store brands versus national brand promotions. *Journal of Marketing*, *65*(1), 71–89. doi:10.1509/jmkg.65.1.71.18132

Ajzen, I. (1985). From intentions to actions: A theory of planned behavior. In J. Kuhl & J. Beckman (Eds.), *Action control: From cognition to behavior* (pp. 11–39). Heidelberg, Germany: Springer. doi:10.1007/978-3-642-69746-3_2

Akerlof, G. (1970). The market for "lemons": Quality uncertainty and the market mechanism. *The Quarterly Journal of Economics*, *84*(3), 488–500. doi:10.2307/1879431

Akroush, M. N., Dahiyat, S. E., Gharaibeh, H. S., & Abu-Lail, B. N. (2011). Customer relationship management implementation: An investigation of a scale's generalizability and its relationship with business performance in a developing country context. *International Journal of Commerce and Management*, *21*(2), 158–191. doi:10.1108/10569211111144355

Albertin, A. (2005). A tecnologia de informação e o indivíduo: Propondo um modelo de adoção de tecnologia para a inclusão digital (Report FGV n.11). School of Management, Getulio Vargas Foundation, Saint Paul, Brazil.

Aleem, A., & Antwi-Boasiako, A. (2011). Internet auction fraud: The evolving nature of online auctions criminality and the mitigating framework to address the threat. *International Journal of Law, Crime and Justice*, *39*(3), 140–160. doi:10.1016/j.ijlcj.2011.05.003

alem Mohammad, A., bin Rashid, B., & bin Tahir, S. (2013). Assessing the influence of customer relationship management (CRM) dimensions on organization performance: An empirical study in the hotel industry. *Journal of Hospitality and Tourism Technology*, *4*(3), 228–247. doi:10.1108/JHTT-01-2013-0002

Alfaro, E., Gámez, M., & García, N. (2006). adabag: Applies Adaboost.M1 and Bagging.

Alge, B. J., Wiethoff, C., & Klein, H. J. (2003). When does the medium matter? Knowledge building experiences and opportunities in decision-making teams. *Organizational Behavior and Human Decision Processes*, *9*(1), 26–37. doi:10.1016/S0749-5978(02)00524-1

Ali, A., Krapfel, R., & LaBahn, D. (1995). Product innovativeness and entry strategy: Impact cycle time and break-even time. *Journal of Product Innovation Management*, *12*(1), 54–70. doi:10.1016/0737-6782(94)00027-D

Allameh, S., Momeni, Z., Esfahani, Z., & Bardeh, M. (2011). An assessment of the effect of information communication technology on human resource productivity of Mobarekeh steel complex in Isfahan Iran. *Procedia Computer Science*, *3*, 1321–1326. doi:10.1016/j.procs.2011.01.010

Allen, D. G., Mahto, R. V., & Otondo, R. F. (2007). Web-based recruitment: Effects of information, organizational brand and attitudes towards a website on applicant attraction. *The Journal of Applied Psychology*, *92*(6), 1696–1708. doi:10.1037/0021-9010.92.6.1696 PMID:18020806

Alm, J., & Melnik, M. (2010). Do eBay sellers comply with state sales taxes? *National Tax Journal*, *63*(2), 215–236. doi:10.17310/ntj.2010.2.02

Almunawar, M. N., Anshari, M. A., & Susanto, H. (2013). Crafting strategies for sustainability: How travel agents should react in facing a disintermediation. *Operations Research*, *13*(3), 317–342. doi:10.1007/s12351-012-0129-7

Al-Olayan, F., & Karande, K. (2000). A Content Analysis of Magazine Advertisements from the United States and the Arab World. *Journal of Advertising*, *29*(3), 69–82. doi:10.1080/00913367.2000.10673618

Amazon Prime Air. (n. d.). *Amazon.com.* Retrieved from http://www.amazon.com/b?node=8037720011

Amber, T., & Roberts, J. (2006). *Beware the Silver Metric: Marketing Performance Measurement Has to Be Multidimensional* (Marketing Science Institute Working Paper Series No. 06-113). Cambridge, MA: Marketing Science Institute.

Amemiya, T. (1984). Tobit models: A survey. *Journal of Econometrics*, *24*(1-2), 3–61. doi:10.1016/0304-4076(84)90074-5

Ampuero, O., & Vila, N. (2006). Consumer perceptions of product packaging. *Journal of Consumer Marketing*, *23*(2), 102–114. doi:10.1108/07363760610655032

Anderson, J. C., & Gerbing, D. W. (1988). Structural equation modeling in practice: A review and recommended two-step approach. *Psychological Bulletin*, *103*(3), 411–423. doi:10.1037/0033-2909.103.3.411

Angeles, R. (2000). Revisiting the Role of Internet-EDI in the Current Electronic Commerce Scene. *Logistics Information Management*, *13*(1), 45–57. doi:10.1108/09576050010306396

Ansari, A., Essegaier, S., & Kohli, R. (2000). Internet Recommendation Systems. *JMR, Journal of Marketing Research*, *37*(3), 363–375. Retrieved from http://www.haas.berkeley.edu/Courses/Spring2000/BA269D/AnsariEssegaierKohli99.pdf doi:10.1509/jmkr.37.3.363.18779

Antón, C., Camarero, C., & Rodríguez, J. (2013). Usefulness, enjoyment and self-image congruence: The adoption of e-book readers. *Psychology and Marketing*, *30*(4), 372–384. doi:10.1002/mar.20612

Antonelli, S., & Santos, A. (2009). Uso da estatística para garantia da qualidade: Um survey com indústria de alimentos baseado no Seis Sigma. Proceedings of the Simpósio de Administração da Produção, Logística e Operações Internacionais. Annals FGV. School of Management, Getulio Vargas Foundation, Saint Paul, Brazil.

Aren, S., Güzel, M., Kabadayı, E., & Alpkan, L. (2013). Factors affecting repurchase intention to shop at the same website. *Procedia: Social and Behavioral Sciences*, *99*, 536–544. doi:10.1016/j.sbspro.2013.10.523

Ariely, D., & Berns, G. S. (2010). Neuromarketing: The Hope and Hype of Neuroimaging in Business. *Nature Reviews. Neuroscience*, *11*(4), 284–292. doi:10.1038/nrn2795 PMID:20197790

Arjaliès, D. L., & Mundy, J. (2012, May). How firms use management control systems to formulate and implement CSR strategy: A levers of control perspective. *Proceedings of the EAA (European Accounting Association)Annual Conference.*

Arksey, H., & Knight, P. (1999). *Interviewing for Social Scientists.* London, UK: Sage.

Arksey, H., & Knight, P. T. (1999). *Interviewing for social scientists: An introductory resource with examples.* London: SAGE.

Armstrong, G., & Kotler, P. (2007). *Principles of Marketing* (12th ed.). New York: Prentice-Hall.

Arndt, R. Z. (2011, November 7). Bluefin mines social media to improve TV analytics. *Fast Company.*

Arndt, J. (1967). Role of product-related conversations in the diffusion of a new product. *Journal of Marketing Research*, *4*(August), 291–295. doi:10.2307/3149462

Arnold, T. J., Fang, E., & Palmatier, R. W. (2011). The effects of customer acquisition and retention orientations on a firm's radical and incremental innovation performance. *Journal of the Academy of Marketing Science*, *39*(2), 234–251. doi:10.1007/s11747-010-0203-8

Ashworth, L., Dacin, P., & Thomson, M. (2009), Why on earth do consumers have relationships with marketers? Toward understanding the functions of brand relationships. Handbook of brand relationships (pp. 82-106).

Askool, S., & Nakata, K. (2011). A conceptual model for acceptance of social CRM systems based on a scoping study. *AI & Society*, *26*(3), 205–220. doi:10.1007/s00146-010-0311-5

Ata, U. Z., & Toker, A. (2012). The effect of customer relationship management adoption in business-to-business markets. *Journal of Business and Industrial Marketing*, *27*(6), 497–507. doi:10.1108/08858621211251497

Atuahene-Gima, K. (1995). An exploratory analysis of the impact of market orientation on new product performance. *Journal of Product Innovation Management*, *12*(4), 275–293. doi:10.1016/0737-6782(95)00027-Q

Atuahene-Gima, K. (1996). Market orientation and innovation. *Journal of Business Research*, *35*(2), 93–103. doi:10.1016/0148-2963(95)00051-8

Atuahene-Gima, K., & Evangelista, F. U. (2000). Cross-Functional Influence in New Product Development: An Exploratory Study of Marketing and R&D Perspectives. *Management Science*, *46*(10), 1269–1284. doi:10.1287/mnsc.46.10.1269.12273

Audretsch, D. B. (1995). Firm Profitability, Growth and Innovation. *Review of Industrial Organization*, *10*(5), 579–588. doi:10.1007/BF01026883

Aungst, S. G., & Wilson, D. T. (2005). A primer for navigating the shoals of applying wireless technology to marketing problems. *Journal of Business and Industrial Marketing*, *20*(2), 59–69. doi:10.1108/08858620510583650

Austin, T. (2013). The Disruptive Era of Smart Machines Is Upon Us. *Gartner*. Retrieved from http://www.gartner.com/doc/2598620

Avlonitis, G. J., & Indounas, K. A. (2006). Pricing practices of service organizations. *Journal of Services Marketing*, *20*(5), 346–356. doi:10.1108/08876040610679954

Ayres, I. (2008). *Super Crunchers: Why Thinking-By-Numbers is the New Way To Be Smart*. Bantam.

Azmat, F., & Ha, H. (2013). Corporate social responsibility, customer trust, and loyalty: Perspectives from a developing country. *Thunderbird International Business Review*, *55*(3), 253–270. doi:10.1002/tie.21542

Backaitis, V. (2014, January 12). Will IBM's Watson Change the Customer Experience? Beyond Customer Experience Management - What your CMS really needs to deliver. *CMS Wire*. Retrieved from http://www.cmswire.com/cms/big-data/will-ibms-watson-change-the-customer-experience-nrf14-023767.php

Baden, D., & Harwood, I. A. (2013). Terminology matters: A critical exploration of corporate social responsibility terms. *Journal of Business Ethics*, *116*(3), 615–627. doi:10.1007/s10551-012-1498-9

Baecke, P., & den Poel, D. V. (2011). Data augmentation by predicting spending pleasure using commercially available external data. *Journal of Intelligent Information Systems*, *36*(3), 367–383. doi:10.1007/s10844-009-0111-x

Baesens, B., Viaene, S., Van den Poel, D., Vanthienen, J., & Dedene, G. (2002). Bayesian neural network learning for repeat purchase modelling in direct marketing. *European Journal of Operational Research*, *138*(1), 191–211. doi:10.1016/S0377-2217(01)00129-1

Bagozzi, R., & Yi, Y. (1988). On the evaluation of structural equation models. *Journal of the Academy of Marketing Science*, *16*(1), 74–94. doi:10.1007/BF02723327

Bajari, P., & Hortacsu, A. (2003). The winner's curse, reserve prices, and endogenous entry: Empirical insights from eBay auctions. *The Rand Journal of Economics*, *34*(2), 329–355. doi:10.2307/1593721

Bajari, P., & Hortacsu, A. (2004). Economic insights from internet auctions. *Journal of Economic Literature*, *42*(2), 457–486. doi:10.1257/0022051041409075

Bakos, Y. (1998). The emerging role of electronic marketplaces on the internet. *Communications of the ACM*, *41*(8), 35–42. doi:10.1145/280324.280330

Balabanis, G., & Craven, S. (1997). Consumer Confusion from Own Brand Lookalikes: An Exploratory Investigation. *Journal of Marketing Management*, *13*(4), 299–313. doi:10.1080/0267257X.1997.9964474

Balachandra, R., & Friar, J. H. (1997). Factors for Success in R&D Projects and New Product Innovation: A Conceptual Framework. *IEEE Transactions on Engineering Management*, *44*(3), 267–287. doi:10.1109/17.618169

Bandettini, P. A. (2012). Twenty Years of Functional MRI: The Science and the Stories. *NeuroImage*, *62*(2), 575–588. doi:10.1016/j.neuroimage.2012.04.026 PMID:22542637

Bandura, A. (1986). *Social foundations of thought and action: A social cognitive theory*. Englewood Cliffs, New Jersey: Prentice Hall.

Bapna, R., Goes, P., & Gupta, A. (2001). Insights and analyses of online auctions. *Communications of the ACM*, *44*(11), 42–50. doi:10.1145/384150.384160

Barquette, S., & Chaoubah, A. (2007). *Pesquisa de marketing*. Saint Paul, Brazil: Saraiva Publisher.

Bartikowski, B., & Singh, N. (2014). Doing e-business in France: Drivers of online trust in business-to-consumer websites. *Global Business and Organizational Excellence*, *33*(4), 28–36. doi:10.1002/joe.21551

Barua, A., Konana, P., Whinston, A. B., & Yin, F. (2004). An empirical investigation of net-enabled business value. *Management Information Systems Quarterly*, *28*(4), 585–620.

Batra, R., & Ray, M. (1985). How Advertising Works at Contact. In L. F. Alwitt & A. A. Mitchell (Eds.), *Psychological Processes and Advertising Effects* (pp. 13–44). Hillsdale, NJ: Lawrence Erlbaum Associates.

Battor, M., & Battor, M. (2010). The impact on innovation and performance advantages: Testing a mediated model. *Journal of Marketing Management*, *26*(9-10), 842–857. doi:10.1080/02672570903498843

Bauer, R. (2004) Kein Bedarf für Plastikräder. *Freitag*. Retrieved from http:// www.freitag.de/2004/43/04431801.php

Bauer, E., & Kohavi, R. (1999). An empirical comparison of voting classification algorithms: Bagging, boosting, and variants. *Machine Learning*, *36*(1/2), 105–139. doi:10.1023/A:1007515423169

Bauer, H. H., Grether, M., & Leach, M. (2002). Building customer relations over the internet. *Industrial Marketing Management*, *31*(2), 155–163. doi:10.1016/S0019-8501(01)00186-9

Baumann, J., & Meunier-FitzHugh, K. L. (2014). Trust as a facilitator of co-creation in customer-salesperson interaction: An imperative for the realization of episodic and relational value? *AMS Review*, *40*(1-2), 5–20. doi:10.1007/s13162-013-0039-8

Baumeister, R., & Leary, M. (1995). The need to belong: Desire for interpersonal attachments as a fundamental human motivation. *Psychological Bulletin*, *117*(3), 497–529. doi:10.1037/0033-2909.117.3.497 PMID:7777651

Baumeister, R., & Tice, D. (1990). Anxiety and social exclusion. *Journal of Social and Clinical Psychology*, *9*(2), 165–195. doi:10.1521/jscp.1990.9.2.165

Baumeister, R., & Twenge, J. (2003). *The social self*. Handbook of Psychology. doi:10.1002/0471264385.wei0514

Beak, T. H., & Morimoto, M. (2012). Stay away from me: Examining the determinants of consumer avoidance of personalized advertising. *Journal of Advertising*, *41*(1), 59–76. doi:10.2753/JOA0091-3367410105

Bebbington, J., Larrinaga, C., & Moneva, J. M. (2008). Corporate social reporting and reputation risk management. *Accounting, Auditing & Accountability Journal*, *21*(3), 337–361. doi:10.1108/09513570810863932

Becker, S. (2013). Why You Cannot Map Attention: A Relational Theory of Attention and Eye Movements. *Australian Psychologist*, *48*(6), 389–398. doi:10.1111/ap.12028

Beitelspacher, L. S., Richey, R. G., & Reynolds, K. E. (2011). Exploring a new perspective on service efficiency: Service culture in retail organizations. *Journal of Services Marketing*, *25*(3), 215–228. doi:10.1108/08876041111129191

Belanche, D., Casaló, L. V., & Guinalíu, M. (2012). Website usability, consumer satisfaction and the intention to use a website: The moderating effect of perceived risk. *Journal of Retailing and Consumer Services*, *19*(1), 124–132. doi:10.1016/j.jretconser.2011.11.001

Bella, A., Ferri, C., Hernández-Orallo, J., & Ramírez-Quintana, M. J. (2011). Using negotiable features for prescription problems. *Computing*, *91*(2), 135–168. doi:10.1007/s00607-010-0129-5

Belleghem, S., Thijs, D., & De Ruyck, T. (2012). Social media around the word 2012. Retrieved from http://www.slideshare.net/InSitesConsulting/social-media-around-the-world-2012-by-insites-consulting

Bennett, R. C., & Cooper, R. G. (1979). Beyond the Marketing Concept. *Business Horizons*, *22*(June), 76–83. doi:10.1016/0007-6813(79)90088-0

Bercea, M. D. (2012). Taking the Pulse of the Market: A Consumer's Decision-Making Algorithm Using Insights from Neuromarketing Research. *Proceedings of theNeuropsychoeconomics Conference* (pp. *42)*.

Berger, J., & Iyengar, R. (2011). *How interests shapes word-of-mouth over different channels* (Marketing Science Institute Working Paper Series No. 11-110). Cambridge, MA: Marketing Science Institute.

Berger, J., & Fitzsimons, G. (2008). Dogs on the Street, Pumas on Your Feet: How Cues in the Environment Influence Product Evaluation and Choice. *Journal of Marketing Research*, *45*(1), 1–14. doi:10.1509/jmkr.45.1.1

Berger, J., & Milkman, K. L. (2012). What makes online content viral? *Journal of Marketing Research*, *49*(April), 192–205. doi:10.1509/jmr.10.0353

Berger, J., & Schwartz, E. (2011). What drives immediate and ongoing word-of-mouth? *JMR, Journal of Marketing Research*, *48*(October), 869–880. doi:10.1509/jmkr.48.5.869

Bernardi, P. (2008). Medindo a predisposição para a tecnologia [PhD Thesis]. School of Management, Getulio Vargas Foundation, Saint Paul, Brazil.

Berry, L. (1983). Relationship Marketing. In L. Berry (2002). Relationship marketing of services - Growing interest, emerging perspectives. *Academy of Marketing Science Journal*, *23*(4), 236–245. PMID:6410122

Berry, L. (2002). Relationship marketing of services: Perspectives from 1983 and 2000. *Journal of Relationship Marketing*, *1*(1), 59–77. doi:10.1300/J366v01n01_05

Berthon, P., Hulbert, J., & Pitt, L. (1999). To serve or to create? Strategic orientations towards customers & innovation. *California Management Review*, *42*(1), 37–58. doi:10.2307/41166018

Bethauer, D. M. (2002). *New Product Development and Delivery Ensuring Successful Products Through Integrated Process Management*. New York, NY: Amacom.

Bhatnagar, A., & Ghose, S. (2004). Segmenting consumers based on the benefits and risks of Internet shopping. *Journal of Business Research*, *57*(12), 1352–1360. doi:10.1016/S0148-2963(03)00067-5

Bhattacharya, C. B., & Bolton, R. N. (2000). Relationship marketing in mass markets. In J. Sheth & A. Parvatiyar (Eds.), *Handbook of relationship marketing* (pp. 327–354). Thousand Oaks, CA: Sage. doi:10.4135/9781452231310.n12

Bhattacharya, C. B., Sen, S., & Korschun, D. (2012). Using corporate social responsibility to win the war for talent. *MIT Sloan Management Review*, *49*(2), 37–44.

Bhattacharya, S., Krishnan, V., & Mahajan, V. (2003). Operationalizing Technology Improvements in Product Development Decison Making. *European Journal of Operational Research*, *149*(1), 102–130. doi:10.1016/S0377-2217(02)00428-9

Bianchi, C., & Andrews, L. (2012). Risk, trust, and consumer online purchasing behaviour: A Chilean perspective. *International Marketing Review*, *29*(3), 253–275. doi:10.1108/02651331211229750

Bichler, M., Kalagnanam, J., Katircioglu, K., King, A. J., Lawrence, R. D., Lee, H. S., & Lu, Y. et al.(2002). Applications of flexible pricing in business-to-business electronic commerce. *IBM Systems Journal*, *41*(2), 287–302. doi:10.1147/sj.412.0287

Bittinger, S. (2001). *Customer Relationship Management in e-Government*. Gartner Research Inc.

Bizcommunity. (2013). South Africa leads in African e-commerce. Retrieved from http://www.bizcommunity.com/Article/196/394/96986.html

Blackburn, R., Furst, S. A., & Rosen, B. (2003). Building a winning virtual team: KSA's, selections, training, and evaluation. In C. B. Gibson & S. G. Cohen (Eds.), *Virtual teams that work: Creating conditions for virtual team effectiveness*. San Francisco: Jossey-Bass.

Blackshaw, P., & Nazzaro, M. (2009). Consumer-Generated Media (CGM) 101: Word-of-mouth in the age of the Web-fortified consumer. In W.G. Mangold, & D.J. Faulds (Ed.). Social media: The new hybrid element of the promotion mix. *Business Horizons*, *52*(4), 357–365.

Blackston, M. (2000). Building Brand Equity by Managing the Brand's Relationship. *Journal of Advertising Research*, *40*(November/December).

Blattberg, R. C., Kim, B.-D., & Neslin, S. A. (2008). *Database marketing: analyzing and managing customers*. New York: Springer.

Blau, J. (2013). Europe's Billion-Euro Brain Research. *Research Technology Management*, *56*(3), 8–10.

Blomqvist, R., Dahl, J., & Haeger, T. (1993). [Relationship Marketing: Strategy and Methods for Service Competition] (In Swedish). Göteborg, Sweden: IHM Förlag.

Boar, B. (2002). *Tecnologia da informação: A arte do planeamento estratégico*. Saint Paul, Brazil: Berkley Publisher.

Bodenberg, T. M. (2001). *Customer relationship management: New ways of keeping the customer satisfied*. New York, NY: The Conference Board.

Bohlmann, J. D., Spanjol, J., Qualls, W. J., & Rosa, J. A. (2013). The interplay of customer and product innovation dynamics: An exploratory study. *Journal of Product Innovation Management*, *30*(2), 228–244. doi:10.1111/j.1540-5885.2012.00962.x

Bolton, G., Katok, E., & Ockenfels, A. (2004). How Effective Are Electronic Reputation Mechanisms? An Experimental Investigation. *Management Science*, *50*(11), 1587–1602. doi:10.1287/mnsc.1030.0199

Bonacich, P. (1987). Power and centrality: A family of measures. *American Journal of Sociology*, *92*(5), 1170–1182. doi:10.1086/228631

Bonds-Raacke, J., & Raacke, J. (2010). MySpace and Facebook: Identifying Dimensions of Uses and Gratifications for Friend Networking Site. *Individual Differences Research*, *8*(1), 27–33.

Bonn, I., & Fisher, J. (2011). Sustainability: The missing ingredient in strategy. *The Journal of Business Strategy*, *32*(1), 5–14. doi:10.1108/02756661111100274

Bonoma, T. (1985). Case Research in marketing: Opportunities, problems and a process. *JMR, Journal of Marketing Research*, *22*(2), 199–208. doi:10.2307/3151365

Boone, L. E., & Kurtz, D. L. (2007). *Contemporary Marketing*. New York, NY: Harcourt College Publisher.

Borghino, D. (2014, May 9). IBM's Watson can now debate any topic. *Gigmag*. Retrieved from http://www.gizmag.com/ibm-watson-debate/31993/

Boulding, W., Staelin, R., Ehret, M., & Johnston, W. J. (2005). A customer relationship management roadmap: What is known, potential pitfalls, and where to go. *Journal of Marketing*, *69*(4), 155–166. doi:10.1509/jmkg.2005.69.4.155

Bounds, G., Yorks, L., Adams, M., & Ranney, G. (1994). *Beyond Total Quality Management*. New York: McGraw-Hill.

Bove, J. (2008). What Makes Shoppers Tick? *Display & Design Ideas*, *20*(3), 76–78.

Bowlby, J. (1969). Attachment and loss: Vol. 1. *Attachment*. New York: Basic Books.

Bowlby, J. (1973). Attachment and loss: Vol. 2. *Separation: Anxiety and anger*. New York: Basic Books.

Boyd, J. (2014, April 23). *Japan's Plan for Centimeter-Resolution GPS*. IEEE Spectrum. Retrieved from http://spectrum.ieee.org/aerospace/satellites/japans-plan-for-centimeterresolution-gps/

Boyd, D. (2007). Why Youth (Heart) Social Network Sites: The Role of Networked Publics in Teenage Social Life. In D. Buckingham (Ed.), *MacArthur Foundation Series on Digital Learning – Youth, Identity, and Digital Media Volume*. Cambridge, MA: MIT Press.

Boyd, D. M., & Ellison, N. B. (2007). Social network sites: Definition, history, and scholarship. *Journal of Computer-Mediated Communication*, *13*(1), 210–230. doi:10.1111/j.1083-6101.2007.00393.x

Boyle, M. J. (2004). Using CRM software effectively. *The CPA Journal*, *74*(7), 17.

Bradshaw, D., & Brash, C. (2001). Managing customer relationships in the e-business world: How to personalize computer relationships for increased profitability. *International Journal of Retail & Distribution Management*, *29*(12), 520–529. doi:10.1108/09590550110696969

Brady, M., Saren, M., & Tzokas, N. (2002). Integrating information technology into marketing practice–the IT reality of contemporary marketing practice. *Journal of Marketing Management* 18.5(6), 555-577.

Breidert, C. (2005). *Estimation of willingness-to-pay, Theory, measurement, and application* [Doctoral thesis]. Vienna University of Economics and Business. Retrieved from http://epub.wu.ac.at/1934/

Breiman, L. (1996). Bagging predictors. *Machine Learning*, *24*(2), 123–140. doi:10.1007/BF00058655

Breiman, L. (2001). Random forests. *Machine Learning*, *45*(1), 5–32. doi:10.1023/A:1010933404324

Breiman, L., Friedman, J., Olshen, R. A., & Stone, C. J. (1984). *Classification and regression trees*. Belmont, CA: Wadsworth international group.

Brewton, J., & Schiemann, W. (2003). Measurement: The missing ingredient in today's CRM strategy. *Coastal Management*, *17*(1), 5–14.

Brint, A. T. (2003). Investigating buyer and seller strategies in online auctions. *The Journal of the Operational Research Society*, *54*(11), 1177–1188. doi:10.1057/palgrave.jors.2601629

Britsch, J., Schacht, S., & Mädche, A. (2012). Anything relationship management. *Business & Information Systems Engineering*, *4*(2), 85–87. doi:10.1007/s12599-012-0208-6

Broadband Commission. (2013). *The state of broadband 2013: Universalizing broadband.* Geneva, Switzerland: The Broadband Commission.

Brodie, R. J., Hollebeek, L. D., Juric, B., & Ilic, A. (2011). Customer Engagement: Conceptual Domain, Fundamental Propositions, and Implications for Research. *Journal of Service Research*, *13*(3), 252–271. doi:10.1177/1094670511411703

Brodie, R. J., Llic, A., Juric, B., & Hollebeek, L. (2011). Consumer Engagement in Virtual Brand Communities: An Exploratory Analysis. *Journal of Business Research*. doi:10.1016/j.jbusres.2011.07.029

Brodie, R. J., Winklhofer, H., Coviello, N. E., & Johnston, W. J. (2007). Is e-marketing coming of age? An examination of the penetration of e-marketing and firm performance. *Journal of Interactive Marketing*, *21*(1), 2–21. doi:10.1002/dir.20071

Brodie, R., Coviello, N., & Winklhofer, H. (2008). Investigating Contemporary Marketing Practices: A Review of the First Decade of the CMP Research Program. *Journal of Business and Industrial Marketing*, *23*(2), 84–94. doi:10.1108/08858620810850191

Brown, B., & Sikes, J. (2012). Minding Your Digital Business: McKinsey Global Survey Results. *McKinsey and Company Research Report.*

Brown, S. L., & Eisenhardt, K. M. (1995). Product development: Past research, present findings, and future directions. Academy of Management Review, 20(2), 343–378.

Brown, J. J., & Reingen, P. H. (1987). Social ties and word-of-mouth referral behavior. *The Journal of Consumer Research*, *14*(December), 350–362. doi:10.1086/209118

Brown, J., & Morgan, J. (2006). Reputation in online markets: The market for trust. *California Management Review*, *49*(1), 61–81. doi:10.2307/41166371

Bruce, M., Leverick, F., Littler, D., & Wilson, D. (1996). The changing scope and substance of marketing - the impact of IT. Proceedings from the European Academy of Marketing Conference - Marketing for an Expanding Europe, Budapest (Vol. 1, 185-204). University of Economic Science.

Bruce, N., Haruvy, E., & Rao, R. (2004). Seller rating, price and default in online auctions. *Journal of Interactive Marketing*, *18*(4), 37–50. doi:10.1002/dir.20021

Brüggenwirth, B. (2006). The CSR brand positioning grid. In *Jonker, J & de White, J., Management Models for Corporate Social Responsibility* (pp. 140–146). Berlin: Springer Berlin Heidelberg. doi:10.1007/3-540-33247-2_17

Brunner, C. B., Esch, F. R., & Kinscher, N. (2012). Communicating corporate social responsibility: Empty promises or smart strategy? *Advances in Advertising Research*, *3*(1), 105–117. doi:10.1007/978-3-8349-4291-3_9

Bruque, S., & Moyano, J. (2007). Organisational determinants of information technology adoption and implementation in SMEs: The case of family and cooperative firms. *Technovation*, *27*(5), 241–253. doi:10.1016/j.technovation.2006.12.003

Bryll, R., Gutierrez-Osuna, R., & Quek, F. (2003). Attribute bagging: Improving accuracy of classifier ensembles by using random feature subsets. *Pattern Recognition*, *36*(6), 1291–1302. doi:10.1016/S0031-3203(02)00121-8

Brynjolfsson, E. (2010). The four ways IT is revolutionizing innovation. Mit Sloan Management Review. Retrieved from http://sloanreview.mit.edu/article/it-innovation-brynjolfsson-article/

Brynjolfsson, E., & McAfee, A. (2014). *The Second Machine Age: Work, Progress, and Prosperity in a Time of Brilliant Technologies*. New York, New York: W. W. Norton & Company.

Buckinx, W., & Van den Poel, D. (2005). Customer base analysis: Partial defection of behaviourally loyal clients in a non-contractual FMCG retail setting. *European Journal of Operational Research*, *164*(1), 252–268. doi:10.1016/j.ejor.2003.12.010

Bueren, A., Schierholz, R., Kolbe, L. M., & Brenner, W. (2005). Improving performance of customer-processes with knowledge management. *Business Process Management Journal*, *11*(5), 573–588. doi:10.1108/14637150510619894

Bühlmann, P. (2002, Jul 15-19). *Bagging, subagging and Bragging for improving some prediction algorithms.* Paper presented at the International Conference on Recent Advances and Trends in NonParametric Statistics, Iraklion, Greece. doi:10.1016/B978-044451378-6/50002-8

Buil, I., deChernatony, L., & Martinez, E. (2013). Examining the Role of Advertising and Sales Promotions in Brand Equity Creation. *Journal of Business Research*, *66*(1), 115–122. doi:10.1016/j.jbusres.2011.07.030

Burez, J., & Van den Poel, D. (2007). CRM at a pay-TV company: Using analytical models to reduce customer attrition by targeted marketing for subscription services. *Expert Systems with Applications*, *32*(2), 277–288. doi:10.1016/j.eswa.2005.11.037

Burez, J., & Van den Poel, D. (2008). Separating financial from commercial customer churn: A modeling step towards resolving the conflict between the sales and credit department. *Expert Systems with Applications*, *35*(1-2), 497–514. doi:10.1016/j.eswa.2007.07.036

Burez, J., & Van den Poel, D. (2009). Handling class imbalance in customer churn prediction. *Expert Systems with Applications*, *36*(3), 4626–4636. doi:10.1016/j.eswa.2008.05.027

Burgess, J. (2008). All Your Chocolate Rain Are Belong to Us?' Viral Video, YouTube and the Dynamics of Participatory Culture. In Video Vortex Reader: Responses to YouTube (pp. 101-109). Amsterdam, Institute of Network Cultures.

Burns, W. (2013, February 27). Nine Business Applications for Google Glass. *Forbes*. Retrieved from http://www.forbes.com/sites/willburns/2013/02/27/nine-business-applications-for-google-glass-love-ideasicle/

Burns, A., & Bush, R. (2014). *Marketing research.* Boston: Pearson Education.

Bush, V. (1945, July 1). As We May Think. *The Atlantic*. Retrieved from http://www.theatlantic.com/magazine/archive/1945/07/as-we-may-think/303881/

Butler, S. (2000). Changing the game: CRM in the e-world. *The Journal of Business Strategy*, *21*(2), 13–14. doi:10.1108/eb040067

Buttle, F. (2009). *Customer Relationship Management* (2nd ed.). Burlinton, USA: Butterworth-Heinemann, Ltd.

Büyüközkan, G., & Feyzıoğlu, O. (2004). A fuzzy-logic-based decision-making approach for new product development. International Journal of Production Economics, 90(1), 27–45. doi:10.1016/S0925-5273(02)00330-4 doi:10.1016/S0925-5273(02)00330-4

Byrne, B. M. (2009). *Structural equation modeling with AMOS: Basic concepts, applications and programming.* New York: Taylor and Francis Group.

Cable, D. M., & Graham, M. E. (2000). The determinants of job-seekers reputation perceptions. *Journal of Organizational Behavior*, *21*(8), 929–947. doi:10.1002/1099-1379(200012)21:8<929::AID-JOB63>3.0.CO;2-O

Cabral, L., & Hortacsu, A. (2010). The dynamics of seller reputation: Evidence from eBay. *The Journal of Industrial Economics*, *58*(1), 54–78. doi:10.1111/j.1467-6451.2010.00405.x

Caffyn, J. (1964). Psychological Laboratory Techniques in Copy Research. *Journal of Advertising Research*, *4*(4), 45–50.

Caillaud, B., & Mezzetti, C. (2004). Equilibrium reserve prices in sequential ascending auctions. *Journal of Economic Theory*, *117*(1), 78–95. doi:10.1016/j.jet.2003.11.002

Calabrese, A., Costa, R., Menichini, T., & Rosati, F. (2013). Does corporate social responsibility hit the mark? A stakeholder oriented methodology for CSR assessment. *Knowledge and Process Management*, *20*(2), 77–89. doi:10.1002/kpm.1406

Calantone, R. J., Di Benedetto, A., & Song, M. (2011). Expecting Marketing Activities and New Product Launch Execution to Be Different in the U.S. and China: An Empirical Study. International Journal of China Marketing, 2(1), 14–44.

Calantone, R. J., Garcia, R., & Droge, C. (2003). The Effects of Environmental Turbulence on New Product Development Strategy Planning. *Journal of Product Innovation Management*, *20*(2), 90–103. doi:10.1111/1540-5885.2002003

Caldentey, R., & Vulcano, G. (2007). Online auction and list price revenue management. *Management Science*, *53*(5), 795–813. doi:10.1287/mnsc.1060.0646

Callcott, M. F., & Lee, W. N. (1994). A content analysis of animation and animated Spokes - characters in television commercials. *Journal of Advertising*, *23*(4), 1–12. doi:10.1080/00913367.1943.10673455

Camarero, C., & San Jose, R. (2011). Social and attitudinal determinants of viral marketing dynamics. *Computers in Human Behavior*, *27*(6), 2292–2300. doi:10.1016/j.chb.2011.07.008

Campbell, J. L. (2007). Why would corporations behave in socially responsible ways? An institutional theory of corporate social responsibility. *Academy of Management Review*, *32*(3), 946–967. doi:10.5465/AMR.2007.25275684

Campbell, M. C. (1999). "Why did you do that?" The important role of inferred motive in perceptions of price fairness. *Journal of Product and Brand Management*, *8*(2), 145–152. doi:10.1108/10610429910266995

Cappelli, P. (2001). Making the most of on-line recruiting. *Harvard Business Review*, *79*, 139–146. PMID:11246921

Carricano, M., Trinquecoste, J.-F., & Mondejar, J.-A. (2010). The rise of the pricing function: Origins and perspectives. *Journal of Product and Brand Management*, *19*(7), 468–476. doi:10.1108/10610421011086883

Carroll, A. B. (1979). A three-dimensional conceptual model of corporate performance. *Academy of Management Review*, *4*(4), 497–505.

Carroll, A. B. (1999). Corporate social responsibility: Evolution of a definitional construct. *Business & Society*, *38*(3), 268–295. doi:10.1177/000765039903800303

Carroll, A. B., & Shabana, K. M. (2010). The business case for corporate social responsibility: A review of concepts, research and practice. *International Journal of Management Reviews*, *12*(1), 85–105. doi:10.1111/j.1468-2370.2009.00275.x

Carter, B., & Marketo. (2013). Contagious Content: What people share on Facebook and why they share it. Retrieved from http://www.marketo.com/_assets/uploads/Contagious-Content.pdf

Casarotti, M., Lisi, M., Umiltà, C., & Zorzi, M. (2012). Paying Attention through Eye Movements: A Computational Investigation of the Premotor Theory of Spatial Attention. *Journal of Cognitive Neuroscience*, *24*(7), 1519–1531. doi:10.1162/jocn_a_00231 PMID:22452561

Cassarro, A. (2011). *Sistemas de informações para tomadas de decisões*. Saint Paul, Brazil: Cengage Learning.

Castiello, U., Becchio, C., Zoia, S., Nelini, C., Sartori, L., Blason, L., & Gallese, V. et al. (2010). Wired to Be Social: The Ontogeny of Human Interaction. *PLoS ONE*, *5*(10), e13199. doi:10.1371/journal.pone.0013199 PMID:20949058

Chaffey, D. (2008). E-Marketing. In M. J. Baker & S. Hart (Eds.), *The Marketing Book* (pp. 502–524). London: Butterworth, Heinemann. doi:10.1016/B978-0-7506-8566-5.50029-7

Cha, M., Kwak, H., Rodriguez, P., Ahn, Y., & Moon, S. (2009). *I Tube, You Tube, Everybody Tubes: Analyzing the World's Largest User Generated Content Video System*. Barcelona, Spain: Telefonica Research.

Chamberlin, B. (n. d.). *Cognitive Computing Trends to Watch in2014*. Retrieved from http://www.billchamberlin.com/downloads/cognitive-computing-a-2014-horizonwatching-trend-report/

Chang, H. H., & Chen, S. W. (2009). Consumer perception of interface quality, security, and loyalty in electronic commerce. *Information & Management*, *46*(7), 411–417. doi:10.1016/j.im.2009.08.002

Chang, H., & Ku, P. (2009). Implementation of relationship quality for CRM performance: Acquisition of BPR and organizational learning. *Total Quality Management*, *20*(3), 327–348. doi:10.1080/14783360902719758

Chang, S. H., Wang, K. Y., Chih, W. H., & Tsai, W. H. (2012). Building customer commitment in business-to-business markets. *Industrial Marketing Management*, *41*(6), 940–950. doi:10.1016/j.indmarman.2011.11.026

Chang, T. Z., & Chen, S. J. (1998). Market orientation, service quality & business profitability: A conceptual model & empirical evidence. *Journal of Services Marketing*, *12*(4), 246–264. doi:10.1108/08876049810226937

Chan, J. O. (2005). Toward a unified view of customer relationship management. *Journal of American Academy of Business*, *6*(1), 32–38.

Chebbi, I., Dustdar, S., & Tata, S. (2006). The view-based approach to dynamic inter-organizational workflow cooperation. *Data & Knowledge Engineering*, *56*(2), 139–173. doi:10.1016/j.datak.2005.03.008

Chen, Y.-J., & Kirmani, A. (2011). *Persuading others online: The consumer as media planner* (University of Maryland working paper).

Chen, G., Liu, C., & Tjosvold, D. (2005). Conflict management for effective top management teams & innovation in China. *Journal of Management Studies*, *42*(2), 277–300. doi:10.1111/j.1467-6486.2005.00497.x

Cheng, J. H., Chen, F. Y., & Chang, Y. H. (2008). Airline relationship quality: An examination of Taiwanese passengers. *Tourism Management*, *29*(3), 487–499. doi:10.1016/j.tourman.2007.05.015

Cheng, L. Y., Yang, C. C., & Teng, H. M. (2013). An integrated model for customer relationship management: An analysis and empirical study. *Human Factors and Ergonomics in Manufacturing & Service Industries*, *23*(5), 462–481. doi:10.1002/hfm.20343

Cheng, L. Y., & Yang, C. W. (2014). Conceptual analysis and implementation of an integrated CRM system for service providers. *Service Business*, *7*(2), 307–328. doi:10.1007/s11628-012-0160-z

Chen, I. J., & Popovich, K. (2003). Understanding customer relationship management (CRM): People, process and technology. *Business Process Management Journal*, *9*(5), 672–688. doi:10.1108/14637150310496758

Chen, J., & Ching, R. (2007). The effects of Information and Communication Technology on Customer Relationship Management and customer lock-in. *International Journal of Electronic Business*, *5*(5), 478–498. doi:10.1504/IJEB.2007.015446

Chen, K. Y., & Chang, M. L. (2013). User acceptance of 'near field communication' mobile phone service: An investigation based on the unified theory of acceptance and use of technology model. *Service Industries Journal*, *33*(6), 609–623. doi:10.1080/02642069.2011.622369

Chen, Y. S., & Chang, C. H. (2013). Greenwash and green trust: The mediation effects of green consumer confusion and green perceived risk. *Journal of Business Ethics*, *114*(3), 489–500. doi:10.1007/s10551-012-1360-0

Chevalier, J. A., & Mayzlin, D. (2006). The effect of word-of-mouth on sales: Online book reviews. *JMR, Journal of Marketing Research*, *43*(August), 345–354. doi:10.1509/jmkr.43.3.345

Chiang, I., & Hsieh, C. (2011). Exploring the impacts of blog marketing on consumers. *International Journal (Toronto, Ont.)*, *39*(9), 1245–1250.

Chiou, J. S., & Ting, C. C. (2011). Will you spend more money and time on internet shopping when the product and situation are right? *Computers in Human Behavior*, *27*(1), 203–208. doi:10.1016/j.chb.2010.07.037

Choi, T.-M., Liu, N., Liu, S.-C., Mak, J., & To, Y.-T. (2010). Fast Fashion Brand Extensions: An Empirical Study of Consumer Preferences. *Journal of Brand Management*, *17*(7), 472–487. doi:10.1057/bm.2010.8

Christensen, C. M., & Overdorf, M. (2000). Meeting the Challenge of Disruptive Change. *Harvard Business Review*, *78*, 67–76.

Christopher, M. (2011). *Logistics and supply chain management* (4th ed.). New York: FT-Prentice Hall.

Christy, R., Oliver, G., & Penn, J. (1996). Relationship marketing in consumer markets. *Journal of Marketing Management*, *12*(1-3), 175–187. doi:10.1080/0267257X.1996.9964407

Chryssochoidis, G., & Wong, V. (1998). Rolling Out New Products across Country Markets: An Empirical Study of Causes & Delays. *Journal of Product Innovation Management*, *15*(1), 16–41. doi:10.1016/S0737-6782(97)00065-9

Chu, S. C. (2011). Viral Advertising in social media: Participation in Facebook groups and responses among college-aged users. *Journal of Interactive Advertising*, *12*(1), 30–43. doi:10.1080/15252019.2011.10722189

Chu, S. C., & Kim, Y. (2011). Determinants of consumer engagement in electronic word-of-mouth (eWOM) in social networking sites. *International Journal of Advertising*, *30*(1), 47–75. doi:10.2501/IJA-30-1-047-075

Ciborra, C., & Failla, A. (2000). Infrastructure as a process: The case of CRM in IBM. In C. Ciborra (Ed.), *From control to drift: The dynamics of corporate information infrastructures* (pp. 105–124). Oxford, UK: Oxford University Press.

Ciegis, R., Ramanauskiene, J., & Martinkus, B. (2009). The concept of sustainable development and its use for sustainability scenarios. *Inzinerine Ekonomika-Engineering Economics*, *2*(62), 28–37.

Cober, R. T., Brown, D. J., Levy, P. E., Cober, A. B., & Keeping, L. M. (2003). Organizational websites: Website content and style as determinants of organizational attractiveness. *International Journal of Selection and Assessment*, *11*(2/3), 158–169. doi:10.1111/1468-2389.00239

Cohen, H. (2011, March 29). *72 Marketing Definitions*. Retrieved from http://heidicohen.com/marketing-definition/

Cohen, M. (2003). Uso da informação na economia de informação: Um estudo na indústria do Estado de São Paulo [PhD Thesis]. School of Management, Getulio Vargas Foundation, Saint Paul, Brazil.

Cohen, M. A., Eliasberg, J., & Ho, T. H. (1996). New product development: The performance & time-to-market tradeoff. *Management Science*, *42*(2), 173–186. doi:10.1287/mnsc.42.2.173

Cohn, J., Ambadar, Z., & Ekman, P. (2006). In J.A. Coan, & J.B. Allen (Eds.), *The Handbook of Emotion Elicitation and Assessment*. New York, NY: Oxford University Press.

Collins, N. & Butler, P. (1995). "Marketing Public Sector Services: Concepts and characteristics", *Journal of Marketing Management*, (11), 83-96.

Collins, N., & Butler, P. (2002). The Marketplace, e-Government and e-Democracy. *Irish Marketing Review*, *15*(2), 86–94.

Compeau, D. R., & Higgins, C. A. (1995). Computer self-efficacy: Development of a measure and initial test. *Management Information Systems Quarterly*, *19*(2), 189–211. doi:10.2307/249688

Constantinides, E. (2006). The marketing mix revisited: Towards the 21st Century marketing. *Journal of Marketing Management*, *22*(3-4), 407–438. doi:10.1362/026725706776861190

Cooke, M., & Buckley, N. (2008). Web 2.0, social networks and the future of market research. *International Journal of Market Research*, *50*(2), 267–292.

Cooper, L. (2013). Wired for Sound. *Marketing Week*. Retrieved from http://www.marketingweek.co.uk/trends/wired-for-sound/4006678.article

Cooper, M. J., Upton, N., & Seaman, S. (2005). Customer relationship management: A comparative analysis of family and nonfamily business practices. *Journal of Small Business Management*, *43*(3), 242–256. doi:10.1111/j.1540-627X.2005.00136.x

Cooper, R. (1988). Pre-development activities determined new product success. *Industrial Marketing Management*, *17*(3), 237–247. doi:10.1016/0019-8501(88)90007-7

Cooper, R. G. (1996). New Products: What Separates the Winners from the Losers. In *The PDMA Handbook of New Product Development*. New York: John Wiley.

Cooper, R. G., & Kleinschmidt, E. J. (1994). Determinants of timeliness in product development. *Journal of Product Innovation Management*, *11*(5), 381–396. doi:10.1016/0737-6782(94)90028-0

Correa, T., Hinsley, A., & De-Zuniga, H. (2010). Who interacts on the web? The interaction of users personality and social media use. *Computers in Human Behavior*, *26*(2), 247–253. doi:10.1016/j.chb.2009.09.003

Corritore, C. L., Kracher, B., & Wiedenbeck, S. (2003). On-line trust: Concepts, evolving themes, a model. *International Journal of Human-Computer Studies*, *58*(6), 737–758. doi:10.1016/S1071-5819(03)00041-7

Costa, A. (2007). Os paradoxos da carreira de tecnologia da informação no século XXI: Um estudo empírico exploratório [Master Dissertation]. School of Management, Getulio Vargas Foundation, Saint Paul, Brazil.

Costanza, R., & Patten, B. C. (1995). Defining and predicting sustainability. *Ecological Economics*, *15*(3), 193–196. doi:10.1016/0921-8009(95)00048-8

Coussement, K., & Van denPoel, D. (2009). Improving customer attrition prediction by integrating emotions from client/company interaction emails and evaluating multiple classifiers. *Expert Systems with Applications*, *36*(3), 6127–6134. doi:10.1016/j.eswa.2008.07.021

Coussement, K., Benoit, D. F., & Van den Poel, D. (2010). Improved marketing decision making in a customer churn prediction context using generalized additive models. *Expert Systems with Applications*, *37*(3), 2132–2143. doi:10.1016/j.eswa.2009.07.029

Coussement, K., & Van den Poel, D. (2008a). Churn prediction in subscription services: An application of support vector machines while comparing two parameter-selection techniques. *Expert Systems with Applications*, *34*(1), 313–327. doi:10.1016/j.eswa.2006.09.038

Coussement, K., & Van den Poel, D. (2008b). Integrating the voice of customers through call center emails into a decision support system for chum prediction. *Information & Management*, *45*(3), 164–174. doi:10.1016/j.im.2008.01.005

Cova, B., Giordano, A., & Pallera, M. (2008). Marketing non convenzionale. Il Sole 24 Ore, Milano.

Coviello, N., Milley, R., & Marcolin, B. (2001). Understanding IT-enabled interactivity in contemporary marketing. *Journal of Interactive Marketing*, *15*(4), 18–33. doi:10.1002/dir.1020

Cox, D., & Good, R. (1967). How to build a marketing information system. *Harvard Business Review*, *45*(3), 145–154.

Craig, A. W., Loureiro, Y. K., Wood, S., & Vendemia, J. M. (2012). Suspicious Minds: Exploring Neural Processes during Exposure to Deceptive Advertising. *Journal of Marketing Research*, *49*(3), 361–372. doi:10.1509/jmr.09.0007

Craig, S. D., D'Mello, S., Witherspoon, A., & Graesser, A. (2008). Emote Aloud during Learning with Autotutor: Applying The Facial Action Coding System to Cognitive-Affective States During Learning. *Cognition and Emotion*, *22*(5), 777–788. doi:10.1080/02699930701516759

Cramer, J., Van Der Heijden, A., & Jonker, J. (2006). Corporate social responsibility: Making sense through thinking and acting. *Business Ethics (Oxford, England)*, *15*(4), 380–389. doi:10.1111/j.1467-8608.2006.00459.x

Creusen, M. E. H., & Schoormans, J. P. L. (2005). The different roles of product appearance in consumer choice. *Journal of Product Innovation Management*, *22*(1), 63–81. doi:10.1111/j.0737-6782.2005.00103.x

Cristopher, M., Payne, A., & Ballantine, D. (1994). *Relationship marketing* (2nd ed.). Burlinton, USA: Butterworth-Heinemann, Ltd.

Croteau, A. M., & Li, P. (2003). Critical Success Factors of CRM Technological Initiatives. *Canadian Journal of Administrative Sciences*, *20*(1), 21–34. doi:10.1111/j.1936-4490.2003.tb00303.x

Culnal, M., J., McHugh, P. J., & Zubillaga, J. I. (2010). How large U.S. Companies can use twitter and other Social Media to gain business value. *University of Minnesota*, 9(4), 243-259.

Cunha, A. (2009). A influência da linguagem no processo decisório. Retrieved from http://www.artigonal.com/gerencia-artigos/a-influencia-da-linguagem-no-processo-decisorio-1115309.html

Cushman & Wakefield. (2013). Global perspective on retail: Online retailing. Retrieved from http://www.cushmanwakefield.com/~/media/global-reports/Global%20Perspective%20on%20Retail%201st%20July%202013.ashx

Dagger, T. S., David, M. E., & Ng, S. (2011). Do relationship benefits and maintenance drive commitment and loyalty? *Journal of Services Marketing*, *25*(4), 273–281. doi:10.1108/08876041111143104

Dahl, R. (2010). Green washing: Do you know what you're buying? *Environmental Health Perspectives*, *118*(6), 246–252. doi:10.1289/ehp.118-a246 PMID:20515714

Dahlsrud, A. (2008). How corporate social responsibility is defined: An analysis of 37 definitions. *Corporate Social Responsibility and Environmental Management*, *15*(1), 1–13. doi:10.1002/csr.132

D'Alessandro, S., Girardi, A., & Tiangsoongnern, L. (2012). Perceived risk and trust as antecedents of online purchasing behavior in the USA gemstone industry. *Asia Pacific Journal of Marketing and Logistics*, *24*(3), 433–460. doi:10.1108/13555851211237902

Damasio, A. R. (2005). *Descartes' Error: Emotion, Reason, and the Human Brain.* New York, NY: Penguin Books.

Daniel, E., Wilson, H., & McDonald, M. (2003). Towards a map of Marketing Information Systems: An inductive study. *European Journal of Marketing*, *37*(5/6), 821–847. doi:10.1108/03090560310465161

Davenport, T. H., Harris, J. G., & Kohli, A. K. (2001). How do they know their customers so well? *MIT Sloan Management Review*, *42*(2), 63–73.

Davila, T. (2000). An empirical study on the drivers of management control systems' design in new product development. *Accounting, Organizations and Society*, *25*(4-5), 383–409. doi:10.1016/S0361-3682(99)00034-3

Davis, D. F., & Herr, P. M. (2014). From Bye to Buy: Homophones as a Phonological Route to Priming. *The Journal of Consumer Research*, *40*(6), 1063–1077. doi:10.1086/673960

Davis, K. (1960). Can business afford to ignore social responsibilities? *California Management Review*, *2*(3), 70–76. doi:10.2307/41166246

Day, G. S. (1994). The capabilities of market-driven organizations. *Journal of Marketing*, *58*(4), 37. doi:10.2307/1251915

De Bock, K. W., & Van den Poel, D. (2010). *Ensembles of Probability Estimation Trees for Customer Churn Prediction.* Paper presented at the 23rd International Conference on Industrial Engineering and Other Applications of Applied Intelligent Systems (IEA/AIE 2010), Cordoba, Spain. doi:10.1007/978-3-642-13025-0_7

De Bock, K. W., & Van den Poel, D. (2011). An empirical evaluation of rotation-based ensemble classifiers for customer churn prediction. *Expert Systems with Applications*, *38*(10), 12293–12301. doi:10.1016/j.eswa.2011.04.007

De Bruyn, A., & Lilien, G. L. (2008). A Multi-Stage Model of Word of Mouth Through Viral Marketing. *International Journal of Research in Marketing*, *25*(3), 143–225. doi:10.1016/j.ijresmar.2008.03.004

De Goede, M. E., Van Vianen, A.E.M., & Kiene, U.-C. (2011). Attracting applicants on the web: PO fit, industry culture stereotypes and website design. *International Journal of Selection and Assessment*, *19*(1), 51–61. doi:10.1111/j.1468-2389.2010.00534.x

De Melo, C. M., Kenny, P., & Gratch, J. (2010). Influence of Autonomic Signals on Perception of Emotions in Embodied Agents. *Applied Artificial Intelligence*, *24*(6), 494–509. doi:10.1080/08839514.2010.492159

de Mooij, M., & Hofstede, G. (2002). Convergence and divergence in consumer behavior: Implications for international retailing. *Journal of Retailing*, *78*(1), 61–69. doi:10.1016/S0022-4359(01)00067-7

de Vries, L., Gensler, S., & Leeflang, P. S. H. (2012). Popularity of Brand Posts on Brand Fan Pages: An Investigation of the Effects of Social Media Marketing. *Journal of Interactive Marketing*, *26*(2), 83–91. doi:10.1016/j.intmar.2012.01.003

De Vroey, M. (2009). A Marshall-Walras Divide? A Critical Review of the Prevailing Viewpoints. *History of Political Economy*, *41*(4), 709–736. doi:10.1215/00182702-2009-038

Del Missier, F., Mäntylä, T., Hansson, P., Bruine de Bruin, W., Parker, A. M., & Nilsson, L.-G. (2013). The Multifold Relationship between Memory and Decision Making: An Individual-Differences Study. *Journal of Experimental Psychology. Learning, Memory, and Cognition*, *39*(5), 1344–1364. doi:10.1037/a0032379 PMID:23565790

Delgado-Ballester, E., Navarro, A., & Sicilia, M. (2012). Revitalising brands through communication messages: The role of brand familiarity. *European Journal of Marketing*, *46*(1/2), 31–51. doi:10.1108/03090561211189220

Dellarocas, C. (2003). The digitalization of word-of-mouth: Promise and challenges of online reputation measures. *Management Science*, *49*, 1407–1424. doi:10.1287/mnsc.49.10.1407.17308

DellaVigna, S. (2009). Psychology and Economics: Evidence from the Field. *Journal of Economic Literature*, *47*(2), 315–372. doi:10.1257/jel.47.2.315

Delmas, M. A., & Burbano, V. C. (2011). The drivers of greenwashing. *California Management Review*, *54*(1), 1–38.

Denison, D., Lief, C., & Ward, J. (2004). Culture in family-owned enterprises: Recognizing and leveraging unique strengths. *Family Business Review*, *17*(1), 61–70. doi:10.1111/j.1741-6248.2004.00004.x

Denzin, N. K. (1978). *The research act: a theoretical introduction to sociological methods*. New York: McGraw-Hill.

Deshpande, R., & Farley, J. (2000). Market-Focused Organisational Transformation in China. *Journal of Global Marketing*, *14*(1-2), 7–35. doi:10.1300/J042v14n01_02

Deshpande, R., & Farley, J. U. (1999). Corporate Culture & Market Orientation: Comparing Indian & Japanese Firm. *Journal of International Marketing*, *7*(4), 111–127.

Deshpande, R., Farley, J. U., & Webster, F. (1993). Corporate Culture, Customer Orientation, & Innovativeness in Japanese Firms: A Quadrad Analysis. *Journal of Marketing*, *57*(1), 23–37. doi:10.2307/1252055

Detric, P. (2010). Demand Effects on Positive Response Distortion by Police Officer Applicants on the Revised NEO Personality Inventory. *Journal of Personality Assessment*, *92*(5), 410–415. doi:10.1080/00223891.2010.497401 PMID:20706927

Deuze, M. (2007). *Media work*. Malden, MA: Polity.

Devaraj, S., Krajewski, L., & Wei, J. C. (2007). Impact of eBusiness technologies on operational performance: The role of production information integration in the supply chain. *Journal of Operations Management*, *25*(6), 1199–1216. doi:10.1016/j.jom.2007.01.002

Dewally, M., & Ederington, L. (2006). Reputation, certification, warranties, and information asymmetries: Lessons from the online comic book market. *The Journal of Business*, *79*(2), 693–730. doi:10.1086/499169

Dewan, S., & Hsu, V. (2004). Adverse selection in electronic markets: Evidence from online stamp auctions. *The Journal of Industrial Economics*, *52*(4), 497–516. doi:10.1111/j.0022-1821.2004.00237.x

Dietterich, T. G. (2000). An experimental comparison of three methods for constructing ensembles of decision trees: Bagging, boosting, and randomization. *Machine Learning*, *40*(2), 139–157. doi:10.1023/A:1007607513941

DigitasLBi. (2014). M-commerce, social media and ROPO (research online, purchase offline) lead retail trends, according to DigitasLBi's Global Survey. Retrieved from http://www.digitaslbi.com/news/global/m-commerce-social-media-and-ropo-research-online-purchase-offline-lead-retail-trends-according-to-digitaslbis-global-survey/

Dillon, W. R., Madden, T. J., Kirmani, A., & Mukherjee, S. (2001). Understanding what's in a brand rating: A model for assessing brand and attribute effects. *JMR, Journal of Marketing Research*, *28*(4), 415–429. doi:10.1509/jmkr.38.4.415.18910

Dimitriadis, S. (2010). Testing perceived relational benefits as satisfaction and behavioral outcomes drivers. *International Journal of Bank Marketing*, *28*(4), 297–213. doi:10.1108/02652321011054981

Dimofte, C. V. (2010). Implicit Measures of Consumer Cognition: A Review. *Psychology and Marketing*, *27*(10), 921–937. doi:10.1002/mar.20366

Dimoka, A., Hong, Y., & Pavlou, P. A. (2012). On product uncertainty in online markets: Theory and evidence. *Management Information Systems Quarterly*, *36*(2), 395–426.

Dini, F., & Spagnolo, G. (2009). Buying reputation on eBay: Do recent changes help? *International Journal of Electronic Business*, *7*(6), 581–598. doi:10.1504/IJEB.2009.029048

Divol, R., Edelman, D., & Sarrazin, H. (2012). Demystifying Social Media. *The McKinsey Quarterly*, *26*(2), 66–77.

Djamasbi, S., Siegel, M., Skorinko, J., & Tullis, T. (2011). Online Viewing and Aesthetic Preferences of Generation Y and the Baby Boom Generation: Testing User Web Site Experience through Eye Tracking. *International Journal of Electronic Commerce*, *15*(4), 121–158. doi:10.2753/JEC1086-4415150404

Dobele, A., Toleman, D., & Beverland, M. (2005). Controlled infection! Spreading the brand message through viral marketing. *Business Horizons*, *48*(2), 143–149. doi:10.1016/j.bushor.2004.10.011

Dogruer, N., Menevi, I., & Eyyam, R. (2011). What is the motivation for using Facebook? *Procedia: Social and Behavioral Sciences*, *15*, 2642–2646. doi:10.1016/j.sbspro.2011.04.162

Dolan, R. J., & Moon, Y. (2000). Pricing and market making on the internet. *Journal of Interactive Marketing*, *14*(2), 56–69. doi:10.1002/(SICI)1520-6653(200021)14:2<56::AID-DIR5>3.0.CO;2-4

Dolekoglu, C., Albayrak, M., Kara, A., & Keskin, G. (2008). Analysis of Consumer Perceptions and Preferences towards Store Brands Versus National Brands: An Exploratory Study in an Emerging Market. *Journal of Euromarketing*, *17*(2), 109–125. doi:10.1080/10496480802134787

Donaldson, B., & O' Toole, T. (2002). *Strategic marketing relationship*. Chichester, UK: John Wiley & Sons.

Dorsch, M. J., Swanson, S. R., & Kelley, S. W. (1998). The role of relationship quality in the satisfaction of vendors as perceived by customers. *Journal of the Academy of Marketing Science*, *26*(2), 128–142. doi:10.1177/0092070398262004

Dowling, G. (2002). Customer Relationship Management: In B2C Markets, Often Less is More. *California Management Review*, *44*(3), 87–104. doi:10.2307/41166134

Dowling, G. R., & Staelin, R. (1994). A model of perceived risk and intended risk-handling activity. *The Journal of Consumer Research*, *21*(1), 119–134. doi:10.1086/209386

Duan, W., Gu, B., & Whinston, A. B. (2008). The Dynamics of Online Word-of-Mouth and Product Sales—An Empirical Investigation of the Movie Industry. *Journal of Retailing*, *84*(2), 233–242. doi:10.1016/j.jretai.2008.04.005

Dubois, A., & Gadde, L. E. (2002). Systematic combining: An abductive approach to case research. *Journal of Business Research*, *55*(7), 553–560. doi:10.1016/S0148-2963(00)00195-8

Dubois, A., & Gibbert, M. (2010). From complexity to transparency: Managing the interplay between theory, method and empirical phenomena in IMM case studies. *Industrial Marketing Management*, *39*(1), 129–136. doi:10.1016/j.indmarman.2009.08.003

Duda, R. O., Hart, P. E., & D.G., S. (2001). *Pattern classification* (second ed.): John Wiley & Sons Inc.

Durmuşoğlu, S. S., Calantone, R. J., & McNally, R. C. (2013). Ordered to Innovate: A Longitudinal Examination of the Early Periods of a New Product Development Process Implementation in a Manufacturing Firm. *Journal of Product Innovation Management*, *30*(4), 712–731. doi:10.1111/jpim.12016

Dwoskin, E. (2014, January 13). What Secrets Your Phone Is Sharing About You: Businesses Use Sensors to Track Customers, Build Shopper Profiles. *Wall Street Journal*.

Dwyer, C., Hiltz, S., & Passerini, K. (2007). *Trust and Privacy Concern Within Social Networking Sites: A Comparison of Facebook and MySpace*. AMCIS.

Eagle, S. (2012). Learning in the early years: Social interactions around picture books, puzzles and digital technologies. *Computers & Education*, *59*(1), 38–49. doi:10.1016/j.compedu.2011.10.013

Easley, D., & Kleinberg, J. (2010). *From the book networks, crowds, and markets: reasoning about a highly connected world*. Cambridge University Press. doi:10.1017/CBO9780511761942

Eastlick, M. A., Lotz, S. L., & Warrington, P. (2006). Understanding online B-to-C relationships: An integrated model of privacy concerns, trust, and commitment. *Journal of Business Research*, *59*(8), 877–886. doi:10.1016/j.jbusres.2006.02.006

Eaton, D. H. (2002). Valuing information: Evidence from guitar auctions on eBay. Working Paper. Murray, KY: Murray State University.

Eaton, K. (2012, June 7). Does your phone know how happy you are? The emotion recognition industry comes giddily of age. *Fast Company*.

eBay Inc., (2002). *eBay Announces Fourth Quarter and Year End 2001 Financial Results*. Retrieved from http://investor.ebayinc.com/financial_releases.cfm

eBay Inc., (2014). *eBay Reports Fourth Quarter and Full Year 2013 Results*. Retrieved from http://investor.ebayinc.com/financial_releases.cfm

Edmondson, A. C., & Nembhard, I. M. (2009). Product development & learning in project teams: The challenges are the benefits. *Journal of Product Innovation Management*, *26*(2), 123–138. doi:10.1111/j.1540-5885.2009.00341.x

Edwards, J. (2014). Facebook Inc. Actually Has 2.2 Billion Users Now – Roughly One Third of the Entire Population of Earth. *Business Insider*. Retrieved from http://www.businessinsider.com/facebook-inc-has-22-billion-users-2014-7

Egan, J. (2003). Back to the Future: Divergence in Relationship marketing Research. *Marketing Theory*, *3*(1), 145–157. doi:10.1177/1470593103003001008

Eisenbeiss, M., Corneließen, M., Backhaus, K., & Hoyer, W. D. (2014). Nonlinear and asymmetric returns on customer satisfaction: Do they vary across situations and consumers? *Journal of the Academy of Marketing Science*, *42*(3), 242–263. doi:10.1007/s11747-013-0366-1

Eisenhardt, K. (1989). Building theories from case study research. *Academy of Management Review*, *14*(4), 532–550.

Eisenhardt, K. M., & Bhatia, M. M. (2002). Organizational Complexity & Computation. In J. A. C. Baum (Ed.), *Companion to Organizations* (pp. 442–466). Oxford: Blackwell.

Ekman, P. (1992). An Argument for Basic Emotions. *Cognition and Emotion*, *6*(3), 169–200. doi:10.1080/02699939208411068

Ekman, P., & Friesen, W. V. (1978). *Facial Action Coding System*. Palo Alto, CA: Consulting Psychologists Press.

El Ghoul, S., Guedhami, O., Kwok, C. C., & Mishra, D. R. (2011). Does corporate social responsibility affect the cost of capital? *Journal of Banking & Finance*, *35*(9), 2388–2406. doi:10.1016/j.jbankfin.2011.02.007

Eley, B., & Tilley, S. (2009). *Online marketing inside out*. Melbourne: SitePoint.

Elliott, J. (2012). *An introduction to sustainable development*. London: Routledge.

Ellis, L., & Bastin, C. (2011). Corporate social responsibility in times of recession: Changing discourses and implications for policy and practice. *Corporate Social Responsibility and Environmental Management*, *18*(5), 294–305. doi:10.1002/csr.254

Elmuti, D., Jia, H., & Gray, D. (2009). Customer relationship management strategic application and organizational effectiveness: An empirical investigation. *Journal of Strategic Marketing*, *17*(1), 75–96. doi:10.1080/09652540802619301

E-marketer. (2014). Global B2C ecommerce sales to hit $1.5 trillion this year driven by growth in emerging markets. Retrieved from http://www.emarketer.com/Articles/Print.aspx?R=1010575

Emmelhainz, M. A. (1993). *EDI: a total management guide* (2nd ed.). New York: Van Nostrand Reinhold.

Enzing, C. M., Batterink, M. H., Janszen, F. H., & Omta, S. O. (2011). Where innovation processes make a difference in products' short-& long-term market success. *British Food Journal*, *113*(7), 812–837. doi:10.1108/00070701111148379

Epps, S. (2013, June 2). Five Ways Google Glass Will Change Marketing. *Forbes*. Retrieved from http://www.forbes.com/sites/onmarketing/2013/07/02/five-ways-google-glass-will-change-marketing/

Erickson, G. M., & Johansson, J. K. (1985). The role of price in multi-attribute product evaluations. *The Journal of Consumer Research*, *12*(2), 195–199. doi:10.1086/208508

Ernst, H., Hoyer, W. D., Krafft, M., & Krieger, K. (2011). Customer relationship management and company performance: The mediating role of new product performance. *Journal of the Academy of Marketing Science*, *39*(2), 290–306. doi:10.1007/s11747-010-0194-5

Ernst, H., Hoyer, W. D., & Rübsaamen, C. (2010). Sales, marketing, & research-and-development cooperation across new product development stages: Implications for success. *Journal of Marketing*, *74*(5), 80–92. doi:10.1509/jmkg.74.5.80

Etzel, M. J., Walker, B. J., & Stanton, W. J. (2001). *Marketing* (12th ed.). New York: McGraw Hill/Irwin.

Evans, D. (2010). *Social Media Marketing: The next generation of user engagement*. Indianapolis, Ind: Wiley Pub.

Evans, D., & Mckee, J. (2010). *Social media marketing: The next generation of business engagement*. Indianapolis, Indiana: John Wiley& Sons, Inc.

Faber, N., Jorna, R., & Van Engelen, J. (2005). The sustainability of "sustainability" – a study into the conceptual foundations of the notion of "sustainability". *Journal of Environmental Assessment Policy and Management*, *7*(1), 1–33. doi:10.1142/S1464333205001955

Facebook Reports First Quarter 2014 Results (2014). Retrieved from http://investor.fb.com/releasedetail.cfm?ReleaseID=842071

Farhoomand, A. F., & Drury, D. H. (2002). Overload. *Communications of the ACM*, *45*(10), 127–131. doi:10.1145/570907.570909

Farris, P. W., Bendle, N. T., Pfeifer, P. E., & Reibstein, D. J. (2006). *Marketing Metrics: 50+ Metrics Every Executive Should Master*. Upper Saddle River, NJ: Prentice Hall.

Farrokhnia, F., & Richards, C. K. (2013). The accountability challenge to global e-commerce: The need to overcome the developed-developing country divide in WTO e-commerce policies. *Advances in Sustainability and Environmental Justice*, *12*, 161–181. doi:10.1108/S2051-5030(2013)0000012012

Feick, L., & Higie, R. A. (1992). The effects of preference heterogeneity and source characteristics on ad processing and judgments about endorsers. *Journal of Advertising*, *21*(2), 9–24. doi:10.1080/00913367.1992.10673364

Fenwick, T., & Bierema, L. (2008). Corporate social responsibility: Issues for human resource development professionals. *International Journal of Training and Development*, *12*(1), 24–35. doi:10.1111/j.1468-2419.2007.00293.x

Fernandes, S. (2013). Main differentiating issues in aligning information systems with business performance. *International Journal of Information Systems in the Service Sector*, *5*(2), 17–29. doi:10.4018/jisss.2013040102

Fernando, M. (2010). Corporate social responsibility in the wake of the Asian tsunami: Effect of time on the genuineness of CSR initiatives. *European Management Journal*, *28*(1), 68–79. doi:10.1016/j.emj.2009.08.002

Ferreira, M., & Serra, F. (2009). *Casos de estudo: usar, escrever e estudar*. Lisboa: Lidel - Edições Técnicas, Lda.

Festinger, L. (1954). A theory of social comparison processes. *Human Relations*, *7*(2), 117–140. doi:10.1177/001872675400700202

Fidelman, M. (2013, September 4). IBM's Watson Set To Revolutionize Marketing. *Forbes*. Retrieved from http://www.forbes.com/sites/markfidelman/2013/09/04/ibms-watson-set-to-revolutionize-marketing/

Filipe Lages, L., & Montgomery, D. B. (2004). Export performance as an antecedent of export commitment & marketing strategy adaptation. *European Journal of Marketing*, *38*(9/10), 1186–1214. doi:10.1108/03090560410548933

Fiocca, R. (1982). Account portfolio analysis for strategy development. *Industrial Marketing Management*, *11*(1), 53–62. doi:10.1016/0019-8501(82)90034-7

Firat, A. Fuat. (1991). Consumption and Gender: A Common History. Gender and Consumer Behavior. First Conference Proceedings (pp. 378-386). Salt Lake City, UT: University of Utah Printing Service

Fletcher, D. (2002). A network perspective of culture organizing and "professional management" in small, family business. *Journal of Business and Enterprise Development*, *9*(4), 400–415. doi:10.1108/14626000210450577

Flight, M.H. (2011). Memory: The Foundations of Accurate Recall. *Nature Reviews. Neuroscience*, *12*(7), 372–373. doi:10.1038/nrn3055 PMID:21610731

Fogel, J., & Nehmad, E. (2009). Internet social network communities: Risk taking, trust and privacy concerns. *Computers in Human Behavior*, *25*(1), 153–160. doi:10.1016/j.chb.2008.08.006

Forza, C., & Filippini, R. (1998). TQM impact on quality conformance and customer satisfaction: A causal model. *International Journal of Production Economics*, *55*(1), 1–20. doi:10.1016/S0925-5273(98)00007-3

Forza, C., Salvador, F., & Rungtusanatham, M. (2005). Coordinating product design, process design, & supply chain design decisions: Part B. Coordinating approaches, tradeoffs, & future research directions. *Journal of Operations Management*, *23*(3), 319–324. doi:10.1016/j.jom.2004.10.001

Fossas-Olalla, M., Lopez-Sanchez, J. I., & Minguela-Rata, B. (2010). Cooperation with suppliers as a source of innovation. *African Journal of Business Management*, *4*(6), 3491–3499.

Fournier, S., Dobscha, S., & Mick, D. (1998). Preventing the premature death of relationship marketing. *Harvard Business Review*, *76*(1), 42–43. PMID:10176918

Frambach, R. T., Prabhu, J., & Verhallen, T. M. M. (2003). The influence of business strategy on new product activity: The role of marketing orientation. *International Journal of Research in Marketing*, *20*(4), 377–397. doi:10.1016/j.ijresmar.2003.03.003

Frank, E., Holmes, G., Pfahringer, B., Reutemann, P., & Witten, I. H. (2009). The WEKA Data Mining Software: An Update. *SIGKDD Explorations*, *1*(1).

Frenzen, J. K., & Davis, H. L. (1990). Purchasing behavior in embedded markets. *The Journal of Consumer Research*, *17*(1), 1–12. doi:10.1086/208532

Freund, Y., & Schapire, R. E. (1997). A decision-theoretic generalization of on-line learning and an application to boosting. *Journal of Computer and System Sciences*, *55*(1), 119–139. doi:10.1006/jcss.1997.1504

Frey, C. B., & Osborne, M. A. (2013, September 17). *The Future of Employment: How Susceptible are Jobs to Computerisation?* Retrieved from http://www.oxfordmartin.ox.ac.uk/downloads/academic/The-Future-of-Employment.pdf

Frosch, R. (1996). The customer for R&D is always wrong! *Research-Technology Management*, *39*(6), 22–27.

Frynas, J. G. (2005). The false developmental promise of corporate social responsibility: Evidence from multinational oil companies. *International Affairs*, *81*(3), 581–598. doi:10.1111/j.1468-2346.2005.00470.x

Fugate, D. L. (2007). Neuromarketing: A Layman's Look at Neuroscience and Its Potential Application to Marketing Practice. *Journal of Consumer Marketing*, *24*(7), 385–394. doi:10.1108/07363760710834807

Fujinoki, H., Chelmecki, C. A., & Henry, D. M. (2014). Fail-safe security architecture to prevent privacy leaks from e-commerce servers. *Journal of Internet Services and Information Security*, *4*(2), 38–54.

Furlow, N. E. (2010). Greenwashing in the new millennium. *Journal of Applied Business & Economics*, *10*(6), 1–4.

Gaete, L. (2010). Análise da resistência a sistemas de informação: A perceção dos gestores de tecnologia da informação acerca de sistemas ERP [Master Dissertation]. School of Management, Getulio Vargas Foundation, Saint Paul, Brazil.

Gakhal, B., & Senior, C. (2008). Examining the Influence of Fame in the Presence of Beauty: An Electrodermal 'Neuromarketing' Study. *Journal of Consumer Behaviour*, *7*(4/5), 331–341. doi:10.1002/cb.255

Galbreath, J. (2009). Building corporate social responsibility into strategy. *European Business Review*, *21*(2), 109–127. doi:10.1108/09555340910940123

Galbreath, J., & Rogers, T. (1999). Customer Relationship Leadership: A leadership and motivation model for the twenty-first century business. *The TQM Magazine*, *11*(2), 161–171. doi:10.1108/09544789910262734

Gallaugher, J. (2013). *Information Systems: A Manager's Guide to Harnessing Technology, v. 2.0*. Flat World Knowledge.

Gallego, G., & Van Ryzin, G. (1997). A Multi-product dynamic pricing problem and its applications to network yield management. *Operations Research*, *45*(1), 24–41. doi:10.1287/opre.45.1.24

Gao, T., Rohm, A. J., Sultan, F., & Huang, S. (2012). Antecedents of consumer attitudes toward mobile marketing: A comparative study of youth markets in the United States and China. *Thunderbird International Business Review*, *54*(2), 211–224. doi:10.1002/tie.21452

Gao, Y., & Wu, X. (2010). A cognitive model of trust in e-commerce: Evidence from a field study in China. *Journal of Applied Business Research*, *26*(1), 37–44.

Garbarino, E., & Johnson, M. (1999). The Different Roles of Satisfaction, Trust and Commitment for and Transactional Consumers. *Journal of Marketing*, *63*, 70–87. doi:10.2307/1251946

Garbarino, E., & Lee, O. F. (2003). Dynamic pricing in internet retail: Effects on consumer trust. *Psychology and Marketing*, *20*(6), 495–513. doi:10.1002/mar.10084

García-Murillo, M., & Annabi, H. (2002). Customer knowledge management. *The Journal of the Operational Research Society*, *53*(8), 875–884. doi:10.1057/palgrave.jors.2601365

Garfinkel, R., Gopal, R., Tripathi, A., & Yin, F. (2006). Design of a shopbot and recommender system for bundle purchases. *Decision Support Systems*, *42*(3), 1974–1986. doi:10.1016/j.dss.2006.05.005

Garrido-Moreno, A., & Padilla-Meléndez, A. (2011). Analyzing the impact of knowledge management on CRM success: The mediating effects of organizational factors. *International Journal of Information Management*, *31*(5), 437–444. doi:10.1016/j.ijinfomgt.2011.01.002

Gartner Group. (2000). Key Issues in E-Government Strategy and Management. *Research notes¸ Key issues*

Gaskins, J. (2013). Confirmatory factor. Retrieved from http://statwiki.kolobkreations.com/wiki/Confirmatory_Factor_Analysis

Gay, R., Charlesworth, A., & Esen, R. (2007). *Online Marketing: A customer-led approach*. New York, NY: Oxford University Press.

Gebhard, A. (2003). *Rapid Prototyping*. Munich, Germany: Hanser-Gardner Publication. doi:10.3139/9783446402690

Gefen, D., Straub, D., & Bourdreau, M. (2000). Structural equation modeling and regression: Guidelines for research practice. *Communications of the Association for Information Systems*, *4*, 1–79.

Geib, M., Kolbe, L. M., & Brenner, W. (2006). CRM collaboration in financial services networks: A multi-case analysis. *Journal of Enterprise Information Management*, *19*(6), 591–607. doi:10.1108/17410390610708481

Geiger, I., Durand, A., Saab, S., Kleinaltenkamp, M., Baxter, R., & Lee, Y. (2012). The Bonding Effects of Relationship Value and Switching Costs in Industrial Buyer–Seller Relationships: An Investigation into Role Differences. *Industrial Marketing Management*, *41*(1), 82–93. doi:10.1016/j.indmarman.2011.11.013

Genco, S., Pohlmann, A., & Steidl, P. (2013). *Neuromarketing for Dummies*. Mississauga, ON: John Wiley & Sons Canada.

Geoffrion, A. M., & Krishnan, R. (2003). E-Business and management science: Mutual impacts (Part 1 of 2). *Management Science*, *49*(10), 1275–1286. doi:10.1287/mnsc.49.10.1275.17311

Giannakos, M., Chorianopoulos, K., Giotopoulos, K., & Vlamos, P. (2013). Using Facebook out of habit. *Behaviour & Information Technology*, *32*(6), 594–602. doi:10.1080/0144929X.2012.659218

Gibbs, J. L., & Kraemer, K. L. (2004). A cross-country investigation of the determinants of scope of e-commerce use: An institutional approach. *Electronic Markets*, *14*(2), 124–137. doi:10.1080/10196780410001675077

Gibson, C. B., & Cohen, S. G. (2003). *Virtual teams that work: Creating conditions for virtual team effectiveness. San Fransisco*. Jossey-Bass.

Giglio, F. (2010). Implicações dos meios digitais na comunicação de marketing (XIII Semead -Management seminars). University of Saint Paul, Brazil.

Gijsbrechts, E. (1993). Prices and pricing research in consumer marketing: Some recent developments. *International Journal of Research in Marketing*, *10*(2), 115–151. doi:10.1016/0167-8116(93)90001-F

Gil, A. (2008). *Métodos e técnicas de pesquisa social*. Saint Paul, Brazil: Atlas Publisher.

Gilaninia, S., Almani, A., Pournaserani, A., & Javad, S. (2011). Relationship Marketing: A New Approach to Marketing in the Third Millennium. *Australian Journal of Basic and Applied Sciences*, *5*(5), 787–799.

Gilbert, D. (1997). *Intelligent Agents: The Right Information at the Right Time*. IBM Corp.

Glady, N., Baesens, B., & Croux, C. (2009). Modeling churn using customer lifetime value. *European Journal of Operational Research*, *197*(1), 402–411. doi:10.1016/j.ejor.2008.06.027

Glavič, P., & Lukman, R. (2007). Review of sustainability terms and their definitions. *Journal of Cleaner Production*, *15*(18), 1875–1885. doi:10.1016/j.jclepro.2006.12.006

Glynn, C., Huge, M., & Hoffman, L. (2012). All the news that's fit to post: A profile of news use on social networking sites. *Computers in Human Behavior*, *28*(1), 113–119. doi:10.1016/j.chb.2011.08.017

Godes, D., & Mayzlin, D. (2004). Using online conversations to study word-of-mouth communication. *Marketing Science*, *23*(4), 545–560. doi:10.1287/mksc.1040.0071

Godes, D., & Mayzlin, D. (2009). Firm-created word-of-mouth communication: Evidence from a field test. *Marketing Science*, *28*(4), 721–739. doi:10.1287/mksc.1080.0444

Godoy, A. S. (1995). Introdução à pesquisa qualitativa e suas possibilidades. *Revista de Administração de Empresas*, 35, 20-29.

Goh, K. M., Heng, C. S., & Lin, Z. (2013). Social Media Brand Community and Consumer Behavior: Qualifying the Relative Impact of User and Marketer Generated Contents. *Information Systems Research*, *24*(1), 88–107. doi:10.1287/isre.1120.0469

Goldenberg, J., Han, S., Lehmann, D. R., & Hong, W. J. (2009). The role of hubs in the adoption process. *Journal of Marketing*, *73*(2), 1–13. doi:10.1509/jmkg.73.2.1

Goldenberg, J., Libai, B., & Muller, E. (2001). Talk the network: A complex systems look at the underlying process of word of mouth. *Marketing Letters*, *12*(3), 211–223. doi:10.1023/A:1011122126881

Golicic, S. L., Davis, D. F., McCarthy, T. M., & Mentzer, J. T. (2002). The impact of e-commerce on supply chain relationships. *International Journal of Physical Distribution & Logistics Management*, *32*(10), 851–871. doi:10.1108/09600030210455447

GoodGuide Delivered To Your Phone. (n. d.). Retrieved from GoodGuide: http://www.goodguide.com/about/mobile

Goodhue, D. L., Wixom, B. H., & Watson, H. J. (2002). Realizing business benefits through CRM: Hitting the right target in the right way. *MIS Quarterly Executive*, *1*(2), 79–94.

Gordon, S., & Gordon, J. (2006). *Sistemas de informação: Uma abordagem gerencial*. Rio de Janeiro, Brazil: LTC Publisher.

Gossner, M. M. (2013). From Content Marketing to Story Advertising? *Social Media Today*. Retrieved from http://socialmediatoday.com/martinmeyergossner/1876956/content-marketing-story-advertising

Goulian, C., & Mersereau, A. (2000). Performance measurement-implementing a corporate scorecard. *Ivey Business Journal*, *65*(1), 48–54.

Grace, D., & O'Cass, A. (2005). Examining the Effects of Service Brand Communications on Brand Evaluation. *Journal of Product and Brand Management*, *14*(2), 106–116. doi:10.1108/10610420510592581

Graeml, A., & Csillag, J. (2006) An application of e-mail survey using a word form. Proceedings of the VIIth Annual Conference of Poms, Boston, USA.

Granovetter, M. S. (1973). The strength of weak ties. *American Journal of Sociology*, *78*(6), 1360–1380. doi:10.1086/225469

Gray, S., & Jennings, R. (2008). How are young people using social media? Retrieved from http://www.slideshare.net/diusgovuk/how-are-young-people-using-social-media-presentation

Gray, C. (2006). Absorptive capacity, knowledge management and innovation in entrepreneurial small firms. *International Journal of Entrepreneurial Behaviour & Research*, *12*(6), 345–360. doi:10.1108/13552550610710144

Greenberg, D. A. (2007). The Secret Strategies Behind Many Viral Videos. *Techcrunch*. Retrieved from http://www.techcrunch.com/2007/11/22/the-secret-strategies-behind-many-viral-videos/

Greenberg, P. (2010). CRM at the speed of light: Social CRM strategies, tools, and techniques for engaging your customers (4th ed.). New York, NY: McGraw Hill.

Greenberg, M. R. (2014). Energy policy and research: The underappreciation of trust. *Energy Research & Social Science*, *1*(29), 152–160. doi:10.1016/j.erss.2014.02.004

Greenberg, P. (2010). *CRM at the speed of light: social CRM strategies, tools, and techniques for engaging your customers* (4th ed.). USA: The McGraw-Hill Companies.

Greenberg, P. (2010). The impact of CRM 2.0 on customer insight. *Journal of Business and Industrial Marketing*, *25*(6), 410–419. doi:10.1108/08858621011066008

Gregg, A. P., & Klymowsky, J. (2013). The Implicit Association Test in Market Research: Potentials and Pitfalls. *Psychology and Marketing*, *30*(7), 588–601. doi:10.1002/mar.20630

Gregg, A. P., Klymowsky, J., Owens, D., & Perryman, A. (2013). Let Their Fingers Do The Talking? Using The Implicit Association Test in Market Research. *International Journal of Market Research*, *55*(4), 2–14. doi:10.2501/IJMR-2013-013

Gregg, P., Jewell, S., & Tonks, I. (2012). Executive pay and performance: Did bankers' bonuses cause the crisis? *International Review of Finance*, *12*(1), 89–122. doi:10.1111/j.1468-2443.2011.01136.x

Greitemeyer, T., Schulz-Hardt, S., Brodbeck, F. C., & Frey, D. (2006). Information Sampling & Group Decision Making: The Effects of an Advocacy Decision Procedure & Task Experience. *Journal of Experimental Psychology*, *12*(1), 31–42. PMID:16536657

Grewal, R., Chakravarty, A., & Saini, A. (2010). Governance mechanisms in business-to-business electronic markets. *Journal of Marketing*, *74*(4), 45–62. doi:10.1509/jmkg.74.4.45

Grieger, M. (2003). Electronic marketplaces: A literature review and a call for supply chain management research. *European Journal of Operational Research*, *144*(2), 280–294. doi:10.1016/S0377-2217(02)00394-6

Griffin, A., & Hauser, J. R. (1996). Integrating R&D & Marketing: A Review & Analysis of the Literature. *Journal of Product Innovation Management*, *13*(3), 191–215. doi:10.1111/1540-5885.1330191

Grigoroudis, E., Tsitsiridi, E., & Zopounidis, C. (2013). Linking customer satisfaction, employee appraisal, and business performance: An evaluation methodology in the banking sector. *Annals of Operations Research*, *205*(1), 5–27. doi:10.1007/s10479-012-1206-2

Grönroos, C. (1980). Designing a long range marketing strategy for services. *Long Range Planning*, *13*(2), 36–42. doi:10.1016/0024-6301(80)90030-8

Gronroos, C. (1990). *Service management and marketing: Managing the moments of truth in service competition*. Lexington, MA: Lexington Books.

Grönroos, C. (1994). From Marketing Mix to Relationship Marketing: Towards a Paradigm Shift in Marketing. *Management Decision*, *32*(2), 4–20. doi:10.1108/00251749410054774

Grönroos, C. (1995). Relationship marketing: The strategy continuum. *Journal of the Academy of Marketing Science*, *23*(4), 252–254. doi:10.1007/BF02893863

Grönroos, C. (1996). Relationship marketing: Strategic and tactical implications. *Management Decision*, *34*(3), 5–14. doi:10.1108/00251749610113613

Gruca, T. S., & Rego, L. L. (2005). Customer Satisfaction, Cash Flow, & Shareholder Value. *Journal of Marketing*, *69*(3), 115–130. doi:10.1509/jmkg.69.3.115.66364

Gruen, T. W., Osmonbekov, T., & Czaplewski, A. J. (2006). eWOM: The impact of customer-to customer online know-how exchange on customer value and loyalty. *Journal of Business Research*, *59*(4), 449–456. doi:10.1016/j.jbusres.2005.10.004

Gummesson, E. (1997). Relationship marketing as a paradigm shift: Some conclusions from the 30R approach. *Management Decision*, *35*(4), 267–272. doi:10.1108/00251749710169648

Gummesson, E. (1998). Implementation requires a relationship marketing paradigm. *Academy of Marketing Science. Journal*, *26*(3), 242–249. doi:10.1177/0092070398263006

Gummesson, E. (1999). *Total Relationship Marketing*. London: Butterworth-Heinemann.

Gummesson, E. (2002). Relationship marketing and a new economy: It's time for de-programming. *Journal of Services Marketing*, *16*(7), 585–589. doi:10.1108/08876040210447315

Gummesson, E. (2004). Return on relationships (ROR): The value of relationship marketing and CRM in business-to-business contexts. *Journal of Business and Industrial Marketing*, *19*(2), 136–148. doi:10.1108/08858620410524016

Gunderson, L. (2012, May 11). Amazon's 'dynamic' prices get some static. *The Oregonian.*

Gupta, A. K., & Souder, W. E. (1998). Key drivers of reduced cycle time. *Research Technology Management*, *41*(4), 38–43.

Guttman, R. H., & Maes, P. (1999). Agent-mediated integrative negotiation for retail electronic commerce. *Agent Mediated Electronic Commerce. Lecture Notes in Computer Science*, *1571*, 70–90. doi:10.1007/3-540-48835-9_5

Hair, J., Black, W., Babin, B., & Anderson, R. (2010). *Multivariate data analysis: A global perspective.* New Jersey: Pearson Education.

Hammarkvist, K.-O., Håkansson, H., & Mattsson, L. G. (1982). *Marknadsföring för konkurrenskraft.* Malmö: Liber Förlag.

Hanna, R., Rohm, A., & Crittenden, V. L. (2011). We're all connected: The power of social media ecosystem. *Business Horizons*, *54*(3), 265–273. doi:10.1016/j.bushor.2011.01.007

Hanneman, R. A., & Riddle, M. (2011). Concepts and Measures for Basic Network Analysis. In J. Scott, & P. J. Carrington (Eds.), The SAGE Handbook of Social Network Analysis (pp. 364-367). Thousand Oaks, CA: Sage Ltd.

Hansen, L. K., & Salamon, P. (1990). Neural Network Ensembles. *IEEE Transactions on Pattern Analysis and Machine Intelligence*, *12*(10), 993–1001. doi:10.1109/34.58871

Hanson, V. (2010). Influencing technology adoption by older adults. *Interacting with Computers*, *22*(6), 502–509. doi:10.1016/j.intcom.2010.09.001

Hanson, W. A., & Kalyanam, K. (2007). *Internet marketing & e-commerce.* Mason, OH: Thomson/South-Western.

Han, Y., Yang, F. Z., & Wu, G. (2013). Applying data mining to the customer relationship management in retail trade. *Social Media Retrieval and Mining: Communications in Computer and Information Science*, *387*, 116–124. doi:10.1007/978-3-642-41629-3_10

Hanzaee, K. H., & Farsani, F. T. (2011). The Effects of Brand Image and Perceived Public Relation on Customer Loyalty. *World Applied Sciences Journal*, *13*(2), 277–286.

Harkema, S. (2003). A complex adaptive perspective on learning within innovation projects. *The Learning Organization*, *10*(6), 340–346. doi:10.1108/09696470310497177

Harmon, R. R. (2003). Marketing Information Systems. In H. Bidgoli (Ed.), *Encyclopedia of Information Systems* (Vol. 3, pp. 137–151). New York, NY: Elsevier Science. doi:10.1016/B0-12-227240-4/00110-6

Harrigan, P., Ramsey, E., & Ibbotson, P. (2009). Investigating the e-CRM activities of Irish SMEs. *Journal of Small Business and Enterprise Development*, *16*(3), 443–465. doi:10.1108/14626000910977161

Hastie, T., & Tibshirani, R. (1986). Generalized additive models. *Statistical Science*, *1*(3), 297–318. doi:10.1214/ss/1177013604

Hastie, T., & Tibshirani, R. (1990). *Generalized Additive Models.* London: Chapman and Hall.

Hausman, A. V., & Siekpe, J. S. (2009). The effect of web interface features on consumer online purchase intentions. *Journal of Business Research*, *62*(1), 5–13. doi:10.1016/j.jbusres.2008.01.018

Hawkley, L. C., Bosch, J. A., Engeland, C. G., Marucha, P. T., & Cacioppo, J. T. (2006). tT Loneliness, Dysphoria, Stress, and Immunity: A Role for Cytokines. *Cytokines: Stress and immunity*: 67.

Haythornthwaite, C. (2005). Social networks and Internet connectivity effects. *Information Communication and Society*, *8*(2), 125–147. doi:10.1080/13691180500146185

Heidemann, J., Klier, M., Landherr, A., & Zimmermann, S. (2013). The optimal level of CRM IT investments. *Electronic Markets*, *23*(1), 73–84. doi:10.1007/s12525-012-0096-0

Heinrich, B., Zellner, G., & Leist, S. (2011). Service integrators in business networks: The importance of relationship values. *Electronic Markets*, *21*(4), 215–235. doi:10.1007/s12525-011-0075-x

Helaakoski, H., Kipinä, J., & Haapasalo, H. (2004). An Agent architecture for steel product business network. In ICEIS (4), 467-470.

He, M., Jennings, N. R., & Leung, H.-F. (2003). On agent-mediated electronic commerce. *IEEE Transactions on Knowledge and Data Engineering*, *15*(4), 985–1003. doi:10.1109/TKDE.2003.1209014

Hennig-Thurau, T., Gwinner, K. P., Walsh, G., & GremleR, D. D. (2004). Electronic word-of-mouth via consumer-opinion platforms: What motivates consumers to articulate themselves on the internet? *Journal of Interactive Marketing*, *18*(1), 38–52. doi:10.1002/dir.10073

Hennig-Thurau, T., & Klee, A. (1997). The impact of customer satisfaction and relationship quality and customer retention: A critical reassessment and model development. *Psychology and Marketing*, *14*(8), 737–764. doi:10.1002/(SICI)1520-6793(199712)14:8<737::AID-MAR2>3.0.CO;2-F

Hennig-Thurau, T., Marchand, A., & Marx, P. (2012, September). Can Automated Group Recommender Systems Help Consumers Make Better Choices? *Journal of Marketing*, *76*(5), 89–109. doi:10.1509/jm.10.0537

Hensel, J. (1970). *Physiological Measures of Advertising Effectiveness: A Theoretical and Empirical Investigation* [Doctoral Dissertation]. Ohio State University, School of Business. Retrieved from https://etd.ohiolink.edu/

Heritage, S. (2013). The cutesification of everything makes me want to strangle an elf., *The Guardian*. Retrieved from http://www.theguardian.com/commentisfree/2013/nov/24/cutesification-of-everything-elf-twitter-funny

Herrmann, A., & Wricke, M. (1998). Evaluating multidimensional prices. *Journal of Product and Brand Management*, *7*(2), 161–169. doi:10.1108/10610429810216973

Hew, K. (2011). Students and teachers use of Facebook. *Computers in Human Behavior*, *27*(2), 662–676. doi:10.1016/j.chb.2010.11.020

Hibbard, J., Brunel, F., Dant, R., & Iacobucci, D. (2001). Does relationship marketing age well? *Business Strategy Review*, *12*(4), 29–35. doi:10.1111/1467-8616.00189

Hillebrand, B., Nijholt, J. J., & Nijssen, E. J. (2011). Exploring CRM effectiveness: An institutional theory perspective. *Journal of the Academy of Marketing Science*, *39*(4), 592–608. doi:10.1007/s11747-011-0248-3

Hill, K. (2012, February2). How Target Figured Out A Teen Girl Was Pregnant Before Her Father Did. *Forbes*.

Hine, J. A., & Preuss, L. (2009). Society is out there, organisation is in here: On the perceptions of corporate social responsibility held by different managerial groups. *Journal of Business Ethics*, *88*(2), 381–393. doi:10.1007/s10551-008-9970-2

Hinsz, V. B. (1999). Group decision-making with responses of a quantitative nature: The theory of social decisions schemes for quantities. *Organizational Behavior and Human Decision Processes*, *80*(1), 28–49. doi:10.1006/obhd.1999.2853 PMID:10508567

Hinz, O., Skiera, B., Barrot, C., & Becker, J. U. (2011). Seeding strategies for viral marketing: An empirical comparison. *Journal of Marketing*, *75*(6), 55–71. doi:10.1509/jm.10.0088

Hismanoglu, M. (2011). The integration of information and communication technology into current ELT coursebooks: A critical analysis. *Procedia: Social and Behavioral Sciences*, *15*, 37–45. doi:10.1016/j.sbspro.2011.03.048

Hobson, C. A. (1999). E-negotiations: Creating a framework for online commercial negotiations. *Negotiation Journal*, *15*(3), 201–218. doi:10.1111/j.1571-9979.1999.tb00192.x

Hoffman, D. L., Novak, & Thomas, P. (1996). A new marketing paradigm for electronic Commerce. *The Information Society*. Retrieved from http://www.bus.umich.edu/FacultyResearch/ResearchCenters/centers/Yaffe/downloads/Complete_List_of_Working_Papers/anewmark.pdf

Hoffman, D. L., Novak, T.P., & Chatterjee, P. (1995). Commercial Scenarios for the Web: Opportunities and Challenges. *Journal of Computer-Mediated Communications*, 1(3). Retrieved from http://onlinelibrary.wiley.com/doi/10.1111/j.1083-6101.1995.tb00165.x/full

Hoffman, T., & Kashmeri, S. (2000). Coddling the customer. *Computerworld*, *34*(50), 58–60.

Hofstede, G. (1984). Cultural dimensions in management and planning. *Asia Pacific Journal of Management*, *1*(2), 81–99. doi:10.1007/BF01733682

Hogan, J., & Lodhia, S. (2011). Sustainability reporting and reputation risk management: An Australian case study. *International Journal of Accounting and Information Management*, *19*(3), 267–287. doi:10.1108/18347641111169269

Hollebeek, L. (2011). Demystifying Customer Brand Engagement: Exploring the Loyalty Nexus. *Journal of Marketing Management*, *27*(7-8), 785–807. doi:10.1080/0267257X.2010.500132

Hollensen, S. (2007). Global Marketing, Chapter 20: Global e-marketing. *Pearson*. Retrieved from http://wps.pearsoned.co.uk/ema_uk_he_hollensen_globalmark_4/64/16425/4204992.cw/index.html

Holm, M., Kumar, V., & Rohde, C. (2012). Measuring customer profitability in complex environments: An interdisciplinary contingency framework. *Journal of the Academy of Marketing Science*, *40*(3), 387–401. doi:10.1007/s11747-011-0263-4

Holzner, S. (2008). Facebook Marketing: Leverage Social Media to Grow Your Business. Indianapolis, IN: Que.

Hoofnagle, C.J., King, J., Li, S. & Turow, J. (2010). *How different are young adults from older adults when it comes to information privacy attitudes and policies?* Research Report, November.

Hooper, D. (2007). Getting better all the time. *HR Monthly*, May.

Horne, S. (2003). Needed: A cultural change. *Target Marketing*, *26*(8), 53–56.

Hosmer, D. W., & Lemeshow, S. (2000). Applied Logistic Regression (2nd ed.). John Wiley & Sons Inc.

Ho, T. K.Tin Kam Ho. (1998). The random subspace method for constructing decision forests. *IEEE Transactions on Pattern Analysis and Machine Intelligence*, *20*(8), 832–844. doi:10.1109/34.709601

Houser, D., & Wooders, J. (2006). Reputation in auctions: Theory, and Evidence from eBay. *Journal of Economics & Management Strategy*, *15*(2), 353–369. doi:10.1111/j.1530-9134.2006.00103.x

Howardson, G. M., & Behrend, T. S. (2014). Using the internet to recruit employees: Comparing the effects of usability expectations and objective technological characteristics on internet recruitment outcomes. *Computers in Human Behavior*, *31*, 334–342. doi:10.1016/j.chb.2013.10.057

Hsieh, Y. H., Chen, I. H., & Yuan, S. T. (2014). FCM-based customer expectation-driven service dispatch system. *Soft Computing*, *18*(2), 359–378. doi:10.1007/s00500-013-1063-1

Hughes, D. E., Le Bon, J., & Rapp, A. (2013). Gaining and leveraging customer-based competitive intelligence: The pivotal role of social capital and salesperson adaptive selling skills. *Journal of the Academy of Marketing Science*, *41*(1), 91–110. doi:10.1007/s11747-012-0311-8

Huhns, M. N., & Vidal, J. M. (1999). Online auctions. *IEEE Internet Computing*, *3*(3), 103–105. doi:10.1109/4236.769429

Hus, V. (2011). The use of ICT in the environmental studies subject. *Procedia: Social and Behavioral Sciences*, *15*, 3855–3860. doi:10.1016/j.sbspro.2011.04.385

IBM Watson Engagement Advisor, Transforming the way people and organizations interact over the lifetime of their relationships. (2013, May). *IBM*. Retrieved from http://www-03.ibm.com/innovation/us/watson/pdf/ibm_watson_engagement_brochure.pdf

IBM Watson. (2014, January). Retrieved from IBM: http://www-03.ibm.com/press/us/en/presskit/27297.wss

IELKA. (2014). 10 Recessionary habits changing the Greek consumer in the retail sector. Retrieved from http://www.ielka.gr/?p=1712

Ignatius, J., Leen, J. Y. A., Ramayah, T., Kah Hin, C., & Jantan, M. (2012). The impact of technological learning on NPD outcomes: The moderating effect of project complexity. *Technovation*, *32*(7), 452–463. doi:10.1016/j.technovation.2012.03.003

Iizuka, E. (2003) Um estudo exploratório sobre a exclusão digital e as organizações sem fins lucrativos da cidade de São Paulo [Master Dissertation]. School of Management, Getulio Vargas Foundation, Saint Paul, Brazil.

IMAP. (2010). Retail industry global report. Retrieved from http://www.imap.com/imap/media/article_documents/IMAP_Global_Retail_Industry_Report__BEDF5F30C7201.pdf

Insider, U. (2014). What uniques and pageviews leave out (and why we're measuring attention minutes instead). Retrieved from http://blog.upworthy.com/post/75795679502/what-uniques-and-pageviews-leave-out-and-why-were

International Telecommunication Union [ITU] (2014). ICT statistics. Retrieved from http://www.itu.int/en/ITU-D/Statistics/Pages/default.aspx

iOS7 - Siri. (n. d.). *Apple Computers*. Retrieved from http://www.apple.com/ios/siri/

IPsoft. (2014). http://www.ipsoft.com/what-we-do/amelia/

Iqbal, M. (2011, June 6). An inquiry into "customer engagement" – making the abstract concrete The Customer Blog. Retrieved from http://thecustomerblog.co.uk/2011/06/06/an-inquiry-into-customerengagement-making-the-abstract-concrete/

Iyengar, R., Han, S., & Gupta, S. (2009). Do friends influence purchases in a social network? *Harvard Business School Marketing Unit Working Paper* 09-123.

Iyengar, R., Van den Bulte, C., & Valente, T. W. (2011). Opinion Leadership and Social Contagion in New Product Diffusion. *Marketing Science*, *30*(2), 195–212. doi:10.1287/mksc.1100.0566

Jackson, B. (1985). Building customer relationships that last: How close can industrial markets get to their customers - and for how long? *Harvard Business Review*, *63*, 120–128.

Jain, R., Jain, S., & Dhar, U. (2003). Measuring customer relationship management. *Journal of Service Research*, *2*(2), 97–109.

Jamal, A., Davies, F., Chudry, F., & Al-Marri, M. (2006). Profiling Consumers: A Study of Qatari Consumers' Shopping Motivations. *Journal of Retailing and Consumer Services*, *13*(1), 67–80. doi:10.1016/j.jretconser.2005.08.002

Jamal, A., & Goode, M. H. (2001). Consumers and Brands: A study of the Impact of Self Image Congruence on Brand Preference and Satisfaction. *Marketing Intelligence & Planning*, *19*(7), 482–492. doi:10.1108/02634500110408286

Jamali, D. (2008). A stakeholder approach to corporate social responsibility: A fresh perspective into theory and practice. *Journal of Business Ethics*, *82*(1), 213–231. doi:10.1007/s10551-007-9572-4

Jamali, D., Safieddine, A. M., & Rabbath, M. (2008). Corporate governance and corporate social responsibility synergies and interrelationships. *Corporate Governance: An International Review*, *16*(5), 443–459. doi:10.1111/j.1467-8683.2008.00702.x

Jameson, K. (2010). Flying high in a new age: An investigation into building airline brand equity through the interactivity of social media. Leeds Metropolitan University, April.

Jang, J. H., Kim, S. W., Lee, Y. S., & Kim, J. (2013). The effects of relationship benefit on relationship quality and store loyalty from convergence environments: NPS analysis and moderating effects. *Electronic Commerce Research*, *13*(3), 291–315. doi:10.1007/s10660-013-9117-0

Janita, M. S., & Miranda, F. J. (2013). The antecedents of client loyalty in business-to-business (B2B) electronic marketplaces. *Industrial Marketing Management*, *42*(5), 814–823. doi:10.1016/j.indmarman.2013.01.006

Jannarone, J. (2012, September 17). When Twitter Fans Steer TV. *Wall Street Journal*.

Jansen, B. J., Zhang, M., Sobel, K., & Chowdury, A. (2009). Twitter power: Tweets as electronic word-of-mouth. *Journal of the American Society for Information Science and Technology*, *60*(11), 2169–2188. doi:10.1002/asi.21149

Jap, S. D. (2002). Online reverse auctions: Issues, themes, and prospects for the future. *Journal of the Academy of Marketing Science*, *30*(4), 506–525. doi:10.1177/009207002236925

Jap, S. D. (2003). An exploratory study of the introduction of online reverse auctions. *Journal of Marketing*, *67*(3), 96–107. doi:10.1509/jmkg.67.3.96.18651

Jap, S. D., & Haruvy, E. (2008). Interorganizational relationships and bidding behavior in industrial online reverse auctions. *JMR, Journal of Marketing Research*, *45*(5), 550–561. doi:10.1509/jmkr.45.5.550

Jap, S. D., & Naik, P. A. (2004). Introduction to the special issue on online pricing. *Journal of Interactive Marketing*, *18*(4), 4–6. doi:10.1002/dir.20026

Javor, A., Koller, M., Lee, N., Chamberlain, L., & Ransmayr, G. (2013). Neuromarketing and Consumer Neuroscience: Contributions To Neurology. *BMC Neurology*, *13*(13), 1–12. PMID:23383650

Jayachandran, S., Sharma, S., Kaufman, P., & Raman, P. (2005). The Role of Relational Information Processes and Technology Use in Customer Relationship Management. *Journal of Marketing*, *69*(4), 177–192. doi:10.1509/jmkg.2005.69.4.177

Jayaraman, V., & Baker, T. (2003). The internet as an enabler for dynamic pricing of goods. *IEEE Transactions on Engineering Management*, *50*(4), 470–477. doi:10.1109/TEM.2003.820134

Jefferies, E., Frankish, C., & Noble, K. (2009). Lexical Coherence in Short-Term Memory: Strategic Reconstruction or "Semantic Glue"? *Quarterly Journal of Experimental Psychology*, *62*(10), 1967–1982. doi:10.1080/17470210802697672 PMID:19255945

Jenkins, H. (2009). A 'business opportunity' model of corporate social responsibility for small-and medium-sized enterprises. *Business Ethics (Oxford, England)*, *18*(1), 21–36. doi:10.1111/j.1467-8608.2009.01546.x

Jin, G. Z., & Kato, A. (2008). Price, quality, and reputation: Evidence from an online field experiment. *The Rand Journal of Economics*, *37*(4), 983–1005. doi:10.1111/j.1756-2171.2006.tb00067.x

Jobber, D., & Ellis-Chadwick, F. (1995). *Principles & Practice of Marketing*. Maidenhead: McGraw-Hill, Inc.

Jochem, R. (2011). Sustainability modelling as an enterprise quality requirement. *Current Issues of Business and Law*, *6*(1), 129–140. doi:10.5200/1822-9530.2011.07

Johanson, J., & Mattsson, L. G. (1987). Interorganizational relations in industrial systems: A network approach compared with a transaction cost approach. *International Studies of Management & Organization*, *17*(1), 34–48.

John, G., & Reve, T. (1982). The reliability and validity of key informant data from dyadic relationships in marketing channels. *JMR, Journal of Marketing Research*, *19*(4), 517–524. doi:10.2307/3151724

Johnmark, D. R., Israel, K. J., & Zumbung, D. M. (2014). Celebrity Advertising and the Performance of New Products in Globacom Nigeria Limited. *Interdisciplinary Journal of Contemporary Research in Business*, *6*(4), 1–18.

Johnson, C. (2006, September 17). Cutting Through Advertising Clutter. *CBS News*. Retrieved from http://www.cbsnews.com/news/cutting-through-advertising-clutter/

Johnson, G., Whittington, R., & Scholes, K. (2011). Exploring Corporate Strategy, 9th Edition. Place: Pearson Education Limited.

Johnston, R., & Vitale, M. R. (1988). Creating competitive advantage with interorganizational information systems. *Management Information Systems Quarterly*, *12*(2), 153–165. doi:10.2307/248839

Johnston, W., Leach, M., & Liu, A. (1999). Theory testing using case studies in business-to-business research. *Industrial Marketing Management*, *28*(3), 201–213. doi:10.1016/S0019-8501(98)00040-6

Joinson, A. (2008). *Looking at, looking up or keeping up with people? Motives and uses of Facebook*. Florence, Italy: CHI.

Jøsang, A., & Presti, S. L. (2004). Analysing the relationship between risk and trust. In T. Dimitrakos (Ed.), *Trust Management* (pp. 135–145). Berlin, Heidelberg: Springer. doi:10.1007/978-3-540-24747-0_11

Jothi, P. S., Neelamalar, M., & Prasad, R. S. (2011). Analysis of social networking sites: A study on effective communication strategy in developing brand communication. *Journal of Media and Communication Studies*, *3*(7), 234–242.

Kadushin, C. (2012). *Understanding Social Networks: Theories, Concepts, and Findings*. Oxford, United Kingdom: Oxford University Press.

Kalaignanam, K., & Varadarajan, R. (2012). Offshore outsourcing of customer relationship management: Conceptual model and propositions. *Journal of the Academy of Marketing Science*, *40*(2), 347–363. doi:10.1007/s11747-011-0291-0

Kallinikos, J., & Mariategui, J. C. (2011). Video as Digital Object: Production and Distribution of Video Content in the Internet Media Ecosystem. *The Information Society*, *27*(5), 281–294. doi:10.1080/01972243.2011.607025

Kannabiran, G., Xavier, M. J., & Anantharaaj, A. (2005). Enabling e-Governance through Citizen Relationship Management - Concept, Model and Applications. *Journal of Service Research*, *4*(2), 223–240.

Kaplan, A., & Haenlein, M. (2010). Users of the world, unite! The challenges and opportunities of social media. *Business Horizons*, *53*(1), 59–68. doi:10.1016/j.bushor.2009.09.003

Kaplan, R. S., & Norton, D. P. (1992). The balanced scorecard: Measures that drive performance. *Harvard Business Review*, *70*(1), 71–79. PMID:10119714

Kaplan, R. S., & Norton, D. P. (2001). Transforming the balanced scorecard from performance measurement to strategic management: Part I. *Accounting Horizons*, *15*(1), 87–104. doi:10.2308/acch.2001.15.1.87

Karimi, J., Somers, T. M., & Gupta, Y. P. (2001). Impact of Information Technology Management Practices on Customer Service. *Journal of Management Information Systems*, *17*(4), 125–158.

Kärkkäinen, M., Laukkanen, S., Sarpola, S., & Kemppainen, K. (2007). Roles of interfirm information systems in supply chain management. *International Journal of Physical Distribution & Logistics Management*, *37*(4), 264–286. doi:10.1108/09600030710752505

Karunanithy, M., & Sivesan, S. (2013). An Empirical Study on the Promotional Mix and Brand Equity: Mobile Service Providers. *Industrial Engineering Letters*, *3*(3), 1–9.

Kasemsap, K. (2013d). Practical framework: Creation of causal model of job involvement, career commitment, learning motivation, and learning transfer. *International Journal of the Computer, the Internet and Management, 21*(1), 29-35.

Kasemsap, K. (2013e). Synthesized framework: Establishing a causal model of organizational learning, knowledge management, knowledge-sharing behavior, and organizational performance. *International Journal of the Computer, the Internet and Management, 21*(2), 29-34.

Kasemsap, K. (2014d). The role of knowledge sharing on organisational innovation: An integrated framework. In L. Al-Hakim, & C. Jin (Eds.), Quality innovation: Knowledge, theory, and practices (pp. 247-271). Hershey, PA: IGI Global.

Kasemsap, K. (2013a). Strategic business management: A practical framework and causal model of empowering leadership, team cohesion, knowledge-sharing behavior, and team performance. *Journal of Social and Development Sciences*, *4*(3), 100–106.

Kasemsap, K. (2013b). Unified framework: Constructing a causal model of Six Sigma, organizational learning, organizational innovation, and organizational performance. *The Journal of Interdisciplinary Networks*, *2*(1), 268–273.

Kasemsap, K. (2013c). Innovative framework: Formation of causal model of organizational culture, organizational climate, knowledge management, and job performance. *Journal of International Business Management & Research*, *4*(12), 21–32.

Kasemsap, K. (2014a). The role of brand loyalty on CRM performance: An innovative framework for smart manufacturing. In Z. Luo (Ed.), *Smart manufacturing innovation and transformation: Interconnection and intelligence* (pp. 252–284). Hershey, PA: IGI Global. doi:10.4018/978-1-4666-5836-3.ch010

Kasemsap, K. (2014b). The role of social media in the knowledge-based organizations. In I. Lee (Ed.), *Integrating social media into business practice, applications, management, and models* (pp. 254–275). Hershey, PA: IGI Global. doi:10.4018/978-1-4666-6182-0.ch013

Kasemsap, K. (2014c). Strategic innovation management: An integrative framework and causal model of knowledge management, strategic orientation, organizational innovation, and organizational performance. In P. Ordóñez de Pablos & R. Tennyson (Eds.), *Strategic approaches for human capital management and development in a turbulent economy* (pp. 102–116). Hershey, PA: IGI Global. doi:10.4018/978-1-4666-4530-1.ch007

Kasemsap, K. (2014e). The role of social networking in global business environments. In P. Smith & T. Cockburn (Eds.), *Impact of emerging digital technologies on leadership in global business* (pp. 183–201). Hershey, PA: IGI Global. doi:10.4018/978-1-4666-6134-9.ch010

Kasemsap, K. (2014f). The role of social capital in higher education institutions. In N. Baporikar (Ed.), *Handbook of research on higher education in the MENA region: Policy and practice* (pp. 119–147). Hershey, PA: IGI Global. doi:10.4018/978-1-4666-6198-1.ch007

Kasemsap, K. (2014g). The role of brand management in emerging markets. In I. Samanta (Ed.), *Strategic marketing in fragile economic conditions* (pp. 167–184). Hershey, PA: IGI Global. doi:10.4018/978-1-4666-6232-2.ch009

Kasemsap, K. (2014h). The role of knowledge management on job satisfaction: A systematic framework. In B. Tripathy & D. Acharjya (Eds.), *Advances in secure computing, Internet services, and applications* (pp. 104–127). Hershey, PA: IGI Global. doi:10.4018/978-1-4666-4940-8.ch006

Kasemsap, K. (2014i). Unifying a framework of organizational culture, organizational climate, knowledge management, and job performance. In R. Perez-Castillo & M. Piattini (Eds.), *Uncovering essential software artifacts through business process archeology* (pp. 336–362). Hershey, PA: IGI Global. doi:10.4018/978-1-4666-4667-4.ch013

Kasemsap, K. (2015). Implementing enterprise resource planning. In M. Khosrow-Pour (Ed.), *Encyclopedia of information science and technology* (3rd ed., pp. 798–807). Hershey, PA: IGI Global. doi:10.4018/978-1-4666-5888-2.ch076

Kashi, K., & Zheng, C. (2013). Extending technology acceptance model to the e-recruitment context in Iran. *International Journal of Selection and Assessment*, *23*(1), 122–129.

Kass, G. V. (1980). An Exploratory Technique for Investigating Large Quantities of Categorical Data. *Journal of the Royal Statistical Society. Series C, Applied Statistics*, *29*(2), 119–127.

Katkar, R., & Reiley, D. (2006). Public versus secret reserve prices in eBay auctions: Results from a pokémon field experiment. *Advances in Economic Analysis & Policy*, *6*(2), 1–23.

Kaufman, F. (1966). Data systems that cross company boundaries. *Harvard Business Review*, *44*(1), 141–155.

Kavanagh, S. (2001). Constituent Relationship Management Systems: A Primer for Public Managers. *Government Finance Review*, *1*(5), 35–39.

Kawamoto, D. (2011, February 8). How IBM Built Watson, Its Jeopardy-Playing Supercomputer. *Daily Finance*. Retrieved from http://www.dailyfinance.com/2011/02/08/ibm-supercomputer-watson-jeopardy/

Kaynak, H. (2003). The relationship between total quality management practices and their effects on firm performance. *Journal of Operations Management*, *21*(4), 405–435. doi:10.1016/S0272-6963(03)00004-4

Kellen, V. (2002). *CRM measurement frameworks* (Working paper). DePaul University, Chicago, IL.

Keller, K. L. (2005). *Strategic Brand Management: Building*. Measuring and Managing Brand Equity.

Kelly, J. (2012). Taming Big Data: A Big Data Infographic. *Big Data, Wikibon*. Retrieved from http://wikibon.org/blog/taming-big-data/

Kenning, P., Plassmann, H., & Ahlert, D. (2007). Applications of Functional Magnetic Resonance Imaging for Market Research. *Qualitative Market Research*, *2*(2), 135–152. doi:10.1108/13522750710740817

Keramati, A., Nazari-Shirkouhi, S., Moshki, H., Afshari-Mofrad, M., & Maleki-Berneti, E. (2013). A novel methodology for evaluating the risk of CRM projects in fuzzy environment. *Neural Computing & Applications*, *23*(1), 29–53. doi:10.1007/s00521-012-1216-7

Kesharwani, A., & Singh Bisht, S. (2012). The impact of trust and perceived risk on internet banking adoption in India: An extension of technology acceptance model. *International Journal of Bank Marketing*, *30*(4), 303–322. doi:10.1108/02652321211236923

Ketter, W., Collins, J., Gini, M., Gupta, A., & Schrater, P. (2012). Real-time tactical and strategic sales management for intelligent agents guided by economic regimes. *Information Systems Research*, *23*(4), 1263–1283. doi:10.1287/isre.1110.0415

Khandelwal, K. A., & Mohendra, N. (2010). Espoused organizational values, vision, and corporate social responsibility: Does it matter to organizational members? *Vikalpa*, *35*(3), 19–35.

Khosla, A., Bainbridge, W. A., Torralba, A., & Oliva, A. (2013). Modifying the Memorability of Face Photographs. *International Conference on Computer Vision 2013.*Sydney. doi:10.1109/ICCV.2013.397

Khosla, A., Sarma, A. D., & Hamid, R. (2014). What Makes an Image Popular?*International World Wide Web Conference*. Seoul, Korea.

Khraim, H. S. (2011). The Influence of Brand Loyalty on Cosmetics Buying Behavior of UAE Female Consumers. *International Journal of Marketing Studies*, *3*(2), 123–133.

Kietzmann, J. H., Hermkens, K., Mccarthy, I. P., & Silvestre, B. S. (2011). Social media? Get serious! Understanding the functional building blocks of social media. *Business Horizons*, *54*(3), 241–251. doi:10.1016/j.bushor.2011.01.005

Kim, H. C., Pang, S., Je, H. M., Kim, D., & Bang, S. Y. (2002, Aug 10). *Support vector machine ensemble with bagging.* Paper presented at the 1st International Workshop on Pattern Recognition with Support Vector Machines, Niagara Falls, Canada. doi:10.1007/3-540-45665-1_31

Kim, A., & Ko, E. (2012). Do social media marketing activities enhance customer equity? An empirical study of luxury fashion brand. *Journal of Business Research*, *65*(10), 1480–1486. doi:10.1016/j.jbusres.2011.10.014

Kimble, C., & Bourdon, I. (2013). The link among information technology, business models, and strategic breakthroughs: Examples from Amazon, Dell, and eBay. *Global Business and Organizational Excellence*, *33*(1), 58–68. doi:10.1002/joe.21523

Kim, D., Cavusgil, S. T., & Calantone, R. J. (2006). Information system innovations and supply chain management: Channel relationships and firm performance. *Journal of the Academy of Marketing Science*, *34*(1), 40–54. doi:10.1177/0092070305281619

Kim, G., Chae, B. K., & Olson, D. L. (2013). A support vector machine (SVM) approach to imbalanced datasets of customer responses: Comparison with other customer response models. *Service Business*, *7*(1), 167–182. doi:10.1007/s11628-012-0147-9

Kim, H. M., & Kachersky, L. (2006). Dimensions of price salience: A conceptual framework for perceptions of multi-dimensional prices. *Journal of Product and Brand Management*, *15*(2), 139–147. doi:10.1108/10610420610658974

Kim, H. S., & Kim, Y. G. (2009). A CRM performance measurement framework: Its development process and application. *Industrial Marketing Management*, *38*(4), 477–489. doi:10.1016/j.indmarman.2008.04.008

Kim, H.-C., Pang, S., Je, H.-M., Kim, D., & Yang Bang, S. (2003). Constructing support vector machine ensemble. *Pattern Recognition*, *36*(12), 2757–2767. doi:10.1016/S0031-3203(03)00175-4

Kim, J. W., Choi, J., Qualls, W., & Park, J. (2004). The impact of CRM on firm- and relationship-level performance in distribution networks. *Communications of the Association for Information Systems*, *14*(1), 632–652.

Kim, J., Suh, E., & Hwang, H. (2003). A model for evaluating the effectiveness of CRM using balanced scorecard. *Journal of Interactive Marketing*, *17*(2), 5–19. doi:10.1002/dir.10051

Kim, W., Jeong, O., & Lee, S. (2010). On social Web sites. *Information Systems*, *35*(2), 215–236. doi:10.1016/j.is.2009.08.003

Kim, Y. S. (2006). Toward a successful CRM: Variable selection, sampling, and ensemble. *Decision Support Systems*, *41*(2), 542–553. doi:10.1016/j.dss.2004.09.008

Kincaid, J. W. (2003). *Customer relationship management: Getting it right!* Upper Saddle River, NJ: Prentice-Hall.

Kinon, C. (2010, February 3). Creators of Glee, Modern Family, track fan reaction via Twitter. Retrieved from http://www.nydailynews.com/entertainment/tv-movies/creators-glee-modern-family-track-fan-reaction-twitter-article-1.175907

Klaus, H., Rosemann, M., & Gable, G. G. (2000). What is ERP? *Information Systems Frontiers*, *2*(2), 141–162. doi:10.1023/A:1026543906354

Klemperer, P. D. (1999). Auction theory: A guide to the literature. *Journal of Economic Surveys*, *13*(3), 227–286. doi:10.1111/1467-6419.00083

Klimova, B. (2011). Making academic writing real with ICT. *Procedia Computer Science*, *3*, 133–137. doi:10.1016/j.procs.2010.12.023

Klünder, P. (2006). Planbarer Brückenschlag. *Design Report*, *11*, 26–27.

Kocher, M. G., & Sutter, M. (2006). Time is Money—Time Pressure, Incentives, & the Quality of Decision-Making. *Journal of Economic Behavior & Organization*, *61*(3), 375–392. doi:10.1016/j.jebo.2004.11.013

Ko, H., Jung, J., Kim, J., & Shim, S. W. (2004). Cross-cultural differences in perceived risk of online shopping. *Journal of Interactive Advertising*, *4*(2), 20–29. doi:10.1080/15252019.2004.10722084

Kohlbacher, F. (2008). Knowledge-based New Product Development fostering innovation through knowledge co-creation. *International Journal of Technology Intelligence & Planning*, *4*(3), 326–346. doi:10.1504/IJTIP.2008.020100

Kohli, A. K., & Jaworski, B. J. (1993). Market orientation: Antecedents and consequences. *Journal of marketing: A quarterly publication of the American Marketing Association, 57*(3), 53-70.

Kohli, R., Piontek, F., Ellington, T., VanOsdol, T., Shepard, M., & Brazel, G. (2001). Managing customer relationships through e-business decision support applications: A case of hospital-physician collaboration. *Decision Support Systems*, *32*(2), 171–187. doi:10.1016/S0167-9236(01)00109-9

Kolikant, Y. (2012). Using ICT for school purposes: Is there a student-school disconnect? *Computers & Education*, *59*(3), 907–914. doi:10.1016/j.compedu.2012.04.012

Kolstad, I. (2007). Why firms should not always maximize profits. *Journal of Business Ethics*, *76*(2), 137–145. doi:10.1007/s10551-006-9262-7

Kost, J. (2004). Analyze Government Transactions to Make Them Citizen-Centric. *Gartner Research, Research Notes*, 1-5.

Kotler, P., & Armstrong, G. (2014). Principles of marketing (15th global ed.). Essex: Pearson Education Limited.

Kotler, P. (2000). *Marketing Management Millennium Edition. 10e*. Prentice Hall.

Kotler, P., & Keller, K. (2011). *Marketing Management, 14/E*. Prentice Hall.

Kotler, P., & Keller, K. L. (2011). *Marketing Management* (14th ed.). Upper Saddle River, NJ: Prentice Hall.

Kozinets, R. V., de Valck, K., Wojnicki, A. C., & Wilner, S. J. S. (2010). Networked narratives: Understanding word-of-mouth marketing in online communities. *Journal of Marketing*, *74*(2), 71–89. doi:10.1509/jmkg.74.2.71

Kraljic, P. (1983). Purchasing must become supply management. *Harvard Business Review*, (September-October): 109–117.

Krasnikov, A., Jayachandran, S., & Kumar, V. (2009). The impact of customer relationship management implementation on cost and profit efficiencies: Evidence from the US commercial banking industry. *Journal of Marketing*, *73*(6), 61–76. doi:10.1509/jmkg.73.6.61

Krauss, M. (2002). At many firms, technology obscures CRM. *Marketing News*, *36*(6), 5.

Krishnan, V., & Ulrich, K. T. (2001). Product Development Decisions: A Review of the Literature. *Management Science*, *47*(1), 1–21. doi:10.1287/mnsc.47.1.1.10668

Kroeber-Riel, W. (1979). Activation Research: Psychobiological Approaches in Consumer Research. *The Journal of Consumer Research*, *5*(4), 240–250. doi:10.1086/208736

Kumar, K., & van Hillegersberg, J. (2000). Enterprise resource planning: Introduction. *Communications of the ACM*, *43*(4), 22–26. doi:10.1145/332051.332063

Kumar, N., Scheer, L. K., & Steenkamp, J. E. M. (1995). The effects of supplier fairness on vulnerable resellers. *JMR, Journal of Marketing Research*, *32*(1), 54–65. doi:10.2307/3152110

Kumar, N., Stern, L. W., & Anderson, J. C. (1993). Conducting interorganizational research using key informants. *Academy of Management Journal*, *36*(6), 1633–1651. doi:10.2307/256824

Kumar, V., & Reinartz, W. (2012). *Customer relationship management: concept, strategy, and tools* (2nd ed.). New York, NY: Springer. doi:10.1007/978-3-642-20110-3

Kuncheva, L. I. (2004). *Combining pattern classifiers: methods and algorithms*. Hoboken, New Jersey: John Wiley & Sons. doi:10.1002/0471660264

Kuncheva, L. I., & Rodríguez, J. J. (2007). Classifier ensembles with a random linear oracle. *IEEE Transactions on Knowledge and Data Engineering*, *19*(4), 500–508. doi:10.1109/TKDE.2007.1016

Kuncheva, L. I., & Whitaker, C. J. (2003). Measures of diversity in classifier ensembles and their relationship with the ensemble accuracy. *Machine Learning*, *51*(2), 181–207. doi:10.1023/A:1022859003006

Kung, M., Monroe, K. B., & Cox, J. L. (2002). Pricing on the internet. *Journal of Product and Brand Management*, *11*(5), 274–287. doi:10.1108/10610420210442201

Kunsch, M. (2007). Comunicação organizacional na era digital: Contextos, percursos e possibilidades. *Signo y Pensamiento*, *51*(XXVI), 38–51.

Kuo, T., & Tang, H. (2014). Relationships amongst personality traits, Facebook usages, and leisure activities- A case of Taiwanese college students. *Computers in Human Behavior*, *31*, 13–19. doi:10.1016/j.chb.2013.10.019

Kurt, G., & Hacioglu, G. (2010). Ethics as a customer perceived value driver in the context of online retailing. *African Journal of Business Management*, *4*(5), 672–677.

LaBarbera, P. A., & Tucciarone, J. D. (1995). GSR Reconsidered: A Behavior-Based Approach to Evaluating and Improving the Sales Potency of Advertising. *Journal of Advertising Research*, *35*(5), 33–53.

Laffont, J., & Maskin, E. (1980). Optimal reservation price. *Economics Letters*, *6*(4), 309–313. doi:10.1016/0165-1765(80)90002-6

Lajante, M., Droulers, O., Dondaine, T., & Amarantini, D. (2012). Opening the "Black Box" of Electrodermal Activity in Consumer Neuroscience Research. *Journal of Neuroscience, Psychology, and Economics*, *5*(4), 238–249. doi:10.1037/a0030680

Lamancusa, K. (2003). Emotional Reactions to Color, *Creative Latitude*. Retrieved from http://www.creativelatitude.com/articles/articles_lamacusa_color.html

Lambert, D. M. (2004). *Supply chain management: Processes, partnerships, performance*. Sarasota, FL: Supply Chain Management Institute.

Lambert, D. M. (2010). Customer relationship management as a business process. *Journal of Business and Industrial Marketing*, *25*(1), 4–17. doi:10.1108/08858621011009119

Landwehr, J. R., Wentzel, D., & Herrmann, A. (2012). The Tipping Point of Design: How Product Design & Brands Interact to Affect Consumers' Preferences. *Psychology and Marketing*, *29*(6), 422–433. doi:10.1002/mar.20531

Lane Keller, K., & Moorthi, Y. L. R. (2003). Branding in Developing Markets. *Business Horizons*, *46*(3), 49–59. doi:10.1016/S0007-6813(03)00029-6

Langerak, F. (2001). Effects of market orientation on the behaviors of salespersons & purchasers, channel relationships, & performance of manufacturers. *International Journal of Research in Marketing*, *18*(3), 221–234. doi:10.1016/S0167-8116(01)00040-4

Langerak, F., Hultink, E. J., & Robben, H. S. (2004). The impact of market orientation, product advantage, & launch proficiency on new product performance & organizational performance. *Journal of Product Innovation Management*, *21*(2), 79–94. doi:10.1111/j.0737-6782.2004.00059.x

Lariviere, B., & Van den Poel, D. (2005). Predicting customer retention and profitability by using random forests and regression forests techniques. *Expert Systems with Applications*, *29*(2), 472–484. doi:10.1016/j.eswa.2005.04.043

Larson, C., & LaFasto, F. (1989). *Teamwork: What must go right/What can go wrong. Newberry Park*. Sage.

Lau, A. K. W. (2011). Supplier & customer involvement on new product performance: Contextual factors & an empirical test from manufacturer perspective. *Industrial Management & Data Systems*, *111*(6), 910–942. doi:10.1108/02635571111144973

Lawrence, A. (2011). Is SCRM really a good social media strategy? *Journal of Database Marketing & Customer Strategy Management*, *18*(3), 149–153. doi:10.1057/dbm.2011.22

Lawton, L., & Parasuraman, A. (1980). The Impact of the Marketing Concept on New Product Planning. *Journal of Marketing*, *44*(January), 19–25. doi:10.2307/1250030

Lazarsfeld, P. F., & Merton, R. K. (1954). Friendship as a social process: A substantive and methodological analysis. In M. Berger, T. Abel, & C. H. Page (Eds.), *Freedom and Control in Modern Society. 18- 66*. Van Nostrand, New York.

Lee, J.-S., & Szymanski, B. K. (2006). Auctions as a dynamic pricing mechanism for e-services. In C. Hsu (Ed.), *Service Enterprise Integration* (pp. 131–156). New York: Kluwer.

Lee, L., Amir, O., & Ariely, D. (2009). In Search of Homo Economicus: Cognitive Noise and the Role Of Emotion In Preference Consistency. *The Journal of Consumer Research*, *36*(2), 173–187. doi:10.1086/597160

Leenders, R. Th. A. J. (2002). Modeling Social Influence through Network Autocorrelation: Constructing the Weight Matrix. *Social Networks*, *24*(1), 21–47. doi:10.1016/S0378-8733(01)00049-1

Lemmens, A., & Croux, C. (2006). Bagging and boosting classification trees to predict churn. *JMR, Journal of Marketing Research*, *43*(2), 276–286. doi:10.1509/jmkr.43.2.276

Lenhart, A., Madden, M. (2007), Teens, Privacy, & Online Social Networks. *Pew Internet and American Life Project Report*. Washington.

Lenhart, A., Purcell, K., Smith, A., & Zickuhr, K. (2010). *Social media & mobile Internet use among teens and young adults*. Washington, DC: Pew Research Center.

Lenny Koh, S. C., Demirbag, M., Bayraktar, E., Tatoglu, E., & Zaim, S. (2007). The impact of supply chain management practices on performance of SMEs. *Industrial Management & Data Systems*, *107*(1), 103–124. doi:10.1108/02635570710719089

Leonard-Barton, L., & Doyle, J. L. (1996). Commercializing Technology: Imaginative Understanding of User Needs. In R. S. Rosenbloom & W. J. Spencer (Eds.), *Engines of Innovation* (pp. 177–207). Boston: Harvard Business School Press.

Leong, E., Ewing, M., & Pitt, L. (2002). E-comprehension evaluating B2B websites using readability formulae. *Industrial Marketing Management*, *31*(2), 125–131. doi:10.1016/S0019-8501(01)00184-5

Leonidou, L. C. (1996). Product standardization or adaptation: The Japanese approach. *Journal of Marketing Practice*, *2*(4), 53–71. doi:10.1108/EUM0000000004136

Leonidou, L. C. (1998). Organisational determinants of exporting: Conceptual, methodological, & empirical insights. *Management International Review*, *38*(1), 7–52.

Lepp, A., Barkley, J. E., & Karpinski, A. C. (2014). The relationship between cell phone use, academic performance, anxiety and satisfaction with life in college students. *Computers in Human Behavior*, *31*, 343–350. doi:10.1016/j.chb.2013.10.049

Leung, L., & Lee, P. (2005). Multiple determinants of life quality: The roles of internet activities, use of new media, social support and leisure activities. *Telematics and Informatics*, *22*(3), 161–180. doi:10.1016/j.tele.2004.04.003

Levin, D., & Smith, J. (1996). Optimal reservation prices in auctions. *The Economic Journal*, *106*(438), 1271–1283. doi:10.2307/2235520

Levine, S. (2000). The rise of CRM. *America's Network*, *104*(6), 34.

Levitt, B., & March, J. (1988). Organisational learning. *Annual Review of Sociology*, *14*(1), 319–338. doi:10.1146/annurev.so.14.080188.001535

Levy, M., & Weitz, B. A. (2004). *Retailing management* (5th ed.). New York: McGraw-Hill/Irwin.

Liaw, A., & Wiener, M. (2002). Classification and Regression by randomForest. *R News*, *2*(3), 18–22.

Li, B., & Tang, F.-F. (2011). Online pricing dynamics in internet retailing: The case of the DVD market. *Electronic Commerce Research and Applications*, *10*(2), 227–236. doi:10.1016/j.elerap.2010.06.004

Libai, B., Muller, E., & Peres, R. (2012). *Sources of social value in word-of-mouth programs* (Marketing Science Institute Working Paper Series No. 10-103). Cambridge, MA: Marketing Science Institute.

Li, C., & Bernoff, J. (2008). *Groundswell: winning in the world transformed by social technologies. Boston.* Massachusetts: Harvard Business Press.

Lievens, F., & Harris, M. M. (2005). Research on internet recruiting and testing: Current status and future directions. In C. L. Cooper & L. T. Robertson (Eds.), *International review of industrial/organizational psychology* (pp. 131–165). Chichester, England: John Wiley & Sons. doi:10.1002/0470013346.ch4

Liljander, V., & Strandvik, T. (1995). The nature of customer relationships in services. In T. Swartz, D.E. Bowen, & S.W. Brown (Eds.), Advances in Services Marketing and Management (pp.141-167). London: JAI Press Inc.

Limeira, T. (2005) Marketing de serviços na indústria de tecnologia da informação: Novos desafios e oportunidades. Retrieved from http://bibliotecadigital.fgv.br/dspace/handle/10438/2920

Lin, C. P., Tsai, Y. H., Joe, S. W., & Chiu, C. K. (2012). Modelling the relationship among perceived corporate citizenship, firms' attractiveness, and career success expectation. *Journal of Business Ethics*, *105*(1), 83–93. doi:10.1007/s10551-011-0949-z

Linder, J. C., & Brooks, J. D. (2004). Transforming The Public Sector. *Outlook*, *3*, 74–83.

Lindgreen, A., Palmer, R., Vanhamme, J., & Wouters, J. (2006). A relationship management assessment tool: Questioning, identifying, and prioritizing critical aspects of customer relationships. *Industrial Marketing Management*, *35*(1), 57–71. doi:10.1016/j.indmarman.2005.08.008

Lindgreen, A., & Wynstra, F. (2005). Value in business markets: What do we know? Where are we going? *Industrial Marketing Management*, *34*(7), 732–748. doi:10.1016/j.indmarman.2005.01.001

Ling, R., & Yen, D. C. (2001). Customer relationship management: An analysis framework and implementation strategies. *Journal of Computer Information Systems*, *41*(3), 82–97.

Lin, R.-J., Chen, R.-H., & Kuan-Shun Chiu, K. (2010). Customer relationship management & innovation capability: An empirical study. *Industrial Management & Data Systems*, *110*(1), 111–133. doi:10.1108/02635571011008434

Linthicum, D. S. (2000). *Enterprise application integration*. Addison-Wesley Professional.

Lipnack, J., & Stamps, J. (1999). Virtual teams: The new way to work. *Strategy and Leadership*, *27*(1), 14–19. doi:10.1108/eb054625

Liu, H. Y. (2007). Development of a framework for customer relationship management (CRM) in the banking industry. *International Journal of Management*, *24*(1), 15–32.

Liu, S. (2012). The impact of forced use on customer adoption of self-service technologies. *Computers in Human Behavior*, *28*(4), 1194–1201. doi:10.1016/j.chb.2012.02.002

Liu, S., Turban, E., & Lee, M. K. (2000). Software agents for environmental scanning in electronic commerce. *Information Systems Frontiers*, *2*(1), 85–98. doi:10.1023/A:1010002205248

Liu, Y. (2006). Word of Mouth for Movies: Its Dynamics and Impact on Box Office Revenue. *Journal of Marketing*, *70*(July).

Livingston, J. A. (2005). How valuable is a good reputation? A sample selection model of internet auctions. *The Review of Economics and Statistics*, *87*(3), 453–465. doi:10.1162/0034653054638391

Lo, A. S., Stalcup, L. D., & Lee, A. (2010). Customer relationship management for hotels in Hong Kong. *International Journal of Contemporary Hospitality Management*, *22*(2), 139–159. doi:10.1108/09596111011018151

Locke, R. M., & Romis, M. (2012). Improving work conditions in global supply chains. *MIT Sloan Management Review*, *48*(2), 54–62.

Löfgren, M. (2006). *The Leader of the Pack: A Service Perspective on Packaging & Customer Satisfaction* [Dissertation]. Karlstad University.

Lohr, S. (2013, May 21). I.B.M. Puts Watson to Work in Business. *New York Times*. Retrieved from http://bits.blogs.nytimes.com/2013/05/21/i-b-m-puts-watson-to-work-in-business/?_php=true&_type=blogs&_php=true&_type=blogs&_r=1

Lorenzo-Molo, C. F., & Udani, Z. A. S. (2013). Bringing back the essence of the "S" and "R" to CSR: Understanding the limitations of the merchant trade and the white man's burden. *Journal of Business Ethics*, *117*(1), 123–136. doi:10.1007/s10551-012-1513-1

Lorenzo-Romero, C., Constantinides, E., & Alarcón-del-Amo, M. D. C. (2011). Consumer adoption of social networking sites: Implications for theory and practice. *Journal of Research in Interactive Marketing*, *5*(2), 170–188. doi:10.1108/17505931111187794

Love, L. G., Priem, R. L., & Lumpkin, G. T. (2002). Explicitly articulated strategy & firm performance under alternative levels of centralization. *Journal of Management*, *28*(5), 611–627. doi:10.1177/014920630202800503

Lozano, J. M. (2008). CSR or RSC? (Beyond the Humpty Dumpty syndrome). *Society and Business Review*, *3*(3), 191–206. doi:10.1108/17465680810907288

Lozano, R. (2011). The state of sustainability reporting in universities. *International Journal of Sustainability in Higher Education*, *12*(1), 67–78. doi:10.1108/14676371111098311

Luce, S. (2013). *Global retail report*. Nyon, Switzerland: UNI Global Union.

Luchesa, C., & Neto, A. (2011) Cálculo do tamanho da amostra nas pesquisas em administração. University central library, Curitiba, Brazil.

Lucking-Reiley, D., Bryan, D., Prasad, N., & Reeves, D. (2007). Pennies from eBay: The Determinants of price in online auctions. *The Journal of Industrial Economics*, *55*(2), 223–233. doi:10.1111/j.1467-6451.2007.00309.x

Lung, N., Mak, P., Wan-Cheng, N., Lian-Chen, L., & Cheng, W. (2007). A Semi-automated negotiation process to improve the usability for online marketplaces.*Proceeding of 7th IEEE International Conference on Computer and Information Technology (CIT 2007)* (pp. 253–258). Fukushima, Japan.

Luo, X., Wieseke, J., & Homburg, C. (2012). Incentivizing CEOs to build customer- and employee-firm relations for higher customer satisfaction and firm value. *Journal of the Academy of Marketing Science*, *40*(6), 745–758. doi:10.1007/s11747-011-0290-1

Lusensky, J. (2011). *Sounds like Branding: Using the power of music to turn customers into fans*. Heartbeats International.

Lynch, J., & De Chernatony, L. (2004). The Power of Emotion: Brand Communication in Business –to-Business Markets. *Journal of Brand Management*, *11*(5), 403–419. doi:10.1057/palgrave.bm.2540185

Lyon, T. P., & Maxwell, J. W. (2011). Greenwash: Corporate environmental disclosure under threat of audit. *Journal of Economics & Management Strategy*, *20*(1), 3–41. doi:10.1111/j.1530-9134.2010.00282.x

Maas, K., & Boons, F. (2010). CSR as a strategic activity: Value creation, redistribution and integration. *Innovative CSR: From Risk Management to Value Creation*, *153*(172), 20.

MacInnis, D. J., Moorman, C., & Jaworski, B. J. (1991). Enhancing and Measuring Consumers' Motivation, Opportunity, and Ability to Process Brand Information from Ads. *Journal of Marketing*, *55*(4), 32–53. doi:10.2307/1251955

Maclin, R., & Shavlik, J. W. (1995, Aug 20-25). *Combining the predictions of multiple classifiers: Using competitive learning to initialize neural networks*, Montreal, Canada.

Madia de Souza, F. (2007). *O grande livro do marketing. M.* Saint Paul, Brazil: Books Publisher.

Maidique, M. A., & Zirger, B. J. (1984). A study of success & failure in product innovation: The case of U.S. electronics industry. *IEEE Transactions on Engineering Management*, *EM-31*(4), 192–203. doi:10.1109/TEM.1984.6447537

Maier, R., & Remus, U. (2002). Defining process-oriented knowledge management strategies. *Knowledge and Process Management*, *9*(2), 103–118. doi:10.1002/kpm.136

Maitin-Shepard, J., Cusumano-Towner, M., Lei, J., & Abbeel, P. (2010). Cloth Grasp Point Detection based on Multiple-View Geometric Cues with Application to Robotic Towel Folding. *Proceedings of theInternational Conference on Robotics and Automation*. doi:10.1109/ROBOT.2010.5509439

Makkonen, H., & Vuori, M. (2014). The role of information technology in strategic buyer–supplier relationships. *Industrial Marketing Management*, *43*(6), 1053–1062. doi:10.1016/j.indmarman.2014.05.018

Malhotra, N. (2006). *Pesquisa de marketing: Uma orientação aplicada*. Porto Alegre, Brazil: Bookman Publisher.

Malhotra, N. K., Birks, D. F., & Wills, P. (2012). *Essentials of marketing research*. Harlow: Pearson Education.

Maloff, J. (1997). Extranets: Stretching the net to boost efficiency. *NetGuide*, *4*, 62–68.

Manetti, G., & Becatti, L. (2009). Assurance services for sustainability reports: Standards and empirical evidence. *Journal of Business Ethics*, *87*(1), 289–298. doi:10.1007/s10551-008-9809-x

Mangold, W. G., & Faulds, D. J. (2009). Social media: The new hybrid element of the promotion mix. *Business Horizons*, *52*(4), 357–365. doi:10.1016/j.bushor.2009.03.002

Manickam, S. A., & Sriram, B. (2013). Modeling the Impact of Marketing Information on Consumer Buying Behavior in a Matured Marketing Environment: An Exploratory of the Middle East Consumers. *Journal of Promotion Management*, *19*(1), 1–16. doi:10.1080/10496491.2012.715127

Manteaw, B. (2008). From tokenism to social justice: Rethinking the bottom line for sustainable community development. *Community Development Journal: An International Forum*, *43*(4), 428–443. doi:10.1093/cdj/bsm015

Maon, F., Lindgreen, A., & Swaen, V. (2009). Designing and implementing corporate social responsibility: An integrative framework grounded in theory and practice. *Journal of Business Ethics*, *87*(1), 71–89. doi:10.1007/s10551-008-9804-2

Maon, F., Lindgreen, A., & Swaen, V. (2010). Organizational stages and cultural phases: A critical review and a consolidative model of corporate social responsibility development. *International Journal of Management Reviews*, *12*(1), 20–38. doi:10.1111/j.1468-2370.2009.00278.x

Marche, S., & McNiven, J. D. (2003). E-Government and E-Governance: The Future Isn't What It Used To Be. *Canadian Journal of Administrative Sciences*, *20*(1), 74–86. doi:10.1111/j.1936-4490.2003.tb00306.x

Marktest Bareme. (n. d.). Retrieved from http://www.marktest.com/wap/a/n/id~1a6a.aspx

Marn, M. V., & Rosiello, R. L. (1992). Managing price, gaining profits. *Harvard Business Review*, *70*(5), 84–93. PMID:10121318

Marsden, G., Kimble, M., Nellthorp, J., & Kelly, C. (2010). Sustainability assessment: The definition deficit. *International Journal of Sustainable Transportation*, *4*(4), 189–211. doi:10.1080/15568310902825699

Marshall, G. (2014, April 3). Cortana: everything you need to know about Microsoft's Siri rival. *Techradar*. Retrieved from http://www.techradar.com/us/news/phone-and-communications/mobile-phones/cortana-everything-you-need-to-know-about-microsoft-s-siri-rival-1183607

Marshall, J. D., & Toffel, M. W. (2005). Framing the elusive concept of sustainability: A sustainability hierarchy. *Environmental Science & Technology*, *39*(3), 673–682. doi:10.1021/es040394k PMID:15757326

Martens, D., & Provost, F. (2011). Pseudo-social network targeting from consumer transaction data. *Working paper CeDER-11-05 - New York University - Stern School of Business*.

Martin, J. H., & Grbac, B. (2003). Using supply chain management to leverage a firm's market orientation. *Industrial Marketing Management*, *32*(1), 25–38. doi:10.1016/S0019-8501(01)00192-4

Martin, S., & Scott, J. T. (2000). The nature of innovation market failure & the design of public support for private innovation. *Research Policy*, *29*(4), 437–447. doi:10.1016/S0048-7333(99)00084-0

Martins, L. L., Gilson, L. L., & Maynard, M. T. (2004). Virtual teams: Where do we go from here? *Journal of Management*, *30*(6), 805–835. doi:10.1016/j.jm.2004.05.002

Martin, W. C., Engelland, B. T., & Collier, J. E. (2011). Assessing the Impact of Acquiescence Response Bias on Marketing Data. *Marketing Management Journal*, *21*(1), 31–46.

Maslow, A. H. (1968). Toward a Psychology of Being. New York: John.

Massey, A. P., Montoya-Weiss, M., & Holcom, K. (2001). Re-engineering the customer relationship: Leveraging knowledge assets at IBM. *Decision Support Systems*, *32*(2), 155–170. doi:10.1016/S0167-9236(01)00108-7

Mast, F. W., & Zaltman, G. (2005). A Behavioral Window on the Mind of the Market: An Application of the Response Time Paradigm. *Brain Research Bulletin*, *67*(5), 422–427. doi:10.1016/j.brainresbull.2005.06.004 PMID:16216689

Mata, F., Fuerst, W., & Barney, J. (1995). Information technology and sustained competitive advantage: A resource-based analysis. *Management Information Systems Quarterly*, *19*(4), 487–504. doi:10.2307/249630

Matos, C. (2011) Uma generalização empírica sobre comunicação boca a boca usando metanálise. Retrieved from http://www.scielo.br/pdf/rac/v15n5/a06v15n5.pdf

Mattana, L., Mota, M., Noro, G., Brito, I., & Rocha, S. (2006) Comunicação organizacional on-line: Aplicação estratégica e suas implicações na gestão de uma empresa de base tecnológica. Proceedings of the XXIX Communication Science Congress, University of Brasília, Brazil.

Matten, D., & Moon, J. (2008). "Implicit" and "explicit" CSR: A conceptual framework for a comparative understanding of corporate social responsibility. *Academy of Management Review*, *33*(2), 404–424. doi:10.5465/AMR.2008.31193458

Maule, A. J., Hockey, G. R. J., & Bdzola, L. (2000). Effects of time-Pressure on Decision-Making Under Uncertainty: Changes in Affective State & Information Processing Strategy. *Acta Psychologica*, *104*(3), 283–301. doi:10.1016/S0001-6918(00)00033-0 PMID:10900697

Mauri, M., Cipresso, P., Balgera, A., Villamira, M., & Riva, G. (2011). Why is Facebook so successful? Psychophysiological Measures Describe A Core Flow State While Using Facebook. *Cyberpsychology, Behavior, and Social Networking*, *14*(12), 723–731. doi:10.1089/cyber.2010.0377 PMID:21879884

Mayer, R. C., Davis, J. H., & Schoorman, F. D. (1995). An integrative model of organizational trust. *Academy of Management Review*, *20*(3), 709–734.

Mayfield, A. (2008). *What is Social Media?* Retrieved from http://www.icrossing.com/sites/default/files/what-is-social-media-uk.pdf

McAdam, D. (1986). Recruitment to High-Risk Activism: The Case of Freedom Summer. *American Journal of Sociology*, *92*(1), 64–90. doi:10.1086/228463

McCarthy, I. P., Tsinopoulos, C., Allen, P., & Rose-Anderssen, C. (2006). New product development as a complex adaptive system of decisions. *Journal of Product Innovation Management*, *23*(5), 437–456. doi:10.1111/j.1540-5885.2006.00215.x

McCarthy, J. (1958). Programs with common sense.*Symposium on Mechanization of Thought Processes* (pp. 77-84). Teddington, England: National Physical Laboratory.

McCarty, J. A., & Hastak, M. (2007). Segmentation approaches in data-mining: A comparison of RFM, CHAID, and logistic regression. *Journal of Business Research, 60*, 656-662. Doi:10.1016/j.jbusres.2006.06.015

McClelland, D. C. (1951). *Measuring motivation in phantasy: the achievement motive*. Psycnet APA.

McClure, S. M., Li, J., Tomlin, D., Cypert, K. S., Montague, L. M., & Montague, R. P. (2004). Neural Correlates Of Behavioral Preference For Culturally Familiar Drinks. *Neuron*, *44*(2), 379–387. doi:10.1016/j.neuron.2004.09.019 PMID:15473974

McDonald, C. G., & Slawson, V. C. Jr. (2002). Reputation in an internet auction market. *Economic Inquiry*, *40*(4), 533–650. doi:10.1093/ei/40.4.633

McDonough, E. F. III. (2000). Investigation of Factors Contributing to the Success of Cross-Functional Teams. *Journal of Product Innovation Management*, *17*(3), 221–235. doi:10.1016/S0737-6782(00)00041-2

McElhaney, K. (2009). A strategic approach to corporate social responsibility. *Leader to Leader*, *52*(1), 30–36. doi:10.1002/ltl.327

McGill, J. I., & van Ryzin, G. J. (1999). Revenue management: Research overview and prospects. *Transportation Science*, *33*(2), 233–256. doi:10.1287/trsc.33.2.233

McGovern, T., & Panaro, J. (2004). The human side of customer relationship management. *Benefits Quarterly*, *20*(3), 26–33.

McGuire, J. W. (1963). *Business and society*. New York: McGraw-Hill.

McMahon, J. M., & Cohen, R. (2009). Lost in cyberspace: Ethical decision making in the online environment. *Ethics and Information Technology*, *11*(1), 1–17. doi:10.1007/s10676-008-9165-7

McPherson, J. M., & Smith-Lovin, L. (1987). Homophily in voluntary organizations: Status, distance and the composition of face-to-face groups. *American Sociological Review*, *52*(3), 370–379. doi:10.2307/2095356

McPherson, J., Smith-Lovin, L., & Cook, J. (2001). Birds of a feather: Homophily in social networks. *Annual Review of Sociology*, *27*(1), 415–444. doi:10.1146/annurev.soc.27.1.415

McShane, L., & Cunningham, P. (2012). To thine own self be true? Employees' judgments of the authenticity of their organization's corporate social responsibility program. *Journal of Business Ethics*, *108*(1), 81–100. doi:10.1007/s10551-011-1064-x

McWilliam, G. (2000). Building Stronger Brands through Online Communities. *Sloan Management Review*, *41*(3).

McWilliams, A., Siegel, D. S., & Wright, P. M. (2006). Corporate social responsibility: Strategic implications. *Journal of Management Studies*, *43*(1), 1–18. doi:10.1111/j.1467-6486.2006.00580.x

Meadows-Klue, D. (2008), Falling in Love 2.0: Relationship Marketing for the Facebook Generation. *Journal of Direct, Data and Digital Marketing Practice*, 9(3).

Mebratu, D. (1998). Sustainability and sustainable development: Historical and conceptual review. *Environmental Impact Assessment Review*, *18*(6), 493–520. doi:10.1016/S0195-9255(98)00019-5

Melnik, M. I. (2011). Listing fees and their role on eBay: Evidence from a natural experiment. *Journal of Internet Commerce*, *10*(4), 1–21. doi:10.1080/15332861.2011.622695

Melnik, M. I., & Alm, J. (2002). Does a seller's reputation matter? Evidence from eBay auctions. *The Journal of Industrial Economics*, *50*(3), 337–349. doi:10.1111/1467-6451.00180

Melnik, M. I., & Alm, J. (2005). Seller reputation, information signals, and prices for heterogeneous coins on eBay. *Southern Economic Journal*, *72*(2), 305–328. doi:10.2307/20062113

Melnik, M. I., Richardson, P., & Tompkins, D. (2011). How seller and product characteristics impact promotion on eBay. *Journal of Promotion Management*, *17*(4), 426–437. doi:10.1080/10496491.2011.597317

Melnik, M. I., Xu, Y., & Alm, J. (2009). The choice of opening prices on eBay. *The Manchester School Journal*, *77*(4), 411–429. doi:10.1111/j.1467-9957.2009.02105.x

Menascé, D. A., & Akula, V. (2004). Improving the performance of online auction sites through closing time rescheduling.*Proceedings of the First International Conference on the Quantitative Evaluation of Systems (QEST'04)*, Twente, Netherlands. doi:10.1109/QEST.2004.1348033

Mendoza, L. E., Marius, A., Perez, M., & Griman, A. C. (2007). Critical success factors for a customer relationship management strategy. *Information and Software Technology*, *49*(8), 913–945. doi:10.1016/j.infsof.2006.10.003

Menguc, B., Auh, S., & Uslu, A. (2013). Customer knowledge creation capability and performance in sales teams. *Journal of the Academy of Marketing Science*, *41*(1), 19–39. doi:10.1007/s11747-012-0303-8

Menon, A., & Lukas, B. A. (2004). Antecedents & outcomes of new product development speed: A propositional inventory germane to marketing. *European Journal of Marketing*, *38*(1/2), 209–223. doi:10.1108/03090560410511195

Merler, S., Caprile, B., & Furlanello, C. (2007). Parallelizing AdaBoost by weights dynamics. *Computational Statistics & Data Analysis*, *51*(5), 2487–2498. doi:10.1016/j.csda.2006.09.001

Middlemiss, N. (2003). Authentic not cosmetic: CSR as brand enhancement. *The Journal of Brand Management*, *10*(4), 353–361. doi:10.1057/palgrave.bm.2540130

Mihart, C. (2012). Impact of Integrated Marketing Communication On Consumer Behavior: Effects on Consumer Decision Making Process. *International Journal of Marketing Studies*, *4*(2), 121–129. doi:10.5539/ijms.v4n2p121

Miles, M. B., & Huberman, A. M. (1994). *Qualitative data analysis: An expanded sourcebook*. London: SAGE.

Minami, C., & Dawson, J. (2008). The CRM process in retail and service sector firms in Japan. Loyalty.

Mintzberg, H., Quinn, J., & Ghoshal, S. (1995). *The Strategy Process* (European ed.). London: Prentice Hall.

Mirvis, P. (2011). Unilever's drive for sustainability and CSR–Changing the game. *Organizing for Sustainable Effectiveness*, *1*(34), 41–72. doi:10.1108/S2045-0605(2011)0000001007

Mirza, A., & Al-Abdulkareem, M. (2011). Models of e-learning adopted in the Middle East. *Applied Computing and Informatics*, *9*(2), 83–93. doi:10.1016/j.aci.2011.05.001

Mishra, A. A., & Shah, R. R. (2009). In union lies strength: Collaborative competence in new product development & its performance effects. *Journal of Operations Management*, *27*(4), 324–338. doi:10.1016/j.jom.2008.10.001

Mital, A., Desai, A., Subramanian, A., & Mital, A. (2011). *Product Development: A Structured Approach to Design & Manufacture*. Butterworth-Heinemann.

Mithas, S., & Jones, J. L. (2007). Do auction parameters affect buyer surplus in e-auctions for procurement? *Production and Operations Management POMS*, *16*(4), 455–470. doi:10.1111/j.1937-5956.2007.tb00272.x

Mithas, S., Krishnan, M. S., & Fornell, C. (2005). Why do customer relationship management applications affect customer satisfaction? *Journal of Marketing*, *69*(4), 201–209. doi:10.1509/jmkg.2005.69.4.201

Mittal, V., Frennea, C., & Westbrook, R. A. (2014). Managing customer value in business-to-business markets. *Marketing Review St. Gallen*, *31*(3), 46–54. doi:10.1365/s11621-014-0362-y

Miwa, K., & Terai, H. (2012). Impact of two types of partner, perceived or actual, in human-human and human-agent interaction. *Computers in Human Behavior*, *28*(4), 1286–1297. doi:10.1016/j.chb.2012.02.012

Miyazaki, A. D. (2003). Guest editorial: The psychology of pricing on the internet. *Psychology and Marketing*, *20*(6), 471–476. doi:10.1002/mar.10082

Moe, W. W., & Schweidel, D. A. (2012). Online Product Opinions: Incidence, Evaluation, and Evolution. *Marketing Science*, *31*(3), 372–386. doi:10.1287/mksc.1110.0662

Mohammed, R., Fisher, R. J., Jaworski, B. J., & Paddison, G. (2002). *Internet Marketing: Building Advantage in the Networked Economy*. Boston: McGraw-Hill/Irwin.

Mohammed, S., & Ringseis, E. (2001). Cognitive diversity & consensus in group decision making: The role of inputs, processes & outcomes. *Organizational Behavior and Human Decision Processes*, *85*(2), 310–335. doi:10.1006/obhd.2000.2943 PMID:11461204

Mohebbi, N., Hoseini, M. A., & Esfidani, M. R. (2012). Identification & prioritization of the affecting factors on CRM implementation in edible oil industry. *Journal of Basic and Applied Scientific Research*, *2*(5), 4993–5001.

Mollen, A., & Wilson, H. (2010). Engagement, Telepresence and Interactivity in Online Consumer Experience: Reconciling Scholastic and Managerial Perspectives. *Journal of Business Research. Special Issue on Internet Customer Behavior*, *6*(9-10), 919–925.

Møller, C. (2005). ERP II: A conceptual framework for next-generation enterprise systems? *Journal of Enterprise Information Management*, *18*(4), 483–497. doi:10.1108/17410390510609626

Möller, K., & Wilson, D. (1995). *Business Marketing and interaction and network perspective*. Boston: Kluwer Academic Publishers. doi:10.1007/978-94-011-0645-0

Monczka, R. M., Handfield, R. B., Scannell, T. V., Ragatz, G. L., & Frayer, D. L. (2000). *New Product Development Strategies for Supplier Integration*. Milwaukee, WI: ASQ Quality Press.

Money, R. B., Gilly, M. C., & Graham, J. L. (1998). Explorations of national culture and word-of-mouth referral behavior in the purchase of industrial services in the United States and Japan. *Journal of Marketing*, *62*(4), 76–87. doi:10.2307/1252288

Monroe, K. B. (1973). Buyers' subjective perceptions of price. *JMR, Journal of Marketing Research*, *10*(1), 70–80. doi:10.2307/3149411

Monroe, K. B. (1990). *Pricing: Making profitable decisions* (2nd ed.). New York: McGraw-Hill.

Montoya-Weiss, M. M., & Calantone, R. (1994). Determinants of New Product Performance: A Review & Meta-Analysis. *Journal of Product Innovation Management*, *11*(5), 397–417. doi:10.1016/0737-6782(94)90029-9

Montoya-Weiss, M., Massey, A., & Song, M. (2001). Getting it together: Temporal coordination & conflict management in global virtual teams. *Academy of Management Journal*, *44*(6), 1251–1262. doi:10.2307/3069399

Moore, N., & Steele, J. (1991). *Information-intensive Britain: a critical analysis of the policy issues*. London: Policy Studies Institute.

Moore, S. B., & Manring, S. L. (2009). Strategy development in small and medium sized enterprises for sustainability and increased value creation. *Journal of Cleaner Production*, *17*(2), 276–282. doi:10.1016/j.jclepro.2008.06.004

Moradabadi, Y., Gharehshiran, M., & Amrai, K. (2012). What is the Motivation Student of Iranians for using Facebook? *Procedia: Social and Behavioral Sciences*, *46*, 5192–5195. doi:10.1016/j.sbspro.2012.06.407

Moresi, E. (2003). *Metodologia da Pesquisa*. Universidade Católica de Brasília - UCB.

Morgan, M. S. (2006). Economic Man as Model Man: Ideal Types, Idealization And Caricatures. *Journal of the History of Economic Thought*, *28*(1), 1–27. doi:10.1080/10427710500509763

Morgan, R., & Hunt, S. (1994). The commitment-trust theory of relationship marketing. *Journal of Marketing*, *58*(3), 20–38. doi:10.2307/1252308

Morin, C. (2011). Neuromarketing: The New Science of Consumer Behavior. *Symposium: Consumer Culture in Global Perspective.*

Morris, M. (2011). Sustainability: An exercise in futility. *International Journal of Business and Management*, *7*(2), 36–44.

Mozer, M. C., Wolniewicz, R., Grimes, D. B., Johnson, E., & Kaushansky, H. (2000). Predicting subscriber dissatisfaction and improving retention in the wireless telecommunications industry. *IEEE Transactions on Neural Networks*, *11*(3), 690–696. doi:10.1109/72.846740 PMID:18249796

Mukerjee, K., & Singh, K. (2009). CRM: A strategic approach. *Journal of Management Research*, *8*(2), 65–82.

Mukhopadhyay, T. (1998). How to win with electronic data interchange in information technology and industrial competitiveness. In C. Kemerer (Ed.), How IT Shapes Competition (pp. 91-106). Boston: Kluwer Academic Publishers.

Mukhopadhyay, T., Kekre, S., & Kalathur, S. (1995). Business value of information technology: A study of electronic data interchange. *Management Information Systems Quarterly*, *19*(2), 137–156. doi:10.2307/249685

Müller, E. (2009) O perfil motivacional e a inclinação de carreira do estudante e do profissional da tecnologia da informação [Master Dissertation]. School of Management, Getulio Vargas Foundation, Rio de Janeiro, Brazil.

Murphy, S. A., & Kumar, V. (1997). The front end of new product development: A Canadian survey. *R & D Management*, *27*(1), 5–15. doi:10.1111/1467-9310.00038

Murthy, S. K. (1998). Automatic construction of decision trees from data: A multi-disciplinary survey. *Data Mining and Knowledge Discovery*, *2*(4), 345–389. doi:10.1023/A:1009744630224

Myers, D. G. (1992). *The pursuit of happiness*. New York: Morrow.

Myerson, R. (1981). Optimal auction design. *Mathematics of Operations Research*, *6*(1), 58–73. doi:10.1287/moor.6.1.58

Nahm, Y. E., Ishikawa, H., & Inoue, M. (2013). New rating methods to prioritize customer requirements in QFD with incomplete customer preferences. *International Journal of Advanced Manufacturing Technology*, *65*(9-12), 1587–1604. doi:10.1007/s00170-012-4282-1

Nancarrow, C., Brace, I., & Wright, L. (2001). Tell Me Lies, Tell Me Sweet Little Lies: Dealing With Socially Desirable Responses In Market Research. *Marketing Review*, *2*(1), 55–55. doi:10.1362/1469347012569427

Narahari, Y., Raju, C. V. L., Ravikumar, K., & Shah, S. (2005). Dynamic pricing models for electronic business. *Sadhana*, *30*(2-3), 231–256. doi:10.1007/BF02706246

Narvainen, J., Pulkkinen, K., Kuoppa, P., Tarvainen, M., Lankinen, M., & Lapveteläinen, A., & ... Karhune, L. (2013). Probing Psychophysiology by Pictorial Stimuli of Emotional Content: General Patterns and Personality Effects. *Neuropsychoeconomics Conference Proceedings* (p. 25).

Narver, J. C., & Savitt, R. (1971). *The marketing economy: An analytical approach*. New York: Holt, Rinehart and Winston.

Narver, J. C., & Slater, S. F. (1990). The Effect of a Market Orientation on Business Profitability. *Journal of Marketing*, *54*(4), 20–35. doi:10.2307/1251757

Nasir, S. (2005). The development, change, and transformation of Management Information Systems (MIS): A content analysis of articles published in business and marketing journals. *International Journal of Information Management*, *25*(5), 442–457. doi:10.1016/j.ijinfomgt.2005.06.003

Natale, J. (2014, April 23). IBM Watson Group to transform the consumer shopping experience. Retrieved from http://phys.org/news/2014-04-ibm-watson-group-consumer.html

Naudé, P., Holland, C., & Sudbury, M. (2000). The benefits of IT-based supply chains-strategic or operational? *Journal of Business-To-Business Marketing*, *7*(1), 45–67. doi:10.1300/J033v07n01_03

Naumann, A., Wechsung, I., & Hurtienne, J. (2010). Multimodal interaction: A suitable strategy for including older users? *Interacting with Computers*, *22*(6), 465–474. doi:10.1016/j.intcom.2010.08.005

Ndubisi, N. O. (2003). Service quality: Understanding customer perception and reaction, and its impact on business. *International Journal of Business*, *5*(2), 207–219.

Nedungadi, P., & Hutchinson, W. J. (1985). In C. H. Elizabeth & B. H. Moris (Eds.), *Prototypicality of Brands: Relationships with Brand Awareness, Preference and Usage Advances in Consumer Research (Vol. 12,* pp. 498–503). Provo, UT: Association of Consumer Research.

Neslin, S. A., Gupta, S., Kamakura, W., Lu, J. X., & Mason, C. H. (2006). Defection detection: Measuring and understanding the predictive accuracy of customer churn models. *JMR, Journal of Marketing Research*, *43*(2), 204–211. doi:10.1509/jmkr.43.2.204

Neslin, S. A., Novak, T. P., Baker, K. R., & Hoffman, D. L. (2009). An Optimal Contact Model for Maximizing Online Panel Response Rates. *Management Science*, *55*(5), 727–737. doi:10.1287/mnsc.1080.0969

Neufeld, J. (2009). *Estatística aplicada à administração usando excel.* Saint Paul, Brazil: Prentice Hall Publisher.

Newell, F. (2000). *Loyalty.com: Customer relationship management in the new era of Internet marketing*. New York, NY: McGraw-Hill.

Ngai, E. W. T. (2005). Customer relationship management research (1992-2002): An academic literature review and classification. *Marketing Intelligence & Planning*, *23*(6), 582–605. doi:10.1108/02634500510624147

Ngai, E. W. T., Peng, S., Alexander, P., & Moon, K. K. (2014). Decision support and intelligent systems in the textile and apparel supply chain: An academic review of research articles. *Expert Systems with Applications*, *41*(1), 81–91. doi:10.1016/j.eswa.2013.07.013

Nguyen, T. H., Sherif, J., & Newby, M. (2007). Strategies for successful CRM implementation. *Information Management & Computer Security*, *15*(2), 102–115. doi:10.1108/09685220710748001

Nguyen, T. H., & Waring, T. S. (2013). The adoption of customer relationship management (CRM) technology in SMEs - An empirical study. *Journal of Small Business and Enterprise Development*, *20*(4), 824–848. doi:10.1108/JSBED-01-2012-0013

Nidumolu, R., Prahalad, C. K., & Rangaswami, M. R. (2009). Why sustainability is now the key driver of innovation. *Harvard Business Review*, *87*(9), 56–64.

Nitzan, I., & Libai, B. (2011). Social effects on customer retention. *Journal of Marketing*, *75*(November), 24–38. doi:10.1509/jm.10.0209

Nusca, A. (2013, October 2). The future of retail is dynamic pricing. So why can't we get it right? *ZDNet*.

Nykamp, M. (2001). *The customer differential: The complete guide to implementing customer relationship management*. New York, NY: AMACOM.

O'Malley, L., & Tynan, C. (2000). Relationship marketing in consumer markets–rhetoric or reality? *European Journal of Marketing*, *34*(7), 797–815. doi:10.1108/03090560010331225

OECD. (2003). *The e-Government Imperative, OECD e-Government Studies*. Paris, France: OECD Publication Services.

OECD. (2005). e-Government for better government. OECD e-Government Studies, Paris, France, OECD Publication Services.

Ofir, C., & Winer, R. S. (2002). Pricing: economic and behavioral models. In B. A. Weitz & R. Wensley (Eds.), *Handbook of Marketing* (pp. 267–281). London: Sage Publications. doi:10.4135/9781848608283.n12

Ohme, R. (2009). Special Topics Session: How Neurophysiological Research Contributes to Advertising Research. *American Academy Of Advertising Conference Proceedings* (pp. 55-57).

Ohme, R., Kowalski, J., & Reykowska, D. (2007). Exploring Consumers' Mind Via EEG And EMG Activity.*Neuropsychoeconomics Conference Proceedings* (p. 26).

Ohme, R., Matukin, M., & Pacula-Lesniak, B. (2011). Biometric Measures For Interactive Advertising Research. *Journal of Interactive Advertising*, *11*(2), 60–72. doi:10.1080/15252019.2011.10722185

Ohme, R., Reykowska, D., Wiener, D., & Choromanska, A. (2010). Application of Frontal EEG Asymmetry To Advertising Research. *Journal of Economic Psychology*, *31*(5), 785–793. doi:10.1016/j.joep.2010.03.008

Onditi, A. A. (2012). An Evaluation of Promotional Elements Influencing Sales of an Organization: A Case Study of Sales of Agricultural and Non-Agricultural Products among Women Groups, Homa Bay District, Kenya. *International Journal of Business and Social Science*, *3*(5), 296–313.

Opitz, D. W., & Shavlik, J. W. (1995, Nov 27-30). *Generating accurate and diverse members of a neural-network ensemble*, Denver, Co.

O'Reilly, T. (2007). What is web 2.0: Design patterns and business models for the next generation of software. *Communications & Stratégies*, *65*, 16–37.

Osarenkhoe, A., & Bennani, A. (2007). An exploratory study of implementation of customer relationship management strategy. *Business Process Management Journal*, *13*(1), 139–164. doi:10.1108/14637150710721177

Osofsky, H. M. (2011). Multidimensional governance and the BP deepwater horizon oil spill. *Florida Law Review*, *63*(5), 1077–1121.

Otair, M., & Hattab, E. (2008). An implementation of a new type of online auction. *International Journal of E-Business Research*, *4*(2), 88–102. doi:10.4018/jebr.2008040106

Othman, S., Darus, F., & Arshad, R. (2011). The influence of coercive isomorphism on corporate social responsibility reporting and reputation. *Social Responsibility Journal*, *7*(1), 119–135. doi:10.1108/17471111111114585

Oxenfeldt, A. R. (1973). A Decision-making structure for price decisions. *Journal of Marketing*, *37*(1), 48–53. doi:10.2307/1250774

Ozcaglar-Toulouse, N. (2007). Living for "ethics": Responsible consumption in everyday life. *Research in Consumer Behavior*, *11*(1), 421–436.

Ozer, M. (2005). Factors which influence decision making in new product evaluation. *European Journal of Operational Research, 163*(3), 784–801. doi:10.1016/j.ejor.2003.11.002

Ozgener, S., & Iraz, R. (2006). Customer relationship management in small-medium enterprises: The case of Turkish tourism industry. *Tourism Management, 27*(6), 1356–1363. doi:10.1016/j.tourman.2005.06.011

Özturan, P., Ozsomer, A., & Pieters, R. (2014). The Role of Market Orientation in Advertising Spending During Economic Collapse: The Case of Turkey in 2001. *JMR, Journal of Marketing Research, 51*(2), 139–152. doi:10.1509/jmr.11.0528

Pai, P., & Arnott, D. (2013). User adoption of social networking sites: Eliciting uses and gratifications through a means–end approach. *Computers in Human Behavior, 29*(3), 1039–1053. doi:10.1016/j.chb.2012.06.025

Pallis, G., Zeinalipour-Yazti, D., & Dikaiakos, M. (2011). Online Social Networks: Status and Trends in New Directions in Web Data Management (pp. 213–234). New York, NY: Springer.

Pamsari, M. B., Dehban, M., & Lulemani, H. K. (2013). Assessment of the key success factors of customer relationship management. *Universal Journal of Management and Social Sciences, 3*(4), 23–29.

Pan, S. L., Tan, C. W., & Lim, E. T. K. (2006). Customer relationship management (CRM) in e-government: A relational perspective, *Decision Support Systems*, 42, 237-250. Pang L. & Norris R. (2002), Applying customer relationship management (CRM) to government. *The Journal of Government Financial Management, 51*(1), 40–45.

Pan, S. L., Tan, C. W., & Lim, E. T. K. (2006). Customer relationship management (CRM) in e-government: A relational perspective. *Decision Support Systems, 42*(1), 237–250. doi:10.1016/j.dss.2004.12.001

Pansiri, J., & Temtime, Z. T. (2010). Linking firm and managers' characteristics to perceived critical success factors for innovative entrepreneurial support. *Journal of Small Business and Enterprise Development, 17*(1), 45–59. doi:10.1108/14626001011019125

Pan, Y., Nam, T., Ogara, S., & Lee, S. (2013). Adoption model of mobile-enabled systems in supply chain. *Industrial Management & Data Systems, 113*(2), 171–189. doi:10.1108/02635571311303523

Papazoglou, M. P. (2001). Agent-oriented technology in support of e-business. *Communications of the ACM, 44*(4), 71–77. doi:10.1145/367211.367268

Parens, E., & Johnston, J. (2014). Neuroimaging: Beginning to Appreciate its Complexities. *The Hastings Center Report, 45*(2), s2–s7. doi:10.1002/hast.293 PMID:24634082

Parisi, C., & Hockerts, K. N. (2008). Managerial mindsets and performance measurement systems of CSR-related intangibles. *Measuring Business Excellence, 12*(2), 51–67. doi:10.1108/13683040810881199

Parsa, H. G., & Njite, D. (2008). Psychology of pricing: A review and suggestions. In H. Oh & A. Pizam (Eds.), *Handbook of Hospitality Marketing Management* (pp. 353–380). Oxford, UK: Butterworth-Heinemann. doi:10.1016/B978-0-08-045080-3.50016-0

Partala, T., & Kallinen, A. (2012). Understanding the most satisfying and unsatisfying user experiences: Emotions, psychological needs, and context. *Interacting with Computers, 24*(1), 25–34. doi:10.1016/j.intcom.2011.10.001

Parvatiyar, A., & Sheth, J. N. (2000). The domain and conceptual foundations of relationship marketing. In J. N. Sheth & A. Parvatiyar (Eds.), *Handbook of relationship marketing* (pp. 3–38). Thousand Oaks, CA: Sage. doi:10.4135/9781452231310.n1

Patton, M. (1990). *Qualitative Evaluation and Research Methods*. London, UK: Sage.

Patton, M. Q. (1987). *How to use qualitative methods in evaluation*. London: SAGE.

Pavlou, P. A., Benbasat, I., Krishnan, R., & Dellarocas, C. 2008. *Mitigating product uncertainty in online markets: it and business solutions and research implications.* Paper presented at the 29th International Conference on Information Systems, Paris, France.

Pavlou, P., & Dimoka, A. (2006). The nature and role of feedback text comments in online marketplaces: Implications for trust building, price premiums, and seller differentiation. *Information Systems Research, 17*(4), 392–414. doi:10.1287/isre.1060.0106

Pavon, F., & Brown, I. (2010). Factors influencing the adoption of the world wide web for jobseeking in South Africa. *Journal of International Management, 12*(1), 443–452.

Payne, A., Christopher, M., Clark, M., & Peck, H. (1999). *Relationship marketing for competitive advantage.* Oxford, UK: Butterworth Heinemann.

Payne, A., & Frow, P. (2005). A strategic framework for customer relationship management. *Journal of Marketing, 69*(4), 167-176. doi:10.1509/jmkg.2005.69.4.167

Payne, A., & Frow, P. (2006). Customer relationship management: From strategy to implementation. *Journal of Marketing Management, 22*(1-2), 135–168. doi:10.1362/026725706776022272

Payne, A., & Frow, P. (2013). *Strategic Customer Management: Integrating Relationship Marketing and CRM.* Cambridge University Press. doi:10.1017/CBO9781139057417

Payne, J. W., Bettman, J. R., & Luce, M. F. (1996). When time is money: Decision behaviour under opportunity-cost time pressure. *Organizational Behavior and Human Decision Processes, 66*(2), 131–152. doi:10.1006/obhd.1996.0044

Peixoto, S. (2010). *Web Trends - 10 cases made in web 2.0. Gaia.* Comunicarte Publishing.

Pelling, E., & White, K. M. (2009). The Theory of Planned Behaviour Applied to Young People's Use of Social Networking Websites. *Cyberpsychology & Behavior, 12*(6), 755–759. doi:10.1089/cpb.2009.0109 PMID:19788377

Pels, J. (1999). Exchange relationships in consumer markets? *European Journal of Marketing, 33*(1/2), 19–37. doi:10.1108/03090569910249157

Pempek, T., Yermolayeva, Y., & Calvert, S. (2009). College students' social networking experiences on Facebook. *Journal of Applied Developmental Psychology, 30*(3), 227–238. doi:10.1016/j.appdev.2008.12.010

Peña, J., & Brody, N. (2014). Intentions to hide and unfriend Facebook connections based on perceptions of sender attractiveness and status updates. *Computers in Human Behavior, 31*, 143–150. doi:10.1016/j.chb.2013.10.004

Peppard, J. (2000). Customer relationship management (CRM) in financial services. *European Management Journal, 18*(3), 312–327. doi:10.1016/S0263-2373(00)00013-X

Peppers, D., & Rogers, M. (2011). *Managing customer relationships: a strategic framework* (2nd ed.). Hoboken, New Jersey: John Wiley & Sons, Inc.

Peres, R., Muller, E., & Mahajan, V. (2010). Innovation Diffusion and New Product Growth Models: A Critical Review and Research Directions. *International Journal of Research in Marketing, 27*(2), 91–103. doi:10.1016/j.ijresmar.2009.12.012

Perez, S. (2012). YouTube Reaches 4 Billion Views Per Day. *Techcrunch.* Retrieved from http://techcrunch.com/2012/01/23/youtube-reaches-4-billion-views-per-day/

Perry, C. (1998). Processes of a case study methodology for postgraduate research in marketing. *European Journal of Marketing, 32*(9/10), 785–802. doi:10.1108/03090569810232237

Perry, M., & Bodkin, C. (2002). Fortune 500 manufacturer web sites: Innovative marketing strategies or cyberbrochures? *Industrial Marketing Management*, *31*(2), 133–144. doi:10.1016/S0019-8501(01)00187-0

Petersen, K. J., Handfield, R. B., & Ragatz, G. L. (2005). Supplier integration into new product development: Coordinating product, process & supply chain design. *Journal of Operations Management*, *23*(3-4), 371–388. doi:10.1016/j.jom.2004.07.009

Peters, K., Chen, Y., Kaplan, A. M., Ognibeni, B., & Pauwels, K. (2013). Social media metrics – a framework and guidelines for managing social media. *Journal of Interactive Marketing*, *27*(4), 281–298. doi:10.1016/j.intmar.2013.09.007

Peterson, R. (1995). Relationship marketing and the consumer. *Journal of the Academy of Marketing Science*, *23*(4), 278–278. doi:10.1177/009207039502300407

Pettigrew, A. M. (1990). Longitudinal field research on change: Theory and practice. *Organization Science*, *1*(3), 267–292. doi:10.1287/orsc.1.3.267

Pfeil, U., Arjan, R., & Zaphiris, P. (2009). Age differences in online social networking – A study of user profiles and the social capital divide among teenagers and older users in MySpace. *Computers in Human Behavior*, *25*(3), 643–654. doi:10.1016/j.chb.2008.08.015

Pfieffelman, P. M., Wagner, S. H., & Libkuman, T. (2010). Recruiting on corporate web sites: Perceptions of fit and attraction. *International Journal of Selection and Assessment*, *18*(1), 40–47. doi:10.1111/j.1468-2389.2010.00487.x

Phelps, J. E., Lewis, R., Mobilio, L., Perry, D., & Raman, N. (2004). Viral Marketing or Electronic Word-of-Mouth Advertising: Examining Consumer Responses and Motivations to Pass Along Email. *Journal of Advertising Research*, *44*(4), 333–348.

Philippot, P., Chapelle, G., & Blairy, S. (2002). Respiratory Feedback in the Generation of Emotion. *Cognition and Emotion*, *16*(5), 605–627. doi:10.1080/02699930143000392

Pilchik, R. (2000). Pharmaceutical blister packaging, Part I. *Pharmaceutical technology*, 24(11), 68.

Pinch, T., & Bijker, W. (1992). The social construction of facts and artifacts: or how the sociology of science and the sociology of technology might benefit each other. In W. Bijker & J. Law (Eds.), *Shaping Technology/Building Society* (pp. 17–50). Cambridge, MA: MIT Press.

Pineida, F. (2011). Competencies for the 21st century: Integrating ICT to life, school and economical development. *Procedia: Social and Behavioral Sciences*, *28*, 54–57. doi:10.1016/j.sbspro.2011.11.011

Pinho, José Carlos Martins, & Soares, A.M. (2011). Examining the technology acceptance model in the adoption of social networks. *Journal of Research in Interactive Marketing*, *5*(2), 116–129.

Pinker, E.J., Seidmann, A., & Vakrat, Y. (2003). Managing online auctions: Current business and research issues. *Management Science, 49*(11), 1457-1484.

Pino, C. (2007a). *El Anunciante en la Era de la Saturación Publicitaria: Nuevas Herramientas de Comunicación*. Ámbitos.

Pino, C. (2007b). Nueva Era en la Comunicación Comercial Audiovisual: El Marketing Viral. *Pensar la Publicidad*, *1*(2), 63–76.

Pinto, J. K., & Slevin, D. P. (1987). Critical factors in successful project implementation. *IEEE Transactions on Engineering Management*, *34*(1), 22–27. doi:10.1109/TEM.1987.6498856

Pitt, L. F., Berthon, P., Watson, R. T., & Ewing, M. (2001). Pricing strategy and the net. *Business Horizons*, *44*(2), 45–54. doi:10.1016/S0007-6813(01)80022-7

Pizzagalli, D. A., Sherwood, R. J., Henriques, J. B. & Davidson, R. J. (2005). Frontal Brain Asymmetry and Reward Responsiveness. *Psychological Science (Wiley-Blackwell), 16*(10), 805-813.

Plessis, M. D., & Boon, J. (2004). Knowledge management in e-business and customer relationship management: South African case study findings. *International Journal of Information Management, 24*(1), 73–86. doi:10.1016/j.ijinfomgt.2003.10.002

Podsakoff, P. M., MacKenzie, S. B., Lee, J., & Podsakoff, N. F. (2003). Common method biases in behavioral research: A critical review of the literature and recommended remedies. *The Journal of Applied Psychology, 88*(5), 879–903. doi:10.1037/0021-9010.88.5.879 PMID:14516251

Polizelli, D., & Ozaki, A. (2008). *Sociedade de informação: Os desafios da era da colaboração e da gestão do conhecimento*. Saint Paul, Brazil: Saraiva Publisher.

Pope, J., Annandale, D., & Morrison-Saunders, A. (2004). Conceptualising sustainability assessment. *Environmental Impact Assessment Review, 24*(6), 595–616. doi:10.1016/j.eiar.2004.03.001

Pordata. (n. d.). Retrieved from www.pordata.pt

Portmann, E. (2012). Towards an emergent semantic web. *Tiny Transactions on Computer Science*, 1.

Prahalad, C. K. (1990). The Changing Nature of Worldwide Competition. *Vital Speeches of the Day, 56*, 354–357.

Prinzie, A., & Van den Poel, D. (2008). Random forests for multiclass classification: Random MultiNomial Logit. *Expert Systems with Applications, 34*(3), 1721–1732. doi:10.1016/j.eswa.2007.01.029

Qian, G. (1997). Assessing Product-Market Diversification in US Firms. *Management International Review, 27*(2), 127–149.

Qian, G. (2002). Multinationality, Product Diversification, & Profitability of Emerging US Small & Medium Sized Enterprises. *Journal of Business Venturing, 17*(6), 611–633. doi:10.1016/S0883-9026(01)00080-5

Quan-Haase, A., & Young, A. (2010). Uses and Gratifications of Social Media: A Comparison of Facebook and Instant Messaging. *Bulletin of Science, Technology & Society, 30*(5), 350–361. doi:10.1177/0270467610380009

Quinlan, J. R. (1993). *C4.5: Programs for machine learning*. Morgan Kaufmann Publishers.

Quiroz-Onate, D., & Aitken, M. (2007). Business and human rights: A critical assessment of the notion of CSR and measurement. *Journal of International Trade Law and Policy, 6*(2), 79–90. doi:10.1108/14770020780000559

Qureshi, I., Fang, Y., Ramsey, E., McCole, P., Ibbotson, P., & Compeau, D. (2009). Understanding online customer repurchasing intention and the mediating role of trust–an empirical investigation in two developed countries. *European Journal of Information Systems, 18*(3), 205–222. doi:10.1057/ejis.2009.15

Radosevich, L. (1997). Early adopters hail extranet benefits, dodge pitfalls. *InfoWorld, 19*(23), 65–66.

Rai, A., Pavlou, P., Im, G., & Du, S. (2012). Inter-firm IT capabilities and communications for co-creating relational value: Evidence from the logistics industry. *Management Information Systems Quarterly, 36*(1), 233–262.

Rai, A., & Tang, X. (2010). Leveraging IT capabilities and competitive process capabilities for the management of interorganizational relationship portfolios. *Information Systems Research, 21*(3), 516–542. doi:10.1287/isre.1100.0299

Rainer, R. K., & Cegielsk, C. G. (2011). *Introduction to information systems: Enabling and transforming business* (3rd ed.). Hoboken, NJ: John Wiley & Sons.

Rainie, L., Purcell, K., & Smith, A. (2011). The Social Side of the Internet. *Pew Internet & American Life Project, Washington, DC*. Retrieved from http://www.pewinternet.org/files/old-media/Files/Reports/2011/PIP_Social_Side_of_the_Internet.pdf

Raman, P. & Pashupati, K. (2004). Online privacy: The impact of self-perceived technological competence. *American Marketing Association Educators Proceedings*, 5-6.

Randall, T., & Ulrich, K. (2001). Product Variety, Supply Chain Structure, & Firm Performance: Analysis of the U.S. Bicycle Industry. *Management Science*, *47*(12), 1588–1604. doi:10.1287/mnsc.47.12.1588.10237

Ranganathan, C. (2012). The role of extrinsic cues in consumer decision process in online shopping environments. *Journal of Electronic Commerce in Organizations*, *10*(1), 52–71. doi:10.4018/jeco.2012010104

Rao, V.R. (1984). Pricing research in marketing: the state of the art. *The Journal of Business, 57*(1), *Part 2: Pricing Strategy*, S39-S60.

Rao, V. R., & Kartono, B. (2009). Pricing objectives and strategies: a cross-country survey. In V. R. Rao (Ed.), *Handbook of Pricing Research in Marketing* (pp. 9–36). Massachusetts: Edward Elgar Publishing Limited. doi:10.4337/9781848447448.00009

Rapp, A., Beitelspacher, L. S., Grewal, D., & Hughes, D. E. (2013). Understanding Social Media Effects across Seller, Retailer and Consumer Interaction. *Journal of the Academy of Marketing Science*, *41*(5), 547–566. doi:10.1007/s11747-013-0326-9

Rasch, C., & Teichert, T. (2013). Assessing Consumers' Preferences with Facial Electromyography - Insights from a Discrete Choice Experiment.*Neuropsychoeconomics Conference Proceedings*, 54.

Rashidirad, M., Soltani, E., & Syed, J. (2013). Strategic alignment between competitive strategy and dynamic capability: Conceptual framework and hypothesis development. *Strategic Change*, *22*(3-4), 213–224. doi:10.1002/jsc.1934

Rashotte, L. S. (2006). Social Influence. In G. Ritzer, & J.M. Ryan (Ed.), The Blackwell Encyclopedia of Sociology (Vol. 9, pp. 4426-4429). Oxford: Blackwell Publishing.

Ratnayake, N., Broderick, A. J., & Mitchell, R. C. (2010). A Neurocognitive Approach to Brand Memory. *Journal of Marketing Management*, *26*(13-14), 1295–1318. doi:10.1080/0267257X.2010.522531

Ratten, V. (2012a). Does the Sky have to be the limit? Utilizing Cloud-Based Learning in the Workplace. *Development and Learning Organization*, *26*(5), 21–23. doi:10.1108/14777281211258662

Ratten, V. (2012b). Entrepreneurship, E-Finance and Mobile Banking. *International Journal of Electronic Finance*, *6*(1), 1–12. doi:10.1504/IJEF.2012.046590

Ratten, V. (2013). The evolution of mobile social networks through technological innovation. In A. Brem & E. Viardot (Eds.), *Evolution of Innovation Management* (pp. 132–150). London: Palgrave MacMillan. doi:10.1057/9781137299994.0013

Ratten, V. (2014a). Indian and US consumer purchase intentions of cloud computing services. *Journal of Indian Business Research*, *6*(2), 170–188. doi:10.1108/JIBR-07-2013-0068

Ratten, V. (2014b). Behavioral intentions to adopt technological innovations: The role of trust, innovation and performance. *International Journal of Enterprise Information Systems*, *10*(3), 1–12. doi:10.4018/ijeis.2014070101

Ravaja, N., Somervuori, O., & Salminen, M. (2013). Predicting Purchase Decision: The Role of Hemispheric Asymmetry over the Frontal Cortex. *Journal of Neuroscience, Psychology, and Economics*, *6*(1), 1–13. doi:10.1037/a0029949

Reardon, S. (2014). Brain-Mapping Projects to Join Forces. *Scientific American*. Retrieved from http://www.scientificamerican.com/article/brain-mapping-projects-to-join-forces/

Reddy, R. (2006). Robotics and intelligent systems in support of society. *IEEE Intelligent Systems*, *21*(3), 23–31.

Reed, R., Lemak, D. J., & Montgomery, J. C. (1996). Beyond process: TQM content and firm performance. *Academy of Management Review*, *21*(1), 173–202.

Reedy, J., Schullo, S., & Zimmerman, K. (2001). *Marketing eletrônico*. São Paulo.

Reichheld, F. (1996). *The Loyalty Effect*. Boston: Harvard Business School Press.

Reichheld, F. F. (1996). *The loyalty effect*. Boston, MA: Harvard Business School Press.

Reichheld, F. F., & Sasser, W. E. (1990). Zero defections: Quality comes to services. *Harvard Business Review*, *68*(5), 105–111. PMID:10107082

Reid, D. A., & Plank, R. E. (2000). Business marketing comes of age: A comprehensive review of the literature. *Journal of Business-To-Business Marketing*, *7*(2-3), 9–178. doi:10.1300/J033v07n02_02

Reijonen, H., & Laukkanen, T. (2010). Customer relationship oriented marketing practices in SMEs. *Marketing Intelligence & Planning*, *28*(2), 115–136. doi:10.1108/02634501011029646

Reiley, D. H. (2000). Auctions on the internet: What's being auctioned and how? *The Journal of Industrial Economics*, *48*(3), 227–252. doi:10.1111/1467-6451.00122

Reiley, D. H. (2006). Field experiments on the effects of reserve prices in auctions: More Magic on the Internet. *The Rand Journal of Economics*, *37*(1), 195–211. doi:10.1111/j.1756-2171.2006.tb00012.x

Reinartz, W. J., & Kumar, V. (2000). On the profitability of long-life customers in a noncontractual setting: An empirical investigation and implications for marketing. *Journal of Marketing*, *64*(4), 17–35. doi:10.1509/jmkg.64.4.17.18077

Reinhardt, F. L., Stavins, R. N., & Vietor, R. H. (2008). Corporate social responsibility through an economic lens. *Review of Environmental Economics and Policy*, *2*(2), 219–239. doi:10.1093/reep/ren008

Resnick, P., & Dellarocas, C. (2003). Online Reputation Mechanisms: A Roadmap for Future Research. *Technical report, First Interdisciplinary Symposium on Online Reputation Mechanisms*. Retrieved from http://ccs.mit.edu/dell/symposium.html#publications

Resnick, P., Zeckhauser, R., Swanson, J., & Lockwood, K. (2006). The value of reputation on eBay: A controlled experiment. *Experimental Economics*, *9*(2), 79–101. doi:10.1007/s10683-006-4309-2

Rezende, D. (2011). *Planeamento de sistemas de informação e informática: Guia prático para planear a tecnologia da informação integrada ao planeamento estratégico das organizações*. Saint Paul, Brazil: Atlas Publisher.

Rezende, D., & Abreu, A. (2010). *Tecnologia da informação aplicada a sistemas de informação empresariais*. Saint Paul, Brazil: Atlas Publisher.

Rheingold, H. (2012). *Net smart: how to thrive online*. Cambridge, Massachusetts: MIT Press.

Richards, K. A., & Jones, E. (2008). Customer relationship management: Finding value drivers. *Industrial Marketing Management*, *37*(2), 120–130. doi:10.1016/j.indmarman.2006.08.005

Riley, J., & Samuelson, W. (1981). Optimal auctions. *The American Economic Review*, *71*, 381–392.

Rios, L. (2006) Comércio eletrónico: Variáveis que influenciam a propensão à compra [Master Dissertation]. School of Management, Getulio Vargas Foundation, Rio de Janeiro, Brazil.

Roberts, C. M. (2006). Radio frequency identification (RFID). *Computers & Security*, *25*(1), 18–26. doi:10.1016/j.cose.2005.12.003

Roberts, K., Varki, S., & Brodie, R. (2003). Measuring the quality of relationships in customer services: An empirical study. *European Journal of Marketing*, *37*(1-2), 169–196. doi:10.1108/03090560310454037

Robins, F. (2000). The e-marketing mix. *The Marketing Review*, *1*(2), 249–274. doi:10.1362/1469347002529134

Rodrigues, E. (2008) A interação entre sistemas de informação e o trabalho no setor bancário no Brasil: Uma análise estruturalista [PhD Thesis]. School of Management, Getulio Vargas Foundation, Rio de Janeiro, Brazil.

Roettgers, J. (2013). Online video will be more popular than Facebook and Twitter by 2017. *Gigaom*. Retrieved from http://gigaom.com/2013/05/29/online-video-will-be-more-popular-than-facebook-and-twitter-by-2017/

Rogers, E. (1995). *Diffusion of Innovations*. New York, USA: Free Press.

Rogers, E. M. (1983). *Diffusion of innovations*. New York, NY: Free Press.

Rolland, K. H., & Monteiro, E. (2002). Balancing the local and the global in infrastructural information systems. *The Information Society*, *18*(2), 87–100. doi:10.1080/01972240290075020

Romano, R. (2011) Os impactos do uso de tecnologia da informação e da identificação e captura automática de dados nos processos operacionais do varejo [PhD Thesis]. School of Management, Getulio Vargas Foundation, Saint Paul, Brazil.

Rosen, E. (2000). *The Anatomy of Buzz: How to Create Word-of-Mouth Marketing*. New York: Doubleday Currency.

Ross, C., Orr, E. S., Sisic, M., Arseneault, J. M., Simmering, M. G., & Orr, R. R. (2009). Personality and motivates associated with Facebook use. *Computers in Human Behavior*, *25*(2), 575–586. doi:10.1016/j.chb.2008.12.024

Rostock, F. (2011) O impacto da tecnologia da informação na geração de recursos competitivos nas empresas: Uma abordagem baseada em estudos de caso [PhD Thesis]. School of Management, Getulio Vargas Foundation, Saint Paul, Brazil.

Rubinson, J. (2010). What Behavioral Economics Can Teach Marketing Research. *Journal of Advertising Research*, *50*(2), 114–117. doi:10.2501/S0021849910091269

Rublescki, A. (2009). Webmarketing e cibercliente: o Marketing em tempos de "4Ps+ 2Ds+ 4Cs". *Biblioteca On-line de ciências da comunicação–BOCC*.

Rugfelt, M. (2014, May 1). Artificial Intelligence's Impact on Marketing. *Direct Marketing News*. Retrieved from http://www.dmnews.com/artificial-intelligences-impact-on- marketing/article/344554/

Rumelt, R. P. (1982). Diversification Strategy & Profitability. *Strategic Management Journal*, *3*(4), 359–369. doi:10.1002/smj.4250030407

Rundh, B. (2005). The Multi-Faceted Dimension of Packaging: Marketing Logistic or Marketing Tool? *British Food Journal*, *107*(9), 670–684. doi:10.1108/00070700510615053

Rundh, B. (2009). Packaging Design: Creating Competitive Advantage with Product Packaging. *British Food Journal*, *111*(9), 988–1002. doi:10.1108/00070700910992880

Rusli, E. (2014, April 2014). Firms Use Artificial Intelligence to Tap Shoppers' Views: Analyzing Focus Groups, Surveys, Online Forums and Social Media Provides New Data. *The Wall Street Journal*.

Russell, K. (2014, February 4). IBM Is Using Watson To Psychoanalyze People From Their Tweets. *Business Insider*. Retrieved from http://www.businessinsider.com/ibm-watson-psychoanalyzes-tweets-2014-2#ixzz2sPUJ6cOw

Ryals, L., & Knox, S. (2001). Cross-functional issues in the implementation of relationship marketing through customer relationship management. *European Management Journal*, *19*(5), 534–542. doi:10.1016/S0263-2373(01)00067-6

Ryals, L., & Payne, A. (2001). Customer relationship management in financial services: Towards information-enabled relationship marketing. *Journal of Strategic Management*, *9*(1), 3–27.

Ryals, L., & Payne, A. (2001). Customer Relationship Management in Financial Services: Towards Information-enabled Relationship Marketing. *Journal of Strategic Marketing*, *9*(1), 3–27. doi:10.1080/713775725

Saarijarvi, H., Karjaluoto, H., & Kuusela, H. (2013). Extending customer relationship management: From empowering firms to empowering customers. *Journal of Systems and Information Technology*, *15*(2), 140–158. doi:10.1108/13287261311328877

Saeed, R., Naeem, B., & Naz, U. (2013). Integrated Marketing Communication: A Review Paper. *Interdisciplinary Journal of Contemporary Research in Business*, *5*(5), 124–133.

Sakkthivel, A M. & Babawale, Tinuki. (2011). Are the Same Determinants Influence Customer Satisfaction and Brand Loyalty – An Exploratory Study. *International Journal of Management. Entrepreneurship and Technology*, *1*(1), 93–102.

Sakkthivel, A. M. (2011a). Modeling of Determinants Influence Consumer Behavior towards Different Technology Products. *International Journal of Electronic Finance*, *5*(1), 84–103. doi:10.1504/IJEF.2011.038224

Sakkthivel, A. M. (2011b). Modeling the Impact of Internal and External Variables on Consumer Durables in a Matured Marketing Environment. *International Journal of Electronic Finance*, *5*(4), 316–332. doi:10.1504/IJEF.2011.043346

Sakkthivel, A. M. (2012). Modeling Consumer Choice (Buying) and Switching Behavior in a Restricted Marketing Environment. *International Journal of Electronic Finance*, *6*(1), 35–48. doi:10.1504/IJEF.2012.046592

Sakkthivel, A. M. (2013). Examining the impact of socio-cultural and psychographic/demographic variables on women consumer behaviour: An exploratory study from Arab League countries. *Int. J. Electronic Finance*, *7*(2), 161–175. doi:10.1504/IJEF.2013.057268

Salo, J. (2006), *Business relationship digitalization: a case study from the steel processing industry*, Doctoral dissertation, Oulu University Press, Oulu.

Salo, J. (2012). The role of mobile technology in a buyer-supplier relationship. *Journal of Business and Industrial Marketing*, *27*(7), 554–563. doi:10.1108/08858621211257329

Salo, J., & Karjaluoto, H. (2006). IT—enabled supply chain management. *Contemporary Management Research*, *2*(1), 17–30. doi:10.7903/cmr.76

Salo, J., Lehtimäki, T., Simula, H., & Mäntymäki, M. (2013). Social media marketing in the Scandinavian industrial marketing. *International Journal of Electronic Business Research*, *9*(4), 16–32. doi:10.4018/ijebr.2013100102

Salo, J., & Wendelin, R. (2013). Longitudinal analysis of digital bonding in buyer seller relationships. *Journal of Business-To-Business Marketing*, *20*(1), 1–19. doi:10.1080/1051712X.2012.719179

Salomo, S., Talke, K., & Strecker, N. (2008). Innovation field orientation & its effect on innovativeness & firm performance. *Journal of Product Innovation Management*, *25*(6), 560–576. doi:10.1111/j.1540-5885.2008.00322.x

Salomo, S., Weise, J., & Gemünden, H. G. (2007). NPD planning activities & innovation performance: The mediating role of process management & the moderating effect of product innovativeness. *Journal of Product Innovation Management*, *24*(4), 285–302. doi:10.1111/j.1540-5885.2007.00252.x

Sammler, D., Grigutsch, M., Fritz, T., & Koelsch, S. (2007). Music and Emotion: Electrophysiological Correlates of the Processing of Pleasant and Unpleasant Music. *Psychophysiology*, *44*(2), 293–304. doi:10.1111/j.1469-8986.2007.00497.x PMID:17343712

Samson, D., & Terziovski, M. (1999). The relationship between total quality management practices and operational performance. *Journal of Operations Management*, *17*(4), 393–409. doi:10.1016/S0272-6963(98)00046-1

Sanchez, F. (1999). *Metodologia para la investigacion en marketing y direccion de empresas*. Madrid, Spain: Ediciones Pirámide.

Sánchez, M., Gil, I., & Mollá, A. (2000). Estatus del marketing de relaciones. *Revista Europea de Dirección y Economia de la Empresa*, *9*(3), 47–64.

Sarin, S., & Mahajan, V. (2001). The Effect of Reward Structures on the Performance of Cross-Functional Product Development Teams. *Journal of Marketing*, *62*(2), 35–53. doi:10.1509/jmkg.65.2.35.18252

Saxena, M. (2013, May 21). *How Cognitive Technologies Can Help Transform the Way Companies and Consumers Connect. A Smarter Planet.* Retrieved from http://asmarterplanet.com/blog/2013/05/connect.html

Schaltegger, S., & Wagner, M. (2011). Sustainable entrepreneurship and sustainability innovation: Categories and interactions. *Business Strategy and the Environment*, *20*(4), 222–237. doi:10.1002/bse.682

Scherbaum, C. A., & Meade, A. W. (2013). New directions for measurement in management research. *International Journal of Management Reviews*, *15*(2), 132148. doi:10.1111/ijmr.12003

Scherer, F. M., & Ross, D. (1990). *Industrial Market Structure & Economic Performance*. Boston, Mass: Harvard Business School Press.

Schiele, H. (2006). How to Distinguish Innovative Suppliers? Identifying Innovative Suppliers as New Task for Purchasing. *Industrial Marketing Management*, *35*(2), 925–935. doi:10.1016/j.indmarman.2006.05.003

Schiff, A. (2013, May 21). Just Ask Watson: IBM Unveils the Watson Engagement Advisor. *Direct Marketing News*. Retrieved from http://www.dmnews.com/just-ask-watson-ibm-unveils-the-watson-engagement-advisor/article/294283/

Schindler, R. M. (2012). *Pricing strategies: A marketing approach*. Thousand Oaks, CA: Sage Publications.

Schmidt, J. B., Montoya-Weiss, M. M., & Massey, A. P. (2001). New Product Development Decision-Making Effectiveness: Comparing Individuals, Face-To-Face Teams, & Virtual Teams. *Decision Sciences*, *32*(4), 575–600. doi:10.1111/j.1540-5915.2001.tb00973.x

Schrage, M. (2000). A Go-Go Dot-Com? Not if its stock went-went. *Adweek Magazines' Technology Marketing*, 20(12), 32.

Schreier, M., & Prügl, R. (2008). Extending Lead-User Theory: Antecedents & Consequences of Consumers' Lead Userness*. *Journal of Product Innovation Management*, *25*(4), 331–346. doi:10.1111/j.1540-5885.2008.00305.x

Schubert, P., & Legner, C. (2011). B2B integration in global supply chains: An identification of technical integration scenarios. *The Journal of Strategic Information Systems*, *20*(3), 250–267. doi:10.1016/j.jsis.2011.04.001

Schwenk, H., & Bengio, Y. (2000). Boosting neural networks. *Neural Computation*, *12*(8), 1869–1887. doi:10.1162/089976600300015178 PMID:10953242

Scornavacca, E., Becker, J., & Andraschko, R. (2001) E-survey: Conceção e implementação de um sistema de survey por internet. Proceedings of the National Meeting of the Post-graduation Programs, Rio de Janeiro, Brazil.

Scott, J. P. (2008). *Social Network Analysis* (3rd ed.). Thousand Oaks, CA: Sage Ltd.

Seamans, R., & Zhu, F. (2014). Responses to Entry in Multi-Sided Markets: The Impact of Craigslist on Local Newspapers. *Management Science*, *60*(2), 476–493. doi:10.1287/mnsc.2013.1785

Segal, J. P., Sobczak, A., & Triomphe, C. E. (2003). *Corporate social responsibility and working conditions*. Dublin: European Foundation for the Improvement of Living and Working Conditions.

Segarra-Moliner, J. R., Moliner-Tena, M. A., & Sánchez-Garcia, J. (2013). Relationship quality in business to business: A cross-cultural perspective from universities. *Marketing Intelligence & Planning*, *31*(3), 196–215. doi:10.1108/02634501311324573

Seitanidi, M. M. (2009). Missed opportunities of employee involvement in CSR partnerships. *Corporate Reputation Review*, *12*(2), 90–105. doi:10.1057/crr.2009.7

Sekhar Bhattacharyya, S. (2010). Exploring the concept of strategic corporate social responsibility for an integrated perspective. *European Business Review*, *22*(1), 82–101. doi:10.1108/09555341011009025

Sernau, S. (2014). Social inequality in a global age. Thousand Oaks, California: Sage Publications.

Shah, M. H., Peikari, H. R., & Yasin, N. M. (2014). The determinants of individuals' perceived e-security: Evidence from Malaysia. *International Journal of Information Management*, *34*(1), 48–57. doi:10.1016/j.ijinfomgt.2013.10.001

Shaker, W. (2013). EP016: How to avoid failure & succeed as an online entrepreneur. Retrieved from http://www.williamshaker.com/how-to-avoid-failure-succeed-as-an-online-entrepreneur/

Shapiro, B. P. (1988). What the Hell is 'Market Oriented'? *Harvard Business Review*, *66*, 119–125.

Sharp, Z., & Zaidman, N. (2010). Strategization of CSR. *Journal of Business Ethics*, *93*(1), 51–71. doi:10.1007/s10551-009-0181-2

Shaw, M. (2000). Electronic commerce: state of the art. In M. Shaw, R. Blanning, T. Strader, & A. Whinston (Eds.), Handbook of Electronic Commerce (pp. 3-24). New York: Springer-Verlag. doi:10.1007/978-3-642-58327-8_1

Shaw, M. (2003). *E-Business Management*. New York: Kluwer Academic Publishers.

Sheremata, W. A. (2000). Centrifugal & Centripetal Forcess in Radical New Product Development Under Time Pressure. *Academy of Management Review*, *25*(2), 389–408.

Sheth, J. N. (2000). Relationship marketing: Paradigm shift of shaft? In J. N. Sheth & A. Parvatiyar (Eds.), *Handbook of relationship marketing* (pp. 609–620). Thousand Oaks, CA: Sage. doi:10.4135/9781452231310.n23

Sheth, J. N. (2002). The future of relationship marketing. *Journal of Services Marketing*, *16*(7), 590–592. doi:10.1108/08876040210447324

Sheth, J. N. (2007). Emerging research opportunities for doctoral students in b-to-b marketing. *Journal of Business-To-Business Marketing*, *14*(1), 13–22. doi:10.1300/J033v14n01_02

Sheth, J. N., & Parvatiyar, A. (2001). Customer Relationship Management: Emerging Practice, Process and Discipline. *Journal of Economic and Social Research*, *3*(2), 1–34.

Sheth, J. N., & Sisodia, R. S. (2002). Marketing productivity: Issues and analysis. *Journal of Business Research*, *55*(5), 349–362. doi:10.1016/S0148-2963(00)00164-8

Sheth, J. N., Sisodia, R. S., & Sharma, A. (2000). The antecedents and consequences of customer-centric marketing. *Journal of the Academy of Marketing Science*, *28*(1), 55–66. doi:10.1177/0092070300281006

Sheth, J., & Parvatiyar, A. (1995). Relationship marketing in consumer markets: Antecedents and consequences. *Journal of the Academy of Marketing Science*, *23*(4), 255–271. doi:10.1177/009207039502300405

Sheth, J., & Parvatiyar, A. (2002). Evolving relationship marketing into a discipline. *Journal of Relationship Marketing*, *1*(1), 3–16. doi:10.1300/J366v01n01_02

Shi, J., & Yip, L. (2007). Driving innovation and improving employee capability: The effects of customer knowledge sharing on CRM. *Business Review (Federal Reserve Bank of Philadelphia)*, *7*(1), 107–112.

Shimp, T. A. (2010). *Integrated Marketing Communications in Advertising and Promotion. 8e*. Cengage Learning.

Shipley, D., & Jobber, D. (2001). Integrative pricing via the pricing wheel. *Industrial Marketing Management*, *30*(3), 301–314. doi:10.1016/S0019-8501(99)00098-X

Shiu, J.-L., & Sun, C.-H. D. (2014). The determinants of price in online auctions: More evidence from unbalanced panel data. *Journal of Applied Statistics*, *41*(2), 382–392. doi:10.1080/02664763.2013.839639

Shi, Z., Rui, H., & Whinston, A. (2010). Information sharing in social Broadacst: Evidences from Twitter.*Proceedings of the 21st Workshop on Information Systems and Economics*. New York, NY.

Shocker, A. D., Srivatsava, R. K., & Ruekert, R. W. (1994). Challenges and Opportunities Facing Brand Management: An Introduction to the Special Issue. *JMR, Journal of Marketing Research*, *31*(2), 149–158. doi:10.2307/3152190

Sierra, C. (2004). Agent-mediated electronic commerce. *Autonomous Agents and Multi-Agent Systems*, *9*(3), 285–301. doi:10.1023/B:AGNT.0000038029.82331.c0

Silberstein, R. B., & Nield, G. E. (2008). Brain Activity Correlates of Consumer Brand Choice Shift Associated with Television Advertising. *International Journal of Advertising*, *27*(3), 359–380. doi:10.2501/S0265048708080025

Silva, A., & Silva, L. (2003) Representação mental sobre o atendimento dos profissionais de informática no CEFET. Proceedings of the XXIII National Meeting of Production Engineering, Ouro Preto, Brazil.

Silva, B. (2011) Decisões do uso da tecnologia da informação: Um estudo sobre o efeito das capacidades dinâmicas [PhD Thesis]. School of Management, Getulio Vargas Foundation, Saint Paul, Brazil.

Silva, B., & Pereira, M. (2011). Contributos da escola para a inclusão digital. *Innovación Educativa*, *21*, 223–233.

Silverthorne, S. (2009). *Understanding Users of Social Networks. September 14* (pp. 1–2). Harvard Business Knowledge.

Simms, C., & Trott, P. (2010). Packaging development: A conceptual framework for identifying new product opportunities. *Marketing Theory*, *10*(4), 397–415. doi:10.1177/1470593110382826

Simonson, I., & Rosen, E. (2014). *Absolute value: what really influences customers in the age of (nearly) perfect information*. New York, NY: Harper Collins.

Simpson, J. A. (1987). The dissolution of romantic relationships: Factors involved in relationship stability and emotional distress. *Journal of Personality and Social Psychology*, *53*(4), 683–692. doi:10.1037/0022-3514.53.4.683

Sinar, E. F., Reynolds, D. H., & Paquet, S. L. (2003). Nothing but net corporate image and web-based testing. *International Journal of Selection and Assessment*, *11*(2-3), 150–157. doi:10.1111/1468-2389.00238

Singh, S. N., & Churchill, G. A. Jr. (1986). Using the Theory of Signal Detection to Improve Ad Recognition Testing. *JMR, Journal of Marketing Research*, *23*(4), 327–336. doi:10.2307/3151808

Sin, L. Y. M., Tse, A. C. B., & Yim, F. H. K. (2005). CRM: Conceptualization and scale development. *European Journal of Marketing*, *39*(11-12), 1264–1290. doi:10.1108/03090560510623253

Skouras, T., Avlonitis, G. J., & Indounas, K. A. (2005). Economics and marketing on pricing: How and why do they differ? *Journal of Product and Brand Management*, *14*(6), 362–374. doi:10.1108/10610420510624512

Slater, S. F., & Narver, J. C. (1995). Market orientation and the learning organization. *Journal of Marketing*, *59*(3), 63–74. doi:10.2307/1252120

Slater, S. F., & Narver, J. C. (1998). Customer-led and market-oriented: Let's not confuse the two. *Strategic Management Journal*, *19*(10), 1001–1006. doi:10.1002/(SICI)1097-0266(199810)19:10<1001::AID-SMJ996>3.0.CO;2-4

Smit, E. G., Van Noort, G., & Voorveld, H. (2014). Understanding online behavioral advertising: User knowledge, privacy concerns and online coping behavior in Europe. *Computers in Human Behavior*, *32*, 15–22. doi:10.1016/j.chb.2013.11.008

Smith, J. (2013). The Importance of audio branding, *IAB*. Retrieved from http://www.iabuk.net/blog/the-importance-of-audio-branding

Smith, M. D. (2002). The impact of shopbots on electronic markets. *Journal of the Academy of Marketing Science*, *30*(4), 446–454. doi:10.1177/009207002236916

Smith, M. D., Bailey, J., & Brynjolfsson, E. (1999). Understanding digital markets: Review and assessment. In E. Brynjolfsson & B. Kahin (Eds.), *Understanding the digital economy* (pp. 99–136). Cambridge, MA: MIT Press.

Smith, M. D., & Brynjolfsson, E. (2001). Consumer decision-making at an internet shopbot: Brand stil matters. *The Journal of Industrial Economics*, *49*(4), 541–558. doi:10.1111/1467-6451.00162

Smith, M., & Chang, C. (2010). Improving customer outcomes through the implementation of customer relationship management: Evidence from Taiwan. *Asian Review of Accounting*, *18*(3), 260–285. doi:10.1108/13217341011089658

Smith, P. G., & Reinertsen, D. G. (1991). *Developing Products in Half the Time*. New York: Van Nostr & Reinhold.

Smith, P. R., & Zook, Z. (2011). *Marketing Communications: Integrating offline and online with Social Media. 5e*. KoganPage.

Smith, S., & Caruso, J. (2010). *The ECAR study of undergraduate students and information technology*. Boulder: Colorado Press.

Smith, W., & Kidder, D. (2010). You've been tagged! Then again, maybe not: Employers and Facebook. *Business Horizons*, *53*(5), 491–499. doi:10.1016/j.bushor.2010.04.004

Smock, A., Ellison, N., Lampe, C., & Wohn, D. (2011). Facebook as a toolkit: A uses and gratification approach to unbundling feature use. *Computers in Human Behavior*, *27*(6), 2322–2329. doi:10.1016/j.chb.2011.07.011

Sodero, A. C., Rabinovich, E., & Sinha, R. K. (2013). Drivers and outcomes of open-standard interorganizational information systems assimilation in high-technology supply chains. *Journal of Operations Management*, *31*(6), 330–344. doi:10.1016/j.jom.2013.07.008

Solomon, M. R., Marshall, G. W., & Stuart, E. W. (2006). *Marketing: Real People, Real Choices*. Upper Saddle River, New Jersey, USA: Pearson Prentice Hall.

Song, X. M., & Parry, M. E. (1994). The dimension of industrial new product success & failure in state enterprises in the People's Republic of China. *Journal of Product Innovation Management*, *11*(2), 105–118. doi:10.1111/1540-5885.1120105

Song, X. M., & Parry, M. E. (1997). The determinants of Japanese new product success. *JMR, Journal of Marketing Research*, *34*(1), 64–76. doi:10.2307/3152065

Sousa, C. (2008). Difusão das tecnologias da informação e comunicação: Grupos estratégicos nas empresas portuguesas. *Tourism & Management Studies*, *4*, 125–141.

South African Goverment. (2002). Electronic Communications and Transactions Act No 25.

Southgate, D., Westoby, N., & Page, G. (2010). Creative determinants of viral video viewing. *International Journal of Advertising*, *29*(3), 349–368. doi:10.2501/S0265048710201221

Special, W., & Li-Barber, K. (2012). Self-disclosure and student satisfaction with Facebook. *Computers in Human Behavior*, *28*(2), 624–630. doi:10.1016/j.chb.2011.11.008

Sreedhar, M., Vishag, B., & McDonald, R. E. (2005). Integrated Marketing Communication (IMC) and Brand Identity As Critical Components of Brand Equity Strategy. *Journal of Advertising*, *34*(4), 69–80. doi:10.1080/00913367.2005.10639213

Srinivasan, S. S., Anderson, R., & Ponnavolu, K. (2002). Customer loyalty in e-commerce: An exploration of its antecedents and consequences. *Journal of Retailing*, *78*(1), 41–50. doi:10.1016/S0022-4359(01)00065-3

Stábile, S. (2001) Um estudo sobre a desconexão entre usuários e desenvolvedores de sistemas de informação e sua influência na obtenção de informação pelo decisor [Master Dissertation]. School of Engineering, University of Saint Carlos, Saint Paul, Brazil.

Stake, R. (1995). *The art of case study research*. Thousand Oaks: SAGE.

Standifird, S. (2001). Reputation and e-commerce: eBay auctions and the asymmetrical impact of positive and negative ratings. *Journal of Management*, *27*(3), 279–295. doi:10.1177/014920630102700304

Starkey, M. W., Williams, D., & Stone, M. (2002). The state of customer management performance in Malaysia. *Marketing Intelligence & Planning*, *20*(6), 378–385. doi:10.1108/02634500210445437

Statista. (2014). Forecast for global retail sales growth from 2008 to 2016. Retrieved from http://www.statista.com/statistics/232347/forecast-of-global-retail-sales-growth/

Steiner, G. A. (1971). *Business and Society*. New York: Random House.

Steinhauer, S. R., Siegle, G. J., Condray, R., & Pless, M. (2004). Sympathetic and Parasympathetic Innervation of Pupillary Dilation during Sustained Processing. *International Journal of Psychophysiology*, *52*(1), 77–86. doi:10.1016/j.ijpsycho.2003.12.005 PMID:15003374

Stender, M., & Ritz, T. (2006). Modeling of B2B mobile commerce processes. *International Journal of Production Economics*, *101*(1), 128–139. doi:10.1016/j.ijpe.2005.05.017

Stephen, A. T., & Lehmann, D. R. (2012). Using incentives to encourage word-of-mouth transmissions that lead to fast information diffusion. *SSRN Electronic Journal*, *07/2012*. doi:10.2139/ssrn.2102661

Stern, L., & Kaufmann, P. (1985). Electronic data interchange in selected consumer goods industries: an interorganizational perspective. In R. Buzzell (Ed.), Marketing in an Electronic Age (pp. 52-73). Boston: Harvard Business School Press.

Stevens, G. A., & Burley, J. (2003). Piloting the Rocket of Radical Innovation. *Research Technology Management*, *46*(2), 16–26.

Stevens, L. E., & Fiske, S. T. (1995). Motivation and cognition in social life: A social survival perspective. *Social Cognition*, *13*(3), 189–214. doi:10.1521/soco.1995.13.3.189

Stevenson, W. (2001). *Estatística aplicada à administração*. Saint Paul, Brazil: Harbra Publisher.

Stewart, J. B. (2012, July 27). Behind eBay's comeback. *New York Times.* Retrieved from http://www.nytimes.com/2012/07/28/business/ebays-turnaround-defies-convention-for-internet-companies.html?pagewanted=all&_r=0

Stringfellow, A., Nie, W., & Bowen, D. (2004). CRM: Profiting from understanding customer needs. *Business Horizons*, *47*(5), 45–52. doi:10.1016/j.bushor.2004.07.008

Ströbel, M. (2000a). On auctions as the negotiation paradigm of electronic markets: Success factors, limitations and research directions. *Journal of Electronic Markets*, *10*(1), 39–44. doi:10.1080/10196780050033962

Ströbel, M. (2000b). Effects of electronic markets on negotiation processes.*Proceedings of 8th European Conference on Information Systems, Trends in Information and Communication Systems for the 21st Century, ECIS 2000*, Vienna, Austria.

Stross, R. (2013, February 9). Digital Tags Help Ensure the Price Is Right. *The New York Times.*

Strugatch, W. (2011). Turning values into valuation: Can corporate social responsibility survive hard times and emerge intact? *Journal of Management Development*, *30*(1), 44–48. doi:10.1108/02621711111098352

Subramanian, R., & Gopalakrishna, P. (2001). The market orientation–performance relationship in the context of a developing economy: An empirical analysis. *Journal of Business Research*, *53*(1), 1–13. doi:10.1016/S0148-2963(99)00109-5

Suduc, A., Bîzoi, M., Gorghiu, G., & Gorghiu, L. (2011). Information and communication technologies in science education. *Procedia: Social and Behavioral Sciences*, *15*, 1076–1080. doi:10.1016/j.sbspro.2011.03.241

Su, M., & Hu, Q. (2000). An exploratory study of internet auction business models. *Proceedings of IRMA Conference,*Anchorage, Alaska. (pp. 561-565).

Sundararajan, M. (2010). Physiological Emotions and Entrepreneurial Decisions. *Global Business and Management Research*, *2*(4), 310–322.

Sundar, S. S., & Kalyanaraman, S. (2004). Arousal, Memory, And Impression – Formation effects of animation speed in Web Advertising. *Journal of Advertising*, *33*(1), 7–17. doi:10.1080/00913367.2004.10639152

Sun, J., & Hsu, Y. (2012). An experimental study of learner perceptions of the interactivity of web-based instruction. *Interacting with Computers*, *24*(1), 35–48. doi:10.1016/j.intcom.2011.11.001

Szmigin, I., & Bourne, H. (1998). Consumer in relationship marketing. *Journal of Consumer Marketing*, *15*(6), 544–557. doi:10.1108/07363769810240545

Szykman, S., Sriram, R. D., & Regli, W. C. (2001). The role of knowledge in next-generation product development systems. *Journal of Computing and Information Science in Engineering*, *1*(1), 3–11. doi:10.1115/1.1344238

Tajfel, H. (1970). Aspects of national and ethnic loyalty. *Social Sciences Information. Information Sur les Sciences Sociales*, *9*(3), 119–144. doi:10.1177/053901847000900305

Takahashi, T. (2000). *Sociedade da informação no Brasil. Green book.* Brasília, Brazil: Science and Technology Ministry.

Talbot, D. (2011, October 18). A Social-Media Decoder. *MIT Technology Review.*

Talvinen, J. M. (1995). Information Systems in Marketing. Identifying Opportunities for New Applications. *European Journal of Marketing*, *29*(1), 8–26. doi:10.1108/03090569510075307

Tang, F.-F., & Gan, L. (2004). Pricing convergence between dot.coms and hybrids: Empirical evidence from the online toy market. *Journal of Targeting. Measurement and Analysis for Marketing*, *12*(4), 340–352. doi:10.1057/palgrave.jt.5740121

Taylor, R. S. (1962). Process of Asking Questions. *American Documentation*, *13*(4), 391–396. doi:10.1002/asi.5090130405

Teece, D. J., Pisano, G., & Shuen, A. (1997). Dynamic capabilities & strategic management. *Strategic Management Journal*, *18*(7), 509–533. doi:10.1002/(SICI)1097-0266(199708)18:7<509::AID-SMJ882>3.0.CO;2-Z

Teo, T., Devadoss, P., & Pan, S. (2006). Towards a holistic perspective of customer relationship management (CRM) implementation: A case study of the Housing and Development Board, Singapore. *Decision Support Systems*, *42*(3), 1613–1627. doi:10.1016/j.dss.2006.01.007

The Economist. (2008). Viral Marketing. Retrieved from http://www.economist.com/node/12677019

The Economist. (2009). Friends for Sale: What is a Facebook friend worth? Retrieved from http://www.economist.com/node/14460087

Theis, T., & Tomkin, J. (2012). *Sustainability: A comprehensive foundation*. Houston: Connexions.

Thomas, G. M. (2004). Building the buzz in the hive mind. *Journal of Consumer Behaviour*, *4*(1), 64–72. doi:10.1002/cb.158

Thompson, J., Scott, J. M., & Martin, F. (2014). *Strategic Management: Awareness and Change* (7th ed.). Hampshire, UK: CENGAGE Learning.

Timmermans, S., Bowker, G., & Star, S. L. (1996). Infrastructure and organizational transformation: classifying nurses' work. In W. Orlikowski, G. Walsham, M. Jones, & J. DeGross (Eds.), *Information technology and changes in organizational work* (pp. 344–370). London: Chapman and Hall.

Tosun, L. (2012). Motives for Facebook use and expressing "true self" on the Internet. *Computers in Human Behavior*, *28*(4), 1510–1517. doi:10.1016/j.chb.2012.03.018

Tosun, L., & Lajunen, T. (2010). Does internet use reflect your personality? Relationship between Eysenk's personality dimensions and internet use. *Computers in Human Behavior*, *26*(2), 162–167. doi:10.1016/j.chb.2009.10.010

TrendWatching. (2006). Customer – Made: time to tap into the global brain. Retrieved from http://trendwatching.com/trends/CUSTOMER-MADE.htm

Troy, L. C., Hirunyawipada, T., & Paswan, A. K. (2008). Cross-Functional Integration & New Product Success: An Empirical Investigation of the Findings. *Journal of Marketing*, *72*(6), 132–146. doi:10.1509/jmkg.72.6.132

Trusov, M., Bodapati, A. V., & Bucklin, R. E. (2006). *Your members are also your customers: Marketing for Internet social networks* (Working Paper). University of California, Los Angeles.

Trusov, M., Bodapati, A. V., & Bucklin, R. E. (2010). Determining influential users in internet social networks. *JMR, Journal of Marketing Research*, *47*(4), 643–658. doi:10.1509/jmkr.47.4.643

Trusov, M., Bucklin, R. E., & Pauwels, K. H. (2009). Effects of word-of-mouth versus traditional marketing: Findings from an internet social networking site. *Journal of Marketing*, *73*(5), 90–102. doi:10.1509/jmkg.73.5.90

Tsai, H. H. (2011). Research trends analysis by comparing data mining and customer relationship management through bibliometric methodology. *Scientometrics*, *87*(3), 425–450. doi:10.1007/s11192-011-0353-6

Tsai, Y. C., & Yeh, J. C. (2010). Perceived risk of information security and privacy in online shopping: A study of environmentally sustainable products. *African Journal of Business Management*, *4*(18), 4057–4066.

Tuominen, M., Rajala, A., & Möller, K. (2004). Market-driving versus market-driven: Divergent roles of market orientation in business relationships. *Industrial Marketing Management*, *33*(3), 207–217. doi:10.1016/j.indmarman.2003.10.010

Turban, E. (1997). Auctions and bidding on the internet: An assessment. *Focus Theme*, *7*(4), 7–11.

Turow, J., King, J., Hoofnagle, C., Bleakley, A., & Hennesy, M. (2009). *Americans reject tailored advertising and three activities that enable it.* Annenberg School of Communication Department Papers.

Turunen, T. T., & Toivonen, M. (2011). Organizing customer-oriented service business in manufacturing. *Operations Management Research, 4*(1-2), 74–84. doi:10.1007/s12063-011-0047-5

Tuzhilin, A. (2012). Customer relationship management and Web mining: The next frontier. *Data Mining and Knowledge Discovery, 24*(3), 584–612. doi:10.1007/s10618-012-0256-z

U.S. Department of the Census. (2013). The 2011 E-commerce multi-sector E-Stats report. Retrieved from http://www.census.gov/econ/estats/

Ulrich, K. T. (1995). The Role of Product Architecture in the Manufacturing Firm. *Research Policy, 24*(3), 419–440. doi:10.1016/0048-7333(94)00775-3

Ulrich, K. T., & Eppinger, S. D. (1995). *Product Design & Development* (5th ed.). McGraw-Hill, Inc.

Underwood, R. L. (2003). The communicative power of product packaging: Creating brand identity via lived & mediated experience. *Journal of Marketing Theory and Practice, 10*(4), 58–69.

United Nations Commission on International Trade Law. (1998). *UNCITRAL model law on electronic commerce guide to enactment.* Vienna, Austria: United Nations.

United Nations. (2005). *Global E-government Readiness Report.* From E-government to E-inclusion.

Upbin, B. (2013, February 8). IBM's Watson Gets Its First Piece Of Business In Healthcare. *Forbes.* Retrieved from http://www.forbes.com/sites/bruceupbin/2013/02/08/ibms-watson-gets-its-first-piece-of-business-in-healthcare/

Upbin, B. (2013, May21). IBM's Watson Now A Customer Service Agent, Coming To Smartphones Soon. *Forbes.*

Urberg, K. A., Luo, Q., Pilgrim, C., & Degirmencioglu, S. M. (2003). A two-stage model of peer influence in adolescent substance use: Individual and relationship-specific differences in susceptibility to influence. *Addictive Behaviors, 28*(7), 1243–1256. doi:10.1016/S0306-4603(02)00256-3 PMID:12915166

Valkenburg, P. M., Peter, J., & Schouten, A. P. (2006). Friend networking sites and their relationship to adolescents' well-being and social self-esteem. *Cyberpsychology & Behavior, 9*(5), 584–590. doi:10.1089/cpb.2006.9.584 PMID:17034326

Valle, S., & Avella, L. (2003). Cross-Functionality & Leadership of New Product Development Teams. *European Journal of Innovation Management, 6*(1), 32–47. doi:10.1108/14601060310456319

Van den Bulte, C., & Wuyts, S. (2007). *Social networks and marketing.* Cambridge, MA: Marketing Science Institute.

Van den Poel, D., & Buckinx, W. (2005). Predicting online-purchasing behaviour. *European Journal of Operational Research, 166*(2), 557–575. doi:10.1016/j.ejor.2004.04.022

van der Lans, R., van Bruggen, G., Eliashberg, J., & Wierenga, B. (2010). A viral branching model for predicting the spread of electronic word-of-mouth. *Marketing Science, 29*(2), 348–365. doi:10.1287/mksc.1090.0520

Van Dijck, J. (2009). Media, Culture & Society: Users like you? Theorizing agency in user-generated content. *Media Culture & Society, 31*(1), 41–58. doi:10.1177/0163443708098245

van Doorn, J., Lemon, K. N., Mittal, V., Nass, S., Pick, D., Pirner, P., & Verhoef, P. C. (2010). Customer Engagement Behaviour: Theoretical Foundations and Research Directions. *Journal of Service Research, 13*(3), 253–266. doi:10.1177/1094670510375599 van Knippenberg, D., & Schippers, M. C. (2007). Work group diversity. *Annual Review of Psychology*, *58*(1), 515–541. doi:10.1146/annurev.psych.58.110405.085546 PMID:16903805

Van Noort, G., Kerkhof, P., & Fennis, B. M. (2007). Online versus conventional shopping: Consumers' risk perception and regulatory focus. *Cyberpsychology & Behavior*, *10*(5), 731–733. doi:10.1089/cpb.2007.9959 PMID:17927547

Van Oorschot, K., Sengupta, K., Akkermans, H., & Van Wassenhove, L. (2010). Get Fat Fast: Surviving Stage-Gate® in NPD. *Journal of Product Innovation Management*, *27*(6), 828–839. doi:10.1111/j.1540-5885.2010.00754.x

van Wezel, M., & Potharst, R. (2007). Improved customer choice predictions using ensemble methods. *European Journal of Operational Research*, *181*(1), 436–452. doi:10.1016/j.ejor.2006.05.029

Venkatesh, A. (1980). Changing Roles of Women – A Life Style Analysis. *The Journal of Consumer Research*, *7*(2), 189–197. doi:10.1086/208806

Venkatesh, A. (1998). Cybermarketscapes and consumer freedoms and identities. *European Journal of Marketing*, *32*(7/8), 664–676. doi:10.1108/03090569810224065

Venkatesh, V., Morris, M. G., Davis, G. B., & Davis, F. D. (2003). User acceptance of information technology: Toward a unified view. *Management Information Systems Quarterly*, *27*(3), 425–478.

Verhoef, P. C., & Donkers, B. (2001). Predicting customer potential value: An application in the insurance industry. *Decision Support Systems*, *32*(2), 189–199. doi:10.1016/S0167-9236(01)00110-5

Verzberger, Y. Y. I. (1994). Collective risk taking: The decision making group & organization. Paper presented at the 35th Annual Convention of the International Studies Association, Washington D.C.

Vijayasarathy, L. R., & Jones, J. M. (2001). Do internet shopping aids make a difference? An empirical investigation. *Electronic Markets*, *11*(1), 75–83. doi:10.1080/10196780151105483

Villano, M. (2008). Technology acceptance model 3 and a research agenda on interventions. *Decision Sciences*, *39*(2), 272–315.

Viswesvaran, C. (2003). Introduction to special issue: Role of technology in shaping the future of staffing and assessment. *International Journal of Selection and Assessment*, *11*(2-3), 1078–1112. doi:10.1111/1468-2389.00233

Vitor, D. A., Ayimey, E. K., & Gayibor, R. A. (2013). Does Sales Promotion Influence Buyer Behavior? A Study of PZ Cussons Limited. *British Journal of Economics. Management & Trade*, *3*(2), 141–152.

Vivek, S. D., Beatty, S. E., & Morgan, R. M. (2012). Customer Engagement: Exploring customer relationships beyond purchase. *Journal of Marketing Theory and Practice*, *20*(2), 122–145. doi:10.2753/MTP1069-6679200201

Vlosky, R. P., Fontenot, R., & Blalock, L. (2000). Extranets: Impacts on Business Practices and Relationships. *Journal of Business and Industrial Marketing*, *15*(6), 438–457. doi:10.1108/08858620010349510

vom Berg, B. W., Valdés, A. R., Memari, A., Barakat, N., & Gómez, J. M. (2014). Customer segmentation based on compensatory fuzzy logic within a sustainability CRM for intermodal mobility. *Soft Computing for Business Intelligence: Studies in Computational Intelligence*, *537*, 415–429. doi:10.1007/978-3-642-53737-0_27

Voss, G. B., & Voss, Z. G. (2000). Strategic Orientation & Firm Performance in an Artistic Environment. *Journal of Marketing*, *64*(1), 67–83. doi:10.1509/jmkg.64.1.67.17993

Vries, G., Terwel, B. W., Ellemers, N., & Daamen, D. D. (2013). Sustainability or profitability? How communicated motives for environmental policy affect public perceptions of corporate greenwashing. *Corporate Social Responsibility and Environmental Management*, *1*(2), 1–4.

Waddock, S. (2008). Building a new institutional infrastructure for corporate responsibility. *The Academy of Management Perspectives*, *22*(3), 87–108. doi:10.5465/AMP.2008.34587997

Wagner, M. (2011, January 19). What Does IBM's Watson Mean for Marketing? *The CMO Site*. Retrieved from http://www.thecmosite.com/author.asp?section_id=1137&doc_id=203302

Wahba, G. (1990). *Spline models for observational data*: Society for industrial and applied mathematics.

Walther, J. B. (2004). Language and communication technology: Introduction to the special issue. *Journal of Language and Social Psychology*, *23*(4), 384–396. doi:10.1177/0261927X04269584

Wan, Y., & Peng, Gang (2010). What's next for shopbots? *IEEE Computer Society*, 43(5), 20-26.

Warschauer, M. (2006). *Tecnologia e inclusão social, a exclusão digital em debate*. Saint Paul, Brazil: Senac Publisher.

Wasserman, S., & Faust, K. (1994). *Social Network Analysis: Methods and Applications*. Cambridge, MA: Cambridge University Press. doi:10.1017/CBO9780511815478

Watson, P., Wienand, N., & Worksman, G. (2009). Teaching sustainability: A valid methodology for addressing the associated problematic issues. *PWASET*, *41*(53), 2070–3740.

WCED (World Commission on Environment and Development). (1987). *Our common future*. Oxford: Oxford University Press.

Weaver, P. M., & Rotmans, J. (2006). Integrated sustainability assessment: What is it, why do it and how? *International Journal of Innovation and Sustainable Development*, *1*(4), 284–303. doi:10.1504/IJISD.2006.013732

Webb, D. J., Mohr, L. A., & Harris, K. E. (2008). A re-examination of socially responsible consumption and its measurement. *Journal of Business Research*, *61*(2), 91–98. doi:10.1016/j.jbusres.2007.05.007

Webster, F. E. (2002). Marketing management in changing times. *Marketing Management*, *11*(1), 18–23.

Weigelt, C., & Miller, D. J. (2013). Implications of internal organization structure for firm boundaries. *Strategic Management Journal*, *34*(12), 1411–1434. doi:10.1002/smj.2074

Wen, C., Prybutok, V. R., & Xu, C. (2011). An integrated model for customer online repurchase intention. *Journal of Computer Information Systems*, *52*(1), 14–23.

Wendelin, R. (2004). The nature and change of bonds in industrial business relationships [Doctoral dissertation]. Hanken School of Economics and Business Administration

Wendelin, R. (2011). Bond audit, a method for evaluating business relationships. *Journal of Business and Industrial Marketing*, *26*(3), 211–217. doi:10.1108/08858621111115930

Wenyan, H., & Bolivar, A. (2008). Online auctions efficiency: A survey of eBay auctions. *WWW*, *2008*, 925–933.

Wernerfelt, B. (2005). Product development resources & the scope of the firm. *Journal of Marketing*, *69*(2), 15–23. doi:10.1509/jmkg.69.2.15.60763

Westerman, S. J., Sutherland, E. J., Gardner, P. H., Baig, N., Critchley, C., Hickey, C., & Zervos, Z. et al. (2013). The design of consumer packaging: Effects of manipulations of shape, orientation, & alignment of graphical forms on consumers' assessments. *Food Quality and Preference*, *27*(1), 8–17. doi:10.1016/j.foodqual.2012.05.007

Wheelwright, S. C., & Clark, K. B. (1992). *Creating project plans to focus product development*. Harvard Business School Publishing.

White, A. (2005). *Fade, integrate or transform? The future of CSR* (Issue Paper). Business for Social Responsibility. Retrieved from www.bsr.org

Wigley, S. (2008). Gauging consumers' responses to CSR activities: Does increased awareness make cents? *Public Relations Review*, *34*(3), 306–308. doi:10.1016/j.pubrev.2008.03.034

Wikström, E., & Wigmo, J. (2010). "Social media marketing: What role can social media play as a marketing tool?" Bachelor, Linnaeus University.

Wilkinson, A. (1991). Developing an Expert System on Project Evaluation. *R & D Management*, *21*(1), 19–29. doi:10.1111/j.1467-9310.1991.tb00726.x

Williamson, O. E. (1975). *Markets and hierarchies*. New York, NY: The Free press.

Wilson, R. F. (2000). The six simple principles of viral marketing. *Web Marketing Today*. Retrieved from http://library.softgenx.com/Children/marketing/ViralMarketing.pdf

Wilson, D., & Mummalaneni, V. (1986). Bonding and commitment in buyer-seller relationships: A preliminary conceptualizations. *Journal of Industrial Marketing and Purchasing*, *1*(3), 44–58.

Wilson, H., Daniel, E., & McDonald, M. (2002). Factors for success in customer relationship management (CRM) systems. *Journal of Marketing Management*, *18*(2), 193–219. doi:10.1362/0267257022775918

Wilson, J., & Morgan, J. (2011). Friends or Freeloaders & quest; Encouraging brand conscience and introducing the concept of emotion-based consumer loss mitigation. *Journal of Brand Management*, *18*(9), 659–676. doi:10.1057/bm.2011.4

Wind, J., & Rangaswamy, A. (2000). Customerization: The Next Revolution in Mass Customization (MSI Report No. 00-108). Marketing Science Institute, Cambridge, MA.

Windsor, D. (2001). The future of corporate social responsibility. *The International Journal of Organizational Analysis*, *9*(3), 225–256. doi:10.1108/eb028934

Wind, Y., & Mahajan, V. (2001). *Digital Marketing: Global Strategies from the World's Leading Experts*. Edição de John Wiley and Sons.

Winer, R. S. (2001). A Framework for Customer Relationship Management. *California Management Review*, *43*(4), 89–105. doi:10.2307/41166102

Wise, R., & Morrison, D. (1999). Beyond the exchange--the future of B2B. *Harvard Business Review*, *78*(6), 86–96. PMID:11184979

Witcher, B. J., & Chau, V. S. (2014). *Strategic Management: Principles and Practice* (2nd ed.). Hampshire, UK: CENGAGE Learning.

Wojnicki, A. C., & Godes, D. (2008). *Word-of-mouth as self-enhancement* (HBS Marketing Research Paper No. 06-01). Boston, MA: Harvard Business School Marketing Unit.

Wolf, L., & Morrissey, S. (2013). Brain Initiative Unveiled. *Chemical and Engineering News*, *91*(14), 9–9.

Wolford, J. (2013). eBay Seller Sues Buyer Over Negative Feedback. *WebProNews*. Retrieved from http://www.webpronews.com/ebay-seller-sues-buyer-over-negative-feedback-2013-04

Woodcock, N., Green, A., & Starkey, M. (2011). Social CRM as a business strategy. *Journal of Database Marketing & Customer Strategy Management*, *18*(1), 50–64. doi:10.1057/dbm.2011.7

Woodcock, N., Stone, M., & Foss, B. (2003). *The customer management scorecard: Managing CRM for profit*. London, UK: Kogan Page.

Woodward, B., Davis, D. C., & Hodis, F. A. (2007). The relationship between ethical decision making and ethical reasoning in information technology students. *Journal of Information Systems Education*, *18*(2), 193–202.

Wu, F., Hoon, L. S., & Yuzhu, Z. (2011). Dos and donts for Chinese companies investing in the United States: Lessons from Huawei and Haier. *Thunderbird International Business Review*, *53*(4), 501–515. doi:10.1002/tie.20426

Wu, F., Mahajan, V., & Balasubramanian, S. (2003). An analysis of e-business adoption and its impact on business performance. *Journal of the Academy of Marketing Science*, *31*(4), 425–447. doi:10.1177/0092070303255379

Wu, K. W., Huang, S. Y., Yen, D. C., & Popova, I. (2012). The effect of online privacy policy on consumer privacy concern and trust. *Computers in Human Behavior*, *28*(3), 889–897. doi:10.1016/j.chb.2011.12.008

Wulf, K., Odekerken-Schroder, G., & Iacobucci, D. (2001). Investments in consumer relationships: A cross-country and cross-industry exploration. *Journal of Marketing*, *65*(4), 33–50. doi:10.1509/jmkg.65.4.33.18386

Wurman, P. R. (2001). Dynamic pricing in the virtual marketplace. *IEEE Internet Computing*, *5*(2), 36–42. doi:10.1109/4236.914646

Wurman, R. (2005). *Ansiedade da informação 2: Um guia para quem comunica e dá instruções*. Saint Paul, Brazil: Cultura Publisher.

Xie, Y. Y., Li, X., Ngai, E. W. T., & Ying, W. Y. (2009). Customer churn prediction using improved balanced random forests. *Expert Systems with Applications*, *36*(3), 5445–5449. doi:10.1016/j.eswa.2008.06.121

Xu, M., & Walton, J. (2005). Gaining customer knowledge through analytical CRM. *Industrial Management & Data Systems*, *105*(7), 955–971. doi:10.1108/02635570510616139

Xu, Y., Yen, D. C., Lin, B., & Chou, D. C. (2002). Adopting customer relationship management technology. *Industrial Management & Data Systems*, *102*(8-9), 442–452. doi:10.1108/02635570210445871

Yahaya, S. Y., & Abu-Bakar, N. (2007). New Product Development Management Issues & Decision Making Approaches. *Management Decision*, *45*(7), 1123–1142. doi:10.1108/00251740710773943

Yakup, D., Mucahit, C., & Reyhan, O. (2011). The Impact of Cultural Factors on Consumer Buying Behaviors Examined through an Empirical Study. *International Journal of Business and Social Science*, *2*(5), 109–114.

Yang, L., & Järvenpää, S. (2005). Trust and Radio Frequency Identification (RFID) Adoption within an Alliance.*Proceedings of the 38th Hawaii International Conference on System Sciences*. Hawaii, USA. doi:10.1109/HICSS.2005.643

Yang, Y. H. (2010). Web user behavioral profiling for user identification. *Decision Support Systems*, *49*(3), 261–271. doi:10.1016/j.dss.2010.03.001

Yao, Z., Sarlin, P., Eklund, T., & Back, B. (2014). Combining visual customer segmentation and response modeling. *Neural Computing & Applications*, *25*(1), 123–134. doi:10.1007/s00521-013-1454-3

Yap, C. M., & Souder, W. E. (1994). Factors Influencing New Product Success & Failure in Small Entrepreneurial High-Technology Electronics Firms. *Journal of Product Innovation Management*, *11*(5), 418–432. doi:10.1016/0737-6782(94)90030-2

Yen, C. H., & Lu, H. P. (2008). Effects of e-service quality on loyalty intention: An empirical study in online auction. *Managing Service Quality*, *18*(2), 127–146. doi:10.1108/09604520810859193

Yim, F. H. K., Anderson, R. E., & Swaminathan, S. (2004). Customer relationship management: Its dimensions and effect on customer outcomes. *Journal of Personal Selling & Sales Management*, *24*(4), 263–278.

Yin, R. (1994). *Case Study Research–Design and Methods*. London: SAGE.

Yi, Y. (1990). Cognitive and Affective Priming Effects of the Context for Print Advertisements. *Journal of Advertising*, *19*(2), 40–48. doi:10.1080/00913367.1990.10673186

Youn, S. (2009). Determinants of online privacy concern and its influence on privacy protection behaviors among young adolescents. *The Journal of Consumer Affairs*, *43*(3), 389–418. doi:10.1111/j.1745-6606.2009.01146.x

You, P.-S. (1999). Dynamic pricing in airline seat management for flights with multiple flight legs. *Transportation Science*, *33*(2), 192–206. doi:10.1287/trsc.33.2.192

Ystats. (2013). Africa B2C ecommerce report. Retrieved from http://www.ystats.com/uploads/report_abstracts/1058.pdf?PHPSESSID=2a2ba9548054959d1dfc4668b2754844

Yu, Y., Zhou, Z. H., & Ting, K. M. (2007, Oct 28-31). *Cocktail ensemble for regression*. Paper presented at the 7th IEEE International Conference on Data Mining, Omaha, NE.

Zablah, A. R., Bellenger, D. N., & Johnston, W. J. (2004). An evaluation of divergent perspectives on customer relationship management: Towards a common understanding of an emerging phenomenon. *Industrial Marketing Management*, *33*(6), 475–489. doi:10.1016/j.indmarman.2004.01.006

Zablah, A. R., Bellenger, D. N., & Johnston, W. J. (2004). Customer Relationship Management Implementation Gaps. *Journal of Personal Selling & Sales Management*, *24*(4), 279–295. doi:10.1080/08853134.2004.10749038

Zahay, D., & Griffin, A. (2004). Customer learning processes, strategy selection, and performance in business-to-business service firms. *Decision Sciences*, *35*(2), 169–203. doi:10.1111/j.00117315.2004.02338.x

Zahir, S. (2002). Designing a knowledge-based interface for intelligent shopping agents. *Journal of Computer Information Systems*, *43*(1), 31–41.

Zahra, S. A., & George, G. (2002). Absorptive capacity: A review, reconceptualization, and extension. *Academy of Management Review*, *27*(2), 185–203.

Zaker, R. A., & Ansari, A. A. (2013). Towards improving quality of e-commerce websites in hospitals. Paper presented at the knowledge globalisation conference, Istanbul, Turkey.

Zarrella, D. (2009). *The Social Media Marketing Book*. Sebastopol, Canada: O'Reilly Media, Inc.

Zeithaml, V. A. (1988). Consumer perceptions of price, quality, and value: A means-end model and synthesis of evidence. *Journal of Marketing*, *52*(3), 2–22. doi:10.2307/1251446

Zeithammer, R. (2007). Optimal Selling in Dynamic Auctions: Adaptation versus Commitment. *Marketing Science*, *26*(6), 859–867. doi:10.1287/mksc.1070.0269

Zhang, L., Lee, M. K., Zhang, Z., & Banerjee, P. (2003). Critical success factors of enterprise resource planning systems implementation success in China. *System Sciences -Proceedings of the 36th Annual Hawaii International Conference on* (pp. 10). IEEE. doi:10.1109/HICSS.2003.1174613

Zhang, C. X., & Zhang, J. S. (2008). A local boosting algorithm for solving classification problems. *Computational Statistics & Data Analysis*, *52*(4), 1928–1941. doi:10.1016/j.csda.2007.06.015

Zhang, J., & Duan, Y. (2010). The Impact of Different Types of Market Orientation on Product Innovation Performance. *Management Decision*, *48*(6), 849–867. doi:10.1108/00251741011053433

Zhang, L., Tan, W., Xu, Y., & Tan, G. (2012). Dimensions of consumers' perceived risk and their influences on online consumers' purchasing behaviour. *Communications in Information Science and Management Engineering*, *2*(7), 8–14.

Zhang, X., & Vogel, D. (2011). Electronic commerce in web 3.0: The evidence from emerging economics[IJCSIT]. *International Journal of Computer Science & Information Technology*, *3*(3), 240–254. doi:10.5121/ijcsit.2011.3317

Zhao, X., Huo, B., Selen, W., & Yeung, J. H. Y. (2011). The impact of internal integration and relationship commitment on external integration. *Journal of Operations Management*, *29*(1/2), 17–32. doi:10.1016/j.jom.2010.04.004

Zikopolous, P. C., de Roos, D., Parasuraman, K., Deutsch, T., Corrigan, D., & Giles, J. (2013). Harnessing the Power of Big Data. The IBM Big Data Platform. New York, NY: McGraw-Hill.

Zineldin, M. (2006). The royalty of loyalty: CRM, quality and retention. *Journal of Consumer Marketing*, *23*(7), 430–437. doi:10.1108/07363760610712975

Zubcsek, P. P., & Sarvary, M. (2011). Advertising to a social network. *Quantitative Marketing and Economics*, *9*(1), 71–107. doi:10.1007/s11129-010-9093-9

Zwick, D., & Dholakia, N. (2004). Consumer subjectivity in the age of Internet: The radical concept of marketing control through customer relationship management. *Information and Organization*, *14*(3), 211–236. doi:10.1016/j.infoandorg.2004.01.002

About the Contributors

Theodosios Tsiakis is a Lecturer of Management of Information Systems with the Dept. of Marketing of the Alexandrian Technological Educational Institute of Thessaloniki. He holds a PhD in Information Security Economics from the Univ. of Macedonia, Greece. His research interests include information security economics, risk, trust and human factors. He has published several articles in the above area, as well as in the broader area of Management of Information Systems.

***

Ana Margarida Barreto holds a PhD degree from the New University of Lisbon where she teaches Marketing. She completed fieldwork as a visiting scholar under the auspices of the University of Texas at Austin, University of Westminster, King's College of London, and Columbia University. Her research, among other interests, pertains to measure the effectiveness of digital communication, the relationship between brands and consumers within social networking sites, and the electronic world-of-mouth. Ana Margarida Barreto has worked for five years in communication and advertising, both in Portugal and in Spain. Her research interests also include social contagion, social influence, consumer behavior and neuroeconomics.

Koen W. de Bock obtained a Ph.D. from Ghent University, Belgium, in 2010 and is currently working as a marketing professor at the IÉSEG School of Management with campuses in Lille and Paris, France. He is a visiting professor in MBA programmes of both the University of Stellenbosch Business School (USB) in Cape Town, South Africa, and at the TIAS School for Business and Society, Utrecht, the Netherlands. His courses focus on Digital Marketing and Web Analytics. His research projects involve innovative methods for predictive customer analytics and his work has been published in international journals such as Journal of Business Research, Computational Statistics & Data Analysis and Expert Systems with Applications.

Othman Boujena, is an associate professor of marketing at Neoma Business School (France) and the Head of the research center for Markets, Brands & Experiences (MBE). He is also responsible of the Major in Marketing. He holds a PhD from Aix-Marseille University (IAE Aix Graduate School of Management). He has been a visiting research fellow at New York University in 2013 and Georgia State University in 2005. He teaches consumer behavior, CRM, marketing strategy, and marketing research. His research interests focus on relationship marketing, CRM and sales force automation. He is author/coauthor of several papers in international marketing conferences and journals like AMA, NCSM, Thought

Leadership on the Sales Profession Conference, GSSI Conference, JPSSM journal, ANZMAC, IMP...). He also contributed to many books through chapters on CRM, customer centricity, customer experience and loyalty programs. He also served as a reviewer for many international conferences and journals like Association for Consumer Research (ACR), AMA conference, European Marketing Academy Conference, European ACR, Academy of Marketing, European Management Journal, International Conference of French Marketing Association or Academy of Management.

Marisa Cesário holds a PhD in Economics and is an Assistant Professor at the Faculty of Economics, University of Algarve. She is member of the Research Centre for Spatial and Organizational Dynamics and teaches microeconomics and public economics in undergraduate courses and regional economics and industrial development in master degrees. She published scientific work related with economic geography, globalization, and technological change.

Kristof Coussement is an Associate Professor of Marketing Analytics at the IÉSEG School of Management (Lille/Paris, France) (EQUIS,AACSB). He teaches several marketing courses including "Customer Relationship Management" and "Database Marketing" in which students are taught the theoretical principles of all aspects in operational and analytical CRM and the methodological foundations of predictive marketing modeling. His main research interests are all aspects in Customer Intelligence and Social Media & Online Community Intelligence using data- and text-mining techniques. He has published in international peer-reviewed journals like Decision Support Systems, Information & Management, the European Journal of Operational Research, the Journal of Business Research, the European Journal of Marketing, Computational Statistics & Data Analysis, and Expert Systems with Applications, among others. Improving his 'practical' experience over the years by doing several real-life projects in a different number of industries, his main focus lies on doing profound academic research with a high-added value to business.

Nikolaos Dimitriadis (MBA, PhD) is applying neurological and behavioral sciences in marketing and communications for over a decade. His award-winning, unique methodology for internal communications based on brain-friendly methods has been implemented by multinationals and local companies throughout the SEE region. Nikolaos has enjoyed a 360o experience in practicing marketing since he worked on the client, agency and academic sides. As a consultant, Nikolaos worked with numerous marketing and communications agencies helping them winning and managing important accounts such as Nestle, Holcim, IKEA, and Banca Intesa Sanpaoplo. One of his projects won the two most prestigious international awards in corporate communications (IPRA and SABRE awards, 2009). Nikolaos is frequently invited in SEE to talk about marketing, brand strategy and neuro-communications. He lectures at the University of Sheffield Executive MBA program in SEE and he is also the strategy consultant at DNA Communications, a full-service advertising agency based in Belgrade, Serbia.

Sílvia Fernandes is an Assistant Professor at Faculty of Economics, University of Algarve and holds a PhD in Information Economics. She is member of the Research Centre for Spatial and Organizational Dynamics and teaches information technology, monetary economics, innovation economics and entrepreneurship in undergraduate and master courses. She has publications in books, journals, and conference proceedings related with innovation, information systems, social networks, technological diffusion, and mobile systems.

Sandra Filipe is an Assistant Professor at the Higher Institute of Accounting and Administration of the University of Aveiro (ISCA-UA) since 1999. She is a Bachelor of Management by the Economy Faculty of Coimbra University, in 1996, Master in Management at ISCTE - Business School of Lisbon University Institute, in 2000, and doctoral student in Marketing at ISCTE since 2009. Currently, she is researcher at the Research Unit of Governance, Competitiveness and Public Policy (GOVCOPP) of University of Aveiro. Her main research interests are relationship marketing, behaviour consumer, digital marketing and corporate social responsibility. She has published in several national and international journals.

Ed Forrest is Professor of Marketing and Chair of the Department of Management & Marketing in the College of Business & Public Policy at the University of Alaska Anchorage. Dr. Forrest graduated from the University of Wisconsin, served on the faculty at Florida State University and Griffith University- Queensland, Australia, where he was Head of School- Marketing (1997-2000). He has edited & authored the books - Interactive Marketing-The Future Present; CyberMarketing-Your On-line Consultants; Internet Marketing Intelligence: Research Tools, Techniques & Resources; and The New York Times-Guide to Marketing; Internet Marketing Intelligence: Resources & Techniques." His most recent publications on emerging technologies impact on Marketing include: "Additive Digital Manufacturing: A Paradigm Shift in the Production Process and Its Socio-economic Impacts," in Engineering Management Research, November, 2013; "Mobile Rising: Mobile "Marketing & the Imminent Predominance of the Smartphone," in E-Marketing in Developed and Developing Countries: Emerging Practices (Publisher: IGI Global, April, 2013).

Anka Gorgiev is investigating to what extend neuroscience and behavioral sciences are affecting marketing and its practice. As a practitioner, she worked in marketing communications agency, consulting some of the major brands. She also served as a brand manager for three leading daily newspapers in Serbia. Anka obtained her BA degree in Business Studies (Marketing) and her MA degree in Marketing, Advertising and Public Relations, both from the University of Sheffield. In 2013, Anka started her research as a full-time PhD Candidate in Neuromarketing under the Doctoral Program offered by the University of Sheffield and South East European Research Center.

Giuseppe Granata Graduated in Economics and Ph.D. in Business Management, later he attended a Master science in Business Management at the Business School of Rome. Through his studies in the field of Marketing and, in particular, marketing and communications, has been started active collaboration with organizations and companies both nationally and internationally. Professor of business management, marketing and communications, has been in charge "Business Communication" at the University of Cassino and Southern Lazio – Department of Economics and Law. Lecturer in marketing at the Master science in Marketing and Retail Management. Visiting professor in business management at University of Paris-Est Creteil (Upec) – Faculty of Economics and at the University of Malta. A member editor and reviewer for some journals. There are several publications in the field of management and marketing.

Goetz Greve has been a professor of Marketing at the Hamburg School of Business Administration, Germany, since 2007, and serves as Vice-President of Research & International Affairs. He holds a diploma and a PhD in Business Administration from Christian-Albrechts-University, Kiel, Germany. In his research, Professor Greve focuses on the areas of customer relationship management, sales management, and online marketing. In particular, he explores the fundamental drivers of CRM performance.

His research findings have been published in international and German journals such as the International Journal of Research in Marketing and Marketing Review, St. Gallen. Prof. Greve has published three books in the field of CRM, customer management, and online targeting. He is on the editorial board of the International Journal of Marketing Studies and serves as an ad-hoc reviewer for other journals, such as the European Journal of Marketing and the Journal of Marketing Theory and Practice. Before returning to academia, Goetz Greve worked as a strategy consultant for Accenture and OC&C Strategy Consultants from 2001 to 2007. He conducted marketing strategy and CRM implementation management projects for numerous clients, particularly in financial services, consumer, and media industries.

Nicholas Grigoriou has over 20 years of academic and practical marketing and international marketing experience in the banking, furniture, petroleum and education industries. He was awarded a doctorate degree in philosophy from Swinburne University in 2013. His Ph.D. research investigated how packaged food and beverage exporters make product customisation and standardisation decisions for export to China. His research interests are in new product development and branding. He is on the editorial review board of the International Journal of Business in Emerging Markets. His research has been published at the ANZMAC conference, the Academy of Marketing Science and the World Marketing Congress. In 2004 he published a book titled International Marketing: A Practical Approach for McGraw Hill. In 2014 he adapted Dawn Iacobucci's Marketing Management for the Asian market. The book is published by Cengage Learning (Singapore) and is titled: Marketing Management in Asia.

Bogdan Hoanca, Ph.D., is Professor of Management Information Systems and Director of Graduate Programs at the University of Alaska Anchorage, where he has been teaching since 2002. Before that, he co-founded, developed and sold a start-up that manufactures technology for increasing bandwidth on optical fiber communication links. His current research is on information security, with a particular focus on authentication using eye tracking technologies. He is a co-inventor on three US patents (with a fourth one pending) and has published more than 70 papers, book chapters and case studies. Prof. Hoanca has a Ph.D. in Electrical Engineering from the University of Southern California, a MS from Syracuse University also in Electrical Engineering, and an Electronic Engineering degree from the Polytechnic Institute of Bucharest, in Romania.

Antonios Kaniadakis is a Lecturer in Information Technology Management at Queen Mary University of London, School of Electronic Engineering and Computer Science. He was trained as a Sociologist in Greece and Canada and he received a PhD in Science, Technology & Innovation Studies from the University of Edinburgh. His research focuses on social and economic aspects of information systems innovation, predominantly in the area of finance. He is an experienced ethnographer and has held research and teaching posts at the London School of Economics and Political Science, The Open University and the University of Edinburgh.

Christos Karpasitis obtained his Multimedia and Digital Entertainment Bachelors of Science (BSc) in 2010 from Northumbria University, UK. Additionally, he holds a Master's of Science (MSc) in E-Business and Information Systems from Newcastle University, UK, with a specialization in Internet Marketing. In 2011, as part of his MSc thesis, Christos worked as an E-Marketing Consultant and Developer for Crane Automation & Industrial Suppliers Pty Ltd which is based in Sydney, Australia. In 2012 he worked as an E-Marketing Executive and Multimedia Developer in Eyelevel Cyprus, where his main areas of activity were Content Development, Web Design, Internet Marketing Consultation and Online Marketing Campaign Development. Currently he holds the position of Special Scientist at UCLan Cyprus and at the Department of Communication and Internet Studies at Cyprus University of Technology, where he teaches modules including Interactive Applications, Content Creation, Collective Intelligence, Radio Production, Digital Radio and Information and Knowledge Management. In his free time, Christos produces Digital Music and collaborates with a number of well known Electronic Music Labels from around the globe. He is now a PhD Research Scholar in the field of Multimedia and Internet Marketing. His PhD research focuses on Viral Marketing and Online Word of Mouth (WOM).

Kijpokin Kasemsap received his BEng degree in Mechanical Engineering from King Mongkut's University of Technology Thonburi, his MBA degree from Ramkhamhaeng University, and his DBA degree in Human Resource Management from Suan Sunandha Rajabhat University. He is a Special Lecturer at Faculty of Management Sciences, Suan Sunandha Rajabhat University based in Bangkok, Thailand. He is a Member of the International Association of Engineers (IAENG), the International Association of Engineers and Scientists (IAEST), the International Economics Development and Research Center (IEDRC), the International Association of Computer Science and Information Technology (IACSIT), the International Foundation for Research and Development (IFRD), and the International Innovative Scientific and Research Organization (IISRO). He also serves on the International Advisory Committee (IAC) for International Association of Academicians and Researchers (INAAR). He has numerous original research articles in top international journals, conference proceedings, and book chapters on business management, human resource management, and knowledge management published internationally.

Anastasia Mariussen (PhD) is an Associate Professor at the Oslo School of Management, where she leads the Bachelor programme in Services Management, as well as a number of modules such as digital media and marketing. Anastasia joined the Oslo School of Management after completing her PhD in Affiliate Marketing Performance Measurement at Oxford Brookes University, UK. Anastasia's research interests include digital marketing, affiliate networking, mobile marketing, online distribution, performance measurement and employment of ITC and social media in services.

Mikhail Ion Melnik is an associate professor of economics at Southern Polytechnic State University in Marietta, Georgia, USA. His research areas include online auctions and public finance. His academic research has been published in a number of leading economics journals including The Journal of Industrial Economics, The National Tax Journal, The Southern Economic Journal, The Manchester School Journal, and many others. His research has been featured on Forbes.com, by the American Enterprise Institute, Bloomberg Radio, CNBC, and other outlets. Dr. Melnik is a member of the Bloomberg Survey of economists. He is also the author of a managerial economics text, "The Basics of Economics for a Modern Manager."

Júlio Mendes holds a PhD in Management, with emphasis on strategy and organizational behavior. He is an Assistant Professor at the Faculty of Economics, University of Algarve and is an active board member of the PhD program in Tourism, Master programs in Marketing and Tourism Marketing. His research interests include quality of experience, marketing, consumer behavior, and branding. He is a member of the Research Centre for Spatial and Organizational Dynamics.

Mercy Mpinganjira is an Associate Professor in the Department of Marketing Management at the University of Johannesburg, South Africa. She holds a PhD in Management and a Masters of Business Administration (MBA) from University of Newcastle in Australia as well as a Bachelors' degree (BSc) from University of Malawi. Her current research interests are in E-Marketing as well as Marketing Strategies and Buyer Behavior. She has published widely in both local and international journals with some of her work appearing in leading Journals such as Management Dynamics, International Journal of Emerging Markets, as well as Journal of Innovation and Technology Management. She has also presented some of her research findings at leading international conferences including the Academy of Marketing Science Annual Conference (USA) and the Australia and New Zealand Marketing Academy Conference (ANZMAC). She is a member of various professional bodies including the Academy of World Business Marketing and Management Development.

Tabani Ndlovu is a Fellow of the Institute of Directors (IOD) in the UK, where he also sits on the IOD Nottinghamshire & Derbyshire regional committee. He holds a PhD in Corporate Governance from Oxford Brookes University, an MBA in Corporate Social Responsibility (CSR) from the University of Nottingham, a BCom in Marketing, a PGCTHE and is a Fellow of the Higher Education Academy. He lectures in Marketing, Sustainability and Strategy at the Nottingham Business School. His research interests span sustainability, responsible business practices, corporate governance as well as marketing and internationalisation. Tabani has worked for a number of large international corporations at the senior management / director level and is a co-founder and director of a consultancy business providing sustainability strategy advice to SMEs in the UK's East Midlands region. Outside of academia, Tabani sits on the boards of a number of East Midlands-based organisations and charities.

Kalender Özcan ATILGAN is an Assistant Professor in Business Information Management at the University of Mersin. He received his B.Sc. in industrial engineering from the University of Dokuz Eylul and his M.Sc. in MBA from the University of Dokuz Eylul. He received his Ph.D. in marketing from the University of Cukurova in 2012. His research interests focus on pricing, behavioral pricing, and dynamic pricing. Other research interests include consumer behavior, conspicuous consumption, retailing, branding and brand equity. Prior to his academic studies, Kalender also has work experience as an industrial engineer in an apparel industry. He is a member of American Marketing Association and Marketing and Marketing Researches Association in Turkey.

Giuseppe Pedeliento D.Sc. (Econ. & Bus.Adm.), is currently Post Doctoral Research Fellow in the Department of Management, Economics and Quantitative Methods at the University of Bergamo (Italy) and holds a doctorate in Marketing from the same university. Former visiting researcher and lecturer in Product and Brand Management at the Aalto School of Business (formerly Helsinki School of Economics AACSB, EQUIS, AMBA), and visiting scholar at the University of Washington Bothell, Seattle (USA), Dr. Pedeliento is member of the research staff of ELab-OPRI, the permanent research center on professional service firms of the University of Bergamo. His research include industrial marketing and branding, project marketing, multichannel retailing, consumer behavior and professional service firms.

Vanessa Ratten is an Associate Professor of Entrepreneurship and Innovation in the Department of Management, La Trobe Business School at La Trobe University, Melbourne, Australia. She teaches Entrepreneurial Business Planning, Managing Innovation in Organisations and Entrepreneurship. Dr.

Ratten has previously been on the business faculty of Duquesne University, the University of Queensland, Queensland University of Technology and Deakin University. She has won a Vice Chancellors award for community engagement with innovation and entrepreneurship programs. Dr. Ratten's main research areas are entrepreneurship, innovation and sport.

A.M. Sakkthivel is Full Professor of Marketing and Assistant Dean for Academic and Research, Sur University College, Sur, Sultanate of Oman. He holds MBA and PhD in Business Administration (Marketing). His research interests are consumer behaviour, internet consumer behaviour, marketing information, mobile promotion response behaviour, marketing environments, leisure behaviour styles, advertising tools, retailing trends, modelling customer lifetime life, promotion, mathematical modelling (Metrics). His papers appeared in the International Journal of Mobile Communications (SSCI), the Journal of Promotion Management, the Journal of Services Research, the International Journal of Entrepreneurship and Small Business, the International Journal of Electronic Finance, the Journal of Internet Banking and Commerce, the IIMB Management Review and published a book chapter with IGI-Global, USA etc. to name a few.

Jari Salo, D.Sc. (Econ. & Bus. Adm.), is currently Professor of Marketing at the Oulu Business School (AACSB) in Finland. Salo is head of the doctoral program in marketing. Before joining Oulu Business School Dr. Salo was Professor of Marketing (non-tenured) at the Aalto School of Business (formerly Helsinki School of Economics AACSB, EQUIS, AMBA). Salo has published in Industrial Marketing Management, the International Journal of Information Management, the Journal of Business and Industrial Marketing, the Journal of Business-to-Business Marketing, and the Computers in Human Behavior and Online Information Review. He has over 140 publications. He is the founding editor-in-chief of the Journal of Digital Marketing. Dr. Salo has been active lecturer in eMBA for over 10 years and lectured in Australia and Italy. He has been working with companies such as Nokia, Outotec, Kone and Rautaruukki.

Adriane Setti holds a PhD in Management from the Faculty of Economics, University of Algarve and a master in linguistics from the Federal University of Paraná (Brazil). She teaches communication and Portuguese language in undergraduate and master courses at the Social Studies Foundation in Curitiba (Brazil). Her research interests are related with linguistics, legal language, IT communication, enterprise information systems, IT professionals and profiles.

Amon Simba works within the Division of Management at Nottingham Business School. He obtained his PhD in Entrepreneurship and Strategy from Nottingham Trent University in 2014 where he has been teaching since 2010. He teaches on a range of business management-related modules at MSc and undergraduate levels. His expertise is in the field of Entrepreneurship and Strategy. He supervises both undergraduate and post graduate students. He has interest in supervising PhD and DBA students studying entrepreneurship and strategy with a focus on born-global companies, international entrepreneurship, SMEs & MNEs. He welcomes studies that originate in both developing and developed nations. In the academic year 2013/14 he was nominated for the award of outstanding teaching administered by Nottingham Trent Student Union (NTSU). He enjoys engaging with students and values their contributions as well as the wider business environment. He has published numerous papers in internationally-recognised journals. He is an Editorial Board Member of the Journal of Small Business and Entrepreneurship (JSBE). He is also a reviewer for the European International Business Academy. He has external links with the Swiss Hotel Management University Centre where he conducts guest lectures on research methods on yearly basis.

Dora Simões received her PhD in Informatics Engineering from the Faculty of Engineering of the University of Porto, Portugal, in 2008. She is Assistant Professor, in computer science area, at the Higher Institute of Accounting and Administration – University of Aveiro (ISCA-UA), Portugal. She is researcher at the Communication Sciences and Technologies Centre (CETAC.MEDIA) of University of Aveiro. As part of her doctoral work, she worked as an invited researcher at the Institute of Engineering and Computer Systems of Porto (INESC Porto), between 2003 and 2008, collaborating in European projects. Her current research interests include information and knowledge management, organizational information systems, relationship marketing and collaborative virtual networks. She has published in various conferences and journals, nationals and internationals.

B. Sriram received his Master's degree in Mathematics from Annamalai University, India. Currently he is working for Sur University College, Sultanate of Oman as lecturer since 2004. He is also holding the position of Quality Assurance Officer since 2009. He has 21 years of teaching experience in Mathematics and IT courses. He has published 23 research papers in peer reviewed national and international journals and presented 12 papers in national and international conferences and symposiums. He is an active researcher in his work profile (Quality Assurance), teaching areas (Information Systems and Technology) and in specialization (Mathematics and Education).

Robert Wendelin is currently acting as Senior Advisor for Strategy and Business development for Connected Services at Scania and has formerly acted in different positions at the Volvo Group where he acted as a mentor and developed strategies for Service Management and Telematics. Robert formerly acted as the Executive Director of CERS, Centre for Relationship Marketing and Service Management at Hanken School of Economics in Helsinki, Finland. CERS is the leading international research and knowledge centre in its field. He has also been acting as a Senior Advisor and Board Member regarding strategy, services, marketing and Total Business Solutions in several global and local companies. He earned his Ph.D. from Hanken in 2004 and has combined research and consulting in strategy, services and marketing for 15 years and consulted international firms like Volvo Trucks, ABB, KONE, and Nokia. He has also been an active lecturer for strategy and sales in international MBA programs.

Index

P

R

S

T

U

V

W

www.ingramcontent.com/pod-product-compliance
Lightning Source LLC
LaVergne TN
LVHW060356300926
849162LV00006B/1275